WASSERSTROM
CHICAGO
MARCH '94

STUDIES IN THE HISTORY OF PHILOSOPHY AND RELIGION

STUDIES IN THE HISTORY OF PHILOSOPHY AND RELIGION

HARRY AUSTRYN WOLFSON

Volume One

edited by Isadore Twersky and George H. Williams

Harvard University Press

Cambridge, Massachusetts

London, England

Second Printing 1979

Library of Congress Catalog Card Number 72–86385
ISBN 0–674–84765–2
Printed in the United States of America

FOREWORD

This volume is the second collection of papers and articles by Professor Wolfson; the first was entitled *Religious Philosophy: A Group of Essays* (Harvard University Press, 1961; revised in paperback, Atheneum, 1965). The articles reprinted in both collections should be read with bifocal lenses inasmuch as their general import and purport is twofold. They are intrinsically valuable, constituting substantive original contributions to extensive areas of philosophical scholarship, based on the characteristically Wolfsonian blend of erudition and insight; some of them are full-fledged monographs of exceptional quality. They are also of self-transcending methodological, philological, and phenomenological importance, constituting a true microcosm of the prodigious scholarly achievement of H. A. Wolfson—by *consensus omnium* one of this century's great and creative scholars in the history of philosophy.

For almost forty years [1] Harry Wolfson has devoted himself unreservedly, indeed heroically, to a bold and imaginative project entitled "Structure and Growth of Philosophic Systems from Plato to Spinoza." The fastidiously reasoned, intricately textured thesis underlying this grand project and unifying its many offshoots has been succinctly and lucidly described by Wolfson himself in the preface to *Religious Philosophy:*

> If we are to follow the conventional method of dividing philosophy into ancient, medieval, and modern, then medieval philosophy is to be defined as that system of thought which flourished between pagan Greek philosophy, which knew not of Scripture, and that body of philosophic writings which ever since the seventeenth century has tried to free itself from the influence of Scripture. Medieval philosophy so de-

[1] That is, since his publication of *The Philosophy of Spinoza* in 1934. His first published article, which he later referred to fondly as an "undergraduate essay," was "Maimonides and Hal-Levi: A Study in Typical Jewish Attitudes towards Greek Philosophy in the Middle Ages," *Jewish Quarterly Review,* n.s. 2 (1911): 297–337.

fined was founded by Philo, who lived at the time of the rise of Christianity. Ostensibly Philo is only the interpreter of the Hebrew Scripture in terms of Greek philosophy. But actually he is more than that. He is the interpreter of Greek philosophy in terms of certain fundamental teachings of his Hebrew Scripture, whereby he revolutionized philosophy and remade it into what became the common philosophy of the three religions with cognate Scriptures, Judaism, Christianity, and Islam. This triple scriptural religious philosophy, which was built up by Philo, reigned supreme as a homogeneous, if not a thoroughly unified, system of thought until the seventeenth century, when it was pulled down by Spinoza.

During the ten years following the publication of *The Philosophy of Spinoza,* Wolfson drafted all the volumes of this great series. From that time, all of his philosophical writings—including what has appeared as an occasional piece in a festschrift for an honored colleague or as an annotated and recast printed version of a lecture—are in fact highly structured essays designed for a much larger philosophical edifice, indeed for a complex of major structures housing the history of religious philosophy in the three major religious traditions. This is the master plan for the first collection of papers and articles by Professor Wolfson, and it is in this context and from this perspective that most of the essays in the present collection should be studied. While it is possible to classify these studies in terms of their relation to Greek, Jewish, Christian, and Islamic philosophy or to categorize them along conventional chronological lines—classical, patristic, early medieval, scholastic, Renaissance, and early modern—it is most appropriate to subordinate the material and temporal aspects to the conceptual and group them thematically in terms of their concern with and illumination of such problems as faith and reason, divine attributes, proofs of the existence of God, creation, internal senses, classification of the sciences. Such a view underscores the sweep and comprehensiveness of Wolfson's approach and also illustrates how, in fact, he has moved gracefully from Plato to Spinoza, and beyond; indeed from pre-Socratics to neo-Kantians, from Greek atomists to American pragmatists.

To Philo, Hellenistic Jew of Alexandria, the initiator and pathfinder of "medieval" or "scriptural" philosophy in the broadest sense of religious philosophy that combines Greek thought and categories with some version of divine revelation, Professor Wolfson devoted two volumes, *Philo: Foundations of Religious Philosophy in Judaism, Christianity, and Islam* (Harvard University Press, 1947; fourth printing, revised, 1962). To Spinoza, who, according to Wolfson, definitely ended the pre-eminence in philosophy of the dictates of faith as based upon revelation (over against reason as embodied in philosophy uninstructed and uninhibited by revelation), thus ushering in the modern period in philosophy as a self-contained realm of rational endeavor comparable to Greek philosophy before it was subordinated to the religious enterprise, Wolfson devoted two volumes, *The Philosophy of Spinoza: Unfolding the Latent Processes of His Reasoning* (Harvard University Press, 1934; a paperback edition, Schocken, 1969). For the interpretation of the first Christian philosophico-scriptural synthesis, Professor Wolfson has projected two volumes. The first volume of *The Philosophy of the Church Fathers,* subtitled "Faith, Trinity, Incarnation," appeared in 1956 (Harvard University Press; third, revised edition, 1970); and the second volume, roughly following the major subdivisions of the two-volume *Philo,* is expected to cover the whole range of patristic thought, including the problem of free will, political theory, and eschatology, and to contain an analysis of normative Judaism in the first century. In the present collection there are four essays (9–12) on the creation of the world *ex nihilo,* which will find their final place somewhere, in revised form, in the second volume of *The Church Fathers.* His two-volume study on *The Philosophy of Kalam,* the next major philosophico-scriptural synthesis, is now in press and scheduled for publication in 1973. A separate volume entitled *Kalam Repercussions in Jewish Philosophy* is ready in galleys. It will be quite clear that the largest number of essays in this collection deal with Jewish religious philosophy after the Hellenistic episode represented by Philo—in other words in the period from Saadia to

Spinoza, the period which the young Wolfson, fresh from his Talmudic studies in various yeshivot, set out to explore in depth; in fact, Wolfson regularly insists that he is primarily a "student of medieval Jewish philosophy." His *Crescas' Critique of Aristotle: Problems of Aristotle's Physics in Jewish and Arabic Philosophy* (Harvard University Press, 1929; second printing revised, 1971) is not a part of the grand project, but this rich, propaedeutic work is a model of felicitous translation and exhaustive explication that provides firm support for many of the philosophic explorations found elsewhere. Part of the Wolfsonian project has been the oft-promised "work on Greek philosophy, introductory to [the] series." This work remains unpublished, but its contours and contents are perfectly visible and appreciable not only in the few papers devoted explicitly or primarily to Greek philosophy—two of them appear in this collection: "The Knowability and Describability of God in Plato and Aristotle" and "Albinus and Plotinus on Divine Attributes"—but also in practically every paper and chapter that he has written.

There are no restrictive linguistic, religious, or chronological barriers in Wolfsonian scholarship; his research moves freely and knowingly, with verve and aplomb, across the frontiers of learning. In the present collection, "Notes on Proofs of the Existence of God in Jewish Philosophy," for example, contains a substantive exploration of Book Eight of Aristotle's *Physics*. Plato, Xenophon, Cicero and Lucretius, Bahya ibn Pakuda, Judah ha-Levi, Abraham ibn Daud, Maimonides, and Joseph Albo, Avicenna, and Averroes all appear together in interlocking analyses on two compact pages of this same article. Sometimes the title itself focuses attention on this sweeping conceptual-philological approach, as "The Problem of the Souls of the Spheres from the Byzantine Commentaries on Aristotle through the Arabs and St. Thomas to Kepler," or "The Platonic, Aristotelian and Stoic Theories of Creation in Hallevi and Maimonides," or "The Internal Senses in Latin, Arabic, and Hebrew Philosophic Texts," or "The Amphibolous Terms in Aristotle, Arabic Philosophy and Maimonides," or "The Terms *Taṣawwur* and *Taṣdīq* in Arabic Philosophy and Their

Greek, Latin and Hebrew Equivalents," or "The Double Faith Theory in Saadia, Averroes and St. Thomas." In other cases, the disciplined procedure and shining performance reveal the same scholarly reality without an apriori declaration of intent. His method of textual analysis, a Talmudic method of study transformed in his skilled hands into a sharp and innovative tool of historical-philosophical research, has indeed enabled him to analyze the major problems of philosophy from Plato to Spinoza—and the essays in this collection bear further witness to this imposing fact.

Several of the essays as printed in this volume have undergone revision at the hand of the author.

The third and fourth essays, different in origin and scope from their companion pieces, deserve some special comment. "Philo Judaeus" secures the integrity of the present collection in a special way in that it might best be called the architect's own replica of his monumental work on Philo, except that this essay is not really a miniature of the larger edifice but, far better, a creative distillation of some of the most important aspects of the thought of Philo for the students of the history of religious thought in general and, as it happens, for the readers of this collection in particular. The reader may be alerted to the fact that the eight italicized headings in this essay, which include or postulate what Wolfson has called Philo's Eight Scriptural Presuppositions,[2] represent, roughly, the major chapter headings (iv–xiii) of the two-volume *Philo*. Again, the present collection is immensely enriched by having among its essays a creative distillation of the epoch-making volume on the *Philosophy of the Church Fathers* with the eclectic relations between patristic theology and the various Greek philosophical traditions and revivals succinctly set forth in "Greek Philosophy in Philo and the Church Fathers."[3] Wolfson in *The Church Fathers* makes much of his observation that of the Eight Scriptural Presuppositions of Philo, seven were noticed by the Fathers and six of them *mutatis mutandis* appro-

[2] *Philo,* I, ch. iii, pp. 164–199.

[3] Essay 4 does not attempt to summarize *Church Fathers,* Part IV: "The Anathematized," notably the Gnostics.

priated.[4] Not all six, however—for example, Creation—feature in the first volume of Wolfson's study or hence in the summary thereof either.

It may be said that Professor Wolfson's main achievement for the history of Christian thought lies in the fact that for the first time the whole of the patristic enterprise has been analyzed and ordered as an epoch in the intellectual history of mankind. There have been genetic studies of the thought of this and that Father, of this and that doctrinal complex, and comprehensive presentations of patristic theology, polity, and piety from within the presuppositions of the community of faith; but never before from Catholic, Protestant, or humanistic pen has there been such a vast delineation in such minute detail and exhaustive analysis of the philosophical thought of the Fathers as part of the mind of Greek antiquity. The often disparate and intermittent thinking of more than half a millennium is in *The Church Fathers* and related essays ordered and arrayed. It is as though some massive and yet intricately variegated crystalline structure had been precipitated from the turbulent fluids and acrimonious vials of ancient controversy, from the clouded humors of bygone piety and bigotry, to be turned before our admiring eyes as the glittering essence of the patristic concern.

The achievement is unique also in its dispassionate objectivity. For though his study was projected as part of a magisterial series, he does not impose a pattern of his own; but, brooding over the recalcitrant or chaotic material, he is confident that the immanent or latent structure of thought will become visible to the perceptive eye, which, peering through the changes in vocabulary and verbal formulation, quietly beholds the congruencies and primordial articulations of pure thought. Thus under his steady scrutiny an ancient heretic may be rehabilitated philosophically on one point; but more commonly another heretic, vindicated by modern scholarship, will have been reconsigned to his former place through still more expert reading of the texts; while occasionally an orthodox

[4] *Church Fathers,* p. 81.

Father will have been shown to nod. Professor Wolfson has deeply honored Christianity by scrutinizing its classical texts and reconstructing the fragments of others with a care perhaps never accorded some of them before.

Finally, *The Church Fathers* and related essays are unique because the utter clarity of composition and purity of exposition is the work of a Jew who has examined the main corpus of normative Christian writings from Paul to Augustine in the West with occasional glances into the scholastic periods from John Scotus Erigena to Thomas Aquinas and in the East to John of Damascus and has gladly acknowledged as a philosopher that he has found more than he expected when he laid down his pen on completing *Philo*.

Concerning *Philo* Jean Daniélou of l'Institut Catholique remarked: "we can readily say Professor Wolfson's work is definitive. In his hands the study of Philonic philosophy enters the field of science" (*Theological Studies,* 9:589). And Professor Johannes Quaesten of the Catholic University has said of the *Church Fathers,* "Even if one does not agree with all of the author's conclusions, his book remains one of the most challenging of our times" (*The Thomist,* 35:320).

There are certain salient traits in Wolfson's scholarship. He has always engaged in creative exploration of the entire field of the history of philosophy, discovering and defining new problems, explaining misunderstood conceptions, tracing abstract problems through their terminological footprints, conjecturing and then verifying novel hypotheses. The banal and the trivial were banished from his writing. He was aroused by big problems, unexplored texts—his pioneering study of the unpublished commentaries of Averroes deserves special appraisal—and uncharted areas of philosophy. Those who know him well are able to affirm that he was genuinely frightened at the prospect of producing insignificant, derivative work. He has sought intellectual adventure and romance. He searched for and was fascinated by the origin, structure, and diversity of philosophic systems.

Related to this is the dynamism of his research. He is always expanding and revising, qualifying and refining, subjecting his interpretations and speculations to relentless scrutiny. Although concerned with structure, his scholarship is in perpetual motion. While elaborating "some guiding principles in determining Spinoza's mediaeval sources," he observed: "The hunt for mediaeval Hebrew and Latin sources of Spinoza is an old and venerable game. I myself have done some hunting in this field, and the chase for me has by no means come to an end with the publication of my book on *The Philosophy of Spinoza,* for by its mere publication a book does not become to its maker a closed masoretic text in which the right of emendation is to be exercised only by higher and lower criticism." [5] In a "Note on Maimonides' Classification of the Sciences" he adds with disarming simplicity: "My discussion here supplements, and in a few details revises, my discussion of the same suggestion in . . ." He frequently promises—and fervently hopes—to revise and amplify his study of Spinoza in order to demonstrate more clearly and with an abundance of additional material his opinion about the medieval matrix of Spinoza's thought: the axioms generally assumed to be new are in fact summaries of medieval views and his reasonings are arguments against these views from which he returns to pre-medieval, pagan positions. No sooner was *The Philosophy of Spinoza* off press than Wolfson happily reported that he had "gathered some 300 additional passages . . . some of which call for revision of certain statements in the book or for the improvement of certain infelicities of expression or for the expansion of certain views too briefly expressed." [6] His two volumes on the *Philosophy of the Church Fathers* grew out of his original intention to write a compact monograph of about one hundred pages bridging the gap between Philo and the Kalam philosophers. The forthcoming study of *The Philosophy of Kalam* started as a brief "exposition of certain philosophic views" in early Islamic theology and grew inexorably into a painstaking study of difficult texts and an integrated exposition of their major philosophic problems.

[5] *Jewish Quarterly Review,* n.s. 27 (1937):333.
[6] *Ibid.*

Wolfson's unique learning is sustained by a style of special elegance and eloquence. One could easily and profitably compose a florilegium of witty repartees, animated generalizations, striking epilogues, vigorous prologues, and exhilarating characterizations.

Underlying all his technical scholarly work is a philosophy of the history of philosophy. While his writing is objective and detached, it is not antiquarian or musty; it is seasoned with relevance and insight—all the more forceful and attractive by virtue of its subtlety and unobtrusiveness. If we were to unfold the latent processes of his own scholarly perceptions and reasonings, we would learn much about modern philosophy in its idealistic, romantic, and existentialist versions, about secularism, atheism, and religious belief, about modern interpretations and distortions of classical Jewish thought, and about the advances and reverses of scholarship.

This volume reflects the most basic biographical fact about Wolfson: his life has been one of unflagging commitment, uninterrupted creativity, and truly remarkable achievement. Undoubtedly, details of his achievement will be debated, his interpretation of specific cruxes will be questioned, some of his conjectures will —in the eyes of some—be found lacking in sufficient verification, his overarching thesis about the first-century Jew of Alexandria and the seventeenth-century Jew of Amsterdam as the pivots of "medieval" philosophy may not for various reasons become the accepted scheme of periodization for textbooks in the history of philosophy. Yet Wolfson's scholarship will be viewed with awe and admiration and his impact will be durable. He has added new dimensions to philosophical scholarship and illuminated wide areas of religious thought, plotting the terrain, blazing trails, and erecting guideposts for scores of younger scholars.

The articles included in this volume are reproduced by permission. Thanks are due the journals and publishers involved. We wish also to thank for their able assistance Charles and Judith Berlin.

Isadore Twersky
George H. Williams

CONTENTS

STUDIES IN THE HISTORY OF PHILOSOPHY AND RELIGION

I

THE PLURALITY OF IMMOVABLE MOVERS IN ARISTOTLE, AVERROES, AND ST. THOMAS

IN his great and epoch-making work on Aristotle,[1] Professor Jaeger analyzes the various texts in which the conception of one immovable mover or of many immovable movers is dealt with by Aristotle.

First, there is the fragment of Aristotle's lost dialogue *On Philosophy.*[2] According to that fragment, there is only one solitary immovable mover of the world, a transcendent being, a pure form, completely separated from the celestial spheres.[3] This transcendent immovable mover imparts to the celestial spheres the circular motion which is common to all of them, acting upon them as a final cause. The motions which are peculiar to the planets are due neither to that transcendent immovable mover nor to any other transcendent immovable movers; they are due to souls which are immanent in these planets.[4] This view, in so far as it relates to one transcendent immovable mover, with no reference to what causes the motions of the erratic stars, is maintained in *Metaphysics* XII,[5] which in its original form did not include chapter 8,[6] and it is also assumed in a passage in *On the Motion of Animals.*[7] Both these works were composed before *Physics* VIII.

Then, there is the discussion of the immovable mover in *Physics* VIII, especially chapter 6. In its original form, chapter 6, according to Professor Jaeger, assumed, again, the existence of only one transcendent immovable mover, and it contained no reference at all to what was the cause of the peculiar motions of the planets. But later, when the question of the possibility of a plurality of immovable movers, one for each planetary sphere, was raised in his School, Aristotle inserted three interpolations in that chapter. In one place (258b, 11), after using the expression "something eternal which first imparts motion", he added, "whether one thing or a plurality". In another place (259a, 7–20), after using the expression "first mover", he added that it may be "one" or "more than one" and proceeded, first, to show why "we ought to suppose that there is one rather than many" and that "it is sufficient to assume only one mover" and, second, to prove that the first mover "must be" something that is "one". In still another place (259b, 28–31), he assumes, without saying so explicitly, that besides the immovable mover there is a mover for each planetary sphere and that the mover of each planetary sphere is moved accidentally, and, with these assumptions in his mind, he proceeds to explain how the accidental motion of these movers of the planetary spheres differs from the accidental motion of the souls of terrestrial creatures. In the case of the former, he says, it means being moved not by themselves but by something else, namely, the outer sphere; in the case of the latter it means being moved by themselves, namely, through the change of the place of their bodies.[8] The evidence for the interpolative character of these three passages is primarily linguistic.[9]

Finally, there is the discussion of the immovable mover in *Metaphysics* XII, 8, which in its original form did not include the passage in 1074a, 31–38. In this chapter Aristotle assumes a plurality of immovable movers, as many as the number of the spheres, though he presents this view only as probable and not as necessary. All these immovable movers, like the first immovable mover, are transcendent beings, existing apart from the spheres which are moved by them and, according to Jaeger, they are, unlike the "sphere-movers" in the third interpolated passage in *Physics* VIII, 6, not moved accidentally by the first sphere.[10] But after having advanced the theory of a plurality of transcendent immovable movers, Aristotle, as a sort of self-criticism, noted down on the margin of his manuscript of chapter 8 an argument in support of the uniqueness of the transcendent immovable mover, which is contained in passage 1074a, 31–38. "His faithful editors," says Professor Jaeger, "introduced it into the text", where it stands as a glaring contradiction to the rest of the chapter. The evidence for the interpolative character of this passage is not only its inconsistency with the rest of the chapter but also the fact that it is foreign to its context from a linguistic point of view.[11]

The linguistic evidence marshalled by Jaeger should be quite sufficient to establish the interpolative character of the passages. Still certain questions arise in our mind. With regard to the third interpolation in *Physics* VIII, 6, it would seem strange that Aristotle, on introducing the unexpected movers of the planetary spheres, should not have changed the text somewhere in order to prepare the mind of the reader for this new piece of information. Then, with regard to the interpolation in *Metaphysics* XII, 8, it would seem even stranger that Aristotle's "faithful editors" should have introduced into the text a statement which appears to be so glaringly contradictory to the entire context of the chapter, without trying at least to soften down the contradiction. While indeed editors, and even authors, in their use of scissors and paste may occasionally overlook a grammatical incongruity in gender or number or tense, they are not likely to introduce, without proper warning, something new, which has not been anticipated by the context, or, worse still, to introduce something contradictory to the context, without attempting to revise the original text. Let us then examine these two chapters and see whether the two questions we have raised cannot be answered.

The key to the answer of these two questions is the term "first" used as a qualification of the expression "immovable mover". Whenever the expression "first immovable mover" occurs as a description of the mover of the first outer sphere and is used in the sense of a transcendent being which moves that sphere as a final cause, it is quite obvious that the term "first" is used not in contrast to the souls of animals which, though immovable movers, are not transcendent beings and do not move the animal bodies as final causes, but rather in contrast to immovable movers of the second and third and all the other inner spheres, which, like the first immovable mover, are conceived as transcendent beings that move their respective spheres as final causes. Now in *Physics* VIII, 6, it will be noticed, in the two places where the question of a plurality of movers is raised, the subject of the question is not simply "movers" but rather "first immovable mover"[12] or "first mover".[13] Moreover, when Aristotle concludes that "it is sufficient to assume only one mover" he describes that one mover as the "first of the immovables" (*πρῶτον τῶν ἀκινήτων*).[14] From all these it may be gathered that in this chapter, as it now stands, Aristotle started with the assumption that there were many immovable movers, at the head of which was a first immovable mover, and it is with regard to this first immovable mover that he raised the question whether there was one or more than one and decided that there was one.

The reason why it should occur to Aristotle to raise the question whether there was one or more than one first immovable mover may be found in the following considerations. In *De Caelo*, he debates the question whether there is one world or many worlds.[15] Now, if there were many worlds, there would of course have to be many first immovable movers. In the *Physics*, he refers to those who believe in the existence of an infinite number of worlds.[16] Again, if there were an infinite number of worlds, there would of course have to be an infinite number of first immovable movers. In an extant fragment of his lost dialogue *On Philosophy* he discusses the question whether there is "one first principle (*ἀρχή*) or many" and concludes that there must be one.[17] From the context it may be inferred that the term *arche* is used there with reference to what in the other fragment, quoted above, Aristotle alludes to as the immovable mover of the world and also that the discussion is on the basis of Plato's as well as Aristotle's own theory of the existence of only one world, so that the question discussed in *On Philosophy* is whether on the theory of the existence of one world there was one first principle or many. Similarly in *Metaphysics* XII, 10, Aristotle argues against Speusippus and others who, on the theory of the existence of only one world, "give us many governing principles",[18] and he cites against them the Homeric saying: "The rule of the many is not good; one is the ruler."[19]

It is with all this in the back of his mind that Aristotle, we have reason to believe, raises here the question whether there is one "first immovable mover" or more than one and, if the latter, whether finite or infinite. The question as posed by him is vague enough to apply either to the assumption of many worlds or to that of one world. But, inasmuch as the assumption of an infinite number of worlds has already been disowned by him in the *Physics*[20] and the assumption of many worlds has already been explicitly rejected by him in *De Caelo*,[21] he does not discuss here the question of the plurality of immovable movers on the assumption of more than one world; he discusses it only on the assumption of one world. Thus assuming that there is only one world, he first tries to show, on the basis of the facts by which the existence of an immovable mover is demonstrated, that the assumption of more than one immovable mover, whether infinite or finite, would be a gratuitous assumption.[22] Then, on the basis of the continuity of the motion in this one world, he tries to show that there must be only one first immovable mover.[23]

Aristotle has thus established in the first part of chapter 6 of *Physics* VIII that there is only one "first immovable mover", which is the mover of the outer sphere, and he has also indicated, by his carefully qualifying the "immovable mover" by "first", that there are other immovable movers, which are the movers of the planetary spheres. But having in mind Plato's suggestion in *Laws* X, 898E–899A, that the movers of the heavenly bodies, which to Plato were bare stars, might reside in those bodies after the analogy of souls in animals, he tries to show that neither the first immovable mover nor the immovable movers of the planetary spheres can be conceived after the analogy of souls in animals. His argument falls into two parts. First, with regard to the first immovable mover, he shows that unlike souls in animals, which are moved accidentally, the first immovable mover must be immovable even accidentally (259b, 1–28). Second, with regard to the immovable movers of the planetary spheres, he shows that, though his argument for the denial of accidental motion in the first immovable mover does not apply to these immovable movers of the planetary spheres, still, unlike the accidental motion of souls of animals, which is by themselves, namely, by the bodies in which they reside, the accidental motion of the immovable movers of the planetary spheres is by something else, namely, by the first sphere (259b, 28–31).

What this distinction between the two kinds of accidental motion means is this. Both animals and the planetary spheres have two types of motion: one common to all animals as a class and to all planetary spheres as a class; the other peculiar to each animal as an individual and to each planetary sphere as an individual. The common motion in the case of animals consists in such natural motions as increase, decrease, and respiration, and the cause of these motions is to be found in the atmosphere and the many things that enter into the animal[24]; the common motion in the case of the planetary spheres is their common circular motion round the centre of the world, and the cause of this motion is the circular motion of the outer sphere, that is, the sphere of the fixed stars, which in turn is caused by the first immovable mover. The peculiar motion in the case of animals consists in the various locomotions of individual animals, and the cause of these peculiar motions is to be found in the souls which exist in the bodies of animals; the peculiar motions in the case of the planetary spheres consists in the various motions of the individual planetary spheres which, according to Aristotle, are fifty-five in number,[25] and the cause of these motions of the planetary spheres is to be found in the individual immovable mover of each of these planetary spheres. Now each individual mover of each individual planetary sphere stands in a fixed and constant relation toward the individual planetary sphere in which it causes its peculiar motion, but, inasmuch as each individual planetary sphere is moved round the centre of the world by the circular motion of the outer sphere, the immovable mover of each planetary sphere, whose relation toward that sphere is fixed and is never changed, participates, as it were, in that circular motion round the centre of the world and may thus be said to be moved accidentally. Accordingly, Aristotle says that while both the soul of the animal and the immovable mover of each planetary sphere are moved accidentally, the soul is moved accidentally by the motion which as a mover it produces in the animal, whereas the immovable mover of each planetary sphere is moved accidentally not by the motion which as a mover it produces in the sphere but by the motion produced in the sphere by the outer sphere.

The upshot of all these is that the movers of the individual spheres, like the first mover, do not exist in the spheres of which they are the movers. They are apart from them. They are transcendent beings. Like the first mover, they move their respective spheres as final causes. Still by the very nature of their fixed and constant relation toward the spheres in which they cause their individual motions they participate in the common circular motion round the centre of the world, caused in all these spheres by the outer sphere. It is on this account that Aristotle declares that in contrast to the first immovable mover all the other immovable movers are moved accidentally by something else.

We have thus explained *Physics* VIII, 6. We shall now take up *Metaphysics* XII, 8.

This distinction between the immovability of the first immovable mover and the immovability of the immovable movers of the planetary spheres, made by Aristotle in *Physics* VIII, 6, is assumed by him also in his discussion of the plurality of movers in *Metaphysics* XII, 8. In this chapter, as Jaeger has clearly shown, the planetary movers, though not expressly described as "separated", are still regarded by Aristotle as "existing apart" and as "transcendent".[26] But when we study the phrasing in this chapter carefully we shall find that these planetary movers, though existing apart and transcendent, are still assumed by Aristotle to have accidental motion. In his description of the first immovable mover under the name of "the principle (ἀρχὴ) and the first of beings"[27] or "the first and immovable substance",[28] he says that it is "immovable both essentially (καθ' αὑτὸ) and accidentally (κατὰ συμβεβηκός)",[29] but, when from the fact that the eternal spatial motion of the universe requires a first immovable mover he raises the question whether the eternal spatial motions of the planets similarly require immovable movers, he drops the terms "accidentally" and argues only from the existence of a "first mover" who must be "immovable essentially"[30] to the existence of a "substance" as the mover of each planetary sphere which is also "immovable essentially".[31] Nowhere in the entire chapter does Aristotle describe the movers of the planetary spheres as immovable accidentally. Moreover, nowhere in the entire chapter does he describe these movers of the planetary spheres as first movers, but, reserving the term "first" for that mover which he has already described as "immovable both essentially and accidentally", he describes the other immovable movers, those of whom he did not say that they are immovable also accidentally, as "second [and third and so on] according to the same order as the orbital motions of the stars".[32] This difference of phrasing in the description of these two kinds of movers may at first sight appear to be without any significance. But in the light of the statement made in *Physics* VIII, 6, that the movers of the planetary spheres are movable accidentally by something else, the description here of each of the movers of the planetary spheres as being "immovable essentially" and not as being, like the mover of the sphere of the fixed stars, "immovable both essentially and accidentally" indicates that here, too, Aristotle assumes that the movers of the planetary spheres are movable accidentally, with the qualification, of course, as stated in the third passage in *Physics* VIII, 6, that they are movable accidentally, not by themselves, but by something else.

We shall now take up passage 1074a, 31–38, in *Metaphysics* XII, 8.

Granting, as we have said, that stylistically and grammatically this passage is a later interpolation, based upon what was originally a marginal note by Aristotle himself, we shall try to show that the contention of this passage, namely, that on account of the immateriality of the "immovable first mover" there can be no plurality of immovable movers, does not necessarily contradict his contention throughout the rest of the chapter that there is a plurality of immaterial movers of the planetary spheres. For as in the question raised in the first and second interpolative passages in *Physics* VIII, 6, the contention here is not that there is one "immovable mover", but rather that there is one "first immovable mover", and we shall try to show that the argument by which he disproves the existence of more than one "first immovable mover" does not apply to the existence of more than one "movable mover". The problem here, as in *Physics* VIII, 6, is the same as the problem discussed in his dialogue *On Philosophy* and in *Metaphysics* XII, 10, namely, whether there is one ruling principle of the world or more than one. As in *Physics* VIII, 6, the chief argument for the unity of the first immovable mover rests on the theory of the unity of the world which has been established in *De Caelo*. But, whereas in *Physics* VIII, 6, relying upon his refutation of a plurality of worlds in *De Caelo*, Aristotle does not discuss the possibility of many first immovable movers on the assumption of many worlds, here he does discuss that possibility. Let us then outline the essential points of Aristotle's argument in *De Caelo* against a plurality of worlds upon which the argument here against a plurality of first immovable movers is based.

If there were many worlds, argues Aristotle in *De Caelo*, these many worlds would have to have many centres, and within each world there would have to be concentric celestial spheres moving round their respective centres, and under the celestial spheres in each of these many worlds there would have to be four elements, earth, water, air, fire, some of which would move upward toward the celestial periphery and some downward toward the centre. But these many worlds, Aristotle insists, would have to be "alike in nature",[33] so that the various subcelestial elements as well as the various celestial spheres in them would be many "in number" (ἀριθμῷ) but one "in species" (κατ' εἶδος).[34] When therefore Aristotle in *De Caelo* refutes the existence of many worlds and shows that the world must be one, he means to establish thereby that the world is one both "in number" and "in species". Now the arguments by which he establishes in *De Caelo* the oneness of the world are all what Aristotle elsewhere calls "physical",[35] based as they all are upon considerations of motion, but in the course of his discussion of these physical arguments he says that "the same could also be shown with the aid of discussions which fall under First Philosophy".[36] Here in this interpolated passage in *Metaphysics* XII, 8, 1074a, 31–38, we have that argument which falls under "First Philosophy". Let us try to unfold this argument in all the fulness in which we have reason to believe it formulated itself in the mind of Aristotle.

There cannot be many worlds, he argues, for, if there were many worlds, they would have to have, as already shown in *De Caelo*, the same species of motion, and so the many worlds would have to be many in number but one in species, and consequently the "principle [i.e., the first mover] of each [world] will be one in species [with that of any of the other worlds] but many in number", This, however, is impossible, for "all things which are many in number have matter". There must therefore be only one world, one, as shown in *De Caelo*, both "in species" and "in number". And consequently, he concludes, "the first immovable mover is one both in formula and in number", the term "formula" (λόγος) being used here in the same sense as the term "species" (εἶδος).[37]

In this passage, it will be noticed, the unity in both species and number is established only with regard to the first immovable mover, that first immovable mover which previously in the same chapter he has described as being "immovable both essentially and accidentally". But what about those immovable movers of the planetary spheres which in the same chapter he describes neither as "first" nor as being "immovable both essentially and accidentally"? They are, of course, not to be considered as one both in species and in number. They are many. But in what sense are they many? They cannot be many in number, for they have no matter. They cannot be many in genus, for they all constitute one genus, that of being immaterial and essentially immovable movers. They must of necessity be many in species. But what is the specific difference that sets off each of these movers as a species different from any of the other movers? Inasmuch as the only difference that one can find between these movers is that each of them is the cause of a different kind of motion in a different planetary sphere, their specific difference must inevitably be the difference in the objects to which they are related as the cause of their motion, so that just as "rational animal" and "irrational animal" constitute two species, the differentia between them being "rational" and "irrational", so also "Saturn-mover", "Jupiter-mover", "Mars-mover", and so on, constitute different species, the differentia being "Saturn", "Jupiter", "Mars", and so on, in relation to which these movers are movers. This is exactly in accordance with Aristotle's requirement that in a definition in which the subject in a relative term, as is the term "mover" here, the differentia must also be a term which expresses a relation to something else.[38] It is in this sense of differentia that Aristotle says that the immovable movers are many and that they are numbered as first and second and so on "according to the same order as the orbital motions of the stars".[39] This kind of differentia between the movers of the planetary spheres, arising, as it does from differences in the motions which, as final causes, they produce in different planetary spheres, does not imply matter. They are thus to be described as many in species but not in number, each of them being a species which consists of only one member.

Professor W. D. Ross, in dealing with the difficulty of how a plurality of immaterial movers of the planetary sphere is possible on the basis of Aristotle's own principle that all things which are many in number have matter, suggests tentatively a solution on the assumption that these movers of the planetary spheres "are pure forms *specifically* different, each of them being the sole member of a separate species, as some of the schoolmen maintained that the angels are". But against this tentative solution of his he raises the following objection: "But at that rate there might be specifically different *prime* movers, and Aristotle's argument for the unity of the universe would break down."[40] According to our explanation, however, of Aristotle's conception of the specifically different movers of the planetary, his argument for the unity of the universe would not break down. For the principal point of Aristotle's argument in this passage, as we have seen, is that, on the assumption of a plurality of worlds, all the worlds would have to have one species of motion and would thus be one in species and many in number, with the result that the prime movers of the many worlds would likewise be one in species and many in number; but, being many in number, they would have to have matter. The movers of the planetary spheres, however, can be many in species, without being many in number, in view of the fact that they produce different species of motion in the different planetary spheres and, acting as they do upon these spheres as final causes, they need not be material in order to produce these motions.

Another objection raised by Ross against his tentative solution is as follows: "And this way of escape is not open to Aristotle; for he holds that specific difference implies *a fortiori* numerical difference."[41] This statement is an inference of Aristotle's statement *ὅσα ἀριθμῷ καὶ εἴδει ἕν, ὅσα δ' εἴδει οὐ πάντα ἀριθμῷ*,[42] in which Professor Ross evidently takes the second part of the statement as a universal negative proposition, meaning that whatsoever things are one in species are not one in number, whence he correctly infers that whatsoever things are many in species are *a fortiori* not one but many in number. But the use of the term *πάντα* after the negative *οὐ* shows that Aristotle did not mean the proposition to be a universal negative. It is a particular negative proposition, meaning that "whatsoever things are one in species are *not all* one in number", the implication being that some things which are one in species are also one in number. Again, the opposite of this proposition is that whatsoever things are many in species are *not all* many in number, the implication of which is, again, that some things which are many in species are one in number. Is it not possible that the two implications of this very statement of Aristotle, namely, (1) that there may be single species under which there are no individuals and (2) that there may be many species which are not many in number, refer to the plurality of the movers of the planetary spheres?

In our interpretation of the texts of Aristotle, we have tried to show that, even on the basis of Professor Jaeger's theory that these texts contain later interpolations, which show a gradual development in thought of Aristotle, in the final form of these texts as we have them today there is no difference between *Physics* VIII, 6, and *Metaphysics* XII, 8, and no inconsistency in the latter between the interpolated passage and the rest of the chapter. Throughout his discussion in these two chapters, as they now stand before us, Aristotle assumes one first immovable mover, that is, the mover of the sphere of the fixed stars, and it is this immovable mover which he describes as the first, but besides this first immovable mover, he assumes also other immovable movers, that is, the movers of the planetary spheres, which he does not describe as first. The first mover is one and unique, because it alone is immovable even accidentally and it alone produces only one kind of motion. The manyness of the movers of the planetary spheres consists in their each producing a different kind of motion in a different sphere. This manyness Aristotle would describe as a manyness in species or in formula or in definition, and is a manyness which does not involve matter.

In the course of his discussion of passage 1074a, 31–38 in *Metaphysics* XII, 8, which we have tried to harmonize with the rest of the chapter, Professor Jaeger says that "the keenest thinkers of posterity have racked their brains to understand how an Aristotle could have involved himself in such contradictions".[43] Among those who saw in this passage a contradiction to the rest of the chapter he mentions Plotinus[44] and several modern students of Aristotle.[45] We have already discussed the tentative solution offered by Ross in his edition of Aristotle's *Metaphysics*, which was published one year after the publication of Jaeger's work. Since that time various attempts have been made to remove this contradiction, all of them trying to show in various ways how the many immaterial movers are, as Professor Ross said, "pure forms *specifically* different, each of them being the sole member of a separate species, as some of the schoolmen maintained that the angels are", except that they try to explain what the specific difference between them is. Mansion explains that there is between these immaterial movers "un ordre de subordination, différence de rang".[46] This "différence de rang" is explained by Mugnier as being determined by the difference in the rotations of the various planetary spheres "dont le nombre augmente à mesure que ces sphères sont plus loin du Premier Moteur".[47] Merlan, who advances the interesting theory that the conception of unique species, with regard to both Aristotle's immovable movers and the schoolmen's angels, is traceable to Plato's ideal numbers,[48] explains that between the various immovable movers of Aristotle, as well as between the various ideal numbers of Plato, there is a relationship of "prior and posterior".[49] All these explanations, we shall try to show are along the line of explanations offered by mediaeval commentators on Aristotle. We shall examine here the explanations of Avicenna and Averroës and, in connection with them, we shall make reference also to Maimonides and St. Thomas. The explanation of Aristotle by Avicenna can be ascertained only indirectly from his discussion of views which are traceable to Aristotle; the explanation of Aristotle by Averroës can be ascertained directly from his commentaries on the works of Aristotle.

According to both Avicenna and Averroës, there is a plurality of movers, called Intelligences. These Intelligences are all transcendent beings, existing apart from the spheres to which they impart motion as final causes. They both also proceed on the Aristotelian principle that all things which are many in number have matter. As for the question which would naturally arise from these premises as to how these immaterial transcendent Intelligences can be numbered two alternative answers are provided, one by Avicenna and the other by Averroës.

The answer provided by Avicenna rests upon his conception that the Intelligences form a series of successive emanations, so that there is a causal relation between them, each Intelligence being the cause of an Intelligence emanating from it, and only God, who is at the top of the series, is an uncaused cause. This conception of an emanative causal relationship between immaterial beings, it may be said in passing, is alien to Aristotle. In fact, it is alien to entire Greek philosophy. It is a new conception, derived from the Christian doctrine of the eternal generation of the Logos,[50] and it was introduced into Greek philosophy by Plotinus, who had acquired it from his teacher Ammonius Saccas, who at one time was a Christian. This imposition of the Plotinian conception of immaterial emanation upon Aristotle's conception of the plurality of immaterial movers of the planetary spheres, which Avicenna inherited from Alfarabi, provided a new principle of differentiation within the immaterial movers and hence also a new explanation of their numerability. This new explanation, which is common to all exponents of emanationism in Arabic philosophy, is succinctly summed up by Maimonides in the following proposition:

> Whatever is not a body does not admit of the idea of number except it be a force in a body, for then the individual forces may be numbered together with the matters or the substances in which they exist. It follows, therefore, that separate beings, which are neither bodies nor forces in bodies, do not admit of any idea of number except when they are related to each other as cause and effect.[51]

In other words, there is between the successively emanated intelligences a difference which may be described by the expression "according to prior and posterior" (*secundum prius et posterius*), which, as we shall see later, is used by Averroës, for every emanative Intelligence is prior to the Intelligence emanated from it in that sense of "prior" which, according to Aristotle, applies to a thing which is in any way the cause of the existence of something else.[52] But this priority of cause implies, according to Avicenna, also what Aristotle calls prior in the sense of "that which is better and more honorable (*τιμιώτερον*)",[53] for in a passage where he shows that the Intelligence did not emanate "simultaneously", by which, according to Aristotle's definition of "simultaneous",[54] he means that they emanated in the order of priority and posteriority, he refers to that Intelligence which emanated prior to all the others as "the more excellent than all the others".[55]

Averroës, however, by rejecting the principle of emanation, could no longer find in the Intelligences a distinction of priority in the sense of cause. He did, however, find in them a distinction in the sense of "better and more honorable". Commenting upon Aristotle's statement that "there are substances and one of these is first and another second [and so on] according to the same order of the orbital motions of the stars",[56] he says that "the order of these movers in relation to the first mover is according to the spatial order of the planetary spheres" and this spatial order, which he describes as an order in which some of the spheres, as well as some of their movers, are "prior" to others "according to place" (*secundum locum*), is taken by him to establish in the spheres, as well as in their movers, an order in which some of them are "prior" to others "in nobility" (*nobilitate*).[57] The term *nobilitate* is used here in the Latin translation of Averroës' Long Commentary on the *Metaphysics* as a translation of the Arabic term *bil-sharaf*,[58] the same term which is used in the Arabic translation of the *Categories* as a translation of the term τιμιώτερον (*ashrafu*).[59] The expression "prior in nobility" in the Latin translation of Averroës here thus reflects what Aristotle in the *Categories* calls "prior" in the sense of "more honorable". The same view is expressed by Averroës in his *Tahāfut al-Tahāfut*, where he says that the order of the Intelligences are determined by the order of their position in their respective spheres appointed by God from eternity,[60] by which he undoubtedly means, as in his Long Commentary on the *Metaphysics*, an order of priority in nobility.

Thus, according to both Avicenna and Averroës the difference between the immaterial Intelligences is a difference "according to prior and posterior", except that to Avicenna the "prior" is that which Aristotle describes as being both in the sense of "cause" and in the sense of "more honorable", whereas to Averroës it is only that which Aristotle describes as being in the sense of being "more honorable", for which his Latin translator uses the term "nobler". But here a question arises. Does this difference according to prior and posterior, in either of its two senses mentioned, constitute a specific difference and are the Intelligences on that account to be regarded as different species? The answer to this question, we shall now try to show, may be gathered from several passages in the works of Averroës.

First, there is a passage in his Long Commentary on *De Caelo*. Directly Averroës discusses there the celestial spheres, but towards the end of his discussion he intimates that the conclusion he arrived at applies also to "the natures which move them".[61] The upshot of his discussion is summed up in his formulation of two contrasting views, that of Avicenna and his own.

According to Avicenna, he says, the substance of the celestial bodies, and hence also that of the Intelligences, is "the same in genus and diverse in species" (*idem genere et diversa specie*).[62] The original statement of Avicenna on the subject, directly with reference to the Intelligences, reads: "These Intelligences are not agreeing (*convenientes*; Arabic: *mutaffiḳah*) in species"[63] but are rather "diverse (*diversae*; Arabic: *muḫtalifah*) in species".[64]

According to Averroës' own view, the substance of the sphere is not "diverse in species" but rather "agreeing in species" (*convenientia in specie*). This agreeing in species, however, is "according to prior and posterior and not according to univocation" (*secundum prius et posterius, non secundum univocationem*).[65]

Second, there is a passage in his *Tahāfut al-Tahāfut*. Here, again, directly he deals with the celestial spheres but, on the basis of his statement in the long commentary on *De Caelo*, we may assume that the same view applies also to the Intelligences. This passage reads as follows: "The heavenly bodies are not one in species and many in number but are rather many in species, as would be the case with regard to the individuals of different animals, if there were only one individual of a species."[66]

These two passages, which seem to be contradictory to each other, are really complementary to each other. They contain the following four assertions.

1. The celestial bodies, and hence also the Intelligences, are not diverse in species.

2. But at the same time also they are not one in species.

3. They are to be described as agreeing in species, but not according to univocation.

4. Their agreement in species is according to prior and posterior and hence, while they are neither diverse in species nor many in number, they are many in species.

Let us explain what these four statements mean.

His statement that they are not one species and that they do not agree in species according to univocation reflects Aristotle's illustration of a univocal term by the term "animal" in its application to a man and an ox, by which is meant that a man and an ox are one in genus because the term "animal" is applied to them according to univocation. By the same token, Averroës seems to argue, two individual human beings are one in species because the term "man" is applied to them according to univocation. Hence, he concludes, inasmuch as the celestial bodies, as well as the Intelligences, do not agree in species according to univocation, they are not one in species.

Still he is opposed to their being described as diverse in species. Evidently what he means to say is that they are not as diverse in species as, say, "man" and "ox", who though they are the same in genus, are diverse in species. And the reason given by him for this is that they agree in species. Still this agreement in species is not according to univocation, that is to say, it is not a sameness in species. Whence he concludes that, while they are not diverse in species, they are many in species.

Behind this seemingly verbal quibbling there lurks Aristotle's discussion of the fine distinctions between the terms "same" (*ταὐτό*, *idem*, Arabic: *huwa huwa*), "diverse", (*ἕτερον*, *diversum*, Arabic: *ghair*), and "different" (*διάφορον*, *differens*, Arabic: *muḫälif*).[67] "Same" means "one"; "diverse" is the opposite of "same"; "different" is between "same" and "diverse", and, in Averroës' own words, it means that which "differs in one thing but agrees in another thing".[68] Consequently, since the planetary spheres, as well as the Intelligences, agree in species but, within that species, they differ according to prior and posterior, they are to be described not as diverse in species but only as differing in species; and, as differing in species, which means being neither the "same" in species nor "diverse" in species, they can be described as many in species. What really Averroës means to say is that the spheres as well as the Intelligences are what Porphyry, and after him also Averroës, calls the "last species" (*ἔσχατον εἶδος*, *species ultima*) or "most special species" (*εἰδικώτατον εἶδος*, *species specialissima*),[69] or what are generally known as the "lowest species" (*species infima*). But of these lowest species each species consists of only one member, and hence the spheres, as well as the Intelligences, are many not in number but only in species.

This conception of the spheres and hence also of the Intelligences as being neither the "same in species" nor "diverse in species" but only "many in species", which we have interpreted to mean that they are lowest species, may be derived also from a passage in Averroës' *Epitome of the Metaphysics*. In that passage Averroës tries to show how each one of the Intelligences can be described as "one in number" and that, when so described, it is understood as being "one in number" partly after the analogy of the "individual one" and partly after the analogy of the "specific one". It is after the analogy of the "individual one", in so far as the individual is not predictable of a subject.[70] It is after the analogy of the "specific one", in so far as the species is "an intelligible thing which is one essentially".[71] What all this means is that each Intelligence is a lowest species of which it is the sole member, so that it may be regarded both as a species and as an individual.

The fact that in this passage a lowest species of which there is only one member is said by Averroës to be described as "one in number" after the analogy of the "individual one" will throw light upon the true meaning of a vexatious passage in his Long Commentary on *De Caelo*. In that passage, dealing with the stars, which to Aristotle as well as to him, are of the same substance as the spheres,[72] he says that "all the celestial bodies are of the same (*eiusdem*) nature in species, and the celestial bodies are many individuals (*plura individua*) in species".[73] Taken literally, it is in direct contradiction to the statement quoted above from his *Tahāfut al-Tahāfut* and, verbally at least, would also seem to be in contradiction to the statement quoted above from the same Long Commentary on *De Caelo*. In the light, however, of our interpretation that the spheres, as well as the Intelligences, are to Averroës lowest species and in the light also of his own statement in the *Epitome of the Metaphysics* that a lowest species which consists of a single member is "one in number" after the analogy of the "individual one", the statement here means that the celestial bodies are "of the same nature in species", in the sense that they agree in a higher species, and they are "many individuals in species", in the sense that they are many lowest species, each of them consisting of only one member.

The result of our discussion is that despite the difference between Avicenna and Averroës as to whether the Intelligences are to be described as diverse in species or as many in species, they both agree that, though immaterial, the Intelligences can be numbered by virtue of a relationship of prior and posterior between them, in which the "prior" is conceived of by Avicenna both in the sense of cause and in the sense of greater nobility and by Averroës only in the sense of greater nobility.

The difference between these mediaeval explanations of the plurality of the immaterial immovable movers and our explanation is that according to the mediaeval explanations there is some kind of distinction of prior and posterior in the immaterial movers themselves, whereas according to our explanation there is no distinction at all in the immaterial movers themselves; the distinction between them is only a distinction in their relation to things outside themselves — a distinction of external relation which, as we have shown, does not affect their nature. Now the assumption on the part of the mediaevals of a distinction of prior and posterior, whether that of cause or that of nobility, in the immaterial movers themselves has led to those endless questions as to whether that distinction does not after all imply a relationship of matter and form and also as to whether that relationship of matter and form is compatible with the initial assumption that these immovable movers are immaterial. But to assume, as we do, that the distinction between the immaterial immovable movers is only a distinction in their relation to things outside themselves does not lead to any of those questions.

While the apparent contradiction between passage 1074a, 31–38, and the rest of chapter 8 of *Metaphysics* XII can be removed by these various explanations of the plurality of the immaterial immovable movers, there still remains the question why that passage, which, as Professor Jaeger has shown on purely linguistic grounds, is quite evidently a later addition, was added at all. The entire context of the chapter would lead us to expect that the purpose of this added passage would be an attempt to prove that there is only one first immovable mover, but why a passage with such a purpose should begin with the words, "That, however, there is one world is evident" and end with the words, "Therefore there is only one world", needs an explanation.

The explanation is supplied by St. Thomas in his Commentary on the *Metaphysics*.

On the whole, St. Thomas' explanation of the plurality of the immaterial movers of the spheres rests on both Averroës and Avicenna. To begin with, like Averroës, he rejects Avicenna's explanation based upon the theory of successive emanation, and he does so sometimes by refuting Maimonides' Proposition, quoted above, in which Avicenna's explanation is formulated.[74] Like Averroës, therefore, the distinction he finds between the Intelligences is that which Aristotle describes as prior and posterior in the sense of "better and more honorable" and which he himself describes as a distinction "according to diverse grades" (*secundum diversos gradus*),[75] or, as he says with regard to angels, "according to the greater and smaller perfection of their simple forms, arising from a greater and smaller propinquity to God".[76] But then, unlike Averroës and like Avicenna, he does not hesitate to describe the Intelligences as "diverse" (*diversae*)[77] in species, that is to say, they are not lowest species which agree in a higher species, but are rather simply separate species without any kind of agreement in species. Indeed, very often St. Thomas describes the Intelligences as "different"[78] in species, but when he does so, he means thereby that they are totally different in species, for Aristotle himself sanctions this use of the term "different".[79] Moreover, St. Thomas explicitly quotes Avicenna in support of his statement that "in the immaterial substances there are not many individuals of the same species, but there are as many species as there are individuals".[80] In fact, it would seem that St. Thomas understood Averroës to believe that the Intelligences are many individuals of one species, for he takes Averroës' statement quoted above from his Long Commentary on *De Caelo* to mean literally that the celestial bodies are many individuals of one species, and hence rejects it as being "manifestly false".[81] Still in his Commentary on the *Metaphysics*, in his comment on the passage that "there are substances and one of these is first and another second [and so on] according to the same order as the orbital motions of the stars", he follows Averroës' commentary[82]; and when he comes to state how, in accordance with the order of priority and posteriority in the spheres, there is an order of priority and posteriority in the Intelligences, he uses the term which is used in the Latin translation of the Long Commentary and says that one Intelligence is prior to the other in the sense that it is "nobler" (*noblior*) than the other.[83]

But then, his analysis of the latter part of the chapter (1074a, 17–38) explains the puzzling opening and closing words of 1074a, 31–38. According to his analysis, this latter part of the chapter falls into three parts, each answering a question which occurred to the mind of Aristotle in connection with his statement that there are as many immovable substances and principles as the number of the spheres which are moved by them.[84] The first question which occurred to the mind of Aristotle is, How do we know that there are not immovable substances to which there are no corresponding spheres moved by them? To this the answer is given in passage 1074a, 17–23. The second question which occurred to his mind is, How do we know that there are not more spheres than those observed by astronomers and hence how do we know that there are not more immovable movers than those calculated on the basis of these observations of the astronomers? The answer to this question is given in passage 1074a, 23–31. The third question which occurred to the mind of Aristotle is this: How do we know that there are not other worlds besides ours and hence more spheres than those observed by astronomers in this world of ours and hence also more immaterial movers than those calculated on the basis of the assumption of the existence of only one world? The answer to this question is contained in passage 1074a, 31–38. And because the last question posed was, How do we know that there are not other worlds besides ours? the answer to this question starts with the statement, "That, however, there is one world is evident", and hence ends with the statement, "Therefore there is only one world".

To sum up: We have tried to show how the apparent difference between *Physics* VIII, 6, and *Metaphysics* XII, 8, and the apparent contradiction in the latter can be removed. We have also tried to show how mediaeval interpreters of Aristotle, especially Averroës, explained the apparent contradiction in the latter.

NOTES

1. *Aristoteles: Grundlegung einer Geschichte seiner Entwicklung*, Berlin, 1923. Subsequent page references are to the English translation by R. Robinson, Oxford, 1934.
2. Frg. 236 (*Aristotelis . . . Fragmenta*, ed. V. Rose, 1886).
3. Jaeger, *Aristotle*, pp. 138–152, 348.
4. The problem of the souls of the spheres is not dealt with in this paper. Later views on this problem in Philo, in the Church Fathers, in Algazali, and in mediaeval Jewish philosophy from Saadia to Grama are dealt with in my *Philo* (1947), pp. 363–366, 417–418, and *Crescas' Critique of Aristotle* (1929), pp. 535–538.
5. Jaeger, pp. 221–222.
6. *Ibid.*
7. *Ibid.*, pp. 355–357.
8. *Ibid.*, pp. 357–367.
9. *Ibid.*, pp. 360, 364, 365.
10. *Ibid.*, p. 361 and pp. 346–351.
11. *Ibid.*, pp. 351–353.
12. *Phys.* VIII, 6, 258b, 10–12.
13. *Ibid.*, 259*a*, 6–8.
14. *Ibid.*, 12–13.
15. *De Caelo* I, 8–9.
16. *Phys.* III, 4, 203b, 26.
17. *Frg.* 17.
18. *Metaph.* XII, 10, 1076a, 3.
19. *Ibid.*, 4; *Iliad* II, 204.
20. *Loc. cit.*
21. *Loc. cit.*
22. *Phys.* VIII, 6, 259a, 6–13.
23. *Ibid.*, 13–20.
24. *Ibid.*, 259b, 7–12.
25. Cf. *Metaph.* XII, 8, 1074a, 10–12.
26. Jaeger, p. 361.

27. *Metaph.* XII, 8, 1073a, 23–24.
28. *Ibid.*, 30.
29. *Ibid.*, 24–25.
30. *Ibid.*, 26–27.
31. *Ibid.* Cf. comments in J. Paulus, "La théorie du premier moteur chez Aristote", *Revue de Philosophie*, N.S., 4 (1933), p. 418, nn. 34 and 35, and I. Dockx, "De Theorie van den Onbewogen Beweger bij Aristoteles", *Tijdschrift voor Philosophie*, 1 (1939), p. 771, n. 30.
32. *Ibid.*, 1073b, 1–3; cf. Latin translation of Averroës' Long Commentary on *Metaphysics*, Comm. 44 (in *Aristotelis Opera*, Venice, 1574), fol. 327 E: *et secunda et tertia secundum ordinem orbium.*
33. *De Caelo* I, 8, 276a, 31.
34. *Ibid.*, 277a, 3–4.
35. Cf. *Phys.* III, 5, 204b, 10; *Metaph.* XI, 10, 1066b, 26.
36. *De Caelo* I, 8, 277b, 9–10.
37. Cf. *Metaph.* V, 6, 1016b, 33.
38. *Topica* VI, 6, 145a, 13–18.
39. *Metaph.* XII, 8, 1073b, 1–3.
40. *Aristotle's Metaphysics* (1924), Vol. 1, Introduction, pp. cxxxix–cxl.
41. *Ibid.*, p. cxl.
42. *Metaph.*, V 6, 1016b, 36.
43. Jaeger, p. 353.
44. *Ibid.*, pp. 351–352.
45. *Ibid.*, p. 353, n. 1.
46. A. Mansion, "La genèse de l'œuvre d'Aristote", *Revue Neo-Scolastique de Philosophie* 29 (1927), p. 341.
47. René Mugnier, *La Théorie du Premier Moteur et l'Évolution de la Pensée Aristotélicienne*, 1930, p. 177.
48. Philip Merlan, "Aristotle's Unmoved Movers", *Traditio* 4 (1946), pp. 9–10.
49. *Ibid.*, p. 11.
50. Cf. my discussion in *The Philosophy of The Church Fathers*, I (1956), pp. 287–298 and 202–204.
51. *Moreh Nebukim* II, Introduction, Prop. XVI.
52. *Categ.* 12, 14b, 10–13; *Metaph.* V, 11, 1019a, 1–14.
53. *Categ.* 12, 14b, 4–5.
54. *Categ.* 13, 14b, 24–26.
55. Latin translation of *al-Shifā'*, in Avicenna's *Opera* (Venice, 1508), *Metaph.* IX, 4, fol. 104 vb, ll. 60–62; corresponding passage in *al-Najāt* (Cairo, 1331 A.H.), p. 454, ll. 12–13, and Latin translation in *Avicennae Metaphysices Compendium* by N. Carame (Rome, 1926), p. 194, ll. 17–18.
56. *Metaph.* XII, 8, 1073b, 1–3.
57. Latin translation of Averroës' Long Commentary on *Metaphysics* XII, Comm. 44, fol. 327F; cf. G.
58. Cf. *Averroës: Tafsir ma ba'd at-tabi'at* (ed. M. Bouyges, Vol. III, 1948), p. 1647, l. 3; cf. ll. 14–15.
59. Cf. *Averroës*: *Talkhiç, kitab al-maqoulat* (ed. M. Bouyges, 1932), p. 112, l. 641, on *Categ.* 12, 14b, 7.
60. *Tahāfut al-Tahāfut* III (*Tahafot at-Tahafot*, ed. M. Bouyges, 1930), § 81, p. 186, l. 6-p. 187, l. 3.

61. *In De Caelo* II, Comm. 49, fols. 131 E–132 B.
62. *Ibid.*, fol. 131 L.
63. Latin translation of *al-Shifā'*, in *op. cit.*, fol. 105 ra, l. 18; corresponding passage in *al-Najāt*, p. 455, l. 14, and Carame's Latin translation, in *op. cit.*, p. 196, l. 8.
64. *Ibid.*, fol. 105 rb, ll. 12–13; *al-Najāt*, p. 459, l. 4; Carame, p. 200, l. 20.
65. *Op. cit.*, fol. 132A.
66. *Tahāfut al-Tahāfut* I, § 82, p. 49, ll. 7–9.
67. Metaph. X, 3, and Averroës' Long Commentary X, Comm. 10–12 (both Latin and Arabic in *op. cit.*); cf. *Metaph.* V, 9, and Averroës' *Epitome of the Metaphysics* (Arabic and Spanish in *Averroës: Compendio de Metafisica*, ed. Quirós, 1919), 1, §§ 44 and 48.
68. *Epitome of the Metaphysics* I, § 48.
69. *Porphyrii Isagoge*, ed. A. Busse, 1887, p. 5, l. 5; Latin translation from the Hebrew of Averroës' Middle Commentary, in *op. cit.*, fol. 6 G sqq.
70. Cf. *Categ.* 2, 1b, 3–7.
71. *Epitome of the Metaphysics* I, § 40.
72. Cf. *De Caelo* II, 7, and Averroës, *ad loc.*, Comm. 41, fol. 124.
73. Long Commentary on *De Caelo* II, Comm. 59, fol. 138 F.
74. *Qu. Disp. de Spiritualibus Creaturis*, 8, Obj. and ad 16; *Qu. Disp. de Anima* 3, Obj. and ad 6.
75. *Cont. Gent.* II, 95; cf. *Qu. Disp. de Spir. Creat.* 8, ad 16; *Qu. Disp. de Anima* 3, ad 6.
76. *Qu. Disp. de Spirit. Creat.*, 8 c, Secunda.
77. *Cont. Gent.* II, 95, *Patet etiam; Qu. Disp. de Anima* 3, ad 6.
78. *Sum. Theol.* I, 50. 4; *Qu. Disp. de Spirit, Creat.* 8.
79. Cf. *Metaph.* X, 3, 1054b, 30.
80. *De Ente et Essentia* 5.
81. *Expositio in De Caelo* II, Lectio XVI, No. 9 (Leonine ed., Rome, 1886).
82. *Expositio in Metaphysicam* XII, Lectio IX, No. 2560 (ed. M.-R. Cathala, Turin, 1915).
83. *Ibid.*, No. 2562.
84. *Op. cit.*, 1074a, 14–16.

2

THE PROBLEM OF THE SOULS OF THE SPHERES FROM THE BYZANTINE COMMENTARIES ON ARISTOTLE THROUGH THE ARABS AND ST. THOMAS TO KEPLER

Kepler, who, as we all know, lived under the new heaven created by Copernicus, discusses the question whether the planets are moved by Intelligences or by souls or by nature.[1] His consideration of Intelligences as possible movers of the planets refers to a view held by those who in the Middle Ages lived under the old Ptolemaic heaven, the term Intelligences being, by a complexity of miscegenation, a descendant of what Aristotle describes as incorporeal substances. His consideration of souls or nature as possible movers of the planets touches upon a topic which was made into a problem by the Byzantine Greek commentators of Aristotle.

In this paper I shall try to show how the Byzantine commentators, in their study of the text of Aristotle, were confronted with a certain problem, how they solved that problem, and how their solution of that problem led to other problems and solutions, all of which lingered in philosophic literature down to Kepler.

I

In Aristotle, a distinction is made between external and internal movers of the celestial bodies. The terms external and internal are used here for what Aristotle would have designated by the terms "separate" (χωριστά) and "inseparate" (οὐ χωριστά), that is, "incorporeal" and "corporeal," or for what those of us who like to use more fashionable terms would call "transcendent" and "immanent."

This paper was delivered at the Symposium on "The History of Byzantine Science," held at Dumbarton Oaks in May 1961.

Of these two kinds of movers, the external ones are directly dealt with by Aristotle in his discussion of the substances which move the spheres in *Metaphysics* XII, 8. They are said by him to be of the same kind as that first substance, called mind,[2] which in the preceding chapter is described by him as "eternal and immovable and separate (κεχωρισμένη) from sensible things."[3] Like that first substance, which has been described by him in the preceding chapter as producing motion as a final cause,[4] these substances too may be assumed to produce motion as final causes. But, unlike the first substance, which is said by him to be immovable both essentially and accidentally, these substances, Aristotle intimates, are immovable only essentially but are movable accidentally.[5] The accidental motion which he attributes to these substances is, however, of a special kind. As explained by him in the *Physics*,[6] it is unlike the accidental motion of the souls of animal beings. The souls of animal beings are moved accidentally by the very motions which they produce in their respective spheres; whereas these substances are moved accidentally not by the motions which they themselves produce in their respective spheres but rather by the motions which are produced in those spheres by the first sphere.[7]

With regard to the inner movers of the spheres, however, the Byzantine commentators found in Aristotle two sets of contradictory statements.

In *De Caelo* I, 2, they found that Aristotle, after starting with the statement that "bodies are either simple or compounded; and by simple bodies I mean those which possess a principle of motion in their own nature, such as fire and earth and the species of these, and whatever is akin to them,"[8] leads up to the conclusion that "there must necessarily be some simple body which revolves naturally and in virtue of its own nature with a circular motion."[9] Commenting upon Aristotle's statement about simple bodies, Simplicius says that the expression "simple bodies" is used by Aristotle in contradistinction to "animals," for, while both simple bodies and animals possess a principle of motion, that of the former is "according to nature alone" whereas that of the latter is "according to soul"[10] and, commenting further upon the statement "and whatever is akin to them," he quotes with approval Alexander's interpretation that Aristotle means by it the other two elements "fire" and "air" and also "the fifth body," that is, the celestial element, for the fifth body, Alexander remarks, "is also a natural body." [11] Thus, according to Aristotle in these statements, the circular motion of the celestial bodies, like the rectilinear motion of the sublunar elements, is not by soul but by nature.

Similarly in *De Caelo* II, 1, after rejecting various explanations for the eternity of the motion of the heaven, Aristotle says, "Nor, again, is it conceivable that it should persist eternally by the necessitation of a soul." [12]

Yet in several other places Aristotle explicitly says that the celestial bodies are living beings and hence possess a soul. Thus, in one place he says that "the heaven is animate (ἔμψυχος) and possesses a principle of motion." [13] In another place he says "in dependence upon the heaven all other things have their existence and their life, some more directly, others more obscurely," [14] which, of course, implies that the heaven itself possesses life and hence a soul. In two other passages, speaking of the stars, which the commentators assume not to differ from the spheres in the nature of their motion, Aristotle says: "We," that is to say, we philosophers, "have been thinking of the stars as mere bodies, and as units which possess an order indeed, but are entirely inanimate. We ought, however, to consider them as partaking of action and life" [15] and also that "we must then think of the action of the stars as similar to that of animals and plants." [16]

And so the Byzantine commentators were confronted with two sets of contradictory statements. This gave rise to two interpretations among them.

One interpretation, which is quoted by Simplicius, reads as follows: "Some philosophers who are revered by me think that the heaven is said by Aristotle to be animate (ἔμψυχον) only in the sense that it has life congenital (σύμφυτον) with its body, according to which it has a principle of motion, but not in the sense that it has a rational soul (λογικὴν ψυχήν)." [17]

This passage makes two assertions. First, it asserts that Aristotle's description of the heaven as "animate" should not be taken literally as meaning that, like an animal, the heaven has a soul distinct from its body. It means only that, like an animal, it is moved by a principle of motion which is within itself, but that inner principle of motion is the nature of the body itself, to which life and motion are congenital. Second, it asserts that this denial to the heaven of a soul distinct from its body means not only the denial of a motive soul but also the denial of a rational soul.

Of these two assertions, the first would seem to be only the rephrasing of a statement by Alexander, to be quoted later, that in the case of the heaven "nature is the same as soul." [18] The second assertion, however, does not represent the view of Alexander, for, as we shall see later, while Alexander indeed maintains that the soul of the heaven is the same as its nature and while to that soul, which is the same as nature, he denies a nutritive and sensitive faculty, he does not deny to it a rational faculty; he maintains only that the rational soul of the heaven, like the rational soul of all living beings, is not something distinct from, and other than, the body, but rather a function of the nature of the body of rational living beings.[19] Furthermore, Simplicius usually quotes Alexander by name, and it would therefore seem strange that he should conceal here the identity of Alexander under the vague and general term "some philosophers."

Who, then, were those philosophers revered by Simplicius who specifically denied that heaven had a rational soul?

Let us assemble all those who before Simplicius denied that the heaven had either a soul in general, possibly including a rational soul, or a rational soul in particular and see whether it was they, all or some of them, that Simplicius could be referring to here.

First, there is Anaxagoras, who is said to have been "indicted by Cleon on a charge of impiety, because he declared the sun to be a mass of red-hot metal," [20] which, as we may gather from Augustine, means that he declared that the sun, and for that matter any other heavenly body, was "neither a god nor even a living body." [21]

Second, there are those anonymous philosophers who are hinted at by Philo when, in the course of his attempt to prove the limitation of human reason by the fact that philosophers are in disagreement among themselves, he raises the following question: "Are the stars animate and intelligent, or are they devoid of intelligence and soul?" [22] This evidently shows that Philo had knowledge of certain philosophers who denied that the stars had a rational soul.

Third, there are Democritus and Epicurus. A fragmentary statement in the *De Placitis Philosophorum,* which was completed by modern scholars, reads: "Democritus and Epicurus say that the heavens [are irrational]." [23]

Fourth, there is Basil, who argues that "the heavens are not alive . . . nor the firmament a sensible animal," and from the context it may be further inferred that, like the waters above the heaven, they are not "intelligent beings." [24]

Fifth and finally, there is John Philoponus, a contemporary of Simplicius and often quoted by him, who, speaking not as a philosopher in one of his commentaries on Aristotle but rather as a Christian in a theological work, denies that the heaven is moved by a soul or even by angels.[25] The denial of "a soul" is in opposition to those Aristotelian commentators who, as we shall see, attributed a soul to the heaven; his denial of "angels," however, is in opposition to at least two Christian theologians who described angels as movers of the celestial bodies. Thus Theodore of Mopsuestia, commenting on the verse, "For by Him were all things created, that are in heaven, and that are in earth, visible and invisible, whether they be thrones, or dominions, or principalities, or powers" (Col. 1:16), says that "some of them command the air, some the sun, some the moon, some the stars, and some some others, in order that they may move all things in accordance with the task imposed upon them by God, to the end that things may exist together." [26] Similarly Cosmas in his comment on the verse, "[Wherein in time past you walked according to the course of this world], according to the prince of the power of the air, the spirit that now worketh in the children of disobedience" (Eph. 2:2), says that "some of the angels were commissioned to move the air, some the sun, some the moon, and some the stars." [27]

These, however, whether all or some of them, could not be those whom Simplicius meant by "the philosophers" who were "revered" by him, for the revered philosophers referred to by him were interpreters of Aristotle, whereas all those I have quoted expressed their own opinion. John Philoponus, in addition, would not have been described as "revered" by him. Among interpreters of Aristotle prior to Simplicius, there was none, as far as I know, who explicitly denied that the celestial bodies had a rational soul. I should like to suggest that the philosophers quoted here by Simplicius were associates of his in the school of Athens during the last years of its existence in the sixth century, prior to its being closed by the order of Justinian in 529. Probably the philosophers quoted by Simplicius started as followers of Alexander's interpretation of Aristotle, but then, either unconsciously misunderstanding the real meaning of Alexander's interpretation or consciously departing from it, they attributed to Aristotle the view of directly denying that the heaven had a "rational soul." Hence, according to this interpretation, the true view of Aristotle was contained in the statements that speak of the heaven as being moved by nature; the passages that speak of the heaven as being animate were to be explained in the same spirit.

The other interpretation is that which takes the passages speaking of the heaven as animate to represent the true view of Aristotle. This interpretation is advanced by Simplicius himself in his criticism of those anonymous revered philosophers whom he has quoted. In his criticism, he starts out by saying, "I think I have a right to ask them, in the first place, to take into consideration the fact that Aristotle has said that some things are animate and others natural." [28] This reference by Simplicius to what Aristotle had said was not meant by him to be a verbal quotation, but rather a general reference to Aristotle's distinction between things that have a soul and things that have no soul, which may be gathered from many places in his writings. Then quoting the passage about the stars, reproduced *supra*,[29] he shows that Aristotle himself has rejected the view that stars are "entirely inanimate" (ἀψύχων πάμπαν), maintaining that we ought to consider them as "participating of action and life," upon which he himself remarks that "to act, according to Aristotle, belongs to the rational soul." [30]

Thus, according to Simplicius' interpretation of Aristotle, the celestial bodies have a rational soul. This interpretation has its precedents in the Greek commentaries on Aristotle.

The earliest occurrence of this interpretation is in Theophrastus' lost treatise *On the Heaven,* which is reported by Proclus in his commentary on the *Timaeus* (35 A) as follows: "For he grants that the heaven is animate and on this account divine. For, if it is divine, he says, and has the most excellent manner of being, it is animate, since nothing is esteemed honorable without a soul, as he writes in his treatise *On the Heaven* (περὶ οὐρανοῦ)." [31]

But if this represents Theophrastus' final view on the subject, he must have arrived at it after the composition of his *Metaphysics,* for in the *Metaphysics,*[32] in the course of his discussion of Aristotle's view that the Prime Mover moves the celestial spheres as an object of appetite or desire (τὸ ὀρεκτικὸν),[33] he argues against this view on account of its implication that celestial bodies possess appetence or desire, for which he uses the Greek terms ὄρεξις and ἔφεσις indiscriminately.[34] He starts his argument as follows: "And if appetence or desire (ἔφεσις), especially that towards what is best, involves a soul, then unless one is speaking by way of similitude, the things that move must be possessed of a soul; but . . . ," [35] and here follow the arguments against it. Later, confining himself to the outermost sphere, he says, "One might perhaps raise the question, with reference to the first heaven itself, whether its rotation is of its essence (τῆς οὐσίας . . . or whether . . . its rotation depends on a desire and appetence (ἐφέσει καὶ ὀρέξει) . . . unless indeed appetence (τὸ ὀρέγεσθαι) is congenital (σύμφυτον) with the first heaven." [36] Here then he suggests that, if the rotation of the outermost sphere is not "of its essence," that is to say, is not by nature, but by "desire and appetence," that is to say, by a soul, then the desire or appetence or soul may be assumed to be "congenital" with the body of that sphere. This suggestion is a direct anticipation of the view of Alexander, to which we have briefly referred *supra* [37] and which we shall discuss more fully later.[38]

The next interpretation of Aristotle's attributing souls to the spheres occurs in pseudo-Plutarch's *De Placitis Philosophorum,* which, according to Diels,[39] is based upon a work by a certain Aëtius, who flourished at about A.D. 100. According to this work,

Aristotle held that "the circumambient spheres are animate and living beings" [40] and "he calls the stars animals." [41]

Then comes Alexander of Aphrodisias, who in his commentary on the *Metaphysics,* like Theophrastus in his lost treatise *On the Heaven* quoted *supra,* argues that the heaven is animate, on the grounds, first, that the heaven is the best of all bodies, seeing that the eternal is better than the non-eternal, and, second, that the best of all bodies must be animate, seeing that an animate body is better than an inanimate one.[42]

The attribution of souls to the celestial bodies is also maintained by some Greek Church Fathers who flourished prior to Simplicius, such as Tatian [43] and Origen,[44] who probably reflected interpretations of Aristotle.

With the adoption of those statements in Aristotle which ascribe a soul to the heavens as representing the philosopher's true doctrine, there arose the question of explaining the other passages in which he describes the rotation of the heaven as being by nature. On this, two views were put forward.

First, there was the view of Alexander as quoted by Simplicius in his commentary on the *Physics* from Alexander's lost commentary on Book II of *De Caelo,* which reads as follows: "We shall endeavor to show that in the divine body nature is not one thing and soul another thing, but the soul in it is nature as is the heaviness of the earth and the lightness of the fire." [45] Again, in his commentary on *De Caelo,* without mentioning the source, Simplicius cites Alexander as maintaining that "nature there [in the heaven] is the same as soul." [46] Speaking for himself, in a work which is not extant in the original Greek but exists in an Arabic translation,[47] Alexander starts out by stating that "every natural body has in its essence a principle of motion," which principle of motion he calls "nature" and then adds that everything that is moved essentially by nature, "whether animate (*mutanaffis* = ἔμψυχος) or inanimate is moved by an *ishtiyāq* for something." [48] The same view is later extended by him to the celestial spheres.[49]

The first thing we have to clear up in this passage is to find out what Greek term lies behind the Arabic term *ishtiyāq,* to which the motion of both animate and inanimate things is ascribed. The term *ishtiyāq* ordinarily means "desire" and hence one would be tempted to assume that it renders the Greek ὄρεξις or ἐπιθυμία for these two terms are most often used by Aristotle as sources of motion. But a later statement in the text excludes either of these possibilities. This later statement says that among bodies which are moved by *ishtiyāq* some are more perfect and possess 'a soul,' but in their case the *ishtiyāq* by which their motion is effected "is accompanied by a certain *shahwah,* and of this *shahwah* one aspect is called 'desire' (*shauq*), another is called anger (*ghaḍab*), and still another is called will (*irādah*)." [50] Now the *shahwah* which in Alexander's statement is subdivided into "desire," "anger," and "will" quite evidently reflects Aristotle's statement that "appetence (ὄρεξις) is desire (ἐπιθυμία), anger (θυμός), and will (βούλησις)." [51] Since, according to these two parallel statements, *shahwah* in the passage of Alexander stands for the Greek ὄρεξις,[52] the term *ishtiyāq,* which is said by Alexander to be accompanied by a certain *shahwah,* of which one element is *shauq,* can be neither the Greek ὄρεξις nor the Greek ἐπιθυμία. Moreover, both ὄρεξις and ἐπιθυμία are always used by Aristotle as faculties of the soul and are always applied by him only to animate beings and never, as in Alexander here, to inanimate beings. With regard to ὄρεξις, there is a passage in which Aristotle explicitly denies that it is applicable to inanimate beings. In that passage, alluding to a view according to which numbers have a desire (ἐφίενται) for unity, Aristotle argues that "no-one says distinctly how they desire," and concludes with the challenge: "And how can one suppose that there is appetence (ὄρεξις) where there is no life?" [53]

Hence evidently the Arabic *ishtiyāq* does not stand here for either of these two Greek terms. What Greek term, then, does it stand for?

An answer to this question is to be found in a passage in Aristotle's *Eudemian Ethics*. In that passage, Aristotle first says that "inanimate things," such as "a stone and fire," may be moved "according to nature and their essential impulse (ὁρμήν)," that is to say, they are moved by nature and impulse, when the stone moves downward and fire upward, and are not compelled by some external force to move in directions opposite to these. Then he says that similarly "animate things" may be moved by their own internal "impulse," that is to say, they are moved by impulse, when they are not compelled to move contrary to it by some external force. But then he draws a distinction between inanimate and animate things. In the case of the natural motion of inanimate things, the principle of their motion is simple: it is the aforesaid "impulse." In the case of animate things, the "impulse" is accompanied either by "appetence" (ὄρεξις) or by "appetence" plus "reason" (λόγος).[54]

In these statements, then, the term ὁρμή is used by Aristotle as the source of motion in both inanimate and animate beings, but in the case of animate beings this ὁρμή is accompanied by ὄρεξις. Consequently, when Alexander, in the Arabic version of his work, says that both inanimate and animate beings are moved by *ishtiyāq* and that in the case of animate beings *ishtiyāq* is accompanied by a certain *shahwah,* which we have shown to mean ὄρεξις, the term *ishtiyāq* quite evidently stands for the Greek ὁρμή. Alexander himself, it may be added, explains his use of the Greek term underlying the Arabic *ishtiyāq* in the following statement: "This *ishtiyāq* [in the case of the elements] which proceeds from their natural predisposition (*tahayyu'*) is their inclination (*mayl*) for a thing which is, as it were, suited for them," and that suitable thing for which the elements have an inclination, he goes on to say, is the "natural place which is appropriate" to every one of the four elements.[55] This reflects a passage in Aristotle where, after stating that "we call things heavy and light because they have the power of being moved naturally in a certain way," that is to say, either downward or upward, he adds: "The activities corresponding to these powers have not been given any name, unless it is thought that inclination (ῥοπὴν) is such a name." [56] If we are right in our assumption that *ishtiyāq* is the Greek ὁρμή, then Alexander's explanation of it by ῥοπή would mean that he used these two terms in the same sense. It may be remarked that in the Latin translation of Aristotle both these terms are translated by *impetus*.[57]

Alexander goes on to say that the celestial sphere, because it is the most perfect of bodies, must be animate (*mutanaffisah*),[58] and as such it is moved by a certain "appetence" (*shahwah* =

ὄρεξις).[59] But then he proceeds to point out some differences between sublunar animate bodies and the celestial sphere. First, in the case of sublunar animate bodies, as he has said, the "appetence" results from "desire" and "anger," whereas in the case of the celestial sphere, "desire and anger are separated from the nature of that body." [60] Second, while it is true that some of the sublunar animate bodies enjoy "free choice" (*iḫtiyār*), their free choice results from "anger" and "desire," whereas the free choice of the celestial sphere results from "the love of the good." [61] Finally, he says, the circular motion of the celestial body is indeed "by a nature which is peculiar to it," [62] but "it must not be believed that its nature is something other than soul, and so also it must not be believed, with regard to composite living bodies, that their nature, by reason of its being that of living creatures, is something other than soul," [63] adding, however, that, while in composite animate bodies there is a bodily nature which is different from the nature which is their soul, in the celestial sphere there is only one nature, and that nature is its soul.[64]

Thus Alexander does not deny that the celestial sphere possesses a soul; he contends only that "soul," both in the case of the celestial spheres and in the case of sublunar animate beings, is just a name given to the natures peculiar to them, and it is by these peculiar natures of theirs that they perform their peculiar kinds of motion, which differ from the kinds of motion performed by the natures peculiar to the four elements.

Alexander is opposed by Simplicius. Asserting that soul and nature are not the same, and further maintaining that Aristotle in his apparently contradictory statement really meant that the heaven is moved both by a soul and by nature, he goes on to say: "If somebody asks, how, on the one hand, nature moves the heaven and how, on the other, soul moves it, it is not to be said as Alexander has said, namely, that nature there is the same as soul. For how can it be the same, when nature is a passive power of that which is moved, existing in a subject which is moved, whereas soul is that which causes motion from without (ἔξωθεν). It is, therefore, not to be said that soul and nature in the heaven are the same but rather that the same motion is moved according to both [soul and nature], that is to say, by soul as by something which causes motion from without (ἔξωθεν) and by nature as by a principle inherent in that which is moved." [65] The term "from without" (ἔξωθεν), by which he describes here the motion caused by a soul, should not, in my opinion, be taken literally, for Aristotle quite definitely describes the soul of animals as a "principle of motion in themselves." [66] What Simplicius means by this description is that the soul as the mover of the heaven is something distinct from, and other than, the body of the heaven, in which respect it differs from "nature" which is not anything distinct from, and other than, the body of the heaven. Thus also Aristotle, after describing the soul as a principle of motion in the animal itself, goes on to say that the soul is distinct and different from the body of the animal, which he expresses by saying that in animals "that which causes motion [namely, the soul] is separate (διῃρημένον) from that which suffers motion [namely, the body]." [67]

Further explanation of soul and nature as being the joint movers of the heaven is to be found in a passage in which Simplicius says: "The natural and animate whole is appropriately moved by the soul through nature as a medium, for nature is a certain life, an aptitude and disposition existing in its subject, the body, so as to enable bodies to be moved by a soul, and through itself as a medium nature conveys the motive power of the soul to the body." [68]

Still further in the same passage he tries to justify Aristotle's description of the motion of the heaven as being natural, despite its being moved by a soul, by referring to Aristotle's use of the term "natural" in two passages of his writings. First, he says, his own interpretation of the term "natural" as meaning that the soul of the heaven uses the nature of its body as a medium "is in conformity, I think, with the teaching of Aristotle, for he says that soul is the entelechy of a natural body." [69] Second, he says, the term "natural" may have been used by Aristotle "in the sense of its having a natural and not a violent motion and, according to it, an aptitude to be moved," [70] evidently expecting us to add that this is in conformity with Aristotle's use of the term "natural" (φύσει) as the opposite of "violent" (βίᾳ) and unnatural (παρὰ φύσιν). [71]

This then is Simplicius' explanation of how Aristotle could describe the motion of the heaven as being both by nature and by soul. Sometimes, however, Simplicius, like Alexander as well as Aristotle himself, uses the term "inclination" as the equivalent of the term "nature." Thus he says: "If, therefore, velocity is produced through natural inclinations (φυσικὰς ῥοπάς) and some things are moved upward, on account of having more levity, and others downward, in consequence of having more gravity, it is evident that gravity and levity existing inwardly, as natural powers (φυσικαὶ δυνάμεις), will receive an infinite addition." [72] Here, then, the expression "natural inclinations" is used as the equivalent of the expression "natural powers" as the cause of the upward and downward motions of the elements.

But here a new question came up. Soul in Aristotle is a general term which includes three kinds of soul, with their respective faculties: (1) the vegetable soul, with its faculties of nutrition and reproduction; (2) the animal soul, with its five external senses as well as imagination and memory; (3) the human soul, distinguished by its faculty of reason. When, therefore, the commentators decided that the celestial bodies were, according to Aristotle, moved by souls, they began to play a sort of charade and asked themselves, what kind of a besouled body is a celestial body? Is it a vegetable? Is it an animal? Is it a human being? In answer to this question, they all agreed that it is not a vegetable, for, as Alexander says, the soul of the sphere has no nutritive faculty,[73] and to this there is no opposition. The reason for this is to be found in Aristotle's view that one of the functions of the nutritive faculty is the reproduction of the species [74] and, in fact, he even says that the nutritive faculty is the same as the reproductive faculty.[75] But this faculty of nutrition and reproduction, Aristotle further says, exists in living beings for a definite purpose, its purpose being to preserve the existence of the various species of living beings, seeing that as individuals they are all subject to extinction.[76] Since, therefore, the nutritive faculty is needed only to preserve the species of beings which individually have no eternal existence, it is not needed in celestial bodies, which, according to Aristotle, are individually eternal.[77]

When it came, however, to the question whether the celestial bodies were animals endowed with sensation, two opposite views were expressed by the early Greek commentators and these two views found their partisans among the later Byzantine commentators.

These two views among the early Greek commentators are reflected in two readings in pseudo-Plutarch's *De Placitis Philosophorum*. According to one reading, adopted by Diels on the basis of the testimonia of Eusebius and Cyril of Alexandria, Aristotle is reported to have held the following view: "The whole world is not besouled in every part of it, nor is it rational (λογικόν) and intellectual (νοερόν), nor is it governed by providence in every part of it. Of all of these, however, the heavens are made partakers." [78] From this reading in the first part of the passage, it is quite evident that the heavens are assumed to be partakers only of the "rational" or "intellectual" faculty of the soul. According to some manuscripts, however, and according to Galen, the reading in the first part of the passage is "nor is it sensitive, rational, and intellectual," which makes the heavens partakers also of sensation. Thus from the Doxography of Aëtius we gather that there may have been two interpretations of Aristotle on this point at about the end of the first century.

The same two interpretations of Aristotle are to be found also among his commentators of the early part of the second century, Plutarch of Chaeronea (*ca.* A.D. 46–120) and Alexander of Aphrodisias (fl. 198–211).

Plutarch of Chaeronea, in a passage which is not written in the form of a commentary on Aristotle but which was quite evidently meant to reproduce what was believed to be the view of Aristotle, speaks of the senses of "seeing and hearing" as celestial and divine, which would imply that he attributed to the celestial bodies the sense of seeing and of hearing.[79]

Alexander of Aphrodisias, however, is quoted by Simplicius as maintaining that the soul of heaven has no sensitive faculty any more than it has a nutritive faculty and, inasmuch as any being, if it is to be called animal, must have sensation, he concludes, that the heaven and the stars, though called by Aristotle "animate beings" (ὄντα ἔμψυχα), cannot be called living beings (ζῷα) except in an equivocal sense,[80] that is to say, they are said to possess a soul only in an equivocal sense.

This interpretation of Aristotle is unfolded by Alexander more fully in a comment on a passage of Aristotle's *De Anima,* which is quoted from his lost commentary on that work by Simplicius and Philoponus.[81]

The Aristotelian passage in question consists of four statements:

A. "Sensation is not necessarily present in all living beings" (*De Anima* III, 12, 434a, 22–23), for, as it goes on to say, plants have nutrition but have no sensation.

B. "It is not possible that a body capable of motion but produced by generation should have a soul and a discriminating intelligence without also having sensation" (434b, 2–3), that is to say, no human being can be without sensation.

C. "Nor yet even not produced by generation" (*ἀλλὰ μὴν οὐδὲ ἀγένητον*) (434b, 4–5), that is to say, neither a heavenly body which is capable of motion but is eternal.

D. This is immediately followed by a statement, which Alexander read as follows: "For why should it have (*διὰ τί γὰρ ἕξει*)? Presumably it would be better so either for the soul or for the body. But clearly it would not be better for either, for the soul will not on account of that be better able to think and the body will be no better off" (434b, 5–8).

Now Alexander takes statement *D* to refer, not to statement *C,* which immediately precedes it, but rather to statement *B,* and accordingly interprets the passage as follows: *A* Sensation is not present in plants, *C* nor is it present in the celestial bodies, *D* for why should the celestial bodies have sensation, when it would not do any good either to their souls or to their bodies, for sensation, according to Aristotle, is needed by animals either for the sake of their being or for the sake of their well-being,[82] but the celestial bodies are described by Aristotle as "eternal," as "not being subject to increase and diminution," as "not growing old," as "unchanging in quality," and as "impassive,"[83] and consequently there is nothing which is needed by them either for their being or for their well-being.

A similar division of opinion is to be found also among the Byzantine commentators, such as Plutarch of Athens, Philoponus, Simplicius, Olympiodorus, and Themistius.

Plutarch of Athens, as quoted by both Philoponus[84] and Simplicius[85] from his lost commentary on Aristotle's *De Anima,* differs from Alexander in his interpretation of the passage in *De Anima* II, 12, which we have divided into four statements. He takes statement *D* in that passage to refer to statement *C* which immediately precedes it, but instead of Alexander's reading "For why should it have?", he has the reading "For why should it not have (*διὰ τί γὰρ οὐχ ἕξει*)?" Accordingly, he interprets statements *B, C,* and *D* as follows: *B* Human beings, because they are endowed with reason, cannot be without sensation, *C* nor can the celestial bodies be without sensation, *D* for why should the celestial bodies be without sensation, when the absence of sensation would not add anything that is good either for their soul or their body. He thus finds that Aristotle attributes sensation to the celestial bodies.

Philoponus follows Alexander in interpreting the passage in *De Anima* III, 12, as meaning that sensation is not required by the celestial bodies.[86]

Simplicius in his commentary on *De Anima* [87] interprets the passage quoted above like neither Alexander nor Plutarch of Athens. The passage, to him, does not contain any reference to the celestial bodies. Omitting statement *C,* namely, "Nor yet even not produced by generation," altogether, but following Alexander in the reading of the beginning of statement *D,* namely, "For why should it have?", he interprets the whole statement as follows: For why should a human being have a soul and a discriminating intelligence without also having sensation, when his not having sensation would not add anything that is good either for his soul or for his body? Here, then, Simplicius is opposed to an interpretation which would show that Aristotle attributed sensation to the celestial bodies.

However, elsewhere in his commentary on Aristotle's *De Anima,* Simplicius puts an interpretation upon a vague passage which enables him to infer that Aristotle did attribute sensation to the celestial bodies. In that passage, Aristotle begins with the statement that in plants there is only nutrition and that in animals there is also sensation, appetite, and locomotion, and then goes on to say, "But others, as, for instance, men or other beings similar to or superior to them, if there be any such, possess also the thinking faculty and intellect." [88] Commenting upon this statement, Simplicius says, "By the expression 'superior to them,' Aristotle means demons . . . as well as the celestial bodies, who have both sensation and appetence, which are not passive or roused by objects perceived as they strike the senses from without, but know and arrange all objects as something perceived from within." [89] It may be remarked that Simplicius' inclusion of the celestial bodies among those beings which are superior to men rests upon Aristotle's statement that "there are many other things more godlike in their nature than man, as, most obviously, the elements of which the cosmos is composed," [90] by which elements of which the cosmos is composed are meant the celestial bodies.[91]

In his comment on this passage, then, Simplicius, by taking the beings superior to men to include the celestial bodies, infers that Aristotle attributed to them sensation, though a sensation which is peculiar to themselves and is unlike that of other living bodies.

In still another place, in his commentary on *De Caelo,* Simplicius says, "It is to be wondered that the divine [celestial body] should be perceived by the senses and should be touched, as Alexander admits it to be, and yet should have no sensation. Is it because it is better for bodies not to have sense-perception? But sense-perception is found to belong to the lowest and vilest of animate (ἀψύχοις *sic*!) bodies. Perhaps, therefore, one is to deny [to the celestial bodies] the material and especially passive senses, namely, smell and taste, but to attribute to them the most accurate senses, for, touching each other, the celestial bodies do not touch without sensation, and they see all and hear all." [92] Recalling to our mind that Alexander in his comment on the passage in *De Anima* quoted *supra* tries to show that celestial bodies have no sensation on the ground that neither the soul nor the body of celestial bodies would be better off by the possession of sensation, Simplicius' argument to the effect that Alexander's denial of sensation implies that "it is better for bodies not to have sense-perception," would seem to be directed against this particular interpretation of Alexander's. Simplicius seems to challenge Alexander as follows: You argue that the celestial bodies need no sensation, because sensation is needed either for the being or the well-being of animals, whereas the celestial bodies need nothing either for their being or for their well-being; I argue that the celestial bodies have sensation, because those beings which possess sensation are better than those which do not possess sensation and the celestial bodies are the best of all beings.

A similar attribution to the celestial bodies of some, but not all, of the five senses is to be found in Olympiodorus, but the senses attributed by him to the celestial bodies are somewhat different from those attributed to them by Simplicius. In his commentary on Plato's *Phaedo,* after quoting Proclus as saying that the heavens have only the senses of seeing and hearing, Olympiodorus adds that this is also the view of Aristotle, giving the following explanation: "for of the senses they have only those which contribute to well-being (τὸ εὖ εἶναι), but not those which contribute to being (τὸ εἶναι)." [93]

Thus, according to Simplicius in one of his statements, Aristotle attributes to the celestial bodies the sense of touch, seeing, and hearing, which three senses he calls the most accurate, in contrast to smell and taste, which he describes as "material" and "passive"; whereas according to Olympiodorus, Aristotle attributes to them the senses of seeing and hearing, which he describes as contributing to "well-being," in contrast to smell and taste and touch, which are described as contributing to "being." Neither of these two divisions of the five senses corresponds to any of the divisions made by Aristotle himself. In one place, only touch is described by him as being "indispensable to the being (εἶναι) of an animal"; whereas all the other senses are only for the sake of "its well-being (τοῦ εὖ)." [94] In another place, Aristotle speaks of touch and taste as senses which are "necessary for the animal," [95] that is to say, for the sake of its being, whereas the other three senses are "for the sake of the well-being" of the animal.[96] In still another place, Aristotle speaks of "smelling, hearing, seeing" as existing both "for the sake of preservation" (σωτηρίας ἕνεκεν),[97] that is, "for the sake of being," and "for the sake of well-being" (τοῦ εὖ ἕνεκα).[98] Nowhere in Aristotle is there a distinction like that given by Simplicius, Proclus, and Olympiodorus. However, a distinction like that given here by Proclus and Olympiodorus is found twice in the work of Philo, who quotes it in the name of those whom he calls "the champions of the senses." Leaving out the sense of touch, because, as he says, it is common to the other four senses, he says of sight and hearing that they "are philosophic, and through them a good life is attained by us," and further that they "help the immortal mind" [99] and are the causes "of living well (καλῶς ζῆν)"; [100] whereas of the other two senses, smell and taste, he says that they are "non-philosophic . . . and have been created only for living" [101] or are only "causes of living." [102]

Finally, among the Byzantines there was Themistius, who followed Alexander in ascribing to Aristotle the denial of sensation to the celestial bodies, stating that "the two extreme types of living beings, namely, plants and stars, are bereft of sensation, the former because they are not good enough for that faculty; the latter because they are too good for it." [103]

While all these Byzantine commentators as well as their predecessors differed among themselves as to whether the celestial bodies possessed a sensitive soul, they all agreed that they possessed a rational soul. Aëtius, as we have seen, while denying them sensation, endows them with reason and intelligence. Alexander, who identifies soul with nature, denies them only nutrition and sensation. Simplicius endows them not only with a rational but also with a sensitive faculty. Philoponus who, while speaking for himself as a Christian, denies them a rational soul; speaking as a commentator of Aristotle, denies them on behalf of Aristotle only a sensitive faculty.

II

These were the interpretations of Aristotle's conception of the inner movers of the celestial bodies among his Greek commentators in the sixth century, a century before the rise of Islam. There was, on the one hand, the interpretation of Alexander which held that the celestial bodies were moved by their nature, also called soul, and that soul, which was the same as nature, was without sensation, though having a rational appetite; on the other hand, there was the Simplician interpretation which held that the celestial bodies were moved both by their nature and by a soul and that the soul, which was not the same as the nature, had sensation. About the middle of the eighth century translations from the Greek into Arabic began. In the course of time all the important Greek texts dealing with the inner movers of the spheres were available in Arabic: Aristotle's own works, Pseudo-Plutarch's *De Placitis Philosophorum,* Alexander's commentary on the *Metaphysics,* Themistius' commentaries on *De Caelo, De Anima,* and *Metaphysics,* Simplicius' and Philoponus' commentaries on *De Anima.* No mention is made by bibliographers of an Arabic translation of Olympiodorus' commentary on the *Phaedo* or of Simplicius' commentary on *De Caelo,* but this does not prove that no such translation existed or that the Arabic philosophers had no knowledge of the contents of these commentaries. Ibn Ḥazm, as we shall see, knew of the interpretation of Aristotle contained in them.

Through these translations the problem of the inner movers of the spheres was introduced into Arabic philosophy, where it was made into a subject of debate, which became involved in many other problems. I shall try to isolate the problem of the soul of the spheres from all the other problems to which it became related, and of this isolated problem I shall consider only two phases, namely, whether the soul is the same as nature or not, and whether it has sensation or not; furthermore, I shall deal with these two phases only insofar as they bear a relation to the Byzantine Greek commentaries. As protagonists of this problem in Arabic philosophy I shall take Avicenna and Averroes, but in the course of the discussion I shall introduce the views of other philosophers.

Avicenna begins his discussion of the inner mover, or, as he calls it, the "proximate agent" of the circular motion of the heavens with the statement that it is a "soul," so that the heaven is a living being (*ḥaywān* = *ζῷον*),[104] and proceeds to argue how that proximate agent cannot be a "nature."[105] This quite evidently reflects the view of Simplicius. Like Simplicius, too, he notes the passages in which Aristotle speaks of the motion of the celestial bodies as being by nature. The explanations he offers are again like those of Simplicius. First, their motion is described as being by nature in the sense that it is "not contrary to the necessitation of another nature inherent in their body," so that, while the soul which moves the spheres is not to be described as a "natural power," it is still to be described as a "natural cause."[106] Second, "every [motive] power causes motion through the medium of a certain inclination (*mayl* = ῥοπή)," [107] which inclination "is undoubtedly other than the motion and also other than the power which causes the motion," [108] and this is true also of the circular motion of the celestial bodies, so that in their case also, "the mover constantly produces in the body one inclination after another, and this inclination may very well be called nature, seeing that it is not a soul, nor anything extraneous, nor has it will or choice . . . and consequently, if you call that concept of inclination nature, you may then say that the celestial body is moved by nature." [109]

In this passage, Avicenna shows a knowledge of both Alexander and Simplicius. His discussion of "inclination" (*mayl*) is taken directly from Alexander's *Fī Mabādī' al-Kull,* which work he mentions elsewhere by title.[110] His statement that the celestial bodies are moved by a soul as well as by nature, and his two explanations of how they can be described as being moved by nature are exactly like the views of Simplicius.

Avicenna's opinion that the soul and the nature by which the celestial bodies are moved are two different principles is repeatedly opposed by Averroes in his various works. It happens that Aristotle's statement in *De Caelo* II, 2, 285a, 29, that "the heaven is animate (ἔμψυχος)" is in the Arabic version translated not literally *al-samā' mutanaffisah* but rather freely *al-samā' dhāt nafs,* "the heaven has a soul," so that in the Latin translation of the Arabic this statement reads *coelum habet animam.*[111] Accordingly, in his *Sermo de Substantia Orbis,* after showing that in the celestial sphere there does not exist the ordinary distinction of matter and form, whence also not the ordinary distinction of soul and body, he says: "The heaven is said to have a soul (*coelum habere animam*) only on account of appetence and locomotion which exist in it. It has appetence, however, only because of its being a celestial body that has life in virtue of its essence and is appetent in virtue of its essence, not because of a power in it which is [part of it and hence] divisible by the division of it. . . . Similarly, its motion is said to be due to an immaterial principle which is in it [without being part of it], and not to a principle which is in it as part of it. It is in this way that the celestial body is said to be living and intelligent," that is, it is said to be living and intelligent "in virtue of its essence." [112] This means that in the celestial bodies the soul is the same as their essence or nature.

Averroes expresses himself even more clearly elsewhere when he says that "the nature of this [celestial] body is nothing but the nature of the soul which causes motion in place," [113] and that "the forms of the celestial bodies, and especially the form of the last circumambient [sphere], are each in a certain sense a soul." [114]

Similarly in his Long commentary on the *Metaphysics* he says: "Inasmuch as Aristotle has said that the celestial substances have no matter (*'unṣur*), that is to say, their bodies are not composed of matter and form but are rather composed of body and an animate (*nafsāniyyah, animata*), intelligent form, not indeed as a living being (*nafs, anima* [*l*]) is an animate (*mutanaffis, animata*) thing, for in the latter case a thing is animated by means of a soul and is alive by means of life, but the celestial substances are animate in virtue of their essence and are alive in virtue of their essence." [115] This reflects the interpretation of Alexander, that the soul of the celestial bodies is identical with their nature.

In the light of all this, when in his *Epitome of the Metaphysics,* Averroes argues for the view that a celestial body must be animate and quotes in support of it Alexander's argument to the effect that "it is impossible that the noblest of animate beings should be inanimate," [116] the animatedness which he ascribes to the celestial body means that it possesses a soul which is identical with its nature. He restates Alexander's argument more carefully, without mentioning the name of Alexander, in his *Tahāfut al-Tahāfut*. He starts out by saying: "The soul which is in the celestial body has no subsistence (*qiwām*) in this body"; [117] in other words, it is not a soul in the same sense as soul of any living being. He then goes on to say: "For the celestial body is not in need of a soul for the continuance of its existence as are the bodies of animals; it is in need of a soul not because it is necessary for its existence to be animate but rather because that which is more excellent must necessarily be in a more excellent condition and to be animate is more excellent than not to be animate." [118] Elsewhere in the same work, drawing upon Ghazali's restatement of Avicenna's view as maintaining that that whose motion is not by nature is to be described as a "voluntary and animate" being, and that the celestial bodies are not to be described as "being moved by will," [119] Averroes paraphrases it to read that, "since the celestial body is not moved by nature, it is moved by a soul," to which he adds, evidently as an expression of his own view: "or by a power which resembles a soul," from which he infers "that the soul in the celestial bodies is described by the term soul only equivocally." [120] In other words, in contradistinction to Avicenna who, like Simplicius, endows the celestial bodies with a real soul which is different from their nature, Averroes, like Alexander, endows them with a soul which is identical with their nature and which is called soul only in an equivocal sense. As we have seen *supra,* according to Alexander, the celestial bodies, though described as "animate," are to be called "living beings" only in an equivocal sense, that is to say, they are said to possess a soul only in an equivocal sense.[121]

While on the question of the relation of soul to nature in the celestial bodies Avicenna sides with Simplicius and Averroes sides with Alexander, on the question whether the celestial bodies are moved by sensation both of them follow Alexander. Avicenna, to be sure, in the principal passages in which he discusses the problem of the souls of the spheres, does not definitely say that the souls have no sensation, but his denial of sensation in those passages may be inferred indirectly from his description of the circular motion of the heaven as caused by its proximate mover, the soul. In that description, he first says that "it is a motion due to an intellectual mobile (*'aqliyyah muntaqilah*) will" [122] and then from the fact that "it is impossible for our intellect to suppose such a mobility without the participation of imagination and sensation," [123] he infers that "we are not hindered from thinking that in the soul of the heaven there is also an intellectual power which undergoes that intellectual mobility after having based itself on something resembling imagination (*taḫayyul*)," [124] concluding that "the celestial sphere is moved by a soul, the soul being its proximate mover, and this soul is constantly undergoing change with reference to imagination (*taṣawwur*) and will." [125] Thus, like Alexander, he does not include sensation among the faculties of the soul of the heaven mentioned by him, though, without any precedent, he includes among them imagination—a problem which is outside the scope of our present discussion. Averroes, however, explicitly says that the celestial body is in no need of "a sensitive or imaginative soul." [126] He has an interpretation of his own of that passage in *De Anima* III, 12, 434b, 4–8, which, as we have seen, was differently explained by the Greek commentators. According to his interpretation, this passage, by implication, denies the existence of sensation in the celestial bodies.[127]

Besides Avicenna and Averroes, other Arab philosophers also discussed the problem of the souls of the spheres. Alfarabi, before Avicenna, endowed the celestial body with a soul, but that soul had neither sensation nor imagination.[128] Ibn Ḥazm, a younger contemporary of Avicenna, in a passage which betrays a knowledge of either Proclus or Olympiodorus,[129] or perhaps of Simplicius,[130] says, "Some people claim that the spheres and the stars have intelligence and that they only see and hear but do not taste and smell. This claim, however, is devoid of demonstration." [131] Ghazali, who lived after Avicenna but before Averroes, argues that the view that the heavens possess a soul is not impossible on religious grounds but on rational grounds it can be neither refuted nor demonstrated.[132] Avempace, who was a teacher of Averroes, is quoted as saying that "Aristotle was of the opinion that the sphere is moved by its own self," that is, by its own nature.[133]

Among Jewish philosophers writing in Arabic, Isaac Israeli, a contemporary of Alfarabi, in his description of the process of emanation, says that the celestial sphere, in the course of its emanation from the soul, "becomes intellectual and rational" [134] and from the context it is clear that it is through a union with the soul that the sphere becomes intellectual and rational. In Plotinus' system of emanation, which is the source of the emanational theory of both Alfarabi and Israeli, the heaven is described as an animate (ἔμψυχον) statue [135] and the world-soul is described as communicating movement and life to the heavens.[136] Saadia, another contemporary of Alfarabi, explicitly denies that the heaven is moved by a soul, but he does so not as a follower of those commentators who interpreted Aristotle in this light, but rather as a critic of Aristotle. Rejecting Aristotle's view that the heaven consists of a fifth element, he maintains that it consists of the element of fire, and argues that fire by its own nature moves circularly; hence he concludes that the circular motion of the heaven is by nature.[137] Of special interest is the view of Judah Halevi. In one place, he asserts that the heaven "is an instrument fully employed by the sole will of God, without the intervention of any intermediate causes." [138] In another place, however, dealing with the various orders of angels, he says that some angels "are lasting, and are perhaps those spiritual beings of which the philosophers speak, whose view we are obliged neither to refute nor to adopt," [139] which reminds one of Ghazali's dismissal of the view that the spheres are animate and rational beings as something which can be neither refuted nor demonstrated.[140] Similarly, in still another place, referring to the philosophic view that the celestial spheres are moved by souls and Intelligences and that the Intelligences are identical with the angels of Scripture, Judah Halevi dismisses it as "subtleties profitable only for speculation." [141] There is, however, a passage in which he enumerates the gradation of causes, trying to show how they all culminate in God, and among the gradated causes he mentions also "the causes of the celestial spheres." [142] What these causes are may be gathered from two other passages. In one passage he says that "the divine wise will ordains the rotation of the uppermost sphere, which . . . causes the other spheres to rotate along with it." [143] The same view, as expressed by him in another passage, states that it is God who causes "the uppermost sphere to carry along all the other spheres." [144] This last statement is almost a verbal reproduction of Aristotle's statement that "the sphere of the fixed stars carries along all the other spheres." [145] Inasmuch as, according to Aristotle, each inner sphere is moved by the sphere of the fixed stars through the intermediacy of the sphere immediately enclosing it, we may conclude that, according to Halevi, while the uppermost sphere is moved directly by God, the inner spheres are moved by the uppermost sphere through the intermediacy of the spheres immediately enclosing them. Abraham Ibn Daud [146] and Maimonides,[147] however, follow Alfarabi and Avicenna in ascribing the motion of the celestial bodies to both souls and Intelligences and in identifying the Intelligences with angels. Opposition to the souls of the spheres is also to be found in post-Maimonidean Hebrew philosophic writings.[148]

About twenty-seven years after the death of Averroes (1198), St. Thomas was born (1225–56). By the time St. Thomas composed the works in which he discusses the inner movers of the spheres, such as his commentary on the *Sentences* of Peter Lombard (1254–56), his *Contra Gentiles* (1264), his *Summa Theologica* (1266–73), and his commentary on *De Caelo* (1272), there were already Latin translations of Arabic works in which this problem was discussed, such as the so-called *Metaphysica* of Avicenna, translated by Dominic Gundisalvi from the *Shifā'* = *Sufficientia,* and Averroes' Long commentary on the *Metaphysics* as well as his *Sermo de Substantia Orbis.* But what is most important, there was a Latin translation, made directly from the Greek, of Simplicius' commentary on *De Caelo.*

References to the discussion of this problem in all of these sources are to be found in St. Thomas' Commentary on *De Caelo.* Mentioning Simplicius by name, he quotes his reference to those "who assumed that Aristotle had said that the heaven was animate not because it had a soul but in the sense that it had a certain life complanted (*complantatam* = *σύμφυτον*) with the body, so that there is not any soul in it except the nature of such a body." [149] The reference is quite clearly to those philosophers described by Simplicius as being revered by him.[150] Thomas then quotes Simplicius' refutation of this interpretation and approves of this refutation. Accordingly, he concludes, that "the motion of the heaven is both by its nature and by its soul, but by nature indeed as by a second and passive principle, insofar as a body of such a kind is by nature apt to be so moved, but by soul indeed as by a principal and active principle of motion." [151] This is exactly the view of Simplicius.[152]

He then raises the question whether the soul of the heaven has sensation. Evidently using Simplicius' commentary on the *De Caelo,* he quotes Alexander's view that "in the celestial bodies, if they are animate, the soul has no sensitive power, just as it has no nutritive power, whence they are called living things only in an equivocal sense, namely, on the ground that they have an intellective soul." [153] He also quotes Simplicius' argument why the celestial bodies should have sensation, concluding that "Simplicius therefore admits that the celestial bodies possess three senses, namely, sight, hearing, and touch, but he excludes from them the two other more material senses, namely, smell and taste." [154]

Between these two views, he favors that of the denial of sensation to the celestial body, for which he finds support in Aristotle's *Metaphysics* XII, 7, 1072a, 26–30 and *De Anima* II, 3, 415a, 8–9. Referring to the passage in *De Anima III,* 12, 434b, 4–8, which, as we have seen, was a subject of various interpretations, he gives preference to the interpretation which makes that passage deny sensation to the celestial bodies, mentioning in this connection Themistius and Averroes.[155]

Having established that, "if the celestial bodies are animate, they have an intellect without sensation," he proceeds to show by argument why they need no imagination, at the end of which he says, "And thereby is excluded the opposite view of Avicenna, who in his *Metaphysics* has shown that the soul of the celestial body must have imagination." [156]

So, following the Alexandrian interpretation of Aristotle as it filtered through the Latin translation of Simplicius' commentary on *De Caelo* and the Latin translations of the works of Avicenna, St. Thomas has arrived at the conclusion that the celestial bodies had a rational soul, free of sensation and imagination. This rational soul of the celestial bodies, though without sensation and imagination, had, like the rational soul of man, which is endowed with sensation and imagination, two functions, that of moving (*movere*) and that of understanding (*intelligere*).[157] But, unlike the human soul, which needs the body both for its moving and for its understanding,[158] the soul of the celestial sphere needed the body only for moving but not for understanding.[159] Accordingly, unlike the human soul which is related to the body as its form,[160] the soul of the celestial body, because it needed the body only for the performance of its function as a mover, "need not be united to the body as its form; but by contact of power (*per contactum virtutis*), as a mover is united to that which moves" [161] or, as he subsequently says, "by contact of some apprehending substance" (*ab aliqua substantia apprehendente*).[162] To justify his use of the term contact between the mover and object moved, even when the mover is not a body, he quotes Aristotle's statement to the effect that there is contact between the mover and the object moved even when the mover is not a body, except that, when the mover is not a body, the contact is only on the part of the object moved and not on the part of the mover.[163]

But, while in his *Summa Theologica* he maintains that the soul of the celestial body is united to its body not as its form but rather by a contact of power, in his earlier work, the *Contra Gentiles,* he explicitly says that the soul, or intellectual soul or intellectual substance as he calls it, "is united to the heavenly body as its form." [164] But there is more than that. While in his commentary on *De Caelo,* as well as in his *Contra Gentiles* and *Summa Theologica,* he describes the inner mover of the spheres as a soul, though only an intellectual soul, in his earliest work, the commentary on Peter Lombard's *Sentences,* he explicitly says, concerning the inner movers of the spheres, whom, following Avicenna,[165] he describes as proximate movers, that they are not souls but rather angels.[166] Still, following Aristotle, he believes that, besides inner or proximate movers, the celestial bodies also had outer or remote movers, called by Aristotle immovable substances and by the Arabs Intelligences. Since Thomas called the proximate movers angels, he calls the remote movers also angels. Angels as the movers of the spheres, as we have seen, were postulated by Theodore of Mopsuestia and Cosmas, and this view was rejected by Philoponus.[167] St. Thomas himself quotes St. Augustine as saying that "if the heavenly bodies are animate, their souls belong to the fellowship of angels." [168] This, it may be remarked, is not exactly what St. Augustine says; it is St. Thomas' own interpretation of St. Augustine's statement that "if the luminaries of heaven have spirits which govern them, the question is whether they are vitally inspired by those spirits just as the bodies of animals are animated by souls, or whether those spirits are present in the luminaries without being intermixed with them." [169]

Since both the proximate and the remote movers are called angels by St. Thomas, some differentiation had to be made between them. Accordingly, he calls the former inferior angels and the latter superior angels, and identifies the former with "ministering angels" and the latter with "Cherubim and Seraphim"; and, though he disagrees with Avicenna's identification of angels with Intelligences, he quote him in support of his view that the remote movers of the spheres are superior angels and the proximate movers are ministering angels. His reference to Avicenna reads, *Unde etiam Avicenna* (tract. X, cap. I) *dicit quod intelligentiae apud Philosophos sunt qui lege vocantur superiores Angeli, ut cherubim et seraphim; animae vero orbium dicunt inferiores, qui dicuntur Angeli ministerii.*[170] The Latin translation of the passage in Avicenna's tract. X, cap. I, reads as follows: *In hoc autem primus gradus est angelorum spiritualium spoliatorum, qui vocantur intelligentiae, post haec est ordo angelorum spiritualium qui vocantur animae, et sunt angeli administratores.*[171] From this it can be seen that the statement of St. Thomas is only a paraphrase of the statement of Avicenna, and that, while the proximate movers are called by Avicenna "ministering angels," the terms "cherubim and seraphim" do not occur in Avicenna. They were added by St. Thomas. It is to be noted, however, that Ghazali, in a work unknown to St. Thomas, dealing with the view which St. Thomas ascribes to Avicenna but which Ghazali ascribes to philosophers in general, says,[172] "They assert that the heavenly angels are the souls of the heavens and that the Cherubic angels who are near [to God] [173] are the incorporeal Intelligences, which are substances subsisting by themselves."

On the whole, however, the two classes of angels described by St. Thomas as "superior" and "inferior" correspond to the first and the second of the three hierarchies into which, following Dionysius, he classifies the angels.[174] The "Cherubim and Seraphim," which he identifies here with the "superior angels," are two of the three orders of angels, Seraphim, Cherubim, and Thrones, which are placed in the first hierarchy. His assignment to the "inferior angels" of the role of proximate movers of the spheres and his description of them as "ministering angels" correspond to his description elsewhere of the order of Virtues, which is one of the three orders of angels of the second hierarchy, as the order to which "the movement of the heavenly bodies belongs," which are "the highest of God's ministries" and to which "anything else of a universal and primary nature in the fulfillment of the divine ministry" is fittingly to be ascribed.[175]

In the light of his explanation in his commentary on the *Sentences* that by the "inferior angels," who are the proximate movers of the spheres, he means angels of the order of Virtues, we may suggest that when in his *Summa Theologica* he describes the soul, which is the proximate mover of each of the spheres, as being related to the body of the sphere *per contactum virtutis,* the term *virtutis* is not to be translated by "of power" but rather by "of virtue" and is to be taken to refer to an angel of the order of Virtues; likewise, the statement *per contactum ab aliqua substantia apprehendente* should refer to the same kind of angel.

Let us now turn to Kepler, to whom we referred at the beginning of this paper. In his discussion of this problem we note two stages of development.

The first stage is in his *De Rebus Astrologicis,* published in 1602. David Fabricius had asked Kepler what he thought of the Intelligences of the stars. As for himself, Fabricius says, he thinks the belief in Intelligences as movers of the spheres to be nonsense, though, he adds, "if you say angels and devils, I accept and understand."[176] This quite evidently reflects the view that denied Intelligences as the remote movers of the spheres, but admitted angels.

In his answer, Kepler says: "A certain power presides over the stars, able to grasp (*capax*) the geometry of the globe, capable of causing motion. . . . I cannot call it other than Intelligence (*intelligentiam*) or mind (*mentem*)."[177]

In this passage Kepler admits the existence of only one mover of the stars. From the fact that he calls it Intelligence and describes it as presiding over the stars it is quite clear that Kepler's one mover of the stars is what traditionally would be described as an immaterial mover who moves the stars as their final cause. No mention is made by him here of an inner mover of the stars, which would traditionally be called soul. But when he ascribes to this Intelligence the functions of (1) grasping, that is, of understanding, and of (2) causing motion, he ascribes to it exactly the two functions which St. Thomas ascribed to the souls of the spheres. In other words, he ascribes to his one Intelligence the function ascribed by St. Thomas to the souls of the spheres.

The second stage may be seen in Kepler's *De Stella Nova Serpentarii,* published in 1606. "The motive faculties of the stars," he says, "partake to some extent of mind, as though they understand (*intelligant*), imagine (*imaginentur*), and grasp or strive after (*affectent*) their course, not indeed by a certain ratiocination (*ratiocinando*), as we human beings do, but by an inborn power (*ingenita vi*), one which at the very beginning of creation was made instinct with them. So also do the animal faculties of natural things possess a certain understanding (without, to be sure, any ratiocination) of their end, toward which they direct all their actions." [178]

In this passage there is no longer one single separate Intelligence which presides over all the stars and moves them all as their final cause, but rather each of the many stars is moved by an "inborn (*ingenita*) power." The term *ingenita* quite evidently reflects the term *σύμφυτον* used by those unnamed philosophers revered by Simplicius, which in the Latin version of Simplicius used by St. Thomas was translated, as we have seen, by *complanata*. But while the term *ingenita* used by Kepler in this connection undoubtedly goes back either directly or indirectly to that Greek term in Simplicius, his full description of the "inborn power" bears an eclectic character, being made up of phrases borrowed from Simplicius, perhaps as quoted by St. Thomas, as well as of phrases borrowed from St. Thomas himself and from Avicenna, perhaps, again, as quoted by St. Thomas. In St. Thomas, the heaven is said to be moved by a soul which is "appetent and intelligent (*appetens et intelligens*)"; [179] in Avicenna, as quoted by St. Thomas, the soul of the celestial sphere is said to have "an imaginative faculty" (*vim imaginativam*); [180] in those anonymous philosophers revered by Simplicius, the celestial sphere is said not to have a "rational soul" (*animam rationalem* = *λογικὴν ψυχήν*).[181] Combining all these, Kepler, in the passage quoted, first says that the stars, in being moved by that "inborn power," are moved by it "as if they understand (*intelligant*), imagine (*imaginentur*), and grasp or strive after (*affectunt*) their course." This reflects the description of the soul of the sphere found in St. Thomas and in Avicenna. But then, paying homage to those anonymous philosophers revered by Simplicius, who explicitly denied the heaven a "rational soul," he adds: "but not indeed by a certain ratiocination (*ratiocinando*) as human beings do."

Thus, like the unnamed philosophers revered by Simplicius, Kepler starts by describing the inner mover of each star as an "inborn power." But then, this "inborn power" is described like the soul in Avicenna, and partly also like the soul in St. Thomas, as having appetence, imagination, and intelligence. Then, again, like those unnamed revered philosophers, he denies that this intelligence implies a ratiocinative soul.

The same view is restated by Kepler in his *Epitome Astronomiae Copernicanae,* published in 1618–21. Here we have a full-dress discussion of the problem.

He begins by restating the view of Aristotle on the spheres and their movements,[182] and in the course of his restatement he refers to "the later philosophers, whom the Arabs seem to have followed," [183] and to Avicenna.[184] In his restatement, he mentions Aristotle's distinction between the outer and inner movers of the spheres. The outer movers are said by him to have been described by Aristotle as "separate and immovable principles" or as "separate minds and even as gods," [185] the latter statement being explained by him elsewhere by a reference to "Book XII of the Metaphysics, Chapter 8," where, he says, Aristotle "built up the most sublime part of his philosophy, that about the gods and the number of them." [186] The Aristotelian inner movers of the spheres are described by him as "motor souls" which are "tightly bound to the spheres and informing them, in order that they might assist the Intelligences somewhat." [187]

In his criticism of Aristotle, his main purpose is to eliminate the outer mover but to retain the inner movers and to define the nature of those inner movers.[188] Inasmuch, however, as Kepler abolished the Aristotelian theory of spheres, which was held by all the Byzantine and mediaeval commentators on Aristotle, the inner movers with which he is concerned are inner movers of the sun, which is said by him to revolve around its own axis, and of the planets, which are said by him to revolve by the rotation of the sun through a certain power emitted by it.[189]

In the course of his discussion he indifferently refers to these inner movers by such terms as "angels," [190] "rational creatures," [191] "natural powers," [192] and "souls" [193]—terms which we have already encountered in previous discussions of the subject. But when he comes to formulate his own view on the subject, he first expresses himself as follows: "This rotation comes from one sole motor: whether it be a quality of the body or an offshoot of the soul born with the body." [194] Later he rephrases the same view as follows: "But the celestial movements are not the work of mind but of nature, that is, of the natural powers of the bodies, or else of the soul acting uniformly in accordance with those bodily powers." [195] Of the two alternatives, which he mentions in both these passages, the first reflects the view of Alexander, according to which the inner mover of the celestial body is the nature of the body, which may be called soul; the second reflects the view of Simplicius, according to which the inner mover of the celestial body is both a soul and a nature, both of them coöperating in producing the movement, the former as an active cause and the latter as a passive cause.

Finally, fearing lest his accounting for the movements of the planets by their solely inner movers and his denial of separate Intelligences or minds as outer movers might lead some to suspect him of denying the existence of God, he hastens to declare, at the conclusion of his discussion, that in denying that "the celestial movements are the work of a mind" he does not deny the existence of "Mind the Creator" (*mens creatrix*), for, whether one believes that the planets are moved by a mind or whether one believes that they are moved by "material necessity," one must still believe that it was God by whom the mind or the material necessity was created at the creation of the world.[196]

[1] Cf. *infra,* at notes 177, 193, 194, 195.

[2] *Metaph.* XII, 8, 1073a, 14.

[3] *Ibid.* XII, 7, 1073a, 3–5.

[4] *Ibid.,* 1072b, 1ff.

[5] *Ibid.* XII, 8, 1073a, 23–25, 26–27, 31–34. Cf. my paper "The Plurality of Immovable Movers in Aristotle and Averroes," *Harvard Studies in Classical Philology,* 63 (1958), p. 238. Above, pages 1–21.

[6] Phys. VIII, 6, 259b, 28–31.

[7] *Art. cit.* (*supra,* note 5), p. 237.

[8] *De Caelo* I, 2, 268b, 27–29.

[9] *Ibid.,* 269a, 5–7.

[10] *Simplicius in De Caelo* I, 2, ed. I. L. Heiberg (1884), p. 16, lines 11–14.

[11] *Ibid.*, lines 21–26.
[12] *De Caelo* II, 1, 284a, 27–28.
[13] *Ibid.* II, 2, 285a, 29–30.
[14] *Ibid.* I, 9, 279a, 28–30.
[15] *Ibid.* II, 12, 292a, 20–21.
[16] *Ibid.*, 292b, 1–2.
[17] *Simplicius in De Caelo* II, 2, p. 388, lines 16–19.
[18] Cf. *infra,* at note 46.
[19] Cf. *infra,* the concluding paragraph after note 64, and notes 80–83.
[20] Diogenes Laërtius, II, 12; cf. Plutarch, *Pericles* 32; *Nicias,* 23.
[21] Augustine, *De Civ. Dei* XVIII, 41.
[22] *De Somniis* I, 4, 22.
[23] Cf. Diels, *Doxographi Graeci*^{2}, V, 20, 2, p. 432a, lines 9–10, and Diels' note *ad loc.*
[24] *Hexaemeron,* hom. III, 9 (PG 29, 76 A); cf. John of Damasacus, *De Fid. Orth.* II, 6 (PG 94, 885 AB).
[25] *De Opificio Mundi* VI, 2, ed. G. Reichhardt (1897), pp. 28, 17ff., 231, 11. 3ff.
[26] *Theodori Mopsuesteni in Epistolas B. Pauli Commentarii,* ed. H. B. Swete, I (1880), pp. 270–271. "Theodoros" is mentioned by Philoponus himself in *op. cit.,* p. 28, line 20.
[27] *The Christian Topography of Cosmas Indicopleustes,* ed. E. O. Winstedt (1909), 117 D; cf. 152 D, 301 C; 405 D, 429 A. For this reference to Cosmas I am indebted to Prof. Milton V. Anastos.
[28] *Simplicius in De Caelo* II, 2, p. 388, lines 19–20.
[29] *De Caelo* II, 12, 292a, 19–21.
[30] *Simplicius in De Caelo* II, 2, p. 388, lines 20–25.
[31] *Procli commentarius in Platonis Timaeum,* ed. C. E. Chr. Schneider (1847), p. 418 AB; ed. E. Diehl (1903–06), II, 122, lines 13–17.
[32] *Theophrastus*: *Metaphysics,* with translation, commentary and introduction by W. D. Ross and F. H. Fobes (1929).
[33] *Metaph.* XII, 7, 1072a, 26.
[34] *Op. cit.*, 5a, 24 and 28, and 6a, 9. Cf. ἐφατόν in *Phys.* I, 9, 192a, 17, used as the equivalent of ὀρεκτικόν in *Metaph.* XII, 7, 1072a, 26. Cf. also the use of ἐφίενται and ὄρεξις in *Eth. Eud.* I, 8, 1218a, 24–28, quoted *infra,* at note 53.
[35] *Op. cit.*, 5a, 28–5b, 2ff.
[36] *Ibid.*, 6a, 5–10; cf. use of the term σύμφυτον in quotation *supra,* at note 17.
[37] Cf. *supra,* at note 18.
[38] Cf. *infra,* at notes 45–64.
[39] H. Diels, *Doxographi Graeci,*^{2} Prolegomena.
[40] *Ibid.* II, 3, 4, p. 330a, lines 9–10.
[41] *Ibid.* V, 20, 1, p. 432a, lines 6–7.
[42] *Alexander in Metaphysica* XII, 6, ed. M. Hayduck (1891), p. 686, lines 11–14.
[43] *Oratio ad Graecos,* Cap. 12.
[44] *De Principiis* I, 7, 2–3.
[45] *Simplicius in Physica* VIII, 4, ed. H. Diels (1895), p. 1219, lines 3–5.
[46] *Simplicius in De Caelo* II, 2, p. 387, line 14.
[47] *Fī Mabādī' al-Kull in Arisṭū 'inda al-'Arab,* ed. A. Badawi (1947), pp. 253–277; cf. S. Pines, "A Refutation of Galen by Alexander of Aphrodisias and the Theory of Motion," *Isis,* 52 (March 1961), pp. 21–54, of which pp. 43–45 deal with the texts quoted here.
[48] *Ibid.*, p. 253, lines 20–23.
[49] Cf. *infra,* at notes 58–59.
[50] *Op. cit.*, p. 204, lines 9–12.
[51] *De Anima* II, 2, 414b, 2.

[52] In the Arabic translation of *De Anima,* ed. A. Badawi (1954), both ὄρεξις and ἐπιθυμία in this statement are translated by *shahwah.* Similarly in *De Anima* II, 2, 414b, 5–6, the statement "this [ἐπιθυμία] is an ὄρεξις for what is pleasurable" is translated into Arabic by "*shahwah* is a *shahwah* for a pleasurable thing." In *De Anima* III, 10, 333a, 25–26, however, the statement that "ἐπιθυμία is a species of ὄρεξις" is translated by "*shahwah* is a species of *shauq.*" So also in *De Anima* III, 9, 432b, 3, τὸ ὀρεκτικόν is translated by *al-shauq.* Evidently there was no consistency in the Arabic translation of these Greek terms.

[53] *Eth. Eud.* I, 8, 1218a, 24–28.

[54] *Ibid.* II, 8, 1224a, 16–30.

[55] *Op. cit.,* p. 254, lines 6–7.

[56] *De Caelo* IV, 1, 307b, 31–33.

[57] See Index volume to Didot's edition of Aristotle, s.v. "Impetus" (p. 389a).

[58] *Op. cit.,* p. 254, lines 13–16.

[59] *Ibid.,* line 19.

[60] *Ibid.,* lines 19–20.

[61] *Ibid.,* p. 255, lines 1–5.

[62] *Ibid.,* lines 17–18.

[63] *Ibid.,* lines 20–23.

[64] *Ibid.,* p. 255, line 22–p. 256, line 8.

[65] *Simplicius in De Caelo* II, 2, p. 387, lines 12–19.

[66] *Phys.* VIII, 4, 254b, 16.

[67] *Ibid.,* 31–32.

[68] *Simplicius in De Caelo* II, 1, p. 381, lines 31–35.

[69] *Ibid.,* ll. 35–36; cf. *De Anima* II, 1, 412b, 5–6.

[70] *Ibid.,* p. 382, lines 11–13.

[71] *Phys.* VIII, 4, 254b, 13–14.

[72] *Simplicius in De Caelo* I, 8, p. 263, lines 18–21.

[73] *Ibid.* II, 8, p. 463, line 5.

[74] *De Anima* II, 4, 415a, 25–26.

[75] *Ibid.,* 416a, 19.

[76] *Ibid.,* 415b, 1–7.

[77] *De Caelo* I, 3, 270b, 1ff.

[78] H. Diels, *Doxographi Graeci*², II, 3, p. 330, lines 5–8.

[79] Plutarch, *De Musica,* 25.

[80] *Simplicius in de Caelo* II, 8, p. 463, lines 3–6. See explanation of this expression *infra,* at note 153.

[81] *Simplicius in De Anima* III, 12, ed. M. Hayduck (1882), pp. 319–321; *Philoponus in De Anima* III, 12, ed. M. Hayduck (1897), pp. 395–396; cf. Fr. Ad. Trendelenburg (1833), Ad. Torstrik (1862), E. Wallace (1882), G. Rodier (1900), and R. D. Hicks (1907) in their commentaries on *De Anima,* dealing with III, 12, 434b, 9–24.

[82] *De Anima* III, 12, 434b, 9–26.

[83] *De Caelo* I, 3, 270b, 1–2.

[84] *Philoponus in De Anima* III, 12, p. 599, line 35; cf. Zeller, *Phil. d. Griech.,* III, 2⁴, p. 809, note 2.

[85] *Simplicius in De Anima* III, 12, p. 320, line 29.

[86] *Philoponus in De Anima* III, 12, p. 595, line 39–p. 596, line 12. Cf. Hicks (p. 578) on *De Anima* 434b, 5.

[87] *Simplicius in De Anima* III, 12, p. 320, lines 9ff.

[88] *De Anima* II, 3, 414b, 18–19.

[89] *Simplicius in De Anima* II, 3, p. 106, lines 25–29.

[90] *Eth. Nic.* VI, 7, 1141a, 34–1141b, 2.

[91] Cf. J. A. Stewart, *Notes on the Nichomachean Ethics* (1892), *ad loc.* (II, p. 58).

[92] *Simplicius in De Caelo* II, 9, p. 463, lines 6–12.

[93] *Olympiodori philosophi in Platonis Phaedonem commentaria,* ed. William Norvin (1913), p. 26, lines 22–27, quoted in *Aristolis Fragmenta,* ed. Didot, p. 38, § 26 (48); ed. Bekker, p. 1481, § 39. Cf. G. Rodier's note on *De Anima* III, 12, 434b, 3 (II, p. 568).

[94] *De Anima* III, 13, 435b, 17–25.

[95] *Ibid.* III, 12, 434b, 21–23.

[96] *Ibid.*, 24.

[97] *De Sensu* 1, 436b, 20.

[98] *Ibid.*, 437a, 1.

[99] *Qu. in Gen.* III, 5, ed. Ralph Marcus (1953), I, p. 187.

[100] *De Specialibus Legibus* I, 62, 337.

[101] *Qu. in Gen.* III, 5.

[102] *Spec.* I, 62, 337.

[103] *Themistius in De Anima,* ed. R. Heinze (1899), p. 123, lines 29–31.

[104] *Al-Najāt* (A. H. 1331), p. 422, lines 7–9.

[105] *Ibid.*, p. 423, lines 3–12.

[106] *Ibid.*, p. 423, lines 15–18; cf. Simplicius *supra,* at note 70.

[107] *Ibid.*, p. 424, line 1; cf. Simplicius *supra,* at note 69.

[108] *Ibid.*, lines 3–4.

[109] *Ibid.*, lines 5–10.

[110] *Ibid.*, p. 436, lines 10–11. Cf. Maimonides, *Moreh Nebukim* II, 3; M. Steinschneider, *Al-Farabi* (1869), p. 67.

[111] *Averroes in De Caelo* II, Text. 13, *Opera Aristotelis* (Venice, 1574), V, p. 102 B, also quoted in Averroes' comment on it (p. 102 E), though in the course of his discussion he uses for it the term *animatum* (p. 102 F). Elsewhere in *De Caelo* I, 7, 275b, 26 (Text. 72), and II, 9, 291a, 23 (Text 56), ἔμψυχον is translated *animatum.*

[112] *Sermo de Substantia Orbis,* cap. 1 (*Opera,* IX, p. 5 HI).

[113] *Ibid.*, cap. 2 (p. 6 C).

[114] *Ibid.* (p. 6 FG).

[115] *Averros: tafsir maba'd at-tabi'at,* ed. M. Bouyges (1938–1948), VIII, Comm. 12, p. 1077, line 19–p. 1078, line 4. Latin: *Opera* VIII, Comm. 12, p. 220 GH.

[116] Arabic text in *Averroes*: *Compendio de Metafisica* IV, 6–7, ed. Carlos Quiros Rodriguez (1913). Cf. notes on p. 241 in S. van den Bergh's German translation, *Die Epitome der Metaphysik des Averroes* (1924).

[117] *Tahāfut al-Tahāfut* IV, ed. M. Bouyges (1930), § 18, p. 271, lines 7–8.

[118] *Ibid.*, lines 8–11.

[119] *Ibid.*, § 1, p. 470, lines 4–13; cf. Ghazali, *Tahāfut al- Falāsifah* XIV, ed. M. Bouyges (1927), §§ 4–6, p. 240, line 8–p. 241, line 8.

[120] *Ibid.*, p. 473, lines 3–5.

[121] Cf. *supra,* at note 80 and *infra,* at note 153.

[122] *Najāt*, p. 425, line 17; Latin in *Avicenne . . . opera* (Venice, 1508), p. 102c, lines 58–59: *potest autem putari quod illa voluntas est intelligibilis mobilis.*

[123] *Ibid.*, p. 427, lines 16–17; Latin, p. 102d, lines 32–33; *intellectioni nostrae non est potentia ponere hanc transmutatione' ι nisi communione imaginationi et sensui.*

[124] *Ibid.*, p. 428, lines 3–4; Latin, p. 102d, lines 37–39: *nos non negamus ibi etiam esse virtutem intelligibilem quae moveatur hac transmutatione intelligibile, sed postquam inititur similitudini imaginationis.*

[125] *Ibid.*, p. 428, lines 7–8; Latin, p. 102c, lines 42–44: *coelum movetur per animam, et anima est proprinquus principium sui motus, sed in illa renovatur imaginatio et voluntas.*

[126] *Sermo de Substantia Orbis,* 2, p. 6 HI.

[127] Averroes, *In III De Anima,* Comm. 61, ed. F. S. Crawford (1953), p. 535.

[128] *Kitāb al-Siyāsāt al-Madaniyyah* (Hyderabad, A. H. 1346), p. 25, lines 12–13.
[129] Cf. *supra,* at note 93.
[130] Cf. *supra,* at note 92.
[131] Ibn Ḥazm, *Fiṣal fī al-Milal* (Cairo, A. H. 1317–27), V, p. 36, lines 17–18.
[132] Ghazali, *Tahāfut al-Falāsifah* XIV, §§ 1 ff., pp. 239ff.; cf. XVI, §§ 1–2, p. 255, line 4–p. 256, line 3.
[133] Quoted by Shem-ṭob Falaquera in his *Moreh ha-Moreh* II, 4, pp. 80–82.
[134] Latin from the Arabic: *Liber Definitionum* in *Omnia Opera Ysaac* (1515), fol. IIIb, line 63: *et factus est per illud intellectualis et rationalis.* Hebrew from the Arabic: *Sefer ha-Gebulim,* ed. H. Hirschfeld, in *Festchrift zum achtzigsten Geburtstage Moritz Steinschneider's* (1896), p. 137.
[135] *Enn.* III, 2, 14.
[136] *Ibid.,* V, 1, 2.
[137] *Emunot ve-De'ot* I, 3, 8th Theory of Creation; Arabic text edited by S. Landauer (1881), p. 59, line 2ff.
[138] *Cuzari* IV, 3, ed. H. Hirschfeld (1887), Arabic, p. 234, lines 8–9; Hebrew, p. 235, lines 8–9.
[139] *Ibid.,* p. 244, lines 2–3; p. 245, lines 7–9.
[140] Cf. *supra,* at note 132.
[141] *Op. cit.,* V, 21, p. 354, lines 15–27; p. 355, lines 16–28.
[142] *Ibid.* V, 20, p. 338, lines 11–12; p. 339, line 8.
[143] *Ibid.,* V, 2, p. 296, lines 17–19; p. 297, lines 18–20.
[144] *Ibid.,* II, 6, p. 74, lines 23–27; p. 75, lines 23–27.
[145] *Metaph.* XII, 8, 1073b, 25–26.
[146] *Emunah Ramah* I, 8, pp. 41–43.
[147] *Moreh Nebukim* II, 4.
[148] Cf. my *Crescas' Critique of Aristotle* (1929), pp. 77–78, 237, 535–538.
[149] St. Thomas, *In II De Caelo,* Lectio III, 2.
[150] Cf. *supra,* at note 17.
[151] St. Thomas, *loc. cit.*
[152] Cf. *supra,* at notes 65, 68.
[153] St. Thomas, *In II De Caelo,* Lectio XIII, 4. Cf. *supra,* at notes 80, 121.
[154] *Ibid.*
[155] *Ibid.,* Lectio XIII, 5–6; cf. St. Thomas, *In III De Anima,* Lectio XVII, and *supra,* at notes 103, 126, 127.
[156] *Ibid.,* Lectio XIII, 8. The reference to Avicenna's *Metaphysics* is to those passages quoted *supra,* at notes 123–125.
[157] *Sum. Theol.* I, 70, 3c; I, 76, 1c.
[158] *Ibid.,* I, 76, 1c.
[159] *Ibid.,* I, 70, 3c.
[160] *Ibid.,* I, 76, 1c.
[161] *Ibid.,* I, 70, 3c.
[162] *Ibid.*
[163] *Phys.* VIII, 5, 258a, 20–22.
[164] *Cont. Gent.* II, 70.
[165] Cf. *supra,* at notes 104, 125.
[166] St. Thomas, *In II Sent.,* dist. XIV, art. 3c: *Et ideo angelos, qui movent orbes proxime, possumus motores dicere, non formas, vel animas.*
[167] Cf. *supra,* at notes 25–27.
[168] *Sum. Theol.* I, 70, 3c.
[169] *De Genesi ad Litteram* II, xvii, 38 (PL 34, 279–280).
[170] *In II Sent.,* dist. XIV, art. 3c.
[171] *Avicenne . . . opera* (Venice, 1508), fol. 107d, lines 47–51; (Venice, 1495), fol. [38d].

[172] Ghazali, *Tahāfut al-Falāsifah* XVI, § 1, p. 255, lines 4–6, quoted in Averroes, *Tahāfut al-Tahāfut* XVI, § 1, p. 494, lines 10–11.

[173] Cf. Koranic expression: "the angels who are near [to God]" (Surah 4:170).

[174] *Cont. Gent.* III, 80; *Sum. Theol.* I, 108.

[175] *Cont. Gent.* III, 80, *Secunda autem ab operante.*

[176] *Re Rebus Astrologicis, Opera Omnia* (Frankfurt-am-Main and Erlangen, 1858–71), I, p. 319.

[177] *Ibid.*

[178] *De Stella Nova* XXVIII, *Opera,* II, p. 719.

[179] St. Thomas, *In II De Caelo,* Lectio III, No. 2.

[180] *Ibid.*, Lectio XIII, No. 8.

[181] *Ibid.*, Lectio III, No. 2.

[182] *Epitome* IV, ii, 2, *Opera,* VI, p. 339.

[183] *Ibid.*

[184] *Ibid.*, p. 341.

[185] *Ibid.*, p. 339.

[186] *Ibid.* IV, Praefatio, pp. 304–305.

[187] *Ibid.* IV, ii, 2, p. 339.

[188] *Ibid.*, p. 340.

[189] *Ibid.*, pp. 343–344.

[190] *Ibid.*, p. 340.

[191] *Ibid.*

[192] *Ibid.*

[193] *Ibid.* IV, ii, 3, p. 343.

[194] *Ibid.* IV, iii, 1, p. 371.

[195] *Ibid.*, p. 372.

[196] *Ibid.*, p. 373.

3

PHILO JUDAEUS

The Jewish Hellenistic philosopher Philo Judaeus (fl. 20 B.C.–A.D. 40) was the son of a wealthy and prominent Alexandrian family. He was well educated in both Judaism and Greek philosophy. Little is known about the actual events of his life except that in A.D. 40 the Jewish community of Alexandria sent him as the head of a delegation to Emperor Caligula to seek redress from the wrongs which the gentile population inflicted upon the Jews. His *Legacy to Gaius* tells the story of this mission. Although he also wrote moral and philosophic treatises on problems then current, the main bulk of his writings are philosophic discourses on certain topics of the Hebrew Scripture. In content they are, on the one hand, an attempt to interpret the scriptural teachings in terms of Greek philosophy and, on the other, an attempt to revise Greek philosophy in the light of those scriptural traditions.

The scriptural teachings with which Philo set out to revise Greek philosophy contained certain definite conceptions of the nature of God and his relation to the world but only vague allusions to the structure and composition of the world. In dealing with the latter, therefore, he felt free to select from the various views of Greek philosophers whichever seemed to him the most reasonable, although occasionally he supported the selection by a scriptural citation. In dealing with the conception of God, however, he approached Greek philosophic views critically, rejecting those which were diametrically opposed to his scriptural traditions and interpreting or modifying those which were plastic enough to lend themselves to remolding.

God, Platonic ideas, creation. Of the various conceptions of God in Greek philosophy, Philo found that the most compatible with scriptural teaching was Plato's conception, in the *Timaeus,* of a God who had existed from eternity without a world and then, after he had brought the world into existence, continued to exist as an incorporeal being over and above the corporeal world. But to Plato, in the *Timaeus,* besides the eternal God, there were also eternal ideas. Philo had no objection to the existence of ideas as such, for he held that there was a scriptural tradition for the existence of ideas. But he could not accept the eternity of the ideas, for, according to his scriptural belief, God alone is eternal. By a method of harmonization that had been used in Judaism in reconciling inconsistencies in Scripture, Philo reconciled the *Timaeus* with the scriptural tradition by endowing the ideas with a twofold stage of existence: first, from eternity they existed as thoughts of God; then, prior to the creation of the world they were created by God as real beings. He may have found support for the need of such a harmonization in the many conflicting statements about the ideas in Plato's dialogues.

The ideas, which in Plato are always spoken of as a mere aggregation, are integrated by Philo into what he terms "an intelligible world," an expression that does not occur in extant Greek philosophic writings before him. Then, following a statement by Aristotle that the "thinking soul" (that is, nous), "is the place of forms" (that is, ideas), Philo places the intelligible world of ideas in a nous, which, under the influence of scriptural vocabulary, he surnamed Logos. Accordingly, he speaks also of the Logos as having the aforementioned two stages of existence.

For the same reason that he could not accept the view that the ideas are eternal, Philo also could not accept the view commonly held by contemporary students of Plato that the pre-existent matter out of which, in the *Timaeus,* the world was created was eternal. But as a philosopher he did not like to reject altogether the reputable Platonic conception of a pre-existent matter. And so here, too, he solved the difficulty by the method of harmonization. There was indeed a pre-existent matter, but that pre-existent matter was created. There were thus to him two creations, the creation of the pre-existent matter out of nothing and the creation of the world out of that pre-existent matter. For this too, it can be shown, he may have found support in certain texts of Plato.

In the *Timaeus,* Plato describes the creation of the world as an act which God "willed" (ἐβουλήθη), and similarly the indestructibility of the world is described by him as being due to the "will" (βούλησις) of God. Presumably, by will in its application to God, Plato here means the necessary expression of God's nature, so that the creation of the world, and of this particular world of ours, was an act that could not be otherwise; and similarly the indestructibility of the world is something that cannot be otherwise. Philo, however, following the scriptural conception of God as an all-powerful free agent, takes the will by which God created the world to mean that had God willed, he could have either not created the world or created another kind of world. And similarly, if it be his will, he can destroy the world, although, on the basis of a scriptural verse, Philo believed that God would not destroy it.

Laws of nature, miracles, providence. The scriptural conception of God as an all-powerful free agent is extended by Philo to the governance of the world.

Finding scriptural support for the belief in causality and in the existence of certain laws of nature current among Greek philosophers, except the Epicureans, Philo conceived of God's governance of the world as being effected by intermediary causes and by laws of nature which God had implanted in the world at the time of its creation. He even tried his hand at classifying the laws of nature which happen to be mentioned by various Greek philosophers. But in opposition to the Greek philosophers, to whom these laws of nature were inexorable, he maintained that God has the power to infringe upon the laws of his own making and create what are known as miracles. These miracles, however, are not created arbitrarily. They are always created with design and wisdom for the good of deserving individuals or deserving groups of individuals or mankind as a whole, for, to Philo, God governs by direct supervision not only the world as a whole but also the individual human beings within the world. To express this particular departure of his from the generality of Greek philosophers, Philo gave a new meaning to the Greek term πρόνοια, "providence." To those Greek philosophers who made use of this term it meant universal providence, that is, the unalterable operation of the inexorable laws of nature whereby the continuity and uniformity of the various natural processes in the world are preserved. To Philo it means individual providence, that is, the suspension of the laws of nature by the will and wisdom and goodness of God for the sake of human beings whose life or welfare is threatened by the ordinary operation of those laws of nature. With this conception of individual providence, Philo takes up the discussion of the human soul.

Soul and will. On the whole, Philo's conception of the soul is made up of statements derived from various dialogues of Plato. He distinguishes between irrational souls, which are created together with the bodies of both men and animals, and rational souls, which were created at the creation of the world, prior to the creation of bodies. Of these pre-existent rational souls, some remain bodiless but others become invested with bodies. The former are identified by Philo with the angels of Scripture. Having in mind certain passages in Plato where such unbodied souls are identified with the popular Greek religious notions of demons and heroes, but knowing that Plato himself and also Aristotle and the Stoics dismissed these popular notions as mere myths, Philo says that the angels of Moses are what philosophers call demons and heroes, but he warns the reader not to take the existence of angels as mere myths. With regard to the pre-existent rational souls that become embodied, he says, following Plato, that they are equal in number to the stars and are to be placed in newly born human beings whose bodies are already endowed with irrational souls. Again following Plato, Philo says that the irrational souls die with the bodies, whereas the rational souls are immortal. But he differs from Plato in his conception of the immortality of the soul. To Plato, the soul is immortal by nature and is also indestructible by nature. To Philo, immortality is a grace with which the soul was endowed by the will and power of God, and consequently it can be destroyed by the will and power of God if it has proved itself unworthy of the grace bestowed upon it.

A similar revision was also introduced by Philo into the Greek philosophic conception of the human will. In Greek philosophy, a distinction is made between voluntary and involuntary acts. But since all the Greek philosophers, except the Epicureans, believed in causality and in the inexorability of the laws of nature, for them the human will, to which they ascribed the so-called voluntary acts, is itself determined by causes and is subject to those inexorable laws of nature which govern the universe, including man, who is part of it.[1] To all of them, except the Epicureans, no human act was free in the sense that it could be otherwise. The term "voluntary" was used by them only as a description of an act which is performed with knowledge and without external compulsion. To all of them, therefore, there was no free will except in the sense of what may be called relative free will. To Philo, however, just as God in his exercise of individual providence may see fit to infringe upon the laws of nature and create miracles, so has he also seen fit to endow man with the miraculous power to infringe upon the laws of his own nature, so that by the mere exercise of his will man may choose to act contrary to all the forces in his nature. This conception of free will is what may be called absolute free will.

Knowledge. Philo also revised the philosophic conception of human knowledge, including the philosophic conceptions of man's knowledge of God. Human knowledge, like all other events in the world, including human actions, is, according to Philo, under the direct supervision of God. Like all other events in the world, which are to Philo either natural, in the sense that they are operated by God through the laws of nature which he has implanted in the world, or supernatural, in the sense that they are miraculously created by God in infringement upon those laws of nature, so also human knowledge is either natural or supernatural, called by Philo "prophetic," that is, divinely revealed.

Under natural knowledge, Philo deals with all those various types of knowledge from sensation to ratiocination that are dealt with by Greek philosophers, especially Plato and the Stoics. He presents prophetic knowledge as a substitute for that type of knowledge which in Greek philosophy is placed above the various senso-ratiocinative types of knowledge and is described as recollection by Plato, as the primary immediate principles by Aristotle, and as the primary conceptions by the Stoics. Like all miracles, prophetic knowledge is part of God's exercise of his providence over individuals, groups of individuals, or mankind in general. An example of prophetic knowledge due to God's exercise of his providence over individuals is Philo's account of his own experience: often, in the course of his investigation of certain philosophic problems, after all the ordinary processes of reasoning had failed him, he attained the desired knowledge miraculously by divine inspiration. An example of prophetic knowledge due to God's exercise of his providence over a group of individuals, as well as over mankind in general, is Philo's recounting of the revelation of the law of Moses.

Man's knowledge of God. Corresponding to the two kinds of human knowledge are two ways by which, according to Philo, man may arrive at a knowledge of God—an indirect ratiocinative way and a direct divinely revealed way. Philo describes the indirect way as the knowledge of the existence of God which the "world teaches" us, and he deals with the various proofs for the existence of God advanced by Greek philosophers. Most acceptable to him is the Platonic form of the cosmological proof in the *Timaeus,* inasmuch as it is based on the premise of a created world. He modifies the Aristotelian form of the cosmological proof so as to establish the existence of a prime mover, not of the motion of the world but of its existence. He similarly modifies the Stoic proof from the human mind to establish the existence not of a corporeal God immanent in the world but of an incorporeal God above the world.

In his discussion of the direct way of knowing God, however, Philo makes no mention of the Stoic proof of the innateness of the idea of God. His own direct way of knowing God he describes as a "clear vision of the Uncreated One." But as he goes on to explain it, this direct way of knowing God is only another version of the various indirect ways of knowing him and is similarly based upon the contemplation of the world. The difference between the indirect and direct ways is this: in the case of the various indirect ways, both the knowledge of the world and of the existence of God derived therefrom are attained laboriously by the slow process of observation and logical reasoning; in the case of the direct way, both the knowledge of the world and of the existence of God derived therefrom are flashed upon the mind suddenly and simultaneously by divine inspiration.

But the knowledge of God which man may gain by either of these two ways is, according to Philo, only a knowledge of his existence, not a knowledge of his essence; for as Philo maintains, "it is wholly impossible that God according to his essence should be known to any creature." God is thus said by him to be "unnamable" (ἀκατονόμαστος), "ineffable" (ἄρρητος), and "incomprehensible" (ἀκατάληπτος). This distinction between the knowability of God's existence and the unknowability of his essence does not occur in Greek philosophy prior to Philo. In fact, in none of the extant Greek philosophic literature prior to Philo do the terms "unnamable," "ineffable," and "incomprehensible," in the sense of incomprehensible by the mind, occur as predications of God. Moreover, it can be shown that both Plato and Aristotle held that God was knowable and describable according to his essence. Philo was thus the first to introduce this view into the history of philosophy, and he had arrived at it neither by Scripture alone nor by philosophy alone. He had arrived at it by a combination of the scriptural teaching of the unlikeness of God to anything else and the philosophic teaching that the essence of a thing is known through the definition of the thing in terms of genus and specific difference, which means that the essence of a thing is known only through its likeness to other things in genus and species. Since God is unlike anything else, he is, as Philo says, "the most generic being" (τὸ γενικώτατον), that is, the *summum genus,* and hence he cannot be defined and cannot be known.

As a corollary of this conception of the unknowability and ineffability of God, it would have to follow that one could not properly speak of God except in negative terms, that is, in terms which describe his unlikeness to other things. But still Scripture repeatedly uses positive terms as descriptions of God. All such terms, explains Philo, whatever their external grammatical form, whether adjectives or verbs, are to be taken as having the meaning of what Aristotle calls property, and the various terms by which God is described are to be taken as mere verbal variations of the property of God to act, in which he is unlike all other beings. For to act is the unique property of God; the property of all created beings is to suffer action.

Theocratic government. Philo widened the meaning of the conception of natural law in its application to laws governing human society. To Greek philosophers, with the exception of the Sophists, this application of the conception of natural law (or, as they would say, law in accordance with nature) meant that certain laws enacted by philosophers in accordance with what they described as reason or virtue were also in a limited sense in accordance with nature, that is to say, in the mere sense that they were in accordance with certain impulses, capacities, rational desires which exist in men by nature. The Greek philosophers assumed, however, that no law enacted for the government of men, even when enacted by philosophers in accordance with reason and virtue, can be regarded as natural law in the sense of its being fully in harmony with the eternal and all-embracing laws of nature by which the world is governed. Philo agrees with the philosophers as to the limited sense in which enacted human law may be regarded as natural law but argues that a law revealed by God, who is the creator of the world (as, to Philo, the law of Moses was), is fully in harmony with the laws of nature, which God himself has implanted in the world for its governance. To Philo, therefore, natural law came to mean a divinely revealed law.

This widened conception of natural law led Philo to answer the question raised by Greek philosophers as to what was the best form of government. To both Plato and Aristotle no form of government based upon fixed law can be the best form of government, and Plato explicitly maintains that the best form of government is that of wise rulers who are truly possessed of science, whether they rule according to law or without law and whether they rule with or without the consent of the governed.

Against this, Philo argues that the best form of government is that based upon fixed law, not indeed upon man-made fixed law, but upon a divinely revealed fixed law. In a state governed by such a divinely revealed law, every individual has his primary allegiance to God and to the law revealed by God. Whatever human authority exists, whether secular, governing the relation of man to man, or religious, governing the relation of man to God, that authority is derived from the law and functions only as an instrument of the application of the law and its interpretation. Such a state, whatever its external form of government, is really ruled by God, and Philo came near coining the term "theocracy" as a description of it; the term was actually so coined and used later, by Flavius Josephus. But Philo preferred to describe it by the term "democracy," which he uses not in its ordinary sense, as a description of a special form of government in contradistinction to that of monarchy and aristocracy, but rather as a description of a special principle of government, namely, the principle of equality before the law, which to him may be adopted and practiced by any form of government.

Virtue. In the course of his attempt to analyze the laws of Moses in terms of Greek philosophy, Philo injects himself into the controversy between the Peripatetics and the Stoics over the definition of virtue. Guided by scriptural tradition, he sides with Aristotle in defining virtue as a mean between two vices; hence, in opposition to the Stoics, he maintains that virtue is not the extirpation of all the emotions, that some emotions are good, that there is a difference of degree of importance between various virtues and various vices, and that the generality of human beings are neither completely virtuous nor completely wicked but are in a state which is intermediate between these two extremes and are always subject to improvement. He maintains, however, that by the grace of God some exceptional persons may be born with a thoroughly sinless nature.

Following Plato and Aristotle, both of whom include under the virtue of justice certain other virtues which they consider akin to justice, but guided also by scriptural tradition, Philo includes under justice two virtues that are entirely new and are never mentioned in any of the lists of virtues recorded under the names of Greek philosophers. Thus, on the basis of the scriptural verse (Genesis 15.6) that "Abraham had faith (*ἐπίστευσεν*) in God and it was counted to him for justice (*δικαιοσύνην*)," Philo inincludes "faith" (*πίστις*), which he takes to mean faith in the revealed teachings of Scripture, as a virtue under what the philosophers call the virtue of justice. Similarly, because the Hebrew term *ṣedaḳah* in Scripture is translated in the Septuagint both by *δικαιοσύνη*, "justice" (Genesis 18.19) and by *ἐλέημοσύνη*, "mercy," "alms" (Deuteronomy 6.25, 24.13), Philo includes "humanity" (*φιλανθροπία*), in the sense of giving help to those who are in need of it, as a virtue under the philosophic virtue of justice. But on the basis of Scripture only, without any support from philosophy, he describes also "repentance" (*μετάνοια*) as a virtue. In

Greek philosophy, repentance is regarded as a weakness rather than as a virtue.

His scripturally based conception of free will as absolute led Philo to give a new meaning to the voluntariness of virtue and the voluntariness of the emotion of desire as used in Greek philosophy. Both Aristotle and the Stoics, using the term "vountary" in the relative sense of free will, agree that virtue is voluntary, but they disagree as to the voluntariness of the emotions. To Aristotle, all emotions are involuntary, except the emotions of desire and anger, the latter of which by the time of Philo was subsumed under desire; to the Stoics, all emotions are voluntary. Philo, however, using the term "vountary" in its revised sense of absolute free will, maintains that in this revised sense the term "voluntary" is to be applied, as in Aristotle, to virtue and to the emotion of desire.

Philo similarly gave a new meaning to the philosophic advice that virtue is to be practiced for its own sake. To Plato, Aristotle, and the Stoics, this advice was meant to serve as a principle of guidance to those who, like themselves, did not believe in individual providence and were not impressed by the explanations offered in the popular Greek religious theodicies as to why virtue is not always rewarded and vice not always punished. The reason underlying this advice was that since there is no certainty as to what external goods or evils would follow the practice of either virtue or vice, it is preferable for man to take his chance on the practice of virtue. This reasoning was presumably based on the common human experience that it is easier for one to induce in himself a feeling of happiness in the misery that may follow a life of virtue than it is to induce in himself a feeling of happiness in the misery, and sometimes even in the joy, that may follow a life of vice. To Philo, however, the advice to practice virtue for its own sake is based upon his belief that providence is individual; that, despite common observation to the contrary, no virtue goes unrewarded; that acts of virtue are of graded merits; and that the reward is always in accordance with the merit of the act. With all this in the back of his mind, Philo's advice to practice virtue for its own sake (which he expresses in a different context by the statement that man is to serve God out of love and not out of expectation of a reward) means that such a practice of virtue is of the highest degree of merit, and the reward for it, which ultimately is of a spiritual nature in the hereafter, will be in accordance with its merit.

Philosophy of history. Finally, Philo's belief in God as a free agent who acts by will and design in the world as a whole, as well as in the life of individual human beings, has led him to a theo-teleological philosophy of history. Alluding to passages in Polybius' *Histories,* in which the rise and fall of cities, nations, and countries are explained by analogy to the Stoic conception of cosmic history as a cyclical process which goes on infinitely, by necessity and for no purpose, Philo describes the cyclical changes in human history as being guided by "the divine Logos" according to a preconceived plan and toward a goal which is to be reached in the course of time. The preconceived plan and goal is that ultimately "the whole world may become, as it were, one city and enjoy the best of polities, a democracy." His description of the ultimate best of polities is an elaboration of the Messianic prophecies of Isaiah and Micah as to what will come to pass in the end of days.

This is a brief sypnosis of Philo's revision of Greek philosophic conceptions of the nature of God and his relation to the world and man. The historical significance of Philo is that his revision became the foundation of the common philosophy of the three religions with cognate Scriptures—Judaism, Christianity, and Islam. This triple religious philosophy, which originated with Philo, reigned supreme as a homogeneous, if not a completely unified, system of thought until the seventeenth century, when it was overthrown by Spinoza, for the philosophy of Spinoza, properly understood, is primarily a criticism of the common elements in this triple religious philosophy.

[1]Similar to the Epicurean view of free will, which is consequent to a denial of causality, is a view held by the Stoic Chrysippus. According to him, the eternal necessary internexus of causes does by its nature cease to function at certain actions in the world and similarly at the will of man, so that, with the cessation of causality, man's action is free. Cf. Cicero, *De Fato* 17, 19, 43, and my *The Philosophy of the Kalam,* pp. 692–693, nn. 68, 69, 69a.

4

GREEK PHILOSOPHY IN PHILO AND THE CHURCH FATHERS

SCRIPTURE AND PHILOSOPHY [1]

When, at about the middle of the 2nd century A.D., philosophically trained gentiles began to flock to Christianity—invariably, as they confess, by becoming acquainted with the teachings of Scripture—they formed a conception of the relation between philosophy and Scripture like that which about a century earlier was formed by the scripturally trained Philo on his becoming acquainted with the teachings of the philosophers. Philosophy and Scripture were held by them to contain two kinds of wisdom. One is that which Paul calls the 'wisdom of men' [2] or the wisdom 'which the Greeks seek after'.[3] The other is that which, again, Paul calls 'the wisdom of God' [4] and which, speaking of the particular gospel of his preaching, he describes as coming to him 'through the revelation of Jesus Christ',[5] but which the Fathers of the Church, if they were to speak of the matters dealt with by them in their own preachings, would describe as coming to them through the revelation of the two Testaments; for to all of them, as to Irenaeus, both Testaments are the revelations of one and the same Householder'.[6] Like Philo, they could not help observing striking similarities between some of the humanly discovered wisdom and the divinely revealed wisdom, such, for instance, as between the teachings of the philosophers and the teachings of the prophets about the unity of God, between their respective denunciations of the worship of images, between their respective condemnations of certain evil religious practices, and between their respective preoccupations with the problem of the righteous or virtuous conduct of men.[7]

These striking similarities seemed to the Fathers, as they did to Philo, to require an explanation. The explanation which they formally advanced, like the explanation which is informally suggested by Philo in various places in his works, is based upon the assumption that the similarities of the philosophic teachings to the prophetic teachings are also in some indirect way of divine origin. This single explanation is presented by the Fathers in three different forms. Sometimes they say that these similarities are borrowings on the part of the philosophers from the Scripture; sometimes they describe them as the discoveries of the philosophers by that power of reasoning which has been implanted in them by God; but sometimes they variously express themselves to the effect that philosophy is God's special gift to the Greeks by way of human reason as Scripture is to the Jews by way of direct revelation. In Philo the view that philosophy, like Scripture, was a special gift of God is indirectly suggested in two statements. In one of these he describes the Law as the words 'which God showers from . . . heaven' [8] and in the other he says that 'it is heaven which has showered philosophy upon us'.[9] Among the Church Fathers this is hinted at by Justin Martyr in his description of philosophy as that which 'is sent down to us',[10] but Clement of Alexandria—who in one passage, reflecting Philo's statement, only says that philosophy has come down 'from God to men . . . in the same way in which showers fall down on the good land' [11]—says in another passage that 'philosophy . . . was a schoolmaster to bring the Hellenic mind to Christ, as the Law was to bring the Hebrews'; [12] and in still another passage, having in mind the description of the Law as a covenant between God and Israel,[13] he says that 'philosophy especially was given to the Greeks as a covenant peculiar to them'.[14]

The belief in the divine origin of Scripture, which implies a belief in its completeness and perfection, led the Fathers, as it had led Philo, to the further belief that, in addition to the obviously striking similarities between the teachings of philosophy and Scripture, many more of the teachings of philosophy, which human reason and experience have found to be true, must have their similarities in the teaching of Scripture. Conditions of life made it necessary for the Fathers, as they did for Philo, to put this further belief of theirs to practical use. For in the Roman world the Christians were exposed to all the charges and accusations which had been levelled previously against the Hellenistic Jews, especially the charge of atheism, which was evoked by the Christian continuation of the Hellenistic Jewish attack upon polytheism, idolatry, and the various forms of heathen worship. If their rejection of the Law had exempted them from the ridicule heaped upon the Jews for their observance of the rite of circumcision and the dietary laws and the Sabbath, the particular form of their religious organization and the particular mode of their religious propaganda brought upon them new accusations, such as infanticide, cannibalism, incest, and disloyalty to the state.[15] Following the kind of defence that had already been developed among the Hellenistic Jews, the Fathers tried to show that in their attack upon polytheism and idolatry and the various forms of heathen worship they were merely following in the footsteps of the best pagan philosophers and that their doctrines, though outlandish, were in agreement with the teachings found in philosophy.

And so the Fathers of the Church, like Philo before them, entered upon their systematic undertaking to show how, behind the homely language in which Scripture likes to express itself, there are hidden the teachings of the philosophers couched in the obscure technical terms coined in their Academy, Lyceum, and Porch. When opponents among the Fathers quoted, against their attempt to philosophize Scripture, Paul's warning against being spoiled 'through philosophy and vain deceit',[16] they argued that the warning was only against the use of that kind of philosophy which is vain deceit but not against true philosophy, which conforms, or can be made to conform, with the teaching of Scripture.[17] The method used by the Fathers, and before them by Philo, in their common effort to invest the language of Scripture with meanings other than its literal meaning, is described by them as being allegorical.

The so-called 'typological allegory.' Now it happens that, before Philo and the Church Fathers, a similar allegorical interpretation of texts had been used by various Greek philosophers with reference to the mythologies in Homer and Hesiod. One would therefore naturally expect the existence of some relation between the earlier and the later uses of this method of interpretation. What that relation actually was may be determined by three sets of facts.

First, in Greek philosophy, as far as written records are concerned, the term 'allegorical' as a description of the philosophical interpretation of mythology occurs for the first time in the work of a certain Stoic named Heraclitus,[18] who is supposed to have been a contemporary of Philo's. Before him this method was described by Theagenes of Rhegium as "physical and ethical'[19] and by Plato and Xenophon as the 'underlying meaning' (ὑπόνοια *hyponoia*).[20] In Philo, the combined terms 'physical and ethical' and the Greek term for 'underlying meaning' and various grammatical forms of the term 'allegory' are all used as a description of his non-literal interpretation of scriptural texts to which he gives philosophical meanings. In addition, Philo uses, as a description of his non-literal interpretation, a number of other terms, some of which occur in Heraclitus either in combination with the term allegory or in the sense of allegory; but, among those other terms used by Philo are included the terms 'type' (τύπος *typos*) and 'shadow' (σκιά *skia*) and 'parable' (παραβολή *parabolē*),[21] none of which occurs in Heraclitus in any connection with allegory. There are also in Philo non-literal interpretations of scriptural texts in which the new meanings given by him are not philosophical but rather those common in the non-literal Midrashic interpretations used by the rabbis, among which there is his use once or twice of that particular kind of Midrashic interpretation which may be described as predictive, that is, as predicting some future event. The antiquity of this kind of Midrashic interpretation is attested by its use in the recently discovered Dead Sea Scrolls.

Second, in Christianity, the non-literal interpretation of scriptural texts designated by the term allegorical did not begin with the Church Fathers. It began with Paul. But with Paul the non-literal allegorical interpretations of scriptural texts are not of the philosophical kind; they are all of the Midrashic kind, and mainly of that Midrashic kind of interpretation which we have described as predictive. Then also, in addition to his use of the term 'allegory',[22] Paul uses, like Philo, the terms 'type'[23] and 'shadow'.[24] It is on the basis of his use of the term 'type' that students of Christianity refer to Paul's predictive kind of interpretation as typological allegory and regard it as an innovation introduced by Paul. Moreover, in the Epistle to the Hebrews, which is traditionally attributed to Paul, the Midrashic kind of predictive interpretation is described not only by the Philonic term 'shadow'[25] but also by the Philonic term 'parable'.[26]

Third, the first occurrence in the Church Fathers of non-literal interpretations of scriptural texts was of texts of the Old Testament, and the interpretations used were all of the Midrashic predictive kind, like that used by Paul. In Barnabas this is described by the term 'type', used by Paul and Philo, and in Justin Martyr it is described not only by the term 'type' but also by the term 'parable', used in the Epistle to the Hebrews and in Philo, and, in addition, by the terms 'symbol' (*σύμβολον symbolon*) and 'tropology' (*τροπολογία tropologia*), both of which are used by Philo, the latter term in its adjectival form 'tropical' (*τροπική tropikē*). The first to introduce non-literal interpretations of the philosophical kind in its application to texts of both the Old and the New Testament is Clement of Alexandria. From that time on, the philosophical kind of interpretation is used by the Fathers alongside of the Midrashic kind of predictive interpretation, the so-called 'typological allegory'. The terms used by them as descriptions of both these kinds of non-literal interpretations are, besides a few new terms, all terms used by Philo, to whom also some of their non-literal interpretation of Old Testament texts can be traced.[27]

From all this it may be gathered that the allegorical interpretation did not come to the Fathers directly from Greek philosophy; it came to them from Philo, partly through the Pauline writings, though in the course of its use by them it came into direct contact with the allegorical method, as used in Greek philosophy, and was affected by it.

The handmaid of theology. Their common belief that the wisdom of Scripture was directly revealed by God in contrast to the wisdom of philosophy which was the product of human reason, though not without the help and foresight of God, led both Philo and the Fathers to the principle of the subordination of philosophy to Scripture or, as it came to be known, the subordination of reason to faith. Scripture, in their view, contained certain beliefs which, though rationally undemonstrable, are fundamental, and to these philosophy, whenever it happened to disagree with them, had to yield. Now, in Greek philosophy, the view that there was a subordinate relationship between the encyclical studies and philosophy, in the limited sense that the former were serviceable and useful to the latter, had been expressed by the application to them respectively of the terms 'handmaids' (θεράπαιναι *therapainai*) and 'mistress' (δέσποινα *despoina*).[28] With this in the back of his mind, Philo, in his allegorical interpretation of the story of Sarah and Hagar, takes Hagar, the handmaid, to symbolize the encyclical studies, and Sarah, the mistress, to symbolize wisdom, which he uses in the sense of Scripture. Philo thus concludes: 'Just as encyclical culture is the handmaid (δούλη *doulē* = θεραπαινὶς *therapainis*) of philosophy, so also is philosophy the handmaid of wisdom.' [29] The same allegorical interpretation of the story of Sarah and Hagar is reproduced by Clement of Alexandria in a passage in which he mentions Philo. Thus, quoting the verse in which Abraham says to Sarah: 'Behold, thy maid is in thy hand; deal with her as it pleases thee,' [30] he interprets it allegorically: 'I embrace worldly culture as a younger maid and as a handmaid (θεραπαινίδα *therapainida*), but thy knowledge I honour and reverence as a full-grown mistress (δέσποιναν *despoinan*).' [31] Again, like Philo, Clement says: 'As the encyclical branches of study contribute to philosophy, which is their mistress (δέσποινα *despoina*), so also philosophy itself co-operates for the acquisition of wisdom. . . . Wisdom is therefore the mistress (κυρία *kyria*) of philosophy, as philosophy is of preparatory culture.' [32] Following Philo or Clement of Alexandria, the same allegorical interpretation of the story of Sarah and Hagar and the same ancillary conception of the relation of philosophy to Scripture is reproduced in various forms by other Fathers. John of Damascus, after alluding to that ancillary conception in his statement that 'it is fitting for the queen to be served by certain handmaids (ἅβραις *habrais*)', goes on to say: 'Let us, therefore, accept the (philosophers') sayings in so far as they serve the truth, but reject the impiety' that is in them.[33]

The ancillary relationship of philosophy to Scripture, or of reason to faith, thus had for Philo and the Fathers two different meanings, corresponding to two different kinds of scriptural teachings with which philosophy was to be brought into relation. First, with regard to scriptural teachings with which philosophy was in agreement, it meant that philosophy was to be used in the explanation and the justification of those teachings for the benefit of those who stood in need of such explanations and justifications. Second, with regard to those scriptural teachings with which philosophy was in disagreement, it meant that philosophy had to be rejected.

Of these two meanings, the second, referring as it does to scriptural teachings which were in conflict with philosophy, was accepted by the Fathers without any qualification. But in regard to the first meaning, referring as it does to scriptural teachings which could be rationally supported by philosophy, the question arose whether mere faith in those teachings was sufficient without the use of rational philosophic support.

In answer to this question, three views appeared among the Fathers. To some of them, of whom Tertullian was the spokesman, simple faith was self-sufficient. To others, of whom Origen was the spokesman, simple faith was inferior to rationalized faith. To still others, of whom Clement of Alexandria was the spokesman, simple faith and rationalized faith were equal. The last view found support in the philosophic use of the term 'faith' as a technical epistemological term. It happens that in a number of passages Aristotle uses the term 'faith' (*πίστις pistis*) as a designation both of undemonstrated immediate knowledge and of demonstrated derivative knowledge; and Simplicius, long after the time of Clement of Alexandria, is evidently following an old Peripatetic tradition when, in commenting on Aristotle's statement that 'anyone syllogizing may believe',[34] he says: 'Faith is twofold, the one without demonstration . . . the other after demonstration.'[35] Now some of the Aristotelian passages in which the term 'faith' is used in those two senses are quoted by Clement in several passages of his *Stromateis*. Then, in one passage, reflecting all these passages, he says that (1) 'faith in God' is 'obedience to the commandments', but that (2) 'demonstration . . . produces scientific faith (*ἐπιστημονικὴ πίστις epistēmonikē pistis*) which becomes "knowledge" (*γνῶσις gnōsis*)',[36] or, as he says in another place, 'knowledge is a sure and strong demonstration of what is received by faith'.[37]

This, then, was the common attitude of Philo and the Fathers toward philosophy. How that attitude manifested itself in their actual use of philosophy in their interpretation of Scripture may be illustrated by an analysis (1) of their common use of the Platonic Theory of Ideas in their respective treatments of their common belief in a Logos, and (2) of the Fathers' use of philosophy in their treatment of the ramifications of their particular conception of the Logos into the Christian doctrines of the Trinity and the Incarnation.

THE LOGOS AND THE PLATONIC IDEAS [38]

Philo, who, on the basis of Scripture supplemented by Jewish tradition, believed that, before the creation of the world, God created certain incorporeal things after the pattern of which He subsequently created corporeal things in this created world, identified this belief of his with the Platonic Theory of Ideas. But in Plato he found contradictory statements with regard to the origin of the Ideas. In some of these statements the Ideas are described as uncreated and coeternal with God; in others they are described as created by God; and in still others the language used lends itself to the interpretation that they are mere thoughts of God. Harmonizing these conflicting statements, Philo arrived at a view according to which the Ideas had existed from eternity as thoughts of God; but that, when God was about to create the world, He created the Ideas as incorporeal patterns for the corporeal things of which the world was to consist. Then in Plato he found that the incorporeal Ideas were integrated into what Plato calls an 'intelligible animal', in contrast to the corporeal world which he calls the 'visible animal'.[39] To Philo, however, who, unlike Plato, did not believe that the corporeal world possessed a soul, the term 'animal' did not seem to be an appropriate description of it. He therefore changed the term 'animal' in both descriptions to the term 'world,' and thus the contrast between the integrated Ideas and the corporeal world became a contrast between the 'intelligible world' and the 'visible world.' Then, also, Philo found in Aristotle a reference to a saying, evidently of some Platonists, that 'the thinking soul' is 'the place of Forms',[40] that is, of Ideas. Under the combined influence of two precedents—on the one hand the Greek use of the term *logos,* meaning, literally, 'word', in the sense of what Aristotle calls here 'the thinking soul' and in the sense of Plato's statement that all animals and plants and inanimate substances 'are created by a *logos* [that is, a reason] and a divine knowledge which comes from God',[41] and on the other hand the scriptural statement (Psalm xxxiii 6 in the Septuagint version) that 'by the *logos* of the Lord the heavens were established'[42]—Philo came to describe the Logos as the place of the intelligible world of Ideas by which the world was created.

The Logos, together with the intelligible world of Ideas within it, thus had, for Philo, two stages of existence; first, as existing within God and hence identical with Him; second, as a real being which came into existence by an act of creation. That, according to Philo, the Logos, together with the intelligible world of Ideas within it, entered upon its second stage of existence by an act of creation, like that by which the visible world came into existence, may be gathered from Philo's description of the Logos as 'older (πρεσβύτερος *presbyteros*) than all things which were the objects of creation',[43] and likewise from his description of the intelligible world as being 'older' in comparison with the visible world as being 'younger' (νεώτερος *neōteros*).[44] Now the terms 'older' and 'younger' are evidently used here by Philo in the same sense in which they are used by Plato in his description of the universal soul as being not 'younger' (νεωτέρα *neōtera*) than the world but rather 'older' (πρεσβυτέρα *presbytera*) than it.[45] But this description by Plato of the universal soul and the world as being respectively older and younger makes a comparison between two created things, since, for Plato, the universal soul, like the world, is created. Consequently, when Philo describes the Logos as being 'older' than all created things and the intelligible world as being 'older' than the 'younger' visible world, the implication is that, for him, the Logos as well as the intelligible world is created in the sense in which the visible world and all things in it are said to be created. Accordingly, Philo's description of the Logos as 'the firstborn son' of God[46] is to be taken as having carried, for him, the same sense as his description of righteous human beings as 'sons of God'.[47] Philo is using the phrase, not in the sense of being begotten of God but rather in the sense of being created by God. Therefore when Philo says of the Logos that it is 'neither uncreated as God is not created as you are' [48] he means by this that, though the Logos was created like all created beings, still, as an incorporeal being, its creation was not like that of man, who was created, as Scripture says, out of dust from the earth.[49]

Since the Logos is said by Philo, in the passage just quoted, to be not uncreated, as God is, the Logos cannot be called God. Accordingly, when Philo himself happens to intepret the term 'God' in Genesis xxxi 13 as referring to the Logos, he hastens to explain that this does not mean that there are 'two Gods'; for, as he goes on to say, 'He that is truly God is one, but those that are improperly so called are more than one.' [50] And so also, when Philo himself happens to describe the Logos as 'a second God' [51] or as 'second to God',[52] this description of the Logos means simply that it is 'divine' (θεῖος *theios*), which is Philo's usual description of the Logos.[53]

In the beginning was the Word. Among the Fathers, speculation about the Logos hinged upon the word *Logos* in the Prologue to the Gospel according to St. John, where it is used as a designation of the pre-existent Christ who subsequently became flesh and where it is described as 'the only begotten from the Father' [54] and as 'God'.[55] Whatever these two descriptions of the Logos may have meant originally when used by John, the Church Fathers, from the earliest times, beginning with those Fathers described as Apostolic, took them to mean literally that the Logos was begotten or generated out of the essence of God and that it was God in the sense that the Father, its begetter, was God. Somewhat later, however, beginning with those philosophizing Fathers called Apologists, two questions arose with regard to this Johannine Logos. First, while all of them believed that the Logos as a real being was not created by God but was generated out of His essence, the question arose among them as to when that generation had taken place. Second, the Fathers somehow came to believe that the Logos of John, like the Logos of Philo, was some kind of version of the Platonic Theory of Ideas, and so the question arose among them as to whether the implication of the Johannine Logos-ized version of that theory, namely, that the Ideas were generated together with the Logos out of the essence of God, represented the Theory of Ideas as originally conceived of by Plato.

The first question—the question when the generation of the Logos had taken place—gave rise to two theories. The first of these two theories to arise was a two-stages theory of existence like that held by Philo, except that the entrance of the Logos upon its second stage of existence, when it became a real being after it had been from eternity a thought of God's, was effected, not by its being created by God, but by its being generated from His essence. The exponents of this theory were such Greek Fathers as Justin Martyr, Tatian, Athenagoras, Theophilus, Hippolytus, and Clement of Alexandria, and such Latin Fathers as Tertullian, Novatian, Lactantius, and, much later, Zeno of Verona. This theory's opposite was a single-stage theory of existence known as that of eternal generation. This was introduced, for different reasons, by Irenaeus and Origen, and it is this single-stage theory that was tacitly recognized as the established Christian belief, though the two-stages theory was never formally anathematized and hence was never branded as being heretical. As representative examples of the manner in which the two-stages theory of existence was presented by its adherents among the Fathers, we may quote two brief statements, one written in Greek by Theophilus and the other written in Latin by Tertullian. As presented by Theophilus, it reads that 'before anything came into being', the Logos was God's 'own mind and thought . . . but, when God wished to make all that He determined on, He begot the Logos as something uttered, "the firstborn of all creation" '.[56] As presented by Tertullian, the theory reads that, 'before all things God was alone', though not without that Reason or Logos 'which He had in Himself'; [57] but, 'as soon as God willed to produce' the world 'He first brought forth the Logos itself'.[58]

When exactly the Platonic Ideas were read into the Johannine Logos is not clear. Justin Martyr says that, before he became a Christian, the Platonic 'conception of incorporeals quite overpowered me and the contemplation of Ideas furnished my mind with wings',[59] but he does not tell us whether, after his conversion to Christianity, he abandoned his belief in Platonic Ideas altogether or whether he has only given them another interpretation. About twenty-five years later, Athenagoras, referring to the Logos during its first stage of existence, says that 'the Son of God is the

Logos of the Father in Idea and in operation, for after the pattern of Him and through Him were all things made'; but, then, referring to the Logos during the second stage of its existence, he says that 'He came forth to be the Idea and operating power of all material things'.[60]

Athenagoras does not tell us how his conception of the Ideas is related to that of Plato. His contemporary Irenaeus, however, makes it clear that his Logos-ized Theory of the Ideas was unlike that of Plato. Plato's Theory of Ideas in their integration is represented by Irenaeus as a belief in the existence of a 'pattern' (*exemplum*) by the side of matter and God, and this, he says, is the basis of the Gnostic theory of aeons. Both of these theories he rejects. His own view is that God 'receives from Himself the pattern (*exemplum*) and form (*figurationem*) of those things which are made',[61] by which he means that the Ideas come from God Himself; for they are contained in the Logos, and the Logos, according to Irenaeus, is eternally generated from the essence of God. Similarly Tertullian makes the Platonic Theory of Ideas the source of the Gnostic theory of aeons, both of which he rejects. As for his own conception of Ideas Tertullian starts out by saying that the Latin term *sensus*, 'mind' or 'thought', means the same as the Greek term *Logos* and the Latin term *sermo*.[62] He then goes on to say: 'As soon as God willed to bring forth . . . the things which He, together with His . . . Logos, had devised within Himself, He first brought forth the Logos itself . . . in order that all things might be made through that through which they had been planned and devised, yea, and already made, in so far as they were in the mind of God (*in dei sensu*).'[63] From this it may be inferred that the Ideas, which are said by Tertullian to have existed 'in the mind of God', existed in the Logos of God.

Plato Philonized and Johannized. While Irenaeus and Tertullian regarded the Johannine Logos-ized Theory of Ideas as something different from the Theory of Ideas as conceived by Plato himself, Clement of Alexandria and Augustine regarded them as being the same.

Clement's view with regard to the relation of the Johannine Logos-ized Theory of Ideas to the Platonic Theory of Ideas may be gathered from the following passages.

In one passage,[64] Clement makes three statements. First, on the basis of a quotation from John, he identifies John's 'Logos' with 'truth.' Second, on the basis of a quotation from the *Phaedrus,* he shows that Plato identified 'truth' with 'an Idea', that is to say, with the totality of Ideas. Third, 'an Idea', Clement says, is that which 'the Barbarians have termed the Logos of God', by which, as it can be shown, he means that the Jews, as represented by Philo, have defined the Logos as being the totality of Ideas. Here then we have an identification of the Logos-ized Theory of Ideas of John with that of Philo, and the identification of both of these with the Platonic Theory of Ideas.

In another passage,[65] after ascribing to 'the Barbarian philosophy' what is known to us as the Philonic contrast between 'the intelligible world' and 'the sensible world' and also as the Philonic interpretation of the account of the first day of creation as referring to the creation of 'the intelligible world,' Clement says: "Does not Plato hence appear to have left the Ideas of living creatures in the intelligible world, and to make intelligible objects into sensible species according to their genera?' Here then we have a suggestion that Plato's account of creation in the *Timaeus* is based on the Book of Genesis, the interpretation of which by Philo was accepted by Clement as its true meaning.

In still another passage,[66] the Philonic statement that God is 'the incorporeal dwelling-place (χώρα *chōra*) of incorporeal Ideas' [67] (reproduced by Clement in the formula that God is 'the dwelling-place of Ideas'), is attributed by Clement to Plato, who, Clement says, 'has learned from Moses that He was a place (τόπος *topos* which contained all things'. The Moses to whom Clement traces the view which he attributes to Plato is really Philo, who interpreted the term 'place' in the verse 'and he saw the place afar off' [68] as referring to God,[69] explaining that God is called place 'by reason of His containing all things'.[70]

Thus Clement of Alexandria first identifies both the Johannine and the Philonic Logos-ized Theories of Ideas with the Platonic Theory of Ideas and then shows how the Platonic Theory of Ideas was derived from the teachings of Moses as interpreted by Philo.

Augustine, at one time, tried to prove the existence of an intelligible world beyond the world of sense from Jesus' saying: 'My kingdom is not of this world.' [71] When later he retracted this interpretation of the verse, he still argued for the existence of an intelligible world of Ideas within the Logos, which to him was eternally generated from the essence of God.[72] This conception of a Logos-ized Theory of Ideas is constantly treated by Augustine as if it were the same as the original Platonic theory. In one place he gives direct expression to this view, and that is in his *Commentary on John,* where he says, without any qualification, that 'in the books of the philosophers' it is also to be found 'that God has an only begotten Son, by whom all things are'.[73]

THE TRINITY AND PHILOSOPHY [74]

Philo, as we have seen,[75] after interpreting the term God in a certain scriptural verse as referring to the Logos, hastened to explain that this does not imply the existence of 'two Gods', arguing that 'He who is truly God is one', so that, whenever he himself happens to apply the term God to the Logos, he uses it loosely in the sense of divine. In the light of this, when the Fathers insisted that the Logos is God in the true sense of the term God, the implication was that there were two Gods. And so, when the Nicene Creed started with the affirmation of a belief 'in one God' and then went on to affirm that the Logos, to whom it refers as 'the Son of God' and the 'only-begotten', is 'God of God', there was a simultaneous affirmation of a belief in one God and of a belief in two Gods, or rather of a belief in one God who was two Gods. Moreover, when the Holy Spirit, who in Justin Martyr is described only as that whom 'we worship and adore',[76] was ultimately declared to be God, the simultaneous affirmation became that of a belief in one God and of a belief in three Gods, or, again, rather of a belief in one God who was three Gods. How to explain and to justify such a conception of a triune deity became a matter of discussion among the Fathers from Justin Martyr to John of Damascus. To all these philosophically trained Fathers this conception of a triune deity seemed to be in violation of what came to be called the Law of Contradiction, which, as formulated by Aristotle in terms that he attributes to Heraclitus, reads: 'It is impossible for contrary attributes to belong at the same time to the same subject.' [77]

Two attempts at solving the problem were made in the course of its history, one by denying the reality of the Logos and the Holy Spirit and the other by denying their Godhood. The first solution had at least eight successive sponsors. One of them, Sabellius, is said to have maintained that 'Father and Son are the same' [78] and that the terms Father and Son and Holy Spirit are merely actions (*ἐνέργειαι energeiai*) or names (*ὀνομασίαι onomasiai*) and are to be compared to 'the light and the heat and the circular form in the sun'.[79] The second solution, offered by Arius, was in effect a return to the Philonic view [80] that the Logos, as well as the Holy Spirit, was not generated from the essence of God but rather was created by God, and that therefore, like anything created by God, it was not God. Both these solutions were anathematized and were branded as heretical.

Most of the Fathers, however, adhering as they did to the established Christian belief in a triune God, tried to defend this belief. Their defence of it consisted primarily in the assertion that the two doctrines, Generation and Trinity, are two ineffable and incomprehensible mysteries, which are not subject to any of the criteria of human reason. Still, while not attempting to probe into the rationality of these mysteries, they tried to explain them and to make them intelligible and to clear them of the most obvious objections, and this they did by the use of philosophic terminology and philosophic concepts. Here are a few examples.

First, wishing to express their opposition to those who claimed that Father and Son and Holy Spirit are only names, they argued that these members of the Trinity are distinguished from each other 'in number' (*ἀριθμῷ arithmō*) and not 'in name only'.[81] What they meant to say is that each member of the Trinity is what Aristotle would call a real individual being (*τὸ ἄτομον to atọmon*); for a real individual being is described by Aristotle as being 'one in number' (*ἓν ἀριθμῷ hen arithmō*).[82]

Second, in order to explain how, on the basis of their belief that the Logos was generated out of the essence of God, they were justified in believing that it is God, they drew upon Aristotle's statement that 'it is the most natural function of all living things . . . to reproduce their species, animal producing animal and plant plant',[83] as also 'man begets man' (another quotation from

Aristotle).[84] Thus Augustine, in his argument against the Arian theologian Maximinus, quotes Aristotle's statement that 'man begets man', with his own addition 'and dog dog', and he then challenges his opponent as follows: 'For you see that a corruptible creature can beget an offspring like itself, and yet you believe that God, the Father almighty, could not beget His only-begotten Son except with a nature of an inferior kind.'[85]

Third, in their attempt to show that, while the conception of a triune God is a mystery which cannot be solved by human reason, it is still free of the charge of its being a violation of what Aristotle could have called the Law of Contradiction, the Fathers try to show that even philosophers sometimes allow the simultaneous description of a thing as being both one and many. In this connection they draw upon Aristotle's enumeration of various ways in which things which are many may legitimately be called one without any violation of the Law of Contradiction. Two of these ways are especially selected by the Fathers as useful for their purpose. One is that which Aristotle describes as the unity of species or of genus, illustrated by the example of several distinct human beings who may be described as being one because of their belonging to the same species man or to the same genus animal.[86] Thus Basil explains that the three members of the Trinity, each of them God, may be said to be one God, in the same way as 'Peter, Andrew, John, and James' are said to be 'one man'[87] or 'one animal.'[88] The other way is that which Aristotle calls the unity of substratum, illustrated by the example of oil and wine which may be described as one because of their common 'substratum' (ὑποκείμενον *hypokeimenon*), which is water.[89] Thus, according to Augustine, the three members of the Trinity, each of them God, may be said to be one God, in the same way as we say of three golden statues: 'three statues, one gold'.[90]

In search of a philosophical nomenclature. Having thus explained how philosophically the three members of the Trinity, despite their each being God, may still be described as one God, the Fathers began to look in the stockpile of philosophic terminology for two good technical terms, of which one would be used as a designation of the reality of the distinctness of each member of the Trinity as an individual and the other would be used as a designation of their underlying common unity. The first two Fathers who dealt with this problem, Origen in Greek and Tertullian in Latin, experimented with various terms.

As a designation of the reality of the distinctness of each member of the Trinity as an individual, the following Greek terms were suggested by Origen:

1. πρᾶγμα (*pragma*),[91] 'thing', evidently based upon a statement by Aristotle in which the Greek term for 'thing' is contrasted with the Greek term for 'name'.[92]

2. οὐσία (*ousia*),[93] which is usually translated either literally as 'essence' or conventionally as 'substance'. This term *ousia*, according to Aristotle, may be used either in the sense of 'primary *ousia*', that is, 'individual', or in the sense of 'secondary *ousia*', that is, 'species' or 'genus'.[94] Here it is quite evidently used by Origen in the sense of 'primary *ousia*'.

3. ὑποκείμενον *hypokeimenon*. In Aristotle, as we have seen, this term is used in the sense of 'substratum'. Origen, however, says that the Son is distinct from the Father 'according to *ousia* and *hypokeimenon*',[95] which shows that he uses it in the sense of 'primary *ousia*' and 'individual'. This use of the term may have been suggested to him by a passage in Aristotle in which the term ὑποκείμενα (*hypokeimena*) is contrasted with the term καθόλου (*katholou*), 'universal'.[96]

4. ὑπόστασις, *hypostasis*. In a passage in which Origen criticizes those whom he at first describes as maintaining that the Father and the Son are 'one . . . in *hypokeimenon*', he then repeats the same criticism by describing them as denying that the Father and the Son are 'different . . . according to *hypostases*'.[97] This shows that he uses the term *hypostasis*, as he uses the term *hypokeimenon*, in the sense of 'individual' and 'primary *ousia*.' That such a use of the term *hypostasis* was already known by the time of Origen may be inferred from a passage in Hippolytus in which, evidently drawing upon some older source, he describes Aristotle's terms 'individual' and 'primary *ousia*' by the expression 'hypostatic *ousia*' (οὐσία ὑποστατική).[98]

In Latin, Tertullian suggests the following terms:

1. *res*,[99] which is a literal translation of the Greek πρᾶγμα (*pragma*).

2. *substantia,*[100] which may be used here either as an etymological translation of the Greek ὑπόστασις (*hypostasis*) or as a conventionalized translation of the Greek οὐσία (*ousia*). In either case, it is used here by Tertullian in the sense of 'primary *ousia.*'

3. *persona,*[101] which has its counterpart in the corresponding Greek term used by Tertullian's contemporary Hippolytus.[102] This term has no technical philosophic background. But both in Latin and in Greek it has the meaning of 'individual'.

As a designation of the underlying common unity of the three persons of the Trinity, Origen uses again the term *ousia.*[103] In this case he undoubtedly uses it in the sense of 'secondary *ousia*', that is, species or genus. Similarly, Tertullian uses again the term *substantia,*[104] as a translation of either *hypostasis* or *ousia,* but in either case it is in the sense of 'secondary *ousia.*' It is quite possible, however, that, if employed here as a translation of *hypostasis,* it might be used in the sense of 'substratum', to which the term *hypostasis* lends itself and in which sense it is used later in the Nicene Creed.

Ultimately, in Greek, the Cappadocians adopted the formula μία οὐσία, τρεῖς ὑποστάσεις (*mia ousia, treis hypostaseis*), of which, says Augustine, the Latin translation should be *una essentia vel substantia, tres personae,* and not *una essentia, tres substantiae*. Augustine's objection to the latter rendering was on the ground, as he says, that 'with us it is the already established usage that by *essentia* we understand the same thing that is understood by *substantia*'.[105] Augustine's *essentia vel substantia,* it may be remarked, reflects, in reverse order, the terms used in the phrase *ex alia substantia aut essentia* in the Latin translation of the Greek phrase ἐξ ἑτέρας ὑποστάσεως ἢ οὐσίας (*ex heteras hypostaseōs ē ousias*) in the Nicene Creed, where, as here by Augustine, these two terms are used in the sense of 'substratum'.

THE INCARNATION AND PHILOSOPHY[106]

In both Philo and John, the Logos is said to be that through which God created the world. In Philo, however, at the creation of the world the Logos is said to have been caused by God to become immanent in the world and to be used by God as that through which He operates the laws of nature in it. In its immanence the Logos is thus described by Philo as 'extending itself from the midst [of the world] to its utmost bounds'; [107] as being 'such a bond of the universe as nothing can break',[108] as being that which 'holds together and administers all things',[109] and as being 'the ruler and steersman of all'.[110] It is to be remarked that some of the terms used by Philo in describing his immanent Logos are used by Plato and by the Stoics in describing their respective world souls.

So also the Fathers—evidently taking John's statement that the Logos 'was in the world',[111] which follows his earlier statement that 'all things were made through' the Logos,[112] to mean that, after the creation of the world, the Logos became immanent in it—conceived of this Johannine immanent Logos as that through which God operates His laws of nature in the world. The Fathers thus apply to this immanent Logos the following descriptions: God 'set in order all things through him'; [113] through the Logos, the world 'is set in order and kept in being'; [114] the Logos 'is called the governing principle because he rules and is master of all things fashioned by him'; [115] the Logos 'orders all things in accordance with the Father's will and holds the helm of the universe in the best way'.[116]

For Philo the career of the Logos comes to an end on its becoming immanent in the world. For the Fathers, however, its career does not end there. For them, about 3760 years and three months after the creation of the world, if we combine the traditional date for the Christian era with the traditional Jewish date for the era of creation, or 5500 years after the creation, if we follow the calculation current among the Church Fathers, or 4004 years after creation, if we follow the chronology of Archbishop Ussher, Jesus was born and thereby the Logos entered a new stage of existence. In John that new stage of existence is described by the statement: 'And the Logos became flesh.' [117] In other parts of the New Testament, however, the pre-existent Christ whom John calls Logos is described as having 'a body' prepared for him [118] or as 'becoming in the likeness of men' [119] and as 'being found in fashion as a man'.[120] This enfleshment, that is, incarnation (*σάρκωσις sarkōsis*) or embodiment (*ἐνσωμάτωσις ensōmatōsis*) or humanation (*ἐνανθρώπησις enanthrōpēsis*) of the Logos, like its

Generation and the Trinity, was declared by the Fathers to be an ineffable and incomprehensible mystery. Still, under a complexity of influences again, like the mystery of the Generation of the Logos and the mystery of the Trinity, it was presented and explained and justified by the use of the philosophic terminology and philosophic concepts and reasoning.

This complexity of influences falls into three parts.

First, in Philo, the relation of the immanent Logos to the body of the world is described in terms of an analogy with the relation of the soul to the body in man. Thus, having in mind his own interpretation of the phrase 'garments (*χιτῶνας chitōnas*) of skin' in Genesis iii 21 to mean the body in which the soul abides, and interpreting the term 'garments' (*ἱμάτια himatia*) in Leviticus xxi 10 to mean the world in which the immanent Logos abides,[121] Philo compares the relation of the immanent Logos to the world to the relation of the soul to the body.[122] Then, also, having in mind the term 'houses' used in the Book of Job (iv 19) as a description of human bodies in their relation to human souls, Philo describes man's body as 'house',[123] and he similarly describes the world in its relation to God, who abides in it through the immanent Logos, as 'house'[124] and 'temple'.[125] So also, in Paul, the human body in its relation to the soul is described as 'house'[126] and as 'tabernacle';[127] and, in John, the Logos, which became flesh, is said to have 'tabernacled among us'[128] and the body of Jesus in which the Logos is incarnate is described as 'temple'.[129]

Second, in Aristotle, the soul is contrasted with the body as form is with matter,[130] and form and matter are each described as an *ousia* or a nature.[131] Accordingly in the language of Aristotle soul and body could be described as two *ousiai* or two natures. Similarly, Philo contrasts God, whom he describes as a 'simple nature',[132] with man who, he says, is made up of many things, among them 'soul and body', and this implies that soul and body are two natures.

Third, according to Aristotle, soul and body, though each an *ousia* and a nature, are 'one'[133] and so also any given man, though consisting of a soul and a body, is to be described as a 'primary *ousia*'[134] and as an 'individual'[135] and as 'one in number'[136]—

terms which, as we have seen, are used by the Fathers as the equivalent of the terms 'person' and *hypostasis*.[137] The question raised by Aristotle—why soul and body are one[138] and hence why man is one[139]—is answered by Aristotle himself in his own comparison of the relation between soul and body with the relation between matter and form. In discussing the relation of form to matter, Aristotle says in one place that the form is the source from which a thing derives its individuality and its name, so that a thing whose matter is bronze and whose form is statue is called statue.[140] So also, in the case of soul in its relation to body, Aristotle says in another place that it is 'the intellectual element' in man that 'is generally thought to be a man's real self'.[141] The same view is re-echoed by Philo in his statement that 'the mind in each of us is rightfully and in the true sense the man'.[142] It is re-echoed again later by Plotinus in his statements that 'the soul of man is man'[143] or 'the soul of man is man himself'[144] or 'the real man coincides with the rational soul'.[145]

And the Word became flesh. With all these precedents in the back of their minds, all the Fathers, however else they may differ with regard to the relation of the incarnate Logos to that in which it is incarnate, agree in comparing that relation to the relation of soul to body. They all describe that in which the Logos is incarnate by various Greek or Latin terms which mean 'house' or 'tabernacle' or 'temple' or 'garment'.[146]

But, as we have seen, that in which the Logos was incarnate is described in the New Testament as being 'flesh' or 'body' and as being 'man'. Now man, whom philosophers define as a rational animal, possesses a soul which they describe as rational. Accordingly, the Fathers were divided on the question as to whether that in which the Logos was incarnate was a man who possessed a rational soul or only a body which was without a soul.

The view commonly held by the Fathers was that that in which the Logos was incarnate was a man endowed with a rational soul. Since it was generally assumed that the relation of the Logos to the man in Jesus was analogous to the relation of the soul to the body in man, and since philosophically the soul and body in man constituted two natures or two *ousiai,* Jesus is said to possess two natures or two *ousiai,* corresponding to the Logos and to the humanity in him. Then, also, since man, though consisting of two natures, is one individual or person, so also Jesus, though consisting of two natures, is one person; and, since that which makes man one person is his soul, so also that which makes Jesus one person is the Logos in him.

As illustrations of how all this is expressed by the Fathers, we may quote a few representative statements. The analogy of soul and body is exemplified in a statement of Augustine's, which reads: 'The Son of God, who is the Logos of God, has man, as soul has body. . . . What is man? A rational soul having a body. What is Christ? The Logos of God having man.' [147] The doctrine of the two *ousiai* or natures appears in Melito of Sardis when he describes the 'God' and the 'perfect man' in Jesus as being 'two *ousiai*'.[148] Origen refers to the divine and the human in Jesus as being 'the nature of that deity' and 'that human nature'.[149] Tertullian, using the Latin *substantia* for the Greek *ousia,* says of Jesus that he has 'two substances' or 'two natures'.[150] The doctrine of the one person appears in Augustine when he says: 'Just as soul is united to the body in unity of person so as to constitute man, so in the same way is God united to man in unity of person so as to constitute Christ'.[151]

A dissenting view was advanced in the latter part of the 4th century by Apollinaris. On purely theological grounds, he started with the belief that that in which the Logos was incarnate could not be a complete man possessing a rational soul.[152] It had to be a body. At first, it is reported, he believed that the body had neither a rational nor an irrational soul, but then he changed his mind and maintained that the body had no rational soul but had an irrational soul. This change of mind may be explained as being due to a change in his philosophic position on a problem with regard to man's irrational soul.[153] According to Aristotle and the Stoics, and also Plato in all but one of his dialogues, the so-called irrational soul in man is only a faculty of his soul, so that his body is without an irrational soul. It is this view which Apollinaris at first followed. According to Plato in the *Timaeus* and Philo in his interpretation of the account of the creation of man in Genesis ii 7, the irrational soul of man is part of his body, together with which it was created, though, according to Philo, it is also united with man's rational soul and is part thereof.[154] This is the view that Apollinaris adopted on second thoughts. Since, according to Apollinaris, Jesus had no rational soul, he had no human nature; there was in him only a divine nature, corresponding to the Logos in him.

The difference of opinion on the question whether Jesus had two natures or one nature produced the two positions known as Dyophysitism and Monophysitism, and it led logically to a difference of opinion on the question whether Jesus had two wills or one will, which produced the two positions known as Dyotheletism and Monotheletism. Those who believed that Jesus had two natures believed also that he had two wills, whereas those who believed that Jesus had only one nature believed also that he had only one will.

Among the Dyophysites, however, there was one, Pyrrhus of Alexandria, who, in spite of his belief that Jesus had two natures, maintained that he had only one will, the divine will. He debated on this subject with Maximus Confessor.[155] Among the arguments by which Pyrrhus supported his view there was one in which, having in mind statements by Aristotle to the effect that action in accordance with one's nature may be described as necessary [156] and hence as compulsory [157] and involuntary,[158] he started out by saying that 'what is natural is entirely necessary', and on the basis of this he went on to argue that, if, as it is claimed, there must be two wills in Jesus to correspond to his two natures, then these wills will each be natural, and, being natural, they will be necessary and compulsory, and thus Jesus would act without freedom of the will. Maximus' refutation of this argument may be restated as follows: Aristotle, in one of the statements which Pyrrhus had in mind,[159] does indeed say that necessity applies to action according to one's own nature, but immediately after that he himself adds that 'of the products of (man's) reason some are never due to . . . necessity'. On the basis of this, Maximus concludes that, inasmuch as Jesus had only a rational soul, the corresponding nature and will of which were, as was maintained by those who believed in two natures and two wills, always in harmony with the nature and will of the Logos in him, his actions in accordance with these two natures and wills in him were not performed by necessity, and hence not by compulsion. They were completely free.

The Christian Fathers as selective philosophers. This is how Philo and the Fathers used philosophy in the discussion of their common belief in a Logos, and how the Fathers used it in the discussion of the Trinity and the Incarnation; and this, one may find, is also how they used philosophy in the discussion of their common or particular conceptions of all the various scriptural teachings, ranging from the creation of the world to its future in the end of days. In all these attempts of theirs to apply philosophy to problems arising from scriptural teaching, one will find that the Fathers as well as Philo did not approach their task as partisans of any of the various schools of Greek philosophy. Their speculations on all such problems did not turn on contrasts between the different systems within philosophy; they turned only on a contrast between Scripture and philosophy. Within philosophy itself there were, for them, only doctrines which were in agreement with Scripture and doctrines which were in disagreement with Scripture, though on certain doctrines they found that some philosophers were in agreement with Scripture more often than others. In battling among themselves, the Fathers did not battle as followers of certain opposing schools of Greek philosophy; they battled only as advocates of opposing interpretations of Scripture. Their opposing interpretations of Scripture, however, were sometimes influenced by philosophic considerations or were supported by philosophic arguments, and it is in this way, therefore, that the Fathers are found occasionally to have aligned themselves with certain philosophic attitudes on certain particular problems. But it would be altogether wrong historically to arrange the Fathers into groups, to dress them up in the uniforms of the Academy and the Lyceum and the Porch, to march them under the school banners of Plato and Aristotle and the Stoics, and to make them sing the schools' respective school songs.

1. *Cf.* my *Philo* 4th ed. Cambridge Mass. 1968 vol. 1 p. 2–199; and *The Philosophy of the Church Fathers* 2nd ed. Cambridge Mass. vol. 1 p. 1–140.
2. I Cor. ii 5.
3. I Cor. i 22.
4. I Cor. i 21, 24.

5. Gal. i 12.
6. *Adversus Haereses* IV 9, 1.
7. *Cf. Philo* vol. I p. 17–19.
8. *Legum Allegoria* III 56, 162.
9. *Specialibus Legibus* III 34, 185.
10. *Dialogus* 2.
11. *Stromateis* I 7 (*Patrologia Graeca* I||| 732B).
12. *Ibid.* I 5 (717D).
13. Deut. v 2.
14. *Strom.* VI 8 (*PG* IX 288C).
15. Tertullian *Apologeticus* chapters 1, 4, 5, 7 and 20.
16. Col. ii 8.
17. Origen *Contra Celsum* I *Praefatio* 5; Augustine *Confessions* VIII 2, 3.
18. Heraclitus *Quaestions Homericae* ed. F. Oelmann, Leipzig 1910.
19. *Cf.* H. Diels *Die Fragmente der Vorsakratiker* 5th ed. Berlin 1922, 8 Theagenes 2.
20. Xenophon *Symposium* 3, 6; Plato *Republic* II 378D.
21. *Cf. Church Fathers* vol. I p. 30–1.
22. Gal. iv 24.
23. Rom. v 14; I Cor. x 11.
24. Col. ii 16–17.
25. Heb. x 1.
26. Heb. ix 9.
27. *Cf. Church Fathers* vol. I p. 43–72.
28. H. F. von Arnim *Stoicorum Veterum Fragmenta* Leipzig 1903–5 vol. I 349–50.
29. *De Congressu* 14, 78–80.
30. Gen. xvi 6.
31. *Strom.* I 5 (*PG* VIII 725B).
32. *Ibid* (721B–724A).
33. *Dialectica* I (*PG* XCIV 532B).
34. *De Caelo* I 2, 269b 13–14.
35. *Simplicius in De Caelo* ed. I. L. Heiberg, Berlin 1894 p. 55: 11, 3–4.
36. *Strom* II 11 (*PG* VIII 985A), but see note 4 *ad. loc.*, and Stahlin's edition of the *Stromateis* Leipzig 1906 p. 139: II, 5–6.
37. *Ibid.* VII 10 (*PG* IX 481A).
38. *Cf. Philo* vol. I p. 200–294; *Church Fathers* vol. I p. 192–286; and my *Religious Philosophy* Cambridge, Mass. 1961 p. 27–49.
39. *Timaeus* 39E and 30D.
40. *De Anima* III 4, 429a, 27–8.
41. *Sophist* 265C.
42. In the Septuagint version this is Psalm xxxii.
43. *De Migratione* 1, 6.
44. *De Opificio* 4, 16.
45. *Timaeus* 34C.
46. *De Agricultura* 12, 51.
47. *De Confusione* 28, 145.
48. *Quis Heres* 42, 206.
49. Gen. ii 7.
50. *De Somniis* I 39, 227–9.
51. *Quaestiones in Genesin* II 62.
52. Leg. *All.* II 21, 86.
53. *De Abrahamo* 41, 244 and *passim.*
54. John i 14.
55. John i 1.

56. *Ad Autolycum* II 22.
57. *Adversus Praxeam* 5
58. *Ibid.* 6.
59. *Ibid.* 2.
60. *Supplicatio* 10.
61. *Adv. Haer.* II 16, 3.
62. *Adv. Praxeam* 5.
63. *Ibid.* 6.
64. *Strom.* V 3 (*PG* IX 32B–33A).
65. *Ibid.* V 14 (137A).
66. *Ibid.* V 11 (112A).
67. *Cf. De Cherubim* 14, 49.
68. Gen. xxii 4.
69. *De Somniis* I 11, 64.
70. *Ibid.* 65.
71. John xviii in *De Ordine* I 11, 32.
72. *Retractiones* I 3, 2.
73. *In Joannis Evangelium* 2, 4.
74. *Cf. Church Fathers* vol. I p. 287–363.
75. *Cf.* above at notes 50–53.
76. *First Apologia* 6.
77. *Metaphysics* IV 3, 1005b 26–7.
78. Athanasius *Fourth Oratio Contra Arianos* 2 (*PG* XXVI 469C).
79. Epiphanius *Adversus Haereses Panarium* Heresy 62 (*PG* XLI 1052B).
80. *Cf. Religious Philosophy* p. 126–46.
81. *Dialogus* 128.
82. *Categories* 2, 1b 6–7.
83. *De Anima* II 4, 415a 26–9.
84. *Met.* VII 7, 1032a 25.
85. *Contra Maximinum* II 6.
86. *Met.* V 6, 1016a 32–3, combined with 1016b 31–2, and *Cat.* 3, 1b 10–15 and 5, 2a 14–19.
87. *Epistula* 38, 1 (*PG* XXXII 325B); *cf.* 38, 3 (328A).
88. *Epistula* 236, 6 (884A).
89. *Met.* V 6, 1016a 17–24.
90. *De Trinitate* VII 6, 11 (*Patrologia Latina* XLII 994).
91. *Contra Celsum* VIII 12 (*PG* XI 1533C).
92. *Sophistical Refutations* 17, 175a 8–9.
93. *De Oratione* 15 (*PG* XI 465A).
94. *Cat.* 5, 3b 10–18.
95. *De Oratione loc. cit.*
96. *Met.* I 2, 982a 21–3.
97. *In Joannem* X 21 (*PG* XIV 376B).
98. *Refutatio Omnium Haeresium* ed. P. Wendland, Berlin 1918 VII 18, 1–2.
99. *Adv. Praxeam* 7.
100. *Ibid.*
101. *Ibid.*
102. *Contra Haeresin Noeti* 7 and 14.
103. *In Joannem* 10, 21 (*PG* XIV 376B).
104. *Apol.* 21 (*PL* I 399A).
105. *De Trinitate* V 8, 10–19.
106. *Cf. Church Fathers* vol. I p. 364–493.
107. *De Plantatione* 2, 9.
108. *Ibid.*

109. *Vita Mosis* II 26, 133.
110. *De Cherub.* II, 36; *De Migratione* I, 6.
111. John i 10.
112. John i 3.
113. Justin Martyr *Second Apologia* 6.
114. Athenagoras *Supplicatio* 10.
115. Theophilus *Ad Autolycum* II 10.
116. Clement of Alexandria *Strom.* VII 2 (*PG* IX 408B).
117. John i 14.
118. Heb x 5; *cf.* Col. ii 9.
119. Phil. ii 7.
120. Phil. ii 28.
121. *Quaest. in Gen.* I 53; *cf. Philo* vol. I p. 118.
122. *De Fuga* 20, 122.
123. *De Somniis* I 20, 122.
124. *De Posteritate* 2, 5.
125. *Spec. Leg.* I 12, 66.
126. II Cor. v 1.
127. *Ibid. Cf.* Wisdom of Solomon ix 15 and Plato Axiochus 366A.
128. John i 14.
129. John ii 23.
130. *De Anima* II 1, 412a 16–20.
131. *Met.* V 4, 1015a 7–13.
132. *Leg. All* II 1, 1.
133. *De Anima* II 1, 410b 6.
134. *Cat* 5, 2a 11–13.
135. *Ibid.* 2, 1b 6.
136. *Ibid* 6–7.
137. *Cf* above at notes 32 and 91–102.
138. *Met* XII 10, 1075b 34–6.
139. *Ibid.* VIII 5, 1045a 14.
140. *Ibid.* VII 10, 1035a 7–9.
141. *Nicomachaean Ethics* IX 4, 1166a 16–17.
142. *Quis Heres* 48, 231.
143. *Ennead* III 5, 5.
144. *Ibid.* IV 7, 1.
145. *Ibid* I 1, 7.
146. *Cf. Church Fathers* vol. I p. 367–9.
147. *In Joannis Evangelium* 19, 15; *cf. Epistula* 137, 3, 11.
148. *Fragmenta* 7 (*PG* V 1221A).
149. *De Principiis* I 2, 1.
150. *De Carne Christi* 5.
151. *Epistula* 137, 3, 11.
152. *Cf Religious Philosophy* p. 147–9.
153. *Cf. ibid.* p. 149–53.
154. *Cf. Philo* vol. I p. 386–7, and *Leg. All.* I 12, 32.
155. *Cf. Church Fathers* vol. I p. 484–6.
156. *Posterior Analytics* II 11, 94b 37–95a 1.
157. *Met.* V 5, 1015a 29.
158. *Eth. Nic.* III 1, 1109b 35.
159. *Anal. Post.* II 11, 95a 3–5.

5

THE KNOWABILITY AND DESCRIBABILITY OF GOD IN PLATO AND ARISTOTLE

THE conception of God as a being who is above knowledge and description has been common in religious philosophy ever since Philo. This conception is generally represented as a philosophic principle, though also supported by appropriate Scriptural quotations. But how far back in the history of philosophy it can be traced is a question which has never been satisfactorily answered. In this paper we shall try to find out whether this conception of God as unknowable and indescribable is to be found in Plato and Aristotle.[1]

I

It may be true that Plato is the first systematic theologian.[2] But if so, his theology has the peculiar characteristic that it dwells more on what may be considered the subordinates of God than on God himself. Compared with the part played by the ideas in the Platonic system of philosophy that of God seems rather insignificant. In fact, whenever in approaching Plato from the direction of the subsequent history of philosophy we wish to ascertain his view on any phase of the conception of God which in later speculation became a subject of articulate discussion, we have to derive it indirectly from what he says about the ideas. For, with the exception of the *Laws,* throughout his dialogues Plato treats of God either as one of the ideas, a supreme idea, the idea of the good, or as a being outside the ideas, a Demiurge, who cannot, however, but be of the same nature as the ideas. In the speculations of the subsequent history of philosophy, the basic

[1] As a chapter in a work on Greek philosophy, introductory to a series of studies on religious philosophy of which two volumes on Philo are now in press, this paper contains general statements on certain moot points which are fully discussed in other parts of the studies.

[2] E. Caird, *The Evolution of Theology in the Greek Philosophers,* 1923 ed., p. 58.

principle in the conception of God which is assumed to lead to the conclusion that He is unknowable and indescribable is the belief in His incorporeality, simplicity, and immutability. In Plato this belief is directly asserted with regard to the ideas. The ideas, according to him, are incorporeal,[3] they are "invisible and imperceptible by the sense,"[4] they are separate from the things which participate in them,[5] they are assumed to exist (*εἶναι*) each absolutely for itself,[6] they are one in kind or simple (*μονοειδές*),[7] they are each for ever in the same state (*κατὰ ταὐτά*) immovably,[8] they do not admit of any change[9] or alteration.[10] Indirectly, from his criticism of the popular conception of the gods, it may be inferred that his own God, whether one of the ideas or a being above the ideas, would also be described by him in the same terms as the ideas. Thus speaking of the popular conception of the gods, he argues, evidently from his own conception of God, that "it is impossible even for a god to wish to alter himself, but, as it appears, each of them, being of the fairest and best possible, abides for ever simply in his own form,"[11] that they "cannot be supposed to have either joy or sorrow,"[12] nor can they be supposed to grieve or laugh,[13] nor, finally, are they "easy to win over when bribed by offerings and prayer"[14] nor do they "betray justice for the sake of gifts offered by unjust men."[15]

But the very same passages in which Plato asserts the incorporeality and simplicity and immutability of the ideas also seem to imply that he would not hesitate to describe all these ideas by such predicates as "existent," "simple," and "for ever the same." Still more directly does he show his readiness to describe God, who is either one of the ideas or a being like the ideas but above them, by such predicates as

[3] *Soph.* 246B.
[4] *Tim.* 52A.
[5] *Parm.* 130B.
[6] *Phaedo* 100B; cf. *Parm.* 128E; *Rep.* VI 507B.
[7] *Phaedo* 78D.
[8] *Tim.* 38A.
[9] *Phaedo* 78D.
[10] *Ibid.*
[11] *Rep.* II 381C.
[12] *Phileb.* 33B.
[13] *Rep.* III 388C, E.
[14] *Laws* X 885B.
[15] *Ibid.* X 907A; cf. *Rep.* II 364B.

"good" (ἀγαθός)[16] and "wise" (σοφός)[17] and "simple" (ἁπλοῦς)[18] and "true" (ἀληθής)[19] and "most righteous" (δικαιότατος).[20] Now the application of such predicates to ideas, on the basis of Plato's own particular theory of predication, would seem to clash with his conception of the ideas as being each simple and indivisible in their nature. According to this particular theory of Plato, whenever any term is predicated of a subject, that subject is assumed to participate in the idea designated by the term predicated of it. When, for instance, a man is described as living and rational and good and great, it means that the man so described participates in the ideas of life, rationality, goodness, and greatness, so that the essence of that man cannot be considered as something simple and indivisible; it must be considered as consisting of all those ideas in which it participates. By the same token, ideas also are said to participate in all the other ideas which are predicated of them. When, for instance, the idea of the good is said to be existent and one, it means that the idea of the good participates in the ideas of existence and oneness, and hence it further means that the idea of the good, if so described, is not simple, as it is assumed to be, but is rather a composite of three ideas, goodness, existence, and unity. Now if all this is to be implied in the description of ideas by any positive terms, how then can ideas, which are assumed to be simple, be described by any such terms?

This question is dealt with by Plato himself in two of his dialogues, in the *Parmenides* and in the *Sophist*.

In the *Parmenides*[21] the question is raised with regard to the application of opposite terms, such as unity and multiplicity, likeness and unlikeness, both to sensible objects and to ideas. In the discussion of this question, a distinction is made by Socrates, who acts as spokesman for Plato, between terms predicated of sensible objects and terms predicated of ideas. In the case of sensible objects, he says, it is possible to predicate of them opposite terms, for sensible objects are composite objects, they consist of a variety of parts, and this variety of parts makes it possible for them to have a variety of respects and a

[16] *Tim.* 29E; *Rep.* II 379A.

[17] *Phaedr.* 278D.

[18] *Rep.* II 382E.

[19] *Ibid.*

[20] *Theaet.* 176C.

[21] *Parm.* 129A–130A.

variety of relations. They may therefore at the very same time, but in different respects or in different relations, participate in such opposite ideas as unity and multiplicity, likeness and unlikeness, greatness and littleness. Moreover, we may add here for Plato, sensible objects are also changeable, and they may therefore participate in opposite ideas at different times. Not so, however, is the case of ideas. Ideas are absolutely simple in their nature; there is no composition and no complexity in them. Whatever they are they are so always and in every respect and in every relation. Being absolutely simple, without any variety in their nature with respect to other things or in relation to other things, they cannot at the same time be described by opposite terms, for to be so described would mean to participate in opposite ideas, but that would run counter to the simplicity of their nature. Moreover, such a contrariness to their nature, we may add here for Plato, would do violence to the law of contradiction, which, as stated by Plato himself, reads that "the same thing will never do or suffer opposites in the same respect in relation to the same thing and at the same time." [22] Nor can ideas be described by opposite terms successively, at different times, for ideas are absolutely unchangeable, and what they are at one time they must be at all other times.

But it will be noticed that only the description of ideas by terms which are opposites (ἐναντία) is said here to be incompatible with their internal unity. Nothing is said here with regard to the description of ideas by terms which are not opposites. The question may therefore be raised whether this mention of terms which are opposites is deliberate, meaning thereby that terms which are not opposites can be predicated of ideas, or whether the mention of terms which are opposites is only accidental and the same reasoning, from the simplicity of ideas, would exclude also the predication of terms which are not opposites.

An answer to this question is to be found in the *Sophist*. After rejecting the view that ideas cannot be described at all and after also rejecting the view that ideas can be described by all terms indiscriminately, the spokesman for Plato in this question states that some ideas can be mingled (συμμείγνυσθαι) with other ideas, have a share

[22] *Rep.* IV 436B; cf. X 602E; *Phaedo* 102E; *Theaet.* 188A.

(μεταλαμβάνειν) in them, communicate (ἐπικοινωνεῖν) with them, and participate (μετέχειν) in them, whereas other ideas do not admit of any such mingling or sharing or intercommunion or participation.[23] For the purpose of illustration[24] he takes the ideas of existence, motion, rest, sameness, and difference. Among these five ideas, he says, the idea of motion, for instance, can participate in the ideas of existence, sameness, and difference, but not in the idea of rest, and consequently we can say of motion that it is existent, that it is the same, i.e., the same with itself, and that it is different, i.e., different from other ideas, but we cannot say that it is rest, for that would result in a contradiction. By the same token, it may be assumed, Plato would allow the description of any other idea by terms which are not opposites. Thus the idea of man could be described, according to him, by the terms animal and rational.

This is as much as we can gather from Plato with regard to the question. He is conscious of the fact that there is some difficulty in describing ideas by positive predicates. But this does not force him to the conclusion that ideas must be indescribable. He rather adopts the view that, while they are indescribable by predicates which are opposites, they are describable by predicates which are not opposites. Now, logically, the difference between predicates which are opposite terms and predicates which are not opposite terms is that the former do violence to the law of contradiction, whereas the latter do no such violence. But with respect to the simplicity of the nature of the idea, the predication of terms which are not opposite would seem to break up that simplicity just as much as the predication of terms which are opposites. When, for instance, the idea of motion is described as "existent" and as "the same with itself," there is indeed no violation here of the law of contradiction, but still if you assume that the idea of motion is simple, even though you do not expressly predicate of it the term simple, then, upon its being made to participate in the ideas of existence and sameness, that simplicity is at once broken up.

[23] *Soph.* 251E–253E.

[24] Cf. F. M. Cornford, *Plato's Theory of Knowledge*, 1935, pp. 273–285, on the question whether these ideas were used by Plato merely for illustrative purposes or whether they were meant by him to constitute a list of categories.

This difficulty, it must be admitted, is not altogether insurmountable. In the later history of philosophy, a similar difficulty with respect to the application of predicates to God is anwered in a variety of ways. But all we want to do at present is simply to call attention to the fact that Plato's statement with regard to the describability of the ideas by terms which are not opposites is open to objection and that Plato has made no attempt to remove that objection.

Since, according to Plato, ideas are describable, it follows that they are also knowable. More directly is the knowability of the ideas expressed by him in such statements as that being (οὐσία), i.e., the totality of ideas, is known by the intelligence [25] and that after proper preparation we can ultimately arrive at a knowledge of "what the essence of beauty is." [26] He admits, of course, that we do not sufficiently know the good [27] and that "in the region of the known the last thing to be seen, and seen only with an effort, is the idea of the good;" [28] but this does not mean that it is unknowable.

If in the passage quoted the good is that which Plato means by God, then we have here a direct statement by him that God, even though He cannot be sufficiently known and it requires effort to know Him, can still be known. If, however, by God he means a Demiurge who is above the ideas, there is still another passage in which he directly states that his demiurgic God can be known. The passage in question reads that "the Maker and Father of this All it is a hard task to find, and having found him, it would be impossible to declare him to all men (εἰς πάντας ἀδύνατον λέγειν)." [29] The meaning of this passage, we take it, is not that God cannot be declared, i.e., that He is indescribable, but rather that He cannot be declared to *all men*, because, as he has said in the passages previously quoted, it requires certain specific preparation to arrive at a knowledge of the idea and that our knowledge of it is not quite complete and can be attained only by effort. It is only later, in Christianity, after the Church Fathers had adopted from Philo the view with regard to the ineffability of God, that this statement of Plato gave rise to the question

[25] *Soph.* 248E.
[26] *Sympos.* 211C.
[27] *Rep.* VI 505A.
[28] *Ibid.*, VII 517B.
[29] *Tim.* 28C.

whether it was meant to assert the ineffability of God. Clement of Alexandria takes it to mean that God is ineffable, "for," he asks, "how can that be effable (ῥητόν) which is neither genus, nor difference, nor species, nor individual, nor number?" [30] So was also the interpretation of this passage of Plato by Celsus.[31] In opposition to Celsus, however, Origen argues that from the wording of Plato's statement it is to be inferred that "he does not speak of God as ineffable (ἄρρητον) and unnamable (ἀκατονόμαστον); on the contrary, he implies that He is effable and that there are a few to whom he may be declared." [32] Origen's interpretation, in view of our discussion, is more in accordance with what one may have reason to believe to be the correct view of Plato.

Against this conception of the knowability of the ideas Plato himself raises two objections.

One of these objections occurs in the *Parmenides*. Starting out with the assumption that the knowable is relative to knowledge (ἐπιστήμη), Parmenides compares the relation between the knowable and knowledge to the relation between master and slave. He then maintains that in the relationship between master and slave the two correlatives must belong to the same level of existence. If the term "master" means the idea of mastership so must also the term "slave" mean the idea of slavery, and *vice versa*. Similarly, if the term "master" means a particular man who is master so also must the term "slave" mean a particular man who is slave, and again *vice versa*. By the same token, he argues, if the knowable is an idea, then the knowledge of which this knowable is the correlative must likewise be ideal knowledge, and, conversely also, if the knowledge is a particular kind of knowledge, then the corresponding knowable must likewise be a particular object. But the knowledge within us is never ideal knowledge; it is always a particular kind of knowledge. Consequently the object of our knowledge must always be some particular

[30] *Stromata* V 12 (PG, IX 121A); cf. quotation from Plato on p. 116B.

[31] Origen, *Contra Celsum* VII 42 (PG, XI 1481C–1484A).

[32] *Ibid.* VII 43 (PG, XI 1481C). Josephus (*Contra Apion.* II 31, 224) takes this passage in the *Timaeus* to mean that "it is not safe to divulge the truth about God to the ignorant mob."

thing; it can never be an idea; and consequently, he concludes, ideas can never be known.[33] No answer is given here by Plato to this objection, though what his answer to this would be could be gathered from other parts in his writings.

The second objection occurs in the *Sophist* and is put in the mouth of the Stranger from Elea. To be known, he says, means to be passive (*πάσχειν*) and hence to be moved (*κινεῖσθαι*), and consequently being (*οὐσία*), if eternally active (*ποιεῖν*) and at rest, must be unknown, for, if known, it cannot be eternally active and at rest.[34] The same Eleatic Stranger answers this dilemma by maintaining that "being" is neither at rest exclusively nor in motion exclusively, but that it consists of both, and consequently it can be known.[35] This answer, however, is said by him to be in opposition to "the theory of those who say that the All is at rest, whether as a unity or in many forms." [36] By this last statement he means that his answer is in opposition to both the view of the Eleatics, who champion the theory of one being, and the view of those, including Plato, who champion the theory of "many forms." [37] What Plato's own answer would be to this objection is not stated.

In Plato, then, we find three passages with regard to the question as to the describability and knowability of the idea. First, there is the statement that ideas can be described by terms which are not opposites, even though thereby the idea described participates in the ideas predicated of it. Second, there is an objection raised against the knowability of ideas on the ground of an analogy between the relation of the knowable to knowledge and the relation of master to slave. Third, there is another objection raised against the knowability of ideas on the ground of an analogy between the relation of the knowable to knowledge and the relation of the passive and movable to the active. No explanation is given by him how, with his theory of participation, terms which are not opposites can be predicated of ideas, nor are answers given to the two questions raised against the knowability of ideas. We shall now try to show how in

[33] *Parm.* 133B–134C.
[34] *Soph.* 248D–E.
[35] *Ibid.* 248E–249D.
[36] *Ibid.* 249C.
[37] Cf. Cornford, *op. cit.*, pp. 242–248.

Aristotle we may find a refutation of Plato's statement with regard to the describability of ideas as well as answers to the two objections raised against the knowability of ideas.

II

With his abolition of all those incorporeal beings which Plato calls ideas, but retaining that incorporeal being which he calls God, Aristotle transfers to God all that which Plato says about the incorporeality and simplicity and immutability of the ideas. By the very same proof by which he establishes that God exists he also establishes that He "is indivisible and is without parts and without magnitude," [38] that He is immaterial,[39] unchangeable and unalterable and unmodifiable.[40] Indeed there are other incorporeal beings, the substances which move the spheres, but these are not gods. How they differ from God and what their relation to God is we shall discuss elsewhere.

Now the term one, according to Aristotle, lends itself to many meanings. It is always relative, according to him, to the term indivisible, "for," as he says, "in general those things that do not admit of division are one in so far as they do not admit of it." [41] Accordingly, inasmuch as a thing may be indivisible in some respect but divisible in another a thing may be called one in some particular respect even though it may be divisible into many in some other respect. Thus, for instance, any concrete being, such as "musical Coriscus," may be called one, even though any such concrete being is divisible into substance and accident.[42] Again, any quantity which is continuous by nature, such as space and time and motion, may be called one, even though every such continuous quantity is infinitely divisible.[43] Then also material objects which are different, such, for instance, as oil and wine, may be called one on account of the unity of their constituent element, which in this case is water, even though every element is itself divisible into matter and form.[44] Again, material objects which are different, such, for instance, as man and horse and dog, may be all

[38] *Phys.* VIII 10, 267b, 25–26.
[39] *Metaph.* XII 6, 1071b, 21.
[40] *De Caelo* I 9, 279a, 19–21.
[41] *Metaph.* V 6, 1016b, 3–5.
[42] *Ibid.*, 1015b, 16–34.
[43] *Ibid.*, 1016a, 4–9.
[44] *Ibid.*, 17–24.

called one on account of the genus animal to which they belong, even though every genus is divisible into species.[45] Finally, different individuals, such as Socrates and Plato, may be called one on account of the unity of their definition as man, even though every definition is divisible into genus and difference.[46] Consequently, when Aristotle describes God as one and indivisible it is necessary to find out in which of the various meanings he uses these terms with reference to God. Does he mean that God is one only in the sense that as an incorporeal being He is indivisible into substance and accident or into elements or into matter and form, or does he also mean that He is one in the sense that He is indivisible also into genus and species?

No direct answer is given by Aristotle to this question. We can only try to find what his answer to this question would be, by studying the terms which he predicates of God and by trying to see whether these terms are applied by him to God as genera and species or not.

There are certain terms which Aristotle definitely predicates of God. God is described by him as "causing motion," as "thinking," as "living," as "being pleased," as "most good," and as "eternal." [47] But in attributing these terms to God he is careful to point out that God is unlike corporeal beings which are described by the same terms. Corporeal beings which are described as causing motion are themselves being moved while causing motion; God, as an incorporeal being, is an immovable mover.[48] Corporeal beings which are described as thinking have something external to themselves as the object of their thought; God has only himself as the object of His thought.[49] Corporeal beings which are described as living possess a life which consists of nutrition, growth, and sensation; God's life consists only of the actuality of His own thought.[50] Corporeal beings which are described as being pleased are pleased only at the satisfaction of a want; God's pleasure consists in the actuality of His own life.[51] Corporeal beings which are described as being good have a goodness which is acquired by them from without; God's goodness consists in His

[45] *Ibid.*, 24–32.

[46] *Ibid.*, 32–1016b, 9.

[47] *Ibid.*, XII 7.

[48] *Ibid.*, 1072b, 1–3.

[49] *Ibid.*, 18–22.

[50] *Ibid.*, 26–27.

[51] *Ibid.*, 14–18.

contemplation of Himself.[52] Corporeal beings which are described as eternal are eternal in the sense that their motion has no beginning and no end; God is eternal in the sense of the continuity of His duration which is motionless.[53] All these terms are thus predicated, according to Aristotle, both of God and of corporeal beings with a certain difference. Being predicated of God, they must of necessity fall under Aristotle's fourfold classification of predicables. They must be either genera, or species, or properties, or accidents.[54] Now in their predication of God they cannot, of course, be accidents, for accidents are to be found only in corporeal objects. But are they properties of God or are they genera and species? In other words, when God is described as an immovable mover, does the predicate constitute a property of God or does it constitute a genus and species and hence a definition of God? With Philo, as we shall see, this question is raised and it is definitely stated by him that the predicates of God are not genera and species but only properties, and that view becomes predominant in subsequent discussions of the problem. In Aristotle there is no discussion of the problem. Whatever answer we may attempt to find for this problem must be based only upon the consideration whether his conception of the unity and incorporeality of God is consistent with the divisibility into genus and species. Now so far as the unity of God is concerned, we know of Aristotle's statement that a thing may be called one even if it is divisible into genus and species. As far as the incorporeality of God is concerned, we know that it excludes only divisibility into corporeal parts or into substance and accident or into matter and form. We know furthermore that genera and species, according to Aristotle, have no real existence, and consequently such statements of his as those which assert that the parts of a definition are prior to the subject defined [55] or that they are causes of it [56] do not mean that they are really prior to the subject defined or that they are really causes of it. From all this we may

[52] *Ibid.*, 22–24.
[53] *Ibid.*, 29–30.
[54] *Topica* I, 101b, 17–25.
[55] *Ibid.* VI 4, 141a, 26–27.
[56] *Anal. Post.* II 10, 93b, 38–39; *De Anima* II 2, 413a, 13–16.

infer that to Aristotle such predications of God as "immovable mover" could constitute definitions consisting of genera and species.

That God, according to Aristotle, can be defined in terms of genus and species may be more directly derived from *Metaphysics* XII, 8, where he deals with the application of the term "one" to "the first" (*τὸ πρῶτον*),[57] to the "principle of each sphere" (*ἡ περὶ ἕκαστον ἀρχή*),[58] and to "men" (*ἄνθρωποι*).[59] By "the first" Aristotle means here God or the first immovable mover and by the "principle of each sphere" he means here the other immovable movers of the spheres which later came to be known as Intelligences. Accordingly, Aristotle deals here with the application of the term "one" to God and the other "immovable movers," on the one hand, and to men, who may be called "movable movers," on the other. Now with regard to men, as, e.g., Socrates and Plato, he says that they are one in definition (*λόγος*) and species (*εἶδος*) but many in number (*ἀριθμός*),[60] and he further explains that that which breaks up a single species into numerically many individuals is matter, for "whatsoever things are many have matter."[61] Accordingly if you have a species of beings, such, e.g., as the immovable movers of the spheres and God, who are without matter, they cannot be broken up into numerically many individuals.[62] By this Aristotle would not deny that they will be many; he would only deny that they can be many in number, according to his own technical use of the term many in number, which must imply matter. How they are to be considered many, if not in number, is a question which becomes in the course of time a subject of controversy, with which we shall deal elsewhere.

For our present purpose the concluding statement of Aristotle is of utmost importance. He says: "But the first essence has no matter, for it is complete reality. So the immovable first mover is one both in formula (i.e., definition) and number."[63] The implication of this statement is that though God is "one in number," He is also "one in definition" and can therefore be described in terms of genus and

[57] *Metaph.* XII 8, 1074a, 36.
[58] *Ibid.*, 32–33.
[59] *Ibid.*, 32.
[60] *Ibid.*, 34, 32, 33.
[61] *Ibid.*, 33–34.
[62] *Ibid.*, 31–35.
[63] *Metaph.* XII 8, 1074a, 35–37.

species. What this means may be explained as follows. There is a genus "mover." Under this genus there are two species, "movable" and "immovable." The species "movable mover" includes corporeal beings, such as men, who constitute individuals which are many "in number." The species "immovable mover" includes God and the moving principles of the spheres. Both God and the moving principles of the spheres are immovable, but there is the following difference in their immovability. God is immovable absolutely; the principles of the spheres, however, have what Aristotle calls "accidental motion by something else." [64] Still all of them, the principles of the spheres no less than God, are immaterial, and consequently the differences between them do not constitute individual differences and do not make them many in number. The differences between them are specific differences and they are many only in species, each of them constituting what came to be known later as a unique species. Consequently God and the immovable principles of the spheres have each a common genus and a specific difference and all of them, including God, can thus be defined.

Aristotle's view as to the describability or definabilty of God, despite His being simple and indivisible in His nature, thus rests on his own theory that the universal terms, genus and species, by which God can be defined have no real existence and therefore their use as predicates of God does not introduce a real division into the simple and indivisible essence of God. The case of God is to him like the case of any definiend, the unity of which, despite the two distinct elements of genus and species in the definition, is explained by him on the ground that the relation of genus to species is analogous to the relation of matter to form, the two of which, being inseparable from each other, coalesce into a perfect unity.[65] Indeed, the question might be raised with regard to God, who is immaterial, how there could be within Him a distinction of matter and form such as must inevitably be implied in a definition. But to this Aristotle would answer that

[64] *Phys.* VIII 6, 259b, 29. According to W. Jaeger, *Aristotle* (Engl. tr., 1934), p. 361, in *Metaph.* XII 8, the planetary movers are not assumed to have that accidental motion which is attributed to them in *Phys.* VIII 6, 259b, 28–31.

[65] *Metaph.* VIII 6, 1045a, 29; cf. V 28, 1024b, 8–9; VII 12, 1038a, 5–6.

matter may be either intelligible (νοητή) or sensible (αἰσθητή),[66] and while indeed in God there can be no sensible matter, there can be in him the distinction of genus and species, even though it implies a logical distinction between intelligible matter and form. This is undoubtedly how Aristotle would have answered the question, though in the subsequent development of his teachings some of his followers were reluctant to allow themselves such an answer on behalf of their master.

Following this line of reasoning Aristotle then pits his own theory of universals against Plato's theory of ideas and argues that, if ideas are assumed to have real existence and if also things defined are assumed to participate in those ideas designated by the predicates which form their definition, then it will inevitably follow that the thing defined will at the same time be one and many. The arguments which Aristotle advances are many and varied; in all of them he tries to show from various angles the multiplicity of difficulties that must follow from Plato's position;[67] but after he has completed all these varied arguments he seems to challenge directly Plato's statement, quoted above, that ideas can participate in other ideas, provided they are not opposites, and this without any deleterious effects upon their simplicity and internal unity. "What then is it," asks Aristotle, "that makes man one; why is he one and not many, e.g., animal plus biped, especially if there are, as some say, an ideal animal and an ideal biped? Why are not those ideas the ideal man, so that men would exist by participation not in man, nor in one idea, but in two, animal and biped? And in general, man would be not one but more than one thing, animal and biped." [68] The implication of this statement is quite evident. According to Plato, he argues, any idea, such, e.g., as the idea of "man," could not be described by any terms at all, not only by terms which are opposites, let us say "mortality" and "immortality," but also by those which are not opposites, such as "animality" and "rationality."

Since God to Aristotle, as we have been trying to show, can be de-

[66] *Ibid.* VIII 6, 1045a, 34.
[67] *Ibid.* VII 13, 1038b, 6–15, 1040b, 4.
[68] *Ibid.* VIII 6, 1045a, 14–20 (W. D. Ross's translation).

fined in terms of genus and species, God to him can be known. For a definition, according to him, is a rational formula which expresses the essence of a thing [69] and such a rational formula yields scientific knowledge.[70]

In admitting the knowability of God Aristotle must have become aware of the objections raised in the *Parmenides* and the *Sophist* against the knowability of ideas. In two passages, we shall now try to show, Aristotle provides answers to these two objections.

The answer to the objection raised in the *Parmenides* is to be found in his discussion of the meaning of the term relation in *Categories*, ch. 7. Parmenides, as will be recalled, compares the relation between the known and knowledge to the relation between master and slave. Without mentioning Parmenides or referring to Plato, Aristotle tries to point out a difference between these two kinds of relation. In the case of master and slave, he says, the two correlative terms are simultaneous in nature (*ἅμα τῇ φύσει*),[71] whereas in the case of knowledge and the known the correlative terms are not simultaneous in nature. To be simultaneous in nature, as he explains it in the same passage, means two things. First, it means that the existence of either one of the correlatives implies the existence of the other, or, as he states later in his formal definition of "simultaneous in nature," the existence of either one of the correlatives involves that of the other, but neither of them is the cause of the existence of the other.[72] Second, it means that the correlatives are mutually subversive,[73] that is to say, with the disappearance of either one of the correlatives the other also disappears. It is in both these senses, Aristotle maintains, that the correlatives "master" and "slave" are simultaneous in nature, for the existence of one implies the existence of the other and the disappearance of the one implies the disappearance of the other. The correlatives "knowledge" and the "object known," however, are not simultaneous in nature, for, as says Aristotle, an object of knowledge may exist

[69] *Topica* I 5, 101b, 39; *Anal. Post.* II 10, 93b, 29.
[70] *Metaph.* IX 2, 1046, 7–8.
[71] *Categ.* Ch. 7, 7b, 15.
[72] *Ibid.* Ch. 13, 14b, 27–29.
[73] *Ibid.* Ch. 7, 7b, 19–20.

prior to the existence of any knowledge of it and it may continue to exist even after the knowledge of it has disappeared.[74]

In the light of this distinction between the relation of master and slave and the relation of knowledge and the knowable, we shall now see how Aristotle would refute Parmenides' argument for the unknowability of ideas and hence also for the unknowability of God. While indeed, Aristotle would say, God as an object of knowledge is correlative with knowledge, still, unlike master and slave, they are not simultaneous in nature, inasmuch as the existence of God does not necessarily imply a knowledge of His existence and inasmuch also as God continues to exist even after knowledge of Him disappears. By the same token, he would continue to argue, unlike the relationship between master and slave, in which the relation must be either between the ideas of mastery and slavery or between a sensible master and slave, the relation between God and knowledge, not being a relation between correlatives simultaneous in nature, does not have to be a relation between God and a type of knowledge which is as independent of corporeal limitations as the essence of God. We may have a knowledge of God or the ideas even if the essence of the object known in either case transcends the corporeal limits of our knowledge, for in the same manner also, he would argue, may the object of our knowledge always transcend the temporal limits of our knowledge and have existence prior to it and continue to exist after it.

The answer to the objection raised in the *Sophist* occurs in *Metaphysics* V, 15. The objection, as will be recalled, maintains that the relation of the knowable to knowledge is like the relation of the passive to the active. In opposition to this, though without mentioning the *Sophist*, Aristotle maintains that the relation of the knowable to knowledge is a different kind of relation from that of the passive to the active. There are three kinds of relation, he says, (1) the relation of that which exceeds to that which is exceeded, (2) the relation of the active to the passive, and (3) the relation of the "knowable" (*ἐπιστητόν*) to "knowledge" (*ἐπιστήμη*) or of the "sensible (*αἰσθητόν*) to "sensation" (*αἴσθησις*).[75] This formal threefold division of relation

[74] *Ibid.*, 15–35.

[75] *Metaph.* V 15, 1020b, 26–32.

clearly indicates that Aristotle did not consider the relation of the knowable to knowledge to be the same as the relation of the passive to the active. To be known, according to Aristotle, does not necessarily mean to be passive and hence to be moved. Quite on the contrary, it can be shown from Aristotle's own statements in other places that in the relation of the knowable to knowledge it is the former that is considered by him as active and the latter as passive. Thus speaking of the distinction between the "sensible" (*αἰσθητόν*) and sensation (*αἴσθησις*),[76] he refers to the former as "the substrata which produce (*ποιεῖ*) the sensation"[77] and as "that which causes motion" (*τὸ κινοῦν*).[78] Still more explicitly does this come out in a passage in which he refers to the sensible object in its relation to sensation as that which causes motion and is not itself moved.[79] And what he says of sensation is true also of any other kind of knowledge.

With his belief in the knowability of God, the distinction between the unknowability of God's essence and the knowability of His existence, which was later introduced by Philo[80] and thereafter followed by other philosophers, does not exist in Aristotle. On the contrary, to him the knowledge of the existence of a thing inevitably leads to a knowledge of its essence. This view is explicitly expressed by him in the statement that "as we know the existence of a thing (*ὅτι ἔστιν*), so also do we know its essence (*τὸ τί ἐστιν*)."[81] No exception is made by Aristotle in the case of God. And consequently to the extent that the existence of God can be demonstrated, to that extent also can His essence be known. The existence of God is held by Aristotle to be demonstrable, and he himself advanced several demonstrations.

We have thus shown that neither in Plato nor in Aristotle is there any suggestion of the principle of the unknowability and the indescribability of God. This principle, as we shall try to show elsewhere, was introduced by Philo, who was led to it by a combination of reasons both rational and historical.

[76] *Ibid.* IV, 5, 1010b, 30–31.
[77] *Ibid.*, 33–34.
[78] *Ibid.*, 37.
[79] *De Anima* II 2, 426a, 2–9; and cf. G. Rodier's note in his edition, *ad loc.*
[80] *Spec. Leg.* I 6, §32.
[81] *Anal. Post.* II 8, 93a, 28–29.

6

ALBINUS AND PLOTINUS ON DIVINE ATTRIBUTES

ON two previous occasions I tried to show how neither Plato nor Aristotle held that God was unknowable, ineffable, and unnameable,[1] how the tentative objections against the unknowability of the ideas raised in the Parmenides and Sophist are answered by Aristotle,[2] how in the extant literature of Greek philosophy prior to Philo there is no conception of a God who is unknowable and unnameable and ineffable,[3] how Philo arrived at the conception of an unknowable, ineffable, and unnameable God,[4] how he may have meant it to be either an interpretation of Plato or something in opposition to him,[5] and how the description of God as ineffable found in Albinus and Plotinus may have been due to the influence of Philo.[6] We may add here that, though Plotinus attributes his conception of a hierarchy of three hypostases to Parmenides as reported by Plato [7] and though it is also to that Parmenides that he may refer by the pronoun "he" in his statement, "he says that it (the One) cannot be spoken (ῥητὸν) or described (γραπτόν)," [8] neither the views which he attributes to Plato nor the language which he quotes from him are those of Plato. They are rather those of older interpreters of Plato,[9] and among them Philo is to be included.[10]

[1] "The Knowability and Describability of God in Plato and Aristotle," Harvard Studies in Classical Philology, 56–57 (1947), 233-249. Above, pages 98–114.

[2] Ibid., pp. 239–249.

[3] Cf. Philo, II, pp. 113–117.

[4] Ibid., II, pp. 118–126.

[5] Ibid., II, pp. 117–118; 112–113.

[6] Ibid., II, pp. 158–160.

[7] Enn., V, I, 8 (23–27). The numbers within parentheses in the references to the Enneads are to the numbered lines in E. Bréhier's edition (Plotin: Ennéades, 1924–1938).

[8] Ibid., VI, 9, 4 (11–12); cf. Parmenides 142A. (In Philo, II, p. 160, n. 78, and p. 484, this reference to the Enneads is misprinted "V, 9, 4").

[9] Cf. É. Bréhier, Plotin: Ennéades, V, p. 13; VI, 2, p. 176, n. 1; A. E. Taylor, The Parmenides of Plato, pp. 145 ff.; E. R. Dodds, "The Parmenides of Plato and the Origin of the Neoplatonic 'One,'" The Classical Quarterly 22 (1928), pp. 129–142; A. H. Armstrong, The Architecture of the Intelligible Universe in the Philosophy of Plotinus, pp. 14–28.

[10] It is only fair to warn the reader that there are scholars who believe with E. R. Dodds that "that Plotinus himself could take . . . Philo . . . as an author-

Now in Philo the view that God is ineffable (ἄρρητος), unnameable (ἀκατονόμαστος), and incomprehensible (ἀκατάληπτος) [11] leads him to the conclusion that, while the existence of God can be known from the things created by Him, His essence cannot be known,[12] and therefore the question is raised by him how one can speak of God, or rather how one is to interpret the predicates by which God is described in Scripture.[13] The problem as it presented itself to the mind of Philo is that those predicates cannot be any of the terms which usually constitute predicates, for they can be neither accidents, nor genera, nor species.[14] Plotinus, in a similar way, immediately after his statement that God is "ineffable" (ἄρρητον),[15] that "he has no name (οὔτε ὄνομα αὐτοῦ),[16] and that "he cannot be grasped by thought" (οὔτε ἐστὶ νόησις αὐτοῦ),[17] asks: "How then are we to speak of Him?" [18] The problem as it presented itself to his mind is stated in two passages. In one passage, after stating that all questions refer either to essence or quality (that is, accident) or cause or existence, he shows first that God has neither accident nor cause and, then, like Philo, he says in effect that, while the existence of God can be known from the things which proceed from Him, His essence cannot be known.[19] In another passage he argues that God cannot be of the same genus with other beings, for in that case "He would differ from them only in property (ἰδίῳ) or specific difference

ity I find it hard to believe" (art. cit., p. 140, n. I) and "that any attempt to extract a coherent system from Philo seems to me foredoomed to failure; his ecclecticism is that of the jackdaw rather than the philosopher" (ibid., p. 132, n. I). But there are others, such as E. Vacherot (Histoire critique de l'Ecole d'Alexandrie, I, 1846, pp. 166–167); H. Guyot (L'infinité divine depuis Philon le Juif jusqu'à Plotin, 1906, pp. 99–100; Les Reminiscences de Philon le Juif chez Plotin, 1906); and long before them the Church Father Eusebius of Caesarea (Historia Ecclesiastica II, 4, 2; cf. Philo, II, p. 158), who believe that Plotinus could have been influenced by Philo, or that he was actually influenced by him either directly or indirectly. As for the jackdawish ecclecticism of Philo, see discussion in Philo, I, pp. 97–115.

[11] Philo, II, p. 111.

[12] Ibid., II, p. 73.

[13] Ibid., II, p. 127.

[14] Ibid., II, pp. 130–131; 109–110.

[15] Enn., V, 3, 13 (I).

[16] Ibid., (4).

[17] Ibid., (37).

[18] Ibid., V, 3, 14 (I).

[19] Ibid., VI, 8, 11 (5–13).

(διαφορᾷ) or accident (προσθήκῃ)." [20] In other words, like Philo, he contends that the predicates of God can be neither accidents nor genera nor species. And so also, before him, Albinus, after stating that God is ineffable (ἄρρητος) [21] and that hence He is "not genus (γένος) nor species (εἶδος) nor difference (διαφορά)," [22] begins to discuss the various ways in which one may form a thought or conception (νόησις) of God.[23] Evidently he was troubled by a problem, and that problem, as we shall see, was a twofold problem, one part being how we are to speak of God.

The answer given by Philo, formally, is that all the predicates of God in Scripture describe Him only by what is known of Him by the proofs of His existence. Now the proofs of existence establish only the fact that there is something beyond the world which is the cause of it and which acts upon everything in it. Accordingly, he takes all the descriptions of God in Scripture to refer only to the causal relation of God to the world, that is, to His actions. Informally, however, Philo adds another theory of divine predicates, and that is negations. For following the scriptural example, which says "God is not like a man," [24] Philo uses many negative descriptions of God, all of which are taken by him to emphasize the unlikeness of God to things in the world.[25] Still Philo does not say outright that, as a result of the unknowability and ineffability of God, He is to be described by negations. Nor does he apply the principle of negation as an interpretation of those predicates in Scripture which are couched in positive form.

In Albinus and Plotinus, however, negation is mentioned explicitly as one of the ways of predicating of God. In Albinus, there is a threefold classification of the methods by which we can form a conception of God, and one of these is negation.[26] In Plotinus, there are two classifications. In one of them,[27] like Albinus, he

[20] Ibid., V, 5, 13 (21–23).

[21] Didaskalikos, X, 3 and 4. The section numbers are those of the edition of the Didaskalikos in Fr. Dübner, Platonis Opera, vol. III, 1873, pp. 228–258; Pierre Louis, Albinos: Epitomé, 1945.

[22] Ibid., X, 4.

[23] Ibid., X, 5–6.

[24] Num. 23:19; cf. Philo, II, p. 97.

[25] Philo, II, pp. 126–127.

[26] Didask., X, 5–6.

[27] Enn., VI, 7, 36.

enumerates three methods by which we can form a conception of God, and these three methods correspond in vocabulary, though not in the order of their arrangement, to those enumerated by Albinus. In the other classification,[28] he deals with the ways in which we can speak of God, and here, again, despite the vagueness of the text, one can make out that the ways enumerated by him are three, and that they are the same three that are enumerated by Albinus and also by himself in his first passage, though couched in different language and arranged in a different order.

"The first method of forming a conception of God," says Albinus, "will be by the abstraction (ἀφαίρεσις, literally, "taking away," "removing") of these [sensible predicates mentioned before], in the same way as we form a conception of a point by its abstraction from the sensible, namely, by first forming the conception of a surface, then that of a line, and finally that of a point." [29]

The passage as it stands would seem to deal not with the manner in which we can speak of God, but rather with the method by which we can arrive at a conception of God, that is to say, the method by which we can arrive at a belief in the existence of God. But we shall try to show, on the basis of what we have reason to believe is the source of Albinus' statement here, that its purpose is to explain not only the method by which we can prove the existence of God but also the manner in which we can speak of God.

In al-Nairīzī's Arabic commentary on Euclid's Elements, in his comment on Euclid's definition of a point as that "which has no part," [30] there is a quotation from Simplicius' lost Greek commentary on the Elements, which reads as follows: "Euclid thus defined a point negatively because it was arrived at by the abstraction of surface from body, and by the abstraction of line from surface, and by the abstraction of point from line. Since then body has three dimensions it follows that a point [arrived at after successively eliminating all three dimensions] has none of the

[28] Ibid., V, 3, 14.

[29] Didask., X, 5. See comments on this passage in E. R. Dodds, Proclus: The Elements of Theology, p. 312; R. E. Witt, Albinus and the History of Middle Platonism, p. 132.

[30] Euclid, Elements, I, Def. 1.

dimensions, and has no part." [31] In other words, in this comment, the method of forming the conception of a point by successive abstractions of surface and line and point is used by Simplicius as an explanation of the question why Euclid has defined a point in negative, rather than in positive, terms.

It will be noticed that the description of the successive abstractions of surface, line, and point in Simplicius (6th cent. A.D.) is exactly the same as that used in the passage we have quoted from Albinus (2nd cent. A.D.). We have, therefore, reason to believe that the statement of Albinus here is only a fragment of a comment on Euclid's definition of a point which, like the passage of Simplicius, tried to explain Euclid's negative definition of a point. Accordingly, in his application of this statement here as an explanation of our conception of God, what he means to explain is not only how we can form a conception of God but also how we can describe God, and, with regard to the latter, his explanation is that we can describe God negatively, in the same way as Euclid defines a point negatively.

That this is how Plotinus understood Albinus is evident from the two passages in his Enneads, which correspond to this passage in Albinus. In his first passage, dealing, as does Albinus, with the methods by which we may form a conception of God, he says, using the same term as Albinus, that one of these methods consists of "abstractions" (ἀφαιρέσεις).[32] In his second passage, answering directly the question as to how we are to speak of God

[31] Cf. Anaratii in decem libros priores Elementorum Euclidis commentarii ex interpretatione Gherardi Cremonensis, ed. M. Curtze, 1899, p. 2, ll. 19–23: Dixit propterea Sambelichius: Punctum ideo negando Euclides diffinivit, diminutione superficiei a corpore, et diminutione linee a superficie, et diminutione puncti a linea. Cum ergo corpus sit tres habens dimensiones, punctus necessario nullum earum habet, nec habet partem." Quoted in T. L. Heath, The Thirteen Books of Euclid's Elements, p. 157. This passage is missing in the edition of the Arabic text by R. O. Besthorn et J. L. Heiberg under the title of Codex Leidensis 399, I. Euclidis Elementa . . . cum commentariis al-Narizii, 1893, p. 8. I take it that the term *diminutio* in the Latin, which Heath has translated by "detaching" but which I have changed to "abstraction," reflects the Greek ἀφαίρεσις (cf. below n. 93), probably through the Arabic *naqṣ*, for the Greek verb ἀφαιρέω has also the meaning of "to diminish." The Arabic verb *naqaṣ* as a translation of the Greek ἀφαιρεῖν occurs in the Arabic translation of Aristotle's Metaphysics (See M. Bouyges, "Index alphabétiques," p. 269, Nos. 1413–1414, in his edition of Averroes: Tafsir ma ba'ad at-tabi'at, Vol. III, 1948).

[32] Enn., VI, 7, 36 (7).

and evidently in explanation of the meaning of the term "abstractions," he says as follows: "Though we do not grasp Him by knowledge, we do not completely fail to grasp Him; we grasp Him enough to say something about Him, without, however, expressing Him himself; for we say what He is not, but what He is we do not say." [33] That the statement in this second passage, namely, that we say of God "what He is not" was meant to be an explanation of the term "abstractions" used by him in his first passage, may be gathered from a third passage, where, dealing again with the question of how God can be spoken of, he says explicitly that "everything that is said of God is only by way of abstraction." [34]

From the fact that the term *aphairesis*, which we have translated by "abstraction," but which literally means "taking away," "removing," is explained by Plotinus to mean that we predicate of God "what He is not" but not "what He is," we may infer that it is used by him, and also by Albinus before him, as the equivalent of the term *apophasis* (ἀπόφασις), which is used by Aristotle in the technical sense of "negation" in a logical proposition.

Now in Aristotle, "negation" in its strictly technical sense of a logical negation is contrasted with the term "privation" (στέρησις) or "privative negation" (στερητικὴ ἀπόφασις).[35] "Privation" or "privative negation" refers only to an affirmative proposition in which the predicate is a privative term, such as "the man is blind," and it is used only with reference to a subject of which, under normal conditions, the opposite of the privative term in question could be predicated, as, for instance, the "man" who is said to be "blind" could normally have been "seeing." "Negation," on the other hand, refers to a proposition which is negative in quality, and in such a proposition the negation of the predicate is possible even of a subject of which that predicate never could be affirmed, as, for instance, the proposition "the wall is not seeing." [36] Accordingly, when Aristotle says that "as a brute

[33] Ibid., V, 3, 14 (4–7).

[34] Ibid., VI, 8, 11 (34–35).

[35] Metaph., IV, 2, 1004a, 14–16; IV, 6, 1011b, 18ff; X, 5, 1056a, 15–18.

[36] The example of "wall," which is used by Maimonides as an illustration of the difference between "privation" and "negation" Millot ha-Higgayon, ch. 11; Moreh Nebukim I, 58) is taken, as I have shown from Alexander's commentary

has no vice and virtue, so neither has a God; but his state is more precious than virtue, and that of a brute is something different in kind from vice,"[37] he means thereby that such propositions as "the gods are not virtuous" or "brutes are not virtuous" are not "privations" but rather "negations," inasmuch as the negation of virtue of them does not imply that gods and brutes can be described as wicked. The assumption is that they are excluded from both virtue and wickedness, gods on account of their being above virtue and wickedness, and brutes on account of their being below virtue and wickedness. Though neither Albinus nor Plotinus says directly that by *aphairesis* he means technically the same thing that Aristotle means by *apophasis* in contradistinction to *steresis*, many statements made by them clearly show that this was their view. Thus, for instance, Albinus says that God can be described neither as bad nor as good,[38] and Plotinus similarly says that God is "neither what is movable nor what is at rest,"[39] that He "neither knows anything nor is there anything of which he is ignorant,"[40] and that He "has neither the not-good nor the good."[41] The implication of all these statements is that both Albinus and Plotinus use the term *aphairesis* in the technical sense of Aristotle's *apophasis.*

"The second method of forming a conception of God," continues Albinus, "is by way of analogy, to be explained as follows. In the case of the sun, its relation to the sense of sight and to the objects seen is such that, without being itself the sense of sight, it imparts to that sense the power to see and to the objects of sight the power to be seen. Of the same nature is the relation that the First Mind bears to the faculty of thinking in our soul and to the objects of our thought, for, without being itself the faculty of thinking, it imparts to that faculty the power to think and to

---

on Aristotle's Metaphysics IV, 6, 1011b, 15 ff. (ed. M. Hayduck, p. 327, ll. 18–20). Cf. "Maimonides on Negative Attributes," Louis Ginzberg Jubilee Volume (1945), pp. 425, 427.

[37] Eth. Nic., VII, 1, 1145a, 25–27.

[38] Didask., X, 4.

[39] Enn., VI, 9, 3 (42).

[40] Ibid., VI, 9, 6 (48–49).

[41] Ibid., V, 5, 13 (5).

the objects of thought the power to be thought of, and that by its bringing to light the truth which is inherent in the latter." [42]

This analogy between the first mind or God and the sun, it may be remarked,[43] is taken from Plato's analogy between the idea of good, which is "the cause of science and of truth," [44] though it is not itself science and truth,[45] and the sun, which "imparts to the visibles not only the power of visibility but also generation and growth and nurture, though it is not itself generation." [46] Now in Plato this analogy is used as an explanation not of the specific problem of how one can speak of the idea of good but rather of the more general problem of how one can come to the knowledge of the existence of the idea of good. Albinus, however, may be taken to use this second method of analogy, just as he has used the first method of negation, as an explanation also of how one can speak of God. What Albinus, therefore, means to say here is that, while one cannot speak of the essence of God, one can speak of His causal relation to the world or of His actions in the world, and hence also of his existence, for it is from the analogy of sight and visibility and the sun that we know that there is a God who has a causal relation to the world, and it is, therefore, this causal relation of God to the world that we can speak of.

So also, in the corresponding passages of Plotinus, the analogy is used both as a method by which we arrive at a knowledge of the existence of God and as a manner in which we can speak of God. Thus, in his first passage, he says that we are led to a knowledge of the existence of God by "analogies" (*ἀναλογίαι*).[47] In his second passage, in answer to the question of how we are to speak of God and quite evidently in correspondence to what Albinus and he himself in the first passage call "analogy," he says as follows: "There is nothing to prevent us from grasping Him, even though we are incapable of expressing Him in words. An illustration

[42] Didask., X, 5.

[43] Cf. reference to Plato in J. Freudenthal, Hellenistische Studien, Heft 3: Der Platoniker Albinos und der falsche Alkinoos, p. 285, and in Pierre Louis, op. cit., p. 60, n. 143.

[44] Rep., VI, 508 E.

[45] Ibid., 509 B.

[46] Ibid.

[47] Enn., VI, 7, 36 (7).

thereof is the case of those who are inspired and possessed. They know only that much, that they have within themselves something greater than themselves, without, however, knowing what it is. But from their agitations and utterances they receive a certain feeling of the Cause which produces those agitations and utterances, even though they differ from that Cause. In this manner also, it seems, is our relation to God. When we acquire a pure intellect, we feel that God is the Mind within, who furnishes essence and other things of the same order, but is not himself these things, for He is something superior to that which we call being; He is too ample and too great to be called by us being; He is superior to reason, intellect, and sense; He imparts these things, but is none of them." [48]

This passage, though it does not contain the term analogy is parallel to the passage about analogy in Albinus and to his own use of the term analogy in his first passage. The analogy here, to be sure, is not between sight, in its relation to the sun, and the human mind, in its relation to God; but rather between inspiration, in its relation to God, and thinking, in its relation to God. Still the principle which this analogy is trying to establish is like that in the analogy used by Albinus, namely, that, though God is not identical with the human mind, there is still a causal relation between God and man's thinking. What Plotinus means to say here is that, though we cannot speak of the essence of God, we can still speak of His causal relation to our mind, inasmuch as it is from His causal relation to our mind that we arrive at a knowledge of the existence of God.[49]

"The third method of forming a conception of God," concludes Albinus, "is of this kind. Whenever man beholds that which is beautiful in bodies, he passes on from that to the beauty that is in the soul, then to the beauty that is in morals and laws, then to the vast sea of beauty, after which he discerns the good itself, the lovable itself, the desirable itself, which, as if it were light, brings brightness and illumination to the soul in its effort thus to ascend. Together with his beholding all this, man forms also

[48] Ibid., V, 3, 14 (8–19).

[49] On the proof of the existence of God from the human mind, see Philo, II, pp. 78 ff.

a conception of God in his mind, [without, however, beholding Him, and this] on account of the exaltedness of His position." [50]

This passage is based upon a passage in Plato,[51] in which he tries to show how by starting with the contemplation of "beautiful bodies" [52] one passes on to "the beauty which is in souls," [53] then to "the beauty which is in morals and laws," [54] then to "the vast sea of beauty," [55] until finally he arrives at the notion of "the beautiful itself" [56] and becomes "the friend of God." [57] Now here, again, in Plato, this description of the successive gradation of knowledge is not used as an explanation of the specific problem of how one can speak of absolute beauty, but rather of the more general problem of how one can come to the knowledge of the existence of absolute beauty. Still in Albinus, again, as before, we may assume, it is used also as an explanation of the latter problem. How this description of the successive gradation of knowledge can be used as a solution of the problem of how one can speak of God may be gathered from the two corresponding passages in Plotinus.

In the first of these passages Plotinus merely says that we are led to a knowledge of God by "the knowledge of things proceeding from it and certain grades of ascension." [58] But in the second passage, directly in answer to the question of how we can speak of God, he says: "We speak of Him from things which are after Him." [59] In other words, just as we arrive at a knowledge of His existence by the contemplation of the gradation of things in the world, that is, the causally interconnected things, which proceed from God and of which He is the cause,[60] so also, in speaking of

[50] Didask., X, 6. The last sentence in this quotation reads: *τούτῳ δὲ καὶ θεὸν συνεπινοεῖ διὰ τὴν ἐν τῷ τιμίῳ ὑπεροχήν*. Pierre Louis (op. cit., p. 62) translates it: "à ces idées on ajoute alors celle de Dieu, qui se distingue par son excéllence."

[51] Cf. reference to Plato in J. Freudenthal, op. cit., p. 286, and in Pierre Louis, loc. cit., n. 144.

[52] Sympos., 210A.

[53] Ibid., 210B.

[54] Ibid., 210C.

[55] Ibid., 210D.

[56] Ibid., 211C.

[57] Ibid., 212A.

[58] Enn., VI, 7, 36 (7–8).

[59] Ibid., V, 3, 14 (7–8).

[60] The reference here is to the Aristotelian proof for the existence of God from the interconnection of all things in the world as cause and effect. Cf. Phys. VIII, 4–5.

God, we describe Him in His causal relation to these things in the world which proceed from Him.

The three kinds of divine predicates enumerated by Albinus and Plotinus are thus reducible to two kinds, negations and actions, for the predicates described as analogies and as certain grades of ascension are really one type of predicate, both of them, as we have seen, describing God in His causal relation to the world or His actions. And so in one passage, where he summarizes his view, Plotinus mentions only two kinds of predicates. "If anyone attributes to Him anything at all," he says, "be it essence or intelligence or beauty, by that attribution one takes away from Him His nature of being the Good. Therefore, let us take away everything from Him and let us affirm nothing of Him . . . And so also, let us not attribute to Him any of the things posterior to Him or inferior to Him, but let us bear in mind that, being above all of them, He is their cause, without being Himself any of them." [61] In other words, let us describe God only by negations or by his causal relation to things posterior and inferior to Him.

But, according to Albinus and Plotinus, not only can God be described by predicates which are negative and active in form, but He can also be described by predicates which are positive or non-active in form, provided they are understood as being negative or active in meaning. While neither Albinus nor Plotinus explicitly discuss this point, we may gather that this is their view from certain statements they make. Thus Albinus describes God by the predicate "complete in himself" (*αὐτοτελής*) but explains it to have the negative meaning of "without want" (*ἀπροσδεής*).[62] Similarly Plotinus describes God by the predicates "one" (*ἕν*) and self-sufficient (*αὐτάρκης*) but explains the former to mean "indivisible" (*ἀμέριστος*) [63] and the latter "not in want" (*ἀνενδεής*).[64] Thus, again, Albinus describes God by the predicates "good" (*ἀγαθός*) and "truth" (*ἀλήθεια*) but explains the former to mean that "He does good (*εὐεργετεῖ*) to everything according to its [receptive] ability and is the cause (*αἴτιος*) of every good," [65]

[61] Enn., V, 5, 13 (9–20).
[62] Didask., X, 3.
[63] Enn., VI, 9, 5 (38–41).
[64] Ibid., VI, 9, 6 (24–26).
[65] Didask., X, 3.

and the latter that "He is the principle (ἀρχή) of every truth." [66] Similarly Plotinus attributes to God the terms "good" and "thinking activity" (νόησις), but he explains the former to mean that "He is good for other things, if they are able to receive some part of it," [67] and the latter that "it is the cause which makes some other being think." [68] It is this also, we may assume, that Plotinus means by his statement that "one must say that He lives, if indeed He gives life." [69] The meaning of this statement is that one must not say that He lives except in the sense of His being the cause of life.

These three methods enumerated by Albinus and by Plotinus as leading to a knowledge of God are described by Plotinus as methods of scientific knowledge (ἐπιστήμη) or of thinking (νόησις).[70] In contradistinction to these methods of scientific knowledge, however, Plotinus mentions another method which he calls vision (θέα, θέαμα).[71] Of these various methods, that of vision is described by him as being "superior" to those of scientific knowledge,[72] and scientific knowledge is described by him as being "prior" to vision,[73] that is, as being preparatory and hence inferior to vision. He also tells us what means are to be employed in order to attain to vision. They are "purifications and virtues and refinements and ascents to the intelligible, abiding therein and feasting there on its delights." [74]

Now the distinction between these two kinds of knowledge, the indirect and the direct, scientific knowledge and vision, is not new with Plotinus. By his time there were already two types of such a distinction, that of Plato and that of Philo. Both Plato and Philo, the former with reference to the ideas and the latter with reference to God, find that there is a distinction between indirect knowledge attained by reason and direct knowledge attained by vision. The former, according to both of them, is ultimately based

[66] Ibid.
[67] Enn., VI, 9, 6 (40–42).
[68] Ibid., (53–54).
[69] Ibid., III, 9, 9 (17–18).
[70] Ibid., VI, 9, 4 (2).
[71] Ibid., (14, 17).
[72] Ibid., (3).
[73] Ibid., VI, 7, 36 (4).
[74] Ibid., (8–10).

upon sense perception; the latter is completely supersensible. But, though Philo is undoubtedly dependent upon Plato in his description of his direct knowledge of the vision of God, there is still a difference between him and Plato as to the nature of that direct knowledge of vision. The difference is as follows: To Plato the vision of the ideas comes by recollection; to Philo the vision of God comes by revelation.[75] To Plato, again, it comes naturally to any one who is properly prepared to receive it; to Philo, while proper preparation is necessary, it comes as an act of divine grace.[76] Plotinus seems to have been conscious of the difference between these two types of supersensible vision and to have consciously aligned himself with Plato as against Philo. Consequently, in his presentation of his own view, while reminiscently making use of Philonic phrases, he gives them a non-Philonic meaning.[77] Reminiscences of Philonic phraseology are to be found, for instance, in one passage where he speaks not only of the soul as ascending by its own power to the good but also of the Good as that which "causes the thinking soul to move towards it, so that in its motion it sees the Good," [78] or in another passage where, in describing the desire of the soul for intelligible objects, he says that "each intelligible object becomes an object of desire only when the Good makes it glitter, by giving graces (χάριτας), as it were, to desired objects and love to those who desire." [79] All this sounds like Philo's description of the vision of God in his statements that God called Moses and spoke to him "so that he might receive the clear vision of God from the First Cause himself" [80] and that "it was impossible for anyone to comprehend by his own unassisted power the truly Existent, unless He himself revealed and manifested himself to him." [81] Still, despite the language he uses, Plotinus could not have meant by it literally that his God comes to the assistance of man in gaining a knowledge of Him, for in opposition to Philo, he says explicitly that God acts

[75] Cf. Philo, II, pp. 83–85; 92.
[76] Ibid., II, pp. 47–51.
[77] On the analogies and differences between Philo's and Plotinus' conceptions of vision see R. Arnou, Le Désir de Dieu dans la Philosophie de Plotin, pp. 224–227.
[78] Enn., V, 6, 5 (7–8).
[79] Ibid., VI, 7, 22 (6–7).
[80] Leg. All., III, 33, 102.
[81] Abr., 17, 80.

without "will" (οὐδὲ βουληθέντος) [82] and in opposition, again, to Philo, he denies the scriptural story of the creation of the world by design and purpose.[83] Moreover, in opposition even to Aristotle, his God has no "knowledge of himself," [84] no "thinking" and no "consciousness." [85] Plotinus' vision of God, therefore, unlike that of Philo, can have no element of grace in it.

But here a question comes up. Vision is said by Plotinus to be superior as well as posterior to scientific knowledge [86] and, furthermore, the predicates of God which are derived from scientific knowledge, those predicates which are negations and causal relations, are described by him as only "directing us toward Him and rousing us to pass from reasons into vision." [87] Are we then to infer that, according to Plotinus, vision gives man a complete knowledge of God's essence? Now, in Philo, as we have shown,[88] the vision of God does not give man a complete knowledge of God's essence, though the knowledge it does give is greater than that given by rational demonstration. A similar view, we believe, can be shown to have been held also by Plotinus. For, in one passage, in a description of those who have a direct vision of God, to whom he refers as those who are able "to harmonize with Him and, as it were, to lay hold of Him and to touch Him," [89] he says that "they can see Him so far as He is visible according to His nature." [90] Not all the essence of God, then, becomes known to those who have a vision of Him. Then, in another passage, in a description of what is supposed to be the vision of the Good, he speaks only of the vision of the light that radiates from the Good.[91] Thus, again, it is not the essence of the Good itself in its entirety that becomes known to those who have a vision of it, but only the light that radiates from it.

In our foregoing analysis of the treatment of divine attributes

[82] Enn., V, 1, 6 (26).
[83] Ibid., V, 8, 7.
[84] Ibid., VI, 7, 38 (10).
[85] Ibid., VI, 9, 6 (51).
[86] Cf. above, n. 72.
[87] Enn., VI, 9, 4 (13–14).
[88] Cf. Philo, II, pp. 91–92, 149
[89] Enn., VI, 9, 4 (26–27).
[90] Ibid., (29–30).
[91] Ibid., VI, 7, 36.

in Albinus and Plotinus, and especially in the latter, we have tried to bring out certain advances made upon Philo's treatment of the same subject. To begin with, there is, in both Albinus and Plotinus, a formal classification of the attributes, in which negations are included. Then there is an indication that both of them use the term negation in its strictly Aristotelian sense, as opposed to privation. Then, also, both of them use the terms negation and causal relation not only with reference to predicates which are negative or causative in form but also with reference to predicates which, though not negative and not causative in form, are taken as much in meaning. From now on formal classifications of divine attributes, with the inclusion of negation as one of the types of attributes and the use of negation in the technical Aristotelian sense of the term and also the application of negation to predicates which are positive and non-active in form, become common characteristics of the treatment of divine attributes in religious philosophic literature, be it Christian or Moslem or Jewish, though further developments, of course, are to be found in later literature, especially in the works of Maimonides.[92] In all these Plotinus is to be considered the proximate source, though the ultimate source of the entire problem of divine attributes is to be found in Philo.

As an example of the continuity of tradition from Albinus and Plotinus throughout Greek and Latin and Arabic and Hebrew philosophic literature, we may take the Greek term *aphairesis*, which, as we have seen, is used by both Albinus and Plotinus in the technical sense of logical negation and as the equivalent of the term *apophasis* as used by Aristotle. Now neither in Plato nor in Aristotle nor in the Stoics is the term *aphairesis* used in the logical sense of *apophasis*. In Aristotle the only technical meaning that the term *aphairesis* has, beyond its ordinary meaning of "taking away" or "subtraction," is that of "abstraction" with reference to mathematical concepts.[93] But once this term has acquired the technical sense of logical negation with Albinus and

[92] Cf. my papers "The Aristotelian Predicables and Maimonides' Division of Attributes" in Essays and Studies in Memory of Linda R. Miller (1938), pp. 201–234; "Maimonides on Negative Attributes" in Louis Ginzberg Memorial Volume (1945), pp. 411–446.

[93] H. Bonitz, Index Aristotelicus, s. v.

Plotinus it continues to be used in that sense throughout Greek, Arabic, Hebrew, and Latin philosophic literature, especially in connection with divine attributes. Thus in Christian Greek literature, the term *aphairesis* is used interchangeably with the term *apophasis*, in connection with divine attributes, by both Dionysius the Areopagite [94] and John of Damascus.[95] In Arabic and Hebrew philosophic texts, while the Arabic term *salb*, Hebrew *shelilah*, usually translates the Aristotelian *apophasis* [96] and the same term is also used as a description of divine attributes which are negative,[97] still the Arabic *nafy*, which reflects the Greek *aphairesis* [98] and of which the Hebrew translations are *harḥaḳah*, *biṭṭul*, and *silluḳ* is used in connection with the negative attributes in an identical expression which occurs both in Maimonides [99] and in Averroes.[100] And so also in mediaeval Latin philosophy, the term *remotio*, used in the sense of *negatio*, in the expression *via remotionis*, is a translation of the Greek *aphairesis*.[101]

[94] De Divinis Nominibus II, 4 (PG 3, 641 A); De Mystica Theologia II (1000B).

[95] De Fide Orthodoxa I, 4 (PG 94, 800 BC).

[96] Cf. Die Hermeneutik des Aristoteles in der arabischen Übersetzung des Isḥāḳ ibn Ḥonain, ed. Isidor Pollak, Glossar, p. 42, s.v.

[97] Cf. Maimonides, Moreh Nebukim I, 58.

[98] In the Arabic translation of Aristotle's Metaphysics IX, 3, 1047a, 14, the Arabic verb *nafa* translates the Greek *ἐξαιρεῖν* (cf. ed. Bouyges cited above, p. 269, No. 1410), which means the same as *ἀφαιρεῖν*.

[99] Moreh Nebukim, I, 51, Arabic: *nafy al-ṣifāt*; Hebrew: *harḥakat ha-to'arim* (Ibn Tibbon); *biṭṭul ha-middot* (Ḥarizi). Cf. also Ḥobot ha-Lebabot, I, 10, Arabic text, ed. A. S. Yahuda, p. 72, ll. 6 and 9: *al-sawālib min ṣifāt;* Hebrew: *ha-shollot be-middot* and *wa-kull mā yunfa 'anhu min al-ṣifāt*; Hebrew: *we-kal ha-meruḥakot mi-mennu min ha-middot.*

[100] Tahafot al-Tahafot, VI, 19, p. 320, l. 11 (ed. M. Bouyges): *min nafy al-ṣifāt*; Hebrew: *be-silluḳ ha-to'arim* (Kalonymus ben David ben Todros).

[101] Cf. Thomas Aquinas, Contra Gentiles, I, 14. I do not think Munk is right in taking the Latin *remotio* to be a translation of the Arabic *nafy* (cf. Le Guide des Egarés, I, 58, p. 239, n.). He has overlooked the Greek *aphairesis*.

7

NEGATIVE ATTRIBUTES IN THE CHURCH FATHERS AND THE GNOSTIC BASILIDES

By the time the Fathers of the Church began to offer negation as a solution of the problem of divine attributes, the theory of negative attributes had already been dealt with by Philo, Albinus, and Plotinus. All three of them, starting with the assumption that God is ineffable, found that one way of describing God was by means of negative attributes. In their treatment of this type of attributes, however, there is a difference between Philo on the one hand and Albinus and Plotinus on the other.

In Philo, the use of negative attributes in the description of God, such as describing God as being invisible, incomprehensible, unnamable, ineffable, and the like, is presented only as a way of expressing the scriptural principle of the unlikeness between God and all other beings.[1] In contradistinction to his own treatment of affirmative attributes, which is cast by him in a framework of the Aristotelian theories of logical propositions and predicables,[2] Philo's treatment of negative attributes is free of any logical implications.

In Albinus and Plotinus, however, negative attributes are treated after the manner of Aristotle's logical propositions of the negative quality.[3] To begin with, corresponding to the term "negation" (ἀπόφασις) in its technical sense as used by Aristotle in contrast to the term "privation" (στέρησις), both Albinus and Plotinus use the term "remotion" (ἀφαίρεσις). Then, the contrast between "remotion" (or "negation") and "privation" is conceived of by them, after Aristotle and his commentator Alexander, as a contrast between a proposition in which the opposite

[1] Cf. my Philo, II, p. 98 ff., 126 ff.

[2] Ibid., pp. 130 ff.

[3] Cf. my paper "Albinus and Plotinus on Divine Attributes," Harvard Theological Review, 45 (1952), 115–130. Above, pages 115–130.

of the predicate negated can under no conceivable circumstances be affirmed of the subject and a proposition in which the opposite of the predicate negated can under certain conceivable circumstances be affirmed of the subject. Accordingly, with reference to God, both Albinus and Plotinus maintain that the negation of any predicate of God does not mean that its opposite can be predicated of Him; it rather means the exclusion of God from the universe of discourse of the predicate in question. In other words, the negative attributes of God are what Aristotle calls technically "negations" and not what he calls technically "privations." Then also, to both Albinus and Plotinus negations can be expressed not only by propositions which are negative in quality, such as "God is not divisible," but also by propositions which are affirmative in quality but in which the predicate is negative in form, such as "God is indivisible." Moreover, to both Albinus and Plotinus, God may be described not only by predicates which are negative in form, such as "indivisible," but also by predicates which, though positive in form, are understood to be negative in meaning, as when, for instance, the term "simple" is understood to mean "indivisible." Then, further, in Plotinus, negation in the sense of being excluded from the universe of discourse of certain predicates may be expressed by saying that God is "before" or "beyond" or "above" those predicates. He thus says that God is "neither what is movable nor what is at rest," because He is "before (πρό) motion and before rest," [4] and also that He "neither knows anything nor is there anything of which He is ignorant," [5] because He is beyond (ἐπέκεινα) thought and knowledge,[6] and similarly that He "has neither the not-good nor the good," [7] because "He is above good (ὑπεράγαθον)." [8] Finally, in Albinus, the method of forming a conception of God as well as describing God by negation is compared to the method of our forming the conception as well as the definition of a mathematical point. "The first method of forming a conception of God," he says, "will be by the remotion (ἀφαίρεσιν) of these [sensible

[4] Enn. VI, 9, 3 (ed. E. Bréhier, ll. 42, 44).
[5] Ibid. VI, 9, 6 (48–49).
[6] Ibid. V, 6, 6 (31 ff.).
[7] Ibid. V, 5, 13 (5).
[8] Ibid. VI, 9, 6 (40).

predicates from God], in the same way as we form a conception of a point by its abstraction (ἀφαίρεσιν), from the sensible, namely, by first forming the conception of a surface, then that of a line, and finally that of a point." [9] In this passage, as we have tried to explain elsewhere,[10] Albinus means to show that God is to be described negatively in the same way as a point is defined by Euclid negatively as that "which has no part." [11]

These two methods of dealing with negative attributes, namely, the Philonic method of using negation only as an expression of the scriptural principle of the unlikeness of God with other beings and the Albino-Plotinian method of using negation in the Aristotelian technical sense of negative propositions, are to be found in the Church Fathers. Here we shall give a few representative illustrations of the latter kind of use of negation by the Church Fathers, with which we shall contrast, on one point, the use of negation by Basilides.

In Clement of Alexandria's treatment of the problem of divine attributes we have a typical example of the combination of Philo and Albinus and Aristotle. Reflecting Philo's statements that, on account of the scriptural doctrine of the unlikeness of God, anthropomorphic expressions in Scripture are to be understood as having been introduced "for the instruction of the many (τῶν πολλῶν)" [12] and are not to be taken literally but rather figuratively,[13] Clement starts out his discussion of divine attributes by stating that "the most of men (οἱ πλεῖστοι τῶν ἀνθρώπων)" think of God after the analogy of themselves and, in the course of his discussion, he reminds his readers that the anthropomorphic appellations in Scriptures were not taken by "the Hebrews" literally but that "certain of these appellations were used more piously in an allegorical sense." [14] Then, as he goes on, he intimates that besides those appellations which are to be taken allegorically there are others which are to be taken negatively and, paraphrasing Albinus, he tries to show how, by a process

[9] Didaskalikos, X, 5 (ed. Fr. Dübner, p. 239, ll. 19–23; ed. P. Lewis, p. 61).
[10] Cf. "Albinus and Plotinus on Divine Attributes," op. cit., pp. 118–119.
[11] Euclid, Elements, I, Def. 1.
[12] Immut. 11, 54.
[13] Sacr. 30, 101.
[14] Strom. V, 11[68] (PG 9, 104 AB).

of abstraction like that by which we arrive at the conceptions of surface and line and point we may also arrive at some conception of God, namely "knowing not what He is but what He is not." [15] But in the course of his discussion, after describing the manner of arriving at the conception of point, which, as we have said, alludes to Euclid's negative definition of point, he adds: "For the point which remains is a unit (μονὰς), so to speak, having position, from which, if we take away position, there is the conception of unit." [16] This additional statement about a "unit" reflects Aristotle's negative definition of "unit" as that "which is not divisible in any dimension and is without position." [17]

A greater use of the Albino-Plotinian method of treatment of negative attributes is to be found in Gregory of Nyssa. In one passage he says that "we either convey the idea of goodness by the negation (ἀποφάσεως) of badness, or *vice versa* by the remotion (ἀφαιρέσει) of the good we convey the idea of the bad." [18] Here, like Albinus and Plotinus, he uses the term *aphairesis* as the equivalent of the term *apophasis*. In another passage he indicates that, again like Albinus and Plotinus, he takes propositions which are affirmative in form but in which the predicates are terms with alpha privative to be the equivalent of negative propositions, for he says that the proposition "God is incorruptible" means that "in the incorruptible corruption is not found," [19] that is to say, it is the equivalent of the proposition "God is not corruptible." In still another passage, after stating that the divine nature is ineffable,[20] he continues as follows: "Wherefore, in order that the superexcellent nature should not seem to have any relationship with these things below, in attempting to describe the divine nature, we have made use of notions and words which separate it from them," such, for instance, as the terms "pretemporal" (προαιώνιον), "beginningless" (ἄναρχον), "end-

[15] Ibid. V, 11[71] (108 B–109 A). On this analogy between Clement and Albinus, see H. Chadwick, Origen: Contra Celsum VII, 42 (1953), p. 429, n. 4.
[16] Ibid. (109 A).
[17] Metaph. V, 6, 1016b, 25.
[18] De Anima et Resurrectione (PG 46, 40 B).
[19] Cont. Eunom. XII (PG 45, 953 BC).
[20] Ibid. (1104 B).

less" (ἀτελεύτητον), and similar other terms formed with alpha privative.[21] From his inclusion of the term προαιώνιον in this list it may be inferred that, like Plotinus, he treated terms with the Greek prefix *pro* as the equivalent of terms with the Greek alpha privative. But evidently being aware that there was some question, as we shall see,[22] whether affirmative propositions in which the predicates are terms with alpha privative are to be considered as privations or as negations, he says, after his enumeration of the above-mentioned examples of such predicates, that all those who are so inclined may coin similar other predicates, "calling them privatives (στερητικά) or remotives (ἀφαιρετικά) or whatever pleases them." [23] What he means to say is that, whatever others may think of propositions with such predicates, he follows Plotinus in regarding them as negations. Finally, like Albinus and Plotinus, he allows to affirm of God even terms which are positive in form, provided they are taken to have a negative meaning. He thus says: "It amounts to the same whether we speak of God as 'unsusceptible (ἀνεπίδεκτον) of evil' or whether we call Him 'good,' whether we confess that 'He is immortal (ἀθάνατον)' or whether we say that 'He ever liveth,' for we understand no difference in the sense of these terms, but we signify one and the same thing by both, though one may seem to convey the notion of affirmation (θέσιν) and the other of negation (ἀναίρεσιν)." [24]

A similar use of the Albino-Plotinian method of treatment of negative attributes is to be found in pseudo-Dionysius the Areopagite and, following him, John of Damascus. The direct source of Dionysius, we may assume, was Plotinus.

To begin with, like Plotinus, Dionysius uses the term *aphairesis* in the sense of negation. Thus in a passage, in which he begins with the statement that "it is not possible either to express or to conceive what the One . . . is," [25] he concludes with the statement that "the godlike minds . . . celebrate Him most ap-

[21] Ibid. (1104 D–1105 A).
[22] Cf. below at nn. 52–57.
[23] Cont. Eunom. XII (1105 A).
[24] Ibid. (953 D).
[25] De Divinis Nominibus I, 5 (PG 3, 593 B).

propriately through the remotion (ἀφαιρέσεως) of all things." [26] Such a "remotion," as in Plotinus, is expressed by him in two ways: (1) by negative propositions, such as, for instance, "God is not a body" or that "He is not in place" or that "He is not seen," [27] and the like, and (2) by affirmative propositions in which the predicate is prefixed by alpha privative, such, for instance, as "God is inconceivable (ἀδιανόητος)" or "ineffable (ἄῤῥητος)" [28] or "invisible (ἀόρατος)" or "incomprehensible (ἀπερίληπτος)," [29] and the like.

In John of Damascus the same view is expressed in the following passage: "In the case of God, however, it is impossible to explain what He is in essence, and it befits us the rather to hold discourse about his remotion (ἀφαιρέσεως) from all things." [30] Elsewhere these discourses about God by means of "remotion" are said by him to be discourses "by means of 'negation'" (ἀποφαντικῶς).[31] He furthermore indicates that this negation may be expressed either by an affirmative proposition in which the predicate has as its prefix an alpha privative, such as "God is incorruptible," or by a negative proposition such as "God is not corruptible." He thus says: "Further the terms beginningless, incorruptible, unbegotten, as also uncreated, incorporeal, unseeable, and so forth, explain what He is not, that is to say, they tell us that His existence had no beginning, that He is not corruptible, nor created, nor corporeal, nor visible." [32]

Then, again like Plotinus, Dionysius tries to show that by remotion he means here the absolute exclusion of God from the universe of the predicates in question. Thus in a passage, in which he started by saying that it is our duty to negate (ἀποφάσκειν) all attributes of the One, he proceeds to say that we are "not to consider the negations (ἀποφάσεις) to be in opposition to the affirmations (καταφάσεσιν), but far rather that the One, which is above every remotion (ἀφαίρεσιν) and affirmation

[26] Ibid. (593 BC).
[27] De Mystica Theologia IV (PG 3, 1040 D).
[28] De Divin. Nomin. 1, 1 (PG 3, 588 B).
[29] Ibid. I, 2 (588 C).
[30] De Fide Orthodoxa I, 4 (PG 94, 800 B).
[31] Ibid. I, 12 (845 C).
[32] Ibid. I, 9 (837 A B).

(θέσιν), is above privations (στερήσεις)." [33] In this passage, we take it, alluding to Aristotle's distinction between "negation" and "privation" and using the terms *apophasis* and *aphairesis* indiscriminately, Dionysius tries to show that negative attributes in the case of God are to be taken not as the negation of an opposite but rather as the exclusion from the universe of a discourse. In another place he expresses the same view in his terse statement that God is "the affirmation of all, the remotion of all, that which is above all affirmation and remotion." [34] This conception of "negation" or "remotion" in the sense of the exclusion from a universe of discourse is sometimes described by him as a "preëminent remotion" (ὑπεροχικὴ ἀφαίρεσις).[35]

In John of Damascus the same view is expressed in his own explanation of what he means by the phrase "His remotion from all things." It means, he says, that God "does not belong to the class of existing things, not that He is as nonexistent, but that He is above all existing things, nay even above existence itself." [36] Similarly, speaking of such divine predicates as "unsubstantial, timeless, beginningless, invisible," he says that all such terms mean "not that God is inferior to anything or lacking in anything . . . but that He preëminently surpasses (ὑπεροχικῶς . . . ἐξῄρηται) all things, for He is not one of the things that exist, but over all things." [37]

Finally, while negative attributes are those by which, as Dionysius says, God can be celebrated "most appropriately," still, like Philo, as well as Albinus and Plotinus, he believes that God must also be celebrated by certain positive attributes, seeing that we cannot directly negate of God such terms as those which, when used with reference to us, express certain perfections. For, he argues in effect, while it can be said that God "is not a body, nor has shape, or form, or quality, or quantity, or bulk; nor is in a place, nor is seen, nor has sensible contact, nor perceives, nor is perceived by the senses, nor has disorder and confusion, as being vexed by earthly passions, nor is powerless, as being sub-

[33] De Myst. Theol. I, 2 (1000 B).
[34] De Divin. Nomin. II, 4 (641 A).
[35] Ibid. II, 3 (640 B).
[36] De Fide Orth. I, 4 (800 B).
[37] Ibid. I, 12 (845 C D).

ject to casualties of sense," still it cannot be said that "He is unsubstantial or lifeless or irrational or unintelligent." [38] God must inevitably be described as "substantial," "living," "rational," "intelligent," and the like. But all such affirmative attributes, he explains after Philo [39] and Albinus and Plotinus,[40] are to be taken to express a causal relation between God and the world.[41] But, in addition to this, all these positive attributes, when combined with the prefix *hyper*, may, as in Plotinus, acquire the logical significance of negation, in the sense of exclusion from a universe of discourse. "The names, then, common to the whole Deity," he says, . . . "are the super-good (ὑπεράγαθον), the super-God (ὑπέρθεον), the super-substantial (ὑπερούσιον), the super-living (ὑπέρζωον), the super-wise (ὑπέρσοφον), and whatever else belongs to the preëminent remotion." [42] Moreover, again as in Plotinus, the prefix *hyper* must not necessarily be actually expressed. Any laudatory terms, though positive in form, may be predicated of God, provided they are understood to be used in a preëminent sense and indirectly in a negative sense. Thus referring to the passage which we have just quoted, Dionysius says: "In the treatise *De Divinis Nominibus* [I have set forth] how He is named good, how He is named being, how He is named life and wisdom and power, and whatever belongs to the intelligible nomenclature of God." [43]

In John of Damascus the same view is expressed in a passage, where, after explaining the significance of negative attributes, he says: "But there are other terms which are predicated of God affirmatively," [44] such, for instance, as "being," "substance," "cause," "reason," "rational," "life," "living," "power," "powerful," [45] and the like. Such terms, he explains, mean to express a causal relation between God and the world.[46] He then goes on to say: "But the sweetest names are a combination of both [that

[38] De Myst. Theol. IV (1040 D).
[39] Cf. Philo, II, pp. 133 ff.
[40] Cf. "Albinus and Plotinus on Divine Attributes," op. cit., pp. 121 ff.
[41] De Divin. Nomin. I, 5 (593 C D); De Myst. Theol. I, 2 (1000 B), et passim.
[42] De Divin. Nomin. II, 3 (640 B).
[43] De Myst. Theol. III (1033 A).
[44] De Fide Orth. I, 12 (848 A).
[45] Ibid.
[46] Ibid. I, 12 (848 B); cf. I, 9 (836 A).

is, of both affirmation and negation], for example, the super-substantial (ὑπερούσιος) substance, the super-divine (ὑπέρθεος) Divinity, the super-principial (ὑπεράρχιος) principle, and the like. Further, there are some affirmations about God which have the force of a preëminent negation (ὑπεροχικῆς ἀποφάσεως), as, for example, darkness, for this does not imply that God is dark and not light, but rather that He is above light." [47]

In all the discussions of attributes, from Philo to John of Damascus, an affirmative proposition, in which the term "God" is the subject and some adjective prefixed by the alpha privative, or by its Latin equivalent the inseparable particle *in*, is the predicate, has the value of a negative proposition in the sense of the exclusion of the subject from the universe of discourse of the predicate. Thus to all of them, one can say not only "God is not effable" but also "God is ineffable," and the meaning of the latter proposition would be the exclusion of God from the universe of discourse of effability.

A view quite the opposite of this is reported by Hippolytus in the name of the Gnostic Basilides. "For, he says," writes Hippolytus, "that which is named [ineffable] is not absolutely ineffable, since we call one thing ineffable and another not even ineffable. For that which is not even ineffable is not named ineffable, but is, he says, above every name that is named." [48]

In this statement, then, Basilides is represented as agreeing with Plotinus and the Fathers on two points but disagreeing with them on a third point. He agrees with them that, whatever term is predicated of God, it must be predicated of Him as a negation in the sense of His exclusion from the universe of discourse of that predicate. Then he also agrees with them that such a negation may be expressed by affirming that God is above some particular predicate. But he disagrees with them as to whether such a negation can be also expressed by an affirmative proposition with a negative predicate, such as "God is ineffable." According to Plotinus and the Fathers, such a negation can be expressed by a proposition of this type. According to Basilides, a proposition like "God is ineffable" does not express such a

[47] Ibid. (848 B); cf. I, 4 (800 C).
[48] Hippolytus, Refutatio Omnium Haeresium VII, 20, 3 (ed. P. Wendland).

negation, or, as he puts it, it does not mean "absolutely ineffable." In order to express such a negation, he contends, one would have to say "God is not even ineffable." The point at issue between them, then, is that, according to Plotinus and the Fathers, an affirmative proposition in which the predicate is negative in form is the equivalent of what Aristotle calls a negative proposition, whereas, according to Basilides, it is the equivalent of what Aristotle calls a privative proposition.

We may ask ourselves, what is the cause of this difference?

The cause of this difference, it seems to us, may be found in a difference in the interpretation of Aristotle.

The distinction between "privation" and "negation," to which there is a definite allusion in Aristotle,[49] has been illustrated by Alexander of Aphrodisias by two examples. The example for "privation" is an affirmative proposition of which the predicate is a term which is negative only in meaning but not in form, such as the proposition "A is blind." In this case, the subject A must be some one who could naturally possess sight but happens to be blind, as, for instance, man, but it could not be something which could never naturally possess sight, as, for instance, wall. The example for "negation" is a negative proposition, such as the proposition "A is not seeing." In this case, the subject A may be even something which naturally could never have sight, as, for instance, wall.[50] It may be remarked, in passing, that the illustration for "privation" from the term "blind" given by Alexander is based upon a text in Aristotle; [51] the illustration given by him for "negation" is not found in Aristotle. But how about an affirmative proposition in which the predicate is privative both in form and in meaning, such as, for instance, "A is sightless (ἄδερκτος)," would that be a "privation" or a "negation"? In Aristotle there are various statements on this point. On the one hand, the proposition "A is toothless (νωδός)" is taken by him to be a "privation." [52] But, on the other hand, such propositions as "a voice is invisible (ἀόρατος)" [53] and "a unit . . . is indi-

[49] Metaph. IV, 2, 1004a, 10–16.

[50] Alexander in Metaphysica, ed. M. Hayduck, p. 327, ll. 18–20.

[51] Categ. 10, 12a, 27–34.

[52] Ibid. 10, 12a, 31–34.

[53] Phys. III, 5, 204a, 13–14; V, 2, 206b, 10–11; Metaph. XI, 10, 1066a, 36.

visible (ἀδιαίρετος) in quantity" [54] and "is positionless (ἄθετος)" [55] are used by him as "negations." From these statements, apparently contradictory, one would be justified to conclude that affirmative propositions with negative predicates had with Aristotle the meaning of both privations and negations. This conclusion is strengthened by the statement, made by Aristotle, that "the immobility (ἀκινησία) of that to which motion belongs [by nature] is rest," [56] the implication of which is that the immobility of that to which motion does not belong by nature is not rest but rather something which is a negation of both motion and rest. From this statement and its implication one may infer that the term "immobile," when used in a proposition in which the subject is "man," is a privation but, when used in a proposition in which the subject is "God," is a negation. In the history of the interpretation of Aristotle, it may be added in passing, two views may be found. One, that of the Stoics and Boethius, takes such propositions as privations; the other, that of Avicenna and Averroes, takes them as negations.[57]

In the light of this discussion, then, we may assume that when Philo, Albinus, Plotinus, and the Church Fathers allow the use of affirmative propositions with predicates negative in form, it is because they take a proposition of this type to be a "negation" and, as a negation, it has here the meaning of the exclusion of God from the universe of effability. When Basilides, however, does not allow the use of the proposition "God is ineffable," we may assume that it is because he takes a proposition of this type to be a "privation," and, as a "privation," it would imply that God, who by His own nature could be effable, just happens to be ineffable. It would not mean, he says in effect, that God is "absolutely ineffable." He therefore insists upon a proposition that is unmistakably a negation, such as "God is not even ineffable." We may further assume that he would allow also such a proposition as "God is not effable," which in Aristotle is definitely taken as a "negation." The reason why he uses the proposition

[54] Metaph. XIV, 2, 1089b, 35–36.

[55] Ibid. V, 6, 1016b, 30.

[56] Phys. III, 2, 202a, 4–5.

[57] Cf. my paper "Infinite and Privative Judgments in Aristotle, Averroes, and Kant," Philosophy and Phenomenological Research, 8 (1947), 173–187.

"God is not even ineffable" is obviously in order to place himself directly in opposition to those before him who did use the proposition "God is ineffable." As to who were those before him who used the expression "God is ineffable," it depends upon whether Hippolytus' report of the teachings in the name of Basilides is authentic or not. If authentic, then the only one who before Basilides, that is, before the reign of Hadrian (117–138), is known to have used that expression is Philo,[58] and it is Philo, therefore, whom he had in mind in his opposition to the use of the term "ineffable" as a predicate of God.

Towards the end of the chapter in which he has restated the view of Basilides, as quoted by us above, Hippolytus says that "Aristotle, born many generations before Basilides, was the first to discourse, in the Categories, upon the subject of equivocal terms (*ὁμώνυμα*), which these men [that is, Basilides and his son Isidore] expound as their own and as a novelty." [59] It is not quite clear what he means by this statement. If he means that, besides negative predications, Basilides and his son allowed also affirmative predications, provided only that the positive terms affirmed of God were taken in an equivocal sense, then Basilides may be considered as being the first to introduce the equivocal interpretation of divine predicates. Apart from this vague statement, Maimonides, as I have shown elsewhere, was the first to state explicitly that all positive terms affirmed of God are to be taken not only as being negative in meaning but as also being equivocal in meaning,[60] and this view of his was made the target of attack, in Latin philosophy, by Thomas Aquinas [61] and, in Hebrew philosophy, by Gersonides.[62]

[58] Cf. Philo, II, pp. 110 ff.

[59] Hippolytus, op. cit. VII, 20, 5; cf. Categ. 1, 1a, 1–6.

[60] Cf. my papers "Maimonides on Negative Attributes," Louis Ginzberg Jubilee Volume, 1945, pp. 411–446, "Maimonides and Gersonides on Divine Attributes as Ambiguous Terms," Mordecai M. Kaplan Jubilee Volume, 1953, pp. 515–530.

[61] Sum. Theol. I, 13, 2c; cf. Cont. Gent. I, 33.

[62] Milhamot Adonai III, 3.

8

AVICENNA, ALGAZALI, AND AVERROES ON DIVINE ATTRIBUTES

I. Avicenna and Alfarabi

The problem of divine attributes in Avicenna rests on two presuppositions. First, the unity of God means not only a denial of a plurality of deities but also a denial of any kind of composition in the nature of God, including the composition of genus and differentia. Second, genera and species and differentiae, that is, universals, are neither real beings nor mere names, but have in them enough of reality to make their affirmation of God incompatible with His unity.

His conception of the unity of God is stated by Avicenna in a passage where he says that the unity of God means two things. In the first place, God is one in the sense that there can be no two Gods, whether (a) mutually dependent upon each other[1] or (b) equal to each other or (c) contrary to each other.[2] In the second place, it means simplicity, which excludes (1) divisibility into «parts of quantity»[3] and (2) divisibility into «parts of definition or formula, whether these parts are related to each other like (a) matter and form or (b) in some other manner, provided only that each part of the formula which explains the meaning of the term defined by it signifies a thing which in existence differs essentially from another thing»,[4] so that the simplicity of God may be said to exclude three kinds of divisibility, namely, that of (1) «quantity», that of (2) «principles», i. e., matter and form, and that of «formula», i. e., definition.[5]

1. *al-Najāt*, III p. 369, ll. 13-14, Cairo, 1331 A. H. (Latin : *Avicennae Metaphysices Compendium*, by N. Carame, Rome, 1926, (p. 71).
2. *Ibid.*, III, p. 374, ll. 3-4 (L : p. 78).
3. *Ibid.*, III, p. 371, l. 3 (L : p. 72, ll. 24-25).
4. *Ibid.*, III, p. 371, ll. 3-6 (L : p. 72, l. 25; p. 73, l. 4).
5. *Ibid.*, III, p. 372, l. 5 (L : p. 74, ll. 5-6.

Before Avicenna, exactly the same conception of the unity of God was laid down by Alfarabi. The term «one» when applied to God, he says, means two things.[6] First, it means that besides God there can be no other being, either one (a) who is more perfect than God and upon whom God is dependent,[7] or (b) one who is equal with God[8] or (c) one who is contrary to God.[9] Second, it means that in the essence of God there is no divisibility such as would result if the attributes by which God is described in discourse were assumed to designate parts in His essence after the analogy of (a) the parts of a definition, which are assumed to be the causes of the existence of the definitum in the same way as (b) matter and form are the causes of the thing that consists of them, and still less is there in the essence of God (c) quantitative divisibility.[10]

After Avicenna, the twofold conception of the unity of God is reproduced by Algazali in the name of those whom he refers to as «the philosophers.» The external conception of the unity of God is restated by him in his contention that the philosophers are unable to «establish a proof that God is one and that it is not possible to assume the existence of two Necessary Beings each of whom is without cause».[11] The internal conception of the unity of God is reproduced by him in his statement that it means «the remotion of plurality in every respect», under which he specifically enumerates the remotion of five kinds of plurality : (a) the plurality arising from a division, whether actually (*fi'lan*) or conceptually (*wahman*), into quantitative parts; (b) the plurality arising from a division, intellectually (*fī al-'aql*), into matter and form; (c) the plurality of essence and attributes; (d) the plurality of genus and differentia, which, again, is only

6. *Kitāb al-Siyāsāt al-Madaniyyah*, p. 14, ll. 19-20, and p. 15, ll. 7-8, Hyderabad, 1346 A. H. (Hebrew : *Sefer ha-Hathalot*, in Z. Filipowski's *Sefer ha-Asif*, Leipzig, 1849, p. 11, ll. 26-27, and p. 12, l. 8).

7. *Ibid.*, p. 13, ll. 15-19 (H : p. 10, ll. 24-28).

8. *Ibid.*, p. 13, l. 19; p. 14, l. 11 (H : p. 10, l. 28; p. 11, l. 16).

9. *Ibid.*, p. 14, ll. 12-19 (H : p. 11, ll. 16-26).

10. *Ibid.*, p. 14, l. 20; p. 15, l. 8 (H : p. 11, l. 27; p. 12, l. 8); cf. *Fuṣuṣ al-Ḥikam*, in *Alfārābī's philosophische Abhandlungen*, ed. Fr. Dietrici, 1890, p. 68, ll. 5-6.

11. *Tahāfut al-Falāsifah* (ed. M. Bouyges), v, p. 143, ll. 2-3 (Latin : in *Averrois Destructio Destructionum Philosophiae Algazelis*, v, p. 74 A, in *Aristotelis opera*, vol. IX, Venice, 1573); cf. *Maqāṣid al-Falasifah*, II, p. 140, l. 15; p. 141, l. 14, Cairo, n. d. (Latin : *Algazel's Metaphysics*, ed. J. T. Muckle, 1933, p. 54, l. 24; p. 55, l. 13).

an «intellectual plurality», and (e) the plurality of essence and existence.[12]

Ultimately this conception of the unity of God goes back to Philo. Not only does Philo formally distinguish within the concept of the unity of God between numerical unity and simplicity,[13] for which indeed he already had before him the example of Aristotle,[14] but he also conceives of the simplicity of God as excluding the distinction of genus and differentia, for which he had no precedent in Greek philosophy. In Greek philosophy before him the simplicity of God, which was a corollary of the incorporeality of God, would exclude only the divisibility of God into (a) body and soul, (b) the four elements, (c) substance and accident, and (d) matter and form. It would not exclude the distinction of genus and differentia and hence it would not exclude definition. It was Philo who, by combining (a) the philosophic principle of the immateriality of God with the scriptural principle of (b) the unlikeness of God to anything in the world, and (c) the scriptural statement that God has not revealed His name to those to whom He appeared, and also (d) the scriptural laws prohibiting mention of the proper name of God, taking the name of God in vain, and in general treating lightly the word «God», arrived at the principle that God is ineffable in the sense of His being indefinable.[15]

The non-nominalistic as well as the non-realistic conception of universals is stated by Avicenna in two passages. In one passage, he aligns himself with those who stood opposed to extreme realism. Thus reflecting Aristotle's statements that the universal is non-existent[16] or that it is not a substance[17] and that «the earliest universal is in the soul»,[18] he says that «no universal or general idea is in existence, for the actual existence of a universal or general idea is only in the intellect, and that is the form which exists in the intellect, whose actual or potential relation to every singular thing is the same».[19] In another

12. *Ibid.*, v, 11-17, p. 149, l. 3; p. 152, l. 10 (L : p. 76 B-H).
13. Cf. *Philo : Foundations of Religious Phylosophy in Judaism, Christianity and Islam*, by H. A. Wolfson, 2nd Printing Revised, 1948, I, pp. 171-173.
14. Cf. *Ibid.*, II, p. 99.
15. *Ibid.*, II, pp. 94-126.
16. *De Anima*, I, 1, 402b, 7-8; *Metaph.*, XII, 5, 1071a, 19.
17. *Metaph.*, VII, 10, 1035b, 28.
18. *Anal. Post.*, II, 19, 100a, 16.
19. *Najāt*, III, p. 360, l. 14; p. 361, l. 1 (L : p. 59, ll. 22-25).

passage he aligns himself with those who stood opposed to extreme nominalism, describing what he means exactly by his statement that universals exist only in the intellect. The genus or universal, he says, has three stages of existence : first, before the many (*qabl al-kathra, ante multitudinem*), when it is in the wisdom of God; second, in the many (*fī al-qathra, in multiplicitate*), when our mind has yet to abstract it from the particular things; third, after the many (*ba'd al-qathra, post multiplicitatem*), when it already exists as an intelligible being in our mind. These three stages of the genus or universal are described by him respectively as (a) the natural genus (*jins ṭabī'iyy, genus naturale*), (b) the intellectual genus (*jins 'aqliyy, genus intellectum*) and (c) the logical genus (*jins manṭiqiyy, genus logicum*).[20] This last kind of universal, though in our mind, was not invented by our mind as a fiction. It is not a mere name. Our mind has discovered within the particular things the traces of those divine exemplars which were in the mind of God before He implanted them within those particular things as something immanent in them.

According to the testimony of Albertus Magnus, the threefold stage theory of universals was held before Avicenna also by Alfarabi.[21] Though in the writings of Alfarabi there is no explicit formulation of these threefold stages in universals such as is found in Avicenna, the implication of this threefold division is certainly to be found in his philosophy.[22] The Avicennian formulation of this theory, however, is to be found in Ammonius, who in his commentary on Porphyry's *Isagoge* says in the exact words used later by Avicenna that «genera are of a threefold nature : some of them are prior to the many (πρὸ τῶν πολλῶν) and others are in the many (ἐν τοῖς πολλοῖς) and still others are posterior to the many (ἐπὶ τοῖς πολλοῖς).»[23] In Ammonius' commentaries on Porphyry's *Isagoge* and Aristotle's *Categories* one may find also the terms «natural genus», «intellectual genus», and «logical genus» used by Avicenna as a description of the

20. Cf. I. MADKOUR, *L'Organon d'Aristote dans le monde arabe*, 1934, p. 151, quoting *al-Shifā'*, Teheran, 1393 A. H., fol. 8a, ll. 44-46; C. PRANTL, *Geschichte der Logik*, II, 1885, pp. 354-357, quoting *Avicennae opera*, Venice, 1508, fol. 12rv.

21. *De Praedicabilibus*, IX, 3; cf. PRANTL, *op. cit.*, II, p. 313, n. 25.

22. MADKOUR, *loc. cit.*

23. *Ammonius in Porphyrii Isagogen* (ed. A. Busse), p. 68, l. 25; p. 69, l. 1; cf. p. 104, ll. 28 ff.

three stages in universals, though their application to these three stages in Ammonius does not exactly agree with that found later in Avicenna. According to Ammonius, the universal «before the many» is to be called «the intelligible genus» (γένος νοητὸν),[24] that «in the many» is to be called «sensible genus» (γένος αἰσθητόν)[25] or «natural genus» (γένος φυσικόν),[26] and that «after the many» is to be called «postgenerated genus» (γένος ὑστερογενές) or «intellectual (i. e., logical) genus» (γένος ἐννοηματικόν).[27] The meaning of this threefold distinction is explained by Ammonius by the following illustration. Let there be a signet-ring, upon which is engraved the image of Achilles. Let the impression of that image be made upon many wax-tablets. Let some one look upon these wax-tablets and retain the image impressed upon them in his mind. That image of Achilles, therefore, has three stages : in the signet-ring it is prior to the many; in the wax-tablets it is in the many; and in the mind of the beholder it is posterior to the many and of posterior origin. Similarly, by assuming that in the mind of God, there are exemplar ideas of all things that are to be created and that are to be known by men, then in the mind of God they are prior to the many, in things they are in the many, and in the mind of men they are posterior to the many.[28]

The universals in the mind of man are said by Ammonius to have some existence apart from bodies (σωμάτων χωριστά), in view of the fact that they do not subsist in the body but in the soul, but still they are not absolutely separable from the body.[29] On this point, he says, the view presented by him differs from both Aristotle and Plato, for to Aristotle universals have no existence at all apart from matter, whereas to Plato they exist absolutely apart from matter.[30] In contradistinction to Ammonius, however, Avicenna seems to present this theory of the threefold stages in universals as an interpretation of Aristotle and evidently as a means of bringing about a harmonization

24. *Ammonius in Categorias* (ed. A. Busse), p. 41, l. 9.
25. *Ibid.*, p. 41, ll. 10-11.
26. *Ammonius in Isagogen*, p. 119, l. 8.
27. *In Categorias*, p. 9, l. 9; *In Isagogen*, p. 69, ll. 4 and 6; cf. also p. 41, ll. 19-20; p. 42, l. 13.
28. *In Isagogen*, p. 41, ll. 13 ff.
29. *Ibid.*, p. 42, ll. 13-15.
30. *Ibid.*, p. 42, ll. 23-24.

between Plato and Aristotle, an attempt which in Alfarabi was open and outspoken.[31]

With these two presuppositions as a starting point, nothing could be predicated of God. For predicables, according to Porphyry's classification of predicables which is followed by Avicenna, must be either one of these five : genus, species, differentia, property, and accident.[32] Certainly no predicate of God can be an accident; nor, as we have seen, can it be a genus or species or differentia. The question, therefore, remains whether it can be a property. No direct answer is given by Avicenna. But we shall try to show that indirectly an answer to this question is implied in his statement that all terms predicated of God are to be taken as being predicated of Him «in virtue of His essence» (*bi-dhātihi*) or more correctly, in this particular instance, «in virtue of himself».

This Arabic term, in its meaning of «in virtue of himself», is a literal translation of the Greek καθ' αὐτό. Thus Aristotle's statement that «God's actuality in virtue of itself (καθ' αὐτὴν) is life most good and most eternal»,[33] is paraphrased in Arabic to read «God is living in virtue of himself (*bi-dhātihi*) and is of eternal duration in virtue of himself».[34] Now the Greek καθ' αὐτό, for which we shall use here the Latin *per se*, is used by Aristotle in the following five senses :[35] (1) as designating the entire essence of a thing, as e. g., man is *per se* a rational animal; (2) as designating only part of the essence of a thing, as, e. g., man is *per se* an animal; (3) as designating the accident of a thing, as, e. g., a surface is *per se* white; (4) as designating that which is *per se* and not by some cause, as, e. g., man is man *per se*; (5) as designating «whatever attributes belong to a thing alone and *qua* alone»,[36] or what Aristotle calls elsewhere «property» (ἴδιον).[37] But of these five senses of the Greek καθ' αὐτό, and hence also of the Arabic *bi-dhātihi*, the first four could not have been meant by Avicenna, when he said that all predicates are

31. Cf. *Kitāb al-jam' bain ra'iyy al-ḥakīmain Aflāṭun al-ilāhiyy wa-Arisṭuṭalis*, pp. 27-29, in *Alfarabi's philosophische Abhandlungen*, ed. F. Dieterici, 1890.
32. *Najāt*, I, p. 12, ll. 7-8; cf. *Porphyrii Isagoge et in Aristotelis Categorias Commentarium* (ed. Busse), p. 1, ll. 3-4.
33. *Metaph.*, XII, 7, 1072*b*, 27-28.
34. SHAHRASTĀNĪ (éd. W. Cureton), p. 315, ll. 13-14.
35. *Metaph.*, V, 18, 1022a, 24-36.
36. *Ibid.*, 1022a, 35.
37. Cf. *Top.*, I, 5, 102a, 18-19; 22-23; V, I, 128b, 35; V, 2, 130b, 11-12.

applied to God *bi-dhātihi*, for certainly he would not admit that they are definitions or genera or accidents, nor quite evidently are they repetitions of the word God as in the statement «man is man *per se*». Avicenna must have therefore used the term *bi-dhātihi* in its fifth sense, meaning thereby that the divine predicates are properties.

The reason why Avicenna allows properties to be used as predicates of God is again Aristotelian. For, according to Aristotle, a property is not a genus nor a species nor a differentia nor a definition nor an accident. It is not a genus or species, because, when predicated of a thing, it «belongs to that thing alone»[38] and cannot «possibly belong to something else».[39] It is not a differentia, because, unlike a differentia, it is not predicated of a subject according to participation.[40] It is not a definition, because, unlike a definition, it does not show the essence of the subject.[41] Finally, it is not an accident, because, unlike an accident, it belongs to the subject «in virtue of itself» (καθ' αὑτό)[42] and it can be eternal, if its subject is eternal.[43] As an example of a predicate which is a property Aristotle takes the phrase «having its angles equal to two right angles» in its predication of a triangle.[44] In pursuance with this Aristotelian conception of a property, Avicenna felt himself justified in maintaining that the predicates of God can be all taken in the sense of properties.

Here, again, before Avicenna, the same view was expressed by Alfarabi in his statement that all the predicates of God indicate something that is «in virtue of himself» (*fī dhātihi*).[45] After Avicenna, it is reproduced by Algazali in the name of «the philosophers» in his statement that, according to them, all the predicates of God are to be understood as applying to Him «in virtue of himself» so that «God is knowing» means that «He is knowing

38. *Ibid.*, I, 5, 102a, 18-19.
39. *Ibid.*, 22-23.
40. *Ibid.*, V, 4, 132a, 5-6; 132b, 36-133a, 1.
41. *Ibid.*, I, 5, 101b, 39; V, 3, 131b, 38-132a, 1.
42. *Metaph*, V, 30, 1025a, 30-34.
43. *Ibid.*, 32-33.
44. *Ibid.*, 32.
45. *Siyāsāt*, p. 19, l. 16 (H : p. 15, l. 29 : *be'azmuto*). I take the Arabic *fī dhātihi* here to reflect the Greek καθ' αὑτό and not the Greek ἐν τῇ οὐσίᾳ, for the latter, according to Aristotle, refers to a definition (cf. *Metaph.*, V, 30, 1025a, 31-32). Cf. the expression *bi-jauharihi wa-dhāthihi wa-dhalik fī nafsihi*, on p. 16, l. 14, quoted below, note 55.

in virtue of himself» (*bi-dhātihi*).[46] But ultimately, again, it goes back to Philo who, after excluding from the essence of God any internal plurality and divisibility, declares all the predicates of God found in Scripture to designate His properties.[47]

But a property, according to Aristotle, belongs only to the subject of which it is predicated and cannot possibly belong to anything else.[48] How then can the terms predicated of God in the Scriptures be taken as properties, when as a matter of fact they are all terms which in ordinary speech are predicated also of other beings'? The general answer to this question in the history of religions philosophy was that the terms predicated of God, though predicated also of other beings, are still to be considered as properties because of the peculiarity of meaning in which they are used when they are applied to God. This peculiarity of meaning is twofold. First, terms, which in their application to all other beings may be accidents of various kinds, in their application to God are all to be considered as properties and to be reduced to the single property of action. Second, terms, which in their application to all other beings are positive in form as well as in meaning, in their application to God, though positive in form, are to be considered as negative in meaning. Historically, the first explanation is traceable to Philo;[49] the second to Albinus and Plotinus.[50]

By the time of Avicenna, these two explanations of why terms predicated of God can be called properties were already commonplaces. They are expressed, though not clearly, by Alfarabi in a passage in which the divine predicates, all of which, as we have seen, are taken by him as properties, are divided into the following two types : (1) «those which show what belongs to Him in virtue of himself (or in virtue of His essence), and not in virtue of His being related to some other thing»; (2) «those which show what belongs to Him by His relation to some other thing outside himself».[51] Now by the second type of predi-

46. *Maqāṣid*, II, 3, p. 152, l. 8 (L : p. 64, l. 18 : «Ergo necessario est sciens se ipsum» is incorrect. It should be changed to read «per se ipsum.»)
47. Cf. *Philo*, II, pp. 130-134.
48. *Top.*, I, 5, 102a, 18-23.
49. Cf. *Philo*, II, pp. 132-138.
50. Cf. my paper *Albinus and Plotinus on Divine Attributes*, «Harvard Theological Review», XLV (1952), pp. 115-130.
51. *Siyāsat*, p. 19, ll. 15-18 (H : p. 15, l. 27; p. 16, l. 1. The Hebrew text here is defective).

cates, the relational, he means actions, using the term relation in the sense of what Aristotle calls the relation of «the active to the passive»[52] or the relation of «agent to patient».[53] Alfarabi illustrates this type of predicates by the terms «justice» (*al-'adl*) and «generosity» (*al-jūd*).[54] As for the predicates of the first type, the non-relational, Alfarabi gives here no further explanation than his statement that they «show what belongs to Him in virtue of His essence». But elsewhere, in trying to explain how all the excellencies which are predicated of God are predicated of Him «in virtue of His substance and His essence, that is, in virtue of His own self»,[55] he says with regard to the predicate of wisdom that «God is wise not by a wisdom which He has acquired by a knowledge of something else outside His essence, but in His own essence there is a sufficiency for His becoming wise through His knowledge of that essence».[56] In other words, non-relational predicates, like wisdom, are affirmed of God as belonging to His essence only in the sense of denying that they are acquired by Him from something external to His essence, that is to say, they are negations.

So also Avicenna, after he has laid down the general principle that all the predicates are properties, explains that as properties they do not show the essence of God; they show only His existence. And even as showing the existence of God they show it only by describing the actions of God or by describing His unlikeness to other beings, so that, even when predicates are adjectival or positive in form, they are to be interpreted as actions or as negations in meaning. «If you investigate the truth», he says, «you will find that the first and direct description of the Necessary Being is that He is and exists. As for the other descriptions, some of them are those by which this existence is determined by way of relation and others are those by which this existence is determined by way of negation».[57] Avicenna then goes on to give examples of these two kinds of predicates and their various combinations. Examples of predicates

52. *Metaph.*, V, 15, 1020b, 30.
53. *Phys.*, III, 1, 200b, 30.
54. *Siyāsat*, p. 19, l. 28, where the printed text errouneously reads *al-jaur*, «violence», for *al-jūd*, «generosity» (H : p. 16, l. 1 : *veha-meṭib*).
55. *Ibid.*, p. 16, l. 14 (H : p. 13, ll. 12-13).
56. *Ibid.*, p. 16, ll. 10-11 (H : p. 13, ll. 7-9).
57. *Najāt*, III, p. 410, ll. 3-6 (L : pp. 129-130).

to be interpreted as negations are «substance» (*jauhar*), «one» (*wāḥid*) and «intellect» (*'aql*), though the last one, he adds, contains also some part of relation. Examples of predicates to be interpreted as relations are «first» (*awwal*), «powerful» (*qādir*), and «living» (*ḥayy*). Examples of predicates to be interpreted both as relations and negations are «willing» (*murīd*) and «generous» (*jawād*). An example of a predicate to be interpreted either as a relation or a negation is the term «good» (*ḫair*).[58]

After Avicenna, the same view is reproduced by Algazali in the name of «the philosophers». «They maintain», he says, «that the essence of the First Principle is one and that the multiplicity of terms predicated of Him describe only the relation of something to Him or His relation to something or else the negation of something with respect to Him».[59] He then proceeds to give examples of these two kinds of interpretation and their various combinations. Examples of predicates to be interpreted as negations are «substance» (*jauhar*), «one» (*wāḥid*), «eternal *a parte ante*» (*qadīm*), «eternal *a parte post*» (*bāqin*), and «intellect» (*'aql*). Examples of predicates to be interpreted as relations are : «first» (*awwal*), «principle» (*mabda'*), «creator» (*ḫāliq*), «agent» (*fā'il*), «maker» (*bāri*), «knowing» (*'ālim*), «powerful» (*qādir*), and «living» (*ḥayy*). Examples of predicates to be interpreted both as negations and relations are «necessary of existence» (*wājib al-wujūd*), «loving» (*'āshiq*), «pleasant» (*ladhīdh*), «willing» (*murīd*), and «generous» (*jawād*). An example of a predicate to be interpreted either as negation or as a relation is the term «good» (*ḫair*).[60]

But then still another question must have arisen in the mind of both Alfarabi and Avicenna. All these terms, predicated of God in a peculiar sense, be it as actions or as negations, are also predicated both of God and of other beings in a general sense. Accordingly, all these terms are applied to God and other beings as common terms with a certain difference of meaning. Now a predicate which affirms of a subject that which it has in common with other things and that by which it differs from other things is said to consist of a genus and differentia and as such to cons-

58. *Ibid.*, III, p. 410, l. 7 - p. 411, l. 8 (L : pp. 130-131).

59. *Tahāfut al-Falāsifah*, V, 19, p. 153, ll. 5-6 (L : p. 78 D); cf. *Maqāṣid*, II, 3, p. 150, ll. 8-9, 15-16 (L : p. 62, ll. 23-24; p. 62, ll. 8-9).

60. *Ibid.*, V, 20-37 (L : p. 78 C, p. 80 A). Cf. *Maqāṣid*, II, 3, p. 151, ll. 1-6 (L : p. 63, ll. 13-21).

titute a definition. But God is assumed to have no genus and no difference and hence no definition.

In anticipation of this question both Alfarabi and Avicenna try to show that these common terms applied to God and other beings with a difference of meaning are not genera and differentiae and hence they do not constitute definitions. Their view on the subject may be reconstructed from passages in Alfarabi and Avicenna and also from those passages in Algazali in which he restates the views of «the philosophers». All these passages may be taken as complementing one another.

In Alfarabi there is the statement that the common terms which are predicated both of God and of other beings are predicated of God «firstly» (*awwalan*)[61] or «in a prior manner» (*bi-aqdam al-anḥā'*)[62] and of other beings «secondly» (*thāniyan*)[63] or «in a posterior manner» (*bi-anḥā' muta'aḫḫirah*).[64] This statement is explained by him to mean that terms which are predicated both of God and of other beings are predicated of other beings only in either of the following two senses : (a) in the sense that they derive the perfection implied by the predicate in question from God as their cause of whom they are effects, and this is true in the case of the terms «existent» and «one»;[65] or (b) in the sense that they derive the perfection implied in the predicate in question from God as their exemplar by reason of their assimilation to Him.[66]

In Avicenna there is the statement that the term «one» is predicated of God and of other beings below Him «in an ambiguous sense » (*bil-tashkīk*).[67]

In Algazali's restatement of the views of «the philosophers», these two explanations of Alfarabi and Avicenna are combined. «If one says : Is not the term existent predicated of both the Necessary Being and other beings besides Him? Accordingly, existence is a general term and the Necessary Being and other beings are thus ranged under a genus. But these other beings must inevitably be distinguished from Him by some differentia.

61. *Siyāsāt*, p. 20, l. 11 (H : p. 16, l. 18).
62. *Ibid.*, p. 20, l. 17 (H : p. 16, l. 26).
63. *Ibid.*, p. 20, l. 11 (H : p. 16, l. 18).
64. *Ibid.*, p. 20, l. 18 (H : p. 16, l. 27).
65. *Ibid.*, p. 20, ll. 11-14 (H : p. 16, ll. 19-23).
66. *Ibid.*, p. 20, ll. 14-17 (H : p. 16, ll. 23-26).
67. *Tafsīr al-Ṣamadiyyah*, 20, l. 1 (quoted in Goichon, *Lexique de la langue philosophique d'Ibn Sīnā*, p. 162, § 328).

It follows therefore that He has a definition. To Him the answer is as follows : No, God has no definition, inasmuch as existence is applied to Him and to other beings by way of priority (*al-taqaddum*) and posteriority (*al-ta'aḫḫur*), for also with reference to substances and accidents, as we have shown, the term existence applies to them in a similar manner. Consequently, the term existence is not predicated by way of univocality (*al-tawāṭu'*), and whatever is not predicated by way of univocality is not a genus.»[68] In another work of his, again restating the view of «the philosophers», Algazali tries to explain how the terms «existent», «substance», and «cause», in their predication of both God and other beings are none of them a genus. They are each, he says, a «consequent» (*lāzim*)[69] and not a genus. He illustrates the difference between a genus and a consequent by difference between the term «animal» (*ḥayy*) and the term «born» (*maulūd*) or «created» (*maḫlūq*) in their predication of man.[70] Furthermore, he says, since the term «existent» is not a genus but rather a consequent, the definition of substance as «that which is existent not in a subject» is only a description (*rasm*) and not a definition (*ḥadd*). The difference between a description and a definition is explained by him by the difference between the statement «a triangle is that whose angles are equal to two right angles» and the statement «a triangle is a figure contained by three sides».[71] The former of these two statements, it may be added, is used by Aristotle as an illustration of what he regards as a property in contradistinction to a definition,[72] whereas the latter is a paraphrase of Euclid's definition of a triangle.[73]

With regard to this distinction between a definition and a description, Avicenna himself says that a definition is that which consists of a genus and a differentia,[74] whereas a description is that which consists of «accidents and properties»,[75] by which, as may be judged from the context, he means that it contains a

68. *Maqāṣid*, II, 2, p. 145, ll. 1-7 (L : p. 58, ll. 3-11).
69. *Tahāfut al-Falāsifah*, VII, 1 (L : p. 92 L M).
70. *Ibid.*, VII, 2 (L : p. 93 A).
71. *Ibid.*, VII, 4-5 (L : p. 93 A B).
72. *Metaph.*, V, 30, 1025a, 30-32.
73. *Elements*, I, Def. 19.
74. *Kitāb al-'Ishārāt wal-Tanbīhāt* (ed. J. Forget), p. 17, ll. 4-5.
75. *Ibid.*, p. 18, ll. 17-18.

property[76] either in place of the genus or in place of the differentia. He illustrates it by three statements[77] in each of which the predicate is taken by him to consist of a genus and a property, namely, (1) «man is an animal that walks on two feet, has straight nails, and is risible by nature»; (2) «a triangle is a figure which has three angles»; (3) «a triangle is a figure whose angles are equal to two right angles». All these three illustrations are derived from Aristotle. (1) «An animal that walks on two feet» is said by Aristotle to be the definition of man,[78] but «walking on two feet» is said by him to be a property of man,[79] and so are also having «straight nails»[80] and being «risible»[81] said by him to be properties of man. (2) «A figure which has three angles» as the definition of a triangle is probably Avicenna's own interpretation of the vague statement «as, e. g., the meaning of what is called triangle» used by Aristotle as an illustration of a nominal definition,[82] for in another place,[83] as an illustration of a nominal definition or, as he calls it there, a «definition which explains the meaning of a term (*al-ḥadd al-shāriḥ li-maʿna al-'ism*)», he refers to Euclid's definition of an isosceles triangle as «that which has two of its sides alone equal».[84] (3) «A figure whose angles are equal to two right angles» is said by Aristotle to belong to a triangle «in virtue of itself but is not in its essence,»[85] by which he means that it is the «property» of a triangle but not its «definition».

The cumulative impression of all these statements is (1) that the divine attributes, such, for instance, as «existence», «unity», «substance», and «cause», are predicated of God and of other beings not in a «univocal» sense but rather in an «ambiguous» sense, that is to say, «according to priority and posteriority»; (2) that, as such, they are not genera but rather «properties» or «con-

76. The term «accidents» here in the expression «accidents and properties», I take it, is loosely used, after Aristotle (*Metaph.*, v, 30, 1025a, 30-32), as another word for «properties». Cf. Avicenna's own discussion of «property» in *Najāt*, I, pp. 14-15.

77. *'Ishārāt*, p. 19, ll. 2-6, quoted in CARRA DE VAUX, *Avicenne*, pp. 175-176; GOICHON, *Introduction à Avicenne*, p. 26 (1); MADKOUR, *op. cit.*, p. 120.

78. *Top.*, I, 4, 101b, 30-31.

79. *Ibid.*, v, 4, 133b, 8.

80. *Historia Animalium*, III, 9, 517a, 33-517b, 2.

81. *De Partibus Animalium*, III, 10, 673a, 8.

82. *Anal. Post.*, II, 10, 93b, 29-32.

83. *Najāt*, I, p. 130, l. 16-p. 131, l. 2.

84. *Elements*, I, Def. 20.

85. *Metaph.*, v, 30, 1025a, 31-32.

sequents», which two terms are evidently used by these Arabic philosophers as equivalents; and (3) that, being «properties» or «consequents», they constitute not «definitions» but rather «descriptions».

Now of these three distinctions, the first distinction, that between predicates which are applied «univocally» and predicates which are applied «ambiguously» or «according to the prior and the posterior», reflects Aristotle's statement that neither «being» nor «unity» is the genus of a thing,[86] that «the genus is always predicated of its species univocally»,[87] and that «being», and for that matter also «unity», is predicated neither «univocally» nor «in the same manner [that is, univocally]»,[88] though, as I have shown elsewhere,[89] the term «ambiguous» and the expression «according to prior and posterior» have their origin in the Commentaries of Alexander Aphrodisiensis. Similarly the second distinction, that between «genera» and «consequents» and between «genera» and «properties», reflects the distinction made by Aristotle between «genus» (γένος) and «consequent» (τὸ παρακολουθοῦν)[90] and between «genus» and «property».[91] The third distinction, however, that between «definition» and «description» is not found in Aristotle. Its origin, it has been shown, is in the Stoics and Galen, where it is used in opposition to Aristotle.[92] But why a distinction, which was originally used in opposition to Aristotle, should come to be used as an interpretation of him, requires an explanation. In Aristotle himself, the only term which he uses in contradistinction to «definition» (ὁρισμός) is the term «definitory» (ὁρικός), by which he means the explanation of one term by the use of some other synonymous term, such as in the sentence «the 'beautiful' is 'becoming'».[93] Otherwise he uses the term «definition» in a general sense, under which he distinguishes four kinds of definition, one nominal kind of definition and three real kinds of definitions.[94] Now the distinction between defini-

86. *Top.*, IV, 6, 127a, 28 ff.
87. *Ibid.*, 127b, 7-8.
88. *Metaph.*, VII, 4, 1030a, 34-35.
89. Cf. my paper *The Amphibolous Terms in Aristotle, Arabic Philosophy, and Maimonides*, «Harvard Theological Review», XXXI(1938), 151–173. Below, pages 455–477.
90. *Top.*, IV, 5, 125b, 28 ff.
91. Cf. above nn. 38 and 39.
92. Cf. MADKOUR, *op. cit.*, pp. 119-120.
93. *Top.*, I, 5, 102a, 5-6.
94. *Anal. Post.*, II, 10, 93b, 29-94a, 14.

tion and description in Arabic philosophy corresponds neither to Aristotle's general distinction between a real and a nominal definition nor to any of his subdivisions of a real definition. Of the examples used for a description, as we have seen, one is what Aristotle calls simply definition without any qualification,[95] one is what Aristotle would call a nominal definition,[96] and one is what Aristotle would not call definition at all.[97] If, despite this, Arabic philosophers saw it necessary to introduce this distinction into Aristotle, there must have been a reason for it. What then was that reason?

The reason seems to have been twofold.

In the first place, the distinction was introduced into Aristotle in order to remove a certain inconsistency in his writings. A definition, says Aristotle, consists of a genus and a differentia.[98] «Walking on two feet», he also says, is a property of man.[99] A differentia, he further says, belongs to the essence of the subject[100] and hence differs from a property.[101] And yet he says that «an animal walking on two feet» is the definition of man[102] and refers to «walking on two feet» as a «differentia».[103] It is in answer to this inconsistency that Avicenna and others have suggested that Aristotle uses the terms «definition» and «differentia» rather loosely and that, when he says that «an animal walking on two feet» is the definition of man, he means by definition what the Stoics call description; but, as we have seen, they extend the use of the term «description» to include also what Aristotle calls «nominal definition».

In the second place, the distinction was introduced in order to remove the contradiction between the view generally accepted among the Arabic philosophers that God has no definition and the fact that certain statements made about God by Aristotle do imply a definition of God.[104] Thus a definition of God in terms of genus and differentia is implied in Aristotle's contention,

95. Cf. above n. 78.
96. Cf. above n. 82.
97. Cf. above n. 85 and also nn. 44 and 72.
98. *Top.*, I, 8, 103b, 15-16.
99. *Ibid.*, V, 4, 133b, 8.
100. *Ibid.*, I, 18, 108b, 4-6.
101. *Ibid.*, V, 4, 133a, 19 and 21.
102. *Ibid.*, I, 4, 101b, 30-31.
103. *Ibid.*, IV, 2, 122b, 16-17.
104. Cf. my paper *The Knowability and Describability of God in Plato and Aristotle*, «Harvard Studies in Classical Philology», XLVI-XLVII (1947), 233-249. Above, pages 98–114.

for instance, that God is causing motion but is himself immovable,[105] or that He is thinking but only of himself,[106] or that He is living but only by the actuality of His thought,[107] or that He is pleased but only by the actuality of His own life.[108] It is, again, in answer to this contradiction that Avicenna and others have suggested that these various forms of the definition of God found in Aristotle are not forms of a real definition but only of what the Stoics and Galen call a description. Whether this is a true interpretation of Aristotle is quite a different matter. In the ultimate analysis it will depend upon whether their interpretation of Aristotle's conception of universals is true or not.

II. Algazali

In his criticism of Alfarabi's and Avicenna's theory of attributes, which he ascribes generally to «the philosophers», Algazali makes the main target of his attack the rigid conception of the simplicity of God which he rightly conceives to be the basic premise for the denial of the existence of real attributes in God. This rigid conception of the simplicity of God, he takes it, is derived from Avicenna's proof for the existence of God as «The Necessary Being» (*wājib al-wujūd* : literally : «The Necessary of Existence») based upon the conception of the possible (*al-mumkin*) and the necessary (*al-wājib*). And so, after reproducing this proof of Avicenna in the name of the philosophers in general,[109] he tries to show that the conception of God as it emerges from this proof means only the existence of a being who has no cause external to himself but not that of a being who has within himself no composition of essence and attributes or of any other kind of composition.

The principal passage in which he states his view reads as follows : «The term 'possible' as well as the term 'necessary' is an obscure term. Undoubtedly what is to be meant by 'necessary' is that which has no cause for its existence and what is

105. *Metaph.*, XII, 1072b, 1-3. On the use of a negation as a differentia, see *Top.*, VI, 6, 143b, 29-144a, 4.
106. *Ibid.*, 18-20.
107. *Ibid.*, 26-27.
108. *Ibid.*, 14-18.
109. *Tahāfut al-Falāsifah*, IV, 11 (L : p. 71, 1).

to be meant by 'possible' is that which has a cause for its existence. But if this is what is to be meant by these terms, let us then return to their basic meaning and say : Every single thing [within the world] is to be described as possible, in the sense that it has a cause superadded to its essence, but the world as a whole is not to be described as possible, in view of the fact that it has no cause superadded to its essence and external to it. But if the term 'possible' is taken to mean something other than that we have taken it to mean, then it will be something incomprehensible.»[110]

The same contention is repeated by him in several other places. In one place he says : «We have already explained that the expression 'the necessary of existence' is loaded with many meanings and that undoubtedly what is to be meant by it is the remotion of a cause.»[111] In another place he challenges «the philosophers» to say whether they do not mean «by the expression 'the necessary of existence' that which has no efficient cause.»[112] In still another place he contends that the proof for the existence of God from possibility and necessity «points only to the fact that the chain of cause and effect must come to an end; but, as for the grandiloquent things which they have invented as requisite for the description of 'the necessary of existence', there is no proof by which it can be established.»[113] In two other places he briefly restates this view by saying that «the proof establishes only the termination of the concatenation of causes»[114] or that «the demonstration establishes only the termination of the chain.»[115] Finally, speaking of the misuse which, according to him, his opponents made of the expression «the necessary of existence», he says : «The meaning of the expression 'the necessary of existence' and the expression 'the possible of existence' is not clear and hence the misconceived and deceptive meanings which they read into these expressions. Let us then return to what is their basic meaning, and that is the remotion and the affirmation of a cause.»[116]

110. *Ibid.*, IV, 12 (L : p. 72 B C).
111. *Ibid.*, V, 3, p. 144, ll. 10-11 (L : p. 74 D).
112. *Ibid.*, VI, 7, p. 166, l. 6 (L : p. 81 I).
113. *Ibid.*, VII, 8-9, p. 189, ll. 3-5 (L : p. 94 I).
114. *Ibid.*, VIII, 3, p. 196, ll. 7-8 (L : p. 98 G).
115. *Ibid.*, X, 3, p. 207, l. 10 (L : p. 103 L).
116. *Ibd.*, X, 5, p. 208, ll. 5-6 (L : p. 104 B).

With this as his interpretation of the meaning of the expression «the necessary of existence», he tries to show how God who is conceived by the philosophers as a being who is necessary of existence can still be conceived as having attributes. When the question is raised whether any kind of attributes can exist in God, he argues, the answer is not to be based upon the irrelevant conception of the absolute simplicity of God or upon the erroneous conception of God as «the necessary of existence» but rather upon the conception of God as a being who has no cause. If it can be shown that the existence of attributes in God is incompatible with our conception of Him as an uncaused being, then the existence of attributes must be rejected. But if such an incompatibility cannot be shown, then the existence of attributes is not to be rejected.

He then tries to show that there is no incompatibility between the existence of attributes and the conception of an uncaused deity. The philosophers, he says, first enumerate three possible kinds of relation that may obtain between the essence of God and His attributes, if attributes are assumed to exist : first, the essence and the attributes are independent of each other; second, they are each dependent upon the other; third, the essence is not dependent upon the attributes but the attributes are dependent upon the essence, and then they try to show how every one of these three possible relations is to be rejected as incompatible with the conception of God as one and as necessary of existence.[117] Now, of these three possibilities, the second is not discussed by Algazali at all. With regard to the first, while he does not approve of this possibility, he denies the cogency of the philosophers' argument which rejects it on the ground of their peculiar conception of God as a being who is necessary of existence.[118] The third possibility is described by him as «the best».[119] He finds it in agreement with his own conception of attributes and undertakes to defend it against the attack of the philosophers.

His defense is based upon his own revised conception of the expression «the necessary of existence». Addressing himself to «the philosophers», he says : «If the expression 'the necessary

117. *Ibid.*, VI, 4 (L : p. 81 D-F).
118. *Ibid.*, VI, 5, p. 165, l. 12-; p. 166, l. 2 (L : p. 81 H).
119. *Ibid.*, VI, 5, p. 165, l. 11; p. 166, l. 2 (L : p. 81 H).

of existence' is, as it should be, taken by you to mean that which has no efficient cause, then what reason have you to derive therefrom that God has no attributes? Why should it be impossible to say just as the essence of Him Who is Necessary of Existence is eternal and has no sufficient cause, so also His attribute exists with Him from eternity and has no efficient cause»;[120] and «just as the mind is capable of the conception of an eternal Being who has no cause for His existence, so it is also capable of the conception of an eternal Being endowed with attributes who has no cause for the existence of both His essence and His attributes.»[121]

By the same reasoning he also tries to show that the conception of God as a being who is necessary of existence does not exclude from Him the distinction of genus and differentia[122] and of essence and existence.[123] He goes still further to show that this philosophic conception of God as a being who is necessary of existence is of itself insufficient to prove the unity of God[124] as well as His incorporeality.[125] In other words, not only the simplicity of God but also His unity and incorporeality cannot be established by the conception of necessity of existence. It is only by vitiating the basic meaning of that conception, by taking it to mean absolute simplicity instead of mere uncausedness, and by reasoning from that unwarranted conception of absolute simplicity, that the philosophers, by a sort of vicious intellectualism, have erroneously denied the true doctrine of divine attributes and have blunderingly tried to support by false reasoning the true doctrine of the unity and incorporeality of God.

III. Averroes

Averroes' criticism of Algazali's theory of attributes is to be found in two works, the *Kitāb al-Kashf 'an Manāhij al-Adillah fī 'Aqā'id al-Millah*[126] and the *Tahāfut al-Tahāfut*.[127] In the

120. *Ibid.*, VI, 7, p. 166, ll. 6-8 (L : p. 81 I).
121. *Ibid.*, VI, 12 (L : p. 82 B).
122. *Ibid.*, VII, p. 185, ll. 2-3 (L : p. 92 L).
123. *Ibid.*, VIII, p. 195, ll. 2-4 (L : p. 98 B).
124. *Ibid.*, V, p. 143, ll. 2-3 (L : p. 74 A).
125. *Ibid.*, IX, p. 200, ll. 2-3 (L : p. 100 G).
126. Ed. M. J. Müller, under the title of *Philosophie und Theologie von Averroes*, 1895, pp. 27-131.
127. Ed. M. Bouyges; Latin : cf. above. n. 11.

former work, he criticizes Algazali indirectly, through his criticism of the Ash'arites, whose view is adopted and defended by Algazali in his *Tahāfut al-Falāsifah*. In the latter work, his criticism is directly aimed at Algazali, though the work contains also some critical comments on Avicenna.

In the *Manāhij*, Averroes deals with two main views which have arisen in the Kalām with regard to divine attributes, the view of the Ash'arites and the view of the Mu'tazilites. According to the Ash'arites, he says, the attributes are «real» (*ma'nawiyyah*),[128] «superadded (*zā'idah*) to the essence»,[129] each of these attributes «subsisting» (*qā'im*) in the essence.[130] The formula used by them in expressing their conception of attributes is that «He knows with a knowledge superadded to His essence and He lives with a life superadded to His essence.»[131] As contrasted with this view of the Ash'arites, the view of the Mu'tazilites is represented by him by the use of the following three formulae: First, «the attributes are the essence.»[132] Second, they are «attributes of the very self» (*ṣifāt nafsiyyah*), which expression is explained as meaning «attributes whereby the essence is described in virtue of itself (*li-nafsihā*) and not in virtue of something else subsisting in the essence and superadded to it.»[133] Third, «the essence and the attributes are one and the same thing.»[134]

Of these two views reproduced by him, that of the Ash'arites is clear enough. It represents exactly the main features of what is generally known as the Ash'arite theory of attributes. But his restatement of the view of Mu'tazilites contains a certain vaguness which calls for clarification. For it will be noticed that the second formula ascribed by him to the Mu'tazilites states that the essence is described by attributes «in virtue of itself (*li-nafsihā*).» Now this formula, with the term *li-nafsihi*, has indeed been used by such representative Mu'tazilites as Najjār,[135] Naẓẓām,[136] and 'Allāf,[137] and the same formula, but with

128. *Manāhij*, p. 56, l. 4.
129. *Ibid.*, ll. 3 and 7.
130. *Ibid.*, l. 6.
131. *Ibid.*, ll. 7-8.
132. *Ibid.*, l. 4.
133. *Ibid.*, ll. 4-5.
134. *Ibid.*, l. 17.
135. AL-SHAHRASTĀNĪ, p. 62, l. 2.
136. AL-ASH'ARĪ (ed. H. Ritter), p. 486, l. 12 (*bi-nafsihi*); cf. SHAHRASTĀNĪ, p. 34, l. 17 (*li-dhātihi*).
137. ASH'ARĪ, p. 177, l. 14.

the equivalent term *li-dhātihi*, has been used by Jubbā'ī[138] and Abū Hāshim.[139] But, while all of them have used this same formula, they are known to have used it in two distinct senses. Naẓẓām and Jubbā'ī are said to have used it in the sense of the denial of the existence of attributes in any sense whatsoever,[140] whereas 'Allāf and Abū Hāshim have used it not in the sense of an absolute denial of the existence of attributes but rather in the sense of the denial of their subsisting in the essence as something superadded to it, affirming, however, their existence as something identical with the essence,[141] the kind of existence which Abū Hāshim ascribes to what he calls modes (*aḥwāl*).[142] The question may therefore be raised as to which of these two Mu'tazilite views are reproduced here by Averroes.

In answer to this question we may say that internal evidence seems to point to the conclusion that Averroes has meant to reproduce here the theory of modes which has been hinted at by 'Allāf and explicitly stated by Abū Hāshim. First, the other two formulae reproduced here by Averroes in the name of the Mu'tazilites, namely, that «the attributes are the essence» or that «the essence and the attributes are one and the same thing», are exactly the same as the formula used by 'Allāf.[143] Second, Averroes' criticism of the Mu'tazilite view, which we shall reproduce soon, will also show that it is the theory of modes that he has meant to reproduce under the name of the Mu'tazilites.

Together with his statement of these two views, Averroes also criticizes them.

In his criticism of the Ash'arites, Averroes confronts them with two alternatives, either of which, he argues, will lead them into a difficulty. If they say that the essence and the attributes are independent of each other,[144] then they are each a God and there is thus a plurality of Gods, after the manner of the Christian belief in the Trinity, which is condemned in the Koran.[145]

138. Shahrastānī, p. 55, l. 20.
139. *Ibid.*, p. 56, l. 2.
140. *Ibid.*, p. 34, ll. 17-18; p. 55, l. 20; p. 56, l. 1.
141. *Ibid.*, p. 34, l. 18.
142. *Ibid.*, p. 34, l. 20; p. 56, ll. 2-12.
143. Ash'arī, p. 165, ll. 5-6; Baghdādī, p. 108, ll. 7-8; Shahrastānī, p. 34, ll. 13-14.
144. Cf. above at n. 117.
145. *Manāhij*, p. 56, ll. 11-14, quoting *Koran*, v, 77.

And if they say, as they, and also Algazali,[146] in fact do, that the essence subsists by itself and the attributes subsist in the essence, then the essence is a subject and the attributes are accidents and God is thus composed of subject and accidents and as such He must be a body.[147] These arguments, it may be added, are not new with Averroes; from the very beginning of the controversy about attributes, these were the stock arguments hurled against the attributists.

His criticism of the Mu'tazilites, it can be shown, is directed against the theory of modes and it reproduces, in fact, one of the stock arguments that was raised against Abū Hāshim's theory of modes. This stock argument, as found in the literature prior to Averroes, contends that the theory of modes is contrary to the law of contradiction or to the law of excluded middle. As contrary to the law of contradiction it is phrased as follows : «According to the opinion of those who maintain the theory of modes, the mode can be described neither by existence nor by nonexistence, but his, as you know, is a self-contradiction and an absurdity.»[148] As contrary to the law of excluded middle, it is phrased as follows : «To explain the difference in the terms attributed to God by the assumption of a mode is false, for the assumption of an attribute which can be described neither by existence nor by nonexistence is the assumption of something which is in the middle between existence and nonexistence, between affirmation and negation, but this is something absurd.»[149] Reflecting this stock objection to the theory of modes, Averroes rephrases it in his own way as follows : «And so also the view of the Mu'tazilites on this question, namely, that the essence and the attributes are one and the same thing, is far removed from the axiomatic notions, nay it is to be thought of as being opposed to them. For it is considered to be one of the axiomatic notions that knowledge must be other than the knower and that it is not possible for knowledge to be identical with the knower, unless it were possible for one of the correlative terms to be taken as a synonym, as, for instance, for the terms father and son to have the very same meaning.»[150] What Averroes means to say

146. Cf. above at n. 119.
147. *Manāhij*, ll. 8-10; 14-16.
148. SHAHRASTĀNĪ, p. 57, ll. 5-6.
149. *Ibid.*, p. 67, ll. 2-3.
150. *Manāhij*, p. 56, ll. 16-20.

is that the predicates of God, say the predicate «knowing», cannot be said by Abū Hāshim to be identical with the essence of God and hence to be nonexistent by itself, when he has already declared it to be a mode and as such not to be nonexistent by itself.

With his rejection of the view of the Ash'arites, which is also that of Algazali, and with his rejection also of the theory of modes, which he presents under the name of the Mu'tazilites, Averroes in his *Tahāfut al-Tāhafut*, adopts the view of Avicenna with regard to the problem of divine attributes. He agrees with Avicenna as to the absolute simplicity of God.[151] He agrees with him also that the absolute simplicity of God excludes the five kinds of plurality enumerated by Algazali, namely, (1) quantitative parts; (2) matter and form; (3) essence and attributes; (4) genus and differentia and hence definition and definitum; and finally (5) essence and existence.[152] He consequently also agrees with Avicenna as to the interpretation of any term predicated of God either as a relation or as a negation or as both a relation and a negation or as either a relation or a negation.[153]

But still, while agreeing with Avicenna on all these main points he makes the following reservations : (1) He rejects Avicenna's proof from necessity and possibility as the ground for the simplicity of God.[154] (2) He differs with Avicenna as to the relation of essence and existence.[155] (3) He differs with him also as to the interpretation of the term intellect as a predicate of God.[156] (4) Finally there is an intimation that he differs with him also as to the use of the terms definition and description.[157]

Of these four reservations made by Averroes, those with regard to the proof from possibility and necessity and the relation between essence and existence and the application of the term intellect to God are special problems in themselves[158] and we shall not discuss them in connection with this problem of

151. *Tahāfut al-Tahāfut*, v, 17-18 (L : p. 76 HI).
152. *Ibid.*, v, 19-35 (L : p. 76 I - 78 B).
153. *Ibid.*, v, 37, p. 310, ll. 3-4 (L : p. 80 B).
154. *Ibid.*, iv, 27-28 (L : p. 71 K - p. 72 B); v, 21-22 (L : p. 76 LM); x, 8-10 (L p. 104 C-F).
155. *Ibid.*, v, 29-34 (L : p. 77 F - p. 78 B); vii, 5-11 (L : p. 93 H - p. 94 E); viii, 2-11 (L : p. 98 H - p. 100 H).
156. *Ibid.*, v, 37, p. 310, ll. 4-9 (L : p. 80 C).
157. *Ibid.*, vii, 4 (L : p. 93 G H).
158. Cf. discussion of these topics in L. Gauthier, *Ibn Rochd (Averroès)*, 1948, pp. 152-156.

attributes. But his implied reservation with regard to the use of the terms definition and description we shall discuss here.

Averroes, on the whole, agrees with Avicenna that there are definitions which are not of the same type of definition as that which is exemplified by «man is a rational animal». Of this other type of definition he mentions, like Algazali,[159] the definition of substance as «that which is existent not in a subject»,[160] and adds to it also Aristotle's definition of soul, which he reproduces, with the omission of one word, as that it is «the entelechy of a natural body furnished with organs.»[161]

He also agrees with Avicenna that while a definition of the type «man is a rational animal» cannot be framed with God as the subject,[162] God can be the subject in a statement of the type «a substance is that which is existent not in a subject.»[163] He still further agrees with Avicenna that terms predicated of God and other beings, such, for instance, as the terms «existent» (*al-maujūd*), «thing» (*al-shai*), «being» (*al-huwiyyah*),[164] and «substance» (*al-dhāt*), are not to be taken as being predicated of them «univocally» (*bi-ṭawāṭu'*)[165] but rather «ambiguously (*bi-tashrik*), that is to say, according to priority (*bi-taqdīm*) and posteriority (*wa-ta'ḫīr*)».[166] But it is to be noted, that unlike Algazali in the text which is the subject of Averroes' discussion, he does not use the term «description» as a designation of this other untrue kind of definition.[167]

A distinction between two kinds of definition, again without the use of the term description for one of them, is also found in his Long Commentary on the *Physics* and *De Anima*. Commenting upon Aristotle's definition of nature,[168] he says : «We have already said that this definition is not said univocally nor equivocally, but according to prior and posterior, and in such

159. Cf. above at n. 71.
160. *Tahāfut al-Tahāfut*, VII, 4, p. 369, l. 11 (L : p. 93 H).
161. *Ibid.*, l. 10; cf. *De Anima*, II, 1, 412b, 5-6.
162. *Ibid.*, ll. 3-6.
163. *Ibid.*, ll. 6-7.
164. *Ibid.*, l. 8. The Arabic *huwiyyah* here reflects the Greek ὄν : cf. AVERROES : *Tafsir ma ba'd at-tabi'at* (ed. M. Bouyges), p. 714, l. 15, corresponding to *Metaph.*, VI, 1, 1026a, 31.
165. *Ibid.*, l. 4.
166. *Ibid.*, ll. 6-7.
167. The list of terms, *hadd*, *rasm*, *sharḥ* and *mafhūm*, in *Tahāfut al-Tahāfut*, III, 132, p. 213, l. 15, does not seem to be of technical significance.
168. *Phys.*, II, 1, 192b, 21-23.

definitions one is to begin with the more general and arrive at peculiar properties, as Aristotle has done in the definition of motion and place.»[169]. A similar comment is to be found on Aristotle's definition of motion. «Since motion», he says, «is not predicated univocally of all the kinds of motion, it has no definition spoken of in a universal sense but only one which is according to the prior and the posterior.»[170] Similarly with regard to Aristotle's definition of the soul he says : «Since genera included in definitions are either univocal, as 'animal' in the definition of 'man', or are spoken of in various senses (*dicta multipliciter*),[171] as being (*ens*), potentiality (*potentia)*, and actuality (*actus*), Aristotle begins to explain the sense in which the genus is to be taken in the definition of soul and says that it is neither equivocal nor univocal.»[172] By its being «neither equivocal nor univocal», Averroes means to say that it is «ambiguous» or «according to priority and posteriority.»[173]

In his Long Commentary on the *Posterior Analytics*[174] Averroes identifies this other kind of definition, that which is not applied «univocally» but rather «according to the prior and the posterior», with what Aristotle calls a nominal definition. Thus commenting upon Aristotle's statement that «one kind of definition will be of what a name signifies... as, e. g., what signifies that which is called triangle»,[175] Averroes gives three examples in illustration of this nominal kind of definition. First, Aristotle's definition of a vacuum as a «place in which there is no body»,[176] in the use of which illustration he is following a suggestion by Themistius.[177] Second, Aristotle's definition of nature which he quotes freely as «the principle of bodies which are being moved or at rest in virtue of themselves.»[178] Third, Euclid's

169. Long Commentary on *Physics*, II, Comm. 3, p. 49, I (Aristotelis opera, vol. IV, Venice, 1574).
170. *Ibid.*, III, Comm. 4, p. 87 B, on *Phys.*, III, I, 200b, 32-201a, 3.
171. Cf. expression πολλαχῶς λέγεται applied by Aristotle to τὸ ὄν, αἰτία, ἀρχή, and στοιχεῖον in *De Anima*, I, 5, 410a, 13; II, 4, 415b, 8-9; *Metaph.*, XII, 5, 1071a, 29-32.
172. Long Commentary on *De Anima*, I, Comm., 30, p. 64 C, on *De Anima*, II, 3, 414b, 20-27 in *Aristotelis opera*, vol. VI, Pars I, Venice, 1574.
173. Cf. my paper on *amphibolous terms* referred to above in n. 89.
174. Long Commentary on *Analytica Posteriora*, II, Comm. 44, pp. 470-471. In *Aristotelis opera*, vol. I, Pars II, Venice, 1574.
175. *Anal. Post.*, II, 10, 93b, 30-32.
176. *Op. cit.*, p. 470 A; cf. *Phys.*, IV, I, 208b, 26-27.
177. *Themistius in Analytica Posteriora* (ed. M. Wallies), p. 51, l. 6.
178. *Op. cit.*, p. 470 B; cf. *Phys.*, II, I, 192b, 21-22.

definition of a triangle as «a figure contained by three sides.»[179] As will be recalled, this Euclidian definition of triangle is used by Algazali as an illustration of a true definition in contradistinction to a description.[180] Averroes, however, must have been following here Philoponus, who in his comment on the same passage of Aristotle quotes this Euclidian definition of a triangle as an illustration of what Aristotle means by a nominal definition.[181] Here, again, the term description is not used.

In his Middle Commentary on the *Topics*, however, Averroes identifies Aristotle's nominal definition with «description». He thus applies there the term «description» to what Aristotle describes as «a statement of the meaning of the name»,[182] illustrating it again by Aristotle's definition of a «vacuum» as a «place in which nothing exists.»[183] He also suggests[184] that that which Aristotle calls «definitory» (ὁρικός), or the explanation of one term by some other synonymous term, such as «the 'becoming' is 'beautiful' »,[185] also resembles a description.

Another place in which Averroes mentions the term «description» is his Epitome of the *Organon*. Using the term definition in a general sense, he applies it to three kinds of statements, which represent three kinds of definition. First, «man is a rational animal»,[186] which definition, he says, consists of genus and differentia. Second, «man is an animal that stands erect and is broad-chested»[187] and «horse is a neighing animal»,[188] each of which definitions is taken by him to consist of a genus and a property, evidently on the ground that standing erect[189] and being broad-chested[190] are said by Aristotle to be properties of man, and neighing[191] is said by him to be the property of a

179. *Op. cit.*, p. 470 D; cf. Euclid, *Elements*, I, Def. 19.
180. Cf. above, nn. 71 and 73.
181. *Joannes Philoponus in Analytica Posteriora cum Anonymo* (ed. M. Wallies), p. 372, ll. 18-19.
182. *Anal. Post.*, II, 10, 93b, 30.
183. *Expositio Media in octo Libros Topicorum*, p. 8, I and M, in *Aristotelis opera*, Vol. I, Pars III, Venice, 1574.
184. *Ibid.*
185. *Top.*, I, 5, 102a, 5-6.
186. Epitome of the Organon : Hebrew : *Kol Meleket Higgayon*, Riva di Trento, 1559, p. 42b, ll. 24-25; Latin : *Epitome in Libros Logicae Aristotelis*, p. 58 D, in *Aristotelis opera*, Vol. I, Pars II, Venice, 1574.
187. *Ibid.*, H : p. 42 b, ll. 25-26; L : p. 58 E.
188. *Ibid.*, H : p. 42b, l. 7; L : p. 58 B.
189. *De Partibus Animalium*, II, 10, 656a, 12-13.
190. *Historia Animalium*, II, 1, 497b, 33-34.
191. *De Audibilibus*, 800a, 25.

horse. Third, «God is the mover of the world»[192] and «God is the form of the universe»,[193] in which definitions the term «mover» and the term «form» are assumed by him to be predicated of God and other beings, like the terms «one» and «existent», not «univocally» but only «ambiguously» and «according to prior and posterior».[194] All these three types of definition are called by him simply definition. Only with reference to the second kind of definition, that which defines man and horse in terms of genus and property, does he say that it might more suitably be called description, in view of the fact that man and horse have another definition, one consisting of genus and differentia; but with reference to the third kind of definition, that which defines God as «the mover of the world» or «the form of the universe», though not expressed in terms of a true genus and hence not a true definition, it is still to be called definition and not description, inasmuch as God can have no true definition expressed in terms of a true genus.[195]

From all this it may be gathered that while Averroes was willing to draw a distinction between various kinds of definition, and this probably for the purpose of removing an inconsistency within Aristotle himself and also for the purpose of reconciling Aristotle's use of definition with regard to God and the prevailing view of the indefinability of God,[196] and while he was also willing to make use of the term description, he still tried to hold on to the original Aristotelian use of the term definition in its most general sense and to restrict the use of the term description either to what Aristotle called a nominal definition or to a definition in terms of genus and property in the case of things which can also be defined in terms of genus and differentia.

192. *Op. cit*, H : p. 42b, l. 20; L : p. 58 D.

193. *Ibid.*,

194. *Ibid.*, H : p. 42b, ll. 14-19; p. 41a, ll. 29-30; L : p. 58 D and A.

195. *Ibid.*, H : p. 42a, ll. 17-20; L : p. 57 M : «Quae vero componuntur ex rebus posterioribus digniores sunt dici descriptiones, nisi de eo, quo non inveniuntur res priores eo, prout dicitur de multis rebus.»

196. Cf. above at nn. 98-108.

9

Plato's Pre-existent Matter in Patristic Philosophy

IN their discussion of the various erroneous theories of the origin of the world, the Fathers of the Church mention a theory that the world was created out of an uncreated matter. As to who was the author of that theory, Theophilus explicitly says that "Plato and those of his school . . . suppose that matter as well as God is uncreated and think that it is coeval with God."[1] Athenagoras, however, includes Plato among "others" whom he describes as maintaining that "God created all things out of a preexistent uncreated matter."[2] A suggestion as to whom Athenagoras might have meant by the "others" is to be found in a statement by Tertullian which attributes to "the Pythagoreans . . . the Stoics" and "Plato" the view that matter is "unborn."[3] It must be remarked, however, that "the Pythagoreans," whom here Tertullian includes among those who believed only in the uncreatedness of a pre-existent matter, are elsewhere described by him, more accurately,[4] as believing in the uncreatedness of the world.[5] As for the Stoics, though their view of an infinite succession of worlds implies a belief in an underlying uncreated matter, they are as a rule treated by the Church Fathers as exponents of a distinct view of their

[1] *Ad Autolycum* II,4 (*PG* 6.1052AB).

[2] *Oratio de incarnatione verbi* 2 (*PG* 25.100A).

[3] *Adversus Valentinianos* 15 (*PL* 2.567A); cf. Clement of Alexandria quoted below at n. 32, who mentions Pythagoras and the Stoics and also Aristotle as those who, like Plato, believed that matter is a first principle, that is, uncreated.

[4] Cf. Zeller, *Phil. d. Griech.* I (6th ed.), 516, n. 4.

[5] *Apologeticus* 11 (*PL* 1.333B).

own. Tertullian, however, represents the Stoics as exponents of the belief in a pre-existent uncreated matter not only in this passage but also in another passage where, after saying that Hermogenes turned away from the Church to the Academy and the Porch, he singles out the Stoics as those from whom, he adds, Hermogenes learned "how to place matter on the same level with the Lord, which matter, too, according to him, had always existed, both unborn and unmade, . . . out of which the Lord afterwards created all things."[6] This treatment of the Stoics as exponents of the belief in a pre-existent uncreated matter seems to reflect a statement by Philo, in which the Stoics are said to believe that "God did not eternally generate prime matter but, making use of matter, He made by means of it the heaven and the earth and also the species of animals and plants and all things."[7]

Most of the Church Fathers, however, in their discussion of those who believe in a pre-existent uncreated matter, do not mention Plato at all. Thus Origen attributes the belief in the uncreatedness of matter to "so many distinguished men."[8] Lactantius, describing the uncreated matter as "a chaos, that is, a confusion of matter and the elements," ascribes it to "the poets," adding that in this "error philosophers also were involved," and as an example of the latter he mentions "Cicero."[9] Maximus, quoted by Eusebius, deals with three conceptions of uncreated matter: (1) God is separate from matter; (2) God is inseparable from matter,[10] and under this he mentions two sub-views: (*a*) "He is united with matter";[11] (*b*) "God exists locally in matter or matter in God."[12] No names are mentioned, but the first view may be identified with that of Plato; (*a*) and (*b*) under the second view correspond to two versions of the Stoic conception of God, the former reflecting the view according to which God is the whole world, the latter reflecting the view that God is something like the artistically working fire, which is described either as pervading through all things or as that which contains the seed of all things.[13] Augustine either mentions no

[6] *Adversus Hermogenem* 1 (*PL* 2.198A).

[7] *De providentia* II,48 (Arnim, *Stoicorum Veterum Fragmenta* I,509, p. 114, ll. 19–21).

[8] *De principiis* II,1, 4, p. 110, 1.11 (ed. Koetschau).

[9] *Divinae institutiones* II,9 (*PL* 6.297A).

[10] *Praeparatio Evangelica* VII,22, 337b (ed. Gifford).

[11] *Ibid.*, 337c.

[12] *Ibid.*, 338a.

[13] *Ibid.* III,9, 100a–103a; Arnim, *op. cit.* I,152–63; II,1021–7.

names at all[14] or ascribes it to the Manichaeans and the ancients.[15] Basil[16] and Gregory of Nyssa[17] mention no names at all.

However, Philo, as I have shown elsewhere, believed that the world was created out of a pre-existent matter which was itself created,[18] and the same view was held by certain Church Fathers. Thus Tatian says that "the Logos, begotten in the beginning, begat in turn the world, having first created for himself the necessary matter," which matter, he subsequently says, "is not, like God, without beginning . . . but brought into existence by the Framer of all things alone."[19] What scriptural basis he had for the belief that the world was created out of a pre-existent created matter he does not say. But Theophilus explains that the "heaven and earth" which were created "in the beginning" (Gen. 1:1) were created out of a preceding matter described in the verse which, according to the Septuagint, reads "and the earth was invisible (ἀόρατος) and unfinished (ἀκατασκεύαστος)" (Gen. 1:2), but that "matter, from which God made and fashioned the world, was in some manner created, being produced by God."[20] It is to Tatian and Theophilus, evidently, that Origen has reference in his statement that "very many, indeed, are of the opinion that the matter of which things are made is itself signified in the language used by Moses in the beginning of Genesis . . . for by the words 'invisible and unfinished' [Gen. 1:2] Moses would seem to mean nothing else than shapeless matter."[21]

It is reasonable to assume that, while Philo and Tatian and Theophilus and Augustine have all been led to this belief by an interpretation of verses in the Book of Genesis, they would not have put such an interpretation on those verses in Genesis unless they believed that Plato taught that the world was created out of a pre-existent created matter and, as philosophers, they wanted to follow Plato. There is nothing in Scripture which should have compelled them to believe in a double creation—the creation of a matter out of nothing

[14] *De civitate Dei* XII,15.
[15] *Contra Faustum Manichaeum* XXI,4.
[16] *Hexaemeron* II,2.
[17] *De hominis opificio* 24.
[18] Cf. my *Philo* I,300–310.
[19] *Oratio adversus Graecos* 5 (*PG* 6.817AB); cf. 12 (829C).
[20] *Ad Autol.* II,10 (1065B).
[21] *De princ.* IV,4,6 (33), p. 357, ll. 6–10.

and the creation of a world out of that matter. In fact, Hermogenes[22] tries to show from the very same verse, Genesis 1:2, that the world was created out of an uncreated matter. Taking the term "earth" in Genesis 1:2, which, according to the Vetus Latina,[23] as according to the Septuagint, reads "and the earth was invisible (*invisibilis*) and unfinished (*incomposita*)," to refer to a pre-existent matter out of which the world was created, he argues that the verb "was" (*erat*) indicates that "it has always existed in the past, being unborn and unmade." Tertullian himself, moreover, tries to show that the invisible and unfinished earth does not mean a pre-existent matter at all but is the same as "the earth" which God created together with the heaven "in the beginning."[24] It is also to be noted that neither Philo nor Tatian nor Augustine explicitly says that Plato believed in a pre-existent uncreated matter. In fact, on a close examination we find that Plato himself does not explicitly say that the matter out of which the world was created was itself uncreated, and it is Plato's vagueness on this point that, as I have suggested, has led Philo to assume a pre-existent created matter out of which the world was created.[25] We may therefore assume that those who interpreted the story of the creation of Genesis as meaning that the world was created out of a pre-existent created matter also assumed that that was the view of Plato, unless, as in the case of Theophilus, they explicitly express themselves to the contrary.

The question, however, may now arise: Is there definite evidence that any of the Fathers did actually interpret Plato's pre-existent matter as created? I think there is.

First, there is Justin Martyr. In one place, he says that "Plato borrowed his statement that God, having altered matter which was shapeless, made the world" from Moses, "through whom the spirit of prophecy" signified "how and from what materials God at first formed the world . . . so that both Plato and they who agree with him, and we ourselves, have learned . . . that by the word of God the whole world was made out of the substance spoken of before by Moses."[26] The pre-existent substance which he finds in the teaching of Moses is, as may be judged from the context, the "earth" described in Genesis

[22] Apud Tertullian, *Adv. Hermog.* 23.

[23] See J. H. Waszink's note *ad loc.* in his translation of this work (p. 57, n. 202).

[24] *Op. cit.*, chs. 24ff.

[25] Cf. *Philo* I (3rd ed.), 304–5.

[26] *Apologia* I,59.

1:2 as being "invisible and unfinished." In another place, he says that "we have been taught that He in the beginning did . . . create all things out of unformed matter."[27] Now while he does not explicitly say that the "unformed matter," out of which both he and Plato, following Moses, believe the world to have been created, was itself created, that certainly was his belief, for elsewhere he says that "God alone is unbegotten" but "all other things after Him are created,"[28] almost the same words used by Tatian in his statement that the pre-existent matter was created.

Second, there is Irenaeus. In one place, he says that the opinion held by the Valentinians that "the Creator formed the world out of previously existing matter" was anticipated by "Anaxagoras, Empedocles, and Plato."[29] In another place, however, in his exposition of the Gnostic views of the Valentinians, he says that "the substance of the matter from which this world was created" consisted of the collection of passions of Achamoth.[30] Now Achamoth is not uncreated. She is one of the Aeons, the last in a succession of Aeons ultimately traceable to one Aeon, called Proarche, Propator, and Bythus, who alone is said to be "eternal and unbegotten."[31] It is thus quite clear that the pre-existent matter of the Valentinians is created. Now, inasmuch as we know that the pre-existent matter, or rather the primitive substances, of both Anaxagoras and Empedocles is uncreated, we may reasonably conclude that, when Irenaeus speaks of their anticipation of the Valentinian pre-existent matter, he means by that anticipation, not an anticipation of the uncreatedness of the pre-existent matter, but only of its pre-existence. It would therefore seem that, unless he believed that the pre-existent matter of Plato was created, he would not have separated the uncreatedness of the pre-existent matter from its pre-existence and speak of Anaxagoras and Empedocles and Plato as forerunners of the Valentinian conception of a matter which is only pre-existent but not uncreated.

Besides these two Church Fathers who, as I tried to show, definitely interpreted Plato's pre-existent matter as created, there were others who either found Plato to be uncertain as to the origin of the pre-existent matter or found him to be vacillating from one opinion

[27] *Ibid.*, 10 (*PG* 6.340C).

[28] *Dialogus cum Tryphone* 5 (488BC).

[29] *Adversus haereses* II,14,4.

[30] *Ibid.* I,4,2.

[31] *Ibid.* I,1,1.

to another as to its origin. Thus, to begin with, there is Clement of Alexandria, who, starting with the statement that Stoic and Plato and Pythagoras and Aristotle do not consider God as the only first principle but suppose matter to be also a first principle, goes on to say that, as for Plato, perhaps he knew that "the true and real first principle was one" and, as for his saying that matter was a principle by the side of God, he quotes Plato's own statement to the effect that to speak with certainty of a first principle of material things is difficult,[32] and he undoubtedly wants the reader to continue with Plato's next statement that what he has to say on that subject is only "probable."[33] Then there is pseudo-Justin Martyr, who, while in two places of his work he attributes to Plato the view that the pre-existent matter is uncreated,[34] in another place finds that, "when Plato has already said that matter is unbegotten, he afterwards says that it is produced."[35] Similarly Epiphanius finds that, while at one time Plato says that matter was produced by God and by powers produced by God, at another time he says that matter is coeval with God."[36] And so we may conclude that it is quite possible that some of those Fathers who speak of a pre-existent uncreated matter, without mentioning the name of Plato, the reason for their not mentioning Plato is that either they were uncertain as to what his view was or that they did not believe that his pre-existent matter was uncreated.

In the light of all this, I think that Bäumker, who has listed all the references to Church Fathers dealing with the problem of the eternal matter, is not right in assuming that all of them, both those who mention Plato and those who do not mention him, understood Plato to believe that his pre-existent matter is uncreated.[37]

Whatever the Church Fathers may have believed with regard to Plato's conception of his pre-existent matter, all of them reject the creation of the world out of a pre-existent uncreated matter, though some of them, as we have seen, admit its creation out of a pre-existent created matter. The main arguments advanced by them against the assumption of a pre-existent uncreated matter, variously phrased though they are, fall into five types.

32 *Stromata* V, 14, 89 (*PG* 9.132AB); cf. *Timaeus* 48 C.

33 *Ibid.* 48 D; cf. 30 B.

34 *Cohortatio ad Graecos* 20 (*PG* 6.277A) and 23 (284A).

35 *Ibid.* 7 (256A).

36 *Adversus haereses Panarium* I,6 (*PG* 41.205A).

37 Clemens Bäumker, *Das Problem der Materie in der griechischen Philosophie*, 143–4.

First, there is an argument based upon a principle derived from Plato's description of God as "the maker and father of this All."[38] With this as a starting point, Theophilus argues that "if God is uncreated and matter is uncreated, God is no longer, according to the Platonists, the creator of all things."[39]

Second, there is an argument based upon two principles derived from Philo's revision of Plato's aforequoted statement that God is "the maker and father of this All" by changing the expression "this All" to the expression "all things intelligible and sensible."[40] The reason that has led him to this revision and the significance of it may be briefly stated as follows: According to Plato, the "this All" of which God is the maker and father refers only to what he describes as the world of sensible (αἰσθητά)[41] and visible (ὁρατά)[42] things, whereas the ideas, which are intelligible[43] and invisible,[44] are said by him to be "ungenerated and indestructible."[45] Thus to him, God, though ungenerated, is not the only ungenerated being. Philo, however, on the basis of his interpretation of the verse, "It is not good that man should be alone" (Gen. 2:18) that "it is good that the Alone should be alone," establishes the principle that from eternity God was alone and hence that God alone is uncreated, so that the invisible or intelligible ideas were created.[46] Accordingly, the Platonic statement that God is "the maker and father of this all" is revised by him to read that God is "the one, who alone is eternal and the Father of all things intelligible and sensible,"[47] or, as he could have said, invisible and visible, for the respective terms in these two pairs of contrasts are used by him, as by Plato, synonymously.

By this Philo has established three principles: (1) God alone is uncreated, whereas all other beings are created by God; (2) nothing is coeternal with God; (3) eternity means deity. Of these three scripturally based Philonic principles, the first and third were adopted by Christianity, the first with the revised meaning that God alone is both

[38] *Tim.* 28 C; cf. *Rep.* X,597D.

[39] *Ad. Autol.* II,4 (1052B).

[40] Cf. below at n. 47.

[41] *Tim.* 28 B.

[42] *Ibid.* 30 A.

[43] *Ibid.* 48 E: παραδείγματος εἶδος . . . νοητόν.

[44] *Ibid.* 52 A: εἶδος . . . ἀόρατον.

[45] *Ibid.* 52 A; cf. *Philebus* 15 B.

[46] Cf. *Philo* I,171–2,200–217.

[47] *De virtutibus* 39, 214.

unbegotten and uncreated, whereas all other beings are either begotten of God or created by God. As for the second principle, it was adopted by those Fathers of the Church known as the Apologists,[48] but, though it was never publicly condemned as heretical, it was ultimately dropped by the Fathers.[49] Thus, when in departure of Philo's second principle, Christianity declared the Word or Son to be coeternal with God the Father, then, in conformity with its own revision of the meaning of Philo's first principle, it declared the Word or Son to be eternally begotten or, as it is usually expressed, eternally generated. This adherence of Christianity to the first Philonic principle, in accordance with its own revised meaning of it, is emphasized in the wording of the first two articles of the Nicene Creed: "We believe in one God, the Father Almighty, maker of all things visible and invisible. And in . . . the Son of God, begotten of the Father." The same reasoning was applied also to the Holy Spirit. The adherence of Christianity to the third of the Philonic principles is illustrated by the fact that John of Damascus, in his disputation with the Muslims, argues that the Word must be God on the ground that it is not created but eternally generated and, being eternally generated, it is coeternal with God, and anything eternal must be God.[50]

This Philonic principle of the identification of eternity with deity is the basis of a set of arguments which are phrased in various forms. Most poignantly is it phrased by Tertullian and Basil. Tertullian argues: "Since this [i.e., eternity] is a property of God, it will belong to God alone," and so will also other eternal properties of God belong to Him alone, and since "it is by possessing these [eternal properties] alone that He is God and by His sole possession of them He is one, if another also shared in the possession, there would then be as many gods as there were possessors of these properties of God."[51] In Basil the argument is phrased as follows: "If matter were uncreated, then it would from the very first be of a rank equal to that of God and would deserve the same veneration."[52] The same argument is implied in Justin Martyr's statement that "God alone is unbegotten and incorrupti-

48 Cf. my *Philosophy of the Church Fathers* I,192–8.

49 *Ibid.*, 198–204, 217–19.

50 *Disceptatio Christiani et Saraceni* (*PG* 94.1586A).

51 *Adv. Hermog.* 4.

52 *Hexaemeron* II, 4 (*PG* 29.32A).

ble and therefore He is God,"[53] and in Theophilus' statement that "nor, so far as their opinions [of an eternal matter] hold, is the monarchy [i.e., the unity] of God established."[54]

Third, there is an argument based upon a principle derived from the Philonic conception of God as the *summum genus* or, as he says, "the most generic" (τὸ γενικώτατον), by which he means that no term can be applied both to God and to another being that would imply that both are different species under the same genus, so that in each of them there would be a distinction of genus and species, for the conception of the absolute simplicity of God, which he was the first to formulate, excludes such a distinction in Him.[55] It is this Philonic principle that is behind an argument against the conception of an uncreated matter used by Dionysius of Alexandria. The gist of his argument is contained in the following passage: "Matter cannot be unoriginate, for matter and God are not the same: but if each is what it properly is, namely, matter and God, while the unoriginate is attached to both, this manifestly is different from each of them, and earlier and higher than both."[56] What he means to say is this: Since God and matter are the same in unoriginateness and differ in Godhood and materiality, then both of them are a species under the genus unoriginateness, and thus originateness is prior to and higher than both.

The same principle, I believe, underlies the argument by Maximus against the view that God is separate from the unoriginate matter, which, as we have suggested, refers to the view of Plato.[57] His argument reads as follows: "But if any one shall affirm that He is separate [from the matter], there must of necessity be something that is intermediate between the two, which also makes their separation evident. For it is impossible that one thing can be proved to be separate from another, when there is no third in which the separation between them is found."[58] I take it that, by the unoriginate God being separate from the unoriginate matter, he means that God is a different species from the matter, both of whom are of the same genus of unoriginateness and that, by the "intermediate" between the two that is required by such a "separation," he means the specific difference. The assumption in

[53] *Dial.* 5 (588 B). [54] *Ad Autol.* II,4 (1052B). [55] Cf. *Philo* II,94–110.
[56] Apud Eusebius, *Praep. Evang.* VII,19, 333d–334a.
[57] Cf. above, after n. 12.
[58] Apud Eusebius, *Praep. Evang.* VII,22, 337d.

this argument is that God cannot be subsumed with anything else under a common genus, because He is the highest genus.

Fourth, there is the principle of the self-sufficiency of God. This conception of God as self-sufficient occurs in Greek literature, including the works of Plato,[59] but Philo, on the basis of a scriptural verse defines it as meaning that "neither before creation was there anything with God, nor, when the world had come into being, does anything take place with Him, for there is absolutely nothing which He needs."[60] This principle, as defined by Philo, is the basis of an argument against a pre-existent uncreated matter phrased by the Church Fathers in various ways. In Theophilus, it occurs in the following form: "What great thing is it if God made the world out of existent materials? For even a human artist, when he gets material from some one, makes of it what he pleases."[61] So also does pseudo-Justin Martyr argue that "the Creator (ποιητής) creates the creature by His own capability and power, being in need of nothing else; but the workman (δημιουργός) frames his production when he has received from matter the capability for his work."[62] The same argument is used by Origen in his statement that those who believe in the eternity of matter of necessity believe that "God could not create anything when nothing existed,"[63] but this can be only the opinion of men "who are altogether ignorant of the power and intelligence of Uncreated Nature."[64] Similarly Athanasius argues that on the assumption of a pre-existent uncreated matter God would be powerless to create without matter and thus He would not be a Creator (ποιητὴς καὶ δημιουργός) but only an artificer (τεχνίτης).[65] Tertullian goes even further to argue that the assumption of a pre-existent uncreated matter carries with it the implication that matter is superior to God, for "on this principle, matter itself, no doubt, was not in want of God, but rather lent itself to God, who was in want of it."[66]

Finally, there is an argument that those who assert that God

[59] *Philebus* 60c, 67a.

[60] Cf. *Philo* I,172.

[61] *Ad Autol.* II,4 (1052B).

[62] *Cohort. ad Graec.* 22 (281B).

[63] *De princ.* II,1,4, p. 110, 11.19–20.

[64] *Ibid.,* 110, 1.25–111, 1.1.

[65] *Orat. de incarn. verbi* 2 (100AB). Cf. above at n. 62 and below at nn. 67 and 71 for the various Patristic uses of the terms δημιουργός and τεχνίτης.

[66] *Adv. Hermog.* 8.

created the world out of a formless, uncreated matter must logically, like the Epicureans, resort to the view that the world came into being by chance and accident. Clearly and fully is this argument stated by Origen in a fragment of his commentary on Genesis, which in its original Greek has been preserved by Eusebius.

He begins by challenging those who believe in a pre-existent uncreated matter to tell him "whether it does not follow from their argument that God by lucky chance found the substance unoriginate, without which, had it not been supplied to Him by its unoriginate character, He could have produced no work at all, but would have continued to be no Creator."[67] Then, evidently referring to Plato's statement to the effect that God has used up the entire pre-existent matter in the creation of the world,[68] he asks his opponents, again, "Whence also came the measurement of just so much of the substratum of matter, as to suffice for the establishment of a world of the actual size?"[69] the implication being that they would again have to resort to a "lucky chance." Furthermore, referring to the general conception of that pre-existent uncreated matter as being devoid of any qualities but still being capable of receiving qualities, he asks once more his opponents, "Whence also has matter become capable of receiving every quality which God wills?"[70] the implication once more being that they would have to resort to a "lucky chance." He concludes his argument with the following statement: "For just as it is absurd in the case of the ordered world, so skillfully contrived, to say [as do the Epicureans] that it has become such without help from a wise Artificer (τεχνίτης), so it is equally unreasonable that the matter, being of such extent, and such quality, and so pliable to the Artificer, the Word of God, has been unoriginate."[71] This part of the argument, as Eusebius suggests, is taken by Origen from Philo's *De providentia*.[72]

This lengthy argument of Origen in his commentary on the Book of Genesis is reflected in his argument in the *De principiis,* in the following statements: (1) Those who assume that the world was created out of an uncreated formless matter, must necessarily assume, with regard

[67] *Praep. Evang.* VII,20, 335ab.
[68] *Tim.* 32 C–33 A.
[69] *Op. et loc. cit.,* 335b.
[70] *Ibid.,* 335c.
[71] *Ibid.,* 335d–336a.
[72] *Ibid.* VII,21, 336b–337a.

to that matter, that "its nature and power were the result of chance,"[73] that is to say, its nature and power to receive every quality which God willed was by a "lucky chance." (2) "I am astonished that they should find fault with those who deny" that the world has a creator, when they themselves say that (*a*) "God could not create anything when nothing existed";[74] (*b*) that the matter "was furnished Him not by His own arrangement, but by accident";[75] (*c*) "that this, which was discovered by chance, was able to suffice Him for an undertaking of so vast an extent."[76]

[73] *De princ.* II,4, p. 110, ll. 12–13.
[74] *Ibid.*, 19–20.
[75] *Ibid.*, 21–22.
[76] *Ibid.*, 22–23.

10

PATRISTIC ARGUMENTS AGAINST THE ETERNITY OF THE WORLD

According to Aristotle himself, all the philosophers before him are agreed that the world was generated,[1] which implies that he was the first to introduce the conception of an ungenerated world; but, according to John Philoponus, Aristotle was only the first among the natural philosophers who discovered a new method to establish the principle that the world had no beginning.[2] Among the Church Fathers, Lactantius sometimes attributes the belief in the eternity of the world explicitly to Aristotle,[3] but sometimes he refers it vaguely to "those who say that the world always existed." [4] Vague references to a belief in the eternity of the world, or to such a belief described as held by some people or by some philosophers, are to be found also in the works of such Fathers as Justin Martyr,[5] Theophilus,[6] Origen,[7] Arnobius,[8] Basil,[9] Augustine,[10] and Diodorus Tarsus.[11] Two pre-Socratic philosophers are mentioned by some Fathers as exponents of the belief in the eternity of the world: Xenophanes [12] by Hippolytus,[13] Eusebius,[14] and Theodoret of Cyrrhus;[15] Pythagoras [16] by Tertullian.[17] Var-

[1] De Caelo I, 10, 279b, 12–13.
[2] De Opificio Mundi, p. 82, lines 10–12 (ed. G. Reichardt, 1897).
[3] Cf. below nn. 44, 56.
[4] Cf. below n. 63.
[5] Cf. below n. 19.
[6] Ad Autolycum II, 4; II, 8.
[7] Cf. below n. 29.
[8] Adversus Nationes II, 56 (PL 5, 898 B).
[9] Cf. below nn. 28, 58.
[10] Cf. below n. 91.
[11] Cf. below n. 25.
[12] Cf. Zeller, Phil d. Griechen, I[6], 663, n. 2.
[13] Refutatio Omnium Haeresium I, 14.
[14] Praeparatio Evangelica I, 8, 23a.
[15] Graecarum Affectionum Curatio IV (PG 83, 900 C).
[16] Cf. Zeller, op. cit., I[6], 516, n. 4.
[17] Apologeticus 11 (Pl 1, 333 B).

Clement of Alexandria's statement that Heraclitus held that "there was a world eternal" besides a world "perishable" (Stromata V, 14 [PG 9, 157 B]) refers to an eternal succession of perishable worlds (cf. De Caelo I, 12, 297b, 14–17, and Zeller, op. cit., I[6], 865–75). This is not the kind of eternity of the world dealt with in this paper.

ious arguments are used by the Fathers in their refutation of this view. These arguments, selected and grouped into six types, are the subject of discussion of the present paper.

ARGUMENT 1

In Plato there is an argument for the creation of the world based upon the fact that the world "can be seen and touched and it has a body" and that as such it belongs to "becoming and creation." [18] A similar argument is used by Justin Martyr when, in answer to "some" who say that the world is "ungenerated," he exclaims: "What reason has one for supposing that a body solid, possessing resistance, composite, changeable, and renewed every day, has not arisen from some source?" [19] Though his use of the term "changeable" would seem to suggest another source, one which will be discussed later,[20] his use of the term "body" as the main fact from which he draws his conclusion, added by his own statement that prior to his conversion to Christianity he found satisfaction in the philosophy of Plato,[21] suggests Plato as the main source of his argument. Like Plato, too, he uses this argument only to prove the originatedness of the world, though as a Christian he certainly believed also in its destructibility and though also he could have demonstrated its destructibility on the basis of Plato's own principle that "all which has been fastened may be loosed" [22] or, as the same principle is expressed by Aristotle, that whatever is generated must be destructible.[23]

ARGUMENT 2

While the preceding argument is based upon an argument by Plato in support of his own belief in the creation of the world, the next argument is based upon a quotation by Aristotle of a tentative objection to his own argument for the eternity of the world from the eternity of motion. The tentative objection reads as

[18] Timaeus 28 B.
[19] Dialogus 5.
[20] Cf. below, Argument 2.
[21] Dialogus 2.
[22] Timaeus 41 A.
[23] De Caelo I, 12, 282b, 3.

follows: "It may be said that no process of change (μεταβολή) is eternal, for the nature of all change is such that it proceeds from something to something, so that every process of change must be bounded by contraries that mark its course, and no motion can go on to infinity." [24] The conclusion expected to be drawn from this is that, inasmuch as no change or motion can be infinite, the world, which consists of things in change and motion, cannot be eternal. Aristotle, of course, answers this tentative objection.

This tentative objection was made into an argument against the eternity of the world by Diodorus Tarsus, who, after having shown that the world is generated from the fact that its constituent elements are subject to change, says: "If anyone should argue that their change (τροπὴν) is ungenerated, he may be answered that this is absolutely impossible, for change is an affection (πάθος) which has a beginning, and one could not say that change is beginningless." [25] It was similarly made into an argument for the creation of the world by John of Damascus, who, starting with the statement that "all things that exist are either created or uncreated," asks, "Who, then, will refuse to grant that all existing things . . . are subject to change (τρέπεσθαι) and alteration and movement of various kinds?" and, expecting a negative answer, he concludes: "Things that are changeable are wholly created." [26] Both of them had thus disregarded Aristotle's answer to the objection.

Basil, however, did not disregard Aristotle's answer. He took notice of it and refuted it and thus by his refutation of it he indirectly transformed the tentative objection into an argument against the eternity of the world.

In his answer to the tentative objection, Aristotle denies the main assumption of the objection, namely, that all the motions in the world are bounded by limits and must therefore be finite and hence cannot be eternal. He tries to show how the motion common to the celestial bodies, being circular, is not bounded by limits and hence is not finite and hence is eternal. To quote: "In

[24] Phys. VIII, 2, 252b, 9–12.

[25] Photius, Bibliotheca 223 (ed. Bekker, 1824, p. 209b, lines 11–14). Cf. Metaph. XII, 2, 1069b, 12: "alteration is change according to affection"; Phys. I, 2, 185a, 34–185b, 1: "Substance or quality or affection cannot be infinite."

[26] De Fide Orthodoxa I, 3 (PG 94, 796 A–C).

rectilinear motion we have a definite beginning, end, and middle, which all have their place in it in such a way that there is a point from which that which is in motion can be said to start and a point at which it can be said to finish its course . . . On the other hand, in circular motion there are no such definite points; for why should any point on the line be a limit rather than any other? Any one point as much as any other is alike a beginning, middle, or end."[27] On the basis of this he concludes that the circular motion of the heavens may be infinite and eternal.

Basil's refutation of this answer is to be discerned in the following passage: "Do not imagine, O man, that those things which are visible are beginningless; and, because of the fact that the [bodies] which move in the heaven move in a circular course, do not believe that the nature [of the motion] of circularly moving bodies is without a beginning." Then, using the analogy of a circle drawn by a draughtsman, he tries to show how the circular motion of the celestial bodies, like the drawn circle, could have a temporal beginning. In such a circle, he says, "it is impossible for us to find out where it begins and where it ends, but we ought not on this account to believe it to be without a beginning. Although we are not sensible of it, it really begins at some point when the draughtsman has begun to draw it at a certain radius from the centre." And here Basil expects us to add that hence the circle had a temporal beginning.

Finally, applying this analogy of a circle drawn by a draughtsman to the circular motions of the celestial bodies, he concludes: "Thus also, because of the fact that the circularly moving celestial bodies always return upon themselves and the regularity of their course is not interrupted by a single pause, you should not vainly imagine to yourself that the world has neither beginning nor end."[28]

ARGUMENT 3

An original argument against the eternity of the world based upon two Aristotelian principles used in support of an anti-Aris-

[27] Phys. VIII, 9, 265a, 29–34.
[28] Hexaemeron I, 3 (PG 29, 9 AB).

totelian principle is advanced by Origen. The argument occurs in a passage where, after expounding the scriptural teaching of creation, he says as follows: "Now, if there be any one who would here oppose either the authority or credibility of our Scripture, we would ask of him whether he asserts that God can, or cannot, comprehend all things? To assert that He cannot, would manifestly be an act of impiety. If then he answers, as he must, that God comprehends all things, it follows from the very fact of their being capable of comprehension, that they are understood to have a beginning and an end, seeing that that which is altogether without any beginning cannot be at all comprehended. For however far understanding may extend, so far is the faculty of comprehending illimitably withdrawn and removed when there is held to be no beginning." [29]

This argument is based upon a combination of three propositions, of which two are explicitly stated and one is only implied. First, there is in this argument the implication of a proposition that an eternal world means an infinite succession of things. This reflects Aristotle's statement that the infinite in his eternal world exhibits itself "in time and in man," [30] that is to say, in an infinite succession of days and an infinite succession of the generations of man. Second, as Origen himself says, "that which is altogether without any beginning cannot be at all comprehended." This reflects Aristotle's statement that "the infinite so far as infinite is unknown." [31] Third, again, as Origen himself says, "God comprehends all things," which is explained by him elsewhere to mean that the object of God's knowledge is both God himself and the things outside himself.[32] This is meant to be in opposition to Aristotle's view that the object of God's knowledge is God himself.[33] Underlying all this is the assumption that in respect of knowing infinite things, God's knowledge is like man's knowledge, which cannot comprehend the infinite. It is to be noted that later, in mediaeval philosophy, the Jewish Maimonides [34] and the Chris-

[29] De Principiis III, 5, 2.
[30] Phys. III, 6, 206a, 25–26.
[31] Ibid. I, 4, 187b, 7.
[32] De Principiis IV, 4, 10 (37).
[33] Metaph. XII, 7, 1072b, 19–21.
[34] Moreh Nebukim III, 20.

tian Thomas Aquinas [35] did not hesitate to say that God knows infinite things: to both of them, in this respect as in any other respect, the knowledge attributed to God is unlike human knowledge, for His knowledge, in this respect as in any other respect, is to be taken, as are all His attributes, either in an equivocal sense, according to Maimonides, or in an eminential and an analogical sense, according to Thomas.

ARGUMENT 4

Two arguments against the eternity of the world by Lactantius are modified versions of two of four arguments, the third and fourth, which Theophrastus, as quoted by Philo, attributes to "those who maintain the generation and destructibility of the world," [36] that is, the Stoics. These two Stoic arguments, together with Theophrastus' refutation of them, may be briefly restated as follows.

The third argument starts with a syllogism, which reads: "Anything the parts of which are all perishable necessarily perishes itself. All the parts of the world are perishable. Therefore, the world itself is perishable." [37] It then proceeds to prove the minor premise by showing how such parts of the world as "earth" and "stones" and "water" and "fire" will perish in various ways.[38] In refutation of this argument, Theophrastus asserts: "The truth surely is not that a thing is destructible if all its parts are destroyed; it is true only of a thing of which all the parts are destroyed together and at the same time." [39] The fourth argument starts with the propositions that the human arts are generated and that they are coeval with the human race, from which it infers that the human race is generated. Then, from the proposition that the human race is generated, it infers that the world is generated. Finally, from the proposition that the world is generated, it infers, on the basis of the Aristotelian principle that whatever is gene-

[35] Summa Theologica I, 14, 12.
[36] De Aeternitate Mundi 23, 117.
[37] Ibid. 24, 121.
[38] Ibid. 24, 125–127.
[39] Ibid. 27, 143.

rated must be destructible,[40] that the world is destructible.[41] In refutation of this argument, Theophrastus tries to show that "it is the height of folly to estimate the age of the human race by the arts." [42]

Lactantius' versions of these two Stoic arguments occur in his Divinae Institutiones in reverse order, the version of the fourth Stoic argument in Book II, Chapter 11, and that of the third argument in Book VII, Chapter 1. This change of order was done by Lactantius advisedly, for, as we shall see, his version of the Stoic third argument presupposes, and is dependent upon, his version of the Stoic fourth argument. We shall, therefore, begin with Lactantius' version of the Stoic fourth argument and list it as Argument 4 of the selected Patristic six arguments.

In his version of the Stoic fourth argument, Lactantius starts with a survey of the various accounts of the origin of man as found in Hebrew Scripture, in Plato, and in Greek mythology.[43]

He then goes on to say as follows: "Aristotle, however, freed himself from labor and trouble by saying that the world always existed and therefore the human race, and the other things which are in it, had no beginning, but always had been and always would be." [44] This restatement of Aristotle's view of the eternity of the world as implying the eternity of the human race is not based upon any statement in Aristotle,[45] though it may be inferred from his use of the example of the generations of man as an illustration of the possibility of an infinite in succession.[46] Prior to Lactantius, Ocellus Lucanus [47] and Diodorus Siculus [48] similarly take the eternity of the world to imply the eternity of the human race. In fact, among the followers of Aristotle the eternity of the world and the eternity of the human race were held to be mutually implicative, so that the Peripatetic Critolaus, as quoted by Philo, starting with the eternity of the human race as a premise, con-

[40] Cf. above n. 23.

[41] De Aeternitate Mundi 24, 130–131.

[42] Ibid. 27, 145.

[43] Divinae Institutiones II, 11 (PL 6, 311 B–315 A).

[44] Ibid. (315 A).

[45] Cf. Zeller, op. cit., II, 2^3, p. 508, n.1.

[46] Phys. III, 6, 206a, 25–27.

[47] De Universi Natura III, 1.

[48] Bibliotheca Historica I, 6, 3; also quoted in Eusebius, Praeparatio Evangelica I, 7, 19a.

cludes that "if man [that is, the human race], a small part of the universe, is eternal, the world must surely be ungenerated and therefore indestructible." [49]

Having thus attributed to Aristotle the view that the eternity of the world implies the eternity of the human race, he undertakes to show that the human race is not eternal. Now, as we have seen, the Stoics in their corresponding fourth argument have tried to prove the non-eternity of the human race from the non-eternity of the arts. Lactantius, however, does not use this Stoic proof, and this evidently because he was aware of Theophrastus' refutation of it. He therefore substitutes for it another proof, one modelled after the Stoic third argument, which, as we have seen, is based on the premise that "anything the parts of which are all perishable necessarily perishes itself." As phrased by him, it reads as follows: "When we all see that each living being separately, which had no previous existence, begins to exist and ceases to exist, it is necessary that the whole race must at some time have begun to exist, and must cease at some time because it had a beginning [50] . . . For that cannot, as a whole, be immortal which consists of mortals." [51]

But evidently being also aware that this substitute proof of his is subject to the same refutation by which Theophrastus has refuted the Stoic third argument after which it is modelled, Lactantius anticipates this possible refutation by providing his readers with an answer for it. His answer is contained in the following passage: "For as we all die individually, it is possible that, by some calamity all may perish simultaneously, either through the unproductiveness of the earth . . . or through the general spread of pestilence . . . or by the conflagration of the world . . . or by a deluge . . . And if it is possible for it to die together, because it dies in parts, it is evident that it had an origin at some time; and as the liability to decay bespeaks a beginning, so also it gives proof of an end. And if these things are true, Aristotle will be unable to maintain that the world had no beginning." [52]

There is more to this statement than meets the eye. Underly-

[49] Philo, De Aeternitate Mundi 11, 55; 13, 69.

[50] Divinae Institutiones II, 11 (315 A).

[51] Ibid. (315 B).

[52] Ibid. (316 A).

ing it, we assume, is Aristotle's statement that "it cannot be true to say that this thing is possible and yet will not be," [53] which, we further assume, is taken by Lactantius to mean that whatever is logically possible must be considered as being actually realizable in infinite time.[54] With this statement of Aristotle as understood by him in the back of his mind, Lactantius challenges all those who use the indestructibility and hence the ungeneratedness of the human race as an argument for the indestructibility and hence the ungeneratedness of the world by addressing them as follows. You claim that the world is indestructible. According to you, then, time is infinite in the future. Now you will all have to admit that there is no logical impossibility in the assumption that some sudden calamity might destroy all human beings together at the same time. Accordingly, you will have to admit that the destruction of the whole human race by some sudden calamity is logically possible. Since this is logically possible, it is actually realizable in infinite time. But, according to your belief, the future time is infinite. Therefore, in that infinite future time of yours, the whole human race is destructible. And so Lactantius concludes his challenge with the words quoted above: "If all these things are true, Aristotle [that is, those followers of Aristotle, such as Critolaus, who use this argument from the indestructibility and ungeneratedness of the human race] will be unable to maintain that the world also itself has no beginning."

Thus Lactantius has transformed the Stoic fourth argument from an argument for the creation of the world into a refutation of an argument for the eternity of the world.

ARGUMENT 5

The Stoic third argument, which in its original form, as we have seen, is aimed directly at proving the destructibility of the world, is extended by Lactantius, again, on the basis of the Aristotelian principle that whatever is generated must be destructible,[55] as an argument in refutation of "Aristotle," who is described by him

[53] Metaph. IX, 4, 1047b, 4–5.

[54] This is how Aristotle's statement is explained by Crescas. Cf. my Crescas' Critique of Aristotle, p. 249 and n. 3 on p. 551.

[55] Cf. above n. 23.

as having said that the world both "had always existed and always would exist." [56] As phrased by Lactantius, the argument reads: "For when we see that earth and water and fire, which are clearly parts of the world, perish, are consumed, and are extinguished, it is understood [that the world is mortal, for] that is as a whole mortal the members of which are mortal. Hence, it follows [that the world did not always exist, for] whatever is liable to destruction must have been produced." [57] From the very wording of Lactantius' version of the argument it is quite evident that it is based upon the Stoic argument as quoted by Philo from Theophrastus, namely, the argument based on the principle that "anything the parts of which are all perishable necessarily perishes itself." Though Theophrastus has refuted this argument, Lactantius makes no reference to it, evidently because, as we have seen, he has already provided an answer for it in his version of the Stoic fourth argument. He must have felt assured that the explanation given by him there for the mortality of the whole human race on account of the mortality of individual human beings could be easily applied as an explanation for the destructibility of its parts and thus constitute a rebuttal of Theophrastus' refutation. And so he left it to his readers to do the application.

An argument like the Stoic third argument, based on the principle that "anything the parts of which are all perishable necessarily perishes itself," is to be discerned in Basil's refutation of the view described by him as that of those who "imagine that the visible world is coeternal with the Creator of all things, with God Himself" [58] or who affirm that "heaven coexists with God from all eternity." [59] By itself this statement might be taken to mean either the Aristotelian or the Plotinian conception of eternity. But from its context I take it to be a restatement in his own words of Aristotle's theory of the eternity of the world to which he has previously referred as the view of anyone who imagines that "those things which are visible are beginningless" [60] and with which he later contrasts a view which can be identified as that of

[56] Divinae Institutiones VII, 1 (PL VI, 735 A — 736 B).
[57] Ibid. (736 B).
[58] Hexaemeron I, 3 (PG 29, 9 C).
[59] Ibid. (12 A).
[60] Ibid. (9 A).

the Neoplatonic eternal emanation.[61] In criticism of this view, he asks of what use is to them all their knowledge of the various branches of mathematics, "if they cannot conceive that a whole of which the parts are subject to corruption and change must of necessity end by itself submitting to the fate of its parts?" [62] We are expected here to conclude that, since the parts of the world are corruptible, the world as a whole is corruptible; and, since the world as a whole is corruptible, the world as a whole was created.

ARGUMENT 6

In addition to these two arguments, Lactantius has a third argument, aimed, as he says, at "those who assert that the world always existed." [63] This argument starts out with an incomplete hypothetical syllogism of which only the major premise is given as follows:

"If the world always existed, it can have no *ratio*."

We are expected here to complete the syllogism:

But the world has a *ratio*;

Therefore, the world did not always exist.

In what sense the term *ratio*, which I have left untranslated, is used here by Lactantius may be gathered from his subsequent discussion in which there occur the following statements.[64] (1) "The world and its parts, as we see, are governed by a wonderful *ratio*." (2) "All things stand together in good order by a most excellent *ratio*." (3) In all these things "a wonderful arrangement (*dispositio*) of a most provident *ratio* shines forth." (4) "The providence of the Supreme God is manifest from the arrangement (*dispositio*) of things." In the course of his discussion he also explains how the governance of things and their standing together and their arrangement, spoken of by him as being effected by a *ratio* or the providence of God, can be demonstrated by the "temperate climate" (*caeli temperatio*),[65] by "the course of the

[61] Ibid. I, 7 (17 BC).

[62] Ibid. I, 3 (12 A).

[63] Divinae Institutiones VII, 3 (745 A).

[64] Ibid. (745 B — 746 A).

[65] Other translations of this expression are: "the framing of the heaven" (William Fletcher, 1871); "l'avvicendarsi delle stagioni" (Gino Mazzoni, 1937); "order in heavens" (Mary Francis McDonald, 1964). But see the same expression as used in the corresponding statement by Cicero quoted below.

stars and of the heavenly bodies, which is uniform even in variety itself (*aequalis in ipsa varietate*)," [66] by "the constant and wonderful arrangement of the seasons," and by "the varied fertility of the soils."

Now Cicero in several places in his De Natura Deorum reproduces various Stoic arguments in proof of what he describes as the belief that "the whole world is ruled and governed by the mind and the *ratio* of the gods" [67] or that "the gods exist" [68] or that "the world and all its parts were set in order at the beginning and have been governed for all time by the providence of the gods." [69] Among the arguments mentioned by him are some which are the same as those used here by Lactantius against the eternity of the world. They are based, as he shows, upon "the greatness of the advantages derived from temperate climate (*caeli temperatio*); the fertility of the soil; [70] . . . the uniformity (*aequibilitas*) of the motion and revolutions of the heaven," [71] and "the succession of the seasons." [72] Since the same arguments are used by both the Stoics and Lactantius in trying to establish the existence of a *ratio* in the world, we may conclude that the term *ratio* is used here by Lactantius in all the shades of meaning it has among the Stoics, namely, reason, plan, order, system, and providence used in the sense of foresight and forethought and hence of purpose. What Lactantius, therefore, has done here is to take the Stoic arguments for a *ratio* in the world, originally used against the theory of chance [73] by which the Epicureans explained both the origin of the world and the generation and destruction of things within the world, and use them against Aristotle's theory of the eternity of the world. In fact, Lactantius himself clearly

[66] The term *aequalis* here, I take it, reflects the Greek ὁμαλῆ in Physics VIII, 9, 265b, 11, so that the phrase *aequalis in ipsa varietate* means that all the celestial bodies are uniform in the circularity of their motions and that each celestial body moves with a uniform velocity, even though they differ among themselves in the direction and the velocity of their motions. Cf. the term *aequabilitas* in the corresponding statement of Cicero quoted below.

[67] De Natura Deorum I, 2, 4.

[68] Ibid. II, 1, 3.

[69] Ibid. II, 30, 75.

[70] Ibid. II, 5, 13.

[71] Ibid., 15.

[72] Ibid. I, 2, 4.

[73] Ibid. II, 5, 15; II, 34, 87; II, 37, 94.

indicates that he was conscious of what he was doing, for immediately after his use of the argument from the existence of a *ratio* in the world against Aristotle's theory of eternity, he uses the same argument against "Epicurus or Democritus,"[74] who, he says, maintained that the world "was produced spontaneously (*sponte*)"[75] . . . "and by his ignorance of *ratio* entirely overthrew the whole *ratio*."[76]

But here a difficulty arises in our mind. It happens that Aristotle had immunized himself against a criticism like that raised later by the Stoics against the Epicurean theory of chance, by differentiating between chance and nature and by maintaining that nature acts for a purpose. Thus in his argument against Empedocles, whom he quotes as saying that most of the parts of animals came to be by chance,[77] and similarly in his argument against Democritus, whom he quotes as saying that the order in the universe came by chance,[78] he tries to show that the orderly regulated recurrence of events in the eternal world is due to nature, which he describes as acting for the sake of something (ἕνεκά του).[79] It would seem strange, therefore, that Lactantius should criticize Aristotle for the very thing for which Aristotle himself had provided an explanation. Let us then study Lactantius' demonstration of the major premise of his incompleted syllogism, which in hypothetical form makes the assertion that an eternal world can have no *ratio*, and see whether somewhere in its wording there is not lurking a refutation of Aristotle's view that the nature of his eternal world acts for a purpose.

Here is how that demonstration reads: "Verily, what could a *ratio* have produced in that which never had a beginning? For before anything is done or constructed, there is need of deliberation (*consilio*), that it may be determined how it should be done; nor

[74] Reflects Cicero's statement (ibid. I, 43, 120): "Democritus, the fountainhead from which Epicurus derived his stream that watered his little garden."

[75] The term *sponte* here is a translation of the Greek αὐτομάτως in the sense of ἀπὸ τύχης. Cicero himself in his De Natura Deorum uses the terms *fortuita* = τὰ ἀπὸ τύχης (II, 5, 15) and *casu* = αὐτομάτως (II, 34, 87; 39, 94) indiscriminately as a description of the Epicurean chance.

[76] Divinae Institutiones VII, 3 (PL 6, 745 B).

[77] Phys. II, 4, 196a, 23–24; 8, 198b, 23–32.

[78] Ibid. II, 4, 196a, 24–28.

[79] Ibid. II, 5, 196b, 17–19; 8, 198b, 10–11; 199a, 3–8.

can anything be done without the foresight of a *ratio*, and thus the *ratio* precedes every work. Therefore, that which has not been made has no *ratio*. But the world has a *ratio* by which it both exists and is governed. Therefore, also, it was made." [80]

The main points in Lactantius' demonstration are two, each of which, as we shall see, reflects some statement of Aristotle. First, deliberation (*consilium*) precedes action — which reflects Aristotle's statements that "we deliberate (βουλευόμεθα) about things that are in our control and are attainable by action" [81] and that "since the object of choice is something within our power which is desired after deliberation, choice (προαίρεσις) will be deliberate desire (βουλευτικὴ ὄρεξις) of things in our power." [82] Second, every work is preceded by *ratio* — which reflects Aristotle's statement, with regard to actions described as good or bad, that "the cause of action (the efficient, not the final) is choice and the cause of choice is desire and *ratio* directed to a certain end (λόγος. ὁ ἕνεκά τινος)." [83] Thus Lactantius' *consilium* reflects Aristotle's "we deliberate about things . . . attainable by action" or his "deliberative desire" or "choice" which precedes and is the cause of action; and Lactantius' *ratio* reflects Aristotle's "*ratio* directed to a certain end."

Now it happens that Aristotle's view that nature acts for a purpose is based upon an analogy drawn by him between acts produced by choice, that is, by "deliberate desire," and acts produced by nature, even though the latter, he admits, are not the result of choice, that is, of deliberate desire.[84] But having thus stated that acts of nature are purposive, even though they are not by "choice," that is, not by "deliberate desire" and hence not by deliberation, he felt the need of explaining why actions which are not by deliberation can be purposive. His explanation is at first stated categorically as follows: "It is absurd to suppose that purpose (ἕνεκά του) is not present because we do not observe the moving agent deliberating (βουλευσάμενον)." [85] Then, having in

[80] Divinae Institutiones VII, 3 (PL 6, 745 A).
[81] Eth. Nic. III, 3, 1112a, 30–31.
[82] Ibid., 113a, 9–11.
[83] Ibid. VI, 2, 1139a, 31–32.
[84] Phys. II, 5, 196b, 17–19.
[85] Ibid. II, 8, 199b, 26–28.

mind his view, as found fully expressed by him in another work, that in certain arts, such, for instance, as the shaping of letters and the spelling of words, there is no deliberation,[86] he adds: "Art does not deliberate either." [87] Accordingly, he goes on to reason: "If the ship-building art were in wood, it would act in a like manner by nature," [88] that is, ships would grow from wood by nature, just as by nature, according to the saying, tall oaks grow from little acorns. Finally he concludes: "If, therefore, purpose is present in art [even when it does not deliberate], it is present in nature [even though it never deliberates]." [89] The cumulative effect of these Aristotelian statements is that the acts of nature, though not deliberative, are still purposive, because purposive action need not be preceded by deliberation, as is evidenced by the action of certain arts, which, though not deliberative, is still purposive. When, therefore, by the side of these Aristotelian statements we place Lactantius' statement that "before anything is done or constructed, there is need of deliberation," it is quite evident that the latter is meant to be a refutation of the former. In direct opposition to Aristotle, Lactantius argues as follows: It is not true that some arts do not deliberate; nay, nothing is done or constructed without being preceded by deliberation, and consequently, in the eternal world of Aristotle, nature, which by Aristotle's own admission does not deliberate, does not act for a purpose.

Here, then, Lactantius gainsays something said by Aristotle and no reason is given for his gainsaying it. Certainly he was not merely trying to be contrary; he must have had some reason. What was his reason?

Let us then try to find out what he could have said and what he would have said if he were asked and urged and prodded to explain himself.

His explanation, I imagine, would have been as follows:

What are those arts of which Aristotle says there is in them no deliberation and which he illustrates by the shaping of letters and

[86] Eth. Nic. III, 3, 1112a, 34 — 1112b, 2.
[87] Phys. II, 8, 199b, 28; cf. Ross in his Commentary *ad loc.*
[88] Ibid., 28–29.
[89] Ibid., 29–30.

the spelling of words? Aristotle himself describes them as arts which are "exact (ἀκριβεῖς) and independent of other arts (αὐτάρκεις)," [90] by which he means arts which are fixed and well-established and are regulated by simple rules which can be easily mastered and which after some practice can be easily followed without the hesitancy of deliberation. But, as for this, while it is true that such arts are performed without deliberation, it is not true that they are not preceded by deliberation. Take, for instance, his own illustration of such arts by the art of shaping letters and spelling words. With regard to this, it is true, indeed, that once it has been conventionally fixed how letters are to be shaped and how words are to be spelled and once a man has practiced for some time how to shape letters and how to spell words, he can do these things without deliberation, but still it was after deliberation that the shaping of letters and the spelling of words were conventionally fixed and it is after some practice, which involves deliberation, that one can shape letters and spell words without deliberation. Or take his statement that, if the art of ship-building were in the wood, ships would grow from the wood without deliberation. If, indeed, the art of ship-building were in the wood, so that ships would grow from the wood without deliberation, then, as in the case of the assumption of a skilled ship-builder, who builds ships without deliberation, it will have to be assumed that some wise master of the art of ship-building has deliberately implanted that art in the wood. In short, if Aristotle's main argument for the nondeliberative purposive action of nature is the analogy of the non-deliberative purposive action observed in certain art, then by the same analogy he must conclude that nature was preceded by deliberation and hence is not eternal, for there is no art, not even those arts of which the performance may be without deliberation, which is not preceded by deliberation.

An argument from order like that used by Lactantius is also used by Augustine against those who say that "the world is eternal and without beginning." But all he says in refutation of this view is the assertion that "the world itself, by its well-ordered changes and movements, and by the fair appearance of all visible

[90] Eth. Nic. II, 3, 1112a, 34 — 1112b, 1.

things, proclaims in silence that it has been created."[91] It is not impossible that the proclamation of its having been created which Augustine attributes to the world is only a reëchoing of Lactantius's argument from the fact that the world has a *ratio* against those who claim that the world always existed.

[91] De Civitate Dei XI, 4, 2.

II

THE IDENTIFICATION OF *EX NIHILO* WITH EMANATION IN GREGORY OF NYSSA

FROM the fourth century on, whenever Church Fathers stressingly point to the distinction between the Word and the world as a distinction between that which was generated from God and that which was created from nothing, they aim, we may assume, not only at the Arian contention that the Word was created from nothing but also at the Plotinian view that the world was generated, that is, emanated, from God. It is this double target that is aimed at by Athanasius in a passage where he contrasts the Word with the world. The Word, he says, is a "generated being" (γέννημα) or a "son" and, as such, he is "the proper offspring (γέννημα) of the essence," "not subject to will," and hence is one who "must always be." In contradistinction to this, the world is a "created thing" (ποίημα), and "created things (τὰ γενητά) cannot be eternal, for they are from nothing," made by God "when He willed (ὅτε ἠθέλησε)."[1] It is also this double target that is aimed at by John of Damascus in a passage where, speaking of the generation of the Word and alluding to its distinction from the creation of the world, he says: "Generation is beginningless and eternal, being the work of nature [that is, not of will] and coming forth of the Father's own essence, . . . while creation, in the case of God, being the work of will, is not co-eternal with God, for it is not natural that that which is brought into existence from nothing should be co-eternal with that which is beginningless and everlasting."[2]

A direct rejection of the theory of emanation as conceived of by the Neoplatonists is to be found in Basil's comment on the verse "In the beginning God made (ἐποίησεν) the heaven and the earth" (Gen. 1:1). Playing upon the use of the word "made," which he contrasts with the words "worked" (ἐνήργησεν) and

[1] *Orationes adversus Arianos* I, 29 (PG 26, 72 A—C).
[2] *De Fide Orthodoxa* I, 8 (PG 94, 813 A).

"formed" (ὑπέστησεν) that could have been used, he rejects the view of "many" who, while imagining that "the world co-existed with God from eternity," still "admit that God is the cause of it, but an involuntary cause, as a body is the cause of the shadow and flame is the cause of the brightness."[3] The term "many" quite evidently refers to Neoplatonists, whose view, exactly as reported here by Basil, may be constructed out of the following statements in Plotinus: (1) "If something exists after the First, it must come from Him either directly or mediately,"[4] by which he means that of all the things that exist after God, Intelligence emanates from God directly, Soul emanates from Him indirectly through Intelligence, and the world emanates from Him also indirectly through Intelligence and Soul. (2) "Since we hold that the world is eternal and has never been without existence," the "Intelligence" — and by the same token also God and the Soul — is "prior" to the world "not as in time" but "in nature," that is to say, it is prior to the world in the sense that it is "the cause of it."[5] (3) "They are wrong . . . who believe that the world was generated by the deliberate will of him who created it,"[6] the implication being that the world came into existence by a process of generation which was without will. (4) Generation is "a radiation of light . . . like the bright light of the sun . . . which is being generated from it" and like the "heat" which radiates from "fire," and other similar examples.[7] Basil, in contradistinction to Plotinus, describes the creation, according to his own belief, as God's bringing things "from nothing into existence."[8]

From all this we gather that, as conceived of by the Fathers, the differences between Neoplatonic emanation and their own traditional belief in creation are three: (1) emanation is from God; creation is from nothing; (2) emanation is an eternal process; creation is an act of time; (3) emanation is by nature; creation is by will. I shall now try to show how Gregory of

[3] *Hexaemeron* I, 7 (PG 29, 17 BC).

[4] *Enneads* V, 8, 12.

[5] *Ibid.* III, 2, 1. On "prior in nature" in the sense of "cause," cf. Aristotle, *Categories*, 12, 14b, 11–13.

[6] *Ibid.* V, 8, 12.

[7] *Ibid.* V, 1, 6. Among the examples used here by Plotinus as illustrations of necessary causality there is no mention of the example of a body and its shadow, which is used by Basil in the passage quoted above at n. 3. But it must have been a common example. It is thus used in the Arabic version of the *Enneads*, the so-called *Theology of Aristotle* (ed. Dieterici, p. 112, l. 10).

[8] *Epistolae* VIII, 11 (PG 32, 264 B).

Nyssa, by making emanation an act in time and of will, has identified it with creation *ex nihilo*, thus probably being the first to make that identification.[9]

Gregory of Nyssa's own conception of creation is fully unfolded in the following statement: "We believe that the power of the divine will is sufficient to bring things from nothing (ἐκ τοῦ μὴ ὄντος) into existence."[10] This statement he subsequently repeats by saying that, according to the commonly accepted doctrine of faith, "the universe came into existence from nothing (ἐκ τοῦ μὴ ὄντος)."[11] It is to be remarked that in both these statements, as well as in the statements quoted above from Athanasius and John of Damascus and Basil, the Greek phrase which I have translated "from nothing" literally means "from non-existence" or "from the non-existent" but, in Patristic literature, that phrase is used in the technical sense of *ex nihilo*, of which the Greek literal equivalent, ἐξ οὐδενός, is used by Hippolytus.[12] Gregory of Nyssa thus explicitly expresses himself as believing in creation *ex nihilo*. Still in the very same context he also says that, according to Holy Scripture, "the genesis of all things is from God (ἐκ τοῦ θεοῦ)."[13]

Now, by itself, Gregory's statement that "the genesis of all things is from God" could be taken to mean that the creation of the world had been in the thought of God from eternity but that when He actually came to create the world He created it out of nothing. However, from the objection quoted by Gregory himself as having been raised against this statement of his, as well as from the way in which he answers that objection, it is quite clear that he means by this statement literally that, according to Scripture, God created the world out of Himself by an emanation like that conceived of by Plotinus, except that in Gregory's use of it the emanation had a beginning in time and it was an act of the divine will.

The objection against his statement that "the genesis of all

[9] For various attempts to identify creation *ex nihilo* with emanation, see my paper, The Meaning of *Ex Nihilo* in the Church Fathers, Arabic and Hebrew Philosophy, and St. Thomas, in *Mediaeval Studies in Honor of Jeremiah Denis Matthias Ford*, 1948, 355–70 (below, pages 207-221); GERSHOM SCHOLEM, Schöpfung aus Nichts und Selbstverschrankung Gottes, in *Eranos* 35 (1957), 87–119; my paper, The Meaning of *Ex Nihilo* in Isaac Israeli, in *Jewish Quarterly Review* 50 N.S. (1959), 1–12 (below, page 222).

[10] *De Hominis Opificio* 23 (PG 44, 212 C).

[11] *Ibid.* 24 (213 C).

[12] *Refutatio Omnium Haeresium* X, 33, 8, p. 290, l. 8 (ed. P. Wendland).

[13] *De Hominis Opificio* 23 (209 C).

things is from God" is ascribed by Gregory of Nyssa to certain "contentious argufiers" (ἐριστικοί), whose own view was that "matter is co-eternal with God." [14] The reference is quite evidently to those well-known followers of Plato who, unlike Plotinus, interpreted the pre-existent matter of their master's teachings to be not as an eternal emanation from God but rather as something independent of God and co-eternal with Him. Their argument against his statement is quoted by Gregory as follows: "If God is in His nature simple and immaterial, without quality, without magnitude, and without composition . . . in what way can matter be born from the immaterial, or a nature which is dimensional from that which is non-dimensional?" [15] His critics then go on to argue that, "if," in order to explain the origination of matter from God, Gregory would say that "something material was in God," then the question is, "How can He be immaterial while including matter in Himself." [16] Gregory's critics thus assume that by his statement that "the genesis of all things is from God" he means emanation from God's essence after the analogy of Plotinus' theory of emanation. In fact, the very objection raised against Gregory's statement reflects a tentative objection raised by Plotinus himself against his own theory of emanation. As phrased by Plotinus, it reads: "How from the One, as we conceive it to be, can any multiplicity or duality or number come into existence," [17] or "How can the variety of things come from the One which is simple and which shows, in its identity, no diversity and no duality?" [18]

That his critics understood correctly the true meaning of his statement may be gathered from Gregory's answer to their objection. His answer falls into two parts, corresponding to the two parts of the objection.

In the first part of his answer, while admitting that he meant by his statement a theory of emanation like that of Plotinus and while admitting also that his statement would imply that matter emanated from God who is immaterial, he sidesteps the objection simply by pleading ignorance of the way in which God moves His wondrous act of creation to perform. To quote: "In obedience to

[14] *Ibid.*
[15] *Ibid.* (209 D — 212 A).
[16] *Ibid.* (212 A).
[17] *Enneads* V, 1, 6.
[18] *Ibid.* V, 2, 1.

the teaching of Scripture, we believe that all things come from God (ἐκ τοῦ θεοῦ); but, as to the question how they were in God, a question beyond our reason, we do not seek to pry into it, believing as we do that all things are within the capacity of God's power, even to bring nothing (τὸ μὴ ὄν) into existence"[19] or, as he expresses himself elsewhere, to bring things "from nothing (ἐκ τοῦ μὴ ὄντος) into existence."[20]

The second part of his answer is introduced by him as follows: "It might perhaps be possible, by some skill in the use of words, to convince those who mock at our statement on the score of matter not to think that there is no answer to their attack on it."[21] The "skill in the use of words," by which he is trying to answer this objection, refers to the argument by which he is trying to show (1) that anything of material existence is a combination of various properties, each of which is an intelligible object (νοητόν); (2) wherever these intelligible properties come to be combined with one another, they produce bodily existence; (3) that it is these intelligible properties that emanate from God, who is an intelligible being (νοητός); (4) that God gives existence to the intelligible properties, so as to enable them to emanate from Him and produce bodily existence; (5) that the combination of these emanated intelligible properties with one another produces the material nature underlying bodily existence.[22] The implication of all this is that, just as the combination of the intelligible properties with one another after their emanation from God produces the crass matter of the various bodies, so also their totality during their existence in God forms an "intelligible matter." Accordingly, what Gregory does in this second part of his answer is to admit, for the sake of argument, that in God there is what Plotinus calls "intelligible matter (ὕλη νοητή), constituted of intelligible properties, but to maintain, in opposition to Plotinus, that the emanation of these intelligible properties from God, as well as their combination and transformation into the crass matter of the corporeal world, was by an act of divine will and in time.

Thus the Christian traditional belief in a volitional and temporal act of creation *ex nihilo* is interpreted by Gregory

[19] *De Hominis Opificio* 23 (212 B).
[20] Cf. above at n. 10.
[21] *De Hominis Opificio* 23 (212 C).
[22] *Ibid.* 24 (212 D — 213 B).

of Nyssa to mean a volitional and temporal act of emanation from God. Now from a comparison of his statement that God brings all things "from nothing (ἐκ τοῦ ὄντος) into existence"[23] and his statement that "all things come from God (ἐκ τοῦ θεοῦ)"[24] it is quite evident that the phrase "from nothing" in the former statement is used by him in the sense of the phrase "from God" in the latter statement. But what does he mean by his use of the term "nothing," of which the underlying Greek μὴ ὄν literally means "non-existence," as a description of God? Certainly he could not mean by it literally that God is nothing in the sense of His being non-existent. What then does he mean by it?

An answer to this query, I believe, is to be found, again, in the second part of his answer to his critics, the part in which his answer may be described as being only *ad hominem*. According to that part of his answer, the term "nothing" in the phrase "from nothing" quite evidently refers to the "intelligible matter" in God prior to its emanation from Him. But here, evidently aware that in Plotinus the "intelligible matter" is described as "existent" (ὄν)[25] and as "substance" (οὐσία),[26] which certainly does not mean that it is "nothing," Gregory makes two statements from which one may infer an explanation for his description of intelligible matter as nothing. In the first of these statements, using the term "qualities" for "properties," that is, "intelligible properties," he says that, if matter is divested of these qualities, then, "by itself, it can in no way at all be grasped by reason."[27] The second statement reads: "If each of these intelligible properties should be taken away from the substratum, then the whole concept of the body would be dissolved,"[28] that is to say, would be reduced to nothing. Though the term matter, which is explicitly mentioned in the first statement and is implied in the second statement, refers to the matter underlying bodies in the world, it may be reasonably assumed that, throughout his discussion of the subject, whatever he says about the matter underlying bodies is true also of the intelligible matter in God prior to its emanation. Thus matter, including the intelligible matter in God prior to its emanation, is described as "nothing" in the sense of its being "by itself" in-

[23] Cf. above at n. 10 (plus at n. 11).
[24] Cf. above at n. 19.
[25] *Enneads* II, 4, 16.
[26] *Ibid.* II, 4, 5.
[27] *De Hominis Opificio* 24 (212 D).
[28] *Ibid.* (213 A).

capable of being "grasped by reason" or incapable of existing in our mind as a "concept"; in short, in the sense of its being incomprehensible.

Thus, according to the second part of his answer, where for the sake of argument Gregory admits that there is in God an intelligible matter, the phrase "from God" in his statement that "the genesis of all things is from God" and the phrase "from nothing" in his statement that "the universe came into existence from nothing" both mean from the intelligible matter, which "intelligible matter" is called by him "nothing" because of its being "incomprehensible." I shall now try to show how also according to the first part of his answer, where the phrase "from God" and "from nothing" in the same two statements of his mean from the essence of God, that "essence of God" is similarly called by him "nothing" because of its being "incomprehensible."

It happens that the incomprehensibility as well as the ineffability of God as to His essence is the common belief of the Fathers, and Gregory of Nyssa himself gives expression to it in his statement that God "cannot be grasped by any term, or by any thought, or by any other mode of comprehension."[29] In the light of this, is it not reasonable to assume that the term "nothing" which is applied by Gregory to God in the first part of his answer is used by him in the sense that there is "nothing" whereby God's essence can be comprehended and described? In fact, about four centuries later, John Scotus Erigena, whose open advocacy of the identification of *ex nihilo* with emanation is exactly like the view which I have tried to elicit from the implications of certain statements in Gregory of Nyssa, explains the term "nothing" in its application to God as being used by him in the sense of the incomprehensibility and the ineffability of God. And here is how Erigena arrives at this explanation.

He begins by stating that "nothing" (*nihil*) means "non-existence" (*non esse*).[30] This, as we have noted above, is the common meaning of "non-existence" (μὴ ὄν) as used by the Greek Fathers. But the fact that Erigena found it necessary to make that statement is significant. It alludes to the two meanings which

[29] *Contra Eunomium* (PG 45, 461 B).
[30] *De Divisione Naturae* III, 5 (PL 122, 634 B).

Aristotle assigns to "non-existence." One is that which he describes as being "non-existence accidentally" (τὸ οὐκ ὂν κατὰ συμβεβηκός), and this he applies to matter. The other is that which he describes as being "non-existence essentially" (καθ' αὑτήν), and this he applies to "privation" (στέρησις), which, in this connection, he uses in the sense of the absence of form,[31] in contrast to "privation" in the sense of "the forcible removal of anything,"[32] and it is with reference to what he considers here as essential non-existence that he says elsewhere that "non-existence" (τὸ μὴ ὄν) is "nothing" (μηδέν).[33] It is, therefore, "non-existence" in its essential sense and as applied by Aristotle to "privation" in the sense of the absence of form that Erigena has reference to in his statement that "nothing" means "non-existence."

He then goes on to show that the term "nothing," which, in his identification of the phrase "from nothing" with the phrase "from God," is applied to God, has the meaning of "privation" in the sense of the absence of form to which Aristotle applies essential non-existence or nothing. But, having in mind Aristotle's statement that "by form I mean the essence of each thing,"[34] he concludes his attempt to explain his use of the term "nothing" as a description of God by saying that that term, in its application to God, "means the privation of the total essence,"[35] that the expression "the privation of the total essence" means "the universal negation of relation, and essence or substance, or accident, and, in general, the negation of all that can be spoken of or thought of,"[36] and that such a "universal negation" is to be applied to God, for God "cannot be spoken of or thought of."[37]

It is by this use of the term "nothing" in the sense of "the negation of all that can be spoken of or thought of" that Gregory of Nyssa, we imagine, would explain his interpretation of the traditional description of creation as being "from nothing" to mean that it is "from God," for God, as it is commonly believed by the Fathers, is in His essence ineffable and incomprehensible.

[31] *Physics* I, 9, 192a, 3–5.
[32] *Metaphysics* V, 27, 1022b, 31.
[33] *De Generatione et Corruptione* I, 3, 318a, 15; cf. *Physics* I, 9, 192a, 5–6.
[34] *Metaphysics* VII, 7, 1032b, 1–2.
[35] *De Divisione Naturae* I, 3 (443 A).
[36] *Ibid.* III, 22 (686 CD).
[37] *Ibid.* I, 15 (463 B).

12

THE MEANING OF *EX NIHILO* IN THE CHURCH FATHERS, ARABIC AND HEBREW PHILOSOPHY, AND ST. THOMAS

WHATEVER the author of the Second Book of Maccabees (7:28) may have meant by the term "not existent" in his statement that God made the heaven and the earth "from things not existent (ἐξ οὐκ ὄντων)," it is clear that the Church Fathers understood it to mean not only a denial of Aristotle's theory of the eternity of the world but also a denial of Plato's theory of the creation of the world from a preëxistent eternal matter. The "not existent" from which the world was made is always explained by them to mean "nothing" and not "matter," and, if the world is made from matter, then matter itself is explained as having been created from "nothing."

With Plotinus, however, a new theory of the origin of the world appeared by the side of the older theories of Plato and Aristotle. The world was no longer conceived, with Plato, as being created from a preëxistent matter which was itself coeternal with God; nor was it conceived, with Aristotle, as being in its completeness coeternal with God; it was now conceived as being eternally generated or emanated from the essence of God. With the appearance of this new conception of the origin of the world the question was raised whether, with the elimination of the element of eternity from the Plotinian theory, the traditional belief in creation *ex nihilo* could not be interpreted to mean the temporal generation of the world from the essence of God.

To the Church Fathers, however, this conception of *ex nihilo* was unacceptable, for to them, quite independently of the view of Plotinus, a distinction was to be made between creation *ex nihilo* and generation from the essence of God, the former to be used with reference to the world and the latter with reference to the Word. Thus Hippolytus, evidently in opposition to the Basilidian Gnostics, distinguishes between the creation of the world from nothing (ἐξ οὐδενός) and the generation of the Word from the Father.[1] Thus also Alexander of Alexandria, arguing against Arius' doctrine of the creation of the Word *ex nihilo*, distinguishes between the world created by God "from things not existent (ἐξ οὐκ ὄντων)" and the Word generated "from the true Father himself."[2] Similarly Athanasius, again arguing against Arius and distinguishing between the world and the Word, says of the former that it was created "from things not existent (ἐξ οὐκ ὄντων)", whereas the latter is of "the essence of the Father."[3] So also John Damascene, evidently with reference to both Arius and Plotinus, distinguishes between the generation of the Word which is from "God's nature" and the creation of the world which is "from the not existent (ἐκ τοῦ μὴ ὄντος)."[4] This distinction is given expression to by St. Augustine, evidently also with reference to both Arius and Plotinus, in the following statements: "They were made from nothing by Thee, not of Thee,"[5] for, if they were made from Thyself, "then they would be equal to Thine Only-begotten, and thereby even to Thee."[6]

Still, in Christianity among those who came under the influence of Plotinus there appeared an attempt to interpret the creation of the world *ex nihilo* as meaning its creation from the essence of God. An inkling of that transformation of *ex nihilo* into *ex essentia Dei* is to be found in Dionysius the Areopagite. He thus speaks of God as one who "produces substances by an outgoing from essence,"[7] of "the birth of all things from God,"[8] and of all things as having gone forth from God.[9] The language is quite explicit. The world is created from the essence of God. But whether this view was presented by him as a new interpretation of the generally accepted theory of *ex nihilo* or whether it was presented by him as a new view in opposition to it is not clear.

The vagueness with which Dionysius has left us on this question is cleared up by his follower John Scotus Erigena. He makes it definitely clear that he takes the expression *ex nihilo* to mean from the essence of God. His reasoning on this subject falls into four stages. First, he tries to show that *nihil* in the traditional expression creation *ex nihilo* means "the privation of the total essence."[10] Second, he explains that by the phrase "the privation of the total essence" he means the "universal negation of all habitude, essence or substance, and accident, and, in general, the negation of all that can be spoken of or thought of."[11] Third, he maintains that such a "universal negation" applies only to God, inasmuch as only God is He who "cannot be spoken of or thought of."[12] Fourth, from all these premises he concludes that the expression "the world was created from nothing" means that the world was created from God:[13] the nothing from which the world was created means God to whom alone may be applied the negation of all that can be spoken of or thought of.

The identification of the religious doctrine of the creation of the world from nothing and Plotinus' doctrine of the emanation of the world from the essence of God is also to be found in Alfarabi. Plotinus' doctrine was known to Alfarabi through the Arabic epitome of the *Enneads*, which appeared under the title of *The Theology of Aristotle*.[14] Referring to the theory of emanation of that work, he says that "in that work it is made clear that God, be He exalted, has created matter from nothing."[15] Now nowhere in the *Theology of Aristotle*, at least in the part of it that has been published, is there any explicit statement that matter was created from nothing. The world, including its matter, is presented in that work as emanating from the essence of God. The fact that Alfarabi ascribes to that work the view that matter was created *ex nihilo* undoubtedly means that in his opinion creation *ex nihilo* meant the same as creation from the essence of God.

Another type of identification of the formula of creation from nothing with Plotinus' doctrine of emanation from the essence of God is to be found, even before Alfarabi, in the Kalam. In the Kalam, we are told by various doxographies, there was a controversy concerning the meaning of the term "not existent (*al-ma'dūm*)."[16] According to one group in the Kalam, the "not existent" is "nothing." According to another group, the "not existent" is "something," and that "something" is variously described as an "object of knowledge" or an "object of memory" or an "object of discourse" or a "substance."[17] The origin and nature of this controversy have been variously explained by students of Arabic philosophy, and there are at least five explanations; but the present writer in a paper published not long ago[18] has tried to show that the controversy had its origin in two different interpretations of the traditional formula for the origin of the world.

This traditional formula must have come to the Arabs from the Greek Church Fathers, among whom the phrase known to us through the Latin as *ex nihilo* was expressed by ἐκ τοῦ μὴ ὄντος, which literally means "from the not existent." Now the Greek τὸ μὴ ὄν, as well as its Arabic equivalent *al-ma'dūm*, as Arabic philosophers of that time could have known from Aristotle, has two meanings. On the one hand, it means "nothing," for, as says Aristotle, "the not existent (τὸ μὴ ὄν) is nothing (μηδέν)" and not a "something (τι)."[19] But, on the other hand, it means "matter," for, again, as says Aristotle, the Platonists who refer to matter as "the great and small" identify it with the not existent (τὸ μὴ ὄν).[20] Consequently, when the philosophers of the Kalam learned of the formula that the world was created from the not existent some of them took it in the sense of "nothing," while others took it in the sense of "matter" and therefore interpreted creation *ex nihilo* as meaning the Platonic theory of creation from a preëxistent matter.

But this latter group, while following Plato in their belief of the creation of the world from a preëxistent matter, describe that preëxistent matter as "something." Now the term "something" is not used by Plato as a description of matter. In Plotinus, however, matter (ὕλη) or the not existent (τὸ μὴ ὄν) is said to be "something" (τι).[21] We may therefore see here the influence of Plotinus. Moreover, this group of the Kalam describe that preëxistent matter also as "substance," as an "object of knowledge," as an "object of memory," and as an "object of discourse." Now, again, none of these terms is used by Plato as a description of his preëxistent matter. In Plotinus, however, the term "substance (οὐσία)" is used as a description of his intelligible matter (ὕλη νοητή),[22] that is to say, the idea of matter, and in Plato the ideas are described as being the object of knowledge (γνῶσις,[23] ἐπιστήμη)[24] and the object of memory or rather of thought (τὸ νοεῖν), inasmuch as "there will be forms of perishable things, for we can have an image of these,"[25] and as enabling us also to carry on a discussion (διαλέγεσθαι)[26]. From all this we may infer that under the influence of Plotinus this group of the Kalam have taken the preëxistent matter from which the world was created to be intelligible matter or the idea of matter. The formula creation *ex nihilo* is thus taken by this group of the Kalam to mean creation from an ideal matter, which ideal matter, we may add here, was further conceived by them to be the totality of ideal atoms.[27] Thus, according to this theory, the creation of the world "from the not existent" means its creation from the ideal matter; but, inasmuch as the ideal matter, under this theory, is an emanation from the essence of God, the creation of the world "from the not existent" means its emanation from the essence of God.

This difference of opinion among the two groups of the Kalam as to the meaning of the formula creation "from the not existent," whether it means from "nothing" or from "something," has created the need among those who believed that creation was from "nothing" to formulate their belief in such a way as to leave no doubt as to its meaning. Saadia, who deals with this problem, suggests that the proper formula is *lā min shai*, literally, "not from thing" and not *min lā shai*, literally, "from not thing."[28] What Saadia means by this puzzling statement is this: In Arabic there are no inseparable negation prefixes.

Consequently, when we have the negative particle *lā*, "not," in juxtaposition to the noun *shai*, "thing," the two words may be translated either by "nothing" or by "no-thing." Now, logically, according to Aristotle, the term "no-thing" is an indefinite or infinite term (ὄνομα ἀόριστον) and, according to his conception of indefinite or infinite propositions, the proposition "A is no-thing" does not mean that "A" by its very nature could not be any thing but "nothing." It only means that "A" which could be "something" happens to be "nothing."[29] Now a thing which could be something and happens to be nothing is not absolute nothing but only relative nothing, and such relative nothing is matter. By the same token, the proposition that "the world was created from no-thing" would mean that it was created from matter. In order, therefore, to avoid any misunderstanding, says Saadia, the formula should not be *min lā shai*, which might be taken to mean "from no-thing," but it should be *lā min shai*, which, meaning literally "not from thing," could not be misunderstood to mean "from no-thing."

Saadia's statement that the formula "not from a thing" is preferable to the formula "from not a thing," will explain why both Alfarabi[30] and Maimonides,[31] in restating the principle of creation *ex nihilo*, use the expression "not from a thing." Neither of them state the reason for their choice of that particular phrasing. Their reason undoubtedly was that given by Saadia.

Another expression used by Maimonides for *ex nihilo* is "after privation" or "after non-existence" (Arabic: *ba'd 'adam;* Hebrew: *aḥar ha-he'eder*).[32] The significance of the use of this expression as a substitute or explanation of the expression *ex nihilo* may be gathered from Aristotle's discussion of the expression "to come from something." This expression, according to Aristotle, may mean either "to come from something (ἐξ οὗ) as from matter"[33] or "to come after a thing (μεθ' ὅ) in time."[34] With this Aristotelian distinction in the use of the preposition "from" in mind, Maimonides seems to argue that the use of the preposition "from" in any formulation of the principle of creation *ex nihilo*, unless it be the formula "not from a thing" or unless the preposition "from" be taken in the sense of "after," would be inappropriate, inasmuch as "from" usually implies the coming of some thing *from* something as *from matter*. He therefore suggests that the formula for *ex nihilo*, however phrased, is to be understood to mean "after privation" or "after non-existence." The term "after" would of course have to be purged of any implication of time, inasmuch as time came into existence only with the creation of time.[35]

In the light of all this we may understand the full significance of St. Thomas' discussion of the expression *ex nihilo* used in the creation of the world. To begin with, he differentiates between the generation of the Son from the "substance of the Father"[36] or "from the essence of the Father,"[37] and the creation of the world "from nothing."[38] This is not only a repercussion of the patristic arguments against Arius but it is also meant to be in opposition to Erigena, whose view, as we have seen, is also the view of Alfarabi. But then he raises the question "whether to create is to make something from nothing."[39] What he means by this question is to point out that the formula "creation from nothing" involves a contradiction in terms. The preposition "from" (*ex*), he says, with evident reference to Aristotle's discussion of this preposition, quoted above, "imports relation of some cause, especially of the material cause, as when we say that a statue is made from bronze, whereas *nothing* cannot be the matter of being."[40] In justification, therefore, of the use of the expression *ex nihilo*, he resorts to the other use of the preposition "from" (*ex*) suggested by Aristotle, namely, that of "after" (*post*). The expression "created from nothing," he says, signifies "only order, as when we say, from morning comes midday, in other words, after morning is midday."[41] Accordingly, the expression "from nothing" means "after nonexistence (*post non esse*)." Here, again, the term "after" is to be understood to have no implication of priority of time, for time was created with the creation of the world. This explanation of St. Thomas' corresponds, as may be seen, to one of Maimonides' two formulations of the principle of *ex nihilo* quoted above, that which in the Latin translation of his work is rendered by *post privationem*.[42] St. Thomas' *post non esse* is Maimonides' *post privationem*, for *non esse* and *privatio* in these two statements mean the same thing and, in fact, the underlying Arabic term *ma'dum* in Maimonides' statement means both "privation" and "nonexistence."

But then St. Thomas proceeds to give another explanation of *ex nihilo*. The proposition "it is made from nothing (*fit ex nihilo*)," he says, may be also taken to mean "it is not made from anything (*non fit ex aliquo*)."[43] This quite evidently corresponds to the other of Maimonides' two formulations of *ex nihilo* quoted above, that which in the Latin translation of his work reads *non est de aliquo*.[44] And this Maimonidean formulation of the belief in creation *ex nihilo* follows, as we have seen, the formulation openly maintained by Saadia and tacitly used also by Alfarabi.

About a century after St. Thomas, the identification of the expression *ex nihilo* with the expression *de essentia Dei* was suggested by Hasdai Crescas. The occasion which had given rise to this identification by Crescas was his attempt to refute Gersonides' arguments against creation *ex nihilo*. In this attempt he starts with an analysis of the Plotinian theory of emanation. This theory, he argues, means that God, who is pure form, causes to come into existence something that is material and absolutely unlike the pure form from which it is supposed to be emanated. This, he further argues, means nothing but that the world came into existence "after privation," or rather "after nonexistence," without any preëxistent matter as its subject. Then he tries to show that the traditional belief in creation *ex nihilo* means nothing but that. In his attempt to establish this last point, he proceeds along the lines of Maimonides and St. Thomas, bringing into play the distinction made by Aristotle between the two meanings of the preposition *ex*, though, again, like Maimonides and St. Thomas, he makes no reference to Aristotle. The expression *ex nihilo*, he says, does not mean that the *nihil* is a subject from which the world came into existence in the same manner as the statue is said to come into existence from the bronze as its subject or its matter. The expression *ex nihilo* rather means that the world came into existence "after privation," or rather "after nonexistence," without any preëxistent matter as its subject. But this, concludes Crescas, is exactly what he has shown to be the meaning of emanation.[45] It must be remarked, however, that the object of Crescas' argument is not to reinstate in religious good standing the doctrine of emanation but rather to show that creation *ex nihilo* is not less rational a belief than the philosophic doctrine of emanation.

In conclusion, attention may be called to the use made by Spinoza of Crescas' identification of emanation from the essence of God with creation from nothing. Dealing with what may be identified as the theory of emanation, Spinoza argues to the effect that the emanation of a material substance from an immaterial substance is impossible on the ground that something cannot come from nothing.[46] The implication is that emanation from the essence of God is taken by him to mean the same as creation from nothing.

1. *Refutatio Omnium Haeresium* x, 33, p. 290, ll. 7-8 (ed. P. Wendland). Cf. vii, 21ff.
2. *Epist.* i, 11 (Migne PG, 18, 564 C).
3. *Orat.* i, 29 (PG, 26, 72 C).
4. *De Fide Orth.* i, 8 (PG, 94, 812 Bf.)
5. *Conf.* xiii, 33, 48.
6. *Ibid.*, xii, 7, 7.
7. *De Divinis Nominibus* v, 8 (PG, 3, 824 C).
8. *Ibid.*, ix, 9 (916 C-D).
9. *Ibid.* (916 D).
10. *De Divis. Nat.* iii, 5 (Migne PL, 122, 634 C-D).
11. *Ibid.*, iii, 22 (686 C).
12. *Ibid.* i, 15 (463 B).
13. *Ibid.*, iii, 22 (686 A-688 A). Cf. H. Bett, *Johannes Scotus Erigena* (1925), pp. 34-36.
14. Fr. Dieterici, *Die sogenannte Theologie des Aristotles*, Arabic, 1882; German, 1883.
15. *Kitāb al-Jam'*, ed. F. Dieterici in *Alfārābi's philosophische Abhandlungen*, 1890, p. 23, ll. 15-16; German translation, p. 37, ll. 27-29.
16. The Arabic term *'adam*, which literally means privation (*στέρησις*), is also used technically in the sense of nonexistence (*μὴ ὄν*).
17. Baghdadi, Cairo, 1910, p. 163, l. 17—p. 164, l. 14.
18. "The Kalam Problem of Non-existence and Saadia's Second Theory of Creation," *Jewish Quarterly Review*, n. s., XXXVI (1946), 371-391.
19. *De Gen. et Corr.* i, 3, 318a, 15.
20. *Phys.*, i, 9, 192a, 6-7.

21. *Enneads* ii, 4, 16.

22. *Ibid.*, ii, 4, 5.

23. *Cratylus* 440 B.

24. *Metaph.* i, 9, 990b, 11-12.

25. *Ibid.*, 14-15.

26. *Parmenides* 135 C.

27. Cf. above n. 18; and "Atomism in Saadia," *J. Q. R.*, n. s., XXXVII (1946), 107-124.

28. Cf. *Commentaire sur le Séfer Yesira par le Gaon Saadya de Fayyoum*, par M. Lambert (1891). Arabic, p. 84, ll. 3-6; French, p. 106, and "The Kalam Problem," pp. 387f.

29. *De Interpr.*, c. 12, 16a, 32. Cf. my paper "Infinite and Privative Judgments in Aristotle, Averroes, and Kant," *Philosophy and Phenomenological Research*, VIII (1947), 173-186.

30. Alfarabi, *loc. cit.*

31. Maimonides, *Moreh Nebukim* ii, 13, Second Theory.

32. *Ibid.*

33. *Metaph.* v, 24, 1023a, 26.

34. *Ibid.*, 1023b, 6.

35. Cf. Maimonides, *Moreh Nebukim* ii, 30.

36. *Sum. Theol.* i, 41, 3c.

37. *Ibid.*, ad 2.

38. *Ibid.*, c.

39. *Ibid.*, i, 45, 1.

40. *Ibid.*, ad 3, The illustration of a statue and bronze occurs in Aristotle (1023a, 29).

41. *Ibid.*, The illustration used by Aristotle is "night comes from day" (1023b, 6).

42. *Rabi Mosei Aegyptij Dux seu Director dubitantium aut perplexorum* (Paris, 1520), lib. ii, cap. xiv, fol. 47a, l. 18.

43. *Sum. Theol.* i, 45, 1, ad. 3.

44. *Loc. cit.*

45. *Or Adonai* iii, i, 5, p. 69a, ll. 4-18 (ed. Vienna, 1859).

46. Cf. my discussion in *The Philosophy of Spinoza* (1934), I, 95, 107, in connection with quotations from *Ethics* i. prop. 6, *Short Treatise* i. 2, and *Epistola* iv.

13

THE MEANING OF *EX NIHILO* IN ISAAC ISRAELI*

In his *Book on the Elements*, Isaac Israeli distinguishes between three kinds of "generation" (*generatio, mithavveh*), one of which, said by him to be peculiar to the action of God, he describes as "creational" (*creabilis, ʿal derek ha-yeṣirah*).[1] This creational generation is described by him as the generation of a thing "from nothing" (*ex nihilo, me-ayin*)[2] or "not from another thing" (*non ex alio, mi-lo dabar*)[3] or "from privation" (*ex privatione, me-ha-heʿder*)[4] or "from the non-existent" (*ex non existente, mi-lo meṣi'ut*).[5] With regard to "privation", Israeli adds that "privation (*privatio, heʿder*) is not something existing in the imagination

* Works of Israeli referred to are:

1. *Sefer ha-Yesodot*, ed. S. Fried, 1900.
2. *Kitāb al-Ḥudūd wa'l-Rusūm*, ed. H. Hirschfeld, *JQR*, 15 (1902–3), 689–93. *Sefer ha-Gebulim*, ed. H. Hirschfeld, *Festschrift zum achtzigsten Geburtstage Moritz Steinschneider's*, 1896, pp. 131–42. Latin of both of these in *Omnia Opera Ysaac*, 1515, *Liber de Elementis*, fols. iv c–x d; *Liber Definitionum*, fols. ii a–iv c.
3. *Sefer ha-Ruaḥ ve-ha-Nefesh*, ed. M. Steinschneider, *Ha-Karmel*, 1 (1871–2), 400–5.
4. *Kitāb al-Jawāhir*, ed. S. M. Stern, *Journal of Jewish Studies*, 6 (1955), 135–45; 7 (1956), 13–29.

English of 2, 3, 4 and an excerpt from 1 in A. Altmann and S. M. Stern, *Isaac Israeli*, 1958.

[1] *Opera*, p. iv d, l. 6; *Yesodot*, p. 8, ll. 1–2; p. 69, l. 22.

[2] *Opera*, p. iv d, l. 7; *Yesodot*, p. 8, ll. 2–3.

[3] *Opera*, p. ix b, l. 14; *Yesodot*, p. 57, l. 5. On the basis of the Latin *non ex alio*, the Arabic read: *lā min shay'in*, and hence the Hebrew should be *lo mi-dabar* and not *mi-lo dabar*. On the difference between these two expressions, see my paper "The Kalam Problem of Non-existence and Saadia's Second Theory of Creation", *JQR*, N.S., 36 (1945–6), 387–91.

[4] *Opera*, p. x b, ll. 26–27; *Yesodot*, p. 69, l. 22.

[5] *Opera*, p. x b, l. 27; *Yesodot*, p. 69, ll. 22–23.

(*in mente*, *be-maḥshabah*) prior to the generation of the things generated from it".[6]

This creation, which he describes as being from nothing, is applied by him to two things: (1) the elements; (2) the soul. But in his description of them as being created *ex nihilo* he uses a language which does not make clear whether he meant that they were created *ex nihilo* in the accepted sense of the expression or whether he meant that they were created out of God himself. With respect to the creation of the four elements, he says: "You will find nothing that preceded them, from which they could have been generated, except the power of God"[7] or that "they were not generated from anything that preceded them, except the power of their Creator".[8] With regard to the creation of the soul, he says: "The soul is not generated from the elements but from the power and might."[9] In all these three passages it is not clear whether he means to say that only the power of the Creator preceded the elements and the soul, and it was that power which created them out of nothing, or whether he means to say that the elements and the soul were created from the power of the Creator, which alone preceded them. In the latter case, the creation of the elements and the soul would be by way of emanation, for, as we shall see later,[10] the expression "created from the will" or "from the power" of God is an expression which is used to describe the process of emanation. With regard to all other things which come into being in the world, Israeli describes them as coming into being in three ways: (1) some of them by "natural generation"; (2) others by "artificial generation"; (3) living things are generated "by way of birth" (*secundum semitam nativitatis*, *'al derek ha-toladah*).[11]

[6] *Opera*, p. x b, ll. 27–28; *Yesodot*, p. 69, ll. 23–24.

[7] *Opera*, p. iv c, ll. 66–67; *Yesodot*, p. 7, ll. 7–8.

[8] *Opera*, p. iv d, ll. 49–50; *Yesodot*, p. 10, ll. 4–5.

[9] *Yesodot*, p. 68, l. 15; *Opera*, p. x a, ll. 66–67: "immo ex creatione et novatione".

[10] Cf. below, at nn. 40–42.

[11] *Opera*, p. iv d, ll. 5–31; *Yesodot*, p. 8, l. 2–p. 9, l. 2.

As in his *Book on the Elements* so also in his *Book of Definitions* Israeli speaks of creation *ex nihilo*. The definition of the Arabic terms *al-ibdāʿ wa'l-iḫtirāʿ* (*conditio et creatio*, *beri'ah viṣirah*), he says, is "the bringing into existence of things existent out of non-existence (*min lays*, *ex non esse*, *me-ayin*)". He then adds:

Perchance one may think that non-existence (*al-lays*, *non esse*, *ayin*) is privation (*al-ʿadam*, *privatio*, *ha-hefḳed*), so we shall let him know this is wrong, and why. Privation takes place only after existence (*wujūd*, *inventio*, *meṣi'ah*). Thus, if a thing exists, and then ceases to exist (*yuʿdam*, *privatur*, *nifḳad*), it is said that such a thing is deprived (*ʿudim*, *privatum*, *nifḳad*), as, for instance, if a man has his sight and then loses it, it is said that he is deprived of his sight. Similarly of everything that exists and is then deprived of existence it is said that such and such a thing is deprived. But no one can say that non-existence (*al-lays*, *non esse*, *ayin*) is deprived, for the non-existent (*al-lays*, *non ens*, [*ayin*]) has no form in the imagination (*al-wahm*, *in mente*, *raʿ-yon*) so as to be described by existence or privation (*wujūd au ʿadam*, *privatum aut mutatum* [= *ʿadam au taghayyur*], *meṣi'ah o hefḳed*).[12]

The extant Arabic text of this passage supplies the missing Arabic vocabulary of the passages we have quoted from the Latin and Hebrew translations of the *Book on the Elements*. Underlying the Latin *creabilis* and the Hebrew *ʿal derek ha-yeṣirah* is the Arabic *ʿalā sabīl al-iḫtirāʿi*, underlying the Latin *nihil* and the Hebrew *ayin* is the Arabic *lays* (*non esse*, *ayin*), and underlying the Latin *privatio* and the Hebrew *heʿder* is the Arabic *ʿadam* (*privatio*, *hefḳed*). But here a difficulty crops up. In the *Book of Definitions*, the terms *lays* and *ʿadam* are definitely said not to be the same, whereas in the *Book on the Elements* they are assumed to be the same, seeing that *ex nihilo* or *me-ayin* is said there to be the same as *ex privatione* or *me-ha-heʿder* and also that *privatio* or *heʿder*, like *lays* in the *Book of Definitions*, is said there not to exist in the imagination. Undoubtedly, therefore,

[12] *Ḥudūd*, p. 693, ll. 5–11; *Opera*, p. iv a, l. 66–p. iv b, l. 6; *Gebulim*, p. 140, ll. 29–34.

there must be some difference of meaning in which either one of these two terms is used by Israeli in these two works of his to account for the apparent contradiction between his two statements. What is that difference of meaning?

The difference of meaning, it may be suggested, is to be found in the use of the Arabic term *ʿadam*. This term is used as a translation of two Greek terms, *μὴ ὄν* and *στέρησις*,[13] each of which is used in two senses. The term *μὴ ὄν* in one of its senses means "nothing" (*μηδέν*)[14] and the term *στέρησις* in one of its senses means "the violent taking away of anything",[15] that is, being deprived of something.[16] We may, therefore, assume that in the two passages, which seem to be contradictory to each other, Israeli uses the term *ʿadam* as the equivalent of these two different Greek terms. In the *Book on the Elements* he uses *ʿadam* as the equivalent of *μὴ ὄν* in the sense of "nothing", and hence he says that it means the same as *lays*, "nothing". In the *Book of Definitions*, however, he uses it, as may be gathered from the context, as the equivalent of *στέρησις* in the sense of "deprivation", and hence he says that it is not the same as *lays*, "nothing".

But then in the *Book of Definitions* there is an outline of the process of creation. The first created being, evidently the one which he would describe as created *ex nihilo*, is, according to this book, "the intellect" (*intelligentia, ha-deʿah*), called also "the upper soul" (*anima alta, ha-nefesh ha-ʿelyonit*).[17] It is described as "the splendor (*splendor, or*) created from the power (*ex virtute, me-ʿoz*) of the Creator without an intermediary"[18] and as "the first substance created from the power (*ex virtute, me-ʿoz*)

[13] Cf. Index D, a, in M. Bouyges' edition of *Averroes: Tafsir ma baʿd aṭ-ṭabiʿat*, s.v. *ʿadam*.

[14] *De Gen. et Corr.* i. 3, 318a, 15.

[15] *Metaph.* v. 22, 1022b, 31–37; cf. ix. 1, 1046a, 34–35.

[16] Cf. my *Crescas' Critique of Aristotle*, pp. 683, 694, 695.

[17] *Opera*, p. ii b, l. 48; *Gebulim*, p. 133, ll. 1–2.

[18] *Opera*, p. ii b, ll. 50–51; *Gebulim*, p. 133, l. 3.

of the Creator without an intermediary",[19] or as "the truly first genus which is created from the power (*ex virtute, me-'oz*) of the Creator without an intermediary".[20] In these passages, quite evidently, the Arabic underlying the Latin *ex virtute* and the Hebrew *me-'oz* was *min ḳudratin*. The question, therefore, is here, again, whether the Arabic *min* should be taken in its literal sense of "from", thus designating the source out of which the intellect was created, or whether it should be taken in the sense of "by", thus indicating the agent by whom it was created. In the former case the creation would be by way of emanation; in the latter case it could be by way of creation *ex nihilo*. The plausibility of the former interpretation recommends itself here by reason of the fact that the creation of all other beings below the intellect is definitely said by Israeli to be by way of emanation. These other beings are, in their descending order of succession: the rational soul, the animal soul, the vegetative soul, and the celestial sphere. Now, in these successive beings, each of the lower ones is described as being "generated from the shadow of the one above it",[21] which means by a process of emanation. Similarly with regard to the four elements, though there is no definite statement that they are generated from the shadow of the sphere, it may be assumed that as in all theories of emanation current in Arabic philosophy they came into being by a process of emanation. Corroborative evidence for this is to be found in Israeli's *Book on Spirit and Soul*, where the procession of things one from another, which begins with the intellect, continues through the rational soul, the animal soul, the vegetative soul, the sphere, and the four elements.[22]

Here, then, we have in Israeli an intermingling of two theories

[19] *Opera*, p. ii c, ll. 27–28; *Gebulim*, p. 133, ll. 29–30.

[20] *Opera*, p. ii c, l. 42; *Gebulim*, p. 134, ll. 2–4.

[21] *Opera*, p. iii a, ll. 56–57, 61–64; p. iii b, ll. 10–13, 24–25; *Gebulim*, p. 136, ll. 30–31, 35; p. 137, ll. 8–9, 12–13.

[22] *Sefer ha-Ruaḥ ve-ha-Nefesh*, pp. 403–4.

of creation. On the one hand, both in the *Book on the Elements* and in the *Book of Definitions* he describes the first act of creation as a creation *ex nihilo*. But, on the other hand, when he comes to describe the first things created, he uses a language which by its common usage would be taken to mean emanation. Moreover, in the *Book of Definitions* as well as in the *Book on Spirit and Soul* the process of coming-into-being after the intellect and through the elements is definitely a process of emanation.

In the history of the interpretation of the philosophy of Isaac Israeli there were two types of explanation.

Neumark admits that the *Book of Definitions* contains a theory of emanation. But he dismisses this work as not representing Israeli's own philosophy. The philosophy which is Israeli's own is to be found only in his *Book on the Elements*. As for this book, he sees in it only the teaching of a doctrine of creation *ex nihilo*. He seems to have noticed no vagueness in the three passages which we have characterized as vague. He paraphrases them to read that they "came into existence out of nonexistence by the creative power of God",[23] thus taking the "power" as the agent of the creation and not as its source. Contrarily, Jakob Guttmann follows the *Book of Definitions* and the *Book on Spirit and Soul* and attributes to Israeli a theory of emanation, including the emanation of the intellect from the power of the Creator.[24] As for Israeli's definition of *al-ibdāʿ wa'l-iḫtirāʿ* as creation *ex nihilo*, which was quite evidently meant by him to be applied to the first act of creation, Jakob Guttmann says that the phrase creation *ex nihilo* only means a denial of an ideal pattern, like that assumed by Plato, in the likeness of which God created the world.[25] Husik

[23] Neumark, *Geschichte der jüdischen Philosophie des Mittelalters*, i. 1 (1907), p. 416; *Toledot ha-Pilosofiah be-Yisra'el*, ii (1929), 90 and 97.

[24] *Die philosophischen Lehren des Isaak ben Salomon Israeli* (1911), pp. 30 ff.

[25] *Ibid.*, p. 33, n. 1, referring to *Yesodot*, p. 57, [l. 5]; *Elementa*, fol. ix b, [ll. 14–15].

similarly describes Israeli's theory of creation as "the Neo-Platonic scheme of emanation as we saw it in Plotinus"; subsequently, however, he adds that "creation in Israeli seems to mean the same as emanation".[26] Julius Guttmann endorses the view of his father in its main contention that "with the concept of creation [*ex nihilo*] he combines the concept of emanation of Neoplatonism".[27] Vajda takes note of Israeli's combination of the traditional theory of creation *ex nihilo* with the theory of emanation and remarks that "the combination of the idea of creation with the theory of emanation is left unaccounted for".[28]

Since the study of Israeli by Vajda in 1947, fragments of Israeli's lost work, the *Book of Substances*, have been discovered. This work begins with the general statement that "the first created things (*al-muḫtarʿāt*)",[29] that is, "first" in the sense of precedence "by nature",[30] are "two simple substances", namely, matter and form, out of which the intellect is composed.[31] This intellect, which is composed of the two first created substances that are prior to it only by nature, is itself then described as "the most noble of all substances . . . and the one nearest to [creation expressed by the Arabic terms] *al-ibdāʿ wa'l-iḫtirāʿ* and most particularly affected by action, without an intermediary, of the power and the will"[32] and as "the emanation (*inbiʿath*) of the light which is created (*al-muḫtarāʿ*) from (*min*) the power and the will"[33] or as "the emanation of the light from the power and the will"[34] or as "the light which emanates from the power and the will without shade and dimness".[35]

Here, then, as in the *Book of Definitions*, the intellect is, on the one hand, described by the Arabic terms for creation (*ibdāʿ*;

[26] Husik, *A History of Mediaeval Jewish Philosophy* (1916), pp. 6 and 13.
[27] Julius Guttmann, *Die Philosophie des Judentums* (1933), p. 99.
[28] Vajda, *Introduction à la pensée juive du moyen âge* (1947), p. 67.
[29] *Kitāb al-Jawāhir*, frg. iv, fol. 4 v.
[30] *Ibid.*, fol. 8 r.
[31] *Ibid.*, fol. 4 v, fol. 8 r.
[32] *Ibid.*, fol. 5 r.
[33] *Ibid.*, fol. 8 r.
[34] *Ibid.*, fol. 8 v.
[35] *Ibid.*, fol. 9 r.

iḫtirāʿ), which Israeli uses technically for creation *ex nihilo*, and, on the other hand, this creation *ex nihilo* is qualified by a phrase in which the Arabic preposition *min* may mean either "from", thus indicating the source of the creation and hence the process may mean emanation, or "by", thus indicating the agent of the creation and hence the process may mean creation *ex nihilo* in its accepted sense. Moreover, the same act which is described as a creation is also described as an emanation.

Then, again, as in the *Book of Definitions*, the process of coming-into-being after the intellect is definitely a process of emanation. In this succession of beings, each of the lower ones is described in terms which mean that it is an emanation from the one above it.[36]

Altmann, in his thorough and sound study of the philosophy of Israeli, has, on the basis of his analysis of the newly discovered fragment of the *Book of Substances*, arrived at the conclusion that the first two substances which constitute the intellect "are created *ex nihilo* by the power and will of God", and that only the "spiritual substances", that is, the rational, animal, and vegetative souls and the sphere, "come into being by way of emanation".[37] He bases his view on the fact that the term "created" which Israeli applies to the first two substances constituting the intellect is that which Israeli has defined as creation *ex nihilo*. As for the qualifying expression "from (*min*) power and will", he takes it, as did Neumark, to mean "by power and will". And as for the statement that the first light "emanates from the power and will", he dismisses it as "a phrase which must be taken *cum grano salis*". In support of all this, he quotes a passage in which a contrast is drawn between the coming-into-being of the intellect and the coming-into-being of the substances below the intellect.[38] The contrast, which is described

[36] *Kitāb al-Jawāhir*, frg. iv, fols. 9 v–10 v.

[37] *Isaac Israeli*, p. 172.

[38] *Ibid.*, p. 171.

by Israeli as one "between an influencing and acting thing and a substantial and essential thing", reads as follows: "The light of wisdom is brought into being from (*min*) the power and the will by way of influence and action, while the light which emanates from the intellect is essential and substantial, like the light and shining of the sun, which emanates from its essence and substantiality."[39] This contrast is taken by Altmann to be a contrast between creation *ex nihilo* and emanation.

Let us take up first the interpretation of the qualifying phrase as meaning "by the power and will". Grammatically, it is to be admitted, the Arabic preposition *min* may be taken to mean "by", but this does not necessarily mean that it must be taken to mean "by" and that hence it is not to be taken to mean emanation. A phrase exactly like that is used by Solomon ibn Gabirol as a description of emanation. Thus, after declaring that "will" (*voluntas*) is identical with "power" (*virtus*),[40] he says that "from it (*ex ea*) is the existence of all things and their constitution"[41] and that "the existence of matter and form is from will (*ex voluntate*)".[42]

Then let us take up the passage in which Israeli is supposed to draw a contrast between creation *ex nihilo* and emanation. The contrast in this passage, it can be shown, is not necessarily a contrast between creation *ex nihilo* and emanation. It may be a contrast between two kinds of emanation, one an emanation immediately from God, which follows directly from the will and power, and the other an emanation from intermediaries, which on the part of those intermediaries is an unconscious act, like the shining of the sun. Such a contrast between two kinds of emanation is known in Arabic philosophy. Those in Arabic philosophy who interpreted Aristotle in terms of emanation

[39] *Kitāb al-Jawāhir*, frg. iii, fol. 3 v.

[40] *Fons Vitae*, v. 39, p. 327, ll. 14–15 (ed. Clemens Baeumker).

[41] *Ibid.*, ll. 16–17.

[42] *Ibid.*, ll. 20–21.

took pains to show that emanation as conceived by Aristotle was not an unconscious, mechanical act on the part of God, like "light emanating from the sun"[43]—the very same analogy used here by Israeli. Though not all of them went so far as to say that Aristotle's kind of emanation, by contrast, was an act of will on the part of God, some did say so. Moreover, the implication of Israeli's statements that the difference between the emanation of the light of wisdom from the power and will and the emanation of the other substances from the power and will consists in the fact that the former is "without an intermediary", while the latter is through an intermediary, corresponds to Ibn Gabirol's statement that "will acts without . . . a means (*sine instrumento*) . . . whereas the intelligible substances act in the opposite manner".[44]

There is thus no clear evidence in the *Book on Substances* that Israeli taught a concept of creation *ex nihilo* in contrast to a concept of emanation. What we have in this work is the same as what we have met with in his other works, a concept of creation described both in terms of *ex nihilo* and in terms of emanation, which unmistakably points to an identification of *ex nihilo* with emanation.

Such an identification of creation *ex nihilo* with emanation is not unknown in the history of philosophy. In Christianity, John Scotus Erigena describes his own theory of emanation as creation *ex nihilo*, and this was probably also the view of Dionysius the Areopagite.[45] In Islam, Alfarabi identifies creation *ex nihilo* with emanation.[46] Similarly Ibn Miskawaih,[47] after outlining

43 *Tahāfut al-Falāsifah*, iii, §§ 3–4, p. 96, l. 10–p. 97, l. 13, and *Tahāfut al-Tahāfut*, iii, §§ 7–9, p. 150, l. 6–p. 151, l. 11; *Moreh Nebukim*, ii. 20; and cf. my paper, "Hallevi and Maimonides on Design, Chance, and Necessity", *Proceedings of the American Academy for Jewish Research*, 11 (1941), 107–8.

44 *Fons Vitae*, iii. 16, p. 113, ll. 21–23; cf. *Keter Malkut*, ix, l. 99 (ed. Israel Davidson).

45 See below, n. 55, paper numbered (2).

46 See below, n. 55, papers numbered (2) and (3).

47 *Al-Fauz al-Aṣghar*, Beirut, A.H. 1319; English by J. W. Sweetman,

in detail a process of emanation,[48] describes that process as a creation "not from a thing" (*lā min shay'in*)[49] or a creation "from non-existence" (*min al-'adamin*).[50] In Judaism, as Graetz has shown, there is a tacit identification of creation *ex nihilo* and emanation in *Sefer Yeṣirah*.[51] A similar identification, as Scholem has shown, occurs in the works of later Cabalists.[52] Solomon ibn Gabirol quite definitely identifies the two, for creation is described by him in *Keter Malkut* as being "from nothing" (*min ha-ayin*),[53] and still, in his *Fons Vitae*, he says: "The creation of things by the Creator, that is, the going out (*exitus*) of forms from the prime source, that is, from the will (*voluntate*) . . . is like the going out (*exitus*) of water emanating (*emanantis*) from its source."[54] And Crescas openly argues for the identification of *ex nihilo* with emanation.[55]

In the light of all this, there is no need of attributing to Israeli an unheard-of hybrid theory—creation *ex nihilo* of the two first substances constituting the intellect and emanation of the spiritual substances below the intellect. The multiplication of theories is to be avoided just as much as the multiplication of hypotheses. Israeli presents no special problem; he is only another one of those who identified *ex nihilo* with emanation.

Islam and Christian Theology, I. i, pp. 93 ff.

48 *Ibid.*, i. 9, p. 28, l. 1–p. 30, l. 10.

49 *Ibid.*, i. 10, p. 30, l. 12.

50 *Ibid.*, p. 32, ll. 6–8.

51 Hirsch (= Heinrich) Graetz, *Gnosticismus und Judenthum* (1846), pp. 111–12, 117, 124–5.

52 G. Scholem, *Major Trends in Jewish Mysticism* (1941), pp. 25–26, 213–14, and nn. 40–41 on p. 394.

53 *Keter Malkut*, ix, l. 97.

54 *Fons Vitae*, v. 41, p. 330, ll. 17–20.

55 First briefly suggested (1) in my paper "The Problem of the Origin of Matter in Mediaeval Jewish Philosophy and Its Analogy in the Modern Problem of the Origin of Life", *Proceedings of the Sixth International Congress of Philosophy*, 1926, p. 606; then more fully discussed in my papers (2) "The Meaning of *ex nihilo* in the Church Fathers, Arabic and Hebrew Philosophy, and St. Thomas", *Mediaeval Studies in Honor of J. D. M. Ford* (1948), pp. 355–69 (above, pages 207–221), and (3) "Aṣilut ve-Yesh me-Ayin," *Sefer Asaf* (1953), pp. 230–6.

In all such identification, the expression creation *ex nihilo* is taken to be a denial that creation was of anything outside of God, primarily a denial that creation was out of a pre-existent eternal matter.[56] What we have here in Israeli is a theory of a volitional and presumably also non-eternal process of emanation in which the first emanated being is described as having been created *ex nihilo* on the ground that it was not created from a pre-existent eternal matter or in the likeness of pre-existent eternal ideal pattern. So also, conversely, both Maimonides and Thomas Aquinas apply the term emanation (*fayḍ*, *shefaʿ*, *emanatio*), used by each of them in a special sense,[57] to their own theory of creation *ex nihilo*,[58] which they directly oppose to the Neoplatonized version of Aristotle's theory of eternity[59] known as the theory of emanation (*fayḍ*, *aṣilut*)[60] in its usual sense of an eternal process.

[56] Even Israeli uses the expression *ex nihilo* not only as a denial of Platonic ideas (cf. above, n. 25) but also as a denial of the Platonic pre-existent eternal matter. See *Opera*, fol. ix b, l. 14: *non ex alio*; *Yesodot*, p. 57, l. 5: *mi-lo dabar*.

[57] *Moreh Nebukim*, ii. 12; i. 69; *In II Sent*. 18, 1, 2 c.

[58] *Moreh Nebukim*, ii. 13, First Theory; *Summ. Theol*. i. 45, 1 c.

[59] *Moreh Nebukim*, ii. 22; *Cont. Gent*. ii. 21, ad *Per hoc*; *Summ. Theol*. i. 45, 5 c.

[60] Avicenna, *Najāt* (Cairo, A.H. 1331), p. 450, l. 8; Judah ha-Levi, *Cuzari*, i. 1 (ed. Hirschfeld, p. 4, l. 10; p. 5, l. 9); iv. 25 (p. 282, l. 3; p. 283, l. 6).

14

The Platonic, Aristotelian and Stoic Theories of Creation in Hallevi and Maimonides

SPEAKING of the story of creation in Scripture, Philo says that in relating it Moses only wished to establish certain "two most essential principles."[1] This view that the story of creation was not meant to lay down a particular theory with regard to the origin of the world, but rather to establish certain essential principles with regard to God's relation to the world and His governance of it, is characteristic of all religious philosophers, whether Jewish, Christian, or Moslem, who after the example of Philo tried to harmonise Scripture and philosophy. This is true also of Judah Hallevi and Moses Maimonides. Despite the difference between them on the general problem of the relation of faith to reason, they both believe that the story of creation was meant only to establish certain essential principles and it is in the light of these principles, and not in accordance with the wording of the story, that they examine the various philosophic theories as to the origin of the world.

Both Hallevi and Maimonides examine three philosophic theories as to the origin of the world, besides creation *ex nihilo*, which is the Jewish doctrine.[2] The three theories which they examine are the following: (i) the creation of the world out of a pre-existent matter, which Hallevi reproduces anonymously[3] and Maimonides repro-

[1] *De Vita Mosis*, ii, 8, 48.
[2] II Macc., vii, 28.
[3] Cf. below, n. 20.

duces in the name of Plato;[4] (ii) the creation and destruction of one world after another, which Aristotle attributes to Empedocles and Heraclitus,[5] and Philo attributes to the Stoics,[6] but which both Hallevi and Maimonides reproduce anonymously;[7] (iii) the eternity of the world, which Hallevi reproduces allusively in the name of "the Philosopher"[8] and Maimonides reproduces directly in the name of Aristotle.[9] With regard to this Aristotelian theory, it may be also observed, both Hallevi and Maimonides are followers of the early Arabic Aristotelians, like Alfarabi and Avicenna, who understood Aristotle's conception of the eternity of the world not in the sense of a world which existed from eternity by the side of God, but rather in the sense of a world which emanated from God eternally.[10] Strictly speaking, this conception of the eternity of the world is more correctly to be described as the eternal generation of the world.

Though both Hallevi and Maimonides believe in creation *ex nihilo,* they admit that such a belief cannot be established by reason. Neither of them agrees with the Kalam, whether the Moslem or the Jewish Kalam,[11] in believing that creation *ex nihilo* can be established definitely by demonstrative reasoning. Hallevi openly declares that "the question of eternity and creation is baffling and the arguments on both sides are evenly balanced."[12] From the context of his discussion it is quite clear that what he refers to here is not the question whether the world came into being by a cause or without a cause but rather the question whether the world, having came into being by a cause, was generated eternally or was generated after it had been in a state of non-existence. Similarly when his spokesman,

4 Cf. below, n. 21.

5 Cf. below, n. 49.

6 Cf. below, n. 40.

7 Cf. below, nn. 39, 48, 53.

8 *Cuzari*, i, 65; cf. i, 62; i, 1.

9 *Moreh Nebukim*, ii, 13 (2).

10 *Cuzari*, i, 1; iv, 25 end; *Moreh Nebukim*, ii, 22.

11 *Moreh Nebukim*, i, 71: "This is the method of every follower of the Kalam among the Moslems on every question of this kind, and similarly of those of our own co-religionists who imitate them." Cf. Saadia, *Emunot we-De'ot*, i, 1.

12 *Cuzari*, i, 67; cf. i, 65.

the Rabbi, at the urgings of the King of the Chazars,[13] is persuaded to reproduce the Kalam stock arguments for creation,[14] he makes it quite clear that he does not subscribe to these arguments and characterises them as being, like all the arguments of the Kalam on other subjects, rather useless and a mere dialectical exercise.[15] More directly Maimonides declares that the creation of the world *ex nihilo* can no more be established by a " decisive demonstration " than the eternity of the world,[16] but, unlike Hallevi, he believes that the former, even on mere speculative grounds, is more probable than the latter.[17] More fully, too, Maimonides goes into a detailed refutation of the Kalam stock arguments for creation *ex nihilo*.[18] Similarly Averroes, who was a contemporary of Maimonides, maintains that the creation of the world, that is to say, creation *ex nihilo*, cannot be demonstrated by reason.[19]

Both Hallevi and Maimonides agree that the Platonic theory of the creation of the world out of a pre-existent matter is compatible with the Scriptural story of creation. Hallevi expresses this view briefly in the statement that " if a believer in the Law finds himself compelled to admit and acknowledge an eternal matter . . . this would not impair his belief that *this* world was created at some particular time, and that Adam and Noah were the first human beings."[20] Maimonides not only says that the Platonic view would

13 *ibid.*, v, 17.

14 *ibid.*, v, 18 (1–3).

15 *ibid.*, v, 16.

16 *Moreh Nebukim*, i, 71.

17 *ibid.*, ii, 18 end; ii, 22, end.

18 *ibid.*, i, 74.

19 *Tahafut al-Tahafut*, i, §175 (ed. M. Bouyges); Latin: *Destructio Destructionum*, i, 33 H (in *Aristotelis opera*, Venice, 1574, vol. ix): " Et rediit quaestio utrum sit possibile, ut sit mundus antiquus, et aeternus, aut innovatus . . . Et non numeratur haec quaestio inter intellectuales." Also viii, §10; Latin: p. 99 GH: " Quod vero existimat secta Assaria quod natura possibilis sit innovata, et creata a nihilo, est id, in quo certant cum eis Philosophi . . . et non constuitur de eo demonstratio."

20 *Cuzari*, i, 67. See discussion of this passage by Kaufmann, " Jehuda Halewi und die Lehre von der Ewigkeit der Welt," *Monatsschrift für Geschichte und Wissenschaft des Judenthums*, 1884, xxxiii, pp. 208–214; and Hirschfeld, " Bemerkung zu S. 208–214," *ibid.*, p. 374–78.

not be " in opposition to the fundamental principles of our religion " but also adds that " many expressions might be found in the Bible and other writings that would confirm and support this theory,"[21] though, for himself, he rejects it as an erroneous view.[22]

Now with regard to those who, following Plato, adopt his theory of a pre-existent matter as their interpretation of the Scriptural story of creation, there is always the question whether that matter is conceived by them as having had an eternal existence independent of God or whether it is conceived by them as having itself been created by God though its creation took place prior to the creation of the world. Philo's position on this question is not clear and whatever view has been attributed to him is based upon indirect inferences.[23] Among the Christian Church Fathers, Tatian,[24] Theophilus,[25] Tertullian[26] and Origen[27] explicitly reject the assumption of an eternal uncreated matter, while Justin Martyr and Athenagoras are vague on this point,[28] and Hermogenes, who was a Christian, though not a Church Father, held that the pre-existent matter was eternal (*semper fuerit*) unborn (*neque nata*) and unmade (*neque facta*)[29] and that " God always had matter co-existent with himself."[30] With regard to Hallevi's and Maimonides' interpretation of Plato's pre-existent matter, which they find to be compatible with Scripture, it can be shown that they both take it to be eternal, unborn and unmade. In the case of Hallevi we can infer it only from his use of the term " eternal "[31] as a description of it. In the case of Maimonides, we have in addition to his use of the term " eternal "[32] also his state-

21 *Moreh Nebukim*, ii, 25.
22 *ibid.*, ii, 26.
23 Cf. Drummond, *Philo Judaeus*, i, p. 299 ff.
24 *Oratio adversus Graecos*, c. 5.
25 *Ad Autolycum*, ii, 4.
26 *Adversus Hermogenem*, cc. 3 ff.
27 *De Principiis*, II, i, 5; II, iv, 3.
28 Cf. Hagenbach, *History of Doctrines*, §47, n. 4
29 Tertullian, *Adversus Hermogenem*, c. 1 end; cf. cc. 2 and 4.
30 *ibid.*, c. 3; cf. Hagenbach, *loc. cit.*, n. 6.
31 *Cuzari*, i, 67.
32 *Moreh Nebukim*, ii, 13 (2); ii, 26.

ment, in characterisation of those who follow the Platonic theory of a pre-existent matter, that "they therefore assume that a certain matter has co-existed with God from eternity in such a manner that neither God existed without that matter nor the matter without God."[33] The same interpretation of the Platonic pre-existent matter is to be found also later in Gersonides, who adopts the Platonic theory as an interpretation of the Scriptural story of creation.[34]

In the history of the problem of creation there is a stock objection against this theory of an eternal pre-existent matter. Such a theory, it is argued, places another eternal being by the side of God and it thus infringes upon the unity of God, for that other eternal being, by virtue of its being eternal, constitutes a deity.[35] This stock objection is met by a stock answer which occurs in Hermogenes, Maimonides and Gersonides. Hermogenes' answer is that, even though matter is eternal like God, it is still not a god, for it is still inferior to God in power, since God is still to be "regarded as the sole Author as well as Lord of all things," so that even eternal matter is to be under His power and authority.[36] Similarly Maimonides, anticipating the stock objection to the eternity of matter, says: "But they do not believe that that eternal matter is of the same order of existence as God; on the contrary, they believe that God is the cause of the existence of that eternal matter and that that eternal matter in its relation to God is like clay, for instance, in its relation to the potter or like iron in its relation to the smith, for God can do with it whatever He pleases."[37] The answer given by Gersonides is the same: "It does not follow," he says, "that if that [formless] body was assumed to be eternal that it would be equal in rank with God, so that like Him it would be a god. The nature of Godhead does not belong to God merely by virtue of the fact that unlike all other

33 *ibid.*, ii, 13 (2). Cf. Munk, *ad loc.* (vol. ii, p. 109, n. 3).

34 *Milhamot Adonai*, VI, ii, 1.

35 Tertullian, *Adversus Hermogenem*, c. 4. Thomas Aquinas, *Contra Gentiles*, ii, p. 38 end. Gersonides, *Milhamot Adonai*, VI, i, 18 (3).

36 Tertullian, *op. cit.*, c. 5.

37 *Moreh Nebukim*, ii, p. 13 (2).

beings He is eternal, for even if all other beings were also assumed to be eternal, God alone would still be God, and this by virtue of the fact that He would still be the governor of all things and the one who has bestowed upon them the law and order which are inherent in all of them."[38]

Both Hallevi and Maimonides discuss also the theory of the succession of worlds, but, while Hallevi accepts this theory as compatible with Scripture, Maimonides rejects it. On the face of it, it would therefore seem that there is a difference between them in this regard. But there are so many angles to this theory and so many vaguenesses in Hallevi's restatement of it that it is possible, as we shall try to show, that there is really no difference between them.

Hallevi presents his view on this theory again in the brief statement that " if the believer of the Law finds himself compelled to admit and acknowledge . . . the existence of many worlds prior to this one, this would not impair his belief that *this* world was created at some particular time, and that Adam and Noah were the first human beings."[39] This brief statement has behind it a long history of the problem, which was started with Philo and was continued among the Church Fathers and found its way also into Arabic philosophy. From Philo's discussion of this theory, which he reproduces in the name of the Stoics, we gather that the successive worlds were assumed by the Stoics to be infinite in number, for he says in effect that the total aggregate of all the successively created worlds constitutes, as it were, one eternal world.[40] This is also St. Augustine's understanding of this theory, as may be gathered from his use of the term " innumerably " (*innumerabiliter*) in his restatement of it.[41] Then again, from Philo's, as well as from Origen's and St. Augustine's, discussion of this problem we gather that this Stoic theory may be conceived either as taking all these successive worlds to be exactly the same in their composition and history or as taking them to be

[38] *Milhamot Adonai*, VI, i, 18 (ad. 3).
[39] *Cuzari*, i, p. 67.
[40] *De Aeternitate Mundi*, iii, 9.
[41] *De Civitate Dei*, xii, 12.

different from each other.[42] Now Philo as well as St. Augustine rejects the theory of the succession of many worlds whether assumed to be different from each other or assumed to be exact repetitions of one and the same world. Origen, however, admits the succession of many worlds provided they are assumed to be different from each other.[43] Furthermore, in addition to this proviso, which is explicitly stated by him, it can also be shown that his admission of the possibility of a succession of worlds rests also on the assumption that these successive worlds are finite in number. We may gather this from two considerations. In the first place, he speaks only of " many ages " (*multa saecula*), by which, as he himself explains, he means many " worlds " (*mundi*), without saying that by " many " he means infinite.[44] In the second place, from the very fact that the pre-existent matter out of which the many successive worlds were created was itself, according to his expressed opinion, as we have seen above, created by God it must be inferred that the successive worlds could not be infinite in number.

In view of this historical background of the problem, we may ask ourselves: What does Hallevi exactly mean by his admission of the possibility of the theory of the successive creations and destructions of worlds? Does he mean to admit its possibility only in the sense that the successive worlds are finite in number? Or does he mean to admit it even on the assumption that the successive worlds are infinite in number?

The question becomes all the more pertinent when we examine Hallevi's statement in the light of certain theories of successive worlds known in Arabic literature, partly from Indian sources[45] and partly

42 Philo, *De Aeternitate Mundi*, xiii, 42–44; Origen, *De Principiis*, II, iii, 1; II, iii, 4; St. Augustine, *De Civitate Dei*, xii, 13. Evidently this is Philo's as well as Origen's and St. Augustine's own interpretation of the Stoics. In the original Stoic view, as may be gathered from the texts cited by Zeller (*Stoics, Epicureans, and Sceptics*, p. 157, n. 4), the successive worlds were taken as being exact reproductions and repetitions of one and the same world.

43 *De Principiis*, II, ii, 4–5.

44 *ibid.*, II, iii, 5.

45 Mas'udi, *Muruj*, ch. 7 (ed. Barbier de Meynard et Pavet de Courteille, i, p. 151 ff.).

from Aristotle's restatement of the view of Empedocles and Heraclitus, which we shall discuss later, and partly also perhaps from Stoic sources.

One of these theories is to be found in the views attributed to the Kharbaniyyah. They are reported to have believed in the succession of one age (*daur*) after another, which presumably, as in the case of Origen, means one world after another. These successive ages continue according to them, for an eternal duration of time (*abad al-dahr*), i.e. they are infinite in number. Finally, during each age " there is created another generation (*quarn ākhar*) of men, animals, and plants."[46] With regard to this last statement, it must be added, it is not clear whether it means an exact repetition of the previous generations or an entirely new generation of a different kind.

Another theory of successive worlds is to be found among the Shiites and the Sufis. Muhammad al-Baqir, one of the twelve Shiite Imams, is reported to have said that " millions of Adams passed away before our father Adam "; and Ibn al-Arabi, speaking for the Sufis, says that " forty thousand years before our Adam there was another Adam."[47] The significance of these statements for our present purpose is that the successive Adams, which undoubtedly means successive worlds, are limited in number. Now Hallevi's statement that the theory of successive worlds is not objectionable because it does not impair the belief that in " this world . . . Adam and Noah were the first human beings," would seem to have reference to the particular version of the theory of successive worlds as found among the Shiites and Sufis, and therefore when he speaks of the possibility of " the existence of many worlds prior to this one," he may mean a finite number of these successive worlds.

If we assume, as we have reason to do, that Hallevi's acceptance of the possibility of successive worlds refers only to a finite number of successive worlds, then Maimonides' rejection of the same theory does not really constitute an opposition to the view of Hallevi, for,

[46] Shahrastani (ed. Cureton), p. 249, 11, 10–11.

[47] Quoted by Muhammad Ali, *Translation of the Holy Quran*, Lahore, 1928, p. lxxv.

as we shall try to show, Maimonides deals with a different conception of this theory.

Maimonides has two references to the theory of the successive worlds.

One of these is presented by him as a subdivision of the second of the three theories of creation which he formally enumerates.[48] A close comparison of the passage of Maimonides with the passage in which Aristotle presents the view of Empedocles and Heraclitus would seem to indicate that the view referred to by Maimonides is that of Empedocles and Heraclitus. For in Aristotle this view is presented as one of three views, of which another one is the Platonic view and all of which assume that the world was generated,[49] with the implied assumption that it was generated from a pre-existent eternal matter. Similarly Maimonides presents this view as the view of one of " several schools," among which the school of Plato is included and all of which assume that the world was generated from a pre-existent eternal matter. Furthermore, Maimonides himself refers to this passage of Aristotle elsewhere in his work.[50] Now the process of successive generations and destructions of worlds as conceived by Empedocles and Heraclitus is described by Aristotle as an eternal process.[51] Consequently when Maimonides says in his description of this view that according to it " the heavens are generated and destroyed and their generation and destruction are like those of all other beings which are under them,"[52] he undoubtedly means that this process of the successive generations and destructions of worlds is infinite and eternal. Moreover, from the fact that he compares the successive worlds to the successive individuals within the world, we may infer that these successive worlds are not assumed to be exactly the same. Both these, as we have seen, are phases of the Stoic view discussed by Philo, Origen and St. Augustine.

The other reference to the theory of successive worlds in Maimon-

[48] *Moreh Nebukim*, ii, 13 (2).

[49] *De Caelo*, I, 10, 279b, 12–13.

[50] *Moreh Nebukim*, ii, 15.

[51] *De Caelo*, I, 10, 279b, 14–17.

[52] *Moreh Nebukim*, ii, 13 (2).

ides is to be found in his discussion of two quotations from the Midrash, one of which states that "the order of the periods of time existed prior to the creation of the world" and the other, which is an inference from the first, states that before the creation of this world "God built worlds and destroyed them."[53] Maimonides rejects this view on the ground that the assumption of the existence of the order of the periods of time before the creation of this world, as well as the assumption of the creation and the destruction of worlds one after the other, implies a belief in the theory of the eternity of the universe. From this criticism we may infer that the successive worlds are conceived by Maimonides as being infinite in number, for otherwise the aggregate of successive worlds would not make eternity. Furthermore, from the second Midrashic statement quoted by Maimonides we may also infer that the successive worlds were conceived by him as being each different from the other, for the reason why God created successive worlds as given in the Midrash is that God was dissatisfied with his earlier attempts.[54] In fact, Maimonides' remark that the second quotation from the Midrash is worse than the first,[55] which is correctly taken by one of his commentators to mean that this second quotation implies imperfections in God's earlier creations,[56] corresponds exactly to Philo's criticism of the assumption that each successive world was a different and an improved world.[57]

Consequently when Maimonides rejects the theory of the succession of worlds he means thereby a theory according to which there was an infinite succession of worlds, the aggregate of which would make one eternal world, but when Hallevi admits the possibility of the theory of the succession of worlds, he may mean thereby only a finite succession of worlds.

53 *ibid.*, ii, 30, referring to *Bereshit Rabbah*, iii, 7.

54 *Bereshit Rabbah*, iii, 7; ix, 2.

55 *Moreh Nebukim*, ii, 30.

56 Moses ben Solomon of Salerno in his unpublished commentary quoted by Munk, *ad. loc.* (vol. ii, p. 233, n. 2).

57 *De Aeternitate Mundi*, xiii, 43–44; cf. also St. Augustine, *De Civitate Dei*, xii, 17.

Both Hallevi and Maimonides agree that there is no decisive proof for Aristotle's theory of the eternity of the world. Concerning the arguments advanced by Aristotle in favour of the eternity of the world Hallevi says that they only establish the theory of eternity as being probable[58] but they do not constitute " evidence " or a " demonstration."[59] About this statement it is not clear whether Hallevi means thereby to reproduce Aristotle's own characterisation of his own arguments or whether he means thereby to express his own personal judgment about the nature of the arguments advanced by Aristotle. Maimonides, however, is more definite in his statement. After expressing his own judgment in one place, that the eternity of the world cannot be established by a " decisive demonstration,"[60] he tells us in another place that Aristotle himself was aware that he had no " demonstration " or " decisive demonstration "[61] for the eternity of the world and that all his arguments and proofs are of the kind that is known as probable arguments.[62] Maimonides refers to Alexander and Galen as having the same view about what Aristotle himself thought about his own arguments.[63] During Maimonides' own time, it may be added, Averroes, with all his objections to the particular arguments raised by Algazali against the eternity of the world, admits that the belief in the eternity of the world cannot be established by reason.[64]

Agreeing as both Hallevi and Maimonides do on the compatibility of the Platonic theory of a pre-existent eternal matter with the Scriptural account of the creation of the world and agreeing as they also

58 *Cuzari*, i, 65. Arabic: *rajaha qiyasatuhu*; Hebrew: *hikri'a heqeshotaw*.

59 *ibid.*, i, 65. Arabic: *'iyan*; *burhan*; Hebrew: *re'iyyah*; *mofet*.

60 *Moreh Nebukim*, i, 71.

61 *ibid.*, ii, 15.

62 *ibid.* Arabic: *al-dala'il . . . allati tabdu wa-tamilu al-nafsu ilaiha akthara*; Hebrew: *ha-ra'ayot . . . asher yera'u we-titteh ha-nefesh alehem yoter*. This reflects Aristotle's definition of τὸ εἰκός in *Analytica Priora*, II, 27, 70a, 3–4, as πρότασις ἔνδοξος.

63 *ibid.* Cf. Galen, *De Hippocratis et Platonis Placitis*, ix, 7; *Opera* (ed. Kühn), v, 780 (Munk, *ad loc.*, vol. ii, p. 127, n. 2). A similar reference to Galen's view as to the impossibility of establishing by proof the eternity of the world occurs also in Algazali's *Tahafut al-Falasifah*, I, i, p. 21, 11, 9 ff. (ed. M. Bouyges).

64 *Tahafut al-Tahafut*, i, 175. Cf. above, n. 19.

do on the inadequacy of the Aristotelian arguments for the eternity of the world, they differ on the question whether Aristotle's theory of the eternity of the world can be reconciled with Scripture.

Hallevi does not discuss this phase of the problem. But two considerations lead us to the conclusion that he did not believe that the Aristotelian theory of eternity could be reconciled with the Scriptural account of creation as he understood it. In the first place, at the beginning of his discussion of the problem of creation he makes a definite reference to Aristotle's theory of eternity,[65] but when he later expresses an indifference, from the religious point of view, to the entire problem of creation and eternity, he merely says, as we have already mentioned before, that there is no objection on grounds of religion either to the theory of a pre-existent eternal matter or to the theory of successive worlds, but no mention is made by him of the Aristotelian view of the eternity of the world. Unless, therefore, we assume that the failure to mention the Aristotelian view was unintentional or else we assume, what is still more unlikely, that under the expression " if a believer in the Law finds himself compelled to admit and acknowledge an eternal matter " he means to include the Aristotelian theory mentioned by him before, we must conclude that the Aristotelian theory of eternity was considered by him objectionable on religious grounds. In the second place, the opening speech of the philosopher at the beginning of the *Cuzari,* which was meant by Hallevi to represent the view of Aristotle on the question of the origin of the world, there is a definite implication that that view is rejected by Hallevi as being contrary to Scripture, despite the fact that it assumes the existence of a God as the cause of the eternally generated world.[66]

Maimonides, however, tries to show the untenability of the Aristotelian theory of the eternity of the world, or at least its inferiority to the theory of creation, on purely rational grounds. He does not assume *a priori* that it is contradictory to Scripture. Quite the contrary, he openly declares: " We do not reject the eternity of the

65 *Cuzari*, i, 64–65.
66 *ibid.*, i, 1.

universe, merely on the ground that certain passages in Scripture confirm its creation," for with regard to these passages it would have been an easy task for us "to interpret those passages in harmony with the theory of the eternity of the universe."[67]

The reason for this difference between Hallevi and Maimonides in their attitude towards the Aristotelian theory of the eternity of the world is to be found in their different conceptions as to what principles are to be derived from the Scriptural story of creation. They both agree that one principle to be derived therefrom is that the world did not come into being by chance but that there is a God who has brought it into existence. They both also agree that another principle to be derived therefrom is that the God who has brought it into existence acts as a free agent and not by the necessity of his nature. But as to whether the Scriptural story of creation meant to teach still a third principle they differ.

To Judah Hallevi there was still a third principle which the Scriptural story of creation meant to teach, for to him the problem of creation was not merely a metaphysical problem but also a historical problem. The problem to him was not only whether the world has a cause which has brought it into existence and whether that cause acts by free will or by the necessity of its nature, but also whether the natural history of the world and the history of the human species in it had a beginning in time. From the Scriptural narrative of creation he derived the principles that not only is there a God, who has brought the world into existence by His free will, but also that there was once a time when this world was not in existence and that there was once a time when men were not in existence. We may gather this from such a statement as that "this world once did not exist, but then came into existence by the will of God at the time He desired."[68] We may gather this also from the wording of his statement of what he believed to be the true conception of creation according to Scripture, namely, the belief that "this world was created at a particular

[67] *Moreh Nebukim*, ii, 25.
[68] *Cuzari*, v, 14.

time and that Adam and Noah were the first human beings."[69] With such a conception of creation he could not logically accept the Aristotelian theory of the eternity of the world with its implication, as he says, that "God never created man" but that "one man was always born from another man,"[70] even if this particular conception of the eternity of the world did imply the existence of a prime cause, and even if it could be assumed, a question which Hallevi does not discuss, that the cause of an eternally generated world could act with free will. This is exactly the reason for Philo's rejection of Aristotle's theory of eternity, even though ostensibly he offers other reasons for his rejection of it.[71] To him, too, the problem of creation is a historical problem in addition to its being a metaphysical one and almost in the words used many centuries later by Hallevi he phrases the Scriptural theory of creation in historical terms, namely, that "there was a time when it was not."[72]

To Maimonides, however, the problem of the origin of the world is purely a metaphysical one, namely, whether it has been brought into existence by a cause or not and whether that cause acts with free will or by the necessity of its nature. From the Scriptural account of creation he derives only two principles, namely, that there is a cause for the existence of the world and that that cause acts with free will. Once the existence of such a free cause is granted, the element of time is non-essential. If it were only logically possible to conceive at once of God as the free cause of the world, as well as of the human species in it, as having existed from eternity, such a conception, according to Maimonides, would be compatible with the true principles that one is to derive from the Scriptural account of creation, even if not with the literalness of its text. Accordingly Maimonides main-

[69] *ibid.*, i, 67. The Arabic expression used here by Hallevi: *hadithun mundh muddatin muhassalah* (Hebrew: *hadash mi-zeman yadu'a*) is a literal translation of the Greek expression ἀπό τινος χρόνου γενόμενον which occurs in Philo's *De Decalogo*, xii, 58. An abridged Arabic translation of Philo's *De Decalogo* is known to have existed (cf. Hirschfeld, "The Arabic Portion of the Cairo Genizah at Cambridge," *Jewish Quarterly Review*, 1905, xvii, pp. 65–66).

[70] *ibid.*, i, 1

[71] *De Opificio Mundi*, ii, 7 ff.; *De Aeternitate Mundi*, iii, 10–12.

[72] *De Decalogo*, xii, 58.

tains that it is not Scriptural texts but logical reasons that have compelled him to accept the view that the world came into being after it had not been. Indeed Maimonides occasionally states the doctrine of creation in historical terms, as when he says, for instance, that "it is a fundamental principle of the Law that the world was created and that of the human species one individual being was created first and that was Adam,"[73] but such statements, as may be always seen from their context, express his view as he has formulated it to himself after he has demonstrated logically that this part of the story of creation, at least, should be taken literally.

The difference between Hallevi and Maimonides as to the theory of the eternal creation of the world, in short, is this: To Maimonides there would be no Scriptural objection to it, if it were logically compatible with free will in God. To Hallevi, on the other hand, there would be Scriptural objection to it, even if on logical grounds it were compatible with free will in God. But as to the question whether Hallevi considered the eternal generation of the world logically compatible with free will in God or not, there is no way of telling. His admission of the possibility of successive worlds, if these worlds were assumed to be infinite in number, would indeed imply his admission also of the possibility of eternal generation. But, as we have seen, Hallevi may have admitted only the possibility of a finite number of successive worlds.

It would be interesting to speculate how Hallevi and Maimonides, in the light of their treatment of these three theories of the origin of the world, would treat the theory of evolution. I imagine that they would at first ask themselves whether this theory implies that the world came into being by chance or by some cause. Among the various interpretations of the process of evolution they would probably find one which would somehow satisfy them that it implies the existence of a cause, which cause they would then proceed to raise to the status of a God. Then they would ask themselves whether this cause or God acts by the necessity of his own nature or by the freedom of his will. Here again among the various interpretations of the

[73] *Moreh Nebuḳim*, iii, 50.

process of evolution they would find at least one which interprets it as a teleological process. They would then proceed to reason therefrom, as in fact they do from the astronomical and biological data of their own time,[74] that this teleology in nature implies free will in God. With Maimonides the inquiry would satisfactorily come to an end at this point, for the world under the theory of evolution, though much over six thousand years old, is not eternal and consequently, according to Maimonides, could have been brought into being by the free will of God. Hallevi, however, would be inclined to reject it on account of its divergence from Scripture on the question of the age of the world. Still, it is quite possible that if he were fully convinced, by the evolutionary evidence, of the greater age of the world, he would add a third statement in the *Cuzari*, which would read as follows: "If, after all, a believer in the Law finds himself compelled to admit and acknowledge that the world and the fullness thereof came into being by that process called evolution, this would not impair his belief that the world was created at a certain time, and that there were first human beings whom Scripture calls Adam and Eve."

74 The present writer has discussed their arguments on this question in "Hallevi and Maimonides on Design, Chance and Necessity," *Proceedings of the American Academy for Jewish Research*, 1941, xi, pp. 105–163.

15

THE INTERNAL SENSES IN LATIN, ARABIC, AND HEBREW PHILOSOPHIC TEXTS

CHAPTER I

Earliest use of the term "internal senses": Augustine, Gregory the Great, Erigena. — Two sets of threefold classifications of internal senses: (*a*) Ḥunain ben Isḥâk, Razi, Isaac Israeli, Pseudo-Baḥya; (*b*) Ibn Gabirol, Ibn Ezra, Maimonides. — Explanation of the origin of the unique fivefold classification of the Iḫwân al-Ṣafâ: analysis of the definition of *διανοητικόν* in John of Damascus. — Explanation of the baffling classification of the internal senses in the Syriac Causa Causarum and the Arabic Sirr al-Ḫalîkah.

In Aristotle there is no general term for those faculties of the soul which he treats of in the Third Book of De Anima and in De Memoria et Reminiscentia to differentiate them as a class from the five senses which he treats of in the Second Book of De Anima. In Latin, Arabic, and Hebrew philosophic texts, however, these post-sensationary faculties, or some of them, or sometimes only one of them, are designated by the term "internal senses,"[1] in contradistinction to the five senses which are designated by the term "external senses."[2] Sometimes instead of "external" the terms "corporeal"[3] and "passive"[4] are used, and instead of "internal" the terms

[1] *sensus interiores* (or *interni*), حواسّ باطنة, חושים (רגשים, הרגשים, הרגשות) פנימים (צפונים, תכונים, נסתרים, נעלמים). See below, nn. 10, 12, 25, 27, 64, 66, and cf. passages quoted in D. Kaufmann, Die Sinne, pp. 46–49.

[2] *exteriores, extreni*, ظاهرة, חצונים, נראים, גלוים, נגלים. See below, n. 27, and cf. Kaufmann, loc. cit.

[3] *corporealis, corporeus*, جسمانىّ, גשמי, גושמני, גופי, חמרי, היולאני. See below, nn. 27, 40, and Ch. II, n. 28, and cf. Kaufmann, loc. cit.

[4] انفعالات, מפעלות, *operatae*, הפעליות, *patibiles*. Cf. below, n. 27.

"spiritual,"[5] "separable,"[6] and "cerebral."[7] Sometimes, too, the term "faculties"[8] or "apprehensions"[9] is used instead of "senses." The use of the terms "internal," "spiritual," and "cerebral" has been explained by the fact that the faculties to which they are applied reside *within* the *brain* and operate *without bodily* organs.[10] In histories of philosophy and psychology the entire subject of the internal senses is usually dismissed by a general statement to the effect that in post-Aristotelian philosophy three or five internal senses are contrasted with the five external senses. But the true history of the internal senses is more complicated than this, and the study of it involves problems in the interpretation of texts, the determination of the exact meaning of terms, and the analysis of certain functions of the soul. In this paper we shall try to trace the entire history of the problem, confining ourselves, however, to classification and terminology, and dealing with the interpretation of texts and the analysis and description of functions only in so far as they are necessary for the determination of the scheme of classification and the meaning of terms.[11]

[5] *spiritualis*, روحاني, רוחני, נפשי. See below, nn. 40, 64, and Ch. II, nn. 28, 73, and cf. Kaufmann, loc. cit.

[6] *distinctus* (= *separabilis*), [مفرق], נבדל. See below, Ch. II, n. 76.

[7] *sensus cerebri, virtutes cerebri.* See below, nn. 10, 14.

[8] *vis, virtus, potentia, facultas*, قوّة, כח. See below, nn. 10, 12.

[9] *apprehensiones*, ادراك, השגות. See below, n. 27.

[10] Averroes, Colliget, II, 20, fol. 30 F (see below, Ch. II, n. 82): "Et virtutes cerebri . . . quamvis non habeant membra vel instrumenta, ipsa tamen habeant propria loca in cerebro." Keckermann (see below, Ch. III, n. 52), Cap. 17, Col. 1522: "Sensus interior est actio sensualis quae intus sit: sive, cuius causae instrumenta immediata sunt collocata intu, in ipso cerebro animalis." Magirus (see below, Ch. III, n. 53), p. 350: "Interiores, qui intra cranium subsistunt."

[11] Two more detailed treatments of the internal senses in the works of two philosophers dealt with here only in a general way will be found in my papers Isaac Israeli on the Internal Senses, in George Alexander Kohut Memorial Volume (1935), and Maimonides on the Internal Senses, in Jewish Quarterly Review, N. S., 25 (1935) Below, pages 315–330, 344–370.

Important studies of the internal senses are to be found in the following works: S. Landauer, Die Psychologie des Ibn Sînâ, in Zeitschrift der Deutschen Morgenländischen Gesellschaft, 29 (1875), pp. 399 ff.; A. Schneider, Die Psychologie Alberts des Grossen, I (1903), pp. 154 ff.; S. Horovitz, Die Psychologie des Aristotelikers Abraham Ibn Daud (1912), in his Die Psychologie bei den jüdischen Religions-Philosophen des Mittelalters von Saadia bis Maimuni (1898–1912), pp. 238 ff.

When the term "internal sense" first appears in Latin philosophic texts it is used as synonymous with a single post-sensationary faculty of the soul. In Augustine, who uses both "internal sense" (*interior sensus*) and "internal faculty" (*interior vis*),[12] these terms are employed as synonymous with Aristotle's "common sense" (κοινὸν αἰσθητήριον), for he invests these terms with some of the functions which in Aristotle are assigned to common sense.[13] Similarly Gregory the Great's "sense of the brain" (*sensus cerebri*), which he describes as presiding within (*qui intrinsecus praesidet*), is also invested with one of the functions of Aristotle's "common sense," and is thus to be understood as a term synonymous with it.[14] In Erigena the sense described as *interior* is identified with the Greek term διάνοια, which, according to his view, stands below *ratio* (λόγος) and *intellectus* (νοῦς) but above the five external senses and imagination.[15]

In Arabic and Hebrew philosophic literature, however, with one possible exception in the case of Arabic literature which we shall discuss later, the term "internal senses" appears from the very beginning as a generic term which includes a variety of post-sensationary faculties. In its simplest form it is used to include three faculties: imagination (φανταστικόν), cogitation (διανοητικόν),[16] and memory (μνημονευτικόν). Now these

[12] Confessiones, I, 20; *De Libero Arbitrio*, II, 3–5; Confessiones, VII, 17. I have been unable to find the use of "internal senses" prior to Augustine. Cicero's *tactus interior* (Acad., II, 7, 20) referred to by R. Eisler (Wörterbuch der philosophischen Begriffe, 4th ed., 1930, under "Wahrnehmung," p. 484) has an entirely different meaning. The statement by M. Dessoir in Abriss einer Geschichte der Psychologie (1911), p. 44, that "Galen unterschied sogar drei innere Sinne" is not quite correct. Galen himself does not use the term "internal sense," though Arabic philosophers in reproducing his classification of the post-sensationary faculties describe them as internal senses. See below, nn. 18, 24.

[13] Cf. The Confessions of Augustine, edited by J. Gibb and W. Montgomery (1908), notes ad loc. cit.

[14] Moralium Libri, sive Expositio in Librum Beati Job, XI, 6 (Migne, LXXV, Col. 957 B). Cf. A. Schneider, Die Erkenntnislehre bei Beginn der Scholastik (1921), p. 32.

[15] De Divisione Naturae, II, 23 (Migne, CXXII, Col. 577 D). Cf. A. Schneider, Die Erkenntnislehre des Johannes Eriugena, I (1921), 64.

[16] Throughout mediaeval Latin texts, as will appear in the course of this paper, *cogitativa* is used as the equivalent of διανοητική. In Albertus Magnus, Summa de

three faculties are to be found in Aristotle's discussion of the faculties which are beyond sensation. Φανταστικόν is discussed by him in De Anima, III, 3. Διανοητικόν is the term which Aristotle himself, in his classification of the faculties of the soul in De Anima, II, 3, 414a, 32, applies to his discussion in De Anima, III, 4–6. Μνημονευτικόν is treated of by Aristotle in his De Memoria et Reminiscentia. We cannot, therefore, agree with the view that the threefold classification of internal senses is of Galenic origin or that there is something peculiarly Galenic in it.[17] Galen's enumeration of these three post-sensationary faculties, precisely like his enumeration of the five senses which precedes it, is nothing but an analysis of Aristotle's De Anima and De Memoria et Reminiscentia, his enumeration of the five senses referring to De Anima, II, 5–12, and his enumeration of the post-sensationary faculties referring to De Anima, III, and De Memoria et Reminiscentia cited above. Like Aristotle, too, Galen does not use the term "internal senses" as a description of these post-sensationary faculties.[18] The fact that Galen does not include in his list common sense, which is discussed by Aristotle in De Anima, III, 1–2, does not militate against our contention, for Aristotle himself, in his enumeration of the faculties of the soul in De Anima, II, 3, 414a, 32, and elsewhere, does not mention common sense, evidently for the reason that he would have included it among the five senses, of which it is the focal point, or else would have identified it with imagination, which is sometimes considered by him a function of common sense. Aristotle himself does not discuss this point, and there is reason to believe that the first two chapters of De Anima, III, which deal with common sense, should be annexed to De Anima, II,

---

Creaturis, II: De Homine (ed. Vivès), Quaest. 38, Art. 3, Solutio, *syllogistica* seems to be used as its equivalent: "Prima dicitur phantasia ab antiquioribus, secunda syllogistica, tertia memorialis."

[17] Cf. S. Horovitz, op. cit., pp. 238 ff., referring to Galen's De Symptomatum Differentiis, Cap. III, in Opera Omnia (ed. D. C. G. Kühn), VII, 56.

[18] Cf. Index in Galeni Libros in Opera Omnia (ed. D. C. G. Kühn), XX. Nor is "internal sense" used in the threefold classification of post-sensationary faculties by Nemesius, De Natura Hominis, Chs. 6, 12, 13, and by John of Damascus, De Fide Orthodoxa, II, 17, 19, 20.

which deals with the five senses.[19] It is indeed true that Ḥunain and Razi, whom we shall soon cite, make mention of Galen in their threefold classifications of the post-sensationary faculties, but upon a close examination of their statements it will be discovered that their references to Galen are only in connection with the localization of these three faculties, in the anterior, middle, and posterior ventricles of the brain respectively,[20] rather than in connection with the enumeration of these faculties.

But the passages in Arabic and Hebrew literature which contain this threefold classification of the internal senses — and we shall refer to it as Galenic for the purpose of identification — do not seem to use the same type of classification, for they do not use the same terminology. On the whole, we may divide them into two groups. One group is represented by the lists given by Ḥunain ben Isḥâk,[21] Razi,[22] Isaac Israeli,[23] and Pseudo-Baḥya.[24] In all of these lists the terms used are accurate translations of the three terms used by Galen, and in the case of Ḥunain and Razi explicit reference is made to him. The other group is represented by the lists given by Ibn Gabirol,[25] Abraham Ibn Ezra,[26] and Maimonides.[27] In these lists

[19] Cf. R. D. Hicks, Aristotle: De Anima, p. 422, and below, Ch. III, n. 22.

[20] Cf. Galen, De Locis Affectis, III, 9, in Opera Omnia (ed. D. C. G. Kühn), VIII, 174 ff. This reference is given in P. de Koning, Trois Traités d'Anatomie Arabes (1903), p. 9, n. 2.

[21] Musere ha-Pilosofim, II, 10 (Lunéville, 1807), p. 15a: (1) ציור, (2) מחשבה, (3) זכרון.

[22] Cf. Al-Manṣûri fi al-Tibb in P. de Koning, Trois Traités d'Anatomie Arabes (1903), p. 9: (1) تخيّل, (2) فكر, (3) ذكر.

[23] Hebrew: Sefer ha-Yesodot, II (ed. S. Fried), 53–55; Latin: Liber de Elementis, II, in Omnia Opera Ysaaci, Lyon, 1515, fol. ix, r:
(1) מצייר, *informatum*; אלפנטסיא, *phantasia.*
(2) מחשבי, *cogitatio.*
(3) זכרון, *memoria.*

[24] Ma'ânî al-Nafs, Ch. 8 (ed. I. Goldziher, 1907, p. 27, ll. 21–23): (1) خيال, (2) فكر, (3) ذكر.

[25] Tiḳḳun Middot ha-Nefesh (Budapest, 1896), p. 11; Arabic: ed. S. S. Wise, The Improvement of the Moral Qualities (1902), p. 4, ll. 19–20: (1) فطرة, הרגשה, (2) فكرة, מחשבה, (3) فهم, בינה. The term used here is "internal" (باطنة, צפונים).

[26] Commentary on Exodus 31, 3: (1) تخيّل, דעת, (2) فكرة, תבונה, (3) حكمة, חכמה.

[27] Moreh Nebukim, I, 47 (46). Arabic: ed. S. Munk, Guide des Égarés (1856–66);

the third term differs from that used by Galen. Instead of "memory," Ibn Gabirol and Maimonides use a term which means "understanding," "comprehension," and Ibn Ezra uses a term which means "wisdom." Furthermore, in Ibn Gabirol's list, the first term, instead of "imagination," is a term which signifies "creation," "natural disposition," "creative power." The lists of Ibn Gabirol and Ibn Ezra, which have been discussed by Horovitz, have been left unexplained by him;[28] the list of Maimonides has not as yet been discussed by anybody in this connection. It is my purpose to show that these three lists are also translations of Galen's classification.

First, with regard to the third internal sense in these three lists, it can be shown, I believe, that the terms by which it is described mean memory, though memory only of a certain kind. For there are two kinds of memory, one belonging to sense-perception or imagination and the other belonging to thought. According to Aristotle, directly memory belongs

---

Latin translation from Judah Ḥarizi's Hebrew version by Augustinus Justinianus, Dux seu Director Dubitantium aut Perplexorum (1520), and from Samuel ibn Tibbon's Hebrew version by Johannis Buxtorf, Fil., Doctor Perplexorum (1629):

(1) تخيّل,	Ḥ: רעיון [דמיוני],	J: *cogitatio assimilativa*
	T: (1) רעיון (2) דמיון,	B: (1) *phantasia*, (2) *imaginatio*
(2) تفكّر,	Ḥ: מחשבה שכלית,	J: *cogitatio intelligibilis*
	T: השתכלות,	B: *cogitatio*
(3) تفهّم	Ḥ: תבונה,	J: *intellectus*
	T: התבוננות,	B: *intelligentia*, sive *intellectio*

The terms used by Maimonides for external and internal senses are as follows:

(1) (*a*) ادراكات جسمانيّة وانفعالات ;	Ḥ: (*a*) השגות גופיות ו(כחות) מפעלות	J: (*a*) *apprehensiones corporales et (virtutes) operatae;*
(*b*) ادراكات حسّيّة ظاهرة ;	(*b*) השגות מורגשות גלויות;	(*b*) *apprehensiones sensibiles manifestae*
	T: (*a*) השגות גשמיות והפעליות;	B: (*a*) *apprehensiones corporales et patibiles;*
	(*b*) השגות חושיות נראות	(*b*) *apprehensiones sensuales externae*
(2) ادراكات باطنة;	Ḥ: השגות פנימיות נעלמות;	J: omitted
	T: השגות פנימיות;	B: *apprehensiones internae*

[28] Cf. S. Horovitz, op. cit., p. 138, n. 138; p. 259, n. 256. Cf. also D. Cassel, Das Buch Kuzari (1869), V, 12, p. 391, n. 2.

to sense-perception or imagination, but indirectly it belongs to thought (*νοούμενον*).[29] In an accidental sense (*κατὰ συμβεβηκός*), he also says, some of the things which are properly objects of scientific knowledge (*ἔνια ὧν ἐπιστάμεθα*) may be objects of memory; and of such intellectual objects of memory, he further states, a person is said to remember that he has learned something (*ἔμαθεν*) or contemplated something (*ἐθεώρησεν*).[30] Similarly, according to Plotinus, there are two kinds of memory: one is the memory of sense-objects (*αἰσθητῶν*), which belongs to imagination;[31] the other is the memory of intellectual conceptions (*νοητῶν, διανοήσεων*), which belongs to reason (λόγος).[32] John of Damascus, following Nemesius, distinguishes between these two kinds of memory and declares that intellectual conceptions (*νοητά*), being perceived only through learning (*μάθησις*) or through natural thinking (*φυσικὴ ἔννοια*), are also remembered through learning or natural thinking.[33] These two kinds of memory are also implied in Isaac Israeli's definitions of memory, where, like Aristotle and John of Damascus, he makes intellectual memory dependent upon investigation, i.e., learning, and contemplation.[34] Averroes, in his discussion of memory, explicitly says that "this faculty is in man by means of cogitation and deliberation."[35] Furthermore, recollection, as distinguished from memory, is according to Aristotle a sort of investigation

[29] De Memoria et Reminiscentia, 1, 450a, 12–14.

[30] Ibid., 2, 451a, 28–29, and 1, 449b, 18–23.

[31] Enneades, IV, iii, 29.

[32] Ibid., 30.

[33] De Fide Orthodoxa, II, 20. Cf. Nemesius, De Natura Hominis, Ch. 13.

[34] Cf. Liber de Elementis, II, in Omnia Opera Ysaaci, Lyon, 1515, fol. ix, r, a; Hebrew: Sefer ha-Yesodot, II (ed. S. Fried), 55; Liber de Definitionibus, ibid., fol. iii, v, b; Arabic: ed. H. Hirschfeld, Jewish Quarterly Review, 15 (1902–03), p. 690; Hebrew: ed. H. Hirschfeld, Festschrift zum achzigsten Geburtstage Moritz Steinschneider's, 1896, Hebrew part, p. 139. Cf. my paper Isaac Israeli on the Internal Senses in George Alexander Kohut Memorial Volume. The terms used by Isaac Israeli are: (1) بحث, חקירה, *indagatio*, (2) نظر, דרישה, *inquisitio*.

[35] Epitome of De Memoria et Reminiscentia (see below, Ch. II, n. 75), fol. 21 G: "ista nam virtus est in homine per cognitionem." Instead of "*per cognitionem*" of the Latin translation the Arabic and Hebrew have: بفكر وروية, במחשבה והשתכלות = *per cogitationem et deliberationem*.

(ζήτησις) and syllogistic reasoning (συλλογισμός), and is therefore found only in man, who has the power of deliberation (βουλευτικόν).[36] In view of all this, we may assume that in these three lists the third term means, or it originally meant, either memory of intellectual conceptions or recollection. The terms signifying "understanding" and "comprehension" used by Ibn Gabirol and Maimonides thus refer to the process of remembering intellectual conceptions, which according to Aristotle and John of Damascus is connected with learning, contemplation, and natural thinking, or else they refer to recollection, which according to Aristotle involves investigation, syllogistic reasoning, and deliberation. The term signifying "wisdom" used by Ibn Ezra refers to the intellectual conceptions themselves which form the contents of intellectual memory, or to the intellectual process involved in recollection, for in the passage referred to above he says: "And 'wisdom' refers to the forms [= intellectual forms] which are stored up in the posterior [ventricle] of the brain in the cranium." In another passage Ibn Ezra speaks definitely of recollection and says: "Know that in the posterior [ventricle] of the brain in the cranium is recollection, and that place is the storehouse of the forms, so that recollection includes memory." [37]

Second, with regard to Ibn Gabirol's use of a term signifying "creation," "natural disposition," and "creative power" where we should expect him to use a term signifying "imagination," the substitution of terms can be explained by the description of imagination found in Maimonides, a similar description of which, we have reason to believe, must have also been known to Ibn Gabirol. In one place, Maimonides refers to imagination as a creation or natural disposition.[38] In another place he says that "every image in our imagination has been created." [39]

36 De Memoria et Reminiscentia, 2, 453a, 9–14.

37 Commentary on Exodus 20, 1 ff.

38 Moreh Nebukim, II, 36. The term used here for "creation" or "natural disposition" is جبلة (יצירה): שלמות הכח המדמה בעקר היצירה.

39 Ibid., I, 46. The term for "created" used here is مخلوقة (ברואה): כי כל צורה מדומה היא ברואה.

In the threefold classifications we have so far studied there is no description of the functions of the various faculties which they mention. All we know about them is that they correspond to the three Greek terms *φαντασία*, *διάνοια*, and *μνῆσις*, and that they are located in the anterior, middle, and posterior hollows of the brain respectively. But then we have a classification by the Iḫwân al-Ṣafâ which not only reproduces the same threefold classification, with the same localization, but adds to it two other faculties and includes also a description of the functions of each of these five faculties. The enumeration of these faculties, which the Iḫwân al-Ṣafâ designate "spiritual senses," in contradistinction to the five senses which they call "corporeal," together with the description of their functions, is as follows: (1) imagination, which (*a*) receives from sense-perception the impressions of the sensible objects and (*b*) assembles them; (2) cogitation, which distinguishes these impressions one from another and knows the true from the false, the right from the wrong, and the useful from the harmful; (3) memory, which preserves these judgments of the cogitative faculty until the time of need and recollection; (4) speaking faculty, the seat of which is in the throat and tongue and the function of which is to communicate the contents of one's mind to others; (5) productive faculty, the seat of which is in the hands and fingers and by means of which the soul produces the art of writing as well as all the other arts.[40]

Now, of these five internal senses the first three are in terminology and localization identical with the threefold classifications we have dealt with before. The description of these three internal senses which is added in this list can be traced to Aristotle. The description of imagination can be easily recognized as being made up of Aristotle's description of imagination and his description of one of the functions of common sense. Thus the first part of the description given by the Iḫwân al-Ṣafâ of imagination, namely, that which retains the

[40] Cf. Fr. Dieterici, Arabic text: Die Abhandlungen der Ichwân Es-Safâ in Auswahl, pp. 468 ff., 269 ff., 220; German translation: Die Anthropologie der Araber, pp. 56 and 38; Die Lehre der Weltseele bei den Arabern, pp. 46–47. The terms used are as follows: (1) متخيّلة, (2) مفكّرة, (3) حافظة, (4) ناطقة, (5) صانعة.

impressions of sense-perception, reflects Aristotle's statements that "sensations and images remain in the sense-organs even when the sensible objects are withdrawn" [41] and that "imaginations remain in us and resemble corresponding sensations."[42] The second part of their description of imagination, namely, that which assembles all the impressions of the various senses, reflects again Aristotle's description of one of the functions of common sense as that which correlates the various impressions of the senses and forms out of them a unified percept.[43] Similarly their description of cogitation can be traced to Aristotle's description of the cogitative soul (διανοητική ψύχη) as the faculty which judges what is good and what is evil, what is to be pursued and what is to be avoided,[44] and also to his description of διάνοια as containing the functions of combination and separation,[45] that is to say, of the cognition of what is true and false.[46] Furthermore, their use of the term "distinguishes" [47] in connection with the cognition of truth and falsehood reflects Aristotle's use of κρίνειν in connection with the cognition of truth and falsehood.[48] Finally, their definition of memory is analogous to what, as we have shown, Aristotle and others have called intellectual memory, as distinguished from sensitive memory, the latter being a function of imagination. But how did the Iḫwân al-Ṣafâ happen to add the other two unprecedented internal senses to these original three?

I wish to make two suggestions with regard to the question.

My first suggestion is that the fivefold classification of internal senses by the Iḫwân al-Ṣafâ is the result of a combination of two threefold classifications, the Galenic and the Stoic, the second of the three terms being the same in both classifications. The Galenic classification has already been reproduced

41 De Anima. III, 2, 425b, 24–25.
42 Ibid., III, 3, 429a, 4–5.
43 De Sensu et Sensibili, 7, 449a, 3–10.
44 De Anima, III, 7, 431a, 14–17.
45 Metaphysics, VI, 1027b, 29–30.
46 Ibid., 25–27.
47 تمييز.
48 De Anima, III, 3, 428a, 2–3.

before. The Stoic classification is as follows: φωνητικόν, διανοητικόν, γεννητικόν.[49] Now, the fourth term in the Iḫwân al-Ṣafâ's list, "speaking" (*nâṭiḳah*), is a literal translation of the first term in the Stoic list, φωνητικόν. As for the fifth term in their list, "productive" (*ṣâni'ah*), it may be taken to represent the third term in the Stoic list, if we assume that that term, γεννητικόν, which means "productive" in the sense of begetting children, was in its transmission into Arabic taken to mean "productive" in the general sense.

My second suggestion rests on the assumption that the classification of the Iḫwân al-Ṣafâ originated in a list of five terms in which the *fourth* term meant what Aristotle calls "theoretical science" (ἐπιστήμη θεωρητική) and the *fifth* term meant what he calls "practical" (πρακτική) and "productive" (ποιητική) sciences. In that original list, I then secondly assume that the *fourth* and *fifth* faculties, which are additional to the original Galenic three, were derived from a current description of the functions of Galen's second faculty, διανοητική. Thirdly, I also assume that the descriptions of the functions of the *fourth* and *fifth* terms in the list of the Iḫwân al-Ṣafâ were added to the original list as a result of a misunderstanding of the meaning of these terms in the original list.

Let me now explain these three points.

(*a*) The fourth term (*nâṭiḳah*) in the Iḫwân al-Ṣafâ is technically the equivalent of the Greek λογική or λογιστική. Now, λογιστική is sometimes used by Aristotle as the equivalent of θεωρητική (cf. De Anima, III, 9, 432b, 26–27), for which the Arabic is *naẓariyyah*[50] or *'ilmiyyah.*[51] It is quite reasonable to assume that a similar interchange of terms took place also in Arabic, and therefore the Iḫwân al-Ṣafâ's *nâṭiḳah* really means "theoretical" and not merely "rational." Again, as I have

[49] Diogenes Laertius, De Vitis, VII, 110. In other sources for γεννητικόν the term σπερματικόν is used. Cf. Diels, Doxographi Graeci, p. 390. But for our purpose here the assumption of the use of the term γεννητικόν is necessary.

[50] نظريّ. Cf. Averroes, Compendio de Metafisica (ed. Carlos Quirós Rodrígues, Madrid, 1919), § 2, Arabic text, p. 1.

[51] علميّة. Cf. my The Classification of Sciences in Mediaeval Jewish Philosophy in Hebrew Union College Jubilee Volume (1925), p. 265.

shown elsewhere,[52] in the Iḫwân al-Ṣafâ the Aristotelian distinction between theoretical and practical has disappeared and in its place there is only the distinction between theoretical and productive, the Aristotelian practical sciences having been placed by them under theology. While elsewhere for "productive" the Iḫwân al-Ṣafâ use the term *'amaliyyah,*[53] the term *ṣâni'ah* used by them here may have the same meaning, especially when contrasted with *nâṭiḳah.*

(*b*) Now, theoretical, practical, and productive sciences are found to have been included among the functions of Galen's διανοητικόν, in a work of a man who was influential in the early history of Arabic philosophy. I refer to John of Damascus. He says: "To διανοητικόν belong [1] judgments (κρίσεις), assents (συγκαταθέσεις), impetuses (ὁρμαί) toward acting, and aversions (ἀφορμαί) toward, and avoidances of, action; [2] and especially considerations with regard to intellectual notions; and [3] virtues, and sciences, principles of arts, deliberation, and choice." [54]

I have purposely inserted numbers in the translation of the passage quoted in order to indicate the three distinct sets of functions which are ascribed in it to διανοητικόν.

The first set of functions of διανοητικόν mentioned here by John of Damascus reflects Aristotle's statements we have quoted above to the effect that διάνοια is the faculty which judges what is true or false, what is good or evil, and decides what is to be pursued or avoided.[55] The terms συγκαταθέσεις, ὁρμαί, and ἀφορμαί used in this passage show the additional influence of the Stoics. The term κρίσεις used here by John of Damascus and the term *tamayyaza* used by the Iḫwân al-Ṣafâ in the description of cognition show a dependence on a common source. Both of them go back to Aristotle's statement that the knowledge of truth and falsehood involves a judgment and is a sort of combination and separation.[56]

52 Cf. ibid., p. 266.

53 عمليّة. Cf. ibid., p. 265.

54 De Fide Orthodoxa, II, 19.

55 Cf. above, nn. 44, 46. Cf. also below on Isaac Israeli, n. 74.

56 Cf. above, nn. 45, 48.

The second and third sets of functions mentioned by John of Damascus under διανοητικόν can be shown to be an elaboration of Aristotle's general statement that "all thought (διάνοια) is either practical or productive or theoretical," [57] for when we closely examine the terms used by John of Damascus we find that they all fall under the three types of thought, or rather the three classes of science, enumerated by Aristotle. Thus, for instance, the knowledge of intellectual notions, which John of Damascus mentions in the second set of functions, corresponds to Aristotle's definition of metaphysics,[58] which is one of his three theoretical sciences. Thus also the terms "virtues" and "deliberation and choice," used in the third set of functions, are borrowed from ethics,[59] which is one of the three Aristotelian practical sciences. Similarly, the terms "sciences" and "arts," mentioned again in the third set of functions, suggest what Aristotle calls productive sciences.[60]

In view of all this, we may assume that the Iḫwân al-Ṣafâ had before them a fivefold classification of the internal senses, containing: (1) imagination, (2) cogitation, (3) memory, (4) *nâṭiḳah*, and (5) *ṣâni'ah*. The first three terms in that list contained also a description of their function, and the description of the third term, "cogitation," corresponded to the description by John of Damascus of the first set of functions of διανοητικόν. The last two terms contained no description, but they were meant to refer respectively to (1) theoretical science and (2) practical and productive sciences, corresponding to the second and third sets of functions of διανοητικόν in John of Damascus' description.

(*c*) We now come to the third and last step in our argument. The fourth term, *nâṭiḳah*, in the list before the Iḫwân al-Ṣafâ, while technically meaning "rational" and hence "theoretical," comes from a word which like the Greek λόγος literally means "speech." Not having before them any description of that

[57] Metaphysics, VI, 1, 1025b, 25.
[58] Ibid., VI, 1, 1026a, 10–11; cf. De Anima, I, 1, 403b, 15–16.
[59] Cf. terms ἀρετή, βούλευσις, προαίρεσις in Nicomachean Ethics, *passim*.
[60] Cf. terms ἐπιστήμη, τέχνη in Metaphysics, I, 1, 981a, 2.

term, the Iḫwân al-Ṣafâ, or somebody else before them, took it in its literal sense and described it as the faculty of speech, the seat of which is in the tongue and the throat. In taking the term *nâṭiḳah* in its literal sense of speech, they were perhaps supported by some such passage as that in John of Damascus in which τὸ λογικόν, i.e., the Greek equivalent of the Arabic *nâṭiḳah*, is said to be divided into internal (ἐνδιάθετον) and expressed (προφορικόν) speech.[61] Similarly with regard to the fifth term, *ṣâni'ah*, not having before them any description of its functions, they took it in its obvious sense of productive art and described it as the power which produces the art of writing as well as the other arts, and the seat of which is in the hands and fingers.

This analysis of διανοητικόν, together with the fact, which we have mentioned above,[62] that Erigena identified the term "internal sense" with διάνοια, will throw light upon two puzzling classifications of the internal senses which scholars have found difficult to explain. One is found in a Syriac work known as Causa Causarum.[63] Using the terms "spiritual" and "internal,"[64] the author of that work enumerates five senses, which are listed here in the transliterated form of the original terms together with their German equivalents as given by the editor and translator of the text: (1) *hauna*, Vernunft, (2) *mada'a*, Verstand, (3) *sukala*, Erkenntniss, (4) *buyuna*, Einsicht, (5) *parushuta* or *ḥushba*, Unterscheidung.[65] The other is found in an Arabic work, entitled Sirr al-Ḫalîkah, which is attributed to Apollonius of Tyana.[66] Using the term

[61] De Fide Orthodoxa, II, 21.

[62] Cf. above, n. 15.

[63] Cf. Karl Kayser, Das Buch von der Erkenntniss der Wahrheit oder der Ursache aller Ursachen, Syriac text (1889), p. 27, l. 17; p. 125, l. 12; p. 126, l. 16; German translation (1893), pp. 35, 160, 162.

[64] ܪ̈ܓܫܐ ܪ̈ܘܚܢܝܐ (p. 125, l. 12; p. 126, l. 16), ܪ̈ܓܫܐ ܠܓܘܝܐ (p. 27, l. 17). For "external senses" the term used is ܪ̈ܓܫܐ ܒܪ̈ܝܐ (p. 27, l. 15).

[65] (1) ܗܘܢܐ, (2) ܡܕܥܐ, (3) ܣܘܟܠܐ, (4) ܒܘܝܢܐ, (5) ܦܪܘܫܘܬܐ (p. 125, l. 12) or ܚܘܫܒܐ (p. 27, l. 17).

[66] Cf. A. J. Sylvestre de Sacy, Le Livre du Secret de la Créature in Notices et Extraits des Manuscrits de la Bibliothèque Nationale, IV (1789), 116.

"internal senses," the author enumerates five senses, which are listed here together with their French equivalents as given by the translator of the text: (1) *fikrah*, pensée, (2) *fitnah*, réflexion, (3) *dikâ'*, intelligence, (4) *himmah*, esprit, (5) *niyah*, jugement.[67] Now these two classifications have proved rather baffling,[68] for while some of the terms contained in them may be made to mean some of those faculties which are conventionally understood by internal senses, they do not on the whole correspond to any of the conventional fivefold classifications of the internal senses which we shall discuss later. But I shall try to show that this difficulty can be removed if we take the term "internal" or "spiritual" senses in these two texts not in its usual meaning but rather in the meaning in which it is taken by Erigena, namely, as identical with *διάνοια*.

In our analysis of the definition of *διανοητικόν* by John of Damascus we have already seen how in one set of terms he virtually reproduces Aristotle's description of *διάνοια* as the function of combination and separation[69] and of the distinction[70] between good and evil[71] and between true and false.[72] More compactly, and evidently following the same passages of Aristotle, Isaac Israeli similarly attributes to the "cogitative faculty," i.e., the *διανοητικόν*, the functions of perscrutation, discernment, and combination,[73] and in another place he attributes to that faculty a somewhat amplified list, containing the following functions: (1) interpretation and discretion, (2) perscrutation, (3) separation and combination, and (4) the knowledge of things according to their truth.[74] All these terms, as will have been noticed, are of the same nature as

[67] (1) فكرة, (2) فطنة, (3) ذكاء, (4) همّة, (5) نيّة.

[68] Cf. A. J. Sylvestre de Sacy, loc. cit., n. *m*, and S. Horovitz, op. cit., p. 257, n. 106; p. 258, n. 107.

[69] Cf. above, n. 45.

[70] Cf. above, nn. 47, 48.

[71] Cf. above, n. 44.

[72] Cf. above, n. 46.

[73] Liber de Elementis, II, fol. ix, r, a: "cogitationis enim est perscrutari et discernere et componere." Sefer ha-Yesodot, II, *55*: לפי שיש לכח המחשבי כח החקירה וההבדל ו[ה]חבור.

[74] Liber de Elementis, III, fol. x, r, a: "intellectualis sensus: qui est (1) interpretatio et discretio, (2) et perscrutatio, (3) et solutio et ligatio, (4) et cognitio rerum

those found in Aristotle and John of Damascus. Now, the five Syriac terms used in the Causa Causarum and the five Arabic terms used in Sirr al-Ḫalîkah, with all their vagueness, do on the whole describe certain functions of thought, and with a little effort one could perhaps conjecturally show that they possess some specific meaning, corresponding to the terms used by Aristotle, John of Damascus, and Isaac Israeli in the description of *διάνοια*. Furthermore, in a work which is extant in Hebrew and conjecturally attributed to Isaac Israeli, reason, by which is meant cogitation, is said to contain the following five functions: (1) *ḥokmah*, wisdom, (2) *binah*, understanding, (3) *hakkarah*, discrimination, (4) *yedi'ah*, knowledge, (5) *ṭub ha-maḥashabah*, good thinking.[75] In this passage, it will be noticed, the five terms correspond almost exactly to the five terms in the Syriac and Arabic passages, three of them being of the same root as the Syriac terms.

That the term "spiritual" or "internal" senses used in Causa Causarum means the thinking faculty can be shown by a study of the context in which it occurs. The author of the work contrasts two views with regard to the constituent faculties of the human soul. According to some philosophers, he says, the rational soul[76] has three faculties,[77] namely, (1) knowing[78] or thinking[79] faculty, which is rationality[80] itself, (2) an-

---

secundum veritate." Sefer ha-Yesodot, III, 68: חוש השכלי אשר הוא (1) ההכרה, (2) והחקירה, (3) וההתר והקישור, (4) והעמידה [= וההתבוננות] על אמתת הענינים.

By "intellectualis sensus" Isaac Israeli means here *διάνοια*. The combination of the terms "intellectualis" and "sensus" can be explained on the ground of Aristotle's own use of the term *αἴσθησις* in the sense of *νοῦς* in Nicomachean Ethics, VI, 11, 143b, 5. The terms "interpretatio," "discretio," "perscrutatio," "investigatio," and their Arabic and Hebrew equivalents I have shown to reflect the Greek *κρίσις*. Cf. my paper Isaac Israeli on the Internal Senses in op. cit.

[75] Sefer ha-Ruaḥ weha-Nefesh le-Rabbi Isaac ha-Ysraeli, ed. M. Steischneider, in Ha-Karmel, I (1871–72), 202: ואם אמרנו חכמה ובינה והכרה וידיעה וטוב המחשבה הנה כל זה מכח השכל. For the use of the term שכל in the sense of *cogitatio*, see above, n. 74.

[76] ܢܦܫܐ ܡܠܝܠܬܐ (p. 125, l. 8) = *λογιστική*.

[77] ܚܝܠܐ (l. 7) = *δύναμις*.

[78] ܝܕܘܥܬܢܘܬܐ (l. 8) = *νόησις*.

[79] ܡܬܪܥܝܢܘܬܐ (l. 8) = *διανόησις*.

[80] ܡܠܝܠܘܬܐ (l. 8) = *λόγος*.

ger,[81] and (3) desire.[82] According to other philosophers, whom the anonymous author himself follows, it has only two faculties, (1) animal faculty [83] and (2) rational faculty,[84] the latter of which is subdivided into five spiritual [85] or internal [86] senses. Now, it is quite evident that the three faculties which he enumerates first correspond to the Platonic tripartite division of the soul: (1) the rational (*λογιστικόν*), (2) the irascible (*θυμοειδές*), (3) the concupiscent (*ἐπιθυμητικόν*).[87] It is also quite evident that his subsequent reduction of the irascible and concupiscent faculties to one animal faculty reflects two statements of Aristotle, first, that concupiscence (*ἐπιθυμία*) and irascibility (*θυμός*) are included under appetency (*ὄρεξις*) and hence under sensation (*αἴσθησις*),[88] and, second, that it is sensation primarily which constitutes the animal (*ζῷον*).[89] But inasmuch as his five spiritual or internal senses are subdivisions of what he calls the knowing or thinking or rational faculty, they cannot of necessity be what is conventionally understood by "internal senses," for the latter, as we have already seen, generally include imagination and memory and sometimes also, as we shall see later, common sense. But neither imagination nor common sense belongs to the knowing, thinking, or rational faculty of the soul, and as for memory, it belongs only accidentally, as we have seen above, to the rational faculty; primarily it belongs to the sensible faculty. It is therefore clear that these internal senses of the Causa Causarum belong, as we have set out to show, to the *διανοητικόν*, so that the term "internal sense" is used there in the same sense as in Erigena.

[81] ܚܡܬܐ (l. 9) = *θυμός*.

[82] ܪܓܬܐ (l. 10) = *ἐπιθυμία*.

[83] ܚܝܐ (l. 10) = *ζωός*.

[84] ܡܠܝܠܐ (l. 10) = *λογιστικός*.

[85] Cf. above, n. 64.

[86] Cf. above, n. 64.

[87] Cf. Zeller, Die Philosophie der Griechen, II, 1 (5th edition, 1922), pp. 844–845.

[88] De Anima, II, 3, 414b, 1–2.

[89] Ibid., II, 2, 413b, 2.

CHAPTER II

Tracing the origin of the *virtus aestimativa* (Arabic: *wahm*) to Aristotle. — How the introduction of *virtus aestimativa* has brought about other changes in the classification of the internal senses: two kinds of compositive imagination. — The *virtus aestimativa* in Alfarabi: his fourfold classification. — The introduction of "common sense": the seven internal faculties. — Avicenna's various fivefold classifications. — Algazali's classifications. — Damiri. — Judah ha-Levi, Baḥya ibn Paḳudah, and Abraham ibn Daud. — Averroes' departure from Avicenna: his fourfold and threefold classifications. — The case of Maimonides. — Post-Maimonidean Hebrew philosophic texts: Joseph Zabara, Zohar, Shem-Ṭob Falaquera, Ruaḥ Ḥen, Gershon ben Solomon, Meir Aldabi, Hillel of Verona.

THE history of the classification of the internal senses, it is said,[1] consists in the rise of the original three Galenic faculties to five by the addition of "common sense" and of what the scholastics call *aestimatio*. This is only partly correct, for, as we have already seen, there was the fivefold classification of the Iḫwân al-Ṣafâ which arose either from the combination of the Galenic and the Stoic threefold classifications or from the breaking up of the Galenic, or rather Aristotelian, διανοητικόν into its constituent elements. Then, also, we shall show that prior to the rise of the original three to five by the addition of "common sense" and "estimation" there was a fourfold classification which arose by the addition of "estimation" only. Incidentally we shall also show that the generally accepted explanation of the origin of the estimative faculty is to be discarded, and a new explanation will be offered. Furthermore, we intend to show how the addition of estimation to the original threefold classification of the internal senses has completely changed the meaning of the Arabic, Hebrew, and Latin terms which represented originally the Greek διανοητικόν, and how it has also introduced a new distinction in the terms representing the Greek φαντασία. Still further, we shall show how with the introduction of "common sense" and "estimation" the original three internal senses rose not to five but to seven, and how these seven were variously combined by different authors and sometimes even by one and the

[1] Cf. S. Horovitz, op. cit., pp. 240–242.

same author to yield a fivefold classification. In connection with this we shall also endeavor to determine the exact meaning of Averroes' views on the internal senses and the scheme of his two classifications. Finally, when we come to deal again with Latin texts we shall show how these various classifications in Arabic literature have given rise to a further development which continued until the time of Kant.

But let us begin our history of the subsequent development of the classification of the internal senses by a discussion of that faculty which in Arabic is known as *wahm* and in scholastic philosophy is known as *aestimatio* or *vis aestimativa*. By definition, estimation is that faculty by which animals instinctively pursue certain things and avoid others — as, for instance, the instinctive action of a lamb in running to another lamb, even if it has never seen it before, and similarly its instinctive action in fleeing from a wolf, even if it has never seen one before. In Aristotle no mention is made of a faculty known as "estimation," but scholars have tried to identify it with what Aristotle calls δόξα.[2] When an objection was raised against this identification on the ground of the fact that the characteristic distinction of the estimative faculty as the equivalent in animals of reason in man does not correspond to δόξα, which according to Aristotle does not exist in animals,[3] reference was made to Porphyry, who reports that according to some philosophers δοξαστικόν is connected with sensation and imagination.[4] The conclusion to be drawn from this reference was that those who connected δοξαστικόν with sensation and imagination would of necessity also attribute it to animals as one of their faculties. This conclusion, however, does not

[2] Cf. A. Schmoelders, Documenta Philosophiae Arabum (1836), pp. 116–118; S. Landauer, Die Psychologie des Ibn Sînâ in Zeitschrift der Deutschen Morgenländischen Gesellschaft, 29 (1875), p. 401, n. 6; S. Horovitz, op. cit., pp. 250–251, n. 93. But this connection between *aestimatio* and δόξα has already been discussed by Albertus Magnus, Liber de Apprehensione, Pars III, § 11: "*Discipulus.* Similitudinem etiam cum opinione habere videtur. *Philosophia* . . . et ideo quidam ex alumnis meis hanc virtutem [= *aestimativam*] credebant opinionem esse." *Opinio* = δόξα. Cf. also D. B. Macdonald, Wahm in Arabic and its Cognates in The Journal of the Royal Asiatic Society (1922), pp. 505–521.

[3] De Anima, III, 3, 428a, 19–22.

[4] Cf. Stobaeus, Eclogae (ed. Wachsmuth), Vol. I, p. 348, and cf. Landauer, loc. cit.

seem to me necessarily to follow from the premise. The mere statement that δοξαστικόν is connected with sensation and imagination does not necessarily mean that it must be possessed by animals; it may only mean that wherever δοξαστικόν exists, that is, in man, it is connected with sensation and imagination. Still less does it explain how the estimative faculty, if it represents Aristotle's δόξα as modified and extended to animals by the philosophers quoted by Porphyry, came to be used primarily as a function peculiar to animals. At best it could only explain why it should be applied also to animals; it does not explain why it should apply primarily to animals. Furthermore, the characteristic description of the estimative faculty as that of the instinctive fears and likes of animals does not correspond to the characteristic descriptions of δόξα which we find in Aristotle.[5]

Another alleged link connecting the estimative faculty with Aristotle's δόξα was discovered in a passage by Philoponus in his commentary on De Anima. Taking up Aristotle's statement that neither δόξα nor πίστις (De An. III, 11, 434a, 10) is to be found in animals, Philoponus raises an objection on the ground that horses have an instinctive fear of the lash. In answer to this objection, he says that this instinctive fear of the horse is not due to conviction (πειθόν) but rather to habit (ἐθισμόν).[6] But this passage, which is taken to establish a link between the estimative faculty and δόξα, seems to me to prove on the contrary that there is no connection between them, since δόξα is explicitly said by Aristotle to be connected with πίστις, whereas the animal faculty under consideration is explicitly said by Philoponus to have no connection with πίστις. Nor can we infer from this passage that *wahm*, or the estimative faculty, is connected in some way with the Greek ἐθισμόν, for there is no etymological connection between these terms. We must therefore look to some other source in Aristotle to account for the rise of the estimative faculty.

[5] On the functions of δόξα, cf. J. Geyser, Die Erkenntnistheorie des Aristoteles, pp. 181 ff.

[6] Cf. Ioannis Philoponi Aristotelis de Animae Libros Commentaria (ed. M. Hayduck), p. 500, ll. 25 ff., and cf. S. Horovitz, op. cit., pp. 250–251, n. 93.

I am going to show that such a source can be found.

The need of introducing *wahm*, or the estimative faculty, as a new faculty arose, it seems to me, out of a desire to supplement a deficiency which seemed to exist in Aristotle's account of the actual motion of pursuit and avoidance which is observed in both man and animals. While pure judgment of what is to be pursued or avoided is attributed by Aristotle to the cogitative soul (ψυχὴ διανοητική), actual pursuit or avoidance, according to him, is determined by the combined action of the appetitive faculty (ὀρεκτικόν) and imagination (φαντασία).[7] Now, imagination is possessed by both man and animal, but in man it may be rational (λογιστική) or deliberative (βουλευτική), whereas in animals it is only sensitive (αἰσθητική). The difference between the motions of pursuit and avoidance caused by these two kinds of imagination, as may be gathered from Aristotle, is as follows: the motion caused by sensitive imagination is a pursuit and avoidance of something that directly causes pleasure and pain, whereas that caused by rational and deliberative imagination may be a pursuit and avoidance of something that may remotely or indirectly cause pleasure and pain, or what Aristotle calls good and evil.[8] Now this explanation of the motion of animals would have been sufficient if animals pursued only that which is directly good and avoided that which is directly bad. But this is contrary to fact. Animal life shows a kind of planning for the attainment of remote pleasure and for the avoidance of remote pain. Aristotle himself describes such a kind of behavior on the part of animals in his Historia Animalium, VIII–IX. Now, sensitive imagination could not accomplish that, for by definition, as we have seen, it can produce only pursuit and avoidance of direct pleasure and pain. It would therefore be necessary to introduce another faculty which would act upon the imagination of animals as the rational or deliberative faculty acts upon the imagination of man.

The suggestion that such a faculty exists in animals is made by Aristotle himself. In one place he says that comparable

[7] De Anima, III, 7, 431a, 14–17, and III, 10, 433b, 27–30.

[8] Ibid., III, 7, 431a, 8–20; III, 10, 433b, 27–11, 434a, 10.

to intelligence (διάνοια) in man there is in animals something equivalent to sagacity (σύνεσις)[9] or a natural faculty (φυσικὴ δύναμις) equivalent to art (τέχνη), wisdom (σοφία), and sagacity (σύνεσις).[10] In another place he describes animals as prudent (φρόνιμος)[11] or as sagacious (συνετός).[12] In still another place he speaks of animals as having a faculty of forethought (προνοητικὴ δύναμις).[13] Now, this faculty of sagacity, prudence, or forethought, which Aristotle attributes to animals as corresponding to intellect in man, accurately corresponds to the description of the Arabic *wahm* and scholastic *aestimatio*. The common element which appears in the description of *wahm* or *aestimatio* in Arabic, Hebrew, and Latin writings is the fact of its being the faculty whereby an animal, without previous experience, perceives the insensible forms connected with the impression of sensible objects, such as the sheep's instinctive perception of hostility and fear at the sight of a wolf or its instinctive perception of friendliness and love at the sight of its young ones. Furthermore, when estimation in animals is combined with imagination it becomes a faculty by which animals are enabled to perform work which in the case of men is ascribed to art and intelligence. Abraham ibn Daud illustrates this by the example of the cochineal insect making almond-shaped structures and of the bee making honeycombs.[14] Similarly in Aristotle the swallow is said to make its nest and the spider its web neither by art (τέχνῃ), nor after inquiry (ζητήσαντα) or deliberation (βουλευσάμενα), nor by intelligence (νῷ), but by nature (φύσει).[15] That animal action which Aristotle attributes to "nature" is the same as what is later described as "estimation" is evident from Averroes' statement that what he, evidently following Aristotle,

9 Historia Animalium, VIII, 1, 588a, 23.

10 Ibid., 29–31.

11 De Partibus Animalium, II, 2, 648a, 5–8.

12 Ibid., II, 4, 650b, 24.

13 Nicomachean Ethics, VI, 7, 1141a, 28.

14 Emunah Ramah, I, 6, p. 29.

15 Physics, II, 8, 199a, 20–30. This Aristotelian view recurs in the writings of the Stoics, Philo, and Cicero. Cf. I. Heinemann, Poseidonios' metaphysische Schriften, II, 464–465.

describes in animals as the work of "nature" is described by Avicenna as "estimation" (cf. below, nn. 79, 80). What happened then is really this: The "natural faculty" with which animals were endowed according to Aristotle was split up into two faculties, one becoming pure estimation and the other becoming estimation combined with imagination. But while estimation exists primarily in animals, taking in them the place of reason in man, it is said to exist also in man and to be often used by man in many of his judgments which are not affected directly by reason.[16]

The introduction of *wahm*, or estimation, to correspond in animals to λογιστική or βουλευτική in man has brought about two other changes in the classification of the internal senses.

In the first place, it has brought about a change in the description of *fikr*, which, as we have seen, was hitherto used as the equivalent of one of the functions of διανοητικόν. From now on, in Arabic as well as in Hebrew and Latin texts which include *fikr* in their classifications, the term *fikr* with its Hebrew and Latin equivalents no longer stands for διάνοια but for διάνοια combined with φαντασία, which may be called φαντασία διανοητική. Though Aristotle uses no such expression, he does use the expression φαντασία λογιστική or βουλευτική, which amounts to the same thing, for διανοητικόν, being a function of νοῦς, is joined with νοῦς by Aristotle (De Anima, II, 3, 414b, 18), and νοῦς is used by him as synonymous with λογιστικόν (ibid., III, 9, 432b, 26). Naturally the function ascribed to *fikr* in its new sense of imagination combined with διάνοια will have to correspond to the function ascribed by Aristotle to διάνοια without imagination, except for such changes as the addition of imagination of necessity will have introduced into it. The faculty of διάνοια uncombined with imagination, as well as the Arabic *fikr* in its earlier usage, as we have seen above, is described by Aristotle as a power of combination and separation;[17] so also now the new usage of *fikr* in the sense of διάνοια combined with imagination is gen-

[16] So stated by Avicenna in Canon (see reference below, n. 31).

[17] Cf. above, Ch. I, nn. 45, 56.

erally described as a power of combination and separation.[18] But the objects which these two faculties are said to combine and separate differ. In the case of διάνοια without imagination, it is the combination and separation of ideas, i.e., the formation of positive or negative judgments. In the case of διάνοια combined with imagination, it is the combination and separation of the images, i.e., the construction out of images of things existent, new composite images of things nonexistent, or the breaking up of images of things existent into images of things nonexistent. A suggestion of this type of imagination is found in Aristotle, when toward the end of his discussion of rational or deliberative imagination (φαντασία λογιστική or βουλευτική), i.e., imagination combined with διάνοια, he says: "Hence we have the power of constructing a single image out of a number of images."[19]

In the second place, it has invested one of the forms of the Arabic word for imagination (*mutaḫayyilah*) with a special meaning. Hitherto, as we have seen in the Iḫwân al-Ṣafâ, *mutaḫayyilah* was used interchangeably with *taḫayyul* and *ḫayâl*[20] as the equivalent of the Greek φαντασία. From now on it will be used, as a rule, as the equivalent of the Greek φαντασία plus *wahm* or *aestimatio*, corresponding in animals to the φαντασία λογιστική or βουλευτική in man. For with the introduction of *wahm* or *aestimatio* as a sort of intelligence in animals and with the new use of *fikr* in the sense of a compositive sort of imagination resulting from the combination of imagination and reason in man, animals, too, were endowed by philosophers with a compositive sort of imagination, which in them was likewise the result of a combination of the faculty of imagination and the faculty of *wahm* or *aestimatio*. That animals are endowed with a faculty of constructing things analogously to the construction of things by human art is

[18] This is what is primarily meant by the expressions تركيب و تفصيل, הרכבה ופירוד, *componendi et dividendi* (Avicenna, Canon; see below, n. 31), which generally occur in Arabic, Hebrew, and Latin texts in the description of this kind of imagination. Cf. below, Ch. III, n. 17. Sometimes, however, these expressions assume a different meaning in certain texts.

[19] De Anima, III, 11, 434a, 9–10.

[20] متخيّلة, تخيّل ; خيال.

recognized by Aristotle in the passage we have quoted above from Physics, I, 8, 199a, 20–30, though he attributes it simply to nature without giving to it any special name. Accordingly, in this new classification, while *fikr* in man reflects Aristotle's φαντασία λογιστική or βουλευτική, *mutaḫayyilah* in animals cannot be said, strictly speaking, to reflect its antithesis φαντασία αἰσθητική.[21] If any Greek equivalent is to be found for it, it would be φαντασία συνετή or φρόνιμη or προνοητική, inasmuch as we have shown that *wahm* represents σύνεσις, φρόνησις, and πρόνοια. In our discussion of the subject we shall henceforth designate these two faculties compositive human imagination and compositive animal imagination. They will differ from imagination proper in that the latter has for its function merely the retention of images, on which account we shall call it retentive imagination. The distinction between retentive and compositive imagination is analogous to the modern distinction between reproductive and productive imagination. But I prefer the terms "compositive" and "retentive" because they preserve the original characteristic terms which occur in the descriptions of these two faculties.

The first to introduce *wahm* into the classification of internal senses,[22] with the consequent changes in the meaning of *mufakkirah* and the addition of another kind of imagination (*mutaḫayyilah*), is Alfarabi. Two classifications are given by

[21] The correspondence of what we have called "compositive human imagination" to φαντασία λογιστική and "compositive animal imagination" to φαντασία αἰσθητική has been generally assumed on the ground of the fact that the former two refer to men and the latter two refer to animals. Cf. S. Landauer, op. cit., p. 400, n. 4; S. Horovitz, op. cit., p. 247, n. 85.

[22] Independently of the internal senses the estimative faculty has already been described by Isaac Israeli in his Liber de Definitionibus, fol. iiii, r, a, and as later in Alfarabi and Avicenna and their followers it is ascribed to animals, in whom it corresponds to reason in men: "Et propter hoc facte sunt bestiae estimantes (ظانّة, וזוממין) non meditantes (متوهّمة, בעלי רעיון)." The term ظنّ, *aestimatio*, זמימות, occurs also in that text. It will have been noticed that the Arabic term used by Isaac Israeli for *aestimatio* is not *wahm* but rather *ẓann*, which is used by Avicenna as the equivalent of *wahm* (see below, n. 43). The term *wahm* (*meditatio*, רעיון, הגות) is used by him as a description of a faculty which is above *aestimatio* but below *cogitatio* (*fikr*, מחשבה). Cf. my paper Isaac Israeli on the Internal Senses in op. cit. See also the discussion of Baḥya ibn Paḳuda, below, nn. 64, 65.

him, one of which contains also a description of each of the faculties in addition to their enumeration,[23] and the other of which contains only an enumeration of terms.[24] In the former, five terms are enumerated and explained as follows: (1) imagination, which, unlike the Iḫwân al-Ṣafâ and like Aristotle, he describes as having only the function of retaining the images of sensible objects; (2) estimation; (3) memory, which, with the introduction of "estimation," he describes as the retention of the forms of "estimation" instead of those of "cogitation" in the description of the Iḫwân al-Ṣafâ; (4) compositive human imagination; (5) compositive animal imagination.[25] But though five terms are enumerated here, Alfarabi probably did not mean to give a fivefold classification of internal senses, but rather, like many others after him, as we shall soon see, he counted compositive human and animal imagination as one, thus having all together four internal senses. That four was the number of internal senses meant by him can be confirmed by his other classification. There he gives only four terms, substituting the *fifth* term of the first classification for its *first*. The terms are as follows: (1) imagination (*mutaḫayyilah*), (2) estimation, (3) memory, (4) compositive human imagination.[26] Now, if we assume that Alfarabi counts compositive human and animal imagination as one faculty, then we may take the first term (*mutaḫayyilah*) in this classification in the sense of "retentive imagination," in which sense it has been used by the Iḫwân al-Ṣafâ, and explain the omission of compositive animal imagination here on the ground of its being

[23] Cf. Risâlat fuṣuṣ al-Ḥukmun, § 36, in Fr. Dieterici's Alfārābī's Philosophische Abhandlungen (1890), pp. 73 ff. German translation (1892), pp. 121 ff.

[24] 'Uyun al-Musâi'il, § 20, in op. cit., p. 63. German translation, p. 105. Cf. also A. Schmoelders, Documenta Philosophiae Arabum (1836), Arabic, p. 32; Latin, p. 54.

[25] (1) مصوّرة, (2) وهم, (3) حافظة, (4) مفكّرة, (5) متخيّلة.

[26] والاحساس الباطنة (1) المتخيّلة, (2) والوهم, (3) والذاكرة, (4) والمفكّرة.

Dieterici erroneously takes المتخيّلة as an adjective and translates the passage as follows (op. cit., p. 105): "sowie die inneren vorstellenden Sinne wie Vermutung, Erinnrung, Nachdenken." Schmoelders (op. cit., p. 55) translates it correctly: "varii sensus interni modi, imaginatio scilicet, informatio, recordatio, cogitatio." Schmoelders' translation of *wahm* by *informatio*, however, is inaccurate.

counted as one faculty with compositive human imagination. But if we assume that Alfarabi counted them in his other classification as two faculties, then however the term *mutaḫayyilah* is taken in this classification, whether in the sense of retentive imagination or in the sense of compositive animal imagination, there will be no adequate explanation for Alfarabi's omission here of one of the five faculties enumerated in the other list. Despite these fourfold classifications, however, Alfarabi sometimes uses the general term imagination to include both retentive and compositive imagination as well as estimation.[27]

In none of the classifications of the internal senses we have thus far discussed is the Aristotelian common sense expressly mentioned, though in Augustine and Gregory the Great two of its functions are ascribed to the internal sense in general and in the Iḫwân al-Ṣafâ one of its functions is included in the description of imagination. Isaac Israeli, who does make mention of common sense, excludes it from both the internal and external senses, or, as he calls them, spiritual and corporeal senses, and makes of it a neutral sense occupying an intermediate position between the two.[28] The first to specifically include common sense in his classification of the internal senses is Avicenna. The characteristic description of common sense which recurs in his writings is analogous to Aristotle's characterization of it as the faculty which distinguishes and compares the data of sense-perception.[29] In the language of Avicenna it is described as the sense wherein the impressions conveyed through the sense-organs are assembled and unified — a descrip-

[27] Cf. Sefer ha-Hatḥalot (in Ẓ. Filipowsky's Sefer ha-Asif, Leipzig, 1849), p. 3: "The imaginative faculty is that which [*a*] retains the impressions of the sensible objects after the latter have disappeared from sense-perception, and [b] combines some of these impressions with others and separates some of them from others. . . . [*c*] Moreover, to this faculty belongs also the apprehension of that which is beneficial or injurious, pleasant or unpleasant." The three functions ascribed here to imagination correspond respectively to (*a*) retentive imagination, (*b*) compositive imagination, and (*c*) estimation.

[28] חוש רוחני, *sensus spiritualis*; חוש גשמי, *sensus corporeus*. Liber de Elementis, II, Latin, fol. ix, r, a; Hebrew, pp. 53–54. Ibid.: "cum sit [*sensus communis*] inter sensum visibilem scilicet corporeum et informatum qui est in anteriori parte cerebri nominatum phantasia, et propter hoc nominatur sensus communis."

[29] De Anima, III, 2, 426b, 8–427a, 16.

tion which, as we have seen, is used also by the Iḫwân al-Ṣafâ and reflects a statement by Aristotle in De Sensu et Sensibili, 7, 449a, 3–10.[30] Its location, in agreement with Galen rather than with Aristotle, is, like that of retentive imagination, in the anterior hollow of the brain.

With this introduction of common sense the classification of the internal senses is completed. There are now all together seven faculties included under the internal senses: (1) common sense, (2) retentive imagination, (3) compositive animal imagination, (4) compositive human imagination, (5) estimation, (6) memory, (7) recollection. The characteristic expressions used in the description of these seven terms are as follows: (1) common sense is the center at which all the senses converge; it distinguishes between the qualities of the different senses; it adds the element of consciousness to sensation; but while it *receives* all the impressions of the senses, it does not *retain* them. (2) Retentive imagination *retains* the impressions of the sensible objects *received* by common sense after the objects have disappeared. (3) Compositive animal and (4) human imagination consists in the construction of new unreal images out of real images. (5) Estimation perceives the insensible forms connected with sensible objects and knows what is to be pursued and what is to be avoided. (6) Memory retains the forms of estimation just as retentive imagination retains the forms of sensible objects. (7) Recollection is the restoration of something to memory after it has been forgotten.

Still, not all of these seven are considered by Avicenna as distinct faculties. Some of them are combined by him to form one faculty, with the result that the seven are reduced to five. But Avicenna does not seem to be decided as to which of these seven faculties should be combined, and consequently various combinations are to be found in his Canon,[31] Al-Shifâ',[32] Al-

[30] Cf. Risâlah fi al-Nafs, Ch. 7 (see below, n. 34) and see above, Ch. I, n. 43.

[31] Canon, Lib. I, Fen I, Doctrina VI, Cap. 5. Arabic text (Rome, 1593), fol. 35; Latin text (Venice, 1582), fol. 27 v; Hebrew text (Naples, 1491).

[32] Al-Shifâ'. Arabic text unavailable at present writing, but scheme of classification and terminology used in it are the same as in Al-Najât. Latin translation of part dealing with soul in Avicenna, De Anima (Pavia, c. 1485), fols. 7d–8a, 28d–34c. Analysis of this work in M. Winter, Über Avicennas Opus egregium de anima (Liber sextus naturalium) (München, 1903).

Najât,[33] and Risâlah fi al-Nafs.[34] These varieties of combination relate (*a*) to common sense and imagination; (*b*) to compositive imagination, both animal and human, and estimation; (*c*) to memory and recollection. We shall comment upon these three types of combination one by one.

(*a*) With regard to common sense and imagination two views are recorded by Avicenna in Canon. According to the philosophers, common sense and imagination are distinct faculties, the former being the *recipient* of the images of things, the latter the *retainer* [35] of the images. According to the physicians, the two constitute a single faculty, though the distinction between the receptive power and the retentive power is still to be observed in it. In Al-Najât, however, he follows the philosophers' view and treats common sense and imagination as two faculties, one receptive and the other retentive, but, curiously enough, he reproduces the Greek word *φαντασία* in Arabic transliteration and makes it synonymous with "common sense," and right after that he uses the Arabic terms *ḫayāl* and *muṣawwizah*, which are translations of the Greek *phantasia*, as one of the functions of common sense.[36] In Risâlah fi al-Nafs, on the other hand, he seems to go even further than the physicians mentioned in Canon, for he not only treats common sense and imagination as one faculty but even identifies them, defining both of them in terms of common sense, and making no mention of any distinction between *reception* and *retention* within it.

Now, who are the physicians to whom Avicenna refers as combining common sense and imagination into one? Naturally one would be inclined to identify them with Galen and his

[33] Al-Najât, II: Physics, p. 45. Published together with Canon, Rome, 1593.

[34] Risâlah fi al-Nafs, Ch. 7. Arabic original with German translation and notes under the title of Die Psychologie des Ibn Sînâ by S. Landauer in Zeitschrift der Deutschen Morgenländischen Gesellschaft, 29 (1875), pp. 335 ff.

[35] "Et quae harum duarum est recipiens (القوة القابلة, הכח המקבל) alia est a custudiente (الحافظة, השומר)."

[36] In Isaac Israeli's Liber de Elementis, II (Latin, fol. ix, r, a; Hebrew, p. 53), the Greek *φαντασία* is correctly identified with imagination: "Et informatum (*imaginatio*, cf. below, Ch. III, p. 116) qui est in anteriori parte cerebri nominatum phantasia." המצייר שהוא בבטן המוקדם שבמח [הנקרא אל] פנטסיא. Cf below, note 42.

followers. But Galen never clearly stated that common sense and imagination were one. In fact the term "common sense" does not occur in his writings. The only evidence one can advance for this identification is the fact that in his enumeration of the faculties of the soul the terms *φαντασία*, *διανοητικόν*, and *μνημονικόν* are mentioned immediately after the five senses, and no mention at all is made of common sense. But for that matter Aristotle himself never includes common sense in his various enumerations of the faculties of the soul,[37] and in one place he says that while the faculty of imagination and that of common sense are identical, they still differ in their essential notion.[38] Furthermore, Isaac Israeli, who was a physician, and according to Maimonides more of a physician than a philosopher,[39] does not, as we have seen, identify common sense and imagination.[40]

Evidently Avicenna does not mean to contrast here the view of any particular physician or of any group of physicians or of physicians in general with that of philosophers in general. What he means to contrast are the two ways in which the internal senses may be viewed, the medical or physiological and the philosophical, without one's necessarily excluding the other. He himself seems to combine in his various writings these two ways, and so also does Averroes, as we shall see later. Now from the physiological point of view the faculties of the soul are regarded only with reference to the bodily organs in which they reside and not with reference to the variety of functions which they perform, for physicians, as says Avicenna in connection with the estimative faculty, concern themselves with faculties of the soul only in so far as a hindrance in their functioning can be traced to an injury in the bodily organs in which they are located. Consequently, if two functionally

[37] Cf. De Anima, II, 3, 414a, 29 ff.; III, 9, 431a, 29 ff.

[38] De Somniis, 1, 459a, 15–17: *καὶ ἔστι μὲν τὸ αὐτὸ τῷ αἰσθητικῷ τὸ φανταστικόν, τὸ δ' εἶναι φανταστικῷ καὶ αἰσθητικῷ ἕτερον*. The term *αἰσθητικῷ* in this passage is generally understood to refer to "common sense." Cf. below, n. 94. For the meaning of *τὸ εἶναι*, see G. Rodier's note on De Anima, II, 1, 412b, 11, in his Aristotle: Traité de l'Ame, II, 180.

[39] Letter to Samuel Ibn Tibbon in Ḳobeẓ Teshubot ha-Rambam we-Iggerotaw, II, 28b.

[40] Cf. above, n. 28.

different faculties of the soul reside in one bodily organ, then physicians will regard them as one faculty, inasmuch as any injury in that organ will affect the two faculties alike. From this point of view, then, common sense and imagination are to be considered as one faculty, inasmuch as the seat of both of them is in the anterior ventricle of the brain, and it is perhaps for this reason that Galen has enumerated only three post-sensationary faculties. From the philosophic point of view, however, a faculty is that which has a distinctive function, irrespective of its location in the brain. For this reason, common sense and imagination are according to them two faculties. If the philosophers themselves, as Avicenna reports, are in doubt as to whether memory and recollection are two distinct faculties, it is because they are in doubt whether these two have distinct functions.

(*b*) With regard to compositive human and animal imagination and estimation, in Canon Avicenna treats them all as one faculty. In Al-Shifâ' and Al-Najât no numbers are given, but from the context it is quite evident that compositive human and animal imagination is treated as one faculty, whereas estimation is treated as a separate faculty. In Risâlah fi al-Nafs, again, no numbers are given, but from the context it is quite certain that estimation is a distinct faculty by itself, and with less certainty it would seem that compositive animal imagination and compositive human imagination are counted as two faculties.

(*c*) Similarly with regard to memory and recollection, in Canon Avicenna refers to a difference of opinion even among philosophers as to whether they constitute one faculty or two faculties; in Al-Shifâ', Al-Najât, and Risâlah fi al-Nafs, however, he makes no distinction between memory and recollection.

In correspondence with this variety of combinations, Avicenna gives in Canon three kinds of classifications of the internal senses. First, a threefold classification: (1) (*a*) common sense and (*b*) imagination (defined in terms of common sense); (2) compositive (*a*) human and (*b*) animal imagination and (*c*) estimation; (3) (*a*) memory and (*b*) recollection. Second, a fourfold classification, by counting common sense and imagination as two. Third, a fivefold classification, by counting memory and recollection as two.[41] In Al-Shifá' and Al-Najât the classification would seem to be fivefold, as follows: (1) common sense, synonymous with the Arabic transliteration of the Greek φαντασία, (2) retentive imagination, (3) compositive (*a*) animal and (*b*) human imagination, (4) estimation, (5) memory and recollection.[42] In Risâlah fi al-Nafs the classification would also seem to be fivefold, but arranged as follows: (1) common sense and imagination, the latter not only identified with common sense but also defined as common sense; (2) compositive animal imagination; (3) estimation; (4) memory and recollection; (5) compositive human imagination.[43]

[41] (1) الحسّ المشترك, החוש המשותף, *sensus communis.*

(2) خيال, דמיון, *phantasia.*

(3) مفكّرة, מחשב, *cogitativa.*

متخيّلة, מדמה, *imaginativa.*

وهميّة, מחשב, *existimativa.*

(4) حافظة, שומר, *conservativa.*

(5) ذكرة, זוכר, *memorialis.*

[42] (1) الحسّ المشترك, *sensus communis.*

فنطاسيا (Shahrastani: بنطاسيا), *phantasia.*

(2) خيال, *imaginatio.*

مصوّرة, *vis formans, virtus formalis.*

(3) متخيّلة, *imaginativa.*

مفكّرة, *cogitativa.*

(4) وهميّة, *aestimativa, extimativa.*

(5) حافظة, *memorialis.*

ذاكرة, *reminiscibilis.*

Winter, op. cit. (above, n. 32), p. 29, n. 1, has failed to see the distinction which we have made here between the identification of the term "common sense" with the Greek term *phantasia* and the identification of the faculties of common sense and imagination.

[43] (1) الحسّ المشترك والمتصوّرة, (2) تخيّل (more likely: متخيّلة, cf. Landauer, op. cit., p. 359, n. 10; but see quotation from Cuzari, III, 5, below, nn. 59, 61), (3) المتوهّمة والظانّة, (4) الحافظة والمتذكّرة, (5) مفكّرة. Landauer (op. cit.) makes of these a threefold classification, as follows: I = our 1; II = our 2 and 3;

The successors of Avicenna follow his example of including common sense in their classifications, and also show his indecision as to its relation to the imaginative faculty; but occasionally, as we shall see, they depart from him in the combination of the various faculties, or in the order of their arrangement, or even in the description of the functions of some of them. Shahrastani's classification [44] is an exact reproduction of the classification in Al-Najât, even to the inclusion of the Arabic transliteration of the Greek *φαντασία* as the synonym of common sense. Algazali differs in his various writings. In Maḳâṣid al-Falâsifah [45] he follows Avicenna's Al-Najât in counting common sense and imagination as two faculties. In his Mîzân al-'Amal [46] and Tahâfut al-Falâsifah,[47] however, he follows Avicenna's Risâlah fi al-Nafs and identifies common sense with imagination. But in departure from all the works of Avicenna, Algazali, as we are now going to show, uses the ordinary Arabic word for memory in a manner which is quite unique.

Hitherto memory has been described after Aristotle as a sort of retentive power like imagination, but unlike imagination, which retains the images of sense-perceptions, it retains either the judgments of the cogitative power (*mufakkirah*), according to the Iḫwân al-Ṣafâ, or the forms of the estimative power (*wahm*), according to Alfarabi and Avicenna.[48] Further-

III = our 4 and 5. But I can see no ground on which his threefold classification is based, unless it was meant to correspond to the Galenic threefold classification. Avicenna's classification here, however, has no relation to the Galenic classification.

[44] Kitâb al-Milal wal-Niḥal, ed. Cureton, pp. 416–417.

[45] Maḳâṣid al-Falâsifah, III: Physics, IV (Cairo, without date), pp. 284–286. Hebrew translation, Kawwanot ha-Pilosofim, MS. Paris, Bibliothèque Nationale, Cod. Heb. 901. Latin translation, Algazel's Metaphysics (ed. J. T. Muckle, Toronto, 1933), pp. 169–171.

[46] Mîzân al-'Amal [IV], Cairo, A. H. 1328, pp. 19–20. Hebrew: Mozene Ẓedeḳ, IV (ed. J. Goldenthal, Leipzig and Paris, 1839), pp. 30–31.

[47] Algazel: Tahafot al-Falasifat, XVIII (ed. M. Bouyges, Beyrouth, 1927), pp. 298–300. Hebrew: Happalat ha-Pilosofim, XVIII, MS. Paris, Bibliothèque Nationale, Cod. Heb. 910. Latin translation in the Latin translation from the Hebrew of Averroes' Destructio Destructionum, In Physicis, II (Venice, 1527).

[48] The contrast between "retentive imagination" and "memory" is expressed in Arabic, Hebrew, and Latin texts by describing the former as خزانة الصور, אוצר

more, the seat of imagination is the anterior ventricle of the brain, whereas the seat of memory is the posterior ventricle of the brain. Then also, in all the Arabic texts which we have hitherto examined, two terms, *ḥâfiẓah* (lit. "conservation") and *ḏâkirah* [49] (lit. "memory"), have been used indiscriminately for memory, though occasionally the latter term had the more specific meaning of "recollection." [50] Now, in Algazali we notice a departure from these usages in all his three works. In Mîzân al-'Amal he follows on the whole Avicenna's Risâlah fi al-Nafs in combining common sense and imagination into one faculty, defining both of them in terms of common sense and as a *receptive* faculty. But departing from the Risâlah fi al-Nafs he includes in his classification also a *retentive* faculty, defined in the same manner as retentive imagination is defined by the Iḫwân al-Ṣafâ, Alfarabi, and Avicenna in his Canon and Al-Najât. But instead of applying to this retentive faculty the term "imagination" he applies to it the term "conservation" (*ḥâfiẓah*), which as we have seen is generally used in the sense of "memory." He further places this faculty of conservation in the anterior ventricle of the brain, where usually retentive imagination is placed. In Maḳâṣid al-Falâsifah, where retentive imagination is treated as a faculty distinct from common sense, the term "conservation" is used as synonymous with it, and the faculty of conservation is again located in the anterior ventricle of the brain. In Tahâfut al-Falâsifah common sense and imagination are identified and "conservation" is defined in terms of retentive imagination,

הצורות, *arca formarum*, and the latter by خزانة المعانى, אוצר העניינים, *arca intentio-num* (cf. below, Ch. III, n. 18). The term *arca* with its Arabic and Hebrew equivalents reflects the Greek ταμεῖον which is used as a description of memory by John of Damascus in De Fide Orthodoxa, II, 20. Instead of *arca* the term *thesaurus* is sometimes used. Cf. below, Ch. III, n. 18.

49 حافظة, ذاكرة. The term *conservatio* with its Arabic and Hebrew equivalents reflect the Greek σωτηρία used in connection with memory by Plato in Philebus 34 A and by John of Damascus in De Fide Orthodoxa, II, 20, and συντήρησις used in connection with memory by Galen in Definitiones Medicae, 124 (Opera Omnia, ed. Kühn, XIX, 381). It may reflect also Aristotle's φαντάσματος ἕξις in De Memoria et Reminiscentia, 1, 451a, 15–16.

50 As, for instance, in Canon, Al-Shifâ', Al-Najât, Risâlah fi al-Nafs.

taking the place of retentive imagination, but the location of conservation is not specified. This use of the term "conservation" (*ḥâfiẓah*) in the sense of "retentive imagination," it may be remarked in passing, is evidently followed also by Damiri in his threefold Galenic classification, where the term "imagination" is replaced by the term "conservation."[51]

Another important difference between Avicenna and Algazali, and in each of them between their various works, is to be found with regard to the location of *wahm*. Avicenna, in several of his works, places it "at the end of the middle hollow of the brain,"[52] but in one work he places it "in the whole brain, but especially at the border line of compositive animal imagination."[53] Algazali in one of his works places it "at the end of the middle hollow of the brain,"[54] but in his two other works he places it together with memory "in the posterior hollow (or part) of the brain."[55]

With this change in the meaning of "conservation," Algazali arranges the internal sense in Mîzân al-'Amal as follows: (1) common sense and imagination, identified and defined in terms of common sense as a recipient power, (2) conservation, defined as retentive imagination and located in the anterior ventricle of the brain, (3) estimation, (4) memory, (5) compositive animal and human imagination.[56] In Tahâfut al-

[51] Damiri's classification is quoted by I. Goldziher, Muhammedanischer Aberglaube über Gedächtnisskraft und Vergesslichkeit in Festschrift zum siebzigsten Geburtstage A. Berliner's (1903), p. 138, n. 4: (1) قوّة الحفظ, (2) قوّة الفكر, (3) قوّة الذكر.

[52] Al-Shifâ', Al-Najât, and also Shahrastani. Latin of Al-Shifâ' (Avicenna, De Anima) reads: "in summo mediae concavitatis cerebri" (fol. 8a). "Summo" here represents the Arabic نهاية and means "extremo" or "extremitate." Winter (op. cit., p. 31) translates it by "oberst (hinterst)." This passage is also quoted in the name of Avicenna by Albertus Magnus in Isagoge in Libros de Anima, Cap. 18.

[53] Risâlah fi al-Nafs, Ch. 7 (op. cit., pp. 360, 402). Cf. also S. Horovitz, op. cit., p. 251, n. 93.

[54] Mîzân al-'Amal, loc. cit.

[55] Maḳâṣid al-Falâsifah, loc. cit.: "estimativa, et memorialis in posteriore parte cerebri"; Tahâfut al-Falâsifah, loc. cit.: "locus eius est ventriculum ultimum cerebri."

[56] (1) خيال, דמיון; حسّ مشترك, חוש משותף.
(2) حافظة, שומר.
(3) وهميّة, רעיוני.
(4) ذاكرة, זוכר.
(5) مفكّرة, חושב, מחשב.
متخيّلة, רעיוני.

Falâsifah he first gives a threefold classification: (1) common sense and imagination, identified and defined in terms of common sense as a recipient power, (2) estimation, (3) compositive animal and human imagination. Then he adds two more: (4) conservation, defined as retentive imagination, and (5) memory.[57] In Maḳâṣid al-Falâsifah his fivefold classification is as follows: (1) common sense, (2) retentive imagination or conservation, (3) estimation, (4) memory, (5) compositive animal and human imagination.[58]

The influence of Avicenna's classifications is to be traced in the writings of Judah ha-Levi, Baḥya ibn Paḳuda, and Abraham ibn Daud.

Judah ha-Levi has two classifications. One is only an enumeration of terms; the other contains also a description of functions. In neither of them is the number five mentioned. But both would seem to contain a fivefold division similar to that of the Risâlah fi al-Nafs, where common sense is identified with imagination, and compositive animal imagination and

57 (1) خياليّة, דמיוני, *imaginativa*.

حسّ مشترك, חוש משותף, *sensus communis*.

(2) وهميّة, מחשבי, *cogitativa*.

(3) متخيّلة, מדמה, *imaginativa*.

مفكّرة, מחשב, *extimativa*.

(4) حافظة, שומר, *conservativa*.

(5) ذاكرة, זוכר, *memorativa*.

Note the reverse use of *cogitativa* and *extimativa* in this Latin translation. This is due to the fact that in Hebrew, from which this Latin translation was made, one and the same term is used in both instances. Cf. also use of *cogitatio* for *aestimatio* in Buxtorf's translation of Cuzari below, nn. 59, 61.

58 (1) حسّ مشترك, חוש משותף, *sensus communis*.

(2) متصوّرة, מצייר, *imaginativa*.

حافظة שומר, *retentiva*.

(3) وهميّة, מחשב, מחשביי, *estimativa*.

(4) ذاكرة, זוכר, *memorialis*.

(5) متخيّلة, מדמה, דמיוני, *fantasia* (erroneously *cogitacio* in MS. Vat. Lat. 4481 as reproduced by Muckle in Algazel's Metaphysics, p. 170; cf. also *cogitativa* on p. 169).

مفكّرة, מחשב, *cogitativa*.

compositive human imagination are counted as two distinct faculties. In his first classification, the order differs somewhat from that of the Risâlah fi al-Nafs. It reads as follows: (1) common sense, (2) compositive animal imagination, (3) estimation, (4) compositive human imagination, (5) memory.[59] In his second classification, the order is the same as that in Risâlah fi al-Nafs, and is as follows: (1) common sense or retentive imagination,[60] (2) compositive animal imagination, (3) estimation, (4) memory, (5) compositive human imagination.[61] But the location of the estimative faculty given in this second classification is a corruption of that in Risâlah fi al-Nafs. It reads: "The seat of estimation is the whole brain, principally the border-line of retentive imagination." [62]

One of the puzzling classifications is that of Baḥya.[63] It contains five terms, but two of these five terms, the *third* and the *fifth*, are not found in the Avicennian lists. If we take

[59] Cuzari, III, 5 (Arabic and Hebrew: Das Buch Al-Chazari, ed. H. Hirschfeld, 1887, pp. 144, 145; Latin translation: Liber Cosri, by J. Buxtorf, Fil., Basel, 1660, p. 158):

(1) حسّ مشترك, הרגשה משתתפת, *sensus communis.*

(2) تخيّل, יצר, *phantasia.*

(3) وهم, רעיון, *cogitatio* (see above, n. 57).

(4) فكر, מחשב, *imaginatio* (note unusual Latin translation).

(5) ذكر, זכרון, *memoria.*

[60] Its definition differs from that of Risâlah fi al-Nafs.

[61] Cuzari, V, 12 (Arabic and Hebrew, pp. 312 ff.; Latin, pp. 343 ff.):

(1) حاسّة مشتركة, הרגשה משתתפת, *sensus communis.*

متصوّرة, יצורי, *imaginatrix, phantasia;* تصوّر, הצטיירות, *formatio.*

(2) متخيّلة, יצרי, *reminiscentia* (so after Moscato), *imaginatrix.*

تخيّل, יצר, *reminiscentia.*

(3) متوهّمة, מחשבי, *cogitativa, cogitatrix* (see above, n. 57).

(4) حافظة, שומר, *retinens, conservatrix.*

مذكّرة, זוכר; تذكّر, זכרון, *memoria.*

(5) مفكّرة, מחשבי (left untranslated).

[62] Cf. above, n. 53.

[63] Ḥobot ha-Lebabot, I, 10 (Arabic: Al-Hidāja 'ilā Farā'id al-Qulūb, ed. A. S. Yahuda, p. 83): (1) ذكر, זכרון, (2) فكر, מחשבה, (3) خاطر, רעיון, (4) ظنّ, ומם, (5) تمييز, הכרה. Cf. D. Kaufmann, Die Theologie des Bachja Ibn Pakuda in Gesammelte Schriften (1910), II, p. 12, n. 1; S. Horovitz, op. cit., p. 256, n. 104.

Baḥya's classification, however, to be of the same type as Judah ha-Levi's first classification, the meaning of its unusual terms can be explained. The *first* and *second* terms in Baḥya offer no difficulty, for they are exactly the same as the *fifth* and *fourth* terms in Judah ha-Levi. The *third* term (*ḫatir*) does not occur in the Avicennian classifications, but inasmuch as the *fourth* term (*ẓann*) is used in both Avicenna's Risâlah fi al-Nafs [64] and Isaac Israeli's Liber de Definitionibus [65] in the sense of estimation, i.e., the *third* term (*wahm*) in Judah ha-Levi, we can take the term *ḫatir* in the sense of compositive animal imagination, i.e., the *second* term (*taḫayyul*) in Judah ha-Levi. Finally, the *fifth* term in Baḥya (*tamayyuz*) has already been shown to refer to common sense [66] and thus corresponds to the *first* term in Judah ha-Levi. Baḥya's list thus contains a fivefold classification like that of Judah ha-Levi's first list, and it runs as follows: (1) memory, (2) compositive human imagination, (3) compositive animal imagination, (4) estimation, (5) common sense.

While Judah ha-Levi and probably also Baḥya follow the classification of the Risâlah fi al-Nafs, Abraham ibn Daud follows that of the Al-Shifâ' and Al-Najât, except that he does not reproduce the transliterated form of the Greek *φαντασία* and use it as synonymous with common sense. The list runs as follows: (1) common sense, (2) retentive imagination, (3) compositive animal and human imagination, (4) estimation, (5) memory.[67]

A departure from the Avicennian type of classification is to be found in Averroes.

[64] Cf. above, n. 43.

[65] Cf. above, n. 22. Judah ibn Tibbon, who translated both Baḥya and Judah ha-Levi into Hebrew, must have taken the term ظنّ, זמם, in the sense of compositive animal imagination, for he translates خاطر by רעיון, which in Judah ha-Levi he uses as a translation of وهم, i.e., estimation.

[66] Cf. S. Horovitz, op. cit., p. 256, n. 104. This is not to be confused with the term مميّز which is used in connection with *διάνοια* (cf. above, Ch. I, nn. 47, 48, 56, and below, n. 73). The application of the term *κρίνειν* to common sense occurs in De Anima, III, 2, 426b, 8 ff., and De Somno et Vigilia, 2, 455a, 17–20.

[67] (1) חוש משותף, (2) מצייר, (3) מדמה, מחשב, (4) רעיוני, (5) זוכר.

Averroes openly rejects the introduction of estimation as a special faculty.[68] He contends that the ancients do not mention it and that it was introduced by Avicenna — a contention which but for the fact that estimation is already used as an internal sense by Alfarabi and independently of the internal senses by Isaac Israeli [69] is quite correct. He further maintains that according to the ancients the unspecified faculty of imagination [70] with which animals are generally assumed to be endowed contains also the function of the estimative faculty. Incidentally it may be remarked that Avicenna himself in his discussion of the estimative faculty in the Canon refers to some persons who call that faculty imagination, and proceeds to say that he has no objection to calling it by that name provided that the function of the estimative faculty is differentiated from the other functions of imagination.[71] This is as much as is definitely stated by Averroes in his Tahâfut al-Tahâfut. But he does not definitely say there that Avicenna's compositive animal imagination (*mutaḫayyilah*) and retentive imagination (*ḫayaliyyah*) are considered by him as one faculty, though this may be implied in the emphasis with which he restates Avicenna's view. Nor does he definitely say that he does not use the term *fikr* in the Avicennian sense of compositive human imagination but rather in its older sense as the equivalent of διανοητικόν or human reason, though indirectly it may be inferred that this is the sense in which he uses that term throughout his discussion in the passage in question.

But that Averroes differs from Avicenna on all these points

[68] Averroes: Tahafot at-Tahafot, II (XVIII) (ed. M. Bouyges, Beyrouth, 1930), pp. 546–547. Latin translation from the Hebrew by Calo Calonymos: Destructio Destructionum, In Physicis, Disputatio II (Venice, 1527).

[69] Cf. above, n. 22.

[70] Throughout his discussion in the passage referred to above in n. 68 Averroes uses the term متخيّلة in the general sense of imagination, which is his own use of the term, though Algazali uses it in the special sense of compositive animal imagination. Cf. below, n. 73.

[71] Cf. Canon, loc. cit.: "Quidam autem hominum sunt qui praesumunt et hanc virtutem [i.e., virtutem existimativam] imaginativam [تخيّل, דמיון] vocant, sed tamen non curamus, quia de nominibus non disputamus, sed intentiones et differentias intelligere debemus." Cf. also Alfarabi's inclusion of the estimative faculty under imagination, above, n. 27.

may be inferred from a passage in his Epitome of De Memoria et Reminiscentia, referred to by him here in Tahâfut al-Tahâfut under the general title of De Sensu et Sensati.[72] That passage contains a fivefold enumeration of the stages of knowledge, the first of which is sense-perception. The subsequent four stages are indirectly a fourfold classification of the "internal" senses, which Averroes here calls "spiritual." They are as follows: (1) common sense, (2) imaginative faculty, (3) cogitative or discriminative faculty, (4) memorative faculty.[73] The fact that both compositive animal imagination and estimation are omitted indicates that he considered them, together with retention, as sub-functions of imagination. Furthermore, the fact that cogitation (*fikr*) is used by him synonymously with the discriminative (*mumayyiz*) faculty, which, as we have seen above, is considered by Aristotle, John of Damascus, and the Iḫwân al-Ṣafâ as a sub-function of διανοητικόν,[74] shows that he took *fikr*, unlike Avicenna, in the sense of human thinking and not in the sense of compositive human imagination. In a passage in his long commentary on De Anima,[75] referring to that

[72] Arabic and Hebrew texts edited by H. Blumberg and to be published in Corpus Commentariorum Averrois in Aristotelem. Latin in Aristotelis omnia quae extant opera. . . . Venetiis, apud Iuntas, VI, Pars 2, 1574, fols. 21 M–22 B.

[73] (1) حسّ مشترك, חוש משותף, *sensus communis.*

(2) متخيّلة, מדמה, *imaginans.*

مصوّر, מצייר, *imaginans.*

(3) مفكّر, מחשב, *cogitativa.*

مميّز, בורר, *distinctiva.*

(4) حافظة, שומר, *conservans.*

ذاكرة, זוכר, *rememorativa, memorans.*

(De Memoria et Reminiscentia: Averrois Paraphrais. Op. cit., fol. 21 M–22 B).

These four stages of knowledge are described by Averroes as spiritual (روحانىّ, רוחני, *spiritualis*), in contrast to the five senses which are described by him as corporeal (جسمانىّ, גשמי, *corporalis*), and they are arranged by him according to their order of spirituality, the fourth being the most spiritual.

The term *distinctiva* with its Arabic and Hebrew equivalents reflects the Greek κριτική which is used by Aristotle as a description of one of the functions of διάνοια. Cf. above, Ch. I, nn. 47, 48, 56.

[74] Cf. above, Ch. I, nn. 45–48, 55, 56.

[75] Hebrew, MS. Berlin 1888.2, to be published in Corpus Commentariorum Aver-

passage in the Epitome of De Memoria et Reminiscentia, Averroes says more directly that Aristotle has posited four stages of "immaterial faculties,"[76] namely, (1) common sense, (2) imagination, (3) cogitation, (4) memory.[77] In De Memoria et Reminiscentia[78] Averroes further states that what man performs by "thought and deliberation" animals perform by "nature."[79] But that "nature," he adds, has no special name; Avicenna, however, calls it "estimation."[80] But, as we have seen, there is another difference between Avicenna and Averroes with regard to estimation. According to Avicenna it is a separate faculty in animals; according to Averroes it is a subfunction of imagination.

But very often Averroes follows those whom Avicenna describes as "physicians" and reduces his fourfold classification of post-sensationary faculties to three, corresponding to the three ventricles of the brain in which they are localized. This threefold classification omits *sensus communis*, evidently because it is in the same ventricle as imagination. The three enumerated sometimes read: (1) *imaginativa*, (2) *cogitativa*, (3) *memorativa*,[81] and sometimes they read: (1) *imaginatio*,

---

rois in Aristotelem. Latin in Aristotelis omnia quae extant opera. . . . Venetiis, apud Iuntas, VI, Pars 1, 1574.

[76] Ibid., Lib. III, § 6, fol. 154 B: "cum posuit virtutes individuales distinctas in quatuor ordinibus," כאשר הניח כחות נבדלים אישיים בארבע מדרגות. I take it that the Latin *distinctus* in this passage reflects the Arabic مفرق and is a mistranslation. It should be *separatas* or *separabiles*. The Hebrew נבדלים may likewise mean both *distinctas* and *separabiles*. *Virtutes distinctas* thus means here *virtutes separabiles*, which is the same as *virtutes spirituales* and hence the equivalent of *sensus spirituales* or *interiores*. Cf. above, Ch. I, nn. 1–8.

[77] (1) חוש משותף, *sensus communis*.
(2) מדמה, *imaginativa*.
(3) מחשבי, *cogitativa* (also described as: "virtus *distinctiva* individualis," אשר יבחין האישים.
(4) שומר, *rememorativa*. For the term *distinctiva* see above, n. 73.

[78] Op. cit., fol. 21 G.

[79] Cf. above, Ch. I, n. 35. For "nature" terms used are: טבע, *natura*. Averroes' statement in this passage is obviously based upon Physics, II, 8, 199a, 20–30, referred to above, n. 16.

[80] وهم, דמיון, *existimatio*.

[81] Long Commentary on De Anima, III, 6, fol. 154 A:
(1) מדמה, *imaginativa*.

(2) *ratio et cogitatio,* (3) *memoria et conservatio.*[82] In another place, after giving a threefold classification, containing (1) *imaginativa,* (2) *cogitativa,* (3) *reminiscibilis et conservativa,* he adds that *cogitativa* is only in man; in beasts *aestimativa* takes its place.[83] As we have seen, this reflects the terminology of Avicenna.

We have already seen above [84] how Maimonides enumerates three internal senses which we have identified with the Galenic imagination, cogitation, and memory. This in itself, however, would not make him depart from Avicenna, whom as a rule he follows, for even with his adoption of Avicenna's fivefold philosophical classification of the internal senses he could still have, as did Averroes, an additional physiological threefold classification. But in our special study of Maimonides on the internal senses we have shown how in several places of his writings, under the general term "imagination," he has described the functions of those internal senses which Avicenna would describe as (1) common sense, (2) retentive imagination, (3) compositive human imagination, (4) compositive animal imagination, (5) estimation. The inclusion of these five internal senses under the term "imagination," we have also tried to show in that study, does not prove that Maimonides aligned himself with Averroes in opposition to Avicenna. Maimonides' comprehensive use of the term "imagination" is followed in a passage which occurs with but a few slight verbal changes in Ruaḥ Ḥen [85] by an uncertain author and in Sha'ar

---

(2) מחשבי, *cogitativa.*
(3) שומר, *rememorativa.*

Ibid., III, 20, fol. 164 C:
(1) מדמה, *imaginativa.*
(2) מחשבי, *cogitativa.*
(3) זוכר, *rememorativa.*

82 Colliget, Lib. III, Cap. 40 (Aristotelis omnia quae extant opera. . . . Venetiis, apud Iuntas, X, 1574, fol. 56 BC).

83 Ibid., Lib. II, Cap. 20 (fol. 30 FG): "Propterea non invenitur haec virtus nisi in homine: et animali bruto concessa fuit aestimativa loco istius."

84 Cf. above, Ch. I, n. 27.

85 Ruaḥ Ḥen, Ch. 2. Hebrew with Latin translation: Ruaḥ ha-Ḥen, Physica Hebraea, Rabbi Aben Tybbon . . . primum edita, et Latina facta. Ioanne Isaac Levita (Coloniae, 1555).

ha-Shamayim [86] by Gershon ben Solomon. This passage, as I have shown in the same study of Maimonides on the internal senses, uses the general term "imagination" to include not only the five functions enumerated by Maimonides but also memory, recollection, and appetency. Thus all the internal senses are subsumed under imagination, a view which anticipates the contention which we shall meet with later in Eustachius a Sancto Paulo.[87]

In Hebrew philosophic texts after Maimonides the classifications of internal senses follow one or the other of the several types of classifications which we have discussed, and if any variation from any given type is discovered among them, it can be explained as due to a combination of various types. Thus Isaac Zabara [88] and the Zohar [89] give a threefold Galenic classification of the internal senses. Shem-Ṭob Falaquera's classification, on the other hand, is of the Avicennian type,[90] and one in which common sense and imagination are treated as two distinct faculties. His description of the function of imagination and common sense, furthermore, reflects also the influence of Algazali, especially of the Maḳâṣid al-Falâsifah. Of compositive human and animal imagination he seems to mention only the latter, but this is evidently due to our defective text.[91]

The influence of Averroes is discerned in a passage of Sha'ar ha-Shamayim,[92] where Averroes is referred to several times. Beginning with a statement of the controversy over the question whether the brain is divided into four or three chambers,[93]

[86] Sha'ar ha-Shamayim, XII (Rödelheim, 1801), p. 76.

[87] Cf. below, Ch. III, n. 59.

[88] Sefer Sha'ashu'im, IX (ed. I. Davidson), p. 103: (1) דמיון, (2) מחשב, (3) זכרון. Bate ha-Nefesh, ibid., p. 156: (1) דמיון, (2) רעיון, (3) זכרון.

[89] Idra Rabba, Exodus, Naso, p. 136a: (1) חכמתא, (2) בינה, (3) דעתא. Cf. Kerem Ḥemed, VIII, 74.

[90] Sefer ha-Nefesh, Ch. 18 (Warsaw, 1881): (1) המשתתף, (2) הדמיון והמצייר, (3) מדמה, [מחשב], (4) והם, (5) השומר והזוכר.

[91] Text to be corrected to read as follows: ואחרי כן הכח הנקרא מדמה [בהקש אל הנפש של בעל חיים והוא הנקרא מחשב] בהקש אל הנפש האנושית.

[92] Sha'ar ha-Shamayim, IX, 49b.

[93] A reflection of this controversy is to be found in Al-Razi (op. cit., above, Ch. I, n. 22), who speaks of imagination as residing in the anterior ventricles (plural, not singular) of the brain.

the author proceeds to state that (1) common sense [94] and (2) retentive imagination are in the anterior two chambers or in the two parts of the single anterior chamber, (3) judgment or cogitation is in the middle chamber, and (4) memory is in the posterior chamber.[95] This is evidently a combination of Averroes' fourfold philosophical classification, as found in his De Memoria et Reminiscentia and De Anima, and his threefold physiological classification, as found in his Colliget. A similar passage occurs also in Meir Aldabi's Shebile Emunah,[96] where he enumerates four faculties, localizing them in the four chambers of the brain: (1) common sense [97] in the first chamber, (2) imagination in the second chamber, (3) judgment or intellect in the third chamber, (4) memory in the fourth chamber.[98] Averroes' enumeration of the five sources of knowledge, in which, as we have seen, the last four correspond to the internal senses, is reproduced by Hillel of Verona,[99] who refers in this connection to Aristotle's De Anima and De Sensu et Sensibili [100] (i.e., Parva Naturalia and more especially De Memoria et Reminiscentia),[101] by which, of course, he means Averroes' commentaries on these works. After mentioning the first stage of knowledge, which he terms "corporeal" and "external," [102] he enumerates the other four stages, which he fails to call "spiritual" and "internal," in the following order: (1) common sense,

94 The term "common sense" is not explicitly used here, but it is clear from the context that this is what is meant by the term בהרגש הפנימי. Cf. Aristotle's use of *αἴσθησις* in Nicomachean Ethics, VI, 8, 1142a, 27–30, and below, Ch. III, nn. 40, 41. Cf. also Aristotle's use of *αἰσθητικόν* in De Somniis, 1, 459a, 15–17, quoted above in n. 38.

95 (1) הרגש פנימי, (2) מדמה, (3) שופט, מחשב, (4) זכרון. I take the passage החכם אבן רשד אמר כי הכח הזה to refer to שופט and not to זכרון which immediately precedes it The term שופט which is defined by the terms מבחין ומברר is the equivalent of Averroes' בורר, *distinctiva* and hence מחשב, *cogitativa*. Cf. above, notes 73, 77.

96 Shebile Emunah, IV, 1.

97 The term "common sense" is not explicitly used here, but it is clear from the context that this is what is meant by the term כח ההרגש. Cf. above, n. 94.

98 (1) כח ההרגש, (2) דמיון, (3) שכל, שופט, (4) זכרון. Cf. above, n. 94. As for the term שכל applied here to *διανοητικόν*, it reflects Aristotle's identification of *διανοητικόν* with *νοῦς* in De Amima, III, 3, 414b, 18.

99 Tagmule ha-Nefesh (Lyck, 1874), p. 7a.

100 אריסטו בספר הנפש ובס' ההרגש והמורגש.

101 Cf. above, n. 72.

102 חוץ לנפש, נשמית.

(2) *phantasia* and also *aestimativa*,[103] (3) intellect, (4) memory.[104] His use of *phantasia* and *aestimativa* as two functions of one faculty rather than two distinct faculties corresponds exactly to the view of Averroes.[105] His use of the term "intellect" for what Averroes calls *cogitativa* and *distinctiva* reflects an accurate understanding of what Averroes' *cogitativa* means in contradistinction to the *cogitativa* as used by Avicenna. So does also Aldabi use the terms "judgment" and "intellect," the former reflecting Averroes' *distinctiva*, as does the term "judgment" in Gershon ben Solomon's classification.[106] In another passage, however, Hillel of Verona identifies *cogitativa* with *aestimativa*.[107] This confusion is due to the influence of the Latin scholastic writings, with which he was acquainted and the Latin terms of which he quotes within his Hebrew text. As we shall see in the next chapter, this confusion occurs in Albertus Magnus and others.

[103] These Latin terms in Hebrew transliteration are used in the text.

[104] (1) חוש משותף, (2) פנטסיע, דמיונית; שטיאומטיבא, שמאית, (3) משכלת, (4) שומר. The term שמאית is a direct translation of the Latin *aestimativa* and does not occur in the works of earlier authors, who had no knowledge of Latin. For the term משכלת see above, n. 98.

[105] Cf. above, nn. 68–70.

[106] Cf. above, n. 95.

[107] Op. cit., p. 21b: מחשבי (קווייטאטיבו); שמאי (אוטיבו).

CHAPTER III

Latin translations of Avicenna's, Algazali's, and Averroes' classifications of the internal senses. — The remarkably careful use of terminology in these translations. — Four types of Avicennian classifications in Albertus Magnus: his discussion of the Averroian classification. — The restatement of the Avicennian and Averroian classifications by Thomas Aquinas: his return to the Augustinian use of the term "internal sense." — Roger Bacon's restatement of the Avicennian classification. — The confusion in the use of the term *cogitativa* by Albertus, Thomas, and Bacon. — General tendencies toward a modification of traditional Arabic classifications in later Latin philosophical texts: Heereboord, Keckermann, Magirus, Zanchius. — The classifications of Eustachius a Sancto Paulo. — Traditional Arabic classifications in early modern philosophy: Descartes, Spinoza, Leibniz. — Ultimate return to the Augustinian use of the term "internal sense": Locke, Kant. — Summary.

THROUGH the Latin translations from the Arabic in the 12th and 13th centuries [1] the Avicennian and Averroian classifications of the internal senses became known to the scholastics. In the 12th century Johannes Hispalensis translated from Avicenna's Al-Shifâ' the section dealing with the soul, which is generally referred to as "VI de naturalibus" or as "De Anima." [2] It was probably also Johannes Hispalensis who translated Algazali's Maḳâṣid al-Falâsifah, the third part of which, dealing with physics and containing the discussion on the soul, is referred to as "Physica." [3] Later in the same century Gerard of Cremona translated Avicenna's Canon. In the course of the 13th century Michael Scotus translated Avicenna's De Animalibus [4] and Averroes' Long Commentary on De Anima, [5] as well as his Epitome of Parva Naturalia, [6] and Bonacosa translated (in 1255) Averroes' Kulliyat under the title of Colliget. [7] Now, Albertus Magnus, Thomas Aquinas, and Roger

[1] Cf. M. Steinschneider, Die europäischen Übersetzungen aus dem Arabischen bis Mitte des 17. Jahrhunderts in Sitzungsberichte der philosophisch-historischen Klasse der Wiener Akademie der Wissenschaften, 149 (1904), 151 (1905).

[2] Cf. above, Ch. II, n. 32, and below, nn. 8, 11, 13.

[3] This part of the Latin translation is included in Algazel's Metaphysics, ed. J. T. Muckle, Toronto, 1933. Cf. above, Ch. II, n. 45.

[4] De Animalibus, Venice, c. 1500.

[5] Cf. above, Ch. II, n. 75.

[6] Cf. above, Ch. II, n. 72.

[7] Cf. above, Ch. II, n. 82.

Bacon have all drawn extensively upon some or all of these Arabic sources in their discussion of the internal senses. Albertus Magnus mentions Avicenna's "VI de Naturalibus,"[8] Algazali's "Physica,"[9] and Averroes' Long Commentary on De Anima and his Epitome of Parva Naturalia.[10] Thomas Aquinas mentions Avicenna's "de Anima" and Averroes' Epitome of Parva Naturalia,[11] quotes from Algazali's "Physica,"[12] and evidences a knowledge of Averroes' Long Commentary on De Anima, as we shall show in our discussion of his use of the term *ratio particularis*. Roger Bacon mentions Avicenna's "de Anima"[13] and "de Animalibus,"[14] and refers also indirectly to his Canon.[15]

Of particular interest to us in the study of these translations is the remarkable care and comparative uniformity with which the technical Arabic terms are rendered into Latin. The Arabic term for common sense, being a literal translation of the Greek *κοινὸν αἰσθητήριον*, is uniformly translated by *sensus communis*. The Arabic terms for retentive imagination and compositive animal imagination are two different forms (*Ḫayâliyyah* and *mutaḫayyilah* respectively) of the same root meaning simply "to imagine" (*ḫâl*). In the Latin translations, these two terms are similarly translated by two different forms of a word meaning simply "imagination," usually one derived from the Greek and the other from the Latin, but sometimes both of them derived from the Latin. Thus in Avicenna's Canon retentive imagination and compositive animal imagination are translated respectively by *phantasia* and *imaginativa*; in Algazali's "Physica" they are translated by *imaginativa* and *phantasia*; and in Avicenna's De Anima they are translated by *imaginatio*

[8] Summa de Creaturis, Pars II: De Homine (ed. Vivès), Quaest. 35, Art. 3: "Avicenna in VI de Naturalibus."

[9] Ibid., Quaest. 35, Art. 2: "Algazel in Physica sua."

[10] Liber de Memoria et Reminiscentia, Tract. I, Cap. 1.

[11] Summa Theologica, Pars I, Quaest. 78, Art. 4, No. 6: "Avicenna in suo libro de Anima."; De Potentiis Animae, Cap. IV: "Unde Algazel dicit."

[12] De Potentiis Animae, Cap. IV: "ut dicit Averroes in lib. suo de Sensu et Sensato."

[13] Opus Majus, V: Perspectiva, Pars I, Dist. I, Cap. II.

[14] Ibid.

[15] Ibid.: "et in libris medicinae."

and *imaginativa*. For retentive imagination the Arabic uses also another term, *mutaṣawwirah*, which is derived from a root meaning "to form" as well as "to imagine" (*taṣwir*), from which also is derived in Arabic the technical word for form (*ṣûrah*). This is literally translated into Latin by *formalis*, which is used in the sense of imagination. Compositive human imagination, for which the Arabic is *mufakkirah*, is invariably translated by *cogitativa*,[16] and so is the same term translated also in Averroes' works, where it means, as we have seen, "human thought" or "reason." The Arabic *wahm* is invariably translated by *aestimatio* (or *extimatio*). The two Arabic terms for memory, *ḥâfiẓah* and *ḏâkirah*, when they are used in the contrasting sense of memory and recollection, are translated respectively either by *conservativa* and *memorialis* (Avicenna, Canon), or by *memorialis* and *reminiscibilis* (Avicenna, De Anima), or by *conservans* and *rememorativa* (Averroes, Parva Naturalia). In Algazali's "Physica," where, as we have shown above, *ḥâfiẓah* is used in the sense of retentive imagination, it is translated by *retentiva*; *dâkirah*, which is used in the general sense of memory, is translated by *memorialis*.

In the light of these remarks we may now examine the classifications of Albertus Magnus, Thomas Aquinas, and Roger Bacon.

In Albertus Magnus we have four kinds of classifications of the internal senses.

First, the classification in Isagoge in Libros de Anima, Cap. XIV–XIX, where he quotes Avicenna to the effect that the internal senses are five. They are arranged by him as follows: (1) common sense, identified with phantasia (*phantasia, quae est sensus communis*), (2) retentive imagination (*imaginatio*), (3) compositive animal imagination (*imaginativa*) and compositive human imagination (*cogitativa*),[17] (4) estimation (*aesti-*

[16] In the late Latin translation from the Hebrew of Averroes' Tahâfut al-Tahâfut (see above, Ch. II, nn. 47, 68) the order is reversed: *fikr* is translated by *aestimatio* and *wahm* by *cogitatio* (see above, Ch. II, n. 57). See also a similar mistranslation of *wahm* in Buxtorf, Cuzari, above, Ch. II, nn. 59, 61.

[17] He calls it also *formativa*: "in quantum autem operatur componendo et dividendo, formativa vocatur" (Cap. 16). Cf. above, Ch. II, n. 18.

mativa), (5) memory and recollection (*memorativa, sive memorabilis; reminiscentia*).

Second, the classification in De Apprehensione, Partes III–IV, where the classification is as follows: (1) *sensus communis*, (2) retentive imagination (*imaginatio, imaginativa, formalis*),[18] (3) estimation (*aestimativa*), (4) compositive animal imagination (*phantasia*) and compositive human imagination (*excogitativa*), (5) memory and recollection (*memoria, reminiscentia*). A similar classification, with but the omission of compositive human imagination, occurs also in his De Anima, Lib. III, Tract. I, Cap. IX.

Third, the classification in De Anima, Lib. II, Tract. IV, Cap. VII, which runs as follows: (1) *sensus communis*, (2) retentive imagination (*imaginatio, virtus formalis*), (3) estimation (*aestimatio*), (4) memory (*memoria*), (5) compositive animal imagination (*phantasia*) and compositive human imagination (*cogitativa*).

Fourth, the classification in Summa de Creaturis, Pars II: De Homine, where common sense is explicitly placed under the external senses (Quaest. XIX: De Visu). The internal senses, assuming that they were meant to be five, are as follows (Quaest. XXXVII–XLI): (1) retentive imagination (*potentia imaginativa, virtus formalis et imaginatio*), (2) compositive animal imagination (*phantasia*) and compositive human imagination (*cogitativa*), (3) estimation (*aestimativa*), (4) memory (*memoria*), (5) recollection (*reminiscentia*).

Our earlier analysis of the classifications of Avicenna and Algazali on the basis of their own original writings will throw light on some very important points, which have hitherto been overlooked in these classifications of Albertus. First, it will show that the difference in the order of the arrangement of the individual senses between the *first*, *second*, and *fourth* classifications, on the one hand, and the *third* classification, on the other, is not accidental, but is due to a difference in the sources used by Albertus, the former three classifications following the order given in Avicenna's Al-Shifâ', and the latter classification follow-

[18] Also: *species, thesaurus formarum* (cf. above, Ch. II, n. 48).

ing the order given in Algazali's Makâṣid al-Falâsifah. Second, it will show that the use of the term *phantasia* in the *first* classification is different from its use in the *second, third,* and *fourth* classifications. In the latter three classifications it stands for compositive animal imagination; in the former classification it reflects the Greek word *φαντασία*, which in Avicenna's Al-Shifâ', as we have seen above, is used as synonymous with common sense, even though common sense and retentive imagination are treated as two distinct faculties. Third, it will also explain how it happened that in Albertus' *second, third,* and *fourth* classifications, as well as in subsequent Latin literature in general, the term *formalis* came to be used as synonymous with *imaginativa.* Finally, the inclusion of common sense under external senses in Albertus' *fourth* classification, which occurs neither in Avicenna nor in Algazali, may be in part at least due to the influence of Isaac Israeli, who does not place common sense under the internal senses but makes it rather an intermediary between the external and internal senses.[19] This work was translated together with his Liber de Definitionibus either by Constantinus Afer in the 11th century or by Gerard of Cremona in the 12th century. The latter work is explicitly mentioned by Albertus in connection with his discussion of memory.[20] It is not quite accurate to say [21] that in his treatment of common sense as an external sense Albertus has departed from Aristotle, for in Aristotle there is no distinction between external and internal senses, nor is there any indication that common sense would have been placed by him under the latter had he made such a distinction.[22]

In Parva Naturalia Albertus Magnus makes three observations on the difference between Avicenna and Averroes in their classifications of the internal senses.

First, he says, Avicenna's *aestimativa* is called by Averroes

[19] Liber de Elementis, II, fol. ix, r, a; Sefer ha-Yesodot, II, 53–54. Cf. my paper Isaac Israeli on the Internal Senses in op. cit.

[20] Summa de Creaturis, Pars II: *De Homine*, Quaest. 40, Art. 1.

[21] Cf. A. Schneider, Die Psychologie Alberts des Grossen, I (1903), 132.

[22] In fact, it has been pointed out that the first two chapters of De Anima, III, which deal with common sense, are more closely connected with the discussion of the external senses in Book II. Cf. R. D. Hicks, Aristotle: De Anima, p. 422.

cogitativa animalium brutorum, or *cogitativa brutorum*.[23] Now, Averroes does not explicitly call Avicenna's *aestimativa* by the terms ascribed to him by Albertus. All that we find in Averroes on this point is as follows: (1) a passage in his Epitome of De Memoria et Reminiscentia where he says that a certain act in the process of imagination (*iudicare . . . ista intentio est istius imaginati*) is performed in man by means of cognition (*per cognitionem*) and in animals by nature (*natura*), and that that faculty in animals has no special name, although Avicenna calls it *aestimativa*;[24] (2) a passage in his Colliget where he says that *virtus cogitativa* is found only in man and that in beasts its place is taken by *aestimativa*.[25] In neither of these passages, it will be noticed, does Averroes use the term *cogitativa brutorum* as the equivalent of Avicenna's *aestimativa*.

Second, in reproducing Averroes' enumeration of the five stages of knowledge, which we have discussed above,[26] the last four, which represent the internal senses, are given by Albertus Magnus as follows: (1) *sensus communis*, (2) *imaginatio*, (3) *virtus distincta*, which Averroes calls *cogitativa brutorum*, (4) *memorativa* (also *conservatio*).[27] In view of the fact that in this passage, as well as in the previous passage, both *aestimativa* and *distincta* are said by Albertus to have been called *cogitativa brutorum* by Averroes, it is quite clear that he takes the term *distincta* to have the same meaning in Averroes as the term *aestimativa* in Avicenna. But as we have already seen above, *virtus distinctiva* in Averroes is used as synonymous with his own use of *virtus cogitativa* (Arabic: *fikr*), that is to

[23] Liber de Memoria et Reminiscentia, Tract. I, Cap. 1: "et hanc quidem Avicenna bene et proprie vocavit *aestimationem*. Averroes autem improprie vocat *cogitativam animalium brutorum*, per quam fugiunt nociva et persequuntur convenientia." Cf. quotation below in n. 27.

[24] Aristotelis omnia quae extant opera. . . . Venetiis, apud Iuntas, VI, Pars 2, fol. 21 G: "ista nam virtus est in homine per cognitionem. . . . Et ista virtus in animalibus non habet nomen: et est illa, quam Avicenna vocat existimationem." Cf. above, Ch. I, n. 35, and Ch. II, n. 79.

[25] Quoted above in Ch. II, n. 83.

[26] Cf. above, Ch. II, nn. 73, 77.

[27] Liber de Memoria et Reminiscentia, Tract. I, Cap. 1: "Quartus locus est in organo *virtutis distinctae*, quam vocat Averroes *cogitativam brutorum*."

say, in the sense of human reason or the discriminative function of human reason.[28]

Third, says Albertus, Avicenna's *virtus formalis vel imaginativa* is called by Averroes *conservans*.[29] This reflects the following passage in Averroes: "Et ista virtus [i.e., facere illam imaginem esse praesentem] invenitur duobus modus. Si nam comprehensio eius fuerit continua, dicetur conservans."[30] Albertus could have quoted with greater pertinency Algazali, who as we have shown above[31] either makes conservation take the place of retentive imagination, as he does in Mîzân al-'Amal and Tahâfut al-Falâsifah, or makes conservation and retentive imagination synonymous terms, as he does in Maḳâṣid al-Falâsifah. The first two works, however, were unknown to Albertus, and as for the last-named work, the Latin translation of it, which he did know, does not happen to render the particular passage in question quite accurately, nor does it use the term *conservans* or *conservativa*. In that Latin translation the passage reads as follows: "Imaginativa est virtus retentiva eius quod impressum fuit sensui communi."[32] A more accurate translation of the passage would read as follows: "Quod ad virtutem imaginativam pertinet, illud verbum est explicatio de conservantis eius quod impressum fuit sensui communi."[33]

While Albertus Magnus in his four kinds of classifications of the internal senses reproduces Avicenna's classification with strict accuracy, no such accuracy is to be found in Thomas Aquinas. Referring specifically to Avicenna's fivefold classification of the internal senses, Thomas enumerates them as follows: (1) *sensus communis*, (2) retentive imagination (*phantasia*), (3) compositive human and animal imagination (*imaginativa*), (4) estimation or cogitation (*aestimativa seu cogitativa*), the former in animals and the latter in man, (5) memory (*me-*

[28] Cf. above, Ch. II, nn. 73, 77, 95.

[29] Liber de Memoria et Reminiscentia, Tract. I, Cap. 1.

[30] De Memoria et Reminiscentia: Averrois Paraphrasis, in op. cit., fol. 21 FG.

[31] Cf. above, Ch. II, nn. 48–51.

[32] Algazel's Metaphysics (ed. J. T. Muckle), p. 170.

[33] وأما القوّة المتصوّرة فعبارة عن الحافظة لما ينطبع فى الحسّ المشترك.

morativa).[34] This does not quite accurately represent Avicenna's classification. In Avicenna, as we have seen, *cogitativa* is taken in the sense of compositive human imagination and is correlated with *imaginativa* in the sense of compositive animal imagination. What Thomas really does here is this: He takes *cogitativa* in the Averroian sense of reason in man and correlates it with the Avicennian *aestimativa* in animals. Thomas evidently was not aware of the difference in the use of *cogitativa* by Avicenna and Averroes.

In his restatement of the view of Averroes,[35] Thomas Aquinas is correct in his general observation that in Averroes' scheme of classification the five Avicennian senses are reduced to four by the combination of retentive imagination and compositive imagination into one faculty. But he is not quite accurate in his description of the details of the scheme. In the first place, he says that according to Averroes compositive imagination is to be found only in man and not in animals.[36] In the second place, he says that according to Averroes *aestimativa* in animals is a distinct faculty corresponding to *cogitativa* in man.[37] As we have seen, *aestimativa* in animals, according to Averroes, is a sub-function of imagination together with retentive and compositive imagination. Thomas' unacquaintance with Averroes' view on the faculty of *aestimatio* is explainable on the ground

[34] Summa Theologica, Pars I, Quaest. 78, Art. 4, No. 6 and Concl.; De Potentiis Animae, Cap. 4. In No. 6 in Summa Theologica the expression "seu cogitativa" does not occur. That the term *imaginativa* which occurs in this Avicennian list between the terms *phantasia* and *aestimativa* is meant by Thomas to include both compositive human imagination and compositive animal imagination is evident from the following statement in Concl. in Summa Theologica: "Avicenna vero ponit quintam potentiam mediam inter aestimativam et imaginativam (= *phantasiam* in this list), quae componit et dividit formas imaginatas . . . Sed ista operatio non apparet in aliis animalibus ab homine, in quo ad hoc sufficit virtus imaginativa (= *phantasia* in this list)."

[35] Summa Theologica, ibid.; De Potentiis Animae, ibid.

[36] Cf. Summa Theologica, loc. cit., Concl.: "Sed ista operatio non apparet in aliis animalibus ab homine, in quo ad hoc sufficit virtus imaginativa. Cui autem hanc actionem attribuit Averroes in libro quodam quem fecit de sensu et sensibilibus." Cf. also De Potentiis Animae, loc. cit.

[37] Cf. Summa Theologica, loc. cit.: "Et ideo quae in aliis animalibus dicitur *aestimativa naturalis*, in homine dicitur *cogitativa*." Cf. also De Potentiis Animae, loc. cit. That this view, which Thomas presents as his own, is also meant by him to represent the view of Averroes, is evident from the context.

of the inaccessibility to him of Averroes' Tahâfut al-Tahâfut, for that work was not translated into Latin until 1328.[38]

Thomas himself follows Averroes' classification as he understood it to be. His fourfold classification, therefore, runs as follows: (1) *sensus communis*, (2) imagination (*phantasia, sive imaginatio*), both retentive and compositive, the latter only in man, (3) estimation in animals corresponding to cogitation in men (*aestimativa, cogitativa*), (4) memory (*memorativa*).[39] For *aestimativa* Thomas uses in Summa Theologica, Pars I, Quaest. LXXVIII, Art. IV, Conclusio, also the term *aestimativa naturalis*. This seems to be a combination of Averroes' *natura* and Avicenna's *aestimatio* (cf. above, Ch. II, nn. 79, 80). For *cogitativa* he also uses in the same work the term *ratio particularis* which he describes in the following words: "Est enim collativa intentionum individualium." This seems to reflect Averroes' term *virtus distinctiva* or *virtus distinctiva individualis* which is used by him as the equivalent of *cogitativa* (cf. above, Ch. II, nn. 73, 77).

Of particular interest is a passage in Thomas which seems to divest the term "internal sense" of its generic meaning as inclusive of several post-sensationary faculties and to identify it with one particular faculty. He identifies it with the term αἴσθησις, in which, according to Aristotle, prudence (φρόνησις) resides, referring to Nicomachean Ethics, VI, 8, 1142a, 27–30.[40] Inasmuch as by αἴσθησις in that passage Aristotle means common sense,[41] Thomas is thus identifying internal sense with common sense, which corresponds to the use made of the term by Augustine.[42]

Roger Bacon shows an unusual historical sense in his treatment of the internal senses. He knows that Aristotle makes

[38] Cf. M. Steinschneider, Die hebraeischen Uebersetzungen des Mittelalters, p. 330.

[39] Cf. op. cit., above, n. 34.

[40] Summa Theologica, Secunda Secundae, Quaest. 47, Art. 3: "Ad tertium dicendum, quod sicut Philosophus dicit in 6 Ethic. (cap. 8, ad fin.), prudentia non consistit in sensu exteriori, quo cognoscimus sensibilia propria, sed in sensu interiori, qui perficitur per memoriam, et per experimentum ad prompte judicandum de particularibus expertis."

[41] Cf. A. Grant, The Ethics of Aristotle, ad. loc. (II, 172, note).

[42] Cf. above, Ch. I, nn. 12–13.

no mention of all the faculties that go under the name of internal senses, except those of common sense, imagination, and memory.[43] He is also conscious of the fact that the Latin translations of Avicenna are likely to lead to a misunderstanding of his views. But when he says that the translators of Avicenna's De Anima, De Animalibus, and Canon have not used a uniform vocabulary,[44] he is not quite right. As we have shown above, the essential part of the vocabulary is remarkably uniform in all the Latin translations.[45] He refers especially to a passage in De Animalibus in which Avicenna is said by him to state that in brutes the estimative faculty takes the place of reason.[46] The passage referred to is probably that found in De Animalibus, Book XIII, which Roger Bacon quotes verbatim in his De Multiplicatione Specierum, Pars III, Cap. II, though he refers to it there as from De Animalibus, Book X.[47] But even without the original Arabic before us, the vocabulary used in that passage does not seem to us to differ from that in the other works of Avicenna.

Bacon's own classification reads as follows: (1) *sensus communis* and *phantasia*, (2) retentive imagination (*imaginatio*), (3) estimation (*aestimativa*), (4) memory (*memorativa*), (5) compositive animal and human imagination (*cogitativa, logistica, rationalis*).[48] Of this classification Bacon himself says that it is taken from Avicenna's De Anima.[49] But certain differences

[43] Opus Majus, V: Perspectiva, Pars I, Dist. I, Cap. V (ed. J. H. Bridges: The 'Opus Majus' of Roger Bacon, II, 9 f.).

[44] Ibid., p. 10: "Et licet translatores librorum Avicennae, ut in illo libro de Anima et in libro de Animalibus et in libris medicinae, aliter transtulerunt et vocabula mutaverunt, ita ut ubique non sit eadem intentio Avicennae translata."

[45] Cf. above, p. 115.

[46] Loc. cit.: "quoniam in libro de Animalibus Avicennae reperitur quod aestimatio est loco rationis in brutis." Cf. quotation from Averroes' Colliget above, Ch. II, n. 83.

[47] Printed in J. H. Bridges, op. cit., II, 510: "Avicenna in decimo de Animalibus dicit. . . . Sed imaginatio et aestimatio non sunt cum motu corporis, vel divisione aliqua in corpore." This passage occurs in Lib. XII of the printed edition of De Animalibus. It must be admitted that this passage resembles rather remotely his reference to the De Animalibus quoted from the Opus Majus in the preceding note. But I could not find any closer passage in the entire work.

[48] Op. cit., Cap. II–V.

[49] Ibid., Cap. V, p. 10: "sed tenenda est ejus sententia in libro de Anima, quia ibi ex principali intentione discuit vires animae, alibi autem magis ex incidenti facit mentionem."

are to be noticed between these two classifications. First, they differ in the order of the arrangement of the individual senses, the *fifth* in Bacon's classification being the *third* in Avicenna's De Anima. Second, in Avicenna's De Anima the term *phantasia* is used as completely synonymous with *sensus communis*; Bacon explains it as a generic term including both (1) *sensus communis* and (2) *imaginatio*.[50] Third, Avicenna's De Anima uses the term *memorialis*; Bacon uses the term *memorativa*. Fourth, and the most important difference, Avicenna's De Anima uses two terms, *imaginativa* and *cogitativa*, as designations respectively of compositive animal imagination and compositive human imagination; Bacon uses the term *cogitativa* (and also *logistica* and *rationalis*) for both compositive animal imagination and compositive human imagination.

Of these three philosophers, as we have seen, Albertus Magnus reproduces the classifications of both Avicenna and Averroes quite accurately, but he misunderstands the meaning of Averroes' use of the term *cogitativa* and with it also his use of the term *distinctiva*. Thomas Aquinas' reproduction of Avicenna's classification likewise reveals a misunderstanding of Avicenna's use of the term *cogitativa*; his reproduction of Averroes' classification reveals merely a misplacement of the term *aestimativa*. Roger Bacon does not reproduce Averroes, but his reproduction of Avicenna reveals again a misuse of the term *cogitativa*, though not the same kind of misuse as that of Thomas Aquinas. It will be noticed that these three philosophers have failed to reproduce with accuracy the use of the term *cogitativa* by either Avicenna or Averroes.

The inaccurate reproduction of Averroes' classification by Thomas Aquinas and similarly the inaccurate reproduction of Avicenna's classification by Roger Bacon appear in the works of Latin authors of a later period. Thus, for instance, Heereboord's fourfold classification of the internal senses is nothing

[50] Ibid., Cap. II, p. 5: "Nam ex secundo de Anima et de Somno et Vigilia et libro de Sensu et Sensato patet quod phantasia et sensus communis sunt idem secundum subjectum, differentes secundum esse, ut Aristoteles dicit, et quod phantasia et imaginatio sunt idem secundum subjectum, differentes secundum esse. Quapropter phantasia comprehendit utramque virtutem, et non differt ab eis nisi sicut totum a parte."

but the Averroian classification as it was understood and adopted by Thomas Aquinas. It reads as follows: (1) *sensus communis*, (2) *phantasia* (including both retentive and compositive imagination), (3) *aestimativa* in animals, corresponding to *cogitativa* in men, (4) *memoria* (and *reminiscentia*).[51] The inaccurate Avicennian classification as given by Roger Bacon seems to be the source of the classifications given by Keckermann,[52] Magirus,[53] and Zanchius.[54] These three authors, however, do not follow Bacon completely. Evidently taking Bacon's hint that in Aristotle only three internal senses are specifically mentioned, they make these three Aristotelian faculties the basis of their classifications. They all thus start with a threefold classification, namely, (1) *sensus communis*, (2) *imaginatio sive phantasia*, (3) *memoria*. It is to be noted that these threefold classifications are different from the Galenic threefold classification which we have discussed above; they are rather, as we have said, the threefold Aristotelian classifications referred to by Roger Bacon. Then all these three authors proceed to discuss *aestimativa* and *cogitativa*.[55] Taking these terms in the sense in which they are used in Bacon's fivefold classifications, they reduce them, as does Averroes, to the status of sub-functions of imagination. Their classifications, we may therefore say, begin with Bacon's reproduction of Avicenna's fivefold classification in which the term *cogitativa* is used in the sense of both compositive animal and compositive human imagination. But knowing, as Bacon did, that of these five faculties only three are directly discussed by Aristotle as distinct faculties, and having evidently become acquainted, through the Latin translations of the Tahâfut al-Tahâfut,[56] with Aver-

[51] Meletamata Philosophica: Philosophia Naturalis, Cap. XIV (Amsterdam, 1680), pp. 900 ff.

[52] D. B. Keckermann, Opera Omnia: Systema Physicum, Lib. III, Cap. 17–19. Geneva, 1614, I, Col. 1522–1526.

[53] J. Magirus, Physiologia Peripatetica, Lib. 6, Cap. 12, Cambridge, 1642, pp. 350 ff.

[54] H. Zanchius, De Operibus Dei intra Spacium Sex Dierum Creatis Opus, Pars III, Lib. II, Cap. III: De Partibus et Potentiis Animae, De Sensibus Internis. 3rd ed. Neustadii in Palatinatu, 1602, pp. 733–739.

[55] Keckermann, Col. 1524 EF; Magirus, p. 352, No. 24; Zanchius, p. 736, Col. 2.

[56] The first translation from the Arabic was made in 1328; the second translation

roes' criticism of Avicenna's views on estimation and compositive animal and human imagination, they return to the original Aristotelian threefold classification, by reducing estimation and compositive human imagination, in accordance with Averroes' criticism of Avicenna, to the status of sub-functions of imagination.

The feeling that the traditional Arabic classifications of the internal senses were too large and that they counted as separate faculties what Aristotle himself would have counted as sub-functions of one faculty is clearly expressed by Eustachius a Sancto Paulo.[57] Beginning with an enumeration of four internal senses like those in the fourfold classification of Thomas Aquinas, namely, (1) *sensus communis*, (2) *phantasia*, (3) *aestimativa sive cogitativa*, and (4) *memoria*, he then argues in turn: first, for their reduction to three by the identification of *aestimativa sive cogitativa* with *phantasia*; second, for their reduction to two by the identification of *memoria* with *phantasia*, for this, he adds, would agree with the view of Aristotle himself, who in De Anima enumerates only *sensus communis* and *phantasia*;[58] third, for their reduction to one by the identification of *sensus communis* with *phantasia*. The term "internal sense" thus becomes with him identical with "imagination," a view which we also meet with in Hebrew philosophic literature.[59]

The same traditional Arabic use of the term "internal sense" with the tendency of reducing the senses which are included under it to a smaller number, and even to one, which we have already met before, is to be found also in modern philosophy. Descartes, in one place, speaks of two internal senses (*sensus interni*), and describes one of them as consisting of our natural appetites (*appetitus naturalis*) and the other as consisting of

from the Hebrew was published in 1527. Cf. M. Steinschneider, op. cit. (above, n. 38), pp. 330, 333.

57 Eustachius a Sancto Paulo, Summa Philosophiae Quadripartita, III: Physica, Pars III, Tract. III, Disp. III, Quaest. 1. Cambridge, 1640, pp. 316–318.

58 Ibid., p. 316: "Probablior adhuc et magis Aristotelica, Duos duntaxat esse Sensus internos, nempe sensum communen et Phantasiam, cum de illis tantum mentionem faciat in lib. De anima."

59 Cf. Ruaḥ Ḥen, Ch. 2, pp. 18–19 (ed. Coloniae, 1555, with Latin translation by I. I. Levita): וההרגש הפנימי הוא הדמיון, *sensus interior est facultas aestimandi* (= *imaginandi*); Gershon ben Solomon, Sha'ar ha-Shamayim, XII: והפנימיות דמיון והוא הכח המדמה.

the emotions of the mind or passions (*animi commotiones, sive pathemata*) and the effects (*affectus*).[60] This would seem to be a novel use of the term. But in another place, where the term "internal sense" is implicitly understood though not explicitly mentioned, he places under it the faculties of "imagination, memory, etc." [61] In still another place imagination is identified by him with common sense, and the latter is contrasted with the external senses.[62] All this can be readily recognized as the reduction to a twofold classification, namely, imagination and memory, of the original threefold classification, namely, common sense, imagination, and memory. The latter classification, as will be recalled, is referred to by Roger Bacon and is adopted by Keckermann, Magirus, and Zanchius. Imagination and memory, as I have shown elsewhere, form also a veiled classification of the internal senses in Spinoza.[63] Imagination only, however, is identified with internal sense (*sens interne*) by Leibniz,[64] a view which, as we have seen, has already been suggested by Eustachius a Sancto Paulo. But when Leibniz proceeds to describe imagination, which he identifies with the internal sense, as the place "where the perceptions of the different external senses find themselves united," we readily recognize in this description Aristotle's description of one of the functions of common sense.[65] What Leibniz, therefore, really does here is not only to identify imagination with common sense, for which he had before him the example of Eustachius a Sancto Paulo and Descartes, but also to define it in terms of common sense. This, as will be recalled, was also done by Avicenna in his Risâlah fi al-Nafs.[66] But evidently unaware of the fact that in his description of imagination he has already indirectly identified it with common sense, Leibniz proceeds to say that

[60] Principia Philosophiae, IV, 190. For another instance of the inclusion of the appetitive faculty among the internal senses, see above, Ch. II, p. 111.

[61] Correspondance, XLVI (Oeuvres, ed. Adam et Tannery, I, p. 263, ll. 6–8).

[62] Meditationes, II (Oeuvres, VII, p. 32, ll. 13–19).

[63] Cf. my The Philosophy of Spinoza, II, 71 ff.

[64] Die philosophischen Schriften von Gottfried Wilhelm Leibniz, ed. C. J. Gerhardt, VI, 501.

[65] De Sensu, 7, 449a, 3 ff. Cf. above, Ch. I, n. 43.

[66] Cf. above, Ch. II, n. 43.

imagination "comprises at once the notions of the particular senses, which are clear but confused, and the notions of the common sense, which are clear and distinct," thus making "imagination" a more extensive term than "common sense." It will be recalled that Roger Bacon takes the Greek term *phantasia,* which Avicenna in his De Anima uses as synonymous with *sensus communis* and as distinct from the Latin term *imaginatio,* and uses it as a more extensive term than *sensus communis* and as including both *sensus communis* and *imaginatio.*[67] What Leibniz seems to be doing here is again this: he uses the term "imagination" in two senses. First, he uses it in the narrow sense of Roger Bacon's *imaginatio,* which Leibniz probably has reference to when he speaks of "the notions of particular senses, which are clear but confused"; second, he uses it in the wider sense of Roger Bacon's *phantasia,* which, as in Roger Bacon, comprises both *imaginatio,* whose notions Leibniz describes as confused, and *sensus communis,* whose notions he describes as distinct. The power of distinguishing between the impressions of the various senses, as will be recalled, is one of the functions of common sense.[68] The term "distinct" used here by Leibniz reflects that definition of common sense.

The history of the traditional use of the term "internal sense" winds up in modern philosophy with its restoration by Locke and Kant, perhaps unbeknown to themselves, to the original meaning with which it started its career in Augustine. Locke identifies internal sense with reflection,[69] which, in its simplest form, means according to him consciousness, or, as he calls it, "perception.[70] Kant defines internal sense (*innerer Sinn*) as "the perception of our own self and of our inner state,"[71] which again is consciousness. But inasmuch as consciousness is, according to Aristotle, one of the functions of common sense,[72] Locke's and Kant's identification of the old

67 Cf. above, n. 50.

68 De Anima, III, 2, 426b, 8-427a, 16. Cf. above, Ch. II, n. 29.

69 Essay concerning Human Understanding, II, 1, § 4.

70 Ibid., II, 9, §§ 1 ff.

71 Kritik der Reinen Vernunft, Transcendentale Asthetik, § 6.

72 De Anima, III, 2, 425b, 12 ff.

term "internal sense" with consciousness is really a return to the view of Augustine, who, as we have seen at the very beginning of our discussion, uses the term "internal sense" as identical with what Aristotle calls common sense and who ascribes to it, among other functions, also that of consciousness.[73]

* * *

Summing up the results of our investigation, we find that the term "internal sense" was at first used in early Latin philosophic texts as a designation of one single post-sensationary faculty, either "common sense" in Augustine and Gregory the Great or διάνοια in Erigena. Then in Arabic philosophy it was used in five different ways:

I. As a designation of διάνοια in Sirr al-Ḫalîkah (and similarly in the Syriac Causa Causarum).

II. As a designation of three post-sensationary faculties, namely, (1) imagination in the most general sense, (2) *fikr* as the equivalent of διάνοια, and (3) memory. These three internal senses are raised to five in the Iḫwân al-Ṣafâ by the addition either of two new post-sensationary faculties from the Stoic list or of two sub-functions of διάνοια.

III. As a designation of five post-sensationary faculties in Alfarabi arrived at (1) by the addition of *wahm* (*aestimatio*), and (2) by the breaking up of imagination into (*a*) retentive imagination, (*b*) compositive animal imagination, and (*c*) compositive human imagination, the last of which transforms the meaning of the Arabic term *fikr* from διάνοια to φαντασία λογιστική or βουλευτική. But by the combination of the two kinds of compositive imagination into one, the five internal senses are reduced to four.

IV. As a designation of seven post-sensationary faculties in Avicenna arrived at by the addition of (1) common sense and (2) recollection to the five of Alfarabi's list. But by various combinations of several of these seven faculties into one, which occur in the writings of Avicenna as well as of his fol-

[73] De Libero Arbitrio, II, 4 (Migne, XXXII, Col. 1246).

lowers, these seven internal senses are reduced, as a rule, to five.[74]

V. As a designation of the same seven faculties reduced to four [75] in Averroes (1) by the combination of *wahm* (*aestimatio*) and the three kinds of imagination into one faculty and (2) by the restoration of the Arabic term *fikr* to its original meaning of *διάνοια*.

In Hebrew philosophic texts, the classification of the internal senses follows the same development as that of the Arabic.

In later Latin philosophic texts, beginning with the translation of the works of Avicenna and Averroes in the 12th century, all the classifications of the internal senses are dominated by the influence of Avicenna and Averroes. But Augustine's use of the term "internal sense" occurs occasionally, and in Locke and Kant it is completely restored.

A table showing at a glance the variety of ways in which Greek terms are translated into Arabic, and from the Arabic into Hebrew and Latin, is given below. Latin terms which are translated from the Arabic indirectly through the Hebrew are marked by asterisks. An asterisk marks also one Hebrew term which was translated from the Latin. The references within the parentheses are to chapters and notes of this paper. Latin terms cited in Chapter III from scholastic writings, though based upon translations from the Arabic, are not included in this table.

φαντασία in its most general sense
- مصوّر (II, 73)
  - מצייר (I, 23; II, 73)
  - informatum (I, 23)
  - imaginans (II, 73)
- [تصوّر]
  - ציור (I, 21)
- [الفنطاسيا]
  - אלפנטסיא (I, 23)
  - phantasia (I, 23)
- خيال (I, 24)
- تخيّل
  - דעת (I, 26)
  - רעיון [דמיוני] (I, 27)
  - רעיון (I, 27)
  - דמיון (I, 27)
  - *cogitatio assimilativa (I, 27)

[74] For a threefold and fourfold classification of these seven internal senses by Avicenna, see above, Ch. II, p. 99.

[75] For a threefold classification of these internal senses by Averroes, see above, Ch. II, p. 109.

- *phantasia (I, 27)
- *imaginatio (I, 27)
- *aestimandi (III, 59)

متخيّلة (I, 40)
- מדמה (II, 73, 77, 81)
- imaginativa (II, 73, 77, 81)

φαντασία, retentive imagination

مصوّرة
- informans (II, 42)
- formalis (II, 42)

متصوّرة
- מצייר (II, 58)
- יצורי (II, 61)
- imaginativa (II, 58)
- *imaginatrix (II, 61)
- *phantasia (II, 61)

تصوّر
- הצטיירות (II, 61)
- *formatio (II, 61)

متخيّلة (II, 26)

خيال
- דמיון (II, 41)
- phantasia (II, 41)
- imaginatio (II, 42)

خياليّة
- דמיוני (II, 57)
- *imaginativa (II, 57)

حافظة
- שומר (II, 58)
- retentiva (II, 58)

حفظ (II, 51)

διάνοια, διανοητικόν

فكر (I, 22, 24)
- רעיון (II, 92)
- שכל (II, 98)

فكرة
- מחשבה (I, 25)
- תבונה (I, 26)

تفكّر
- מחשבה שכלית (I, 27)
- השתכלות (I, 27)
- *cogitatio intelligibilis (I, 27)
- *cogitatio (I, 27)

مفكّرة
- מחשב (II, 73)
- מחשבי (II, 77, 81)
- משכלת (II, 111)
- cogitativa (II, 73, 77, 81)
- cogitans (II, 73)

κριτικόν

مميّز
- בורר (II, 73)
- מברר (II, 95)
- מבחין (II, 77, 95)
- שופט (II, 95, 98)
- distinctiva (II, 73, 77)
- distinguens (II, 73)

φαντασία λογιστική or *βουλευτική*, compositive human imagination

فكر
- מְחַשֵּׁב (II, 59)
- מחשבה (II, 63)
- *imaginatio (II, 59)

مفكّرة
- מחשב (II, 57)
- חושב (II, 56)
- מחשבי (II, 61)
- cogitativa (II, 41, 42, 58)
- *extimativa (II, 57)

σύνεσις, φρόνησις, πρόνοια, estimative faculty

وهم

רעיון (II, 59)
והם (II, 94)
דמיון (II, 80)
existimatio (II, 80)
*cogitatio (II, 59)

وهميّة

מחשב (II, 41, 42, 58)
מחשבי (II, 57)
*שמאי (II, 104, 107)
existimativa (II, 41)
extimativa (II, 42, 58)
aestimativa (II, 41)
*cogitativa (II, 57)

متوهّمة

מחשבי (II, 61)
*cogitativa, *cogitatrix (II, 61)

ظنّ (II, 22, 43, 63)

זמימות (II, 22)
זָמָם (II, 63)
aestimatio (II, 22)

خاطر

רעיון (II, 63)

تخيّل

דמיון (II, 71)
virtus imaginativa (II, 71)

φαντασία [συνετή, φρόνιμη, προνοητική], compositive animal imagination

متخيّلة

מדמה (II, 41, 42)
דמיוני (II, 58)
רעיוני (II, 56)
יצרי (II, 61)
imaginativa (II, 41, 42, 57)
phantasia (II, 58)
*reminiscentia (II, 61)
*imaginatrix (II, 61)

تخيل

יצר (II, 59, 61)
*reminiscentia (II, 61)
*phantasia (II, 59)

μνήμη [αἰσθητῶν], memory of sensible objects

ذكر

זכרון (II, 59; I, 23)
memoria (I, 23; II, 59)

ذاكرة

זוכר (II, 56, 58)
memorialis (II, 58)
rememorativa (II, 81)

مذكّرة

זוכר (II, 61)
*memoria (II, 61)

تذكّر

זכרון (II, 61)
*memoria (II, 61)

حافظة

שומר (II, 41, 42, 57, 73, 77, 81)
conservativa (II, 41)
conservans (II, 73)
memorialis (II, 42)
rememorativa (II, 77, 81)

μνήμη [νοητῶν], memory of intelligible notions

فهم

בינה (I, 25)

حكمة

חכמה (I, 26)

تفهّم
תבונה (I, 27)
התבוננות (I, 27)
*intellectus (I, 27)
*intelligentia (I, 27)
*intellectio (I, 27)

ἀνάμνησις, recollection
ذكرة
זוכר (II, 41)
memorialis (II, 41)
ذاكرة
זוכר (II, 57)
reminiscibilis (II, 42)
memorans (II, 73)
rememorativa (II, 73)
*memorativa (II, 57)
متذكّرة (II, 43)

16

ISAAC ISRAELI ON THE INTERNAL SENSES[1]

In his discussion of the soul in *Liber de Elementis* Isaac Israeli incidentally refers to the distinction between the five senses and the post-sensationary faculties, which throughout medieval philosophy, Arabic, Hebrew, and Latin, are known by the contrasting terms external senses and internal senses. Like his successors the Iḫwân al-Ṣafâ he designates them by the terms "corporeal" and "spiritual"[2] senses, and like his predecessor Ḥunain ibn Isḥâḳ and Razi[3] he divides the spiritual or internal senses into three: (1) imagination, (2) cogitation, (3) memory.[4] This threefold classification of the post-sensationary faculties has been ascribed to Galen on the basis of a reference made to him by both Ḥunain and Razi, and on the basis of a passage in the writings of Galen where after his enumeration of the five senses he mentions three post-sensationary faculties: (1) φανταστικόν, (2) διανοητικόν, (3) μνημονευτικόν[5]. But the reference made to Galen by both Ḥunain and Razi is only in connection with the localization of these three faculties in the various chambers of the brain,[6] and as

[1] The historical and philological generalizations in this paper are based on my monograph "The Internal Senses in Latin, Arabic, and Hebrew Philosophic Texts." *The Harvard Theological Review*, 28 (1935), 69–133.

[2] חוש נשמי, *sensus corporeus*; חוש רוחני, *sensus spiritualis*. *Sefer ha-Yesodot*, II, ed. S. Fried, pp. 53–55; *Liber de Elementis*, II, in *Omnia Opera Isaaci*, Lyon, 1555, fol. IX r a. Cf. Fr. Dieterici, *Die Abhandlungen der Ichwân Es-Safâ in Auswahl*, p. 209: حس روحانى ; حس جسمانى.

I am indebted to Prof. Alexander Marx for making available to me the rare copy of the *Omnia Opera Isaaci* in the Library of the Jewish Theological Seminary and also for directing my attention to the published Arabic fragment of the *Liber de Definitionibus* referred to in subsequent notes.

[3] *Musere ha-Pilosofim*, II, 10; *Al-Mansûri fi al-Ṭibb* in P. de Koning, *Trois Traités d'Anatomie Arabes*, p. 9.

[4] (1) מצייר, *formativus*, *formatus*, אלפנטסיא, *phantasia*, (2) מחשבה, *cogitatio*, (3) זכרון, *memoria*.

[5] *De Symptomatum Differentiis*, Cap. 3, in *Opera Omnia*, ed. D. C. G. Kühn, Vol. 7, p. 56. Cf. Horovitz, *Die Psychologie bei den jüdischen Religions-Philosophen des Mittelalters*, pp. 238 f.

[6] *De Locis Affectis*, III, 9, *ibid.*, Vol. 8, pp. 174 ff.

for Galen's enumeration of the faculties of the soul in the passage referred to, it is nothing but an analysis of the contents of Aristotle's *De Anima* and *Parva Naturalia*, his enumeration of the five senses referring to *De Anima*, II, 5–12, and his enumeration of the three post-sensationary faculties referring to (1) *De Anima*, III, 3, where *φανταστικόν* is discussed, (2) *De Anima*, III, 4–6, where, according to Aristotle's own analysis of the *De Anima* in *De Anima*, II, 3, 414a, 32, the subject matter discussed is *διανοητικόν*, and (3) *De Memoria et Reminiscentia*, where *μνημονευτικόν* is discussed. The fact that Galen does not mention in his list "common sense," which is discussed by Aristotle in *De Anima*, III, 1–2, does not militate against our contention, for Aristotle himself in his enumeration of the faculties of the soul in *De Anima*, II, 3, 414a, 32, and elsewhere, does not mention "common sense," evidently for the reason that he would have included it among the five senses, of which it is the focal point, or else he would have identified it with imagination, the latter of which is sometimes considered by him as a function of the former. Aristotle himself is not clear on that point, and there is reason for annexing the first two chapters of Book III, which deal with common sense, to Book II, which deals with the five senses.[7]

Isaac Israeli, however, does mention common sense[8] and he seems to have a definite view as to where it should be placed. He excludes it from the internal senses, and does not include it among the external senses. Its position, according to him, is that of an intermediary between the two, and he furthermore explains the meaning of the term "common" applied to that sense as derived from the fact that it has something in common with both the external and the internal senses, for he says: "It is an intermediary between the corporeal sense of sight and the imagination, the latter of which resides in the anterior ventricle of the brain and is known as *phantasia*. It is for this reason that it is called 'common sense,' namely, that it receives from the corporeal sense, i.e., the sense of sight, the corporeal characteristics of things and conveys them to the spiritual sense, i.e., imagination."[9]

[7] Cf. R. D. Hicks, *Aristotle: De Anima*, p. 422.

[8] *Loc. cit.*

[9] Hebrew, pp. 53–54; Latin, fol. IX r a;

לפי שהוא אמצעי בין חוש הראות הגשמי ובין המצייר, שהוא בבטן המוקדם שבמוח, הנקרא אלפנטסיא, ולכן נקרא שמו החוש המשותף בעבור שמקבל מהחוש הגשמי, כלומר חוש הראות, גשמות הדברים ויביאם אל החוש הרוחני, כלומר המצייר.

"cum sit medius inter sensum visibilem scilicet corporeum et informatum, qui est in anteriori parte cerebri, nominatum phantasia, ei propter hoc nominatur sensus communis quia recipit a sensu corporeo, [sive] visibili (enim) corporeitatem rerum et procedit cum ea ad sensum spiritualem, sive formatum."

This explanation is rather unique. In Aristotle's works common sense is not merely the conveyer of the impressions of the sense of sight but the focus of the impressions of all the five senses.[10] Equally unique is his assignation to common sense of an intermediate position between the external and the internal senses. In Arabic philosophy, before Avicenna, common sense is not mentioned in the enumeration of internal senses, though one of its functions is included by the Iḫwân al-Ṣafâ among the functions of imagination in their description of the internal senses.[11] When common sense does appear with Avicenna, it is thereafter invariably included among the internal senses, though sometimes it is identified with imagination. This is true of all the classifications modelled after that of Avicenna, which are found in Arabic, Hebrew, and Latin literatures. The only exception to that is one classification by Albertus Magnus, which, though of the Avicennian type, places common sense among the external senses.[12] Undoubtedly Albertus Magnus was influenced by Isaac Israeli, though he does not literally follow him, for Isaac Israeli's *Liber de Definitionibus* is quoted by Albertus Magnus elsewhere in his discussion of the internal senses.[13]

The enumeration of the internal senses, which in Isaac Israeli is mentioned only casually, is naturally not followed by a formal description of their functions. But out of various statements scattered throughout his *Liber de Elementis* and *Liber de Definitionibus* we can build up a full description of these functions. In some respects his statements are interesting both philologically and philosophically.

Of the first internal sense, imagination, two mutually complementary statements are made by Israeli. First, in *Liber de Elementis*, he states that imagination is not completely independent of sense-per-

[10] *De Anima*, III, 2, 426b, 8–427a, 16.

[11] Cf. Dieterici, *op. cit.*, p. 468. Even Alfarabi, who anticipated Avicenna in his inclusion of the estimative faculty among the internal senses, does not mention common sense. He does, however, speak of an unnamed faculty to which he ascribes what is unmistakably the functions of common sense and, like Isaac Israeli, he places it on what he calls the "common boundary" between the external and internal senses. According to Farani's commentary on Alfarabi, some manuscripts have the reading "common sense" instead of "common boundary." Cf. "Risâlat fuṣuṣ al-Ḥikam," §42, in F. Dieterici's *Alfārābī's philosophische Abhandlungen* (1890), p. 75, and M. Horten's "Das Buch der Ringsteine Fârâbî's. Mit Auszügen aus dem Kommentar des Emîr Ismâ'îl el Ḥoseinî el Fârânî," §42, in *Zeitschrift für Assyriolgie*, 18 (1904), p. 284; 20 (1907), p. 323.

[12] *Summa de Creaturis*, Pars II: *De Homine*, Quaest. 19: *De Visu* (ed. Vivés).

[13] *Ibid.*, Quaest. 40, Art. 1.

ception, for it operates upon the sensible forms of corporeal objects,[14] after those forms have been conveyed to it by common sense.[15] This on the whole corresponds to Aristotle's view of imagination as that of a faculty quite different from sense-perception but still dependent upon it.[16] Subsequently, in the Avicennian classification of the internal senses, after common sense has been included among the internal senses, the distinction between common sense and imagination is presented as that between the "receiver" of images and the "retainer"[17] of images. Second, in his *Liber de Definitionibus*, Israeli adds that while imagination differs from reason or thought, it is indispensable to it. "The sensitive faculty, when it perceives things by sensation, implants their forms in the *phantasia*, which is in the front part of the head, and *phantasia* conveys them to the rational soul."[18] This again reflects Aristotle's view that while imagination is different from thought (διάνοια),[19] still images are the objects of thought, for "to the thinking soul images serve as present sensations."[20]

The second internal sense which represents the Greek διανοητικόν is fully defined in *Liber de Definitionibus* and its functions are described in several places in *Liber de Elementis*. The definition in *Liber de Definitionibus* reads as follows: "Cogitation is an intellectual faculty which is supervenient to things, for cogitation is one of the faculties of the intellect, on account of which every cogitative being becomes

[14] *Sefer ha-Yesodot*, II, p. 52; *Liber de Elementis*, II, fol. VIII v b:

והשני, שהדבר כשיהיה גשמי נלקח מהחוש נטבעה צורתו במהירות בבטן המוקדם מן המוח.	"Et secundus est cum sermo fuerit corporeus sumptum a sensu, imprimitur forma ipsius in phantasia velociter."

[15] *Ibid.*, Hebrew, p. 54, Latin, fol. IX r a, quoted above in n. 9.

[16] *De Anima*, III, 3, 428a, 5 ff.; 428b, 11 ff.

[17] قابلة, מקבל, *recipiens*; حافظة, שומר, *custodiens*. Cf. Avicenna, *Canon*, Lib. I, Fen I, Doctrina VI, Cap. 5.

[18] *Ḥibbur Izḥak ha-Rofeh ha-Yisraeli* (*Sefer ha-Gebulim weha-Reshumim*), ed. H. Hirschfeld in *Festschrift zum achzigsten Geburtstage Moritz Steinschneider's*, 1896, Hebrew part, p. 135; *Liber de Definitionibus* in *Omnia Opera Isaaci*, Lyon, 1555, fol. III r a:

כי כח ההרגש כשיראה הדברים בהרגשה יפתח צורתם בפנדסיאה שהיא במקום [המוקדם] של [ה]ראש ותוליכם הפנטסיאה אל נפש השכל.	"cum enim virtus sensibilis praesentat res sensibiliter imprimit formas in phantasia quae est in anteriori parte cerebri et phantasia praeducit ad animam rationalem."

This passage is missing in the fragment of the Arabic original (*Kitab al-Ḥudud wal-Rusum*), ed. H. Hirschfeld in *JQR*, 15 (1902–03), pp. 689–693.

[19] *De Anima*, III, 3, 427b, 14–15.

[20] *Ibid.*, III, 7, 431a, 14–15.

an intelligent being."[21] Now as a mere definition of the underlying Greek word *διάνοια*, this is simple enough. It reflects, in the first place, Aristotle's use of the term *διανοητικόν* as synonymous with *νοῦς*[22] and of the term *διάνοια* as synonymous with *λογισμός*.[23] In the second place, the statement that cogitation "is supervenient to things" reflects a passage in Aristotle where *διάνοια* and *πρᾶγμα* are contrasted. The passage reads: "Falsity and truth are not in things (*πράγμασιν*) . . . but in thought (*διανοίᾳ*).[24] But as a definition of the Arabic term فكر as used in the classifications of the internal senses, this definition of Isaac Israeli is of special significance.

The arabic term فكر as well as its Hebrew equivalent מחשבה and its Latin equivalent *cogitatio*, in its use as an internal sense, has undergone three stages of development. Prior to Alfarabi, and even afterwards whenever it is used in a threefold classification of internal senses, it stands as here in Isaac Israeli for the greek *διάνοια*. After Alfarabi and Avicenna, in all classifications which follow their models, it stands not for *διάνοια* but rather for a special kind of imagination in man which is the combined result of *διάνοια* and *φαντασία* and is described by Aristotle as *φαντασία λογιστική* or *βουλευτική*.[25] Then in Averroes' classification, and in all classifications based upon that of Averroes, it stands again for *διάνοια*. To this generalization the only exception is to be found in the use of *cogitatio* in scholastic reproductions of Averroes' classifications and in the use of *cogitatio* in Roger Bacon's reproduction of Avicenna's classification. In the light of these facts with regard to the subsequent development of the meaning of فكر Isaac Israeli's statement that "cogitation is one of the faculties of the intellect" is of high significance, for it emphasizes the use of فكر as the equivalent of *διάνοια* which is a function of *νοῦς*.

[21] Arabic, p. 690; Hebrew, p. 139; Latin, fol. III v b:

الفكر قوة عقلية تحل
فى الاشياً لان الفكر
قوة من قوات النطق
ولذلك صار كل (אל)
مفكر ناطق.

המחשבה כח דיעני הולך
בדברים, כי המחשבה היא
כח מכחות השכל, ובעבור
זה נעשה כל החשב משכיל.

"Cogitatio est virtus intelligibilis praecedens in rebus, quia cogitatio est una de virtutibus animae rationalis, et propter hoc factus est omnis cogitans rationalis."

On the technical meaning of the Arabic حل, see my *Crescas' Critique of Aristotle*, p. 544, n. 11.

[22] *De Anima*, III, 3, 414b, 18.

[23] *Ibid.*, III, 3, 415a, 8.

[24] *Metaphysics*, VI, 4, 1027b, 25–27.

[25] *De Anima*, III, 10, 433b, 29 ff.

Besides this definition of "cogitation" in *Liber de Definitionibus*, Isaac Israeli, as I have said, also describes its functions in *Liber de Elementis*. In one place, the description explicitly mentions the term "cogitation." It reads as follows: "Cogitation has the power to perscrute, to discern, and to combine."[26] In another place, the term "cogitation" is not mentioned, but it is implied in its context. It reads as follows: "In man . . . in addition to nutrition, growth, motion, and the corporeal sense, there are also the spiritual sense and the power of investigation and discretion."[27] In this passage it is quite clear that by "spiritual sense" Israeli means imagination, which on a previous occasion he refers to as "the spiritual sense,"[28] and that by the power of "investigation and discretion" he means, as in the previous quotation, the cogitative faculty. In a third place, he ascribes these functions to what he calls the "intellectual sense." It reads as follows: "The rational soul has in addition to the natural sense and the animal sense also the intellectual sense which consists of (1) interpretation and discretion, (2) perscrutation, (3) separation and combination, and (4) the cognition of things according to their truth.[29] In this passage it is clear that by "natural sense" he means nutrition and growth which are the functions of the vegetative soul,[30] that by the "animal sense" he means sensation and motion which are the

[26] *Sefer ha-Yesodot*, II, p. 55; *Liber de Elementis*, II, fol. IX r a:

לפי שיש לכח המחשבי כח [1] החקירה, [2] וההבדל, [3] ו[ה]חבור.

"Cogitationis enim est [1] perscrutari et [2] discernere et [3] componere."

[27] *Ibid.*, III, Hebrew, p. 69; Latin, fol. X r b:

ואולם באדם . . . נתחברו בו עם המזון והגידול והתנועה והחוש הגשמי, החוש הרוחני [1] והדרישה והחקירה [2] וההכרה.

"in homine autem . . . aggregatus in ipso cum nutrimento et augmento [et motu] et sensu corporeo, sensus spiritualis et [1] investigatio et [2] discretio."

[28] *Ibid.*, II, Hebrew, p. 54; Latin, fol. IX r a:

ויביאם אל החוש הרוחני כלומר המצייר.

"et procedit cum ea ad sensum spiritualem sive formatum."

[29] *Ibid.*, III, Hebrew, p. 68; Latin, fol. X r a:

והמדברת יש לה עם החוש הטבעי והחוש הנפשי חוש השכלי אשר היא [1] ההכרה, [2] והחקירה [3] וההתר והקשור, [4] והעמידה (וההתבוננות or) על אמיתת העניינים.

"Et rationali inest cum sensu naturali et sensu animali, intellectualis sensus, qui est [1] interpretatio et discretio, et [2] perscrutatio, et [3] solutio et ligatio, et [4] cognitio rerum secundum veritatem."

[30] *Ibid.*, Hebrew, p. 68; Latin, fol. X r a:

ואמנם הצומחת יש לה חוש טבעי שתחוש בו במזונה וגידולה.

"et vegetabili quidem inest sensus naturalis, quo sentit in nutrimento et augmento suo"

Cf. *De Anima*, II, 4, 415a, 22 ff.

functions of the animal soul,[31] and that by the "intellectual sense" he means "cogitation," which, according to his own statement elsewhere,[32] is a function of the rational soul or the intellect. The combination of the term "sense" with the term "intellectual," which would seem rather strange, can be explained on the ground that Aristotle himself is found to have used the term *αἴσθησις* in the sense of *νοῦς* in *Nicomachean Ethics*, VI, 11, 1143b, 5: *τούτων οὖν ἔχειν δεῖ αἴσθησιν, αὕτη δ᾽ ἐστὶ νοῦς*. The term "intellect" (שכל) in the sense of "cogitation" is also to be discerned in *Sefer ha-Ruaḥ weha-Nefesh* ascribed to Isaac Israeli, in the statement that "wisdom, understanding, discrimination, knowledge, and good thinking all belong to the faculty of intellect."[32a]

It is unfortunate that the Arabic text of *Liber de Elementis* is not extant to provide us with the Arabic terms underlying the terms contained in the Latin and Hebrew versions of the three passages quoted. But these Arabic terms can be supplied from the Arabic fragment of *Liber de Definitionibus*.

In these three passages quoted we have *five* Latin terms and *four* Hebrew terms, as follows:

1. *interpretatio et discretio*, הכרה,
2. *discernere*, הבדל,
3. *discretio*, הכרה,
4. *perscrutari*, חקירה,
5. *investigatio*, דרישה וחקירה.

Now the Latin *discretio* occurs in *Liber de Definitionibus* as the equivalent of تمييز הבדלה, whereas the Hebrew חקירה occurs there as the equivalent of بحث, *indagatio*.[33] But inasmuch as the Latin translations of the two works were made by one person whereas the Hebrew translations were made by two persons, we have reason to believe that تمييز rather than بحث is the underlying Arabic term for *discretio* in *Liber de Elementis*. Furthermore, inasmuch as *discernere* and *discretio* are the same word in different forms and also inasmuch

[31] *Ibid.*:

והחיונית יש לה עם החוש הטבעי חוש נפשי שבו תחוש במכאוב הגשמי ותתנועע[1] ברצון.

[1] Changed from והתנועות.

"Et animali inest cum sensu naturali sensus animalis, quo sentit dolorem corporeum et movet voluntarie."

Cf. *De Anima*, II, 5, 416b, 32 ff.

[32] Cf. above n. 21.

[32a] *Sefer ha-Ruah Weba-Nefesh le-Rabbi Yizhak ha-Yisraeli*, ed. M. Steinschneider, *Ha-Karmel*, I (1871–72), 202: ואם אמרני חכמה ובינה והכרה וידיעה וטוב המחשבה כל זה מכח השכל. Cf. my "The Internal Senses, etc.," *op. cit.*, pp. 84 and 112 n. 98.

[33] Arabic, p. 690; Hebrew, p. 139; Latin, fol. III v b.

as *discernere* in *Liber de Elementis* has as its Hebrew equivalent the term הבדל, which term in *Liber de Definitionibus* is used as the equivalent of تمييز, we have reason to believe that the same Arabic word underlies *discernere.* As for the remaining three terms, *interpretatio, perscrutatio,* and *investigatio,* none of them occurs in that part of *Liber de Definitionibus* of which the Arabic is extant. But the term הכרה, which the Hebrew translator of *Liber de Elementis* uses as the equivalent of *interpretatio et discretio,* is used by him in his translation of Algazali's *Mizan al-'Amal* as the equivalent of تمييز in the sense of *discretio,*[34] whereas the Hebrew translator of *Liber de Definitionibus* uses it as the equivalent of معرفة, *cognitio.*[35] As between these two, the term تمييز is preferable here. Furthermore, in that part of *Liber de Definitionibus* of which there is no Arabic extant, the terms (1) *perscrutatio* and *investigatio,* חקירה, (2) *discretio,* הבדלה, and *cognitio,* הכרה, are used together,[36] which shows that *cognitio* represents a different Arabic term than any of the terms represented by the Latin terms used in *Liber de Elementis.* Similarly the Hebrew חקירה, which the Hebrew translator of *Liber de Elementis* uses as the equivalent of *perscrutari,* and also the Hebrew דרישה וחקירה, which he uses as the equivalent of *investigatio,* are both together used by him as the equivalent of بحث in his translation of *Mizan al-'Amal,*[37] whereas the Hebrew translator of *Liber de Definitionibus* uses חקירה as the equivalent of بحث, *indigatio,* and דרישה as the equivalent of نظر, *inquisitio.*[38] As between these two, بحث is preferable, for the ordinary meaning of نظر is that of the Greek θεωρία, *contemplatio,* עיון,[39] and so does the Hebrew translator of *Liber de Elementis* render it in his translation of *Mizan al-'Amal.*[40]

As a result of this discussion we may now give a complete list of

[34] *Mozene Ẓedeḳ,* IV, p. 34; *Mizan al-'Amal,* [IV], p. 22 הנער המכיר, المميز, الصبى, *the boy who is of the age of discretion.*

[35] Arabic, p. 690; Hebrew, p. 139; Latin, fol. III v b.

[36] Cf. Hebrew, pp. 136–137, Latin, fol. III r a-b, quoted below in n. 55

[37] *Mozene Ẓedeḳ,* IV, p. 27; *Mizan al-'Amal,* [IV], p. 17.

[38] Arabic, p. 690; Hebrew, p. 139; Latin, fol. III v b.

[39] Cf. below, discussion of first definition of memory of *Liber de Definitionibus.*

[40] *Mozene Ẓedeḳ,* III, p. 24; *Mizan al-'Amal,* [III], p. 14.

the terms used in the description of the functions of the faculty of *cogitatio*. They are as follows:

(1) يميز, הכרה, הבדל, *discretio, discernere, interpretatio et discretio.*

(2) بحث, חקירה, דרישה וחקירה, *perscrutari, investigatio, indagatio.*

Now both these Arabic terms, together with the other two descriptions of *cogitatio*, namely, (1) separation and combination and (2) the cognition of things according to truth, can be traced to Aristotle's description of διάνοια. The faculty called διάνοια is, according to Aristotle, that in which falsity and truth exist,[41] and truth and falsity, again according to him, depend "on combination and separation"—σύνθεσις (or συμπλοκή) καὶ διαίρεσις.[42] Furthermore, truth and falsehood, says Aristotle, is something which we discern or judge (κρίνομεν).[43] This last statement of Aristotle is reflected in a passage of John Damascenus who directly describes διανοητικόν as that to which judgments (κρίσεις) belong.[44] The terms *discretio, perscrutatio, interpretatio*, and their like, used by Isaac Israeli in his description of "cogitation," thus reflect the term κρίσις which is used by Aristotle indirectly in connection with διάνοια and which by John Damascenus is applied directly to it, just as the terms *solutio et ligatio, componere*, and *cognitio rerum secundum veritatem* reflect the other two statements made by Aristotle in connection with διάνοια.

Of the third internal sense, memory, four definitions are given by Isaac Israeli, one in *Liber de Elementis* and three in *Liber de Definitionibus*. It is my purpose to explain the exact meaning of each definition, and also to show how the four definitions make up one complete definition of memory such as we find in the philosophic literature current at the time of Isaac Israeli. My interpretation of these definitions will assume that Isaac Israeli had before him a description of memory such as we find in John Damascenus' *De Fide Orthodoxa*, II, 20, which in itself can be shown to have been made up of elements drawn from the writings of Aristotle.[45]

[41] *Metaphysics*, VI, 4, 1027b, 25–27.

[42] *Ibid.*, 18–19, 29–30.

[43] *De Anima*, III, 3, 428a, 3–4.

[44] *De Fide Orthodoxa*, II, 19.

[45] John Damascenus' immediate source is Nemesius, *De Natura Hominis*, Cap. 13, to whom reference is made in the printed editions of *De Fide Orthodoxa*.

John Damascenus' definition of memory reads as follows:

Τὸ δὲ μνημονευτικόν ἐστι μνήμης καὶ ἀναμνήσεως αἴτιόν τε καὶ ταμεῖον. Μνήμη γάρ ἐστι φαντασία ἐγκαταλελειμμένη ἀπό τινος αἰσθήσεώς τε καὶ νοήσεως κατ' ἐνέργειαν φαινομένης, ἢ σωτηρία αἰσθήσεώς τε καὶ νοήσεως. Ἡ γὰρ ψυχὴ τῶν μὲν αἰσθητῶν διὰ τῶν αἰσθητηρίων ἀντιλαμβάνεται, ἤγουν αἰσθάνεται, καὶ γίνεται δόξα. τῶν δὲ νοητῶν, διὰ τοῦ νοῦ, καὶ γίνεται νόησις. ὅταν οὖν τοὺς τύπους ὧν τε ἐδόξασεν, ὧν τε ἐνόησε, διασώζῃ, μνημονεύειν λέγεται.

§1. The memorative faculty is the cause and storehouse of memory and recollection. For memory is an image left behind by a sensible perception or a mental reflection which has actually taken place, or it is the conservation of some sensible perception or some mental reflection. When the soul perceives or senses sensible objects by means of the sense-organs, there arises opinion; when it perceives intelligible notions by means of the intellect, there arises thought. Therefore, when it preserves the impressions of the things of which an opinion or thought was formed, the term "to remember" is used.

Δεῖ δὲ γινώσκειν, ὅτι ἡ τῶν νοητῶν ἀντίληψις οὐ γίνεται, εἰ μὴ ἐκ μαθήσεως, ἢ φυσικῆς ἐννοίας, Οὐ γὰρ ἐξ αἰσθήσεως . . .

§2. It must also be known that the apprehension of intelligible notions does not take place except through learning or natural thinking, not by sense-perception . . .

Ἀνάμνησις δὲ λέγεται μνήμης ἀπολομένης ὑπὸ λήθης ἀνάκτησις . . .

§3. Recollection is said of the recovery of a memory which has been lost through forgetfulness . . .

Τὸ μὲν οὖν φανταστικὸν, διὰ τῶν αἰσθήσεων ἀντιλαμβανόμενον τῶν ὑλῶν, παραδίδωσι τῷ διανοητικῷ, ἢ διαλογιστικῷ, ταὐτὸν γὰρ ἀμφότερα, ὃ παραλαβὸν καὶ κρίναν, παραπέμπει τῷ μνημονευτικῷ.

§4. The imaginative faculty delivers the materials, which have been received through the senses, to the cogitative or the discursive faculty (for the two words mean the same), and this receives them and examines (*κρίναν*) them and transmits them to the memorative faculty.

Analyzing this passage of John Damascenus we find that it contains

First, the definition of memory of sense perception (§1).

Second, the definition of memory of intelligible notions (§§1, 2, 4).

The distinction between these two kinds of memory is referred to by Aristotle in *De Memoria et Reminiscentia*, 1, 449b, 18–23, when he says that one who remembers may do so either with reference to scientific knowledge (ἐπιστήμη) or with reference to sense perception (αἴσθησις); in the former case he is said to remember what he learned (ἔμαθεν) or contemplated (ἐθεώρησεν), in the latter case he is said to remember what he heard or saw.

Third, the definition of recollection as distinct from memory (§3).

This again is based upon Aristotle's discussion in *De Memoria et Reminiscentia*, 2, 451a, 18 ff.

Fourth, the description of memory by the term "conservation" (σωτηρία), which he presents as an alternative to the terms "cause" (αἴτιόν) and "storehouse" (ταμεῖον) (§1).

The use of the term σωτηρία as a description of memory reflects Plato's use of that term in the same connection in *Philebus* 34 A and elsewhere. A similar term (συντήρησις) is used by Galen in *Definitiones Medicae*, 124 (*Opera Omnia*, ed. Kühn, Vol. 19, p. 381). It is also in the similar sense of "retention" that Aristotle evidently applies the term ἕξις to memory in *De Memoria et Reminiscentia*, 1, 451a, 16.

The four definitions of memory given by Isaac Israeli correspond exactly to these four statements made by John Damascenus.

The definition in *Liber de Elementis* reads as follows: "And when the imaginative faculty has received from common sense the materiality of things it transmits it to memory and stores it away with it."[46] This evidently is a definition of the memory of sensible objects. Then in *Liber de Definitionibus* he deals with the three other definitions of memory.

The first definition of memory in *Liber de Definitionibus* reads as follows:[47]

حد الذكر درك الاشيا الخامة فى النفس بالبحث وانظر·

תכלית הזכירה דריכות הדברים הנולדים בנפש בחקירה ובדרישה.

Definito memoriæ. Memoria est apprehensio rerum existentium in anima cum indigatione et inquisitione.

"Memory is the apprehension of things which arise in the soul as a result of investigation and research." This is evidently a definition of the memory of "intelligible notions," as John Damascenus calls it,

[46] *Sefer ha-Yesodot*, II, p. 55; *Liber de Elementis*, II, fol. IX r a:

וכשקבל זה המצייר מהחוש המשותף, שלחו אל הזכרון והפקידו אצלו.

"et cum formatus sit recipit etiam illud a sensu communi, ducit ipsam super memoriam et deponit apud eam."

[47] Arabic, p. 690; Hebrew, p. 139; Latin, fol. III v b.

or of "scientific knowledge," as Aristotle calls it. The expression "investigation and research" corresponds to μάθησις and φυσικὴ ἔννοια in John Damascenus and to ἔμαθεν and ἐθεώρησεν in Aristotle. The term بحث, חקירה, *indagatio*, while not a direct translation of μάθησις, used by both John Damascenus and Aristotle, is a close enough equivalent of it. The Arabic term نظر, which the Hebrew and Latin translate here by דרישה and *inquisitio*, is ordinarily used as a translation of the Greek θεωρία (עיון, *contemplatio*) which is exactly the term used by Aristotle and which is probably also what John Damascenus means by φυσικὴ ἔννοια. Furthermore, بحث, as we have shown above, reflects also the Greek κρίσις, and this term in the form of κρίναν is used by John Damascenus here in his description of intellectual memory in the last paragraph of my quotation (§4). It is this definition of memory that is quoted in the name of Isaac Israeli by Albertus Magnus in *Summa de Creaturis*, Pars II: *De Homine*, Quaest. XL, Art. I. In his quotation, the definition, with the omission of only one word, reads as follows: "Isaac in libro de Definitionibus: 'Memoria est comprehensio rerum existentium in anima cum inquisitione.' "

The second definition in *Liber de Definitionibus* reads as follows:[48]

حد التذكر اختلاف شیء ما[49] قد نسی	תכלית הזכרון חלוף דבר מה שכבר נשכח.	*Definitio recordationis. Recordatio est inquisitio adventus rei jam oblitae (a virtute cogitativa).*[50]

"Recollection is the recovery of a thing that has already been forgotten." Its correspondence to John Damascenus' definition of recollection is quite evident. Philologically, in this definition, the terms اختلاف, חלוף, *inquisitio adventus*, are interesting. From the context it is quite evident that اختلاف is to be understood here in the sense of "regaining" or "recovery," thus reflecting the term ἀνάκτησις used in John Damascenus. The Hebrew חלוף is a transliteration as well as a translation of the arabic اختلاف and has been used by the translator in the sense of "recovery" and "regaining" through its association with the Biblical expression יחליפו כח, *renew their strength* (Is. 40.31, 41.1). Thus also Judah ibn Tibbon in Ibn Janaḥ's *Sefer ha-Shorashim* on the root חלף in Ps. 90.5 and 6 translates ویخلق ای یتجدّد [و یتبدّل] by ויחליף כלומר יתחדש ויתחלף.[51]

[48] *Ibid.*

[49] I have changed this reading from שיא, which I take to be a corruption of שי מא.

[50] The phrase "a virtute cogitativa" occurs neither in the Arabic original nor in the Hebrew version.

[51] Cf. *Kitab al-Uṣul*, ed. Ad. Neubauer, Col. 229; *Sefer ha-Shorashim*, ed. W. Bacher, p. 156.

The third definition reads as follows:[52]

حد الحفظ ذكر متصل غير منقسم.	תכלית השמירה הזכירה בלי הפרש ובלי התוך.	*Definitio servatoris. Servatio est memoria continua (non)*[53] *indiscreta.*

"Conservation is a continuous and uninterrupted memory." This reflects the fourth of John Damascenus' statements about memory, where the term "conservation" is used in place of "cause" and "storehouse." It is interesting to note that subsequently, throughout Arabic, Hebrew, and Latin philosophic literatures, both "conservation" and "storehouse"[54] are used in the description of memory. The terms "continuous and uninterrupted," used in this definition, are the terms which differentiate memory from recollection.

As in the case of common sense so also in the case of the estimative faculty Isaac Israeli mentions it and describes it but does not include it among the internal senses. The estimative faculty, to call it by the name by which it is known in scholastic literature, is a faculty which is peculiar to animals and corresponds in them to the rational faculty in men. The first to include this faculty among the internal senses is Alfarabi in which respect he is followed by Avicenna, from whom it has passed on to subsequent Arabic, Hebrew, and Latin philosophic authors. This faculty is placed by Isaac Israeli outside the internal senses, and as far as I could find out he is the first to describe it in the terms by which it became later known as an internal sense. His description of it occurs in *Liber de Definitionibus* and it reads as follows: "Inferior to this order of the rational soul in clearness and sublimity is the animal soul, for it is generated from the shadow of the rational soul, on account of which it is removed from the splendor of intelligence and becomes enmeshed in shadow and darkness and is deprived of judgment and discernment and becomes estimative in the true sense of the term and meditative only in the transumptive sense of the term, for it judges a thing only according to appearance and not according to truth. The faculties appropriate to it are sensation, motion, and locomotion. It is for this reason that brute animals are foolhardy and excessively rash, seeking victory and

[52] Arabic, p. 690; Hebrew, p. 139; Latin, fol. III v b.

[53] The Latin should read either "non discreta" or "indiscreta." The reading in the printed edition is evidently the result of an erroneous combination of these two alternative readings.

[54] The common expression for this in Arabic, Hebrew, and Latin is خزانة الصور, אוצר הצורות, *arca formarum.*

power, but without judgment and discernment and knowledge, just as the lion, for instance, seeks to obtain power over all other beasts, without, however, having any judgment and discernment and knowledge of what he does. Evidence that brute animals possess estimation but no judgment is to be found in the case of the ass. When the ass is very thirsty and is led to water, on seeing his own image or some other image in the water, he takes fright and runs away, even though his very life and well-being depend upon the water. Similarly when he sees a lion, he advances toward him, follows him, and rushes at him, with the result that the latter kills him and carries him off as prey. For this reason brute animals receive neither reward nor punishment, inasmuch as they cannot discern or know what action is remunerable, so as to be able to choose to do that which is remunerable and thereby deserve reward for themselves, and not to do something which is contrary to the remunerable and different from it and through which they would incur punishment. This is so because the animal soul is deprived of the power of inquiry and discretion and of the perception of truths and is endowed only with estimation and meditation."[55] Again: "Estimation is a faculty which applies to

[55] Hebrew, pp. 136–137; Latin, fol. III r a-b.

ותחת זו המעלה של נפש השכלית היא הנפש הבהמית, כי היא נולדה מצל הנפש השכלית, ובעבור זה נתרחקה מאור הדיעה ונאחזה בצל ונאפל וסרה מעליה החקירה וההבדלה, זוממת על האמת הוגה על מעבר, שהוא טרנצוציאון בלעז, כי תגלה את הדבר ממראית עין, לא מדרך האמת, ומחזקתה [=ומסגולתה] ההרגשה והתנועה וההעתקה ממקום למקום. ובעבור זה נעשו הבהמות זריזים ומקדימים לרוב ומבקשים [נצחון ו]ממשלה, אך בלי חקירה ובלי הבדלה ובלי הכרה, כמו הארי שהוא מבקש הממשלה על האחרים מהבהמות בלי חקירה ובלי הבדלה ובלי הכרה במה שהוא פועל. ואשר הוא מורה על הבהמות שהם זומומים שאנחנו מוצאים החמור שהוא ברוב צמא, כשיקדים על המים ויראה צורתו במים או צורה אחרת, מתיירא ובורח, ובמים תלויים חייו ובוריו, וכשיראה הארי תובע אותו לבקשו והוא ימיתהו ויאבדהו. ובעבור זה הבהמות לא ישיגו לא גמול ולא חיוב, כי אינם מכירים

"Et inferior quidem anima rationali in claritate et sublimitate ordinis est anima bestialis, quoniam ipsa ex anima rationali generata est, et propter hoc elongat a splendore intelligentie et acquirit umbram et tenebras et privatur perscrutatione et discretione et facta est estimativa secundum veritatem et meditativa secundum transsumptionem, iudicat enim (debite?) [de re ex apparitione non] ex eo ubi est veritas, et ex proprietate eius sunt sensus et motus et permutatio in locis, et propter hoc factae sunt bestiae praesumptuosae multe audaciae victoriam quaerentes et principatum [sed absque investigatione et discretione et cognitione] sicut leo acquirit dominium super alias bestias absque investigatione et discretione et cognitione eius quod facit. Significat autem quod bestiae sunt aestimantes et non discernentes id quod in asino invenitur. Invenimus enim cum ipse ultime sittit, si ad aquam ducatur et videat formam suam in ea

things impossible. It is said that estimation is a judgment concerning a thing with reference to what it appears to be and not with reference to what it is in truth. For this reason brute animals are estimative beings and not meditative beings. They are said to be meditative only in a figurative and metaphorical sense."[56] There is, however, the following observation to be made with regard to the Arabic term used by Israeli in describing the sense in question. In Alfarabi, Avicenna, and all other subsequent Arabic authors, this particular sense is called وهم. In Avicenna it is sometimes called both وهم and ظن.[57] Here Isaac Israeli calls it ظن and uses وهم in the sense of *meditatio*, הגות, רעיון, which is somewhat higher than ظن but lower than فكر,

aut formam alterius, terret ex ea et refugit, et aqua tamen existit eius vita et eius constructio, et cum videat leonem, incedit ad eum et quaerit ipsum et vadit ad ipsum, et ipsum tamen interficit et praedit eum. Propter hoc non consequuntur bestiae retributionem neque poenam, quoniam non discernunt neque sciunt illud quod remuneratur, licet faciant ipsum et mereant retributionem sibi et faciant contrarium ipsius et diversum ab eo et mereant damnationem sibi. Illud quidem quia investigatione privata[e] et discretio[ne] et perceptio[ne] veritatum et quia appropriata[e] sunt cum aestimatione et meditatione."

במה יהיה להם גמול שיבקשוהו לעשותו להזכות בו ולא לעשות כנגד לקבל ממנו חיוב, וזה בעבור שסרה מעליה החקירה וההבדלה [והשגת האמתיות] ונכנסה לזמימות וההגות.

[56] Arabic, p. 691; Hebrew, pp. 139–140; Latin, fol. IV r a:

حد الظن قوة تجول فى الممتنعات ويقال انه (אף) القضا على الشي من الظاهر لا من حيث الحق ولذلك صارت البهائم ظانة لا متوهمة الا ان يقال ذلك فيها على الاستعارة والمجاز

תכלית הזמימות כח הולך בדברים של המנע. ותאמר הזמימות בדין על הדבר מחמת מראית עין, לא מחמת האמת, ובעבור זה נעשו הבהמות זוממין לא בעלי רעיון, אבל יאמר זה בהם לפי פיגורא ומעבר.

"Definitio aestimations. Aestimatio est virtus incedens in impossibilibus. Et dicitur quod aestimatio sit iudicium de re ex apparitione non ex eo ubi est veritas, et propter hoc factae sunt bestiae aestimantes non meditantes nisi illud de eis secundum accommodationem et transumptionem."

[57] Cf. S. Landauer, Die Psychologie des Ibn Sinâ in *ZDMG*, 29 (1875), p. 359, l. 21: المتوهمة واظانة.

מחשבה, *cogitatio*. While the Latin translator has rendered ظن here by *aestimatio*, the term which subsequently became the standard equivalent of وهم in its later use, the Hebrew translator has rendered it by זמימות[58] instead of מחשבה and רעיון which latter two terms by his time were already used as the standard Hebrew equivalents of the Arabic وهم and Latin *aestimatio*.

[58] Thus also Judah ibn Tibbon uses זמם in the same technical sense as a translation of ظن in the enumeration of the internal senses in *Ḥobot ha-Lebabot*, I, 10. See my "The Internal Senses, etc.", *op. cit.*, pp. 105–106. But cf. J. Klatzkin, *Oẓar ha-Munaḥim ha-Pilosofiyim*, s. v.

17

NOTES ON ISAAC ISRAELI'S INTERNAL SENSES

MANY YEARS AGO, I published almost simultaneously, three papers on the internal senses,* a general paper, entitled "The Internal Senses in Latin, Arabic, and Hebrew Philosophic Texts" (*Harvard Theological Review*, 28 [1935], pp. 69-133), and two special papers, entitled "Isaac Israeli on the Internal Senses" (*George A. Kohut Memorial Volume* [1935], pp. 583-598) and "Maimonides on the Internal Senses" (*Jewish Quarterly Review*, N.S., 25 [1935], pp. 441-467). Recently in revising these papers with a view to their republication, with other kindred papers, in book form, I went through the literature published on the subject since 1935. Comments on my treatment of the internal senses in Israeli by S. M. Stern in *Isaac Israeli* by A. Altmann and S. M. Stern, 1958, are of sufficient importance to deserve special treatment. Dr. Stern comments on my treatment of four Arabic terms, *fikr*, *dhikr*, *wahm*, and *ẓann*.

I. *fikr*

In the *Book on the Elements*, Israeli formally divides the senses into external and internal and under internal he enumerates three senses, which in the Latin and Hebrew translations of the non-extant Arabic text are designated as (1) *formativus*, *formatus*, מצייר, *phantasia*, אלפנטסיא, (2) *cogitatio*, מחשבה, and (3) *memoria*, זכרון. *Cogitatio* is described by him there as a faculty "which possesses the power to scrutinize, to separate, and to combine, for it separates the shells of a thing (*rei*, הדבר) from its innermost part." In his *Book of Definitions*, Israeli has also a definition of the Arabic term *fikr*, which in Hebrew and in Latin is again translated respectively by *cogitatio* and מחשבה. Following the Arabic

* Above, pages 250–330; below, pages 344–370.

text, extant in Hebrew characters, I translated this definition to read: "An intellectual faculty which is supervenient to things (תחל פי אלאשיא), for (כי לאן) cogitation is one of the faculties of the intellect, on account of which every cogitative being becomes (צאר, *factus est*, נעשה) an intelligent being" (*art. cit.*, pp. 586-587). Dr. Stern, however, following, in the first part of the definition, the Latin and Hebrew versions, translates it to read: "An intellectual faculty which roves among things (*praecedens in rebus*, הולך בדברים). It is one of the faculties of reason, on account of which every cogitative being is rational" (*op. cit.*, p. 55). The term *fikr* here quite evidently is the *fikr* which in the *Book on the Elements* is classified among the three internal senses, so that the opening statement about cogitation, whether translated "is supervenient to things" or "roves among things", corresponds to the statement "separates the shell of a thing from its innermost part" in the *Book on the Elements*. Now, with regard to the internal senses, I have shown that in the various classifications of these senses found in Arabic, the term *fikr* stands for the Greek διάνοια. Consequently Israeli's definition of *fikr* in both his works stands for the Greek *dianoia* and in both these works the definition of *fikr* or *dianoia* uses a statement which contains the word "thing" or "things."

In the course of my discussion of the Greek sources of the various terms and phrases used by Israeli in his definition of *fikr*, I also wanted to find out the Greek source of his use of the terms "thing" and "things." This I found in a passage *Metaphysics* VI, 4, where Aristotle, starting with the statement that truth and falsehood depend upon "combination and separation" (1027b, 18-19), raises the question of "how it happens that we think things together or apart" (23), that is, in combination and separation; and then goes on to say (25-27) that "falsity and truth are not in things (πράγμασι) ... but in cogitation (διανοίᾳ) ... since the combination and the separation are in cogitation and not in things" (29-31). All these passages I quoted in the course of my discussion, to which may now be added the expression "cogitation about things" (διάνοια κατὰ τῶν πραγμάτων), which occurs in *Rhetorica ad Alexandrum* 15, 1431b, 9-10.

With all this before him, Dr. Stern says: "the exact source of Israeli's definition, which is rather in general terms, is not known." In other words, Dr. Stern, as he expressed himself in a passage to be quoted later, would not be satisfied until some statement was found in which some other author in Arabic prior to Israeli had defined *fikr* in the same or in similar terms. It did not occur to him that Israeli was able to frame his own definitions directly on the basis of Arabic translations of Greek philosophic texts available to him. In fact, there is ample evidence that he often did so.

Toward the end of his discussion of this definition, Dr. Stern says: "Some of Wolfson's comments on Israeli's paragraph are occasioned by the false reading of *taḥillu* instead of the correct *tajūlu* and should therefore be disregarded."

The reference here is to the passage quoted above which I translated "an intellectual faculty which is supervenient to things" and he translated "an intellectual faculty, which roves among things." His comment contains three inaccuracies:

(1) If anything in my discussion were occasioned by what he calls a false reading, it is not "some comments" but only *one* comment, and that is my attempt to explain Israeli's use of the term "things" in his definition of *fikr* on the basis of Aristotle's use of that term in his discussion of *dianoia*.

(2) Even on the assumption that the text which I followed is false and that the translation should read "roves among things" instead of "is supervenient to things," my comment could still be right, for Israeli would still be using the term "things" in his definition of *fikr* and its use could still be explained by Aristotle's use of the term "things" in his discussion of *dianoia*.

(3) Now for his apodeictic assertion of the falsity of the reading *taḥillu*. Here are the facts in the case: The Arabic

text, extant only in Hebrew characters, reads here יתחל פ אלאשיא, which I have translated, "is supervenient to things." The Latin and Hebrew translations read here *praecedens in rebus*, הולך בדברים, which reflects an Arabic تجول ف الاشياء, on which account Dr. Stern translates it "roves among things." Later, in the definition of *ẓann* (as well as of *wahm*), the Latin and Hebrew translations read *incidens in*, הולך ב···, and the transliterated Arabic similarly reads תג̇ול פי, which I translated "applies to" and Dr. Stern again translates "roves among." Now, if in editing the extant Arabic text, the editor chose to change the reading תחל פי here to תג̇ול פי, on the basis of the Latin and Hebrew translations and of the Arabic reading in the definitions of *wahm* and *zann*, he would be within his right to do so. But if he arbitrarily dismissed the reading in the transliterated Arabic text here as false and of no account, he would be wrong, for תחל פי is an admissible reading and makes sense, and for all we know it may represent an original reading. We have no right to assume arbitrarily that the scribe, whose transliteration of an Arabic text into Hebrew characters is contained in our manuscript, or a scribe before him, whose copy of the Arabic text was the basis of his transliteration, either by mere carelessness or by sheer ignorance changed the Arabic ج to ح. That the expression תחל פי אלאשיא here is not an impossible reading may be shown by the fact that the expression אלסאכנה פי אלשי is used by Israeli in the latter part of his definition of *wahm* (p. 691, l. 31).

2. *dhikr*

Memory is dealt with by Israeli as falling into four kinds, which may be described as follow: (1) memory of sensible objects; (2) memory of intelligible notions; (3) memory as the recollection of things forgotten; (4) memory in the sense of conservation. For each of these four kinds he has a definition. The first of these definitions occurs in his *Book on the*

Elements and the last three occur consecutively in his *Book of Definitions*. In an introductory statement, I said: "My interpretation of these definitions will assume that Isaac Israeli had before him a description of memory such as we find in John of Damascus' *De Fide Orthodoxa* II, 20, which in itself can be shown to have been made up of elements drawn from the writings of Aristotle." In a footnote I added that "John of Damascus' immediate source is Nemesius. *De Natura Nominis*, Cap. 13." The reason for the assumption, which I thought would be evident to every reader of my subsequent discussion there, is as follows: (1) While the definitions of all these four phases of memory, can be traced, as I have shown, to various scattered passages in Aristotle, they are all found in the one single passage of John of Damascus. (2) Some of the terms used by Israeli are those used by John of Damascus. (3) The definition of recollection in Israeli is almost a verbal translation of that in John of Damascus. (4) John of Damascus' *De Fide Orthodoxa* was translated into Arabic in the 10th century, probably during the lifetime of Israeli.

All this, which should be evident to any reader who approached my discussion with an open mind, is not evident to our doubting Thomas. Having become convinced by my references to Aristotle that there is nothing new in Israeli's definition, he says: "There is hardly anything in these texts beyond the most commonplace notions concerning memory." He then adds: "the exact sources of Israeli's definitions could not be identified". By his statement that "the exact sources of Israeli's definitions could not be identified" our critic assumes, again, as he expresses himself in a passage to be quoted later, that Israeli's definitions are taken bodily from certain sources and hence thinks that the only problem is to find those sources and that, if these sources turned up, the problem would be solved. This, I believe, is a gratuitous assumption. Israeli, it can be shown from various places in his writing, was able to formulate his own definitions of philosophic concepts directly on the basis of whatever sources of knowledge of Greek philosophy were available to him, even though occasionally he draws upon definitions formulated by others on the basis of Greek sources. Accordingly, throughout my study of his definitions of internal senses, I tried to show how his definitions were directly based upon Aristotelian passages. Should any direct source ever turn up for any of these definitions, then it would only mean that that source was based upon these Aristotelian passages quoted by me. In the case of Israeli's definition of memory, however, I made an exception. Owing to the similarities which, as I pointed out, exist between Israeli's definitions and the passage in John of Damascus and owing to the fact that the work of John of Damascus may have been known to Israeli and owing also to the fact that all kinds of philosophic doxographies existed in Arabic which are no longer extant or which have not yet been published, I said rather cautiously that "my interpretation of these definitions will assume that Isaac Israeli had before him a description of memory *such as we find* in John of Damascus."

3. *wahm* and *ẓann*

The term *wahm*, which ordinarily means "imagination" or "opinion," came to be used with Alfarabi as a designation of one of the senses in a new classification of internal senses. What the newly acquired meaning of this term is may be gathered from the context of passages in which it occurs. On that score there is no doubt. But there is doubt about its origin in Greek sources. In my general paper on the Internal Senses (pp. 86-113), I have given a history of the problem, discussed the various suggestions made as to its Greek origin, and gave my own explanation of its Greek origin. Briefly stated my explanation is this. In Aristotle, a distinction is made between the imagination in human beings and the imagination in brute animals. The former may be rational (λογιστική) or deliberative (βουλευτική), whereas the latter is only sensitive (αἰσθητική). But still irrational animals, according to Aristotle, sometimes act with a kind of sagacity (σύνεσις) which is instinctive with them. This instinctively sagacious imagination of irrational animals was designated in Alfarabi by the term *wahm*, and from that time on this term was used in Arabic classifications of the internal senses as a designation of this particular kind of imagination, in contradistinction to other kinds of imagination which were designated by other terms. Latin translations from the Arabic rendered the term *wahm* by *aestimatio*, and so the term "estimation" came to be used in Scholastic philosophy as a designation of that instinctively sagacious imagination possessed by irrational animals. As the equivalent of *wahm*, and in the same sense, Avicenna happens to use also the term *ẓann*.

With regard to Israeli, I said both in my general paper (p. 93, n. 22) and in my paper on Israeli (1) that the instinctively sagacious imagination of irrational animals, which his contemporary Alfarabi calls *wahm*, Israeli calls *ẓann*, (2) that *wahm* is used by him as a designation of another faculty, and (3) that neither of these faculties is included by him under what in his *Book on the Elements* he describes as internal senses. But, inasmuch as that faculty which he treats under *ẓann* later became one of the internal senses I dealt with it briefly in my paper on Israeli, by merely quoting and translating his discussion of the animal soul (pp. 595-96 and n. 55) and also his definition of *ẓann* (pp. 596-97 and n. 56). With his definition of *wahm* I did not deal at all; I only called attention to his use of that term as differing from its use by Alfarabi and by others after him.

All this, Dr. Stern dismisses curtly with the pronouncement that "Wolfson's studies... have not solved the problem." Whether they have solved the problem or not is a legitimate matter of discussion, but responsible scholars, even those who have earned the right to pontificate—as I hope

Dr. Stern will learn someday—are chary of arrogating to themselves that right. But, then, suggesting a method by which the problem could be solved, he says: "A re-examination of the psychological doctrines of the earlier Islamic philosophers will perhaps elucidate these matters." This Micawberish trustfulness that something will turn up in earlier Islamic philosophy which will solve the problem of the origin of the Alfarabian internal sense *wahm* shows that our critic has not by the time of his expressing this hope fully grasped the nature of the problem about which he is pronouncing snap judgments. The problem is not that of finding the meaning of *wahm*. That is quite clear from the context of the passages in which it is dealt with. The problem is that of discovering a Greek source for it. Should an earlier Islamic text containing the same use of *wahm* turn up it would not solve the problem. The problem would still be what its Greek source was. In one instance, an earlier Islamic text did turn up since the publication of my paper on Israeli in 1935, and that is a passage in a work of al-Kindi, published in 1950-53, which passage our critic has reproduced as the source or as a paralled by Israeli's definition of *Zann*, or rather of the middle part of Israeli's definition of *ẓann*. Does that explain the origin of that part of Israeli's definition? Is there not still the question as to what is the Greek source of al-Kindi's statement? Our critic would have displayed a better understanding of the problem if he had prayed wishfully, though perhaps vainly, for a Greek text to turn up.

But we need not play the Micawber and wait for something to turn up in Greek philosophy to solve problems of origin that may arise in our study of this early period of Arabic philosophy. We can try to solve all such problems with the Greek sources at hand, if we only use the proper method. The proper method to be used in finding the origin of any statement we encounter in the works of any Arabic philosopher of that early period is not to ask ourselves, where in Greek philosophy did that statement come from? but rather to ask ourselves, what could the author of that statement have known of Greek philosophy, either by reading or by hearsay, that led him to make that statement? Employing this method, let us see whether we cannot find the source of our critic's quotation of Avicenna as well as the sources of Israeli's definitions of *wahm* and *ẓann*—definitions which our critic declared to be "rather obscure", and expressed the hope that something would turn up in early Islamic philosophy to clarify them

(a) *Wahm* ordinarily means "imagination" or "opinion." In approaching Israeli's attempt to define this term philosophically, we ask ourselves whether he uses this term technically as reflecting passages in philosophic literature which deal with imagination (φαντασία) or those which deal with opinion (δόξα). We try the former and find it does not work. We try the latter. Let us see what we find.

Suppose Israeli had read in the Arabic translations of Aristotle that "opinion may be true or false" (*De Anima* III, 3, 428a, 19), that "the words 'to be' and 'it is' signify that a thing is true, but the words 'not to be' signify that it is not true but false" (*Metaph.* V, 7, 1017a, 31-32), and that "that which is possible may either be or not be" (*ibid.* IX, 8, 1050b, 11-12). Would not this background of knowledge be sufficient to explain how he came to say that "*wahm* applies to things possible"?

Suppose further that Israeli had read in Aristotle that "opinion implies reason" (*De Anima* III, 3, 428a, 22-23), that "in the case of those that have thinking power" the senses furnish the data "from which arise understanding of both intelligible and practical objects" (*De Sensu* 1, 437a, 1-3), and that "the intelligible objects are in the sensible forms, both the abstractions, as they are called, and all the habits and affections of sensible things" (*De Anima* III, 8, 432a, 4-6). With these passages supposed to be in the back of his mind, one could readily see how Israeli came to make the next statement, in which, using the expression "psychical faculty" in the sense of "rational faculty,"[1] he says that *wahm* "employs the psychical faculty, because the form of things which are communicated to us by sense perception in their matter and their element are communicated to us by the psychical faculty as knowledge abstracted from their matter and their element."

Finally, suppose Israeli had reminded himself of Aristotle's statement that "it is opinion that is concerned with that which may be true or false, and can be otherwise" (*Anal. Post.* I, 33, 89a, 2-3). This would explain why toward the end of his definition he went on to expand his opening statement by adding that *wahm* "is also said of the faculty which is resting in the things concerning which one seeks to find whether it is so-and-so or not."

(b) The term *ẓann* ordinarily means "opinion" and it is commonly used as a translation of the Greek δόξα. But it may also mean "imagination." Inasmuch as we have shown that *wahm* is used by Israeli in the sense of "opinion," we may assume that *ẓann* is used by him in the sense of "imagination." Let us then see how it will work out.

Suppose Israeli had read in Aristotle that "imaginations are for the most part false" (*De Anima* III, 3, 428a, 12) and had also read that certain things are "not only false but also impossible" (*De Caelo* I, 12, 281b, 13-14). Are we not justified in assuming that it is on the basis of these statements that Israeli formulated the first part of his definition, that "*ẓann* is a faculty which applies to things impossible"?

The second part of Israeli's definition of *ẓann*, for which Dr. Stern has quoted a parallel definition from al-Kindi's recently published work, is quite evidently based either upon al-Kindi's definition or upon a definition like that given by al-Kindi, and so let us study first the source of al-Kindi's definition.

[1] In Israeli there is no "psychical faculty" as distinct from sensation and imagination. The psyche or soul, according to him, is divided into the rational soul, the animal soul, and the vegetative soul.

In his definition of *ẓann*, al-Kindi says: "It is a judgment concerning a thing with reference to what it appears to be (*min al-ẓāhir*); it is also said: [it is] not with reference to what is in truth (*al-ḥaqīqah*) and [it is] an explanation without proofs or demonstration (*burhān*); so that this judgment may cease."

It can be shown quite definitely that in this definition al-Kindi uses *ẓann* in the Greek sense of δόξα, "opinion," for it reflects certain passages in Aristotle's *Organon*, the Arabic translation of which, available to al-Kindi, was recently published. [2]

(1) It reflects a passage in *Analytica Priora* II, 16, 65a, 35-37, in which Aristotle contrasts demonstrations (ἀποδείξεις, *al-barāhīn*), which are concerned with things that exist in truth (κατ' ἀλήθειαν, *bi'l-ḥaqīqah*), and dialectical arguments, which are concerned with things that exist according to opinion (κατὰ δόξαν, *bi'l-ẓann*).

(2) It reflects a long discussion in *Topica* I, 1, 100a, 18-101, 1, in which Aristotle distinguishes between a demonstration (ἀπόδειξις, *al-burhān*), which is based on premises which are true (ἀληθῶν, *ṣādiqah*) and dialectical and contentious syllogisms. One kind of contentious syllogism is described by him as that which is constructed "from premises which appear to be resting on generally known opinions (ἐνδόξων) but are not really so." [3] In the Arabic version, the quoted part of this statement reads: "from premises generally known (*dha'i'ah*) in appearance (*fī al-ẓāhir*) but not generally known in truth (*'alā al-ḥaqīqah*)," and "generally known premises" are described in that version as those premises "which all men, or most of them, or all philosophers, or most of them or the most renowned of them, or those of the highest celebrity accept as their opinion (*yaẓinnuhā*)." [4] Of this kind of

[2] *Organon Aristotelis in versione Arabica antiqua*, edidit 'Abdurrahman Badawi, Cahirae, MCMLII.

[3] *Anal. Pr.* I, 1, 100b, 23-25.

[4] Arabic of 100b, 21-23.

contentious syllogism Aristotle says that "it is not a syllogism, for, though in appearance it is a syllogism, it does not lead to a conclusion," [5] which statement quite evidently underlies al-Kindi's statement that "this judgment may cease."

Israeli, however, must have taken the term *ẓann* of al-Kindi's definition to mean "imagination" and so he added that definition to the first part of his own definition of *ẓann*. But it is to be noted that Israeli reproduces only the first part of al-Kindi's definition of *ẓann*, which, as phrased by him, reads: "It is said that *ẓann* is a judgment concerning a thing with reference to what it appears to be and not with reference to what it is in truth." This may mean that the immediate source of this part of Israeli's definition was not al-Kindi but some other doxography, where the same definition of *ẓann* occurred. Perhaps Israeli was led to take *ẓann* of al-Kindi's definition to mean "imagination" by the fact that he had found in Aristotle a similar statement about imagination. In that statement, Aristotle says that "there are false imaginings concerning things of which we hold at the same time a true conception, as, for example, the sun appears only a foot in diameter, but we are convinced that it is larger than the inhabited world," in which case, he adds, in judging the matter by our imagination, "we have abandoned the true opinion which we had about it" (*De Anima* III, 3, 428b, 2-5).

Finally Israeli concludes his definition of *ẓann* or imagination as follows: "For this reason brute animals are imaginative beings but not beings possessed of opinion; they are said to possess opinion only in a figurative and metaphorical sense." This reflects Aristotle's statement that "opinion is attended by conviction... but no brute is ever convinced, though many have imagination" (*De Anima* III, 3, 428a, 19-21).

But Israeli, like his contemporary Alfarabi, knew that brute animals which have imagination but have no reason

[5] Arabic of 101a, 3-4.

or even opinion are said by Aristotle to act sometimes by what he describes as an instinctive sagacity (σύνεσις). This instinctively sagacious imagination is fully described by Israeli, again by the use of the term *ẓann,* in his discussion of the animal soul, referred to above. It is this instinctively sagacious imagination of irrational animals to which, as we have shown, Alfarabi gave the name *wahm* and which in Avicenna is called not only *wahm* but also *ẓann.*

But all this is based, of course, only upon circumstantial evidence; we have no direct testimony of either al-Kindi or Israeli that this is exactly how their minds worked; bread-and-butter scholarship may, therefore, brush it all aside and dismiss it as unconvincing.

18

MAIMONIDES ON THE INTERNAL SENSES[1]

By the term "internal senses" mediaeval philosophers in Arabic, Hebrew, and Latin literatures designate one or some or all of those post-sensationary faculties of the soul which are treated of by Aristotle in the Third Book of *De Anima* and in *De Memoria et Reminiscentia* to differentiate them as a class from the five senses which are called "external senses." An explicit reference to this distinction is made by Maimonides in *Moreh Nebukim*, I, 47, in connection with his discussion of the anthropomorphisms which according to him are implied in the ascription to God not only of the perceptions of the five senses but also of the perceptions of the faculties of imagination, thought, and understanding. Using for what is generally known as "external senses" the terms "corporeal, passive, sensitive, and external apprehensions"[2] and for "internal senses" the term "internal apprehensions"[3] he enumerates under the latter three faculties which literally translated mean: (1) imagination, (2)

[1] The philological and historical generalizations in this paper are based upon my monograph on "The Internal Senses in Latin, Arabic, and Hebrew Philosophic Texts", in *The Harvard Theological Review*, Vol. 28 (1935), pp. 69–133. Above, pages 250–314.

[2] (a) ادراكات جسمانية وانفعالات, Ibn Tibbon: השגות גשמיות והפעליות, Buxtorf: *apprehensiones corporales et patibiles*; Ḥarizi: השגות גופיות ו(כחות) מפעלות, Justinianus: *apprehensiones corporales et (virtutes) operatae.* (b) الادراكات الحسّية الظاهرة, Ibn Tibbon: ההשגות החושיות הנראות, Buxorf: *apprehensiones sensuales externae*; Ḥarizi: ההשגות המורגשות הנלויות, Justinianus: *apprehensiones sensibiles manifestae.*

[3] الادراكات الباطنة, Ibn Tibbon: ההשגות הפנימיות, Buxtorf: *apprehensiones internae*; Ḥarizi: ההשגות הפנימיות הנעלמות, Justinianus: omitted.

cogitation, and (3) understanding.[4] The first two of these three terms are exactly the same as those of the threefold classifications of the internal senses that we find in the writings of Ḥunain ben Isḥak, Razi, Isaac Israeli, and Pseudo-Baḥya, corresponding respectively to the Greek *φανταστικόν, διανοητικόν*, and *μνημονευτικόν* which are found in Galen and Aristotle and those who followed them. Maimonides' third term, however, differs from that used in all the conventional lists of threefold classifications. In all such lists the term "memory" is used instead of the term "understanding" used here by Maimonides.

In my monograph on the internal senses, in an attempt to remove this difference, I have tried to show that the term "understanding" used here by Maimonides is to be taken in the sense of that kind of rational thinking which was generally assumed to be involved in a certain kind of memory and also in recollection. In support of this I have shown how in Aristotle, Plotinus, John of Damascus, Isaac Israeli and Averroes a distinction is made between the memory of sensible objects and the memory of intelligible notions and how the latter is said by them to involve contemplation,[5] learning,[6] natural thinking,[7] intellectual inquiry,[8] cogitation,[9] and deliberation.[10] Furthermore, I have shown how

[4] (a) تخيّل, Ibn Tibbon: (1) רעיון, (2) דמיון, Buxtorf: (1) *phantasia*, (2) *imaginatio*; Ḥarizi: [דמיוני] רעיון, Justinianus: *cogitatio assimilativa*—(b) تفكّر, Ibn Tibbon: השתכלות, Buxtorf: *cogitatio*; Ḥarizi: המחשבה השכלית, Justinianus: *cogitatio intelligibilis*—(c) تفهّم, Ibn Tibbon: התבוננות, Buxtorf: *intelligentia, sive intellectio*; Ḥarizi: חבונה, Justinianus: *intellectus*.

[5] *θεωρία*, نظر, דרישה, *inquisitio*. On this Hebrew and Latin translation of the Arabic term, see my paper "Isaac Israeli on the Internal Senses" in *George Alexander Kohut Memorial Volume*, 1935.

[6] *μάθησις*.

[7] *ἔννοια φυσική*.

[8] بحث, חקירה, *indagatio*.

[9] فكر, מחשבה.

[10] روية, השתכלות.

recollection in contradistinction to memory is according to Aristotle a sort of intellectual inquiry[11] and syllogistic reasoning[12] and is on that account said by him to be found only in man who has the faculty of deliberation.[13] This explanation of the use of the third term in Maimonides' threefold classification of the internal senses has also enabled us to explain the third term in Ibn Gabirol's threefold classification, which is the same as that used by Maimonides, and similarly the third term in Abraham ibn Ezra's threefold classification, which is "wisdom."[14]

In Avicenna's *Canon*[15] this threefold classification of the internal senses, to which Maimonides makes definite reference, is characterized as a medical classification in contradistinction to a more diversified classification which is said by him to be favored by philosophers. What Avicenna means by this distinction between the medical and the philosophical classifications is this: To the physicians an internal faculty of the soul is determined by its location in a certain chamber of the brain and, inasmuch as the so-called internal faculties of the soul, however different they may be as modes of perception, are all localized in three chambers of the brains, they are all regarded as constituting only three internal faculties. To the philosophers, however, a faculty is that which serves as a distinct mode of perception, and consequently, inasmuch as there are more than three such modes of perception, there are more than three internal faculties. Avicenna enumerates altogether seven such internal modes of perception, which may be described

[11] *ζήτησις*.

[12] *συλλογισμός*.

[13] *βουλευτικόν*.

[14] חכמה, حكمة. The terminological difficulties in Ibn Gabirol's and Ibn Ezra's classifications have been pointed out by S. Horovitz, *Die Psychologie bei den jüdischen Religions-Philosophen des Mittelalters*, pp. 256, 259.

[15] *Canon*, Liber I, Fen I, Doctrina VI, Cap. 5.

by the following terms: (1) common sense, (2) retentive imagination, (3) compositive human imagination, (4) compositive animal imagination, (5) estimation, (6) memory, (7) recollection. The Arabic terms by which the three forms of imagination and the faculty of estimation are designated by Avicenna in his various writings are of interest to us here. For retentive imagination the following terms are used by him: خيال, تخيّل, مصوّرة. For compositive human imagination he uses only one term: مفكّرة. For compositive animal imagination he uses متخيّلة and perhaps also تخيّل.[16] For estimation he uses various forms of وهم (وهميّة, متوهّمة) and also the term ظنّ These seven faculties, furthermore, he variously combines to form a fivefold classification, thus reducing some of them to the status of sub-functions of a single faculty. No uniform method of combination, however, is followed either by Avicenna himself in his various works or by his followers.

Nowhere in his writings does Maimonides give us a formal classification of the philosophic list of internal faculties as outlined by Avicenna. This is not to be wondered at. Maimonides' works, with the exception of his *Millot ha-Higgayon*, are not manuals of philosophy. They are discussions of certain philosophical and theological problems in which formal summaries of philosophic views appear only incidentally whenever they are required by the occasion. If the Avicennian classification of the internal senses is not reproduced formally by Maimonides, it is because he had no occasion to do so. But still it is of interest for us to inquire whether he does anywhere in his writings mention any or all of these internal senses of the Avicennian list,

[16] This is the reading in *Risalah fi al-Nafs* (ed. S. Landauer, *Zeitschrift der Deutschen Morgenländischen Gesellschaft*, 29 (1875), p. 359. Landauer suggests the emendation متخيّلة (ibid., n. 10). But the same reading is used several times in *Cuzari*, V, 12 (ed. Hirschfeld, p. 314, ll. 2, 21).

and if he does not explicitly mention them, we should still like to know whether in any of his descriptions of the functions of certain faculties of the soul we cannot discern some of the Avicennian internal senses.

"Common sense" is not explicitly mentioned by Maimonides. But in his discussion of angels in *Moreh Nebukim*, II, 6, we may discern a disguised allusion to it. The passage reads as follows: "In *Midrash Kohelet*[17] it is written: 'When man sleeps, his soul speaks to the angel, and the angel to the cherub.' In this statement it has been made clear to any one who has intelligence and understanding that man's imaginative faculty is also called 'angel,' and that 'cherub' is used for man's intellectual faculty."[18] Now it will have been noticed that in this partial quotation from the Midrash three terms occur, namely, "soul (נפש)," "angel (מלאך)," and "cherub (כרוב)," of which Maimonides explains the last two as referring to imagination and intellect respectively. He does not, however, explain the specific meaning of the term "soul." Among the commentators of Maimonides there is a difference of opinion as to its meaning. Narboni[19] and Efodi[20] take the term "soul" in this passage to refer to common sense. Shem-Ṭob, on the other hand, takes it to refer to the sensitive faculty,[21] and this despite the fact that his comment on the passage in question is bodily taken from Narboni.[22] Of these two interpretations, it seems to me, that of Narboni and Efodi is the correct one, for the

[17] Ecclesiastes Rabbah on 10.20.

[18] וכתוב במדרש קהלת, בשעה שאדם ישן נפשו אומרת למלאך ומלאך אומר לכרוב, הנה כבר בארו למי שיבין וישכיל, שהכח המדמה גם כן יקרא מלאך ושהשכל יקרא כרוב.

[19] והנפש רמז אל החוש המשותף.

[20] נפשו אומרת למלאך, ר"ל שהצורה נופלת ראשונהֵ בחוש המשותף והוא הנפש.

[21] ונפשו היא הנפש המרגשת.

[22] The following passage occurs, with several differences of reading, both in Narboni and Shem-Ṭob: למה שהנפש אחת בנושא רבת הכחות יעיקו ההשגות זו את זו, ובעת היקיצה יעיקו ההשגות החיצוניות לפנימיות, ובעת השינה ישובו הכחות הטבעיות אל התחלתם, ותוכל הנפש להשלים פעלה, ואז יכניעו הכחות המשיגים האחד את האחד בצורות אשר קבלו ביקיצה.

psychological process described by Maimonides in this passage is that of imagination in its relation to dreams, the two of which are connected according to Aristotle,[23] and also in its relation to sensation below it and to intellect above it. Now, according to the psychological concepts underlying this passage, neither dreaming nor imagination is directly connected with the five senses, common sense being interposed between either one of them and the latter. While it is not by sense-perception, says Aristotle, that we perceive d eams,[24] still the affection of dreaming, he argues, must pertain to sense-perception as surely as sleep does,[25] and inasmuch as sleep, according to him, pertains to sense-perception only indirectly through its dependence upon common sense,[26] it must follow that dreams, too, are according to him dependent upon common sense. Similarly imagination, according to Aristotle, belongs to the faculty of common sense, for these two faculties, he says, are in some respect identical.[27] Following this Aristotelian conception of the relation of the imaginative faculty to the faculty of common sense, Arabic philosophers usually describe common sense as the faculty which first receives the impressions of the five senses and then conveys them to the imagination.[28] Furthermore, according to Aristotle, imagination serves as a source of supply to reason. "Without imagination," he says, "intellectual activity is impossible"[29] and "to the thinking soul images serve as present sensations."[30] In view of all this, if we assume with Narboni and Efodi

[23] *De Somniis*, 1, 459a, 14–22; 3, 462a, 16.
[24] Ibid., 1, 458b, 8–9.
[25] Ibid., 1, 459a, 12–14.
[26] *De Somno et Vigilia*, 2, 455a, 4–25.
[27] *De Somniis*, 1, 459a, 15–17.
[28] Cf., e. g., Avicenna, *Al-Najat*, II: Physics, p. 45 (Rome, 1593, together with the *Canon*).
[29] *De Memoria et Reminiscentia*, 1, 449b, 31.
[30] *De Anima*, III, 7, 431a, 14–15.

that by the term "soul" Maimonides means common sense, his psychological interpretation of the midrashic passage follows with technical accuracy the accepted views with regard to the relations between common sense, imagination, and intellect. The first statement that "the soul speaks to the angel" is taken by him as a description of common sense as the purveyor of the impressions of sense-perception to the imagination, and the second statement that "the angel speaks to the cherub" is taken by him as a description of imagination as the purveyor of images to the intellect, by the latter of which they are transformed into intellectual notions.

Another description of the function of common sense may be discerned, I believe, in Maimonides' account of imagination in *Moreh Nebukim*, I, 73, Prop. 10, Note. Imagination is described by him there as having two functions. The second of these two functions will be discussed later. But the first function is of interest to us now. It reads as follows: "Imagination apprehends only the individual, as a composite whole, according as it is apprehended by the senses."[31] Now the first part of this statement, viz., "imagination apprehends only the individual," may be a true description of both imagination and common sense, for the contents of either one of these two faculties are individual in their nature, since abstract universal concepts, according to Aristotle, are formed only by the activity of the intellect. But the second part of the statement, viz., "as a composite whole," does not occur as a description of imagination. It does occur, however, as a description of one of the functions of common sense in the writings of Aristotle and is reproduced by Avicenna and other mediaeval authors. In Aristotle, this function of common sense is described as a

[31] שהדמיון (الخيال) לא ישיג אלא האישי המורכב בכללו לפי מה שישיגוהו החושים.

power which combines the various sensations of sense-perception into one single perception so that a thing which is reported to the individual senses through its individual qualities independent of each other is apprehended as a single whole.[32] Similarly Avicenna describes this function of common sense in his statement that common sense is "a power in which the apprehensions of the four senses are assembled and become therein one form."[33] In view of all this, it is quite evident that the first function ascribed by Maimonides to imagination in the passage quoted above is in fact a description of common sense. That Maimonides should have included common sense in a description of imagination is explicable on the ground of several literary precedents. Aristotle himself defines the faculty of imagination as identical with that of common sense, though the two are different in their essential notion.[34] According to Avicenna, the identity of common sense and imagination is a view commonly held by physicians.[35] Furthermore, Avicenna himself, in his *Risalah fi al-Nafs*, from which we have quoted his definition of common sense, identifies common sense and imagination. The identification of these two faculties is also found in some of the works of Algazali[36] and in the *Cuzari* of Judah ha-Levi.[37] Finally, in the writings of the Iḥwan al-Ṣafa,[38] as I have shown in my mono-

[32] *De Sensu et Sensibili*, 7, 449a, 2–20.

[33] *Risalah fi al-Nafs*, Ch. 7 (op. cit., p. 359, ll. 1–2, and cf. p. 400, n. 2): قوّة اجتمعت فيهم ادراكات الحواسّ الاربع وصارت عندها صورة واحدة.

[34] *De Somniis*, 1, 459a, 15–17.

[35] *Canon*, loc. cit.

[36] *Tahafut al-Falasifah*, XVIII, ed. M. Bouyges, p. 298; *Mizan al-'Amal*, [IV], Cairo, A. H. 1328, p. 19; *Mozene Ẓedeḳ*, IV, p. 30.

[37] *Cuzari*, V, 12.

[38] Cf. Dietirici, Arabic text: *Die Abhandlungen der Ichwân Es-Safâ in Auswahl*, p. 468; German translation: *Die Anthropologie der Araber*, p. 56.

graph on the internal senses, the function of common sense is ascribed, as here in Maimonides, to the faculty of imagination without even the mention of the term common sense.

From these two passages of Maimonides, therefore, we may gather a complete description of one of the functions of common sense. If we combined them into one statement, it would read: It is the faculty which assembles the various impressions of the senses, combines them into a composite whole, and conveys it to the imagination.

A more explicit reference, however, is found in Maimonides to the distinction between retentive imagination and compositive imagination. Speaking of imagination, he says in *Shemonah Peraḳim*: "Imagination is that faculty which (a) retains the impressions of the sensibly perceived objects after the latter have ceased to be in contact with the senses which had perceived them and (b) joins some of them with others and separates some of them from others."[39] In *Moreh Nebukim*, II, 36, the same distinction between the two kinds of imagination is more briefly stated, and, furthermore, compositive imagination is linked up by him there together with man's natural instinct for imitation. The passage reads as follows: "You also know the functions of this imaginative faculty in so far as they consist of the (a) retention of the sensible impressions, and of (b) the combination thereof as well as of the power of imitation which is inherent in his nature."[40] The last statement about imitation reflects Aristotle's statements that "it is innate

[39] והחלק המדמה (المتخيّل) הוא הכח אשר יזכור (تحفظ) רשומים המוחשים אחר העלמם מקרבת החושים אשר השיגום, וירכיב קצתם אל קצתם ויפריד קצתם מקצתם. In this passage, the term ישמור would have been a more accurate translation of the underlying Arabic term than the term יזכור, since the sense described in it is not memory but rather retentive imagination. Similarly in passage quoted below in n. 40.

[40] וכבר ידעת עוד פעלות זה הכח המדמה (المتخيّلة) מזכור (حفظ) המוחשים והרכבתם והחקוי (المحاكاة) אשר בטבעו.

(σύμφυτον) in men from childhood to imitate (μιμεῖσθαι)"[41] and that "imitation" is "natural (κατὰ φύσιν) to us".[42] The Arabic word for imitation used by Maimonides here (المحاكاة) is exactly the word used for the Greek μιμεῖσθαι in the Arabic translation of Aristotle's *Poetica*.[43] Another description of compositive imagination is found in the second function Maimonides ascribes to imagination in the passage which we have partly quoted above from *Moreh Nebukim*, I, 73, Prop. 10, Note, in our discussion of common sense. Starting out with a statement that the higher class of animals, namely, those which have a heart, have also imagination, he at first ascribes to imagination a function which we have identified above as common sense and then he proceeds to ascribe to it a compositive function by saying that it "combines things which in reality exist separately and joins some of them with others and represents them all as one body".[44] Of these three passages in which compositive imagination is described, to judge from their respective contexts, the first two refer to compositive human imagination only, the third refers to both compositive human imagination and compositive animal imagination.

Now it will have been noticed that in all these passages the general terms for imagination used by Maimonides are خيال and متخيّلة, which in the classifications of the internal senses of the Avicennian type, as we have seen, are used respectively in the specific senses of "retentive imagination" and "compositive animal imagination." Maimonides, however, was not without precedent in his use of these terms in a general sense. In such a general sense is the term

[41] *Poetica*, 4, 1448b, 5–6.

[42] Ibid., 20–21.

[43] Cf. D. Margoliouth, *Analecta Orientalia ad Poeticam Aristoteleam*, Arabic text, p. 7, l. 6.

[44] או ירכיב הדברים המפוזרים במציאות, וירכיב קצתם על קצתם, ויעשה מהכל גשם.

خيال used in Pseudo-Baḥya[45] and the term متخيّلة in the Iḥwan al-Ṣafa.[46] So also the term تخيّل which Avicenna, uses in the specific sense of retentive imagination, is used by Maimonides in a general sense in his threefold classification reproduced above.[47] As for retentive imagination, while no specific term is used by Maimonides in connection with it, his description of it contains the term تحفظا in *Shemonah Peraḳim* and حفظا in *Moreh Nebukim.* This term usually occurs in the description of retentive imagination in the writings of Avicenna and his followers. Algazali, in fact, uses the term حافظة, which ordinarily is used for memory, as a designation of retentive imagination.[48] No mention, however, is made by Maimonides in these passages of the term فكر, which is generally used in Arabic philosophy for compositive human imagination. The term, however, is used by him under the form تفكّر in his threefold classification in *Moreh Nebukim,* I, 47. There, however, we shall try to show, it has an entirely different meaning.

The term فكر as used in the classification of internal senses has undergone three stages of development. First, in the early threefold classifications of the internal senses, it is used in the sense of "cogitation" as the equivalent of the Greek *διάνοια.* Second, in the Avicennian type of classification, the term فكر stands for *δάινοια* plus *φαντασία*, which could have therefore been called in Greek *φαντασία διανοητική*, but is actually called by Aristotle *φαντασία λογιστική* (also *βουλευτική*),[49] for *διανοητικόν* is used by Aristotle as synonymous with *νοῦς*[50] and *νοῦς* is used by him as synonymous with *λογιστικόν.*[51]

45 *Ma'ânî al-Nafs,* Ch. 8, ed. Goldziher, p. 27, l. 21.

46 Cf. reference above, n. 38.

47 Cf. above, n. 4.

48 *Mizan al-'Amal,* loc. cit.; *Mozene Ẓedeḳ,* loc. cit.

49 *De Anima,* III, 10, 433b, 29 ff.

50 Ibid., II, 3, 414b, 18.

51 Ibid., III, 9, 432b, 26.

This change in the meaning of فكر occurs as early as in the writings of Alfarabi, and it is to فكر in this sense that we have referred above as compositive human imagination. Third, in the Averroian type of classifications of the internal senses, the term فكر is restored to its original meaning of *διάνοια* and hence as synonymous with *νοῦς* or *λογιστικόν* or any of their functions. It is as the equivalent of *διάνοια*, as it is invariably used in all the threefold classifications of the internal senses, that Maimonides uses the term تفكّر in his own threefold classification.

But the term *διανοητικόν* is also translated by عقل, and Maimonides himself uses the term ناطق, which is the equivalent of عقل, for *διανοητικόν* in his reproduction of Aristotle's general classification of the faculties of the soul.[52] Consequently, since Maimonides uses, as we have seen, the general terms خيال and متخيّلة for the term فكر in the second of its two meanings, we should naturally expect to find him contrasting the terms عقل and خيال or متخيّلة in the same manner as the two meanings of فكر are contrasted with each other. Now, the contrast between these two meanings of فكر corresponds exactly to the contrast between *διάνοια* without imagination and *διάνοια* with imagination. In both its meanings, the term فكر is generally described as the power of combination and separation,[53] for so is also *διάνοια* described by Aristotle as the power of combination and separation.[54] But the objects which it is supposed to combine and separate differ in each case. In the case of فكر as the equivalent of *διάνοια* without imagination, it is the combination and separation of ideas,

[52] *Shemonah Peraḳim*, Ch. 1: הזן והוא הנקרא צומח, המרגיש, המדמה, המתעורר, והשכלי (*διανοητικόν* الناطق). Cf. *De Anima*, II, 3, 413a, 31–32.

[53] The conventional Arabic, Hebrew, and Latin terms for this are: تركيب و تفصيل, הרכבה ופירוד, *componendi et dividendi*. Cf. *Canon*, loc. cit.

[54] The Greek terms for this are: *σύνθεσις* (*συμπλοκή*), *διαίρεσις*. Cf. *Metaphysics*, VI, 4, 1027b, 19, 29–30.

i. e., the formation of positive or negative judgments. In the case of فكر in the sense of *διάνοια* joined to imagination, it is the combination and separation of images, i. e., the construction out of images of things existent new composite images of things non-existent or the breaking up of images of existent things into images of non-existent things. It is this contrast between the two meanings of فكر, or between *διάνοια* without imagination and *διάνοια* with imagination, that Maimonides describes in his contrast between intellect and imagination in *Moreh Nebukim*, I, 73, Prop. 10, Note: "Intellect (عقل)", he says, "analyses composite things and differentiates their parts and forms abstract ideas of them and represents them according to their true reality and in their causal relations", whereas "imagination (خيال) . . . combines things which in reality exist separately and joins some of them together."[55]

The translation of the Greek *διάνοια* by the Arabic فكر and the subsequent change of فكر to mean *διάνοια* plus imagination may be also considered, I believe, as the source of the explanation, which occurs in the writings of Arabic philosophers as well as of Maimonides, as to the divination by dreams.

In my monograph on the internal senses I have shown how the various functions ascribed by Aristotle to *διάνοια* are summed up by John of Damascus in his *De Fide Orthodoxa*, II, 19, and how that passage of John of Damascus, or some similar passage, had influenced the description of فكر in Isaac Israeli[56] and the Iḫwan al-Ṣafa. Now toward the end of the passage, John of Damascus says: "The cogitative faculty (*διανοητικόν*) is also that which in

[55] השכל יפרק המורכבות ויבדיל חלקיהם ויפשיטם ויציירם באמתתם ובסביבותיהם . . . הדמיון . . . ירכיב הדברים המפוזרים במציאות וירכיב קצתם על קצתם.

[56] Cf. also my paper "Isaac Israeli on Internal Senses" in op. cit.

dreams tells us future events, which alone[57] the Pythagoreans, following the Hebrews,[58] declare to be true divinations." This passage is taken by John of Damascus from Nemesius[59] and must represent a widely accepted opinion. In view of the fact that διάνοια was translated by فكر and that فكر came to include imagination and imagination was connected with dreams, one can easily see how such a statement as that of John of Damascus in which διάνοια was said to include the function of divination by dreams could have given rise to those speculations as to the connection between dreams, imagination, and prophecy which we find in Arabic and Jewish philosophy.

Another faculty which in Alfarabi, Avicenna and all their followers in Arabic, Hebrew, and Latin philosophy is included among the internal senses is what is called in Arabic وهم. Avicenna in one place uses for it also the term ظنّ, and this term is also used by Isaac Israeli in the same sense. In Latin that faculty is generally called *aestimatio*. In Hebrew وهم is translated directly from the Arabic by מחשבה, דמיון, רעיון and מְחַשֵּׁב, and indirectly through the Latin by שמאי. The term ظنّ is translated by זמימות or זָמָם. The origin of this faculty in Greek philosophy has been discussed by me in my monograph on the internal senses, where I have tried to show that it does not reflect, as it is generally assumed, the Greek δόξα. But what is of importance for

[57] This statement that the Pythagoreans regard dreams as the only means of true divination is an indirect allusion to their denial of divination by sacrifices. Cf. Plutarch, *De Placitis Philosophorum*, V, 1.

[58] The view expressed here that the Pythagoreans followed the Hebrews reflects the ancient belief as to the oriental origin of Pythagorean philosophy which among Christians, Mohammedans, and Jews was changed into a Hebrew origin. According to Shahrastani (ed. Cureton, p. 265) Pythagoras lived at the time of King Solomon and has derived his knowledge from the teachings of the prophets.

[59] *De Natura Hominis*, Cap. 12. Reference is also given, in the printed editions of *De Fide Orthodoxa*, to the discussion of divination by dreams in the Bible by Gregory of Nyssa, *De Hominis Opificio*, Cap. 13.

us here is the description which is generally given of this faculty. In the first place, it is a faculty which exists primarily in animals and is a function of the animal soul, though like all functions of the animal soul it is also operative in man as an irrational mode of internal perception. In the second place, throughout the literature, estimation is described as a faculty which perceives insensible forms connected with sensible objects, such as the perception on the part of animals of the friendliness or hostility of certain other animals—a perception which is not based upon experience. Among the examples cited in illustration of the functioning of this faculty mention is made of maternal and filial love. Thus Avicenna in his *Canon* illustrates it by the example of the sheep, who, without any previous experience, knows that a wolf is an enemy and that its young one is a friend.[60] In his *Al-Najat* he similarly illustrates it by the example of the sheep who knows that a wolf is to be fled from and that its young one is to be cared for.[61] This last illustration is reproduced verbatim by Algazali in his *Mizan al-'Amal*.[62] In the third place, this estimative faculty together with imagination produces what we have called compositive animal imagination just as the dianoetic faculty together with imagination produces compositive human imagination, i. e., فكر. Finally, the estimative faculty like all the other internal senses, as we shall point out later, belongs to the cognitive faculties of the soul as distinguished from the motive faculty.

Now Maimonides does not explicitly mention this faculty, though in two passages, where he contrasts the perceptions

[60] *Canon*, loc. cit.: بان الذيب عدو والولد حبيب, שהזאב אויב והבן אוהב, *quod lupus est inimicus et filius est dilectus.*

[61] *Al-Najat*, loc. cit.: بان الذيب مهروب منه وان الولد معطوف عليه. The same also in Shahrastani, ed. Cureton, p. 417.

[62] *Mizan al-'Amal*, [IV], p. 20; *Mozene Ẓedeḳ*, IV, pp. 30–31: שהזאב ראוי לברוח ממנו והבן ראוי לרחם עליו. Arabic is the same as in *al-Najat*.

of وهم and ظنّ with intellectual and rational concepts and scientific knowledge,[63] he may have perhaps meant to include under these two terms also the faculty of estimation. But, as we have seen above in the case of the other internal faculties, Maimonides describes the function of the estimative faculty, as illustrated by paternal love, under the general term imagination. Thus in one place he says that "the love and tenderness of the mother for her young ones is not produced by reasoning but by imagination, and this faculty exists not only in man but in most living beings".[64] In another place he says that it is the "imaginative form"[65] which produces parental love.

This last type of imagination which Maimonides illustrates by the example of parental love has been treated by Diesendruck in connection with prophecy in his exhaustive study of Maimonides' theory of prophecy.[66] His conception of the nature of this type of imagination differs from ours. Finding an inconsistency between Maimonides' description of imagination as an irrational faculty and his treatment of it as a somewhat rational faculty through

[63] Cf. *Moreh Nebukim*, I, 74 (6): והיא התבוננות הדמיונות והמחשבות (الاوهام) לא התבוננות המציאות והמושכלות; II, 38: אנשי הכת הג' אשר אין להם דבריות ולא חכמה אלא דמיונות ומחשבות (ظنون) לבד.

[64] Ibid., III, 48: כי אהבת האם ורחמיה על הולד אינו נמשך אחר השכל רק אחר פעל הכח המדמה (المتخيّلة) הנמצא ברוב בעלי חיים.

[65] Ibid., III, 49: הצורה הדמיונית (الخيالية).

[66] "Maimonides' Lehre der Prophetie" in *Jewish Studies in Memory of Israel Abrahams*, 1927, pp. 110 ff. The following statement in *Moreh Nebukim*, II, 36: ושיעקב אבינו לא באתהו נבואה כל ימי אבלו להתעסק כחו המדמה בהפקד יוסף cited by Diesendruck (p. 111, n. 139) does not refer exclusively to the estimative faculty. From the context of the passage it is quite clear that what Maimonides means to say is this: Inasmuch as imagination, in all its variety of meanings, is a faculty connected with the body, any disturbance in the equilibrium of the body, such as is caused by any kind of grief and anger, will interfere with the functioning of the imagination and hence also with the functioning of the prophesying faculty.

which prophecy operates, he tries to show that the imagination which Maimonides associates with prophecy is that kind of imagination which Maimonides illustrates by the example of parental love. This kind of imagination, he says, is superior to all the other kinds of imagination, and it is upon this kind of imagination that the gift of prophecy descends from God through the Active Intellect. Now, we have seen, that the imagination which is illustrated by parental love is what is generally called the estimative faculty, which is a function of the animal soul and has nothing rational about it and cannot therefore be elevated above the other forms of imagination to be directly connected with the Active Intellect. If it is really necessary to confine Maimonides' use of the term imagination in connection with prophecy to one special kind of imagination, and one which will have an element of reason in it, it would rather have to be compositive human imagination, that is, مفكّرة, which by definition is the product of the combined action of reason and imagination. Then also, Diesendruck considers the estimative faculty, in contradistinction to all the other internal senses, as belonging to the motive faculty of the soul.

This Maimonidean fourfold classification of the imaginative faculty is reproduced in disguised form in a passage which occurs with but a few slight verbal differences in two works, the *Ruaḥ Ḥen*[67] of uncertain authorship and Gershon ben Solomon's *Sha'ar ha-Shamayim*.[68] Externally this passage appears to be nothing more than a paraphrase of Maimonides' twofold classification of imagination in the passage quoted above from the *Shemonah Peraḳim*, with the only difference that it includes the appetitive faculty, which is listed by Maimonides as a distinct faculty, under imagina-

[67] *Ruaḥ Ḥen*, Ch. 2.
[68] *Sha'ar ha-Shamayim*, XII, 1.

tion, thus increasing Maimonides' twofold classification of imagination to a threefold classification. But upon a close examination of this passage we shall find that each one of its three classes is sub-divided into two parts, thus making altogether a sixfold classification of imagination. In this sixfold classification, we shall then find, are included not only the four kinds of imagination we have met with in Maimonides but also memory and the appetitive faculty, which Maimonides himself does not include under imagination.

Let us adduce the evidence for our foregoing statement.

The first class of imagination in *Ruaḥ Ḥen* and *Sha'ar ha-Shamayim* reads as follows: "First, imagination is [a] the apprehension of the disposition of sense-perceptions and [b] the combination of some of these sense-perceptions with others at the time of the perception."[69] Now the second part of this passage is indeed nothing but a paraphrase of Maimonides' description of compositive imagination in *Shemonah Peraḳim*. The first part, however, does not occur there. But it will be noticed that it corresponds to the first part of Maimonides' description of imagination we have quoted above from *Moreh Nebukim*, I, 73, Prop. 10, Note. Just as in that passage Maimonides says of imagination that it apprehends the individual thing as a composite whole according as it is apprehended by the senses, so in this passage here imagination is said, in effect, to apprehend the things perceived by the senses according to their "disposition",[70] that is to say, according to their arrangement and order whereby they are formed into united wholes. Now the description of imagination in that passage of *Moreh Nebukim* we have shown to be a description of

69 האחד הוא השגת תכונת המוחשים והרכבתם קצתם על קצתם בעת ההרגש.

70 תכונה = هيئة διάθεσις. Cf. my "Classification of Sciences" in *Hebrew Union College Jubilee Volume*, 1925, p. 302, n

common sense. So also here the passage under consideration is really a description of common sense.

The description of the second class of imagination in *Ruaḥ Ḥen* and *Sha'ar ha-Shamayim* contains also two parts. It reads as follows: "Second, imagination is [a] the conservation of the sense-perceptions and [b] the conservation of the combination of these sense-perceptions in the imaginative faculty after they have disappeared from the senses."[71] Here, again, the first part of the description is only a paraphrase of Maimonides' description of retentive imagination in *Shemonah Peraḳim*. The second part, however, does not occur there. But these two parts of the description of the second class of imagination will be found upon close scrutiny to contain a formal statement of what was generally considered to be the distinction between retentive imagination and memory. Both of them are alike in that they are retentive faculties. They differ, however, in the objects which they are supposed to retain. Retentive imagination is said to retain the forms of the objects perceived by the senses. The technical expression for this in Arabic, Hebrew, and Latin is خزانة الصور, אוצר הצורות, *arca formarum*. Memory, on the other hand, is said to retain the "intentions" formed by the compositive and estimative faculties. The technical term for this is خزانة المعانى, אוצר העניינים, *arca intentionum*. In the passage under consideration, therefore, the first part which reads "the conservation of the sense-perceptions" refers to retentive imagination; the second part which reads "the conservation of the combination of these sense-perceptions" refers to memory. And since the latter part refers to memory, which generally is used in a comprehensive sense to include recollection, the author of the passage adds: "This includes

[71] .והשני שמירת המוחשים ושמירת הרכבתם בדמיון אחר העלמם מן החושים

recollection (וממנו הזכרנות)." I take the term זִכְרָנוּת here to mean "recollection" rather than "memory", though, like Arabic terms derived from the root ذكر, Hebrew terms derived from the root זכר may mean both memory and recollection. Memory in contrast to recollection is usually called in Arabic, Hebrew, and Latin by the terms حافظة, שומר, *conservativa*, from the Greek σωτηρία, ἕξις and συντήρησις applied to memory by Plato, Aristotle, and Galen. Still, while the existence of a distinction between memory and recollection is generally assumed, there is a question as to whether they should be considered as two faculties or as one single faculty. Hence the significance of the comment that recollection is to be included under memory.

Finally, the description of the third class of imagination in *Ruaḥ Ḥen* and *Sha'ar ha-Shamayim* is likewise to be divided into two parts. It reads as follows: "Third, imagination is [a] that appetitive faculty which strives to remove anything that is injurious and to reach after that which is beneficial, for even though a person has perceived by his imagination what is injurious to him or what is pleasurable to him, he is still in need of another faculty to excite him to the action of removing the thing which he has imagined to be against him or of reaching after the thing which he has imagined to be beneficial to him . . . [b] By the same token, an animal's love for its young is a function of the imaginative faculty."[72] Here, too, the first part of the description corresponds to Maimonides' description of the appetitive faculty in *Shemonah Peraḳim*, which Maimonides, as we have mentioned above, does not subordinate to

[72] והג' הוא שמתעורר להרחיק הדבר המזיקו ולכוין את הנאות לו, כי אף על פי שהכיר בדמיונו הדבר ההוא המזיקו או המעננו צריך שיהא בו כח אחר שיעורר אותו להרחיק הדבר שנדמה לו שהוא כנגדו או לכוין אל הדבר שנדמה לו שהוא נאות לו . . . וכן אהבת הבהמה או הוולד שלה היא מפעלת כח המדמה.

imagination. The second part, however, does not occur in the *Shemonah Peraḳim.* But maternal love, as we have seen, is one of the conventional examples used as an illustration of the estimative faculty, which Maimonides, as we have also seen, has included under the general term imagination. By similarly including the estimative faculty under imagination, the authors of *Ruaḥ Ḥen* and *Sha'ar ha-Shamayim* have followed their general method of enriching their paraphrase of Maimonides' classification of the functions of imagination in *Shemonah Peraḳim* by including within it all those other functions which Maimonides elsewhere has included under imagination, and also by including within it the faculty of memory and recollection which is akin to the faculty of imagination. In fact, what the authors of this passage did was to substitute the term "imagination" for the term "internal senses" and to reduce all the internal senses to the status of sub-functions of imagination. That they did so deliberately is evident by their own statement previously that "the internal senses are as a whole called imagination".[73] In this indeed these two authors display a tendency which beginning with Averroes becomes more and more general so that one of the later scholastics, Eustachius a Sancto Paulo,[74] explicitly argues for the reduction of all the internal senses to mere forms of imagination.

But while the inclusion of common sense, memory, recollection, and estimation under the term imagination in *Ruaḥ Ḥen* and *Sha'ar ha-Shamayim* can be thus fully accounted for, the inclusion in these works of the appetitive faculty under imagination needs some further explanation.

In Aristotle and throughout the works of his followers those faculties which became later known as internal senses

[73] החצוניות נקראות בכלל הרגש והפנימיות דמיון.

[74] *Summa Philosophiae Quadripartita*, III: Physica, Pars III, Tract. III, Disp. III, Quaest. I. Cambridge, 1640.

are all considered as belonging to what is called cognitive faculties (γνωριστικόν), in contradistinction to those which are known as motive faculties (κινητικόν).[75] Thus common sense, the various forms of imagination, estimation, memory and recollection are all cognitive faculties. The case of the appetitive faculty, however, is somewhat ambiguous. Its position is somewhat intermediate between the cognitive and motive faculties. While cognition creates desire in the appetitive faculty, the appetitive faculty excites action in the motive faculty. The motive faculty never acts, according to Aristotle, but together with the appetitive faculty added to imagination or intellect.[76] Because of its intermediate position between the cognitive and motive faculties, the appetitive faculty is not considered by Aristotle as a faculty of the same order as the other faculties, for appetency, he says, is found in each faculty.[77] This intermediate position of the appetitive faculty is clearly and succinctly expressed by Abraham ibn Daud in the following passage: "All of them (both the external and the internal senses) are subservient to the appetitive faculty, causing the living being to approach some things and to withdraw from others. There is, however, still another faculty called the motive faculty."[78] Similarly in Maimonides' description of the appetitive faculty in *Shemonah Peraḳim* its intermediate position between the cognitive and the motive faculties and the fact of its not being fully identified with the motive faculty is subtly brought out in the careful phrasing employed by him: "The appetitive part of the soul is that faculty whereby man conceives a desire for a certain thing or a disdain for it, and it is by means of

[75] *De Anima*, III, 3, 427a, 17–19; 9, 432a, 15–17. Cf. also I, 2, 4046, 28.
[76] Ibid., III, 10, 433a, 9 ff.
[77] Ibid. III, 9, 432b, 6–7.
[78] *Emunah Ramah*, I, 6, p. 30: וכלם יעבדו הכח המתעורר, יביאוהו לקרב ולהתרחק. עוד יש בו כח יקרא מניע.

this faculty that he comes to the action of seeking after something or running away from it, or of choosing something or recoiling from it. . . . . The organs of the body, both external and internal, together with their powers, are the instruments of this appetitive faculty."[79] Note that the appetitive faculty is said by Maimonides to be that part of the soul by which man only conceives a desire or disdain and by which he only comes to the action of seeking or avoiding. The implication is that the actual action of seeking and avoiding is the function of the motive faculty, which, though not explicitly mentioned here by Maimonides, is tacitly implied in his statement.

In view of these considerations, while the passage of *Ruaḥ Ḥen* and *Sha'ar ha-Shamayim*, in so far as it includes the appetitive faculty under imagination, departs from Maimonides' scheme of classification in *Shemonah Peraḳim*, its departure is not without justification, for the appetitive faculty, being inseparably associated with the imaginative faculty, could be properly included under it.

But while Maimonides himself does not explicitly include either the appetitive faculty or memory under the term imagination, it is quite clear that he does include under that term all the other internal senses, namely, common sense, retentive imagination, compositive human imagination, compositive animal imagination, and estimation. Now with reference to the subsumption of common sense under imagination, as we have already shown, Maimonides has followed the method which is occasionally used even by Avicenna, despite the latter's explicit statement that to philosophers, as distinguished from physicians, these two constitute

[79] *Shemonah Peraḳim*, Ch. 1: והחלק המתעורר הוא הכח אשר בו ישתוקק האדם לדבר אחד או ימאסהו, ומזה הכח יבא אל פעלות בקשת הדבר והבריחה ממנו ובחירת דבר אחד או התרחק ממנו . . . איברי הגוף הנראים והנסתרים, הם וכחותיהם, כלם כלים לזה הכח המתעורר.

two distinct faculties. But with reference to the subsumption of retentive imagination, the two compositive imaginations, and estimation under the imaginative faculty, some difficulty arises. For a difference of opinion existed on this point between Avicenna and Averroes. While the former considers them philosophically as three distinct faculties, the latter considers them as only sub-functions of a single imaginative faculty. Now the very fact that in *Moreh Nebukim*, II, 36, and in *Shemonah Peraḳim*, Ch. 1, Maimonides definitely describes imagination as containing two functions, the retentive and the compositive, would seem to point to the conclusion that he has on this point departed from Avicenna, adopting a view which is like that held by Averroes. Such indeed is the conclusion arrived at by Moscato in his commentary *Ḳol Yehudah* on *Cuzari*, V, 12,[80] and this conclusion would seem to gain corroboration from the fact that Maimonides includes under imagination also the faculty of estimation.

But I am going to show that, without the assumption of his departure from Avicenna and of his acquaintance with the view of Averroes, Maimonides had two good precedents for classifying these three internal faculties under the general term imagination, thereby also incidentally showing that this case is no exception to the general rule which every student of Maimonides must follow, namely, (a) not to assume a departure on the part of Maimonides from the views of his philosophic predecessors, unless he himself has given definite and unmistakable indications for the justifiability of such an assumption; (2) not to assume a knowledge on his part of any particular view held by Averroes in opposition to Avicenna, unless there is positive proof for it.

[80] ומלבד פעולה זו שזכרנו בכח הזה יחסו אליו פעולה שנית לדעת ן' רשד וסיעתו, והוא פעל ההרכבה וההפרדה הדמיונית . . . וביאר זה המורה בשני פ' ל"ו באמרו, וכבר ידעת עוד פעולת זה הכח המדמה מזכור המוחשים והרכבתם . . . אמנם ו' סינא לא כן ידמה ולא כן יחשוב . . .

First, Avicenna himself has provided Maimonides with a justification for his inclusion of the estimative faculty under the general term imagination. While Avicenna invariably uses the term وهم or ظنّ as a designation of the estimative faculty and while he is described by Averroes,[81] quite inaccurately, as the originator of the use of the term وهم as a designation of the estimative faculty, he is found to be inconsistent with himself with regard to the classification of that faculty. In his *Al-Shifa'*, *Al-Najat*, and *Risalah fi al-Nafs* he classifies the estimative faculty as something distinct from compositive imagination; in his *Canon*, however, he classifies it, even from the philosophic point of view, together with compositive imagination as one faculty. Furthermore, in his *Canon* he does not even insist upon the use of the term وهم in connection with the estimative faculty. He says: "There are some people who use language metaphorically and call this estimative faculty (وهميّة) imagination (تخيّل). They may do so, for we must not quarrel about names. We must, however, understand the meaning of the ideas behind the names and the differentiations between the ideas."[82] Thus Avicenna himself has granted Maimonides leave to include estimation under the imaginative faculty.

Second, it was Alfarabi who provided Maimonides with a literary precedent for the inclusion of all the three faculties, namely, retentive imagination, compositive imagination, and estimation, under the general term imagination. Now Alfarabi himself in two of his works, *Risalat Fuṣuṣ al-*

[81] *Epitome De Memoria et Reminiscentia* in *Aristotelis omnia quae extant opera*, Venice, 1574, Vol. 6, Pars 2, fol. 21 G: "Et illa virtus in animalibus non habet nomen, et est illa, quam Avicenna vocat existimationem (وَهم)".

[82] *Canon*, loc. cit.: ויש אנשים מי שיעבור (*praesumunt*, يتجوز) ויקרא הכח הזה דמיון והרשות בידו כי אין ויכוח בשמות, אבל ראוי שיובנו הענינים וההפרשים.

Ḥukmun, §36[83] and *'Uyun al-Musa'il*, §20,[84] lists retentive imagination, compositive imagination, and estimation as three faculties, each of which is designated by a separate term. Still in his *Sefer ha-Hatḥalot* he describes imagination as follows: "The imaginative faculty is that which [a] retains the impressions of the sensible objects after the latter have disappeared from sense-perception, and [b] combines some of these impressions with others and separates some of them from others . . . [c] Moreover, to this faculty belongs also the apprehension of that which is beneficial or injurious, pleasant or unpleasant."[85] The last part of the passage is a characteristic description of the function of the estimative faculty the like of which is used by Alfarabi himself in his *Risalat Fuṣuṣ al-Ḥukmun*. Thus all the three faculties, retentive imagination, compositive imagination, and estimation, are enumerated by Alfarabi under imagination, without necessarily implying that, like Averroes, he did not consider them as distinct faculties. No such implication must therefore be drawn from Maimonides' subsumption of these three faculties under imagination. Furthermore, Maimonides' classification of the faculties in *Shemonah Peraḳim* contains unmistakable internal evidence of being based on Alfarabi's *Sefer ha-Hatḥalot*.

On the whole, we may conclude, Maimonides' treatment of the internal senses conforms to the general method as it became standardized in the works of Alfarabi and Avicenna. He continues to use the old medical threefold classification of the internal senses into imagination, cogitation, and memory. But by the side of this old medical classification

[83] Cf. Dieterici, *Alfarabi's Philosophische Abhandlungen*, Arabic text, 1890, pp. 73 ff.; German translation, 1892, pp. 121 ff.

[84] Ibid., Arabic, p. 63; German, p. 105.

[85] *Sefer ha-Hatḥalot* in Z. Filipowsky's *Sefer ha-Asif*, Leipzig, 1849, p. 3: והמדמה הוא אשר ישמור רישומי המוחשים אהר העלמם מן החוש וירכיב קצתם אל קצתם ויפריד קצתם מקצתם . . . ולו עם זה השגת המועיל והמזיק והערב ובלתי ערב.

he makes use also, though only indirectly, of the new philosophical classification, with its breaking up of imagination into several kinds of imagination and with its addition of common sense and estimation. The existence of these two classifications side by side is also to be found in the works of Avicenna and Averroes, for the newer classification did not altogether supplant the older one. Again like Alfarabi, and partly also like Avicenna, he allows himself to use the term imagination rather loosely and to include under it not only common sense and the various forms of imagination but also the faculty of estimation.

19

THE TWICE-REVEALED AVERROES

AVERROES was revealed twice to European philosophy: first in the thirteenth century and then in the sixteenth century. In this essay I shall try to recall to our minds the circumstances which had led to each of these revelations and to discuss the problems which they each gave rise to.

I shall first take up the revelation in the thirteenth century.

In the second half of the eighth century, for reasons which need not here be gone into, a fervid activity of translating works on philosophy from the Greek into Arabic was started in Islam. It lasted for about two and a half centuries. During that time, among the many works translated, were almost all the works of Aristotle and many of his Greek commentaries. The study of these translations led to original writings on philosophy, beginning with the works of al-Kindi (d. 820) and ending with those of Averroes (d. 1198). Most of these philosophic works written originally in Arabic consisted of independent systematic treatises; but those of Averroes consisted mainly of commentaries on Aristotle. Of these commentaries, five were written in three forms, known as Long, Middle, and Epitome; ten only in two forms, Middle and Epitome; two only in the form of the Epitome: and one only in that of the Middle.[1] In addition to these, there are many short treatises by Averroes on special topics in Aristotelian philosophy,[2] among them his treatise *De Substantia Orbis*.

his *Quaestiones in Physica*, and his lost *Treatise on the Prime Mover*.[3] Without counting these short treatises and the doubtful commentary on *De Plantis*, and counting *Parva Naturalia* as one and including Porphyry's *Isagoge*, there are thirty-eight commentaries of Averroes on Aristotle.

With the Christian reconquest of Toledo in 1085, a school of translators from the Arabic into Latin was established there shortly after 1130 under the patronage of its archbishop. Before the close of the century, certain Arabic translations of Aristotle and of Greek commentaries on Aristotle, as well as of original Arabic works on philosophy, were translated from the Arabic into Latin.[4] These translations created a demand for other translations from the Arabic. And so in the second decade of the thirteenth century, less than twenty years after the death of Averroes, there began a systematic attempt to translate his commentaries into Latin. The translators who dedicated themselves to this task were Michael Scot and Hermann the German. Both of them had started their work in Toledo and then, either both or only Michael, drifted into the court of Frederick II, the then patron of translations from the Arabic. They produced translations of four of the five long commentaries, those on the *Physica*, *De Caelo*, *De Anima*, and *Metaphysica*. These contained also Latin translations of the Arabic translations of the Greek text of Aristotle, according as they were quoted in these commentaries of Averroes. They produced also translations of the Middle commentaries on four works: *Poetica*, *De Caelo*, *De Generatione et Corruptione*, and *Ethica Nicomachea*; and also a translation of the Epitome of *Parva Naturalia*.[5] A third translator, a contemporary of these two, was William of Luna, who translated Averroes' Middle commentaries on the *Isagoge* of Porphyry, the *Categories*, and *De Interpretatione*; and also his Middle commentaries on *Analytica Priora* and *Analytica Posteriora*.[6] To these three may be added Theodorus Antiochenus, also of the court of Frederick II, who translated Averroes' Prooemium to his Long Commentary on the *Physics*.[7]

The reception of these translations of Averroes' commentaries by Christian philosophers may be described by a term currently in vogue as ambivalent.[8] They praised him as commentator but damned him as theologian. For Averroes occasionally, in his exposition of Aristotle on innocuous problems of philosophy, digresses to pay his respect to certain touchy problems of religion. Already in the thirteenth century, while he was hailed by William of Auvergne (1228–1249) as "the most noble philosopher" (*philosophus nobilissimus*),[9] by St. Thomas as "the Commentator" (*Commentator*),[10] and by Dante as "he who made the grand commentary (*il gran commento*),"[11] he was decried by all of these, as well as by others, for certain heretical views. Special books were written against him and time and again was he publicly condemned. Toward the end of the thirteenth century, Giles of Rome, in his work, *Errores Philosophorum*, devotes a special chapter to the errors of Averroes.[12]

I should like to discuss some of these errors, and to discuss them not for their own sake, as problems of philosophy and theology, but rather as examples illustrating two predicaments, the predicament of language and the predicament of the apperceptive mass, which every student of the history of the transmission of ideas so often encounters in the course of his studies. The manner in which Averroes was received by the Schoolmen is a good illustration of these two predicaments. Transferred as he was from the Arabic world with its Islamic background to the Latin world of mediaeval Christianity, Averroes' vocabulary and pronouncements often invoked in the minds of his new readers associations and meanings springing from an accumulated mass of knowledge quite different in origin and composition. For our purpose here I have selected the first three statements contained in the first of the twelve errors which Giles of Rome found in Averroes.

Here is one statement. To quote: "Because he reviled all law, as is clear from book II of the *Metaphysics* and also from book XI, where he reviles the law of the Christians, that is our Catholic law, and also the law of the Saracens, because they maintain the creation of the universe and that something can be produced out of nothing."

The statement is verbally correct. In his commentary on the *Metaphysics* XII, Comm. 18, in the 1574 Junta edition of Aristotle's works, vol. 8, p. 305 F, Averroes explicitly says that "the *Loquentes* of the three laws which exist today" believe in creation *ex nihilo*, and that he rejects it. It is also true that the *Loquentes* of the three laws or religions maintained creation *ex nihilo*. In Christianity, Patristic and Scholastic philosophers maintain it. Jewish philosophers of the Arabic period, for the most part, describe creation as being *ex nihilo*. In Islam one of the early creeds, the Fikh Akbar II, which may have originated in the middle of the tenth century, says in Article 5: "Allah has not created things from a pre-existing thing."[13] Still, Giles' statement that Averroes, by his denying creation *ex nihilo*, was reviling the Muslim religion just as he was reviling the Christian religion, is not an accurate statement, for the status of the belief in creation *ex nihilo* in Islam was different from that in Christianity and consequently for a Muslim at the time of Averroes to have denied creation *ex nihilo*, as it was rigidly understood in Christianity, and to substitute for it another theory of creation, was not the same as for a Christian at the time of Giles of Rome to come out with such a denial and to substitute for it another theory of creation.

Let us briefly analyze the problem of creation as it emerges from the discussions of this problem in the Arabic philosophic literature. The problem falls into three parts.

First, irrespective of the question whether the present world existed as it now is is from eternity or whether it had come into existence after it had not existed, there is the question whether the world is self-sufficient and causeless or whether it is in some sense dependent upon a cause. The answer, on the basis of the Koran, is that the world is dependent upon a cause, whom the Koran calls God and who is described as Creator.

Second, there is the question whether a Muslim is bound to accept the chronology of the Hebrew Scripture, whereby the age of the present world can be determined by adding to the Christian era either 3760 years, according to the Jewish reckoning, or 5503 years, according to the Patristic reckoning, or 4004 according to Archbishop Ussher's reckoning.[14] The answer is no. The Hebrew scriptural chronology is not mentioned in the Koran, and so a Muslim may believe that the present world is millions of years old. But the Koran does mention that Adam was the first man, and so a Muslim must believe that all mankind is descendant from one man. Accordingly, one of the Twelve Shiite Imams is reported to have said that "millions of Adams passed away before our father Adam" and the Sufis are reported to have said that "forty thousand years before our Adam there was another Adam."[15] Mas'ūdī, speaking for Islam in general, declares that religious philosophers among the Muslims say that "demonstrations may establish the creation of the world" as well as the belief that "the beginning of men is from Adam" but that "it is impossible for us to determine and count up the years," adding that "God has informed us in His Book that He created Adam . . . but He has not furnished us any information with regard to the extent of time that has elapsed since then."[16]

Third, there is also the question whether in the Koran there is an explicit mention of creation *ex nihilo*. The answer is no. Quite the opposite, the Koran says something to the effect that God created the heaven out of smoke (41: 10). Thus as early as the ninth century the question whether the world was created *ex nihilo* or out of a preexistent matter appeared in Islam, as I have shown,[17] under the guise of the discussion of the philosophic problem whether the "nonexistent" is "nothing" or "something," and as late as the twelfth century there was still a discussion as to the meaning of the "smoke" out of which according to the Koran, God created the heaven. Zamakhsharī says that the smoke proceeded from the waters under the throne of God, which throne was one of the things created before the heavens and the earth.[18] Averroes, however, uses this verse to prove that the heavens were created from something eternal.[19]

Orthodox Islam, indeed, decided in favor of creation *ex nihilo* and the phrase *ex nihilo* became standardized, but, standardized though it became, it was interpreted differently, so that a philosopher like Alfarabi, who believed that the world was eternally emanated from the essence of God by the will of God, described that belief of his as a belief in creation *ex nihilo*.[20] And it can be shown, I think, that, while orthodox Islam would reject Alfarabi's interpretation of *ex nihilo*, it would not brand it as heretical. For this I can cite no better authority than Algazali, the great champion of Muslim orthodoxy. In his discussion of the problem of creation, Algazali argues especially against those who believe in the eternal emanation of the world from God by necessity, and it is this view which is branded by him as being "opposed to the religion of the Muslims."[21] He does not discuss the view of the eternal emanation of the world from the will of God and, though he would undoubtedly reject it on the ground of its assertion of the coëternity of the world with God, but his rejection of it, as his rejection of the coëternity of the world with God in general, would be on purely philosophic grounds, for it is to be noted that nowhere in his argument against the mere conception of the eternity of the world, without the added conception of necessity, does he repeat his statement that it is "opposed to the religion of the Muslims."[22] This leniency on the part of Muslim orthodoxy toward such a conception of the coëternity of the world with God is based, I venture to suggest, upon a conception of eternity in its relation to God which is distinctive of orthodox Islam. Eternity, to Muslim orthodoxy, is not a property which is peculiar to God alone, and consequently not everything that is eternal must *ipso facto* be God. It is on this ground that orthodox Islam, despite its insistence upon the absolute unity of God, could justify its belief in the reality of eternal attributes existing in God. It is also on this ground that orthodox Islam, while rejecting the belief in an eternal world, even when conceived of as depending upon the will of God for its existence, could still tolerate such a belief and not consider it as inconsistent with the belief in the absolute unity of God.

As for Averroes, he rejects, indeed, the view that the world is coëternal with God in the sense that it is eternally emanated from God. To him, the world is coëternal with God in the sense that it is eternally moved by God. But this its being eternally moved by God is described by him in religious terms as being eternally "created" (*muḥdath*) by God and, while he disagrees with the orthodox conception of creation *ex nihilo*, he still uses this expression as a description of his own view, insisting that he uses that expression in its right meaning.[23] Similarly, while he denies creation as an act of divine will in the sense in which orthodoxy uses that expression, he still uses that expression as a description of his own view, insisting, again, that he uses it in its right meaning.[24] On logical grounds, I imagine, Algazali would have rejected this view of Averroes, but, on strictly religious grounds, he would have no objection to it. And what is true of "the law of the Saracens," Islam, is true also of the third of "the three laws," Judaism, with regard to the doctrine of creation *ex nihilo*.[25]

The situation in Christianity was different. Whatever reference or allusion there is in the New Testament to the creation of the world, it reflects the Old Testament teaching. In the Old Testament story of creation, there is no explicit statement that creation was *ex nihilo*. Still the Fathers from the earliest times insisted upon creation *ex nihilo*. The proof-text upon which they base their view is II Maccabees vii. 28. But that proof-text does not say that God created heaven and earth ἐκ μηδενός, that is, "out of nothing"; it says that God created them οὐκ ἐξ ὄντων, "not out of things existent," and, as in philosophic Greek οὐκ ὄν or μὴ ὄν may mean matter, the proof-text quoted may mean that He created heaven and earth out of pre-existent matter.[26] The Fathers of the Church, however, had a good theological reason for insisting upon creation *ex nihilo*. The doctrine of the Trinity, which from the earliest time maintained the equality of the first two persons as God and which gradually came to maintain the equality of all the three persons as God, required the denial of the existence of anything coëternal with the triune God. For the belief in the equality of all the three coëternal persons as God meant to the Fathers that eternity spells deity and hence that nothing which is not God could be eternal. It is by this argument that Tertullian rejected the belief in the creation of the world out of a pre-existent eternal matter as urged by Hermogenes.[27] It is for this reason, too, I imagine, that Johannes Scotus Erigena, who interpreted creation *ex nihilo* as a sort of Neoplatonic emanation out of God himself, explaining that God is called *nihil* because of His incomprehensibility and ineffability and of the impossibility of describing Him by any terms,[28] still does not conceive of the creation of the world as an eternal process but maintains that this visible world of changing qualities and quantities and all the other accidents had a temporal beginning.[29]

And so, when Giles of Rome says that Averroes by his belief in the eternity of the world reviled not only the Christian religion but also the Muslim religion, he was passing judgment upon Averroes from an apperceptive mass which is peculiarly Christian and was not shared by Muslim thinkers. In Christianity, creation *ex nihilo* was already an established principle; in Islam, as well as in Judaism, it was still a debatable subject, even though orthodoxy in both these religions was upholding it.

Here is a second statement by Giles of Rome. To quote again: "These vituperations are to be found also in the beginning of book three of the *Physics*, where he holds that some people, because of the contrary habit (*consuetudinem*) of the laws, deny self-evident principles, such as the principle that nothing can be produced out of nothing." What Giles is here accusing Averroes of saying may be restated as follows: "Some people", namely the *Loquentes* of the three religions, to whom, as we have seen, he ascribes elsewhere the belief in creation *ex nihilo*, have arrived at this belief because of their "habit" to follow their respective "laws," and thus, believing as they do in creation *ex nihilo*, they deny the self-evident principle of *ex nihilo nihil fit*.

The reference here to "book three of the *Physics*" should be, as has been pointed out by the editors Koch and Riedl, "book three of the *Metaphysics*," referring to a passage in Averroes on *Metaphysics* II, Comm. 14, p. 34, I-K, which is a comment on Aristotle in *Metaphysics* II, 3, 995a, 3–6.

Let us see what Aristotle says in that passage, what Averroes means in his comment on it, and what Giles makes of that comment.

In the original Greek text, Aristotle says: "How great a force habit (σύνηθες) is, the laws (οἱ νόμοι) make manifest, for in the law the fanciful and the childish, through force of habit, have more influence than our knowledge of them."

Averroes, in his comment on this, says as follows: "And this happens not only in the laws (*in legibus*) but also in the primary notions (*prima cognita* = τὰ πρῶτα νοήματα), as it happens to men who for the first time heard the science of the *Loquentes*, for those *Loquentes*, on account of habit (*propter consuetudinem*) deny the nature of being and truth and deny also necessity in existence and assume that everything is possible."

I shall try to show that Giles misunderstood the meaning of two expressions used in this comment of Averroes. First, he misunderstood the meaning of the expression *in legibus*. Second, he misunderstood the meaning of the expression *prima cognita*.

Let us first take up his misunderstanding of the expression *in legibus*.

The term *lex* in the Latin translation of Averroes' Long Commentary on the *Metaphysics* stands for the following two Arabic words:

(1) *millah* "religion." This use of *lex* occurs in such expressions as "opinio Loquentium in nostra lege et lege Christianorum"[30] and "Loquentes trium legum quac hodie quidem sunt."[31]

(2) *nāmus*, which is only a transliteration into Arabic characters of the Greek νόμος "law." This use of *lex*, in its plural form *leges*, occurs in the Latin phrase *in legibus*, which translates the Arabic *fī al-nawāmis*,[32] which in turn reflects the Greek οἱ νόμοι[33] in the original passage of Aristotle, upon which Averroes commented in the passage now under consideration. Quite evidently the Latin *in legibus* in Averroes' comment is used in the sense of "laws" and not in the sense of "religions."[34]

Giles, however, misled by the frequent use of the term *leges* in the Latin translation of Averroes in the sense of "religions," took it in this passage also to mean religions, and hence he takes this passage of Averroes as a gibe against those whom he elsewhere calls "the *Loquentes* of the three laws which exist today."

Let us now take up his misunderstanding of the meaning of Averroes' expression *prima cognita* "primary notions."

What Averroes means by "the primary notions" and by his statement that "the *Loquentes*, on account of habit deny the nature of being and truth and deny also necessity in existence and assume that every thing is possible" may be established by passages, all available to Latin readers, which expound the Kalam's denial of causality and its explanation of the regularity in the succession of events observed in nature as being due to what they call habit (*'ādah, consuetudo*)[35]—a view with which we have now all become acquainted through Hume's argument against causality.[36] Averroes, in his refutation of this view, argues that the denial of causality would lead to a denial of "the nature of being"; but, he continues, it is "self-evident," that is, it is a "primary notion," that each existent thing has "a nature."[37] From all this it is quite evident, then, that when Averroes says here that the *Loquentes*, on account of "habit," denied the "primary notion" and denied also the "nature of being," the reference is to their denial of causality and not to their affirmation of creation *ex nihilo*. On this point, it may be noted, all the Schoolmen, including Giles himself, with the only exception of Nicolaus of Autrecourt, agree with Averroes in rejecting the view of the *Loquentes*.

And so, because of his misunderstanding of the allusions in the text of Averroes, Giles found heresy in a statement of his, which, if he had understood it properly, he would have applauded.

And here is a third statement in Giles' condemnation of Averroes. To quote once more: "And what is worse, he derisively dubs us and other upholders of the law *Loquentes*, as if to say babblers and people who are moved [to talk] without reason."

No reference to any passage in Averroes, where this alleged error of his is to be found, is given by Giles. The reference, as has been suggested,[38] is undoubtedly to a passage in Averroes on *Metaphysics* III, Comm. 15, p. 55 B, which bears upon a text in Aristotle's *Metaphysics* III, 4, 1000a, 5 ff.

Let us then see what Averroes actually says in his comment on that text of Aristotle.

In the text which occasioned Averroes' comment, Aristotle raises the question whether the principles of perishable things and imperishable things are the same or different. He quotes the opinion "of the school of Hesiod and the theologians (θεολόγοι)." He refutes their opinion, and describes both the school of Hesiod and the theologians as having "thought only of what was plausible to themselves, but treated us with disdain" or as "using words which are familiar to themselves, yet what they have said . . . is above our comprehension." Now in the Arabic translation of the text of Aristotle quoted by Averroes the Greek expression πάντες ὅσοι θεολόγοι is rendered by a phrase which should be literally translated into Latin by "omnes qui loquuntur in rebus divinis, i.e., all those who speak of matters divine.[39] The Latin translation, however, instead of "omnes qui loquuntur in divinis" uses the expression "omnes loquentes in divinis."[40] Then also in Averroes' comment on the text, the Arabic should be translated into Latin to read "intendit per *ei qui loquuntur in divinis* ei qui loquuntur sermonem extra intellectum hominis." Instead, the Latin translation reads: "intendit per *loquentes in Divinis* loquentes sermonem extra intellectum hominis" (p. 55 B). Now the change from *ei qui loquuntur* to *loquentes* is significant. For the term *loquentes*, through the Latin translations of the works of Averroes and Maimonides, became a technical term referring to the Muslim theologians known as the Mutakallimūn. Moreover, the term *Loquentes* was extended by Averroes to include both Jewish and Christian theologians, as when, for instance, he speaks of "the *Loquentes* of the three laws which exist today" (*Loquentes trium legum, quae hodie quidem sunt*)[41] or "the *Loquentes* in our law and the law of the Christians" (*Loquentes in nostra lege et lege Christianorum*).[42] Similarly Maimonides extends the meaning of *Loquentes* to include "the sages of the [Christian] Greek *Loquentes*" (*scitae a sapientibus Graecarum Loquentium*).[43] And so the statement of Averroes in his comment on Aristotle, which in its original Arabic is merely a reproduction of Aristotle's characterization of Greek myth-makers, was misunderstood by Giles and taken to refer, as he says, to "us and other upholders of the law," that is to say, to Christian, Muslim, and Jewish theologians. It is interesting to note that a similar mistake is made by Renan when he says that in "*Met.* XII, Cap. vi" (1071b, 27 = Averroes, Text. 30, p. 314 H; Comm. 30 p. 315 E), θεολόγοι is translated by Averroes "*Motecallemin*" [= *Loquentes*].[44] The Latin translation there of that Greek term is both in the Text and in the Commentary "Loquentes in Divinis," which, without the printer's capitalization, does not mean the Muslim "*Motecallemin*."

Besides this misunderstanding, which is due to the predicament of language, this passage of Giles contains another misunderstanding, which is due to the predicament of the apperceptive mass.

When Giles came upon Averroes' reference to the *Loquentes* of the Christians, he naturally associated these *Loquentes* with the Fathers of the Church. Consequently, when he came upon Averroes' references to "our *Loquentes*" or "the *Loquentes* of the Saracens" or "the *Loquentes* of the three laws," he assumed that the position of the *Loquentes* in Islam was similar to that of the Church Fathers in Christianity. When, therefore, he thought that Averroes derisively dubbed the *Loquentes* babblers and people who speak without reason, he naturally described him as one undermining the authority of the upholders of both these two religions. But here is where Giles was mistaken: he viewed an internal squabble in Islam from a Christian perspective. The position of the *Loquentes* in Islam is not the same as that of the Church Fathers in Christianity. The Church Fathers are those who formulated the fundamental Christian doctrine during the first six Oecumenical Councils. It was they who purged Christianity of the various heresies, and they are constantly cited by the later mediaeval Schoolmen in whatever question of faith that may come up. The term "Holy Fathers," which was first applied by St. Basil to the traditional 318 representatives of the Church who assembled at Nicea, was subsequently applied to all those representatives of the church who flourished to about the middle of the eighth century. Nothing like it is the position of those called *Loquentes* in Islam. If there is any body of religious authorities in Islam corresponding to the Church Fathers in Christianity, it is those who are referred to as the *ṣaḥābah*, "the companions" of the Prophet, and the *tābiʿūn*, "the followers," and the *salaf*, "the ancients." All these are distinguished from the *Mutakallimūn*, the so-called *Loquentes* of the Latin translations from the Arabic. By the time of Averroes, the *Mutakallimūn* were spoken of as being of two kinds. There were the Muʿtazilite *Mutakallimūn* and there were the Ash'arite *Mutakallimūn*. The former were condemned as heretical. As for the latter, while by the time of Averroes they were already established as the exponents of orthodoxy, they did not gain that recognition, without having first been attacked by orthodoxy. The term "*Mutakallimūn*" did not mean to the Muslims at the time of Averroes what the term "Fathers of the Church" meant to Christians. And so when Averroes, as a Muslim, spoke rather derogatorily of the *Loquentes*, he was unlike a Christian of the same period who would speak derogatorily of the Church Fathers.

So much for the first revelation of Averroes.

Taking up now the second revelation, let us again begin by reminding ourselves of the circumstances which have brought about this second revelation.

Despite the repeated condemnation of Averroes for his real or imaginary heresies, his commentaries were widely read and studied and copied. Moreover, they were imitated. The very same persons who damned him for his heresy—Albertus Magnus, Thomas Aquinas, and even Giles of Rome—followed his example and wrote commentaries on Aristotle in his style and manner; and they constantly quoted him. These new commentaries on Aristotle by Schoolmen, despite their freedom from religious error, did not replace Averroes. They only created a greater interest in Aristotle, and with it in Averroes. By the fourteenth century Averroes came to be recognized as the Commentator *par excellence*, and this reputation he continued to enjoy during the fifteenth century.[45] Then a boost came for the commentaries of Averroes from a source unexpected. Nicolaus Leonicus Thomaeus, a celebrated Greek scholar who taught Aristotle at Padua, publicly declared that, with the exception of the Greek commentators, Averroes was the most admirable (*exquisitissimus*) interpreter of Aristotle.[46] Then also, a way was found of removing the sting of heresy from the works of Averroes. In 1495 Niphus published an edition of Averroes' works fringed with antidotal notes. All this led to a demand in the sixteenth century for a complete translation of Averroes.

But by that time, in Europe, it was hard to find copies of the original texts of Averroes' commentaries. Huet (1630–1721) quotes Scaliger (1540–1609) as saying that there was no Arabic copy of Averroes in Europe and that he saw only the various Latin translations, which by that time already existed in print. Huet then adds:[47] "But I myself have seen an Arabic Averroes, which was formerly brought hither, out of the East, by Postellus; and which one would wonder that Scaliger would never hear of, he who was his intimate friend and correspondent in learning." The Arabic Averroes referred to is Averroes' Middle Commentary on the *Organon*, now in Leyden,[48] which contains besides the six books of the *Organon* also the *Rhetoric* and *Poetics*, thus eight of Averroes' thirty-eight commentaries. Since that time, it may be remarked, research in European libraries has discovered one copy each of the Middle Commentary on *De Caelo* and the Long Commentary on *Metaphysics*, again in Leyden, and two copies of the Epitome of the *Organon*, one in Paris and one in Munich, but both of them are in Hebrew characters.

Besides the scarcity of the original Arabic texts of Averroes in Europe, there were at that time in Europe very few people who could translate Arabic philosophic texts. Fortunately, the Jews, who had been expelled from Muslim Spain with the coming of the Almohades at about the middle of the twelfth century, carried with them the works of Averroes to the new countries where they found refuge, Northern Spain and Southern France. Some of these Arabic works, transliterated into Hebrew characters, are still to be found in European libraries. Then, less than a century later, in 1232, these Arabic works of Averroes began to be translated into Hebrew, and in the course of ninety years all of his commentaries, with the possible exception of two, were translated into Hebrew. It is through Latin translations from these Hebrew translations that Averroes revealed himself again to European philosophy. In the sixteenth century editions of Latin translations of Aristotle, those of the Juntas and Cominus de Tridino, which contain also Latin translations of thirty-four of the thirty-eight commentaries of Averroes and of some of his other works, twenty-six of these thirty-four translations were made from the Hebrew, six of them replacing older translations made in the thirteenth century directly from the Arabic.[49] Similarly, his other works contained in the Junta edition, namely, *De Substantia Orbis*, *Destructio Destructionum*, and *Epistola de Intellectu* were translated from the Hebrew, though, again, of some of these works there existed older translations made in the thirteenth century directly from the Arabic. Of chapters 57–59 of *Colliget* V the new translation from the Hebrew is printed by the side of the older Latin translation from the Arabic.

The reception with which Averroes was now met after his second revelation was of a different kind. The old cry of heresy no longer came from the Schoolmen. A new cry was now raised by the Hellenists, questioning the usefulness of Averroes' commentaries. Two conflicting views were expressed. Here are representative examples. On the one hand, the Spanish scholar Juan Luis Vives (1492–1540) said:[50] "He has gained the name of Commentator, though he is very far from explaining his author Aristotle or deserving that title. This would have been too great a task for one of an extraordinary genius, much more for him who had but a moderate one, nay, to say the truth, a mean one. For what qualifications had he for undertaking a commentary on Aristotle? He had no knowledge of antiquity, nor of its several doctrines and sects with which Aristotle everywhere abounds." He then goes on to point at certain errors made by Averroes. But, on the other hand, the German scholar Gerhard Johann Vossius (1577–1649) said:[51] "He was called the Commentator *par excellence*, who, without knowing anything of Greek, penetrated so felicitously into the mind of Aristotle."

These are wholesale condemnation and wholesale praise. A more judicious opinion is given by Bartholomaeus Keckermann (1571–1609), who made a special study of Averroes' works on the *Organon*. He says:[52] "In the *Posterior Analytics*,[53] it appears, Averroes has performed an excellent work, and such as deserves to be immortal. *The Epitome of Logic*,[54] which he wrote [not in the form of a running commentary on a text], is most praiseworthy for many reasons, and his *Logic*[55] is extraordinary (*quaesita*). None of the ancient interpreters seem to hit the sense of Aristotle so happily as this Arabian."

I am not going to debate the question whether Averroes was not often wrong in his interpretation of Aristotle. One may readily admit it. But so were his Greek commentators, Alexander, Themistius, and Simplicius, also often wrong in their interpretations of Aristotle and, to judge by reviews that appear in learned journals on every new book on Aristotle, commentators on Aristotle are still often wrong. Many years ago, on the basis of my studies of Averroes' commentaries and the Hebrew supercommentaries on them, I arrived at this conclusion: "Contrary to the prevalent opinion among students of the history of philosophy, the translations of Aristotle both in Arabic and Hebrew have preserved to a remarkable degree not only clear-cut analyses of the text of Aristotle's works but also the exact meaning of the terminology and forms of expression. The literalness and faithfulness with which the successive translators from one language into another performed their task, coupled with a living tradition of Aristotelian scholarship, which can be shown to have continued uninterruptedly from the days of the Lyceum through the Syriac, Arabic, and Hebrew schools of philosophy, enabled [mediaeval readers] to obtain a pretty accurate knowledge of Aristotle's writings. That knowledge, to be sure, was traditional and one-sided, but the tradition upon which it was based, like the various traditional interpretations of the Bible text before the rise of independent critical scholarship, was clear and definite and suffered comparatively little corruption."[56] The more I followed the history of the transmission of philosophy through translations the more firmly convinced I became of the continuity of an oral tradition accompanying every translation, which served as a sort of oral commentary upon each translation, explaining all the new shades of meanings that were imported into the words of the language of the translation from the language from which they were translated.

Perhaps I could best illustrate this point by a concrete case study. As subject for this case study I shall take a passage of a Latin translation made from the Hebrew translation of one of the commentaries of Averroes—a passage which deals with a problem involving certain technical terms in Greek and certain constructions peculiar to Greek, which are untranslatable into Arabic. I shall act as a sort of supercommentator on Averroes' commentary. First, I will introduce the problem dealt with in the passage in question. Then I will quote the passage in Latin, followed by an English translation. Finally, in my exegesis I will explain what I have done in my translation and why I have done it.

The passage which I have selected is from Averroes' *Epitome of the Organon*. The Latin text is from the Junta edition of 1574–75. The underlying Hebrew text is from an edition of the Hebrew of the *Epitome of the Organon* published at Riva di Trento in 1559. The Arabic text has not yet been published, but it is extant in two manuscripts in Hebrew characters. I have purposely made no effort to secure a photostat of the Arabic text, as I wanted to use this case study also as a test of how far one could go in translating and interpreting texts of Averroes on the basis of the Latin and Hebrew translations where no Arabic texts are extant.

Here is the introductory statement concerning the problem dealt with in the passage to be quoted from Averroes:

From several places in his writings we gather that Aristotle distinguishes between the following three forms of logical propositions:

(1) *ἔστι τυφλό₂ ἄνθρωπος*, Man is blind.[57]
(2) *οὐκ ἔστι δίκαιος ἄνθρωπος*, Man is not just.[58]
(3) *ἔστιν οὐ δίκαιος, ἄνθρωπος*, Man is not-just.[59]

Ammonius, on the basis of certain statements in Aristotle, describes these three types of propositions respectively as "privative" (*στερητικὴ*), "negative" (*ἀποφατικὴ*), and "indefinite" (*ἀόριστος*),[60] the last of which, through a mistranslation of Boethius,[61] is known in Western philosophy as "infinite." With regard to privative and negative propositions, Aristotle draws the following distinction. The negative proposition "A is not seeing" may be used even in cases where the subject "A" is an inanimate object which by nature is incapable of seeing.[62] The privative proposition "A is blind" can be used only in cases where the subject "A" is a living being who by nature is capable of seeing but it happens to be deprived of sight.[63] There is nothing in his writings, however, to indicate as to whether, with respect to that distinction drawn by him between negative and privative propositions, the indefinite proposition belongs to the one or to the other.

The uncertainty as to whether a proposition with a separable negative particle preceding the predicate is regarded by Aristotle as a privative or as a negative proposition becomes all the greater when we find that a proposition with an inseparable negative particle prefixed to the predicate is treated by him both as a privative and as a negative proposition. Thus a proposition of the type of "man is toothless (*νωδός*)" is explicitly described by him as a privative proposition.[64] Similarly from his statement that "the brutes are not to be described as either temperate (*σώφρονα*) or as intemperate (*ἀκόλαστα*)"[65] it is to be inferred that the predicate "intemperate" is used here as a privation, for, if it were used as a negation, it could be predicated of brutes, since by nature brutes are incapable of temperance. The same may be inferred from his statement that the terms "just" (*δίκαιος*) and "unjust" (*ἄδικος*) are contraries between which there is an intermediate, so that the subject may be described as being at once "neither just nor unjust."[66] Here, too, the predicate "unjust" is used as a privation, for, if it were used as a negation, then "unjust" would be "contradictories" (*ἀντιφάσεις*) and not "contraries" (*ἐναντία*),[67] and consequently the statement that the subject may be described as being at once "neither just nor unjust" would be wrong, for it would infringe upon the Law of Excluded Middle.[68] But, then, such statements as "a voice is invisible (*ἀόρατος*)"[69] and "a unit . . . is quantitatively indivisible (*ἀδιαίρετος*)"[70] and "is positionless (*ἄθετος*)"[71] are quite evidently used by Aristotle as negations.

In one place, *Metaphysics* V, 22, predicates with alpha privative, such as *ἄνισον*, "unequal," *ἀόρατον*, "invisible," and *ἄτομτον*, "uncutable," are each called "privation," but are each described as being used either in the technical sense of negation or in the technical sense of privation, depending upon the nature of the subject of which they are predicated.[72] Of the same tenor is also the statement that "the immobility (ἀκινησία) of that to which motion belongs [by nature] is rest (ἠρεμία),"[73] the implication of which is that the immobility of that to which motion does not belong [by nature] is not rest but rather something which is a negation of both motion and rest. In consequence of this view, the term "immobile," when used in a proposition in which the subject is "man," would be a privation but, when used in a proposition in which the subject is "God," would be a negation. This distinction, it may be remarked, would not explain why, in the statement quoted above, the term "intemperate" predicated of brutes is used as a privation.

Both these uses of predicates with the alpha privative are to be found in post-Aristotelian philosophy. Thus the Stoics use the proposition "the man is inhumane (ἀφιλάνθρωπος)" as an illustration of what they call "privative,"[74] and, in Boethius, the typical example of a privative proposition is the proposition *est iniustus* [= ἄδικος] *homo*.[75] In Philo, Albinus, Plotinus, and the Church Fathers, however, various terms with alpha privative are predicated of God in the sense of negation.[76] Arabic students of Aristotle's works could not get any information from the above-quoted "man is toothless (νωδός)" as to how Aristotle used this type of proposition, for in the Arabic translation of the *Categories*, the Greek term νωδός, which is negative both in form and in meaning, being composed of the negative prefix νη and ὀδούς, "tooth," is translated by the Arabic *adrad*, which is positive in form, though negative in meaning.[77] However, from the reading in the Arabic translation of the passage in *Metaphysics* V, 22, quoted above, Arabic students of Aristotle could learn that *lā musāwin* and *lā mubṣar*, which are the equivalents respectively of the Greek ἄνισος, "unequal," and ἀόρατος, "invisible," are used as negations, whereas *lā munkaṭi'*, which is the equivalent of the Greek ἄτμητος, "uncutable," is used either as a negation or as a privation, and so are these terms explained by Averroes in his Long Commentary on the *Metaphysics*.[78]

In the case of this kind of proposition, then, from the fact that Aristotle himself says that it may be used either as negation or as privation, we may reasonably assume that those whom we have quoted as using it either in the one or in the other of these two senses only happen to have occasion to use it in that one particular sense, without thereby excluding the possibility of its use in the other sense.[79] In the case, however, of propositions in which the predicate is preceded by a separable negative particle, concerning the use of which no information is to be found in Aristotle, we note two opposite views among post-Aristotelian philosophers, one by Western philosophers and the other by Averroes, who represents an older Arabic tradition.

The Stoics are reported to have described a proposition, which Aristotle would call "indefinite," as a "privative proposition,"[80] but it is not certain whether they meant it to be taken as an interpretation of Aristotle, or whether they meant it to be taken as a view of their own. So also in Hobbes *homo est non lapis*, which, according to Aristotle, should be described as an indefinite proposition, is described as a negative proposition,[81] but here, again, it is not certain whether this was meant to be in opposition to Aristotle, or whether it was meant to be an interpretation of Aristotle, or whether unknowingly Hobbes confused an indefinite proposition with a negative proposition. Quite certain it is, however, that the use by Kant of what he calls infinite judgment, such as "the soul is not-mortal,"[82] as the equivalent of Aristotle's negative judgment was not meant to be an interpretation of Aristotle, for what he calls negative judgment, such as "the soul is not mortal,"[83] is not used by him as the equivalent of Aristotle's negative judgment but rather as the equivalent of Aristotle's privative judgment. But I imagine it would be heretical to say that Kant unwittingly distorted an old logical distinction; it would be more canonical to say that he discovered an original profound logical distinction. In Averroes, however, Aristotle's indefinite propositions are presented without much ado as privative propositions. Thus commenting on the passage in *De Interpretatione* where Aristotle distinguishes between the negative proposition "man is not just" and the indefinite proposition "man is not-just," he adds: "When we say man is not just, the statement may apply both to a man who is wicked and to a man who is neither wicked nor just, that is, an uncivilized man or boy.

But when we say 'man is not-just,' the statement applies only to a man who is wicked, for our predicate 'not-just' signifies a privation, and privation is the remotion of a habit from a subject in which it would naturally exist at a time when it would naturally exist in it."[84]

But here Averroes and other Arabic writers, dealing with this type of proposition, hint at a certain difficulty which they try to solve in anticipation. The difficulty may be stated as follows. In Greek, the difference between a negative proposition and an indefinite proposition, as may be gathered from the examples used by Aristotle,[85] consists in the difference in the position of the negative particle in the proposition. In a negative proposition, such as *οὐκ ἔστι δίκαιος ἄνθρωπος*, the negative particle is placed before the copula, whereas in a privative proposition, such as the proposition *ἔστιν οὐ δίκαιοςἄνθρωπος*, the particle is placed before the predicate. This is all well and good in Greek, where the copula, with but a few exceptions, is always used. But in Arabic the copula is as a rule omitted. How then could the difference between the two kinds of propositions be expressed? Thus the three Arabic words *Zayd lā basīr*, "Zayd not seeing," may stand either for the negative proposition "Zayd is not seeing" or for the privative proposition "Zayd is not-seeing."

Here is the Latin text in which Averroes deals with the problem:

> Et earum sunt remotivae, et sunt illae, quarum praedicatum est nomen vel verbum imperfectum: sicut si dixerimus Socrates est non sanus: et hoc est in orationibus, quae non usitantur in lingua Arabum. . . . Vis autem nominum inperfectorum in idiomatibus, quae utuntur eis, est vis nominum privativorum, quia dictum nostrum non videns est in gradu dicti nostri caecus: et dictum nostrum non sanum est in gradu dicti nostri aegrum. Quoniam autem non fuerunt ista nomina in lingua Arabum, fuit dictio negationis apud eos ex dictionibus ambiguis, quia ipsi aliquando proferunt ipsam simpliciter, et volunt per eam rem privationis, et aliquando volunt per eam negationem absolutam. Et hoc est, quod cogit homines huius artis loqui per nomina remotiva, quia nos dum non cavemus ea, et imponemus eis istam impositionem, possible est quod erremus, et accipiamus quod est imperfectum loco negationis, et contra.[86]

And here is an English translation in which I put within parentheses Latin terms which I did not translate literally and within brackets explanatory comments which are not to be found in the Latin text underlying the translation:

"Some propositions are transposed (Latin: *remotivae*) and these are those propositions in which the predicate is an indefinite (Latin: *imperfectum*) noun or verb, as when we say, for instance, 'Socrates is [*non sanus*; Hebrew: *lo bari'* = Arabic: *lā ṣaḥīḥ*, used in the sense of] not-healthy.' This occurs in propositions which are not used in the Arabic language. . . . The force of indefinite (Latin: *imperfectorum*) terms in those languages in which they are used is the force of privative terms, for, when we say [*non videns*; Hebrew: *lo ro'eh* = Arabic: *lā baṣīr*, which consists of two words] 'not' and 'seeing' [it may mean 'not-seeing' and as such] it is of the same order as when we say 'blind,' and similarly, when we say [*non sanus*; Hebrew: *lo bari'* = Arabic: *lā ṣaḥīḥ*, which consists of two words] 'not' and 'healthy' (it may mean 'not-healthy' and as such] it is of the same order as when we say 'sick.' Inasmuch as these [indefinite] terms do not exist in the Arabic language, the negative particle [*lā*, 'not,' in the Arabic proposition *lā baṣīr*] is regarded by Arabic logicians as a sort of ambiguous particle, for sometimes they use it in an unrestricted sense [as, e.g., in the expression 'is not-seeing'] and mean thereby privation, and sometimes [they use it differently, as in the expression 'is not seeing'] when they mean thereby absolute negation. It is this consideration that has compelled men of this art [of Logic in the Arabic language] to speak of 'transposed terms' (Latin: *nomina remotiva*), for, if we are not careful about predicates preceded by a negative particle and do not think of the possibility that they may have two meanings, we may err and take some such predicate as indefinite [and hence as a privation], when it should be taken as a negation, and similarly the other way around."

Here is my exegetical supercommentary:

It will be noticed that in my English translation I have rendered the Latin *remotivae* by "transposed" and the Latin *imperfectum* by "indefinite." There is a good reason for these renderings.

Both these Latin terms are possible translations of the underlying Hebrew terms, (1) the Latin *remotivae* of the Hebrew *musarim*; (2) the Latin *imperfectum* of the Hebrew *bilti nishlam* or *bilti magi'a*. Since, however, the context requires that these two terms, or at least one of them, should reflect Aristotle's ἀόριστος, "indefinite," as used by him in *De Interpretatione*, I assumed that behind one of these terms, at least, there would be an Arabic term used as a translation of that Greek term of Aristotle. Fortunately the old Arabic translation of *De Interpretatione* is available in two printed editions.[87] There the Arabic for ἀόριστς is *ghayr muḥaṣṣal*, which would ordinarily mean "not caused to result," "not attained." Inasmuch as these are respectively the ordinary meanings of the Hebrew *bilti nishlam* and *bilti magi'a* underlying the Latin *imperfectum*, we may assume that the underlying Arabic of these Hebrew terms is *ghayr muḥaṣṣal*, which, as we have already seen from the Arabic translation of *De Interpretatione*, is the conventionalized Arabic rendering of the Greek ἀόριστος. On the basis of this I have substituted in my translation the English "indefinite" for the Latin *imperfectum*.

Since the Latin *imperfectum* proved to stand for the Arabic *ghayr muḥaṣṣal*, the other Latin term, *remotivae*, would have to stand for some other Arabic term. But what is that Arabic term? Here our search would have to start from the Hebrew term *musarim* of which Latin *remotivae* is a translation. And so I began to look for the term *musar* in Hebrew works which were translated from the Arabic and of which the Arabic was available in print. I could not find that word in any published Hebrew work of that type.[88] But I found it in a copy of an unpublished Hebrew translation of Algazali's *Maqāṣid al-Falāsifah*[89] in the library of the Jewish Theological Seminary.[90] There the Arabic underlying the Hebrew *musar* is *ma'dūlah*. Now the term *ma'dūlah*, as technically used in logical terminology, has been variously interpreted. John Hispalensis, of the twelfth century, in his Latin translation of Algazali's *Maqāṣid*, as may be gathered from a quotation in Prantl's *Geschichte der Logik* II² (1885), p. 273, n. 60, translated it *privativa*. But this cannot be connected etymologically with *ma'dūlah.* Horten in *Die spekulative und positive Theologie des Islams* (1912), p. 203, translates it *infinita.* This, too, cannot be connected etymologically with *ma'dūlah.* Goichon, in her *Lexique de la langue philosophique d'Ibn Sīnā* (1938), §411, translates it *equivalente.* This has an etymological connection with *ma'dūla,* for *ma'dūlah* comes from a word which means "to be equal," but there is no term in Greek philosophy meaning "equivalent" to be used in the sense in which the Arabic term seems to be used here in this context. What is needed here is a Greek term, underlying this Arabic term, which should have been used as an equivalent of the term ἀόριστος, "indefinite," as used by Aristotle in connection with the subject under discussion. So we went to look for such a term, and lo and behold! Alexander of Aphrodisias in his commentary on *Analytica Priora,* of which there existed an Arabic translation,[91] quotes Theophrastus as having used the expression πρότασις κατὰ μετάθεσιν,[92] "proposition by transposition," that is to say, a proposition in which the negative particle was transposed from a place before the copula to a place before the predicate, as the equivalent of the expression "indefinite proposition." All we needed now was to show how *ma'dūlah* could be used as a translation of κατὰ μετάθεσιν. This was easy, for the verb *'adal,* of which *ma'dūlah* is a passive participle, means not only "to be equal" but also "to deviate." Thus *ma'dūlah* means "deviated" and as such we may assume it was used in the sense of "transposed" as a translation of κατὰ μετάθεσιν. Similarly the Hebrew term *musarim,* of which the Latin translation is *remotivae,* may also mean "turned away" and hence "deviated" and "transposed." Moreover, another unpublished Hebrew translation of Algazali's *Maqāṣid,* of which, again, there is a copy in the library of the Jewish Theological Seminary, translates *ma'dūlah* by *noṭeh,*[93] "turning away," and hence "deviated" and "transposed."

Averroes must have had all this in the back of his mind. He thus speaks of "those languages" in which "indefinite terms" are used, that is to say, in which the copula is used, so that by position of the negative particle one could tell whether the proposition is negative or indefinite. And thus he speaks also of the

Arabic language in which "indefinite terms" are not used, so that there is no way of telling whether certain Arabic propositions are negative or indefinite. What languages he had in mind in his reference to those languages which use "indefinite terms" may be gathered from a parallel passage in Avicenna, which would seem to be the source of the passage of Averroes quoted above. In that parallel passage, Avicenna, after stating that in Arabic the copula is sometimes omitted, refers to "certain languages" in which the copula is always used, and of these languages he specifically mentions "Persian," a language which he knew and of which he quotes a sentence as an illustration.[94] The other language of the "languages" referred to by Avicenna was undoubtedly Greek, which he did not know, but about which, on this particular point there must have been a living tradition among students of Aristotle's *Organon*, with which he was acquainted. Accordingly, "those languages" referred to by Averroes, we may assume, are Greek and Persian, neither of which he knew.

In Arabic, then, there were two terms to designate what Aristotle calls "indefinite" propositions, (1) *ghayr muḥaṣṣal* and (2) *ma'dūlah*, the former being a translation of ἀόριστος used by Aristotle himself; the latter being a translation of κατὰ μετάθεσιν, quoted by Alexander from Theophrastus. The Arabs, as we may gather not only from the passage here of Averroes but also from passages of Avicenna[95] and Algazali,[96] adopted the term *ma'dūlah* as a description of the indefinite proposition. They must have followed Alfarabi who said that "propositions whose predicates are *ghayr muḥaṣṣalah* are called *ma'dūlāt*."[97] To those Arabic philosophers, a single word was preferable to a phrase. Moreover, the phrase *ghayr mūḥaṣṣal* merely told them that a proposition was "indefinite"; the term *ma'dūlah* told them how to recognize a proposition as "indefinite"; it is "indefinite" when it is "transposed." Thus, for instance, in such a proposition as *Zayd lā baṣīr*, literally consisting of three words, "Zayd not seeing," when the copula "is" is mentally supplied before "not," the proposition is negative; but when later it is mentally transposed to before "seeing" the proposition thereby becomes "indefinite."

This is what Averroes means by his statement in the latter part of his passage that "it is this consideration that has compelled men of this art [of logic in the Arabic language] to speak of transposed propositions," where he then goes on to explain in effect how by mentally transposing the mentally supplied copula one could tell that a proposition is "indefinite," that is, "privative," rather than "negative."

This, then, is an example of what is needed for an understanding of a text of Averroes, especially if one has only the Latin translation before him. No wonder that there were different opinions about the value of Averroes after his second revelation.

I have spoken of two revelations—revelations which took place at an interval of four hundred years. In 1931, about four hundred years after the second revelation of Averroes, there was a third revelation. It took place when our Academy adopted its plan for the publication of a *Corpus Commentariorum Averrois in Aristotelem.* There is, however, a difference between the third revelation and its two preceding ones. The first revelation involved translations only. The second revelation involved translations and printing only. The third revelation, as projected in the plan, involves three series of edited texts, each text in each of the three series equipped with three critical apparatuses and a quadrilingual glossary, and supplementary to all these a fourth series of translations with commentaries. The brief exegesis of the Latin passage in Averroes which I have acted out before you will explain why this third revelation of Averroes had to take this elaborate form.

In speaking of the first two revelations, I dealt with their achievements and their receptions. But I feel there must have been a story, a human story, behind the achievements, the story of Michael and Hermann and William and Frederick and Abraham de Balmes and Joannes Franciscus Burana and Jacob Mantinus and the Juntas and Cominus de Tridino. For we of the Academy know that there is a story, a human story, behind the volumes, so splendidly published in our *Corpus*—the story of scholars who, without the patronage of a Frederick, voluntarily gave up their evenings and week-ends, year after year, for the preparation of the thousands of minute items that make up the elaborate and complicated apparatuses and glossaries of their editions; the story of a provost and a dean of a university who allowed us the use of a certain fund under their care for the publication of certain volumes; the story of the president of a foundation who always came to our assistance when we had to meet the printer's bill; and the story of a business man who at a luncheon, after consulting with one of our editors on a matter on which he needed some advice, said: Now that you have done something for me, what can I do for you? And he did. He came just in the nick of time to enable us to publish one of our most expensive volumes. I hope that some future speaker at a future meeting of the Academy, perhaps at the celebration of the completion of the *Corpus* fifty years, or a hundred years, hence, in reporting on the achievement and the reception of this third revelation of Averroes, will also tell the story, the human story, behind the achievement.

POSTSCRIPT

After the original publication of this paper, I secured, through the courtesy of the Mediaeval Academy, a microfilm of the Munich manuscript of the Arabic text of the Epitome of the *Organon*. It verified all my conjectures as to the Arabic terms underlying the Hebrew, and hence also the Latin, translation.

NOTES

1. Cf. M. Bouyges, "Inventaire des textes arabes d'Averroès, *Mélanges de l'Université Saint-Joseph, Beyrouth*, VIII (1922), pp. 13 ff.
2. Cf. Steinschneider, *Die hebräischen Übersetzungen*, §§91–107.
3. Cf. H. A. Wolfson, "Averroes' Lost Treatise on the Prime Mover," *Hebrew Union College Annual*, XXII, 1 (1950–51), 683–710. Below, p. 402.
4. Cf. Steinschneider, "*Die europäischen Übersetzungen aus dem Arabischen*," *Sitzungsberichte d. Wiener Akademie*, CXL (1905), 1–84, under "Gerard von Cremona" (pp. 16 ff.) and "Johannes Hispalensis" (pp. 40 ff.).
5. *Ibid.*, under "Hermannus Alemannus" (pp. 32 f.) and "Michael Scotus" (pp. 55 ff.).
6. *Ibid.*, under "Wilhelmus de Lunis apud Neapolim," p. 80; G. Lacombe, *Aristoteles Latinus*, I, pp. 101–2, 207–10.

7. *Ibid.*, p. 79; *ibid.*, p. 104.

8. Cf. Renan, *Averroès et l' Averroïsme*, 2nd ed. (1861), pp. 205 ff.

9. *Il de Universo* II, 8 (*op.* 1574, p. 851, col. 2).

10. *Sum. Theol.* I, 3, 5 obj. 2.

11. *Inferno* IV, 144. The expression *gran commento* does not simply mean the Great or Long Commentary as distinguished from the "Middle" Commentary or "Epitome," for in the translations of that time these distinctions were not stressed.

12. Cf. *Giles of Rome: Errores Philosophorum*, edited by Josef Koch and translated by John O. Riedl (1944).

13. Cf. Wensinck, *The Muslim Creed*, pp. 94, 190.

14. Cf. my paper, "The Veracity of Scripture in Philo, Halevi, Maimonides, and Spinoza," *Alexander Marx Jubilee Volume* (1950), pp. 622 ff. and in my *Religious Philosophy* (1961), pp. 237 ff.

15. Quoted by Muhammad Ali in his *Translation of the Holy Quran* (Lahore, 1928), p. lxxv.

16. Mas'ūdī, *Les Prairies d'Or*, IV, 110–111 (texte et traduction par C. Barbier de Meynard, 1865).

17. "The Kalam Problem of Nonexistence and Saadia's Second Theory of Creation," *Jewish Quarterly Review*, N.S., XXXVI (1946), 371–391.

18. Quoted by Sale in a note to his translation of the Koran 41: 10.

19. *Faṣl al-Maqāl*, p. 13, ll. 6–7 and 11–12 (ed. M. I. Müller, under the title of *Philosophie und Theologie von Averroes*, 1859; German translation, 1875).

20. Cf. my paper, "The Meaning of *ex nihilo* in the Church Fathers, Arabic and Hebrew Philosophy and St. Thomas," *Mediaeval Studies in Honor of J. D. M. Ford* (1948) p. 358. Above, pages 207–221.

21. *Tahāfut al-Falāsifah* III (ed. Bouyges 1927), §2, p. 96, ll. 1–4 and III, §16, p. 102, l. 13 (English translation in *Averroes: Tahāfut al-Tahāfut*, by Simon van den Bergh (1954), pp. 87 and 96; also in *Al-Gahasali: Tahāfut al Tahāfut*, by Sabih Ahmad Kamali (Lahore, 1958), pp. 63 and 68.

22. *Ibid.* III, §§ 17–28, p. 103, l. 4–p. 109, l. 14 (English: van den Bergh, pp. 96, 97, 98–99, 99–100, 101, 102; Kamali, pp. 68–73).

23. *Tahāfut al-Tahāfut* III (ed. Bouyges, 1930), §§34–38, p. 162, l. 7–p. 165, l. 3 (English: van den Bergh, pp. 96–97, 97–98).

24. *Ibid.* III, §§23-24, p. 157, l. 11–p. 158, l. 12 (English: van den Bergh, pp. 93–94).

25. Cf. my *Philo.* I (1947), pp. 302–303, 324, and my paper, "The Platonic, Aristotelian, and Stoic Theories of Creation in Halevi and Maimonides," *Essays in Honour of Chief Rabbi, the Very Rev. Dr. J. H. Hertz* (1942), pp. 427–442. Above, pages 234–249.

26. Cf. *art. cit.* above (n. 19), p. 379.

27. *Adversus Hermogenem*, ch. 4.

28. Cf. *art. cit.* (above n. 20), pp. 357–358.

29. *De Divisione Naturae* III, 15 (Migne, *P.L.*, CXXII, 665–666).

30. *In XII Metaph.*, Comm. 18, p. 304f.

31. *Ibid.*, p. 305 f.

32. *In II Metaph.*, Text. 14, p. 34 I (Arabic *Tafsīr mā ba'd aṭ-ṭabi'at*, ed. Bouyges, 1938, p. 43, l. 1).

33. *Metaph.* II, 3, 995a, 4.

34. Comment 14 of the Latin translation under discussion is not a translation of the corresponding Comment 14 in the published Arabic text (pp. 43–44). It is an abridgement of it. But the term *nāmūsiyyah* occurs in the Arabic original (p. 43, l. 9).

35. The most likely source from which Schoolmen could have learned of the *Loquentes*' explanation of causality by "habit" (*consuetudo*) is the Latin translation of Maimonides' *Guide of the Perplexed* I, 73 (72), Propositions 6 and 10.

36. Cf. my paper, "Causality and Freedom in Descartes, Leibnitz, and Hume," *Freedom and Experience, Essays Presented to H. M. Kallen* (1947), pp. 108 ff. and in my *Religious Philosophy* (1961), pp. 196 ff.

37. *Tahāfut al-Tahāfut*, Phys. I (XVII), §5, p. 520, l. 9–p. 521, l. 2 (English p. 318).

38. Cf. n. 41, on p. 17, of Koch and Riedl's edition of *Errores Philosophorum*.

39. Arabic of Averroes, *In III Metaph.*, Text. 15, p. 247, l. 2.

40. Latin, *ibid.*, Text 15, p. 54 C.

41. *In XII Metaph.*, Comm. 18, p. 305 f.

42. *Ibid.*, p. 304 f.

43. *Deux seu Director dubitantium aut perplexorum* I, 70, fol. XXIX v, ll. 4–5 (Paris, 1520).

44. *Op. cit.*, n. 2 on pp. 104–105.

45. Cf. Renan, *op. cit.*, p. 317.

46. *Ibid.*, pp. 385–86.

47. Pierre Daniel Huet, *De Claris Interpretibus*, p. 185, which is the second part of his *De Interpretatione Libri Duo* (1860).

This quotation and also quotations in notes 48, 49, 50 below are from Pierre Bayle's *Dictionary Historical and Critical* (*Dictionnaire Historique et Critique*), I, 552–556 (London, 1734). The quotations as well as the references have been checked and, whenever necessary, revised. For this quotation see Bayle, p. 558, n. 83.

48. Cf. Bouyges, *op. cit.* (n. 1 above), p. 10, No. 5.

49. Cf. pp. 93–94 in my paper "Revised Plan for the Publication of a *CORPUS COMMENTARIORUM AVERROIS IN ARISTOTELEM*," *Speculum*, 38 (1963). Below, pages 430–452.

50. Joannes Ludovicus Vives, *De Causis Corruptarum Artium* V, 3, in *Opera Omnia*, VI (1785), 192 (Bayle, p. 552, n. 5).

51. Gerhard Johann Vossius, *De Philosophia et Philosophorum Sectis*, Liber II (1657), p. 90 (Bayle, p. 552 c).

52. Cf. Keckermann, *Systema Systematum*, Part I: *Recognita Logica*, Tract. II, Cap. 2, no. 32 (1613), p. 17 (Bayle, p. 558, n. 87).

53. Of the *Posterior Analytics* there are three Latin translations of the greater part of Book I and two translations of the rest of the work, all of them made from the Hebrew and all of them printed in parallel columns, taking up a volume of 568 folios in the Junta edition of 1574–75. The Arabic test is not extant.

54. This refers to Averroes' *Epitome of the Organon*, which contains Porphyry's *Isagoge* at the beginning and the *Rhetoric* and *Poetics* at the end.

55. This probably refers to Averroes' *Quaesita varia in Logica* and *Epistola Una*, translated from the Hebrew, which in the Junta edition follows the *Epitome in Libros Logicae Aristotelis*.

56. Cf. my *Crescas' Critique of Aristotle* (1929), p. 7.

57. *Categ.* 10, 12a, 31–33.

58. *De Interpret.* 10, 19b, 27–28.

59. *Ibid.*, 28.

60. *Ammonius De Interpretatione*, ed. A. Busse (1897), "Index Verborum," sub *πρότασις*.

61. Boethius on *De Interpretatione*, Secunda Editio III, c. 10 (ed. C. Meiser, II, 277–278).

62. Cf. *Alexander in Metaphysica*, ed. M. Hayduck (1891), p. 327, ll. 18–20.

63. *Categ.* 10, 12a, 27–34.

64. *Categ.* 10, 12a, 31–33.

65. *Eth. Nic.* VII, 7, 1149b, 31–32.

66. *Categ.* 10, 12a, 20–25.

67. *Anal. Post.* I, 2, 72a, 12–14.

68. *Metaph.*, IV, 7, 1011b, 23–24.

69. *Phys.* III, 5, 204a, 13–14; V, 2, 206b, 10–11; *Metaph.* XI, 10, 1066a, 36.

70. *Metaph.*, XIV, 2, 1089b, 35–36.

71. *Ibid.* V, 6, 1016b, 30.

72. *Ibid.*, V, 22, 1022b, 32–1023a, 4.

73. *Phys.* III, 2, 202a, 4–5.

74. Diogenes, VII, 70.

75. Boethius, *op. cit.*, Prima Editio, II, c. 10 (Vol. I, p. 133); Secunda Editio, III, c. 10 (Vol. II, p. 277).

76. Cf. *Philo*, II, pp. 111, 153–154, 158–160.

77. Cf. *Categ.* 10, 12a, 34, in *Organon Aristotelis in Versione Arabica Antiqua*, ed. Badawi, p. 41.

78. Book V, Text. et Comm. 27 (cf. above n. 32).

79. This will explain why in his *Epitome of the Metaphysics* Averroes uses Arabic terms reflecting Greek terms with alpha privative in senses which are only negations (cf. pp. 177–178 in my paper "Infinite and Privative Judgments in Aristotle, Averroes, and Kant," *Philosophy and Phenomenological Research*, 8 (1947).

80. Diogenes, VII, 69; οὐχὶ ἡμέρα ἐστίν.
81. *Opera Latina* (1839), I, 31.
82. *Logik*, §22; *Kr. d. rein. Vern.*[1], p. 70.
83. *Ibid.*
84. Middle Commentary on *De Interpretatione* (*Aristotelis Opera* [Venice, 1574], Vol. I, 1, p. 86 A): "Nam cum dicitur, homo non est iustus, verificatur de homine iniusto et de homine qui non est iniustus neque iustus, qui sive est incivilis vel puer. Sed cum dicitur, homo est non iustus, significat privationem. Privatio autem est ablatio rei ab aliquo, qui nata est inesse, tempore quo nata est in inesse ei."
85. *De Interpret.* 10, 19b, 27–28.
86. *Epitome of De Interpretatione* (*op. cit.*, Vol. I, 2, p. 41, I).
87. *Die Hermaneutik des Aristoteles*, ed. Isidor Pollak (Leipzig, 1913); *Organon Aristotelis*, ed. 'Abdurraḥman Badawi (Cairo, 1952).
88. Klatzkin's *Thesaurus Philosophicus Linguae Hebraicae*, under *musar* quotes only the passage of the *Epitome* here under discussion, and *musar* is translated there *privative*.
89. Cairo, n.d., p. 22, l. 17.
90. MS. Adler, 1015, p. 23a.
91. Cf. Steinschneider, *Die arabischen Übersetzungen aus dem Griechischen* (1897), p. 41.
92. *Alexander in Priora Analytica*, ed. M. Wallies (1883), p. 397, l. 2; cf. Prantl, *Geschichte der Logik*, I (1885), 357–358, nn. 30–33; Zeller, *Die Philosophie der Griechen*, II, 2² (1862), 158, n. 4.
93. MS. Adler, 131, p. 9b.
94. *Kitāb al-'Ishārāt wa'l-Tanbīhāt*, ed. J. Forget (1892), p. 27, l. 20–p. 28, l. 1. French translation: *Livre des Directives et Remarques* by A.-M. Goichon (1951), p. 127. Cf. also Algazali, *Maqāṣid*, p. 22, ll. 13–14, where reference is made to the use of the copula in Persian.
95. *Op. cit.*, p. 27, l. 9; p. 28, l. 9 (French, pp. 125 and 128).
96. *Op. cit.*, p. 22, l. 17.
97. *Alfarabi's Commentary on Aristotle's DE INTERPRETATIONE*, ed. W. Kutsch and S. Marrow, p. 106, l. 17.

20

AVERROES' LOST TREATISE ON THE PRIME MOVER

IN a list of works of Averroes reproduced by Renan from an Arabic manuscript there is mention of a « Treatise on the Prime Mover » (*Kalām lahu 'ala al-muḥarrik al-awwal*).[1] This work is not extant and nothing is known about it. But, as we shall see, I have found references to it in Averroes' Long Commentaries on *Analytica Posteriora* I, Com. 70,[2] and *Physica* VIII, Com. 3.[3] A refutation of that treatise, containing a general description of it, as well as paraphrases of arguments and at least one quotation, is also to be found in a work by Moses ben Joseph al-Lawi, which was written in Arabic and translated into Hebrew.[4] On the basis of this general description and the paraphrases and quotations,[5] with the help of parallel

1 Cf. Renan, *Averroès et l'Averroïsme*², p. 464, l. 13; cf. also Steinschneider, *Hebr. Übers.*, p. 181.

2 Quoted below in n. 25.

3 Quoted below in n. 29.

4 Concerning him, see Steinschneider, *op. cit.*, p. 410.

5 In the quotations from al-Lawi's treatise in this paper, I have followed the manuscript of the Hebrew translation in the Library of the Cathedral of Pamplona in Spain, without giving the variant readings in the Oxford and Leningrad manuscripts, with which years ago I collated the Pamplona manuscript. The Oxford and Leningrad manuscripts are mentioned in Steinschneider (*loc. cit.*). The Pamplona manuscript was first mentioned by Fritz Baer in *Die Juden im christlichen Spanien*, I (1929), p. XVII, n. The reference to this manuscript was brought to my attention by Prof. Alexander Marx and a photostatic copy of it was secured for me in 1931 by Prof. José M. Millás. The original Arabic

passages in the extant writings of Averroes,[6] we shall try to reconstruct the main outline and contents of that lost treatise.

Al-Lawi's general description of the treatise is contained in the following passage :

« Averroes has composed a treatise for the purpose of [1] refuting this method, in which treatise he censures its inventor, namely, Avicenna, and ridicules the method, and [2] argues in favor of the view that the first mover is identical with the Necessary Being. »[7]

The point at issue between Avicenna and Averroes referred to in this passage involves two problems, which, for the sake of simplicity, may be stated in reverse order from that given here by al-Lawi. Both Avicenna and Averroes, following Aristotle, believe that the spheres are each moved by an incorporeal substance which in their language is called Intelligence. The Intelligence which moves the outermost or first sphere is called

of this treatise was recently identified by Prof. Georges Vajda in a Vatican manuscript work by Joseph ben Abraham Ibn Waqār, of which a French translation entitled « Un Champion de l'Avicennisme » was published by him in *Revue Thomiste*, 1948, pp. 480-508. From that French translation it would seem that the Arabic text used by Ibn Waqār differed in a number of places from the Arabic text underlying the three manuscripts of the Hebrew translation.

6 The works of Averroes are cited in the notes of this paper by the following abbreviations :

TMBAT = *Tafsir ma ba‘d at-tabi‘at*, ed. M. Bouyges, Beyrouth, 1938-1948.

‘IMBAT = *‘Ilm ma ba‘d at-tabi‘at*, ed. Carlos Quiros Rodrigues, *Averroes compendio de metafisica*, with Spanish translation, 1919; German translations by Max Horten, *Die Metaphysik des Averroes*, 1912, and by S. van den Bergh, *Die Epitome der Metaphysik des Averroes*, 1924.

TAT = *Tahafot at-tahafot*, ed. M. Bouyges, Beyrouth, 1930.

Quotations from the Latin translations of Averroes are from *Aristotelis opera*, 10 vols., Venice, 1573-76.

7 וזה שאבו אלוליד הניח מאמר כונתו סתירת זה הדרך וגנה מוציאה, והוא אבו עלי, והלעיג עליה, וקיים שהמניע הראשון הוא מחוייב המציאות.

by both of them the « first mover. » But the point at issue between them is whether this first mover is God or not. Avicenna is of the opinion that this first mover is not God and that God is a being beyond it, whom he calls « The Necessary Being » (*wājib al-wujūd,*) [8] or « the First Principle » (*al-mabda' al-awwal*). In opposition to him, Averroes maintains that the first mover is God and hence identical with what Avicenna calls the Necessary Being or the First Principle. Connected with this difference between them, there is another difference. Avicenna, who does not identify the first mover with God, discards also Aristotle's physical proof from motion for the existence of a first mover as a proof for the existence of God. In its stead he has a proof from possibility and necessity, which he describes as a metaphysical proof. In opposition to him, again, Averroes maintains that Aristotle's proof from motion as given in the *Physics* is a proof for the existence of God. In the lost treatise, according to this passage of al-Lawi, these two problems are discussed by Averroes. First, he refutes Avicenna's proof for the existence of God. Second, he tries to show that the first mover is identical with God. [9]

In another passage, referring again to the two main divisions of Averroes' treatise, al-Lawi gives us some further details of the first division. To quote : « In that treatise of his, Averroes opens the discussion by (1) reproducing some of Avicenna's words on this problem. Then (2) he begins to refute him by saying that, even if the propositions used by Avicenna be granted, they would still not lead to the conclusion with

8 Literally « the Necessary of Existence », after the analogy of the scriptural expression « the Ancient of Days » (Dan. 7:13). Similarly, in the Latin translation of this phrase, namely, « necesse esse », the term « esse » is to be taken as a descriptive genitive and as the equivalent of « existentiae ».

9 Cf. analysis of this problem, with reference to Moses al-Lawi's treatise, in my paper « Notes on Proofs of the Existence of God in Jewish Philosophy », *Hebrew Union College Annual*, 1 (1924), pp. 590 ff. Below, pages 561–582.

regard to the thesis in question. And thereupon he undertakes to substantiate, to his own satisfaction, this statement of his. »[10]

In still another place he says :

« Furthermore, after having mentioned at the beginning that, even if the propositions used by Avicenna in this method be granted, they would not lead us to his conclusion with regard to the thesis in question, namely, the establishment of the Necessary Being, and after having finished what in his opinion was a substantiation of that statement of his, Averroes began to refute the propositions which were made use of in this method. »[11]

Besides these fragmentary outlines which furnish us with general headings of various topics, al-Lawi's treatise reproduces individual arguments under each of these headings and also supplies us with Averroes' concluding statement of his treatise. Bringing all these fragmentary outlines and individual arguments and conclusion together, we have the following outline of the structure of Averroes' lost Treatise on the Prime Mover.

A. Refutation of Avicenna's Proof for the Existence of God.
  1. Restatement of Avicenna's proof (Fragm. 1).
  2. Censure of Avicenna and ridicule of his proof (Fragm. 2).
  3. Formal fallacies of Avicenna's proof :
     (a) On the basis of his premises, even granting that they are true, he failed to show that his proof is metaphysical and not physical (Fragm. 3).
     (b) Again, on the basis of his premises, even granting that they are true, his proof is not a scientific demonstration (Fragm. 4).
  4. Material fallacy of Avicenna's proof : the defect in his premises (Fragm. 5).

B. Refutation of Avicenna's view that God is a being beyond the first mover.

10 Text quoted below in nn. 12 and 21.

11 Text quoted below in n. 46.

1. Criticism of the proposition that from one simple being only one simple being can proceed (Fragm. 6).
2. The assumption of a God beyond the first mover introduces a superfluity in nature (Fragm. 7).
3. The variety of objects of knowledge in the understanding of the first emanation is not sufficient to explain the plurality of beings that proceed from it (Fragm. 8).

C. Conclusion (Fragm. 9).

Fragment 1

« In that treatise of his Averroes opens the discussion by reproducing some of Avicenna's words on this problem ». [12]

Averroes' reproduction of « some of Avicenna's words » probably consisted of a brief summary of Avicenna's proof for the existence of God, such, for instance, as is given by Algazali in his *Tahāfut al-Falāsifah*. Averroes himself in his *Tahāfut al-Tahāfut* gives a nod of approval to this summary. [13] As summarized by Agazali, the proof reads as follows : « It is argued that every one of the individual causes [within the world] is either possible with reference to its own essence or necessary. Now, if each one of them were necessary, then it would not be in need of any cause. And if each of them is possible, then the universe as a whole is to be described as possible. But inasmuch as everything that is possible is in need of a cause superadded to its essence, it follows that the world as a whole is in need of a cause extraneous to itself. » [14]

Fragment 2

« He censures the inventor of this method, namely, Avicenna, and ridicules the method. » [15]

12 אבו אלוליד פתח אותו מאמר שלו באשר קיים קצת דברי אבו עלי בזאת השאלה. אחר כך לקח לסתור אותו ואמר עד שאלו קובל לאבו עלי ההקדמות אשר עשה לא הביאו לקיום הדרוש. אחר כך לקח לאמת זה כפי דעתו.

13 Cf. *TAT* IV, 27, p. 276, 11. 10-11.

14 *Tahāfut al-Falāsifah* IV, 11, p. 138, ll. 9-12.

15 Text quoted above in n. 7.

This statement, we take it, refers not to the general character of Averroes' criticism but rather to a specific passage in it. What that passage was, al-Lawi does not tell us. But from the nature of Averroes' references to Avicenna in his other works, where he speaks of « Avicenna and others » as those « who have perverted the view of men of divine science so that it became something fantastic »,[16] it may be inferred that his censure and ridicule here was similarly some statement to the effect that Avicenna misrepresented the views of Aristotle.

Fragment 3

« Then he begins to refute him by saying, that even if the propositions used by Avicenna be granted, they would still not lead to the conclusion with regard to the thesis in question. And thereupon he undertakes to substantiate, to his own satisfaction, this statement of his. He reproduces a certain difficulty raised by the Philosopher in Book Capital Alpha of his *Metaphysics*, namely, whether the principle of generated and perishable things is generated and perishable, or eternal.[17] For if it is generated and perishable, it undoubtedly must itself have a principle and the same must be said of that principle, and so on continuously. And if it is eternal, then that which comes into existence through it must likewise be eternal, and not generated and perishable as has been assumed,[18] for were

16 *TAT* III, 72, p. 182, ll. 4-5 : ابن سينا وغيره الذين غيروا مذهب القوم في العلم الالهي حتى صار ظنيا .

17 Cf. *Metaph.* III (B), 4, 1000b, 23-24. al-Lawi's reference here to « Book Capital Alpha » is probably an error. Or it may be explained on the ground that in the Arabic text used by him Book Capital Alpha included the first four chapters of Book Beta, for, in Arabic texts of the *Metaphysics,* Book I was designated as « Small Alpha » (cf. Steinschneider, *Heb. Über.*, p. 163) and « Capital Alpha » consequently came immediately before « Beta, » and thus it may have included the first four chapters of « Beta. »

18 Cf. *ibid.*, 1000b, 24-32, reproduced by Averroes in *'IMBAT* III. 28.

it not assumed to be eternal, there would be the question as to the reason why that which was generated from it was generated at one time rather than another.[19] He then says that this difficulty can be solved only by the fact established in physical science that it is the celestial body which is the cause of generation and corruption and that this body, though eternal, by reason of certain changes of position that occur in its parts, possesses certain changeable dispositions which have a temporal beginning, and it is in virtue of this that the celestial body, though in itself eternal, is the cause of generation and corruption.[20] This is the gist of his statement, even though we

19 This part of the argument is not found in the passage of the *Metaphysics* referred to in the preceding note. But it is found *'IMBAT* III, 29, where it reads as follows : « But he who does not believe in eternal motion will be unable to give a reason why the Creator, exalted be He, who is eternal, created the world after He had been uncreative. » ومن لم يقل بحركة دائمة لم يمكنهم ان يوفوا السبب فى كون البارى تعالى وهو ازلى فاعلا للعالو بعد ان لم يفعل .

This question is also raised by him in his *Kitab al-Kashf* (see below, n. 48), p. 30, ll. 10-12 : « Moreover, if the agent sometimes acts and at other times does not act, then there must be a cause which brings about its being in one of these conditions rather than in the other. »

In Aristotle, the same question is to be found in *De Caelo* I, 12, 283 a, 11-12 (cf. S. van den Bergh, *Die Epitome der Metaphysik des Averroes*, p. 217, n. 3 to p. 80).

20 In *'IMBAT* III, 28, after reproducing the same difficulty that is quoted here in the name of « the Philosopher, » Averroes similarly says : « This difficulty can be solved by what has been said in physical science with regard to the eternal motion of translation. » هذا الشك ينحل بما تبين فى العلم الطبيعى من امر حركة النقلة السرمدية .

By « the eternal motion of translation » he means the eternal circular motion of the celestial spheres. Then, after stating that the spheres are eternal and have no potentiality for destruction, he adds that, despite their eternity, they can be the cause of the transiency of things « on account of the interchange of positions which occurs to them, » . من جهة تبديل الاوضاع التى تعرض لها

have not quoted it verbatim ... [But, adds Averroes,] these beings, namely, the celestial bodies, which are assumed to constitute the proximate cause of generation and corruption, have themselves been shown to be eternal and the causes of generation and corruption only by arguments from physical science. Hence it necessarily follows that the metaphysician cannot prove the existence of the Necessary Being but must accept it from the physicist as granted or else he must compose a proof for it out of the combination of the two sciences. »[21]

What he means by « the variation of position » is explained in *De Gener. et Corr.* II, 10, 336b, 2-9, which passage is meant by his vague reference to « physical science ». The argument contained in that passage and referred to here in the Fragment, as restated by Averroes himself in his *Expositio Media in Libros de Generatione et Corruptione* II, Com. 56, f. 385 I K, reads as follows :

« The cause, therefore, of the continuity of primary generation and corruption is primary motion. The cause, however, of generation and corruption is the fact that the stars and the planets are in motion along that [inclined] circle, whereby they have diverse dispositions with reference to existing things, inasmuch as sometimes they approach and sometimes they retreat, on which account their action is diverse. It therefore follows that, if by retreatment their action destroys, by approachment it produces generation, for contrary effects demand contraries as their causes. »

« Causa ergo continuitatis primae generationis et corruptionis est primus motus. Causa autem generationis et corruptionis est quod moventur stellae et planetae in orbe isto, cum habeant dispositiones diversas entibus, quoniam aliquando approprinquant, aliquando removentur, quare est eorum diversa operatio. Oportet ergo, quod si per elongationem corrumpit, quod per approprinquationem generationem faciat, quia contrariorum contrariae causae. »

21 אחר כך לקח לסתור אותו מאמר עד שאלו קובל לאבו עלי ההקדמות אשר עשה שם לא הביאהו לקיום הדרוש. אחר כך לקח לאמת זה כפי דעתו. והביא ספק זכרו הפילוסוף במאמר האלף הגדולה מספר במה שאחר הטבע, והוא האם התחלת הדברים ההוים ונפסדים הוה נפסדת או נצחית. ואם הוא הוה נפסדת, הנה לה התחלה בלי ספק, ותשוב השאלה בזאת ההתחלה, וכן תמיד. ואם נצחית, חוייב שיהיה מה שימצא

The main point of this argument is to refute Avicenna's claim that his proof of the existence of God is a purely metaphysical proof and is independent of Aristotle's physical proof from motion for the existence of a prime mover. In order to refute this claim of Avicenna, he tries to show how Avicenna's proof of the existence of God must needs depend upon certain physical considerations.

The contention that Avicenna's proof is not purely metaphysical but depends upon motion occurs in several works of Averroes.

In his Long Commentary on the *Physics*, commenting on Aristotle's statement that, « as for the First Principle in respect of form, whether it is one or many and what it is or what they are, the accurate determination thereof is the task of the first philosophy, »[22] he says : « It is to be noted that the existence of that class of beings, namely, beings separated from matter, ought to be demonstrated only in this physical science, and he who says that the first philosophy is that which endeavors to demonstrate the existence of separate beings is in error, for these separate beings are the subjects of the first philosophy, but it has been shown in the *Analytica Posteriora* that it is impossible for any science to demonstrate the existence of its own subject but that it concedes its existence either as something which is self-evident or as something which has been demonstrated in another science. Therefore Avicenna erred exceedingly

ממנה נצחי גם כן, לא הוה נפסד כמו שהונח, ואם לא, למה נתחדש ממנה מה שהתחדש בעת בלתי עת. אמר וזה הספק לא יותר אלה במה שהתבאר בחכמה הטבעית מן שהגשם השמימיי הוא סבת ההויה וההפסד, וזה הגשם אף על פי שהוא נצחי הוא בעל ענינים מתחדשים מחודשים, וזה מצד מה שיקרה לחלקיו מהתחלף המצבים, כי בזה הצד היה סבה להויה ולהפסד, עעם היות עצמו נצחי. זהו ענין מאמרו ואם לא נקיים אותו בלשונו... [והוסיף עוד] שאלה הנמצאות אשר יונחו סבה קרובה להויה ולהפסד, והם הגשמים השמימיים, אמנם יתבאר שהם נצחיים ושהם סבות להויה ולהפסד בחכמה הטבעית. ויתחייב מזה שבעל החכמה האלהית אי אפשר לו קיום מחוייב המציאות, אבל ראוי שיקח זה קבלה מבעל החכמה הטבעית או שיערב באורו משתי החכמות יחדו.

22 *Phys.* I, 9, 192a, 34-36.

when he said that the metaphysician demonstrates the existence of the First Principle, in accordance with which, in his book on metaphysics, he proceeded [to prove the existence of God] by a method which he thought to be necessary and essential in that science and thereby has fallen into a manifest error. »[23]

The reference in the passage quoted is to that passage in the *Analytica Posteriora* which in the Arabic version reads, « It is plainly evident that no master of any art can demonstrate the proper principles of his own art. »[24] Commenting upon this, Averroes says : « That is, by an absolute demonstration which shows cause and existence. For the master of particular arts can demonstrate the causes of his own subject through signs, or *a posteriori,* just as Aristotle did in the *Physics,* where he demonstrated the existence of prime matter and the prime mover, but the only way by which he could demonstrate the existence of the prime mover was through a sign in that science, namely, physical science, and not as it was thought by Avicenna. Whence we have composed a special treatise to show the falsity of the universal method whereby Avicenna thought the metaphysician can prove the existence of a First Principle. »[25]

In another place, commenting on Aristotle's statement in the *Physics* which in the Arabic translation reads : « The

23 *Commentaria Magna in Libros Physicorum,* I, Com. 83, f. 47 FG; « Sed notandum est, quod istud genus entium, esse, scilicet separatum a materia, non debet declaratur nisi in hac scientia naturali. Et qui dicit quod prima philosophia nititur declarare entia separabilia esse, peccat. Haec nam entia sunt subiecta primae philosophiae et declaratus est in in Posterioribus Analyticis quod impossibile est aliquam scientiam declarare suum subiectum esse, sed concedit impsum esse, aut quia manifestum per se aut quia est demonstratum in alia scientia. Unde Avicenna peccavit maxime, cum dixit quod primus philosophus demonstrat primum principium esse et processit in hoc in suo libro de scientia divina per viam quam existimavit esse necessariam et essentialem in illa scientia et peccavit peccato manifesto. »

24 Cf. *Anal. Post.* I, 9, 76a, 16-17, and *Commentaria Magna,* Text. 70, f. 152 F.

25 *Ibid., Commentaria Magna,* Com. 70, f. 154 DF :

question as to what is the disposition of separable form and as to what it is, belongs to the first philosophy, » [26] he says : « The investigation concerning the dispositions of separable forms in so far as they are separable and concerning their essence belongs to the first philosophy and not to physical science. But it is to be noted that the investigation into the existence of these

de Balmes

Id est commonstratione simpliciter, id est commonstratione quae largiatur causam et esse. Artifex namque particularium artium potest demonstratione ostendere sui subiecti causas per signa, prout fecit Aristoteles in commonstrando primam materiam et primum moventem in Physicis Asculationibus, immo non est modus commonstrandi primum moventem esse, nisi per signum in hac, scilicet physica scientia, non sicut opinatus est Avicenna. Unde nos instituimus proprium tractatum in demonstrando corruptelam modi universalis, quo Avicenna putavit quod possit theologus demonstrare primum primum principium esse.

Burana

Intelligit monstratione sufficiente, hoc est monstratione exhibente causam et existentiam. Et hoc quoniam artifices scientiarum particularum possunt monstrare demonstrationem causarum subiecti sui per signa, quemadmodum fecit Aristoteles cum monstravit materiam primam in Auditu Naturali et motorem primum. Sed non est via, qua monstraret existentiam motoris primi, nisi per signum in hac scientia, hoc est in scientia naturali, non quemadmodum existimavit Ben Senae. Iam vero posuimus sermonem ad monstrandam corruptionem viae unisalis, quam opinatus est Ben Senae quod potest artifex scientiae divinae monstrare existentiam primi principij.

Mantinus

Hoc est demonstratione absoluta, quae scilicit praestet causam et esse. Nam possessor artium particularum bene potest demonstrare causas sui subiecti per signa, seu a posteriori, ut fecit Aristoteles in Libro Physicorum, ubi demonstrat materiam primam et primum movens. Sed non potest probare quod primum movens sit, nisi per signum a posteriori in hac scientia, scilicet naturali, non ut putat Avicenna. Nos vero iam edidimus tractatum, in quo probamus falsitatem illius methodi universalis, qua Avicenna putavit metaphysicum posse probare primum principium esse.

[26] Cf. *Phys.* II, 2, 194b, 14-15, and *Commentaria Magna*, Text. 26, f. 58 K).

forms belongs to physical science, and not to the first philosophy, as is fancied by Avicenna, for it is in this science that it becomes manifest that this class of forms do exist and it is only after their existence has been demonstrated that the first philosophy investigates into their essences and dispositions. »[27]

In still another place, commenting upon Aristotle's statement in the *Physics* to the effect that the question whether there is a beginning of motion is important « not only for the study of nature, but also for the investigation of the First Principle, » [28] he says : « For the metaphysician accepts the first moving principles from the physicist, and he has no way to demonstrate the existence of a first mover unless he accepts it as something well-known from the physicist. As for the opinion of Avicenna who thought that the metaphysician ought to demonstrate the existence of the First Principle, it is false and his method of proof, which he imagined to have invented himself, of which he has made use in his book. and in which he was followed by Algazali, is a feeble method and is in no way demonstrative. We, moreover, have composed a special treatise concerning this, and he who would like to learn the difficulties which occur in this method, let him consult the work of Algazali, for many things which he inveighs against others are true. » [29]

27 Cf. *ibid., Commentaria Magna,* Com. 26, f. 59 BC : « Consyderatio autem de dispositionibus formarum abstractarum, secundum quod sunt abstractae, et de quiditatibus earum, est proprie primae philosophiae, non scientiae naturalis. Et notandum quod consyderatio in esse istarum formarum est in scientia naturali, non in prima philosophia, sicut existimat Avicenna, quoniam in hac scientia apparet istud genus formarum esse. Deinde prima philosophia consyderat de quiditatibus et dispositionibus earum. »

28 Cf. *Phys.* VIII, 1, 251a, 5-8.

29 *Commentaria Magna in Libros Physicorum*, VIII, Com. 3, f. 340 EF: « Divinus nam accipit prima principia moventia a naturali, et nullam habet viam ad demonstrandum esse primum motorem, nisi accipiat ipsum pro constanti a naturali. Et quod existimavit Avicenna quod divinus debet

A similar statement occurs also in his Epitome of the *Metaphysics.* « The demonstrations which Avicenna makes use of in his metaphysics to establish the existence of the First Principle are all contentious (*jadaliyyah*) assertions, not altogether true, nor do they prove anything in an appropriate manner (*'ala al-taḫṣīṣ*) ... The metaphysician, therefore, as we have said, accepts the existence of the First Principle from physical science and discusses only the manner in which it is a mover, just as it is from mathematical astronomy that he accepts the number of principles which exist as movers of the spheres. »[30]

A discussion of the same problem, with reference to Avicenna, is to be found also in his Long Commentary on the *Metaphysics,* where he tries to interpret a passage quoted from Alexander of Aphrodisias. As in the passages quoted before from his other commentaries, he brings into play Aristotle's statement in *Analytica Posteriora* that « no master of any art can demonstrate the proper principles of his own art. » Again, as in those other passages, he maintains that this refers only to an attempt to demonstrate « according to the method of an absolute demonstration (*al-burhān al-muṭlaq*), but according to the method which proceeds from posterior propositions to prior propositions or that which is called signs (*al-dalā'il,* σημεῖα) it is possible to demonstrate them. »[31] Then, after indicating

monstrare primum principium esse, est falsum, et via eius, quam finxit ipsum invenisse eam, qua usus est in suo libro, et similiter Algazel sequens ipsum, est via tenuis et non est demonstrativa aliquo modo. Nos autem de hoc fecimus tractatum singularem super hoc, et qui voluerit accipere quaestiones accidentes in ea videat hoc ex libro Algazelis, plures enim quas induxit contra alios verae sunt. »

30 *'IMBAT* I, 8-9 : واما البيانات التى يستعملها ابن سينا فى بيان المبدا الاول فى هذا العلم فهى اقاويل جدلية غير صادقة بالكل وليسر تعطى شيئا على التدميص ... ولذلك يتسلم كما قلنا ماخب هذا العلم وجودوه عن العلم الطبيعى ويعطى الجهة التى بها يكون محركا كما يتسلم عدد وجود المحركين عن مناعة النجوم التعالمية.

31 *TMBAT, Lam* (XII), Com. 5, p. 1423, ll. 6-8 : على طريق البرهان

that Aristotle's proof for the existence of the First Mover is a proof from signs, he says : « And therefore it is impossible to prove the existence of a separable substance except from motion and the methods which have been thought to lead to the existence of the First Mover short of the method of motion are all persuasive [i.e., rhetorical] methods [32] ... But Avicenna... says that the physicist assumes the existence of nature as a hypothesis and that the metaphysician it is who demonstrates it by proof. » [33] Later Averroes remarks that it was a misunderstanding of that passage in Alexander that « has caused Avicenna to err. » [34] Still later, however, Averroes quotes another passage from Alexander in which a view like that later advanced by Avicenna is expressly stated. [35]

In his refutation of Avicenna's contention, Averroes reproduces, from the *Metaphysics*, Aristotle's question with regard to the transiency of sublunar things. The question is reproduced by him rather freely. He then refers to « physical science » as the place where an answer to this question is to be found. The reference is to the *De Generatione et Corruptione*. The answer to the question reproduced by him in this Fragment, in its phraseology, reflects his own commentary on that work of

المطلق واما على طريق المسير من المتاخرات الى المتقدمات وهى التى تسمّى الدلائل فيمكنه ذلك.

32 *Ibid.*, p. 1423, ll. 10-13 : ولذلك لا سبيل الى تبيين وجود جوهر مفارق الا من قبل الحركة والطرق التى يظن بها انها مفضية الى وجود المحرك الاول من غير طريق الحركة هى كلها طرق مقنعة.

33 *Ibid.*, p. 1423, l. 18-p. 1424, l. 2 : واما ابن سينا ... فقال ان صاحب العلم الطبيعى يضع وضعا ان الطبيعة موجودة وان صاحب العلم الالاهى هو الذى يبرهن وجودها.

34 *Ibid.*, p. 1426, l. 12 : وهو الذى غلط ابن سينا

35 *Ibid.*, Com. 6, p. 1429, ll. 1-3. German translation of this passage in J. Freudenthal, *Die durch Averroes erhaltenen Fragmente Alexanders zur Metaphysik des Aristoteles*, p. 74 ll. 13-20.

Aristotle as well as his discussion of that question in his Epitome of the *Metaphysics.*[35a]

The general drift of Averroes' refutation is clear. He wants to show that Avicenna's proof is not, as is claimed for it, purely metaphysical. The argument by which he tries to show this may be restated as follows. One of the essential elements in the conception of God as the Necessary Being is that, while God depends for His existence on nothing else, He is the cause of the existence of everything else, and consequently this is also one of the essential elements in his proof of the existence of God from possibility and necessity. Now among the things included in « everything else », of which God is conceived as being the cause, are also the sublunar transient things which come to be and pass away. Consequently, then, God, who is eternal, is the cause of the existence of these transient things. But here is a difficulty raised by Aristotle himself. How can a being who is eternal be the cause of transient things? The answer to this question, maintains Averroes, is to be found in the Aristotelian theory that the motion of sublunar bodies, though indirectly due to God, is directly due to the motion of the celestial spheres. For, maintains Aristotle, while the motion of these celestial spheres is eternal, within these celestial spheres there are stars and planets, and these stars and planets in the course of their motion sometimes approach sublunar things and sometimes retreat from them, and it is these approachments and retreatments which cause respectively the motions of generations and corruption in sublunar things. Now, continues Averroes, the eternity of the celestial bodies as well as their being, through their approachments and retreatments, the causes of generation and corruption in sublunar things is demonstrated in Aristotle by arguments taken from physics. Hence, he concludes, Avicenna's proof for the existence of God, even if based not exclusively on physical science, draws some of its propositions from that science.

35a Cf. quotations above in n. 20.

Fragment 4

« In the course of that argument Averroes mentioned that the method followed by Avicenna in the proof of the Necessary Being is similar to the method of the Mutakallimūn, by which he means that the propositions used therein are common and inappropriate propositions. »[36]

The charge that Avicenna's proof has its origin in the Kalām is found also in Averroes' *Tahāfut al-Tāhafut*, where, after referring to this method as being that of Alfarabi and Avicenna, he says : « This is a path which was not trod by the ancients and these two men have only followed therein the Mutakallimūn of our religion. »[37] Again : « This demonstration, which Algazali recites in the name of the philosophers, was first ascribed to philosophy by Avicenna on the ground that it was a better method than the methods of the ancients, for he thought that this method proceeded from the essence of being, whereas the methods of the others proceeded from accidents consequent to the First Principle. This method was taken by Avicenna from the Mutakallimūn. »[38] Similarly in his Long Commentary on the *Physics* he says that « the method

36 וזכר אבו אלוליד באותו מאמר שזה הדרך אשר הלך אבו עלי בקיום מחוייב המציאות ידמה דרך המדברים, ירצה שההקדמות הנעשות בו הקדמות כוללות בלתי מיוחסות.

37 *TAT* I, 93, p. 54, ll. 14-15 : وهو مسلك لم يسلكه المتقدمون وانما اتبع هذان الرجلان فيه المتكامين من اهل ملتنا.

38 *TAT* IV, 27, p. 276, ll. 1-4 : هذا البرهان الذى حكاه عن الفلاسفة اول من نقله الى الفلسفة ابن سينا على انه طريق خير من طريق القدماء لانه زعم انه من جوهر الموجود وان طرق القوم من اعراض تابعة المبدأ الاول. وهو طريق اخذه ابن سينا من المتكلمين.

Cf. quotations from Averroes on this subject in Shem-Tob Falaquera, *Moreh ha-Moreh* II, 1, pp. 76-77.

in which Avicenna proceeded in proving the existence of the First Principle is the method of the Mutakallimūn. »[39]

The additional statement here that the Avicennian proof which is of Kalām origin, is based upon « common » and « inappropriate » propositions, is an indirect way of saying that it is not a true scientific demonstration, for a true scientific demonstration, according to Aristotle, must be based upon premises which are appropriate (ἀρχαὶ οἰκεῖαι)[40] and not something common (κοινόν τε).[41] It reflects similar criticisms of Avicenna's proof found in several works of Averroes. Thus in his *Tahāfut al-Tahāfut,* Averroes says with regard to Avicenna's proof that « his argument is persuasive (*maqna'*), [i.e., rhetorical],[42] contentious (*jadaliyy*), and not demonstrative (*la burhāniyy*).[43] » So also in a passage quoted above from his Long Commentary on the *Physics,* he describes it as feeble (*tenuis*) and not demonstrative (*non demonstrativa*).[44] Similarly, in a passage also quoted above from the Epitome of the *Metaphysics,* he describes Avicenna's assertions as « contentious (*jadaliyyah*), as not being « altogether true, » and as not proving anything in an « appropriate manner » (*'ala altaḥṣiṣ*). »[45]

Fragment 5

« Moreover, after having mentioned at the beginning that, even if the propositions used by Avicenna in this method be

[39] *Commentaria Magna in Libros Physicorum,* II, Com. 22, f. 57 B: « Via autem, qua processit Avicenna in probando primum principium, est via loquentium ».

[40] Cf. *Anal. Post.* I, 2, 71b, 23; I, 9, 75b, 38.

[41] Cf. *ibid.* I, 9, 75b, 41.

[42] The Arabic *maqna'* is the Greek πιθανόν and hence it means also « rhetorical », according to the definition of rhetoric in *Rhet.* I, 2, 1355b, 26-27. Cf. *Crescas' Critique of Aristotle,* p. 397.

[43] *TAT* I, 93, p. 54, ll. 12-13: فهو قول مقنع جدلى لا برهانى.

[44] Cf. above n. 29.

[45] Cf. above n. 30.

admitted, they would still not lead to the conclusion with regard to the thesis in question, namely, the establishment of the Necessary Being, and after having finished what in his opinion was a substantiation of that statement of his, Averroes began to refute the propositions which were made use of in this method... He tries to show that our statement that whatever is necessary of existence by virtue of something else, that is, compulsory, is possible of existence by virtue of itself is a fictitious and false proposition. If the proposition is not fictitious and false, he says, one may wonder how a thing could be necessary of existence by virtue of something else, that is, compulsory, and at the same time also be possible of existence by virtue of itself. For as soon as a thing has received from something else compulsion with regard to its form, it can no longer be described as being possible of existence by virtue of itself [with regard to that form], inasmuch as for anything to be possible to exist implies that it is also possible for it not to exist, but the latter possibility cannot be harmonized with that which has been assumed to have come to it by compulsion from something else. This is the gist of his argument, even though we have not quoted it verbatim.» [46]

In this argument Averroes touches upon a fundamental distinction between him and Avicenna in the use of the term possible. Both of them agree that anything whose existence is not dependent upon anything else is to be called necessary of existence by its own essence. Such a being is God. But with

[46] עוד כי אבו אלוליד למה שזכר תחלה, שאפילו היו לו אלו ההקדמות הנעשות בזה הדרך, לא הביאונו אל הדרוש, והוא קיום מחוייב המציאות, והשלים לבאר זה כפי מחשבתו, והתחיל לסתור ההקדמות הנעשות בזה הדרך... וזה שהוא יאמת שאמרנו שכל מה שהוא מחוייב המציאות מזולתו, ר"ל הכרחי, הוא אפשרי המציאות מעצמותו, היה הקדמה דמיונית כוזבת. אמר, ואם לא, איך יהיה הדבר מחוייב המציאות מצד זולתו, ר"ל הכרחי, והוא עם זה אפשר המציאות מצד עצמו. וזה כי כשקבל ההכרחיות בצורתו מהזולת, נמנע שיתואר עם זה בשהוא אפשרי המציאות מעצמותו, כי אפשר שימצא יתחייב לו אפשר שלא ימצא, וזה לא יתקבץ עם מה שהתאמת לו מההכרחיות מצד הזולת. זהו ענין מאמרו, ואם לו נקיימנו בלשונו.

reference to all other beings whose existence depends upon some cause there is a difference of opinion between them. According to Avicenna, such things are to be called necessary by virtue of their cause but possible by virtue of their essence. According to Averroes, such things are to be called necessary (*wājib*, ἀναγκαῖος) in the sense of what Aristotle describes as compulsory (βίαιος, *ḍarūriyy*).[47] The term possible, according to him, is to be applied only to that which, not being yet in existence, may either come into existence or not come into existence, that is to say, whose coming into existence is neither necessary nor impossible. But once a thing has come into existence by some cause, that thing, according to him, has lost its nature as something possible and is to be described only as « necessary » or rather « compulsory. »

In his criticism of Avicenna here, therefore, Averroes pits his own view against that of Avicenna. Starting with his conception of the possible as that which, not having yet come into existence, may either come or not come into existence, he argues that, when a thing has already come into existence by some cause, it has thereby changed its nature and lost the possibility which it had previously possessed.

This argument occurs in several other works of Averroes. First, in his *Kitāb al-Kashf ʿan Manāhij al-Adillah fī ʿAqāʾid al-Millah*, after reproducing Avicenna's view with regard to things possible with respect to their own essence but necessary by reason of their cause, he criticizes it as follows : « This is a most erroneous assertion. That which is possible with respect to its essence and substance becomes necessary by reason of its cause only when its possible nature has been changed into a necessary nature. »[48]

47 Cf. *Metaph.* V, 5, 1015a, 28.

48 Cf. *Philosophie und Theologie von Averroes*, ed. M. J. Müller, p. 39, ll. 11-13 : وهذا قول فى غاية السقوط وذلك ان الممكن فى ذاته وفى جوهره ليمر يمكن ان يعود ضروريا من قبل فاعله الا لو انقلبت طبيعة الممكن الى طبيعة الضرورى.

Second, in his Long Commentary on the *Metaphysics,* he similarly argues : « That the same thing should with respect to its substance be possible of existence and yet should from something else receive necessity of existence is possible only when its nature has been changed. »[49]

Fragment 6

« In his endeavor to contradict this view and to prove that the First Principle is identical with the First Mover, Averroes starts out by showing that the First Principle is not the efficient cause of anything inferior to it but is its cause only by way of form. He supports this contention by the following argument. An efficient cause, he says, is that whose action depends upon its bringing about the transition of the object of its action from non-existence into existence, so that when the object has already passed into existence, the action of the efficient cause no longer depends upon it, for its action depends upon the object only during the latter's transition into existence. Now the process of generation is a finite change, for it is impossible for any generated object to be generated for an infinite time. Accordingly, the action of the efficient cause of such a generation must likewise be finite in respect to time.[50] But no finite action can be ascribed to an eternal being, seeing that an eternal being must exist forever in the same state of its final perfection and cannot therefore be active at one time and not active at another. As this argument establishes, in Averroes' opinion, that the First Principle cannot be an efficient cause, he sets out to refute the view of those who believe that the First Principle is not the same as the First

49 *TMBAT*, Lam (XII), Com. 41, p. 1632, ll. 5-7: لان الشيء الواحد لا يمكن ان يكون من قبل جوهره ممكن الوجود ويقبل من غيره الوجود الضروري الا لو امكن فيه ان ينقلب.

50 Cf. *Phys.* VIII, 10, 266a, 24-266b, 6.

Mover. Those who maintain this view, he says, find support for it in two propositions. First, that the First Principle is simple. Second, that from one cause there can follow only one effect. Now, with regard to the proposition which states that the First Principle is simple, Averroes concedes it to them. But with regard to the proposition which states that from one cause there can follow only one effect, Averroes, while also conceding it, does so only in the case of an efficient cause, that is to say, if an efficient cause is one and simple, that which follows from it must be likewise one and simple. In the case of a cause by way of form, however, he almost does not admit the proposition, namely, that, if such a cause is one and simple, its effect must also be one and simple. » [51]

In this passage Averroes tries to establish two points. First, the First Principle is not an efficient cause but only a formal cause. Second, since it is only a formal cause, it can be, despite its simplicity, the cause of many things, for the principle that from one simple cause only one simple effect can proceed applies only to an efficient cause.

The first point is discussed fully by Averroes both in his

[51] כי הוא למה שרצה לחלוק על זה הדעת ולקיים שההתחלה הראשונה הוא המניע הראשון, התחיל ראשונה וקיים שההתחלה הראשונה איננה סבה פועלת למה שלמטה ממנה, ואמנם הוא סבה לו על דרך הצורה. ונסמך בזה על זאת הטענה, והוא שהפועל הוא אשר תתלה פעולתו בהוצאת הפעול מההעדר אל המציאות, וכאשר יצא אל המציאות לא יתלה בו פעולת הפועל, ואמנם יתלה בו בעת צאתו אל המציאות. ולפי שהיתה ההויה שנוי בעל תכלית, כי אי אפשר שיתהוה ההוה זמן אין תכלית לו, היה פעולת הפועל בעל תכלית מזה הצד, והפעולה הבעלת תכלית אי אפשר שתיוחס לנצחי, כי הנצחי ימצא לעד על שלמותו האחרון, ואיננו אם כן פועל עת ובלתי פועל עת. ולמה שחוייב כפי דעתו מזאת הטענה שההתחלה הראשונה אינה סבה פועלת, לקח לבטל דעת מי שיחשוב שההתחלה הראשונה זולת המניע הראשון, ואמר שהאומרים זה הדעת נשענו בקיום סברתם זאת בשתי הקדמות. אחת מהם שההתחלה הראשונה פשוטה. והשנית שאמנם יתחייב מן העלה האחת עלול אחד. אמנם ההקדמה האומרת שההתחלה הראשונה פשוטה הנה הוא יודה אותה להם. ואמנם ההקדמה האומרת שאמנם יתחייב מהעלה האחת מציאות עלול אחד, הוא גם כן יודה אותה בעלה הפועלת לבד, ר״ל שהסבה הפועלת כשהיתה אחת פשוטה יהיה המתחייב ממנה אחד פשוט, ואמנם בעלה אשר על דרך הצורה כמעט שלא יודה זה, ר״ל שכשהיתה אחת פשוטה שיחוייב שיהיה עלולה אחת פשוטה.

Long Commentary on the *Metaphysics* and in his *Tahāfut al-Tahāfut.* In both these works he tries to show that the First Principle or God is not the creative nor the emanative cause of the world but rather its formal and final cause, in the sense that He is the cause of the unity and order in the world and that He moves the world as its object of understanding and desire. It is in this sense of His being the cause of the unity and order and motion of the world that He may also be called the cause of the existence of the world, that is, its efficient cause, inasmuch as the real existence of the world consists in its unity and order and motion. [52]

The second point is discussed by him directly in his Long Commentary on the *Metaphysics.* Referring to those, like Alfarabi and Avicenna, who from the premise that from one simple cause one simple effect must proceed inferred that God was above the mover of the outermost sphere, he says : « This discourse of theirs is sheer fancy, for in the case under consideration there are no processions (*ṣudūr*) and no consecution (*luzūm*) and no action (*fi'l*) to justify us in bringing into play against it the proposition that from one agent (*fā'il*) only one single action (*al-fi'l*) can follow. » [53] In the sequel he tries to show that the agent in this case is an agent only in the sense of its being a formal and final cause.

Similarly, in the Epitome of the *Metaphysics,* after stating the view of those whom he describes as « the later philosophers of Islam, as Alfarabi and others, » he says : « But there is the following difficulty. When we say that from one there can proceed only one, it is true of an efficient cause (*fā'il*) *qua* efficient cause only but not *qua* a formal cause (*ṣūrah*) or a

52 Cf. *TBMAT*, Lam (XII), Com. 44; *TAT* III, 53, 70-72, 79, 81.

53 *TMBAT*, Lam (XII), Com. 44, p. 1649. ll. 1-3 : وهذا القول هو موهم وذلك انه ليس هنالك صدور ولا لزوم ولا فعل حتى نقول ان الفعل الواحد يلزم ان يكون عن فاعل واحد.

final cause (*ghāyah*), seeing that formal and final causes are also called efficient causes by a certain kind of simile. »[54]

The phraseology in the passage just quoted from the Epitome of the *Metaphysics* will explain the use of the term « almost » by al-Lawi in the present Fragment. Probably in the original text of Averroes' lost treatise, just as in his Epitome of the *Metaphysics,* his statement read something to the effect that « the proposition was true of an efficient cause *qua* efficient cause only, but not of an efficient cause *qua* formal cause, » without saying outright that it was not true of a formal cause. In his paraphrase of this passage, therefore, al-Lawi says that in the case of a formal cause Averroes « almost does not admit the proposition, » the term « almost » having here the meaning of « virtually, » « practically, », or « indirectly. »

Fragment 7

« One of the most amazing things is Averroes' contention here to the effect that if we assume that the First Principle does not act essentially, that is to say, if we assume that the First Principle does not directly move any of the celestial bodies but acts by the intermediacy of that which is inferior to it, then the First Form would be without the action which is appropriate to it and the work of nature would thus be in vain.[55]

The criticism in this passage, as fully stated by Averroes in his Long Commentary on the *Metaphysics,* reads as follows :

54 *'IMBAT* IV, 60 : وفيه خلل وذلك ان قولنا الواحد لا يصدر عنه الا واحد هى صادقة فى الفاعل من حيث هو فاعل فقط لا من حيث هو صورة وغاية فان الصورة والغاية ايضا يقال فيها انها فاعلة بضرب من التشبيه .

55 ומן הדבר היותר נפלא מאמר אבו אלוליד הנה שאנחנו אם הנחנו שהעלה הראשונה אין לה בעצמותה פועל, ר"ל אם הנחנו שההתחלה הראשונה לא תניע דבר מן הגרמים השמימיים, ואמנם תפעל באמצעות מה שלמטה ממנה, היתה הצורה הראשונה שלולת פעולתה המיוחדת בה, ופעל הטבע לבטלה.

« As for the statement of recent philosophers that there is a prime substance who is prior to the mover of the universe, it is absurd, and for the following reason. Any one of these substances [i.e., Intelligences] is a principle of a sensible substance [i.e., a sphere] after the manner of a motive cause (*muḥarrik*) and of a final cause (*ghāyah*) and it is for this reason that Aristotle says that if there were any substances (i.e., Intelligences) which did not cause motion, their action would be in vain (*bāṭil*). »[56] The last statement is not a direct quotation from Aristotle, though Aristotle does say elsewhere in a general way that « nature does nothing in vain. »[57] It is meant to be a paraphrase and interpretation of Aristotle's contention that the number of the Intelligences cannot exceed number of the movements of the spheres.[58] Averroes' paraphrase and explanation of this contention of Aristotle evidently reflects the following paraphrase of the same passage by Themistius : « It is impossible that any divine substance or nature should be in vain (Hebrew : *baṭel*) and without any action, for any substance of that kind, by reason of its having attained to the perfection of everlasting life, is in the highest degree good and is incessant in that activity which is appropriate to it and which comes within the scope of its definition. »[59]

56 *TMBAT*, Lam (XII), Com. 44, p. 1648, 4-8 : واما ما قاله المتاخرون من ان هاهنا جوهرا اول هو اقدم من محرك الكل فهو قول باطل وذلك ان كل جوهر من هذه الجواهر فهو مبدا الجوهر المحسوس على انه محرك وعلى انه غاية ولذلك ما يقول ارسطو انه لو كانت هاهنا جواهر لا تحرك لكان فعلها باطلا .

57 *De Caelo* I, 4, 271a, 33. This is the reading of the text as was known to Averroes. Cf. my paper « Hallevi and Maimonides on Design, Chance, and Necessity », *Proceedings of the American Academy for Jewish Research*, 11 (1941), pp. 158 f.

58 Cf. *Metaph.* XII, 8, 1074a, 17-24.

59 *Themistius in Aristotelis Metaphysica* XII, ed. S. Landauer, Hebrew: p. 24, l. 31 — p. 25, l. 1 (Latin : p. 28, ll. 18-22) : ואי אפשר שיהיה עצם וטבע אלהי בטל אין פועל לו, כי כל עצם זה עניינו, הנה הוא טוב, לא יתרשל בפעולתו המיוחדת בו, הנכנסת בגדרו, על תכלית המעלה, אחר שהשיג בשלמות החיים התמידים.

Fragment 8

« Furthermore, Averroes raises here the following objection against those who say that the First Principle is not identical with the first mover. He says : 'Would that I knew whether that which the mover of the universe understands of the First Principle is a perfection to its essence or is not a perfection to it. If it is a perfection to it, how then could any action be conceived to proceed from it, without regard to the existence of that which is a perfection to it? For the relation of that perfection to it is like that of form to matter and the relation of its essence to the perfection is like that of matter to [form], and, consequently, just as there can be no action on the part of matter except by virtue of its form so there can be no action on the part of that first mover except by virtue of that which it understands of the First Principle.' This is a verbatim quotation of his statement. » [60]

By this argument, Averroes tries to show that if we assume the principle that from one simple being only one simple being can proceed is true, then the emanationists' explanation of the rise of plurality from unity is not a good explanation. For what is their explanation? They say that within the understanding of the first emanation there are two concepts, one in so far as it understands the First Principle and the other in so far as it understands its own essence and that from each of these two concepts there proceeds a different being, so that from the first emanation, who is one, there arise more than one emanation. But, argues Averroes, these two concepts are

60 עוד כי אבו אלוליד יקשה גם כן הנה על האומרים כי ההתחלה הראשונה בלתי המניע הראשון ויאמר מי יתן ואדע האם מה שישכיל מניע הכל מן ההתחלה הראשונה שלמות לעצמותו או איננו שלמות לו. ואם היה שלמות לו, איך יצוייר פועל מסודר ממנו מזולת השגחת מציאות זה השלמות לו, כי זה השלמות יחסו אליו יחס הצורה, ויחס עצמותו אליו יחס החמר, וכמו שמחוייב שלא ימצא פעל לחמר אלא מצד הצורה, כן מחוייב שלא נמצא פעל לזה המניע אלא מצד מה שישכילהו מן הראשון. זהו מאמרו בלשונו.

related to each other as matter and form, and, inasmuch as matter by itself without form is incapable of producing anything, one of the concepts, namely, that which is analogous to matter, cannot produce any being. In other words, the two concepts in the understanding of the first emanation constitute a unity and hence no plurality could emanate from it. Somewhat different is the argument against the duality of concepts within the understanding of the first emanation given by Averroes in his *Tahāfut al-Tahāfut*. Whereas here he contends that the essence of the first emanation and its knowledge of the First Principle are related to each other as matter to form, there he contends that its essence and its knowledge of the First Principle are identical. The passage in question reads as follows : « This, however, is an error according to the fundamental teachings of the philosophers, for according to their teachings the intellect in its act of understanding (*al-'āqil*) and the object of the intellect's understanding (*al-ma'qūl*) are one and the same thing in the case of the human intellect and how much more so must it be in the case of the separate Intelligences. »[61]

An allusion to this criticism may also be found in the Epithome of the *Metaphysics* in the sequel of the passage quoted above, in which a difficulty (*ḥalal*) is raised.[62] The sequel of that passage, according to the Madrid Arabic manuscript, reads as follows : « The thing that is especially to be determined here is whether in (*fī*) one simple thing more than one simple thing may be conceived (*yataṣawwaru*) and by that simple thing more than one thing attain its perfection. If this is impossible, then the difficulty (*al-mus'alah*) is real; if it is possible, the difficulty is not real. We have already discussed

61 *TAT* III, 68, p. 180, ll. 1-3 : وهذا خطأ على أصولهو لان العاقل والمعقول هو شيء واحد فى العقل الانسانى فضلا عن المقول المفارقة .

This passage is quoted by Narboni on *Moreh Nebukim* II, 22, p. 35, ll. 23-25.

62 Cf. above n. 54.

this in another place. »[63] Assuming that the reading of the Arabic manuscript is correct, then the difficulty referred to is like that discussed by him in the lost Treatise on the Prime Mover and in the *Tahāfut al-Tahāfut*, namely, the contention that the knowledge of its cause and the knowledge of its own essence do not constitute in the first emanation a duality of distinct elements. In the Hebrew translation from the Arabic, as well as in the Latin translation from the Hebrew, the reading of the first sentence in the preceding quotation is as follows : « The thing that is especially for us to determine here is whether from (*min*, ex) one simple thing more than one simple thing may proceed (*yesudar*, ordinetur), »[64] which quite evidently implies a different underlying Arabic text, where the reading was عن for فى and يصدر for يتصور. If this reading is assumed to be correct, then the passage is merely a restatement of the difficulty with regard to the distinction between an efficient cause and a formal or a final cause mentioned by him previously and quoted by us above.[65]

Fragment 9

« Averroes finally says that these matters are to be understood according to the manner which he himself has set forth and not according to the manner in which the common run of philosophers are in the habit of interpreting them ».[66]

63 *'IMBAT* IV, 60 : وانما المطاب الخاص بهذا ان يقال هل يمكن ان يتصور فى الشيء الواحد البسيط اكثر من شيء واحد ويستكمل به اكثر من شيء واحد فان امتنع هذا فالمسالة صحيحة فان جاز فالمسالة باطلة.

64 MS. Paris, Bibliothèque Nationale, Cod. Heb. 918, f. 145vl : ואמנם המבוקש המיוחד בזה שנאמר אם אפשר שיסודר מן הדבר האחד הפשוט יותר מדבר אחד. Cf. Latin, f. 393 D : « Sed quaesitum proprium huius rei est, ut dicamus utrum sit possibile, quod ex uno simplici ordinetur plusquam unum. »

65 Cf. above n. 54.

66 והוא יאמר שאלה הדברים יצטרך שיובנו על דרך שזכר, לא כמו שפשט בו מנהג המון הפילוסופים.

So also in his other works Averroes refers in a similar vein to the exponents of the view represented by Avicenna as « the later ones » (*al-mut' aḫḫirūm*) [67] and as « the later ones of the philosophers of Islam » (*al-muta' aḫḫirah min falāsifah al-islām*). [68]

In this paper we have collected the fragments of Averroes' lost Treatise on the Prime Mover, supplementing them with parallel texts from his other writings and also with brief explanatory comments. But the problems touched upon in these Fragments and parallel texts have, both historically and philosophically, much deeper roots and much wider ramifications. Some of these deeper and wider aspects of the problems are dealt with in an unpublished study, by the present writer, on mediaeval philosophy, in which this paper, as originally written, formed one of several appendices.

67 *TMBAT*, Lam (XII), Com. 44, p. 1648, l. 4.

68 *TAT* III, 56, p. 173, l. 7.

21

PLAN FOR THE PUBLICATION OF A *CORPUS COMMENTARIORUM AVERROIS IN ARISTOTELEM*

Averroes as a Naturalized Hebrew and Latin Author

Bibliographers, by the practice of their profession, will always list Averroes among Arabic authors. But if there is a process of naturalization in literature corresponding to that in citizenship, the writings of Averroes belong not so much to the language in which they were written as to the language into which they were translated and through which they exerted their influence upon the course of the world's philosophy. In the original Arabic the career of Averroism was brief. It came to an end with the abrupt disappearance of philosophic activity among the Arabic-speaking peoples, which synchronizes with the death of Averroes. Arabic philosophy, unlike Hebrew and Latin, did not enjoy a fruitful though declining old age. It was cut off in its prime through untoward political conditions. Among his own people Averroes left no disciples to continue his teachings nor an active opposition to keep them alive. His name, it has been pointed out by Renan, is not even mentioned in the standard Arabic works of biography.[1] Of his commentaries on Aristotle the longest and the most important ones are lost in the original language, and of those extant the number of manuscripts is very small and some of them are written in Hebrew characters and have been preserved by Jews. Most of the manuscripts in Arabic characters had been unknown until very recently, when they were dug up in oriental libraries.

NOTE. The original plan, submitted to the Medieval Academy of America, was published in Speculum, VI, 3 (July 1931). This plan is reprinted, with revisions, from Speculum, XXXVII, 1 (January 1963).

The tremendous influence which Averroes' commentaries on Aristotle had upon the history of Western philosophy was achieved through the Hebrew and Latin translations.

The earliest date of completion of a Hebrew translation of an Averroian commentary on Aristotle is 1232,[2] but it has been shown that some translations were made at an earlier date.[3] The latest date of the completion of a Hebrew translation of an Averroian commentary is 1337.[4] Between these two dates, almost all of Averroes' commentaries on Aristotle were translated into Hebrew, and four of the more important ones were translated twice. Ten translators are connected with this task: Jacob Anatolio, Jacob ben Machir Ibn Tibbon, Kalonymus ben Kalonymus, Moses ben Samuel Ibn Tibbon, Moses ben Solomon of Salon, Shem-Tob ben Isaac of Tortosa, Solomon Ibn Ayyub, Todros Todrosi, Zerahiah Gracian, and one whose name is not known. The bulk of the work, however, was done by Moses ben Samuel Ibn Tibbon (flourished between 1240 and 1283) and Kalonymus ben Kalonymus (1286– after 1328).

The popularity which these commentaries enjoyed among Jews is attested by the great number of manuscript copies that are extant to the present day—as, e.g., about twenty of the Epitome of the *Physics*, about eighteen of the Epitome of *De Caelo*, about thirty-six of the Middle Commentary on *De Caelo*, and about twenty-five of the Epitome of *Parva Naturalia*. The intensive study of these commentaries, which was pursued by individual scholars as well as by organized classes in schools, gave rise to critical and interpretative works which may be here referred to indiscriminately as supercommentaries. There are such supercommentaries on almost every commentary of Averroes, the only exceptions being the Epitomes of the *Metaphysics*, the Middle Commentary on *Meteorologica*, and all of the Long Commentaries. On some of the commentaries there is more than one supercommentary, as e.g., about a dozen each on the Middle Commentaries of the *Organon* and *Physics*, five on the Middle Commentary of *De Anima*, and four on the Middle Commentary of the *Metaphysics*. The writing of these supercommentaries continued for about three centuries, from the beginning of the fourteenth to about the end of the sixteenth. Some of the greatest names in Jewish philosophy are represented among the supercommentators, such as Narboni, Gersonides, and various members of the Shem-Tob family.

Besides these direct supercommentaries on Averroes, literary material relevant to the study of Averroes' teachings is to be found in almost every Hebrew philosophic text produced since the early part of the thirteenth century. Beginning with Samuel Ibn Tibbon's commentary on the *Book of Ecclesiastes,* to which a translation of some of Averroes' treatises on the Intellect is appended—and this before the first dated translation of a commentary of Averroes in 1232—there is not a book in Jewish philosophy in which the views of Averroes are not discussed or in which some passage of his writings is not quoted or paraphrased, analyzed, interpreted, and criticized. An example of the use made of the writings of Averroes by independent Hebrew authors and of its importance for the study of Averroes may be found in Crescas' *Or Adonai.*[5]

The first Latin translations of Averroian commentaries on Aristotle appeared in 1230,[6] but it has been suggested that they may have been made earlier.[7] Three names are connected with this activity, those of Michael Scot, Hermann the German, and William de Lunis. All of them flourished during the thirteenth century. Among them they translated fifteen (see below) out of the thirty-eight titles into which we shall divide all of Averroes' commentaries.

The incompleteness of the early Latin translations of Averroes, the loss of the original Arabic texts of his commentaries, the spurious views attributed to Averroes by the so-called Averroists, and the fact that Hebrew literature, through translations, had fallen heir to the entire tradition of Arabic philosophy—all this tended to make European scholars dependent upon Hebrew for a complete and accurate knowledge of Averroes. When, therefore, in the sixteenth century the translation of the works was resumed, all the new translations were made from the Hebrew. Of some works several translations were made; in some instances new translations were made from the Hebrew even when mediaeval translations from the Arabic were in existence. Moreover, his Middle Commentaries on the *Isagoge, Categories* and *De Interpretatione* were supplemented by translations of Gersonides' supercommentaries. The names of these new translators are Elias Cretensis (Elijah Delmedigo), Jacob Mantinus, Abraham de Balmes, Paul Israelita (Ricius or Riccius), Vital Nissus, and Giovanni Francisco Burana.

Inventory of Averroes' Commentaries

There is no authoritative contemporary record as to the number of commentaries written by Averroes. Whatever we know about it has been gathered by modern scholars, particularly Moritz Steinschneider,[8] Maurice Bouyges,[9] and Georges Lacombe,[10] from a study of the extant manuscripts and printed editions in the various languages, particularly Hebrew MSS. Averroes is known to have written his commentaries on all the works of Aristotle accessible to him, including also the *Isagoge* of Porphyry, which was treated by him as an inseparable introduction to Aristotle's *Categories*. In some instances his commentaries are found in three forms, the Epitome, the Middle, and the Long [11] the first of these not being really a commentary in the true sense of the term. In most instances, however, his commentaries are found in two forms, the Epitome and the Middle. In two instances there is only the Epitome and in one instance there is only the Middle.

The following is a complete list of Averroes' commentaries on Aristotle:

Organon

Epitome

1. *Isagoge*
2. *Categories*
3. *De Interpretatione*
4. *Prior Analytics*
5. *Posterior Analytics*
6. *Topics*
7. *Sophistic Elenchi*
8. *Rhetoric*
9. *Poetics*

Middle

10. *Isagoge*
11. *Categories*
12. *De Interpretatione*
13. *Prior Analytics*
14. *Posterior Analytics*
15. *Topics*
16. *Sophistic Elenchi*
17. *Rhetoric*
18. *Poetics*

Long

19. *Posterior Analytics*

Physics

20. Epitome
21. Middle

22. Long

De Caelo

23. Epitome
24. Middle
25. Long

De Generatione et Corruptione

26. Epitome
27. Middle

Meteorologica

28. Epitome
29. Middle

De Animalibus (including only *De Partibus Animalium* and *De Generatione Animalium*)

30. Epitome

De Anima

31. Epitome
32. Middle
33. Long

Parva Naturalia (including only *De Sensu et Sensibili, Memoria et Reminiscentia, De Somno et Vigilia,* and *De Longitudine et Brevitate Vitae*)

34. Epitome

Metaphysics

35. Epitome
36. Middle
37. Long

Nichomachean Ethics

38. Middle

The works of Bouyges, Steinschneider, and Lacombe may also be used as guides to the location of the Arabic, Hebrew, and Latin manuscripts and of the MSS of the Hebrew supercommentaries. Steinschneider has made use of almost all the public and private collections of Hebrew MSS known in his time. The only two collections which he seems to have left out are those of Spain and the Cambridge University Library. Since his time, however, many Hebrew MSS of Averroes have been acquired by Professor Alexander Marx for the Library of the Jewish Theological Seminary from sources unknown to Steinschneider. The Averroes manuscripts of the Joseph Almanzi Collection, which are recorded in Steinschneider's work, are now in Columbia University Library. Several manuscripts of Averroes commentaries are also in the Felix Friedmann Collection in Harvard University Library.

Certain translations and supercommentaries are given by Steinschneider as anonymous. In some instances he tries to identify them. It is not unlikely that when all the MSS are brought together and carefully studied, the identification of some of these anonymous works will become possible and some of Steinschneider's identifications may have to be revised. A few illustrations of what can be done in that direction may be found in the writer's paper, "Isaac ben Shem-Tob's Unknown Commentaries on the *Physics* and His Other Unknown Works," in *Freidus Memorial Volume* (1929), pp. 279–290, Samuel Kurland's paper, "An Unidentified Hebrew Translation of *De Generatione et Corruptione*," in *Proceedings of American Academy for Jewish Research*, v (1933–34), 69–76, and Appendices I and II at the end of this article.

Of the thirty-eight titles of Averroes' commentaries, twenty-eight are extant in the original Arabic. Of these fifteen are in Arabic characters, four both in Arabic and in Hebrew characters, and nine only in Hebrew characters.

Those in Arabic characters are:

Epitome
1. *Physics*
2. *De Caelo*
3. *De Generatione et Corruptione*
4. *Meteorologica*
5. *De Anima*
6. *Metaphysics*

Middle
7. *Categories*
8. *De Interpretatione*
9. *Prior Analytics*
10. *Posterior Analytics*
11. *Topics*
12. *Sophistic Elenchi*
13. *Rhetoric*
14. *Poetics*

Long
15. *Metaphysics*

Those both in Arabic and in Hebrew characters are:

Epitome
1. *Parva Naturalia*

Middle
2. *De Caelo*
3. *De Generatione et Corruptione*
4. *Meteorologica*

Those only in Hebrew characters are:

Epitome:
1. *Isagoge*
2. *Categories*
3. *De Interpretatione*
4. *Prior Analytics*
5. *Posterior Analytics*
6. *Topics*
7. *Sophistic Elenchi*
8. *Rhetoric*
9. *Poetics*
10. *De Anima*

At the time this Plan for the publication of a Corpus of Averroes' commentaries first appeared in the SPECULUM (July 1931), the following commentaries of Averroes in the original Arabic existed in print: (1) Middle Commentary on *Poetics,* by Fausto Lasinio (Pisa, 1872); (2) Epitome of *Metaphysics,* by Mustafa al-Kabbani (Cairo, without date, but at about 1904); (3) Epitome of *Metaphysics,* by Carlos Quiros Rodriguez (Madrid, 1919). To these, since that time, the following have been added: (1) Middle Commentary on *Categories,* by Maurice Bouyges (Beirut, 1932); (2) Long Commentary on *Metaphysics,* by Maurice Bouyges (Beirut, 1938–1948); (3) Epitomes of *Physics, De Caelo, De Generatione et Corruptione, Meteorologica, De Anima,* and *Metaphysics* (Hyderabad, 1366: 1947); (4) Epitome of *De Anima,* by Ahmed Fouad El Ahwani (Cairo, 1950); (5) Epitome of *Parva Naturalia,* by 'Abdurraḥmān Badawi (Cairo, 1954); (6) Middle Commentary on *Rhetoric,* 'Abdurraḥmān Badawi (Cairo, 1960); (7) Epitome of *Parva Naturalia,* by Helmut Gätje (Wiesbaden, 1961).

Hebrew translations from the Arabic are extant of thirty-six out of the thirty-eight commentaries. Those missing are the Long Commentary on *De Caelo* and the Long Commentary on *De Anima,* of neither of which is there the Arabic original; there are only Latin translations made from the Arabic. Whether no Hebrew translation of these two commentaries ever existed or whether they were lost cannot be ascertained. With regard to the Long Commentary on *De Anima,* the question will be discussed below in Appendix I. There is, however, an anonymous Hebrew translation of the Long Commentary on *De Anima* made from the Latin. The identity of the translator will be discussed below in Appendix II.

Out of these thirty-six commentaries of Averroes in Hebrew translation the following existed in print at the time this Plan first appeared in SPECULUM (July 1931): (1) Epitome of the *Organon* (Riva di Trento, 1559); (2) Epitome of *Physics* (Riva di Trento, 1560); (3) Middle Commentary on *Rhetoric,* by J. Goldenthal (Leipzig, 1842); (3) Middle Commentary on *Poetics,* by Fausto Lasinio (Pisa, 1872).

Fifteen out of the thirty-eight commentaries were translated into Latin during the thirteenth century directly from the Arabic. They are:

Epitome
1. *Parva Naturalia*
by Michael Scot
Middle
2. *Isagoge*
3. *Categories*
4. *De Interpretatione*
5. *Prior Analytics*
6. *Posterior Analytics*
by William of Luna
7. *Rhetoric*
8. *Poetics*
9. *Nicomachean Ethics*
by Hermann the German
10. *De Generatione et Corruptione*
11. *Meteorologica*
by Michael Scot
Long
12. *Physics*
13. *De Caelo*
14. *De Anima*
15. *Metaphysics*
by Michael Scot, except for the Prooemium to the *Physics,* which is by Theodorous Antiochenus

Nineteen were translated during the sixteenth century from the Hebrew. The four of which there are no Latin translations are: (1) Epitome of *Physics,* (2) Epitome of *De Caelo,* (3) Epitome of *De Anima,* (4) Middle Commentary on *De Anima.*

The list below contains: (1) all the Latin translations of Averroes' commentaries in the 1575 edition by the Juntas, (2) those in the 1560 edition by Cominus de Tridino which are not in the aforementioned 1575 edition, (3) those in the 1483 edition by Andreas Torresanus de Asula et Bartholomaeus de Blavis which are not in the aforementioned 1560 edition, and (4) those which are only in the 1481 edition of the *Rhetoric* and *Poetics* by Philipus Venetus. Names marked by asterisks are those of mediaeval translators from the Arabic; all the others are names of sixteenth-century translators from the Hebrew.

Organon
Epitome
1. *Isagoge*
2. *Categories*
3. *De Interpretatione*
4. *Prior Analytics*
5. *Posterior Analytics*
6. *Topics*
7. *Sophistic Elenchi*
8. *Rhetoric*

9. *Poetics*
   Nos. 1–9, by Balmes in 1575, of which 1–7 are in Vol. I, ii, and 8–9 in Vol. II, 192D–197.
   No. 4, by Burana, in Vol. I of 1560.

Middle
10. *Isagoge*
11. *Categories*
12. *De Interpretatione*
13. *Prior Analytics*
14. *Posterior Analytics*
15. *Topics*
16. *Sophistic Elenchi*
17. *Rhetoric*
18. *Poetics*
   Nos. 10–12, by Mantinus, in Vol. I of 1575; by *William, in Vol. I of 1560.
   Nos. 13–14, by Burana, in Vol. I, i–ii, of 1575; by *William, in Vol. I, i, of 1483.
   No. 15, by (a) Balmes and by (b) Mantinus, the latter only Books I–IV, both in Vol. I, iii, of 1575.
   No. 16, by Balmes, in Vol. I, iii, of 1575.
   No. 17, by Balmes, in Vol. II of 1575.
   No. 18, by Mantinus in Vol. II of 1575; by Balmes, in Vol. III of 1560; by *Hermann, in 1481.

Long
19. Posterior Analytics
   By (a) Balmes, by (b) Burana, and by (c) Mantinus, the last only Book I, 1, 71a, 1–22, 830b, 10, all in Vol. I, ii, of 1575.

Physics
20. Middle
   By (a) Mantinus, only Books I–III, in Vol. IV of 1575; by (b) Vitalis Dactylomelos, extant only in manuscript (cf. Renan, *Averroes,*[2] p. 382; Steinschneider, *Hebr. Uebers,* p. 986).
21. Long
   By *Michael, minus Prooemium, which was translated by (a) *Thedorus Antiochenus and by

(b) Mantinus, all in Vol. IV of 1575.

De Caelo

22. Middle

By Paulus Israelita, in Vol. V of 1575.

23. Long

By *Michael, in Vol. V of 1575.

De Generatione et Corruptione

24. Epitome

By Vitalis Nisus, in Vol. V of 1575.

25. Middle

By *Michael, in Vol. V of 1575.

Meteorologica

26. Epitome

By Elias Cretensis (Elijah Delmedigo), in Vol. V of 1575.

27. Middle

By Elias Cretensis, only portions of Books I–III; dispersed and embodied in the Epitome; in Vol. V of 1575.

By *Michael, only Book IV, in Vol. V of 1575.

De Animalium (including only *De Partibus Animalium and De Generatione Animalium*)

28. Epitome

By Mantinus, in Vol. VI, i–ii, of 1575.

De Anima

29. Long

By (a) *Michael, but comments 5 and 36 in Book III also by (b) Mantinus, both in Vol. VI, i, of 1575.

Parva Naturalia (including only *De Sensu et Sensibili, Memoria et Reminiscentia, De Somno et Vigilio,* and *De Longitudine et Brevitate Vitae*)

30. Epitome

By *Michael, in Vol. VIII of 1575.

Metaphysics

31. Epitome

By Mantinus, in Vol. VIII of 1575.

32. Middle

By Elias Cretensis, only Books I–VII, in Vol. VIII of 1560.

33. Long

By *Michael, minus Prooemium to Book XII, which is by (a) Paulus Israelita and by (b) Mantinus, all in Vol.

Vol. VIII of 1575.	By *Hermann, in
Nicomachean Ethics	Vol. III of 1575.
34. Middle	

The result of this inventory is that of the thirty-eight commentaries twenty-eight are extant in the original Arabic, and of these fifteen are in Arabic characters, four are both in Arabic and in Hebrew characters, and nine are only in Hebrew characters. Hebrew translations from the Arabic exist of thirty-six out of the thirty-eight commentaries, the two missing are also missing in the Arabic, and of one of the two missing there is a translation from the Latin. Latin translations exist of thirty-four out of the thirty-eight commentaries, and of these fifteen are mediaeval translations made directly from the Arabic, including the two which are missing both in Arabic and in Hebrew; the remaining nineteen are sixteenth-century translations made from the Hebrew. Of these nineteen translated from the Hebrew four were translated two times, one was translated three times, and six were new translations of commentaries of which there had already existed mediaeval Latin translations directly from the Arabic. In addition to Latin translations from the Hebrew of whole commentaries, there are (a) two Latin translations from the Hebrew of Averroes' own Prooemium to one of his Long Commentaries, which was missing in the mediaeval Latin translations from the original Arabic of that commentary; (b) a new Latin translation from the Hebrew of two Comments in a Long Commentary of which a Latin translation from the Arabic already existed in the mediaeval Latin translation of that commentary.

THE PROJECT

The facts brought out in the Inventory convince one beyond any doubt that the publication of a complete and properly edited corpus of Averroes' Commentaries in only one of the three languages is almost impossible. Both the Arabic and the Latin are dependent upon the Hebrew for the filling out of their respective lacunae. All of them—the Arabic, the Hebrew, and the Latin—are dependent upon each other for the establishment of accurate texts—unless we think that the Arabic, Hebrew, and Latin texts can be established independently of each other by merely counting the scribal errors in their respective manuscripts and adding to them some conjectural emendations. Furthermore, the Arabic, the Hebrew, and the Latin are in need of each other for the determination of the exact meaning of words and phrases and in general for the proper study of the text. Without such reciprocal help, the corpus would be only an additional shelf of unintelligible volumes, for the knowledge of Averroes' commentaries expired among the Arabic-speaking peoples with the death of the author at the end of the twelfth century, and among readers of Hebrew and Latin it has lingered only among a few of the initiate since the seventeenth century. Finally, no proper study of the commentaries of Averroes is possible without the help of the Hebrew supercommentaries. Not only do these supercommentaries contain all the important critical, historical, and interpretative material necessary for the study of the subject matter of the commentaries, but owing to their inclusion of great portions of the commentaries in the form of quotations, they are also valuable for the establishment of the text.

The object of the plan, therefore, is to prepare an edition of the commentaries of Averroes simultaneously in the three languages—the language in which they were originally written, the language in which they have been most thoroughly expounded and most completely preserved, and in the language through which they became known to Western philosophy. The edition, furthermore, is to be equipped with all the necessary textual and philological information that may be helpful to anyone who may wish to study these commentaries in their manifold bearings upon the various phases of the history of philosophy.

The method to be followed in editing the work can best be described by showing what critical apparatus, glossaries, and other equipments the edited volumes are expected to have.

CRITICAL APPARATUS

Each of the texts in the three languages is expected to have three critical apparatuses, which may be designated as *A*, *B*, *C*.

Apparatus *A* is to contain the variant readings of the MSS of a given text in one of the three languages. This Apparatus will naturally differ in the three texts, though occasionally the variant readings in the text of one language may be found to have some bearing upon the variant readings of the text of another language, in which case they will be recorded in more than one text.

Apparatus *B* is to show the relation between the Arabic, Hebrew, and Latin texts. This apparatus will be divided into two parts, each part containing translations of the variant readings in the text of one of the other two languages into the language of the text that is being edited. Thus, for instance, in the edition of a Latin text, Apparatus *B* will be subdivided into Latin-Arabic and Latin-Hebrew.

Apparatus *C* is to show the relation of Aristotelian passages contained in Averroes' commentaries to their corresponding Greek texts. Such an Apparatus will be necessary because of the occurrence of Aristotelian passages, in some form or other, in every one of the three series of commentaries. In the Long Commentary the Aristotelian text is given *in extenso* and is on the whole distinguishable from the commentary proper. In the Middle Commentary the Aristotelian texts are either reproduced verbally or given in paraphrase form. Though quotations and paraphrases of Aristotle are supposed to be introduced by the word "dixit," still it is not always possible to distinguish them from the rest of the commentary. In the Epitome, quotations and paraphrases of Aristotle occur only casually. In preparation of this Apparatus, it will be necessary to compare the commentaries with the original works of Aristotle, to mark off, first, all the passages that are supposed to be translations of Aristotle, and, second, all the passages that are supposed to be paraphrases of Aristotle, and then, to mark these two off from each other and both of them from the commentary. The passages which are either translations or paraphrases of Aristotle are to be compared with the original Greek, word for word and phrase for phrase, and the differences discovered are to be recorded in Apparatus *C*.

While these three Apparatuses are to be kept distinct from each other, certain elements may have to be transferred from one Apparatus to another.

TYPOGRAPHICAL DISPOSITION OF TEXT

In printing, the three strata of the text, viz., (1) translations of Aristotle, (2) paraphrases of Aristotle, and (3) Averroes' own comments, are to be indicated by the use of different type or by a difference in spacing between letters or between lines.

REFERENCES TO SOURCES

Not many sources are mentioned by Averroes. But occasionally he refers to works of Aristotle, to some other place in his own commentaries, to Greek commentators of Aristotle, such as Alexander and Themistius, and to earlier Arabic authors, such as Alfarabi, Avicenna, and Avempace. In all such instances the sources are to be identified and whenever a printed edition or manuscript of the source in question exists, proper references are to be supplied.

GLOSSARIES

Each commentary is to have at the end a glossary in four languages, arranged as follows: (1) For the Arabic—Arabic, Hebrew, Latin, Greek. (2) For the Hebrew—Hebrew, Arabic, Latin, Greek. (3) For the Latin—Latin, Arabic, Hebrew, Greek. But in order to make the work also useful to the student of Aristotle, there should be a fourth glossary—Greek, Arabic, Hebrew, Latin, to be printed together with each text of the commentary.

ORGANIZATION OF STAFF

In order to carry out the work effectively it is necessary to have a staff organized along the following lines: (1) Editor-in-Chief, selected from among the (2) Board of Editors, consisting of the following three members: Editor of the Arabic Series, Editor of the Hebrew Series, Editor of the Latin Series; (3) Advisory Board; (4) Editors of the individual works.

While in some cases it may be possible for one editor to edit the same work in the three languages, it is on the whole advisable to have an Arabist, a Hebraist, and a Latinist associated with the edition of any commentary which exists in the three languages. Among the three editors, however, there must be one who has a knowledge of the three languages, so that he may be able to co-ordinate the work on all three texts. It is the belief of the writer that there will be no difficulty in getting properly qualified men in sufficient number to carry out the program as laid out.

PUBLICATION

The polyglot form, with the three texts printed one beside the other or one below the other, would perhaps be most ideal for the publication of this corpus. But practical considerations may make such a plan impossible. Besides, there is nothing tangible to be gained by it. The various apparatuses and glossaries will furnish to the student of any single one of the texts all the information that he may gather from the other two texts. Those few who are able to use themselves all the three texts will find it just as easy to handle three monoglot volumes as one polyglot one.

Consequently, while the editing of the texts must be done simultaneously in the three languages by editors working in association with each other, the publication of the texts may be treated, if necessary, as three independent undertakings. There will be three series of texts and a series of translations and studies:

A. The Arabic Series
B. The Hebrew Series
C. The Latin Series
D. Translations and Studies

Whenever the Hebrew or the Latin possesses several translations of the same text, all the translations are to be printed, either one or all of them critically edited, as the case may require.

A special subdivision of the Hebrew Series will be supercommentaries on Averroes. These will have to be considered as an integral part of the Corpus. Similarly, the Latin Series will have to include the Annotations of Zimara and others as well as the Latin translations of the Hebrew supercommentaries of Gersonides.

While the present plan contemplates an edition of only the commentaries of Averroes, which is to include his *Quaestiones* to the various books of Aristotle, it may be extended to include also the publication of the other works of Averroes and of the works of other Arabic and Jewish philosophers, which happen to exist in Arabic, Hebrew, and Latin.

As the Corpus is to be something more than a mere collection of texts, it should also have room for annotated translations into modern languages of selected commentaries of Averroes and for monographs dealing with certain phases of Averroes' philosophy. The scholars who will be entrusted with the editing of the texts as well as other competent scholars are therefore to be encouraged to undertake translations or independent studies of the works included in the Corpus. Such works are to form a Fourth Series of the Corpus.

APPENDIX I

Was There a Hebrew Translation from the Arabic of Averroes' Long *De Anima?*

STEINSCHNEIDER in his *Hebraeische Uebersetzungen* offered evidence to show that there had existed a Hebrew translation from the Arabic of Averroes' Long Commentary on *De Anima*. We shall examine his evidence.

First, in the Bodleian Library (Neubauer 1353.6) there is a supercommentary by Joseph b. Shem-ṭob on the section dealing with the rational faculty in one of Averroes' commentaries on Aristotle's *De Anima*. The manuscript contains no statement as to which of the three Averroes' commentaries on that work is the subject of the supercommentary. Neubauer in his catalogue of the Bodleian Hebrew manuscripts (1886) simply says "according to Averroes' paraphrase," where the term "paraphrase" is evidently used by him, as it is throughout the catalogue, in the sense of Epitome. Steinschneider in his *Hebraeische Uebersetzungen* (1893) takes it to be the Long Commentary (§ 73, p. 150), on the basis of which he tries to show that in the latter part of the fifteenth century there was still in existence a Hebrew translation from the Arabic of the Long *De Anima,* for at the end of his preface Joseph b. Shem-ṭob promises to write a super commentary on the whole book.

However, on the basis of the incipits quoted by Steinschneider himself (*op. cit.*, nn. 725–730 on pp. 207–208) it can be shown that the commentary used as the subject of the supercommentary here is the Middle Commentary. According to these incipits, the supercommentary is described as a "Treatise on the Rational Faculty." It then begins with a passage which is introduced by the Hebrew word for "He says." Then follows a comment on the foregoing passage, which is introduced by the Hebrew word for "Commentary." Then follows another passage introduced by the Hebrew words for "Says Averroes," and this is followed again, by a passage introduced by the Hebrew word for "Commentary." Finally, there is a passage introduced, again, by the Hebrew words for "Says Averroes." Commenting on these incipits, Steinschneider says that "they agree with the Latin of Averroes' Long Commentary" (*ibid.*, p. 208). This, however, is not so. The description of the supercommentary as a "Treatise on this Rational Faculty," the words "He says," "Says Averroes," and "Commentary," and the passages which follow these words are all taken verbatim from Moses Ibn Tibbon's Hebrew translation of Averroes' Middle Commentary (MS Jewish Theological Seminary.)

It may be added that Joseph b. Shem-tob's statement that there was no supercommentary on the commentary in question (quoted *ibid.*, p. 207, n. 725) applies equally to the Middle Commentary as to the Long Commentary, for at the time that the statement was made there were in existence only some annotations on it by Solomon b. Joseph Enabi (cf. *ibid.*, p. 150).

Second, the Junta editions of 1550 and 1575 contain two Latin translations of Comments 5 and 36 of Averroes' Long Commentary on *De Anima* III, one by Michael Scot made directly from the Arabic and the other by Mantinus made from the Hebrew during the sixteenth century. This is taken by Steinschneider to show that a Hebrew translation from the Arabic of the Long *De Anima* was still in existence during the lifetime of Mantinus (*ibid.*, p. 151). However, this is not conclusive. These two comments happen to deal with problems concerning the intellect and it is therefore quite possible that long before the time of Mantinus they had been detached from the rest of the commentary and translated into Hebrew, having been regarded as independent treatises on the intellect, on a par with other similar treatises on the intellect by Averroes, which exist in Hebrew translation. It may be added, in passing, that Mantinus' translation of Comments 5 and 36 are not made from the Hebrew translation from the Latin Long *De Anima* to be discussed in the next Appendix.

While the evidence advanced by Steinschneider does not prove the existence of a Hebrew translation from the Arabic of the Long *De Anima,* there is the evidence of an eyewitness who testifies to his having seen a Hebrew translation of Book III of the Long *De Anima.* Isaac Abravanel (1437–1508), writing to Saul ha-Kohen Ashkenazi of Candia, in answer to a letter addressed to him on the fifth day of the Second Adar of the year 5266 (2 March 1506), says: "We in these lands have of works of Aristotle, containing his full text (*bi-leshono*) together with the Long Commentaries of Averroes, only the *Posterior Analytics* of the *Organon,* the *Physics,* the Third Book of *De Anima,* and the Tenth Book of the *Metaphysics*" (*She'elot . . . Sha'ul ha-Kohen* [Venice, 1574], p. 15d). This quotation calls for the following comments: First, the phrase "in these lands" refers to Italy, where Abravanel lived after the banishment of the Jews from Spain in 1492. Second, it is to be assumed that the translation of the Long Commentary on the Third Book of *De Anima,* like the translations of the other Long Commentaries mentioned by him, was a translation made directly from the Arabic. Third, according to the catalogues of Hebrew manuscripts in Italian libraries, published long after the time of Abravanel, there is a Long *Posterior Analytics* in Parma, but no Third Book of the Long *De Anima* anywhere. As for the Long Commentaries on the *Physics* and the Tenth Book of the *Metaphysics* mentioned by Abravanel, of the Long *Physics* there were in Turin, before the fire of 1906, only Books I–IV and of the Long *Metaphysics* there are Books VII–X and XII in the Vatican, wrongly ascribed to Alexander (cf. *Hebr. Ueber,* §87, p. 172, n. 488). There can be no question, however, of the trustworthiness of Abravanel's precise statement as to what he had seen in Italy of the Hebrew Long Commentaries. Abravanel was a close student of the Hebrew translations of Averroes' commentaries, to which he refers and upon which he draws so frequently in his own works. His statement is evidently based upon manuscripts he saw in private collections. Many private collections of Hebrew manuscripts existed at that time in Italy.

APPENDIX II

The Identity of the Hebrew Translator from the Latin of Averroes' Long *De Anima*

In 1888 the then Royal Library in Berlin purchased through Ephraim Deinard from the library of Landsberg in Kremenetz, Russia, two manuscripts, one an anonymous Hebrew translation of Averroes' Long Commentary on *De Anima* and the other a Hebrew translation of Averroes' Long Commentary on *Metaphysics* made from the Arabic by Moses ben Solomon of Salon (cf. Steinschneider, *Hebr. Uebers.*, pp. 151, 172). According to a note on the *De Anima* by its former owner, Mendl Landsberg, the manuscript was purchased by him from a bookseller in the month of Nisan of the year 5609 (March–April 1849) and two folios missing in the manuscript were copied for him from another manuscript, which he had located after a long search. Nothing is known about that other manuscript. As a list of manuscripts owned by Bisliches of Brody, which was published in Geiger's *Wissenschaftliche Zeitschrift für jüdische Theologie,* III (1837), 283, contains an item described as "Aristoteles de anima und dessen Metaphysik, übersetzt ins Hebr., mit einem ausführlichen Comm. von Moses ben Salomo aus Xilon [1] in Spanien," Steinschneider suggested that the two manuscripts purchased might be those originally owned by Bisliches (cf. *Die Handschriften-verzeichnisse der königlichen Bibliothek zu Berlin* [1897], §§ 214, 215, p. 64).[2]

The colophon in the Landsberg manuscript of the Long *De Anima* does not give the name of the translator nor does it say from what language it was translated. All that the copyist says in it is that "I Samuel Phinehas, the youngest of the scribes, have written this book of the Long *De Anima* for Abraham di Benevento, completing it on Thursday, second day of the month of Ab, in the year" and here follows a quotation of part of Lamentation 3:27, in which a dotted word amounts to the year 5235 (6 July 1475).[3] It is not clear, however, whether Benevento was the city where the Abraham referred to lived and hence where the manuscript was written or whether it was only the family name of Abraham, and it was some other city where he lived and where the manuscript was written. A comparison of certain passages in this Hebrew translation with those in the Latin translation, supplied by Professor Samuel Rosenblatt, led Professor F. Stuart Crawford, who edited the Latin translation for the Mediaeval Academy, to conclude that the Hebrew translation was made from the Latin translation. Nine of these comparisons are referred to by Crawford in the Prolegomena of his edition (pp. xi–xii). Some of these will be commented upon at the end of this Appendix.

In examining this Hebrew translation of the Long *De Anima* with a view to discovering some clues as to the identity of the translator, I found it contains the following peculiarities.

First, the three Books of the *De Anima* are divided into seventeen Summae (Hebrew *kelalim*) and each Summa is subdivided into chapters (Hebrew *peraḳim*). From Bouyges' edition of Averroes' Long Commentary on *Metaphysics* it may be gathered that no such divisions and subdivisions are used by Averroes in his Long Commentaries. Nor, as I am told by Crawford, are there any such divisions and subdivisions in the manuscripts of the Latin translations of the Long Commentary on *De Anima*. Nor, again, are there such divisions and subdivisions in the 1483 edition of the Latin translations of the Long Commentaries. They do appear, however, in the sixteenth century Latin editions, but, in the case of the Long *De Anima,* which I have examined, they do not agree with those in the Hebrew manuscript.

Second, while the Arabic name Ibn Bājja appears in this Hebrew translation as a transliteration of Avempace, the form in which this name occurs in the Latin translation, the names Empedocles and Hippocrates appear in it in their customary Hebrew transliterations from the Arabic as Ibn Doḳles and Abuḳrat. Similarly the forename of Alexander Aphrodisiensis appears in it as Aleskander, the form used in some Hebrew translations from the Arabic.

Third, the Hebrew term *ḥidah* "riddle" appears in it as a translation of μῦθος in *De Anima,* I, 3, 407b, 22, for which the Arabic translation of *De Anima* has *ḫurāfah,* "fanciful tale," "fable," "superstition" (ed. Badawi, p. 17, l. 22) and the Latin translation from the Arabic in Averroes' Long Commentary has *apologus* (I, 53, ll. 3, 12). It seems that some student of this Hebrew translation, who may have known either the original Greek term or the Latin term, was puzzled by the use of the Hebrew term for "riddle" here, and so he put down between the lines of the manuscript, above the Hebrew word *ḥidah,* the word *apologo,* as if to warn the next user of the manuscript that *ḥidah* here is used in the special sense of the Latinized Greek word *apologus.*

With these peculiarities of the translator to go by, I began to look for some Hebrew translator from the Latin whose translations might show the same or similar peculiarities. Inasmuch as, according to the colophon, the manuscript was written in Italy during the fifteenth century, in order to shorten the search, I began to look for a possible translator of this work among Hebrew translators from the Latin who lived in Italy during the fifteenth century and who translated philosophic works. Baruch ben Isaac Ibn Ya'ish seemed to be the most likely candidate, for among the works which he translated from the Latin into Hebrew there was a Hebrew translation from the Latin of Aristotle's *Metaphysics* (MSS. Bodleian, 1366; Leyden, 33; Bibliothèque Nationale, 891). Further information about him is as follows. In a manuscript of a Hebrew translation of Thomas Aquinas' commentary on the *Metaphysics,* Ibn Ya'ish is referred to by its translator Abraham Naḥmias as still living in 1490 (cf. *Hebr. Uebers.,* p. 158, n. 31b), that is, fifteen years after the date of the manuscript of the Hebrew Long *De Anima.* Then, in a manuscript of a Hebrew translation of a Latin commentary on the *Nicomachean Ethics* (Bibliothèque Nationale, 1001), there is a colophon which reads as follows: "I, Samuel b. Solomon Atortos, have translated it and written it down out of what as I have heard it from the mouth of my teacher, the accomplished and all-around scholar, the divine philosopher, Baruch ben Ya'ish, and finished it in the city of Benevento in the year 5245 (1485)." The meaning of the colophon is not quite clear. It may mean that Ibn Ya'ish was merely helping his student to translate the work from the Latin into Hebrew or it may mean that he orally dictated to his student his own Hebrew translation of the Latin work. But it is quite clear that in 1485, ten years after the manuscript of the Hebrew Long *De Anima* was written by one who describes himself as "the youngest of the scribes" for a certain "Abraham di Benevento,"

Ibn Ya'ish lived in Benevento. This creates a strong probability that already in 1475 he was there, that "the youngest of the scribes" was a student of his, and that this student of his was commissioned by a patron of learning in Benevento, named Abraham, to copy, or perhaps to take down from oral dictation, his master's translation from the Latin of Averroes' Long Commentary on *De Anima*.

This tentative identification of Ibn Ya'ish as the translator in question was finally clinched by finding that his Hebrew translation of Aristotle's *Metaphysics* contains the three peculiarities we have noticed in the anonymous Hebrew translation of Averroes' Long *De Anima*. First, as in the anonymous Hebrew translation of the Long *De Anima* so also in his translation of the *Metaphysics,* each book is broken up into smaller divisions, in this case only into chapters, and this division of each book into chapters is described by him as an innovation which he himself has introduced (see quotation of his statement in Neubauer's catalogue of the Bodleian Hebrew Manuscripts 1366). Second, as in the Long *De Anima* so also in his *Metaphysics,* the name Empedocles appears as Ibn Doḳles. Third, once more, as in the anonymous Long *De Anima* so in his *Metaphysics,* the Greek *μῦθος* in XII, 8, 1074b, 1 and 4, for which the Latin translation has *fabula,* is translated by him from the Latin by the Hebrew *ḥidah* "riddle." [4]

Baruch ben Isaac Ibn Ya'ish is thus the Hebrew translator from the Latin of Averroes' Long Commentary on *De Anima.*

Though this Hebrew Long *De Anima* is undoubtedly a translation from the Latin, some of its readings, rejected for good reasons in the Crawford edition, may represent the original Arabic text.

Here are a few examples:

In I 23, 15 (ed. Crawford), Averroes uses in his comment, according to the Latin reading, the expression "Homerus versificator," whereas according to the Hebrew reading he uses an expression which means "Homerus verificator." The Greek text upon which Averroes' comment rests reads: *διὸ καλῶς ποιῆσαι τὸν Ὅμερου* (*De Anima,* I, 2, 404a, 29), for which the Arabic translation of *De Anima* (ed. Badawi, p. 9, l. 6), if translated into Latin, would read: "et ideo bene fecit Homerus in suis versibus (*aḥsan fī shi'rihi*) cum dixit." But it will be noticed that the Arabic text used here by Averroes, as translated into Latin, reads: "et ideo dixit Homerus, et verum dixit" (I 23, 6–7). This shows that the text of the Arabic translation used here by Averroes, unlike the text of the extant Arabic translation of *De Anima,* did not take the term *ποιῆσαι* in the underlying Greek text in the sense of saying in verse. Consequently the reading "verificatur" in Averroes' comment on it is more likely to represent the original Arabic here than the reading "versificator."

It is to be noted that in his Long Commentary on the *Metaphysics* IV, Comm. 21 (ed. Bouyges, p. 419, ll. 9 and 14), where Averroes definitely uses an Arabic expression meaning "Homerus versificator (*al-shā'ir*)", the term *'εποίησε* applied to Homer in *Metaphysics* IV, 5, 1009b, 28–29, upon which Averroes' comment rests, is translated in the Arabic text used by Averroes by *dhakar fī shi'rihi* (ed. Bouyges, IV, Text. 21, p. 413, l. 11), for which the Latin translation from the Arabic reads: "dixit enim in suis versibus."

In I 29, 5 (ed. Crawford) the Hebrew and the printed editions and manuscripts read: "ignis enim est primorum partium inter elementa." The corresponding Greek reads: *πῦρ . . . καὶ γὰρ . . . λεπτομερέστατόν* (405a, 5–6), for which the Arabic translation of *De Anima* (ed. Badawi, p. 10, l. 17), if translated into Latin, would read: ". . . ignis, quia est subtilissimarum (*daḳīḳah*) partium." On the basis of the Greek, Crawford emended the text to read: "parviorum partium." It is quite possible, however, that the text used by Averroes had the reading "primorum partium inter elementa," for it will be noticed that in his Comment on this text Averroes paraphrases it to read "quia reputabant ignem esse elementum ceterorum elementorum," and this is followed by "et simplicorum partium" (I 29, 16–18), which seems to be an explanation of the preceding statement. Now the expression "elementum ceterorum elementorum" quite evidently implies the reading of "primorum partium inter elementa" in the underlying text. Such a reading of the text and its explanation as added by Averroes in his Comment would reflect Aristotle's statement in *Metaphysics* I, 8, 988b, 35–989a, 2, that fire is held by some to be "the most elementary of all" (*στοιχειωδέστατον πάντων* and hence the "most minute in its parts" (μικρομερέστατον) and the "most subtle" (λεπτότατον).

In I 53, 3 (ed. Crawford) after "Apologus quo utitur Pitagoras," the Hebrew and some Latin manuscripts add: "scilicet apologo quem posuit ad corrigendum animas civium." Though in the Arabic translation of *De Anima* this additional statement does not occur (ed. Badawi, p. 17, l. 22), it is not necessarily an interpolation from Averroes' comment on this text (I 53, 13). It is quite possible that the text used by Averroes contained this additional statement, where it was introduced from Themistius' commentary on *De Anima,* for Themistius, right after quoting Aristotle's κατὰ τοὺς Πυθαγορικοὺς μύθους comments: οἷς ἐκεῖνος μὲν ἐχρῆτο πολιτικῶς (ed. R. Heinze, p. 23, l. 33). The term "utitur" in Averroes "Apologus quo utitur," which has nothing to correspond to it either in the Greek text of Aristotle or in its Arabic translation, shows the influence of the term ἐχρῆτο in Themistius' comment.

1 Cf. Renan, *Averroès et Averroïsme,* 2nd ed. p. 36 ff. He is, however, frequently mentioned by Ibn Khaldūn, who also made abridgments of his works. Cf. F. Rosenthal's translation of *The Muqadimmah,* I, xliv, and Index.

2 Cf. Steinschneider, *Die hebraeischen Uebersetzungen des Mittelalters* (1893), p. 58: Middle Commentary on the *Isagoge* and the first four books of the *Organon* by Jacob Anatolio.

3 *Ibid.*, p. 59.

4 *Ibid.*, p. 63: Middle Commentary on the *Rhetoric* and *Poetics* by Todros Todrosi.

5 Cf. the writer's *Crescas' Critique of Aristotle,* (1929), "Index of Passages," pp. 741–743.

6 Cf. Renan, *op. cit.*, p. 205.

7 *Ibid.*, p. 208.

8 *Die hebraeischen Uebersetzungen des Mittelalters* (1893).

9 *Notes sur les Philosophes Arabes Connus des Latins au Moyen Age* (1922), reprinted from *Mélanges de l'Université Saint-Joseph,* VIII (1922), 13 ff.

10 *Aristoteles Latinus,* I (1939); II (1955).

11 On the question as to the chronological order in which these three types of commentaries were written by Averroes, see Jacob Teicher, "I Commenti de Averroè sul 'De Anima'," *Giornale della Società Asiatica Italiana,* III (1935), 233–256.

NOTES TO APPENDIX II

1 "Xilon" here is a conjectural identification by Julius Fürst, who furnished the list, of the name of the city written in Hebrew as *Shilon.* It is now generally identified as Salon in France.

2 In his *Hebr. Uebers.* (1896), §87, p. 172, however, Steinschneider lists the manuscript of the Long *Metaphysics* purchased by Berlin from the Landsberg collection

and the Bisliches manuscript mentioned in Geiger's *Zeitschrift* as two different manuscripts.

[3] Steinschneider in his above-mentioned catalogue of the Berlin Hebrew manuscripts gives 1497 as the equivalent of the Hebrew *anno mundi* mentioned in the colophon, which is evidently a misprint.

[4] It is to be added that the Greek *μῦθος* is variously translated into Arabic. Though this term in *De Anima* I, 3, 207b, 22, is in the Arabic translation of *De Anima* translated by *ḫurāfah* "fanciful tale," "fable," superstition" (ed. Badawi, p. 17, l. 22), in Averroes' Middle Commentary on *De Anima* it is translated by the Arabic *lughz* "riddle" (MS. Bibliothèque Nationale, Cod. Heb. 1009.3) and hence *ḥidah* in Moses Ibn Tibbon's Hebrew translation of it (MS. Jewish Theological Seminary). In Averroes' Middle Commentary on the *Poetics,* however, in a passage corresponding to *Poetics* 6, 1450a, 4 *μῦθος* is translated by the Arabic *ḫurāfah,* "fanciful tale," "fable," "superstition" (ed. Lasinio, p. 9, l. 5) and hence *sippur tefelut* "superstitious tale" in Todros Todrosi's Hebrew translation of it (ed. Lasinio, p. 7, l. 24) and hence *fabula* in Mantinus' and Balmes' Latin translations from the Hebrew. In Averroes' Long Commentary on the *Metaphysics,* in a passage corresponding to XII, 8, 1074b, 1 and 4, *μῦθος* is translated by the Arabic *aḥādīth* 'tales' (ed. Bouyges, p. 1687, ll. 3 and 4), for which the Latin translation from the Arabic has *fabula* (ed. 1574, p. 333 KM) and the Hebrew translation from the Arabic has *sippur,* "tale" (MS. Ebr. Vat. Urb. 46.1). Averroes in his comment on this text (Comm. 50) uses, as the equivalent of the Arabic *aḥādīth* of the text, two other Arabic terms: (1) *lughz,* "riddle" (p. 1688, ll. 5, 7, 11, 12, 16; p. 1689, l. 4), Latin: *apologus,* but once *fabula;* Hebrew: *ḥidah;* (2) *ramz.* "hint" (p. 1688, l. 11), Latin: *sermo*; Hebrew: *remez,* "hint." Ibn Ya'ish's translation of both the Latin *apologus* in *De Anima* and the Latin *fabula* in *Metaphysics* by the Hebrew *ḥidah* reflects the influence of the Latin and Hebrew translations of Averroes' Long Commentary on *Metaphysics,* reference to the Hebrew translation of which is made by him in his Introduction to his Hebrew translation of the Latin *Metaphysics.*

22

THE AMPHIBOLOUS TERMS IN ARISTOTLE, ARABIC PHILOSOPHY AND MAIMONIDES

IN ARABIC philosophic texts, and following them also in Hebrew philosophic texts, restatements of Aristotle's distinction between 'equivocal' (ὁμώνυμα, *mushtarakah*) and 'univocal' (συνώνυμα, *mutawāṭi'ah*), terms [1] usually contain another type of term which stands midway between these two. It is called 'ambiguous' or 'amphibolous' (ἀμφίβολα, *mushakkikah*) terms, and it is given a meaning which is a sort of moderation of the two meanings of the terms between which it is placed. Now, while each of these three terms occurs in Aristotle and while also the meanings of the terms equivocal and univocal used by the Arabic philosophers are the same as those used for them by Aristotle,[2] nowhere in Aristotle's writings are these terms combined into a threefold classification nor is the meaning of the term amphibolous as used by Aristotle the same as the meaning given to it by the Arabic philosophers. The question before us, therefore, is twofold: First, what is the origin of the formal threefold classification of the terms equivocal, ambiguous, and univocal? Second, what is the origin of the new meaning of the term amphibolous?

An answer to the first question may be found in the *Topics* (I, 15, 106a, 9), where Aristotle distinguishes between terms which have many meanings (πολλαχῶς) and terms which have one meaning only (μοναχῶς), a distinction which evidently corresponds to his distinction in *Categories*, Ch. 1, between 'equivocal' and 'univocal' terms. In commenting upon those terms which Aristotle describes as having many meanings, Alexander remarks that they are also called 'equivocal' (ὁμώνυμα) and 'ambiguous' (ἀμφίβολα).[3] Thus this statement of Aristotle, according to Alexander, implies a combination of the terms equivocal, ambiguous, and univocal into a threefold

[1] Categories, Ch. 1, 1a, 1–12.

[2] Cf. Bonitz, Index Aristotelicus, s. v.

[3] Alexander in Topica, ed. M. Wallies (1891), p. 97, ll. 22–23.

classification. While, indeed, there is no evidence that Alexander's Commentary on the *Topics* was translated into Arabic,[4] it is still reasonable to assume that Arabic students of Aristotle's works could of themselves, without the aid of Alexander, derive from this statement in the *Topics* their threefold classification of the terms equivocal, ambiguous, and univocal.

Once we know that Aristotle himself distinguishes an intermediate type of term which is to be called 'ambiguous,' we shall now be able to find in Aristotle's own writings, with the aid of his Greek commentators, the origin of the various treatments of these intermediate terms in Arabic philosophy. We shall take as a starting point the treatment of ambiguous terms by Alfarabi,[5] and this we shall supplement as well as complement by statements drawn from the treatments of the same subject by Avicenna,[6] Algazali,[7] Averroes[8] and Maimonides.[9]

The description given by Alfarabi of ambiguous terms is that their application to two different things is according to the order of priority and posteriority. This description is the most prevalent in Arabic philosophy. It occurs in Avicenna, Algazali, Averroes, and, after them, in the Hebrew texts that happen to deal with ambiguous terms. The source of this description of ambiguous term is to be found in a passage of Aristotle's *De Anima* with Alexander's comment thereon. In *De Anima* I, 1, 402b, 6–8, Aristotle makes the statement that "if there is a different definition for each separate soul, as for horse and dog, man and god," then the term 'animal,' as the universal, is to be regarded "(*a*) either as nothing (*οὐθέν*) (*b*) or

[4] Cf. Steinschneider, *Die arabischen Uebersetzungen aus dem Griechischen*, §24 (48).

[5] Risālat fī Jawābi Masā'il Su'il 'anhā, § 12, in F. Dieterici, Alfārābī's philosophische Abhandlungen: Arabic (1890), p. 88; German (1892), pp. 145–146.

[6] Najāt: I. Logic (ed. Rome, 1593), p. 23; (ed. Cairo, 1331/1913), p. 142; Shifā': I. Logic, quoted by I. Madkour in his L'Organon d'Aristote dans le monde arabe (1934), pp. 61–62.

[7] Maqāṣid al-Falāsifah: I. Logic, pp. 11–12, II. Metaphysics, p. 106 (Cairo, without date); Mi'yār al-'Ilm (Cairo, 1329/1911), p. 44.

[8] Original Arabic not extant. Hebrew translation: Kol Meleket Higgayon: Mabo, (Riva di Trento, 1559), pp. 2b–3a; Latin translation from the Hebrew: Epitome in Libros Logicae Aristotelis, in Aristotelis Opera (Venice, 1574), Vol. I, Pars II^2, p. 36 I-M.

[9] Millot ha-Higgayon, Ch. 13, ed. L. Roth (1935); Moreh Nebukim, I 56.

as posterior (ὕστερον)." Upon this passage, Alexander in his *Quaestiones* makes the following comment: "If, says Aristotle, these things, namely, horse and dog and man and god, are not of the same genus and 'animal' therefore is not their common genus, then each of them has its own proper definition, with the result that the term 'animal,' which is predicated in common of all of them, (*a*) either does not signify any particular nature and is nothing but an equivoque, (*b*) or, if it does signify anything, is to be taken in the same sense as it is supposed to be in the case of those terms of many meanings (πολλαχῶς λεγόμενα) between which there is the distinction of the prior and the posterior (τὸ πρότερον καὶ ὕστερον)."[10] In this passage, then, Aristotle, as interpreted by Alexander, includes under πολλαχῶς λεγόμενα two types of terms, namely, (*a*) equivocal terms and (*b*) terms which apply to things according to priority and posteriority. Taking this passage together with the passage in the *Topics* where the two types of πολλαχῶς λεγόμενα are (*a*) equivocal terms and (*b*) ambiguous terms, we may conclude that ambiguous terms are terms which apply to things according to priority and posteriority.

This general description of ambiguous terms in Alfarabi is followed by three examples.

The first of these examples reads: "as substance (*jauhar*) and accident (*'araḍ*)." From parallel passages in Avicenna, Algazali and others we may gather that what Alfarabi meant to say is that the term 'being' (*maujūd*) in its application to the terms 'substance' and 'accident' is an ambiguous term, inasmuch as it is applied priorily to substance and posteriorily to accident. The source of this illustration is to be found in Aristotle's discussions in the *Metaphysics* as to the relation of 'being' to the ten categories into which it is divided. The most characteristic passages are as follows: "The term 'being' (τὸ ὄν) bears many meanings (λέγεται πολλαχῶς), but they are all with reference to one, and to one certain nature, and not equivocally."[11] Alexander in his comment on this passage remarks that the term 'being' is between (μεταξύ) equivocal and

10 Alexandri Scripta Minora, ed. I. Bruns (1892), p. 23, ll. 4–9.
11 Metaphysics IV, 2, 1003a, 33–34.

univocal terms.[12] In another place Aristotle says still more clearly that the term 'being' is used neither 'equivocally' (ὁμωνύμως) nor 'in the same sense' (ὡσαύτως);[13] by 'in the same sense' he means here what he elsewhere describes as 'univocally' (συνωνύμως).[14] These statements with regard to the intermediate position of the term 'being' between equivocal and univocal terms, or what Alexander would call for Aristotle an 'ambiguous' term, may be supplemented by other passages in which Aristotle speaks of 'being' as applying 'first' (πρώτως) to 'substance' and then to the other categories, i.e., accidents. The most characteristic passages on this point are the following: "The term 'is' is predicable of all things, not however in the same sense, but of one sort of thing first and of others next."[15] To what things it applies primarily is explained by him elsewhere: "While 'being' has all these senses, obviously that which is first is the 'what,' which indicates the substance of the thing."[16] And, again, "therefore that which is first and is simply (not 'is something') must be substance."[17]

The second example given by Alfarabi for ambiguous terms reads: "as potentiality (*quwwah*) and actuality (*fi'l*)." Here, too, as in the case of his first example, what Alfarabi means to say is that the term 'being' in its application to the terms 'potentiality' and 'actuality' is an ambiguous term, inasmuch as it is applied to them according to priority and posteriority. The source of this example is again Aristotle. In one place, he says that "'being' and 'that which is,' in these cases we have mentioned, sometimes means being potentially, and sometimes being actually."[18] As to whether potentiality or actuality is prior, we have different statements in Aristotle. Thus, in one place, he says: "potentiality is prior to that cause [i.e., the actual cause], and it is not necessary for everything potential to be disposed that way [i.e., to be actual],"[19] and, in another

[12] Alexander in Metaphysica, ed. M. Hayduck (1891), p. 241, l. 8.

[13] Metaphysics VII, 4, 1030a, 34–35.

[14] Cf. the commentaries of Bonitz, Schwegler and Ross ad loc.

[15] Metaphysics VII, 4, 1030a, 21–22. On the terms 'first' and 'next' see below, nn. 27 and 28.

[16] Ibid. VII, 1, 1028a, 13–15.

[17] Ibid., 1028a, 30–31.

[18] Ibid. V, 7, 1017a, 35–b, 2.

[19] Ibid. III, 6, 1003a, 1–2.

place, he says that "it is clear that actuality is prior to potentiality."[20]

A third example given by Alfarabi for ambiguous terms reads: "as prohibition and command."[21] A parallel passage in Avicenna's *Najāt* states that an ambiguous term "is that which applies to a thing and its contrary (*ḍidd*), such as the terms lawful and prohibited."[22] From this parallel passage of Avicenna, then, we gather that Alfarabi's example of 'prohibition and command' is not to be taken as an illustration of his own stated description of an ambiguous term as that which applies to things according to priority and posteriority, but rather as an illustration of a new description, left by him unstated, namely, that an ambiguous term is that which applies to contraries. The example itself, as given by both Alfarabi and Avicenna, seems to be incomplete, just as the previous two examples given by Alfarabi. The term 'law' evidently has to be supplied here just as the term 'being' had to be supplied in the previous two examples. What Alfarabi and Avicenna mean to say is this: The term 'law' in its application to the contraries 'prohibited' and 'lawful' (or 'commanded') is an illustration of this new description of ambiguous terms. So also in Philo's *De Fuga et Inventione* 18, § 95, and 19, § 100, the contraries 'prohibition' (ἀπαγόρευσις) and 'command' (πρόσταξις) are said to be subdivisions of the term 'legislative' (νομοθετική) or 'laws' (νόμοι).

As the previous description and examples so also this new description and example, I shall now try to show, can be traced to Aristotle.

As for the description, it can be traced to that passage in the *Topics* in which, as we have shown above, Aristotle, according to the commentary of Alexander, differentiates between equivocal and ambiguous terms. Aristotle enumerates four kinds of such ambiguous terms. In the second of these four kinds, he says that an ambiguous term is that which is applied to two

[20] Ibid. IX, 8, 1049b, 5.

[21] *al-nahy wal-amr.*

[22] The Cairo edition (p. 142, l. 13) has here: *al-ḥalāl wal-nāhil*, in which, from a comparison with Alfarabi, *al-nāhil* is evidently a corruption of *al-nāhī*. In the Rome edition (p. 23, l. 7) the reading is *al-ḥāmil wal-bāhil*, *pregnant woman and unmarried woman.*

different things which lead to the same end, "as the science of contraries (ἐναντία) is said to be the same (for of contraries the one is no more an end than the other)." [23] Neither Aristotle nor his commentator Alexander, however, uses here the example given by both Alfarabi and Avicenna. Aristotle does not give here any examples at all. Alexander gives three examples: (1) medicine, which is the science of both health and disease, (2) music, which is the science of both harmonized and unharmonized sounds, (3) gymnastics, which is the science of both good bodily condition and bad bodily condition.[24]

But the example of 'law,' which is the science of both 'the prohibited' and 'the commanded' or 'lawful,' used here by Alfarabi and Avicenna, can be traced to another passage of Aristotle which occurs in the *Metaphysics*. In that passage, Aristotle discusses again the term 'being' and tries to show that it is not an equivocal term but rather a term which Alexander would call for him 'ambiguous.' In connection with this, he repeats the statement with regard to contraries which we have just quoted from the *Topics*. He says: "Every pair of contraries is to be examined by one and the same science, and in each pair one term is the privation of the other." [25] This statement leads him to the discussion of the contraries 'just' and 'unjust,' in the course of which discussion he defines the 'just' as one who is "obedient to the laws (νόμοις)" and the 'unjust' as one who is "in some respect deficient" with reference to obedience to the laws.[26] It can be easily seen how Alfarabi's and Avicenna's example of lawfulness and prohibition as an illustration of the ambiguity of terms when applied to contraries may have survived as a reminiscent phrase of Aristotle's discussion of the 'just' and the 'unjust,' in the sense of obedience and disobedience to the laws, in connection with his similar discussion of the ambiguity of terms when applied to contraries. When one recalls that the Greek word for law used by Aristotle in this passage, namely, νόμος, has been adopted into Arabic, where it became *nāmūs*, and is used there in the same sense,

[23] Topics II, 3, 110b, 19–21.

[24] Alexander in Topica, p. 152, ll. 19–20.

[25] Metaphysics XI, 3, 1061a, 18–20.

[26] Ibid., 25–27.

the connection between Alfarabi's and Avicenna's example and the passage in Aristotle becomes still more evident.

As correlated with the distinction of 'priority' (*taqaddum*, πρότερον) and 'posteriority' (*ta'akhkhur*, ὕστερον) already mentioned by Alfarabi and illustrated by the example of the term 'being' in its application to substance and accident, Algazali in his *Mi'yār al-'Ilm*, p. 44, mentions also two other similar distinctions. First, the distinction of 'primary' or 'first' (*awwaliyy*) and 'subsequent' or 'next' (*ākhiriyy*), which he illustrates again by the example of 'being' in its application to a thing to which it belongs essentially (*min dhātihi*) and to a thing to which it belongs by reason of something else (*min ghairihi*). Second, the distinction of 'intensity' (*shiddah*) and 'slightness' (*ḍa'f*), which he illustrates by the example of the term 'whiteness' in its application to 'ivory' (*'āj*) and a 'crown' (*tāj*). Now these two new kinds of distinctions can also be traced to Aristotle. With regard to the first distinction, Algazali's phrase 'primary and subsequent' (*al-awwaliyy wal-ākhiriyy*) reflects the contrasting Greek words πρώτως and ἑπομένως. Furthermore, the example used by Algazali to illustrate these two terms reflects Aristotle's statement that the term 'first' or 'primary' (πρῶτος) applies to things to which 'being' belongs essentially (καθ' αὑτό) as distinguished from things to which it belongs in virtue of something else (κατ' ἄλλο),[27] in the latter case of which he could probably also say that 'being' belongs to those things 'next' or 'subsequently' (ἑπομένως), for in another place he says that 'being' is predicated 'first' (πρώτως) of one sort of thing, i.e., substance, and 'next' (ἑπομένως) of others, i.e., accidents.[28] With regard to the second distinction, Algazali's phrase 'intensity and slightness' (*al-shiddah wal-ḍa'f*) literally reflects the contrasting Greek terms σφόδρα and ἠρέμα which occur often in Aristotle.[29] But from the fact that Algazali uses it here with reference to some difference with which the term 'whiteness' is applied to different white things it may be inferred that it reflects the Greek phrase 'more

[27] Metaphysics VII, 6, 1031b, 13–14.
[28] Ibid. VII, 4, 1030a, 21–22.
[29] Cf., e.g., Topics III, 2, 117b, 23, and see Bonitz, Index Aristotelicus, s.v.

and less' (τὸ μᾶλλον καὶ τὸ ἧττον) which is often used by Aristotle in a similar connection as, e.g., in his statement that "one thing is said to be more (μᾶλλον) or less (ἧττον) white than another."[30] The changing by Algazali, or by somebody else before him, of Aristotle's original phrase 'more or less' into 'intensity or slightness' may at first sight seem to be purely accidental, for the two phrases are sometimes used by Aristotle himself in the same sense.[31] Furthermore, a similar change of terms also occurs in Averroes' Middle Commentary on Aristotle's *Categories* where the term 'more' (*akthar*), which is used in the Arabic translation of Aristotle's text as the literal translation of the Greek μᾶλλον, is changed to the term 'more intense' (*ashadd*).[32] But later, when I shall take up the question whether Aristotle would call 'whiteness' in its application to different white things an 'ambiguous' term, I hope to show that the change of the phrase 'more or less' to 'intensity or slightness' in this particular instance was made for a definite purpose.[33]

In the same place in his *Mi'yār al-'Ilm*, Algazali adds a set of three other examples to illustrate the use of ambiguous terms. (1) A term which applies to different things by virtue of their proceeding from one beginning, as, e.g., the term 'medical' (*ṭibbiyy*) in its application to (*a*) a book (*kitāb*), (*b*) a small knife (*mibḍa'*), and (*c*) a drug (*dawā'*). (2) A term which applies to different things by virtue of their conducting to one end, as, e.g., the term 'healthy' (*ṣiḥḥiyy*) in its application to (*a*) a drug (*dawā'*), (*b*) gymnastics (*riyāḍah*), and (3) venesection (*faṣd*). (3) A term which applies to different things by virtue of their having both one beginning and one end, as, e.g., the application of the term 'divine' (*ilāhiyyah*) to all things. This passage has been traced to Porphyry,[34] who in his reclassification of Aristotle's equivocal terms places under what he calls 'equivocal in meaning' (ὁμώνυμος ἀπὸ διανοίας), (1) terms applied to things proceeding from one source (ἀφ' ἑνός), such, e.g.,

[30] Categories, Ch. 8, 10b, 26.

[31] Cf. Bonitz, Index Aristotelicus, sub μᾶλλον.

[32] Cf. M. Bouyges, Averroes: Talkhiç Kitāb al-Maqoūlat (1932), p. 32, l. 138 of Aristotle's Text and p. 33, l. 1 of Averroes' Commentary; also p. 84, l. 458 of Text and l. 4 of Commentary.

[33] Cf. below, p. 167.

[34] Cf. Baneth, op. cit., p. 37.

as the application of the term 'medical' (ἰατρικός) to (*a*) medical book (βιβλίον ἰατρικόν), (*b*) a drug (φάρμακον), (*c*) a small knife (σμιλίον), and (2) terms applied to different things leading to one end (πρὸς ἕν), such, e.g., as the application of the term 'healthy' (ὑγιεινόν) to (*a*) grain (σιτίον), (*b*) walking (περίπατος) and (*c*) a [hygienic] lecture (ἀνάγνωσμα).[35] Now there is no doubt that part of Algazali's passage is based upon that of Porphyry, but still Porphyry's passage by itself would not account for the peculiar fact that Algazali makes use of these examples as illustrations of ambiguous terms, nor would it explain how Algazali, or whoever was responsible for it, happened to introduce the term 'venesection' which does not occur in Porphyry's passage. In order to be able to account for this particular use made by him of these examples as well as for his use of the term 'venesection,' we must turn again to Aristotle and Alexander, for most of the examples used by Porphyry and Algazali occur also, though in different form, in that passage of the *Topics* where Aristotle discusses what Alexander calls for him ambiguous term. In Aristotle they occur under the first of the four kinds of ambiguous terms enumerated by him there. It is described by him as a term which is applied to different things of which one is an end and the other is a means to that end. Aristotle illustrates it by the example of the term 'medical' in its application both to the science of producing health (ὑγίειαν ποιῆσαι) and to the science of prescribing diet (διαιτῆσαι).[36] Alexander illustrates it by the term 'medical' in its application to health and to those things which produce health, such as diet (δίαιτα), cutting (τομή) and cautery (καῦσις).[37] Now, the term τομή, which means 'cutting' in any kind of surgical operation, may have been taken by some Arabic reader or translator of Alexander in the special sense of 'cutting of vein' (φλεβοτομία) and hence Algazali's 'venesection.' Furthermore, in the *Metaphysics* Aristotle uses the term 'medical' as an illustration not only of its application to different things by virtue of their leading to one end but also of its application to

35 Porphyrius in Categorias, ed. A. Busse (1897), p. 66, ll. 2 ff.

36 Topics II, 3, 110b, 17–19.

37 Alexander in Topica, p. 152, ll. 16–17.

different things by virtue, as he says elsewhere, of their proceeding from one source (ἀφ' ἑνός).[38] He thus says that the term 'medical' applies both to a [medical] discourse (λόγος) and to a small knife (μαχαίριον) on the ground that "the former proceeds from medical science (ἀπὸ τῆς ἰατρικῆς), and the latter is useful to it."[39] Finally, Simplicius, in his commentary on the *Categories*, states definitely that terms applied to things proceeding from one source (ἀφ' ἑνός) or leading to one end (πρὸς ἕν) are neither equivocal nor univocal[40] but that they are intermediate (τὸ μέσον) between equivocal and univocal.[41] In short, they are ambiguous terms.

A further extension of the use of 'ambiguous' terms is to be found in Averroes' Epitome of Porphyry's *Isagoge*.[42] Defining an 'ambiguous'[43] term as that which is applied to different things which are related to one source, as, e.g., one agent,[44] or to one end[45] or to one subject,[46] he divides it into two main divisions of which the first has two subdivisions and the second four subdivisions, as follows:[47]

[38] Nicomachean Ethics I, 6, 1096b, 27–28.

[39] Metaphysics XI, 3, 1061a, 3–5.

[40] Simplicius in Categorias, ed. C. Kalbfleisch (1907), p. 74, ll. 30–31.

[41] Ibid., p. 228, l. 9. Here Simplicius mentions only ἀφ' ἑνός.

[42] Cf. above, n. 8.

[43] *nomina analoga* (p. 36 L). In the Hebrew version: שמות מסופקים (p. 3a), i.e., *nomina ambigua*. On the use of *analoga* for *ambigua*, see below n. 84.

[44] אל התחלה אחת, כמו שייוחס אל פועל אחד, ad principium unum: sicut si comparentur, *ad efficiens unum*. This reflects Aristotle's interpretation of ἀρχή as an efficient cause in Metaphysics VI, 1, 1013a, 7–10.

[45] אל תכלית אחת, *ad finem unum*.

[46] *ad subjectum unum*. In the Hebrew version: אל מקום אחד, i.e., *ad locum unum*. The Hebrew מקום seems to reflect here the Arabic *maḥall* rather than the Arabic *makān* and hence the Latin *subjectum*. The Arabic *maḥall* in Maqāṣid al-Falāsifah: II. Metaphysics, p. 80, is translated into Hebrew by משכן, i.e., מקום (Kawwanot ha-Pilosofim, MS. Paris, Bibliothèque Nationale, Cod. Heb. 901), and into Latin by *subjectum* (Algazel's Metaphysics, ed. J. T. Muckle (1933), p. 6, l. 8). Cf. my Crescas' Critique of Aristotle, p. 577, n. 15.

[47] In the Latin translation the description 'ambiguous' (or as it is called there 'analogous') terms refers only to what I designate here by B. This is due to the fact that the Latin translation contains only one kind of equivocal terms instead of the two kinds found in the Hebrew translation, and consequently the Latin translation takes Averroes' concluding statement "Et istae species, exceptis primis duabus speciebus, sunt notae in nominibus analogis [= ambiguis]," ואלו המינים, לבר המינים הראשונים, יודעו בשמות המסופקים, to refer to B and the clause *exceptis primis duabus speciebus* to refer to the one kind of equivocal terms and to A.

A. (1) [Primitive] terms, such, e.g., as the term 'being' in its application to 'substance,' 'quantity,' 'quality' and the other categories, or the term 'heat' in its application to 'fire' and to other hot objects.[48]

(2) Derivative terms, such, e.g., as the term 'medical' in its application to a 'lancet' and to a 'drug,' the term 'healthy' to 'gymnastics' and 'symptom,' the term 'good' to a 'place' and a 'house' and the term 'true' to 'slavery' and 'wisdom.'[49]

B. (1) Terms applied to things according to the order of priority and posteriority, such, e.g., as the term 'essence' in its application to many of the categories and their species.[50]

[48] Sicut est nomen entis, quod dicitur de substantia, quantitate, et qualitate, et caeteris praedicamentis, et sicut caliditas quae dicitur de igne et caeteris rebus calidis.

כנמצא אשר יאמר על העצם, על הכמות והאיכות, ושאר המאמרות, והחום אשר יאמר על האש ועל שאר הדברים החמים.

In his Tahāfut al-Tahāfut, VII (ed. M. Bouyges, 1930, § 37, pp. 387–388) he adds to these two examples taken from 'being' and 'heat' also the example of 'motion' in its application to locomotion and to other kinds of motion.

[49] Et earum sunt quae dicuntur nomine derivato a nominibus, ut si dixeris phlebotomum medicinalem [et pharmacum medicinale, exercitationem salubrem et signum salubre], (locum bonum et domum bonam, veram servitutem et veram sapientiam).

ומהם מה שיאמר בשם הנגזר משמותיו, כאמרך אזמל רפואיי וסם רפואיי והתעמלות בריאותיי וסימן בריאותיי.

In this Latin quotation, the passage within brackets is supplied from the Hebrew version; that within parentheses is omitted in the Hebrew. The example of the term 'medical' occurs also in Averroes' Epitome of the Metaphysics (cf. Averroes: Compendio de Metafisica, ed. Quirós, 1919, II, § 3, p. 37) where he adds also an example from the term 'military.'

[50] Quaedam comparantur ad ipsam secundum prioritatem et posterioritatem, sicut est comparatio multorum praedicamentorum et specierum eorum ad substantiam.

מהם מה שיהיה יחסם אליהם (במדרגה והקדמה ואיחור) [במדרגת הקדימה והאיחור] כיחס הרבה מהמאמרות ומיניהם אל העצם.

I take the term עצם, *substantia*, in this passage to reflect the Arabic *dhāt*, i.e., the Greek *τὸ τί ἐστι*, rather than the Arabic *jauhar*, i.e., the Greek *οὐσία*, and accordingly Averroes' passage here may be taken to reflect the following passage in Aristotle's Metaphysics VII, 4, 1030a, 17–23: "'Definition,' like the essence of a thing (*τὸ τί ἐστι*), has several meanings, for the essence of a thing in one sense signifies substance (*οὐσία*) and the individual thing, but in another sense signifies each of the categories, quantity, quality, and the like. For as 'being' (*τὸ ἔστιν*) belongs to all things, though not in the same sense, but to one sort of thing primarily and to others consequently, so also 'essence' (*τὸ τί ἐστιν*) belongs to substance absolutely but to the other categories in a sort of way." That the term *substantia* in this passage of Averroes cannot be taken in its literal sense is quite evident from the context.

(2) Terms applied to things according to the same order.[51]

(3) Terms applied to things according to the relation of analogy, such, e.g., as the term 'principle' in its application to the 'heart' of an animal, the 'foundation' of a wall, and the 'upper end' of a road.[52]

(4) Terms applied to things according to a relation of difference, such, e.g., as the term 'vinaceous' in its application to a bunch of grapes and to the color of a face.[53] By this type of ambiguous term Averroes undoubtedly means the same as that which Algazali in his *Mi'yār al-'Ilm*, p. 44, describes as the application of a term to two things according to a difference of 'intensity and slightness' and illustrates by the example of 'whiteness' in its application to ivory and a crown.[54] As to what justification Averroes had in including this kind of terms under ambiguous terms, we shall discuss it in connection with Maimonides.

Averroes' classification, on the whole, as will have been noticed, is, with the exception of the inclusion of analogy, only a different arrangement of the elements which we have already met previously in Alfarabi, Avicenna, and Algazali and the origin of which in Aristotle we have already accounted for. The inclusion of analogy, however, requires some attention. In

[51] Et earum sunt, quarum comparatio ad ipsam est in gradu uno.

ומהם מה שיהיה יחסם אליהם במדרגה אחת.

[52] Et earum sunt quarum comparatio fuerit ad res diversas consimiles, sicut est principium, quod dicitur de corde animalis et de fundamento domus et de extremo viae.

ומהם מה שיהיה מהם אל דברים מתחלפים יחס מתדמה, כמו התחלה אשר יאמר על לב בעל חיים ועל יסוד הקיר ועל קצה הדרך.

The Arabic term underlying מתדמה, *consimilis*, would seem to be *mutashābih* which usually translates the Greek ὅμοιος (cf. Averroes' Epitome of the Metaphysics I, ed. Quirós, p. 25, § 45, last line, and Metaphysics V, 9, 1018a, 15.) But here I take it to reflect the Greek ἀναλογικός on the ground that the examples used here by Averroes are similar to those used by Porphyry (Commentaria in Categorias, ed. A. Busse 1887, p. 65, ll. 31 ff.) as illustrations of analogy.

The enumeration of the various meanings of 'principium' in this passage of Averroes reflects Aristotle's discussion of the various meanings of ἀρχή in Metaphysics VI, 1, 1012b, 34–1013a, 1, and 1013a, 4–7.

[53] Vel erit eis ad rem unam comparatio diversa, ac si diceres uvam vinosam et faciem vinosam.

או שיהיה אל דבר אחד יחס מתחלף, כאמרך ענב ייני ומראה ייני.

[54] Cf. above, nn. 29 and 30.

certain passages Aristotle speaks of analogical terms as if he meant by them the same as equivocal terms, as, e.g., when he maintains that things can be called 'one by analogy' even if they are not of the same genus or category.[55] Now, not to be of the same genus or category and still be described by the same term *analogically* means, by Aristotle's own definition of equivocalness, to be described by that term *equivocally*. Still in one passage he admits that there is some difference, even if only an apparent difference, between these two kinds of terms. "In the case of equivocal terms," he says, "sometimes the different senses in which they are used are far removed from one another . . ., and sometimes again they are nearly related either generically or analogically, with the result that they seem not to be equivocal though they really are." [56] Furthermore, in that passage of the *Topics* where, as we have shown, Aristotle differentiates what Alexander calls ambiguous terms from equivocal terms, there is an indication that analogical terms would be placed by him under ambiguous terms. Toward the end of his discussion there of what is meant by ambiguous terms, Aristotle concludes that "this rule is useful in dealing with relative terms; for cases of this kind are generally cases of relative terms." [57] What he means to say is that relative terms are ambiguous terms. Now analogy is defined by Aristotle as a sort of relation,[58] and consequently analogical terms should according to him be included under ambiguous terms.

Probably the most troublesome description of ambiguous terms is that given by Maimonides in his *Millot ha-Higgayon* and his *Moreh Nebukim*. It differs from all the descriptions we have met with before in two respects. In the first place, in his explanation of ambiguous terms he uses none of the explanations we have thus far found among his predecessors. Instead he gives the following explanation. "An ambiguous term is a term which is applied to two or more objects (*a*) on account of something which they have in common but (*b*) that thing which they have in common does not constitute the essence of

[55] Metaphysics V, 6, 1017a, 2–3.
[56] Physics VII, 4, 249a, 23–25.
[57] Topics II, 3, 111a, 6–7.
[58] Metaphysics V, 6, 1016b, 34–35.

either one of them." [59] Or again: "Terms used ambiguously are those which are applied to two things (*a*) between which there is a similarity in respect to a certain thing and (*b*) that thing in which they are similar is an accident in both of them and does not constitute the essence of either of them." [60] In the second place, the example by which he illustrates the use of ambiguous terms is none of the examples we have thus far met with among his predecessors in illustration of ambiguous terms but rather one based on that which is used by Aristotle in *Categories*, Ch. 1, 1a, 1–6, as an illustration of an equivocal term. As given by Maimonides, the illustration reads as follows: "An example thereof is the term 'man' in its application to a certain Reuben who is by definition endowed with life and rationality and to the corpse of a certain dead person or to the figure of a man made of wood or stone or to the painted picture of a man. The term 'man' is predicated of all of them by virtue of the common element which they possess, namely, the shape and the appearance of man, but that shape and appearance do not constitute the essence of man." [61]

It is my purpose now to show, first, how like all the explanations of ambiguous terms which we have already discussed this explanation of Maimonides can also be traced to Aristotle, and, second, how Maimonides came to transfer Aristotle's illustration for equivocal terms to ambiguous terms.

With regard to Maimonides' general explanation of ambiguous terms, it will be noticed that a similar explanation is implied in some of the examples given by Algazali and Averroes. When Algazali says that 'whiteness' in its application to ivory and to a crown is an ambiguous term, the implication is that ambiguous terms include also terms which indicate some accidental quality which exists in two things, for whiteness, in

[59] Millot ha-Higgayon, Ch. 13.

[60] Moreh Nebukim I, 56.

[61] Millot ha-Higgayon, Ch. 13. There is one notable difference between the original example by Aristotle in Categories, Ch. I, and its reproduction by Maimonides. In Aristotle, it is the term 'animal' that is taken as the subject of the example. In Maimonides, it is the term 'man.' But the substitution of 'man' for 'animal' is also to be found in John of Damascus, Dialectica, Ch. 16 (Migne, Vol. 94, Col. 580), in Avicenna's Shifā' (Cf. Madkour, L'Organon d'Aristote dans le monde arabe, p. 62) and in Algazali's *Mi'yār al-'Ilm*, p. 44.

his example, is an accidental quality in both ivory and a crown. A similar inference is to be drawn also from Averroes' example of the term 'vinaceousness' in its application to grapes and a face, for here, too, vinaceousness is an accident to both grapes and faces. Algazali, Averroes and Maimonides, therefore, despite the differences in the language which they use, express a common view, and this common view, it is reasonable to assume, must ultimately go back to a common source. What is that common source?

The common source, I believe, is again that passage in the *Topics* in which Aristotle discusses what Alexander calls for him ambiguous terms. Of the four types of ambiguous terms enumerated there by Aristotle, the first, second and fourth of which we have already discussed, the third is described by him as a term which is applied to two different things, to one of which it belongs *per se* (καθ' αὑτό) and to the other *per accidens* (κατὰ συμβεβηκός).[62] Of these two expressions, as will be noticed, the second, κατὰ συμβεβηκός, suggests at once the 'accident' which 'does not constitute the essence' spoken of by Maimonides and implied in the examples of 'whiteness' and 'vinaceousness' mentioned by Algazali and Averroes. The first expression, however, namely, καθ' αὑτό, which is generally translated by 'essentially,' would seem to be quite the opposite of the 'accident' which these three authors mention or allude to. But I shall try to show that by καθ' αὑτό here Aristotle refers also to an accident.

The expression καθ' αὑτό, according to Aristotle, has several meanings, of which two are necessary for our present purpose. Sometimes it refers to the genus of a thing and its differentiae and in this sense the expression means that which constitutes the essence or definition of a thing.[63] But sometimes it refers also to accidents, but such accidents as reside 'primarily' (πρώτῳ), i.e., directly, in a thing, even though they do not constitute the essence of the thing. Aristotle illustrates this by the example of 'whiteness' which, though only an accident, is said to reside in surface καθ' ἑαυτήν, in the sense that it resides in it

[62] Topics II, 3, 110b, 21–22.
[63] Metaphysics V, 18, 1022a, 27–29.

primarily or directly.[64] As contrasted with καθ' αὑτό in this latter sense, the expression κατὰ συμβεβηκός means an accident which resides in something in a manner opposite to 'primarily' (πρώτως). The opposite of πρώτως, as we have seen above,[65] is described by Aristotle as ἑπομένως, i.e., *next, secondarily, subsequently, indirectly.*

In the passage of the *Topics* under consideration it is quite evident from the two examples used by Aristotle that the contrasting expressions καθ' αὑτό and κατὰ συμβεβηκός both refer to accidents but that in one case the accident belongs to a thing primarily and in the other case subsequently. Thus, for his first example he takes the phrase 'equal to two right angles' which, according to him, is applied to the angles of a triangle καθ' αὑτό but to the angles of any equilateral figure κατὰ συμβεβηκός, because in the latter case it is so only indirectly, by the mere accident that the equilateral figure happens to be a triangle.[66] Now, we happen to know from another place of his writings, that having its angles equal to two right angles is said by Aristotle to be predicated of a triangle καθ' αὑτό only in the sense that it is a permanent 'accident' of it, but not in the sense that it constitutes its essence (μὴ ἐν τῇ οὐσίᾳ ὄντα).[67] His second example is that of the desire of the sweet-toothed person for sweetness and for wine, in the former case of which it is καθ' αὑτό, i.e., directly, and in the latter case, it is κατὰ συμβεβηκός, i.e., indirectly, because of the accident that the wine happens to be sweet. Here, too, the desire in both cases is only an accident. So interpreted, therefore, Aristotle's third kind of ambiguous terms inevitably refers to a term which indicates some common accident existing in two things, but in one of these things it exists 'primarily' and in the other it exists 'subsequently.'

This is exactly the explanation of ambiguous terms as given by Maimonides and as is also implied, as I have shown, in the examples used by Algazali and Averroes. They all speak of terms which indicate some common accident which exists in two things. Furthermore, a careful examination of the examples

[64] Metaphysics V, 18, 1022a, 29–31.

[65] Cf. above, nn. 27 and 28.

[66] Topics II, 3, 110b, 22–25.

[67] Metaphysics V, 30, 1025a, 30–32.

used by them will show that according to all of them the common accident exists in one of these things primarily and in the other subsequently. This is quite clear in the case of Averroes and Maimonides, for the 'vinaceousness' in Averroes' example belongs to grapes primarily and to a face subsequently, and similarly the human shape and appearance in Maimonides' example belongs to the living man primarily and to the corpse and figure or picture of a man subsequently. In the case of Algazali it is not so obvious. But if we take the term 'crown' in his example to refer to an ivory crown, it will follow that 'whiteness' belongs to ivory primarily and to the ivory crown subsequently. Indeed Algazali describes the difference between the whiteness of the ivory and that of the crown as a difference of 'intensity' and 'slightness' which, as we have shown, corresponds to what Aristotle calls a difference of 'more or less.' But it is quite possible that the change of vocabulary was introduced here intentionally for the purpose of indicating that in the example used the difference between the whiteness of the ivory and the ivory whiteness of the crown is that of 'primarily' and 'subsequently' and not that of 'more' or 'less.'

As for the illustration of ambiguous terms given by Maimonides, it can be explained, I believe, by the combination of the following circumstances: (*a*) The infrequency of the use of Aristotle's example of a real man and the picture of a man as an illustration of equivocal terms in Arabic philosophy. (*b*) The change of meaning in an Arabic term which originally in Arabic translations of Aristotle's works was used for the Greek term meaning 'equivocal.' (*c*) The double meaning of the term under which Algazali includes the example from a real man and the picture of a man.

(*a*) It is noteworthy that most of the Arabic original treatises on logic prior to Maimonides do not use the Aristotelian example from a real man and the picture of a man as an illustration for equivocal terms. Instead they use as an illustration the Arabic term '*ain* which means 'eye' and 'spring of water.' [68] In this indeed they had the precedent of post-Aristotelian Greek

[68] Additional meanings of the term '*ain* are given in Najāt (p. 142) and in Maqāṣid al-Falāsifah (p. 11).

philosophers who had similarly substituted for Aristotle's example the example of a word which has several unrelated meanings. Thus Philo uses the example of the term 'dog' which means a terrestrial animal, a marine monster and a celestial star.[69] The Neoplatonic commentators on Aristotle, such as Porphyry, Simplicius, Dexippus, Ammonius, Philoponus, Olympiodorus and Elias, all use such illustrations as Ajax, which refers to both the son of Oileus and the son of Telamon, and Alexander, which refers to both the son of Priam and the son of Philip.[70] Similarly John of Damascus, though in one place he reproduces the Aristotelian illustration,[71] in another place uses the illustration of 'dog' which means both a terrestrial and a marine dog.[72] The texts in which the example of a real man and the picture of a man does occur are: (*a*) The Arabic translation of Aristotle's *Categories*. (*b*) Avicenna's *Shifā'*. (3) Algazali's *Mi'yār al-'Ilm*, where, however, it occurs not as an illustration of equivocal terms but as in Porphyry's commentary on the *Categories* and as in John of Damascus' *Dialectica* as an illustration of terms which he calls *mutashābih*, reflecting the term ὁμοιότης used by Porphyry[73] and John of Damascus.[74] If we assume now that the direct source of Maimonides' example of a real man and the picture of a man was either the Arabic translation of Aristotle's *Categories* or Algazali's *Mi'yār al-'Ilm*, we shall be able to explain how Maimonides came to use that example as an illustration of ambiguous terms.

(*b*) In the Arabic translation of the *Categories*, in that passage where the example of a real man and the picture of a man occurs, the term used for 'equivocal' is not the term *mushtarak*, which is generally used by Maimonides, but rather the term *muttafiq*.[75] We further observe that while both the term

[69] De Plantatione Noe 37, § 151.

[70] Cf. their respective commentaries on Categories, Ch. 1, 1a, 1 ff., in Commentaria in Aristotelem Graeca.

[71] Dialectica, Ch. 16 (Migne, Vol. 94, Col. 580).

[72] Ibid., Ch. 30 (ibid., Col. 596).

[73] Porphyrius in Categorias, p. 65, ll. 25–30 and cf. l. 19.

[74] Dialectica, Ch. 30.

[75] Cf. M. Bouyges, op. cit., p. 6, l. 2 of Aristotle's Text.

mushtarak and the term *muttafiq* are used as translations of the Greek term for 'equivocal' in the early Arabic translation of Aristotle's *De Interpretatione*[76] as well as by such an early Arabic philosopher as Alfarabi,[77] later philosophers, such as Avicenna and Algazali, use only the term *mushtarak* in that sense. From this we have reason to infer that the term *muttafiq* in the course of time had lost its meaning of 'equivocal.' This inference may be confirmed by the fact that Averroes, in his Middle Commentary on the *Categories*, after reproducing from the old translation of the *Categories* the term "*muttafiqah*" found it necessary to add: "that is, *mushtarakah*."[78] But more than that. Not only has the term *muttafiq* lost its meaning of 'equivocal' but it has also acquired a new meaning, that of 'ambiguous,' for which the term generally used was *mushakkik*. Thus Algazali in two places in his *Maqāṣid al-Falāsifah*, in the Logic (pp. 11–12) and the Metaphysics (p. 44), uses *muttafiq*[79] as well as *mushakkik* in the sense of 'ambiguous,' and in the Logic he uses the former as the main term. Thus the changed meaning of the term *muttafiqah* used in the Arabic translation of Aristotle's *Categories* may furnish the explanation for the use made by Maimonides of Aristotle's example for equivocal terms as an example for ambiguous terms.

(*c*) Or, the explanation may be furnished by the duplicity of meaning of the term *mutashābih* under which Algazali reproduces the example of a real man and the picture of a man in his *Mi'yār al-'Ilm*. This term means both 'similar' and 'ambiguous.' If we assume therefore that Maimonides has drawn upon this work for his example of a real man and the

[76] Cf. "Glossar" under these two terms in Isidor Pollak, Die Hermeneutik des Aristoteles in der arabischen Übersetzung des Isḥāq ibn Ḥonain (Leipzig, 1913).

[77] Op. cit.

[78] Cf. M. Bouyges, op. cit., p. 6, l. 4.

[79] Translated into Hebrew by נאות (Kawwanot ha-Pilosofim, Ms. Paris, Bibliothèque Nationale, Cod. Heb. 901). In the Latin translation (Algazel's Metaphysics, ed. J. T. Muckle, 1933, p. 26, ll. 9–10) the term *muttafiq* is rendered "eo quod aptatur omnibus," which follows immediately the statement "et vocatur nomen ambiguum," and it is thus taken not as an alternative of the term *mushakkik* (*ambiguum*) but rather as an explanation of it. The Arabic as printed should be rendered "aut vocatur nomen aptum." Evidently the Latin translation is based upon a different reading of the Arabic text.

picture of a man, it is quite possible that he took the term *mutashābih* in both these meanings. He therefore combined it with the term *mushakkik* and placed under it the example of a real man and the picture of a man. Traces of such a combination are to be noticed in *Moreh Nebukim* I, 56, where in his description of terms used 'ambiguously' (*bi-tashkīk*) he maintains that "ambiguous terms imply a certain similarity (*tashābuh*)." The plausibility of this assumption may be further supported by the fact that the Arabic term for 'similarity' (*ishtibāh*) was taken in the sense of 'ambiguity' by a mediaeval Latin translator from the Arabic in a passage which is the ultimate underlying source of the passage in Algazali under consideration. This passage in Algazali is unmistakably based upon a passage in which Porphyry describes what he calls ὁμώνυμος καθ' ὁμοιότητα.[80] But Porphyry's passage itself is undoubtedly based upon a passage in Aristotle's *Physics* VII, 4, 249a, 23–24, which says that "in the case of equivocal terms . . . sometimes there is a certain similarity (τινα ὁμοιότητα) between them." Now in the old Latin translation of the *Physics* made from the Arabic, this passage reads as follows: "Aequivocarum . . . alia autem in eis est *ambiguitas*." [81] It is quite evident that the Greek ὁμοιότης here could not have become the Latin *ambiguitas* unless we assume that the intermediate Arabic term was *ishtibāh* which means both 'similarity' and 'ambiguity' and that the Latin translator took it in the sense of ambiguity. Similarly in the Latin translation of Averroes' Long Commentary on this passage the term *ambiguitas*[82] undoubtedly reflects the Arabic *ishtibāh*.

If we assume therefore that Maimonides has learned of the

[80] Porphyrius in Categorias, p. 65, l. 19, cf. Baneth, op. cit., p. 37.

[81] Aristotelis Opera (Venice, 1574), Vol. IV, p. 331 E.

[82] Ibid., p. 331 I–K. Incidentally, it may be noted that as in the case of the term *mutashābih* so also in the case of the term *mushkil*, from its original meaning of 'similar' it came to mean 'ambiguous' (cf. Lane's Arabic-English Lexicon, s.v.) in which sense it is used by Alfarabi in his description of ambiguous terms (loc. cit.), though in this case of Alfarabi it may be a corruption of *mushakkik*, as has been suggested by Baneth (op. cit., p. 38, n. 18). An indirect suggestion as to some sort of association between the terms 'similar' and 'ambiguous' may be discerned in the statement "habet quamdam similitudinem atque ambiguitatem" in Boetii in Librum De Interpretatione Editio Secunda (Migne, Vol. 64, Col. 466 B; ed. Meiser, p. 143, ll. 15–16).

example of a real man and the picture of a man either from the Arabic translation of the *Categories* or from Algazali's *Mi'yār al-'Ilm*, we can easily see how he came to use that example as an illustration for ambiguous terms.

We have seen thus that the Arabic term *mushakkik* both historically, as a translation of the Greek ἀμφίβολος, and etymologically, as a derivative of the Arabic root *shakk*, to doubt, is to be translated in any language by a term which means 'doubtful' or 'ambiguous.' Now, in Hebrew it is always correctly translated by *mesuppaq*. In Latin translations from the Arabic, however, there is no uniformity in the term used for *mushakkik*. In the old mediaeval translations it is on the whole correctly rendered by *ambiguus*.[83] But in the 15th century Latin translations from the Hebrew it is often translated by *analogicus*.[84] Similarly in modern translations from the Arabic the term *mushakkik* is also often translated by 'analogical.'[85]

The reason for this, it seems to me, is to be found in St. Thomas Aquinas and the other scholastic writers who follow his vocabulary. In Thomas Aquinas the term *analogia*, with its derivative forms, has many meanings, based upon various sources, and among them are included some of those mean-

[83] Cf. Algazel's Metaphysics, ed. J. T. Muckle (1933), p. 26, l. 9, corresponding to p. 106, l. 15 of *Maqāṣid al-Falāsifah*, and the old mediaeval Latin translation of Maimonides' Moreh Nebukim (Dux seu Director Dubitantium aut Perplexorum, Paris, 1520), I, 55 of Ḥarizi's version (corresponding to I, 56 of Ibn Tibbon's version).

[84] Cf. Latin translation of Averroes' Epitome of the Organon, made from the Hebrew by Abraham de Balmes, quoted above in n. 43; Latin translation of Averroes' Epitome of the Metaphysics, made from the Hebrew by Mantinus, in Aristotelis Opera (Venice, 1574), Vol. VIII, p. 359 K and p. 364 A; Latin translation of Maimonides' Millot ha-Higgayon, made from the Hebrew by Munster (Logica Sapientis Rabbi Simeonis, Basel, 1527), Ch. 13; Hebrew and Latin texts quoted in I. Husik, Judah Messer Leon's Commentary on the "Vetus Logica" (1906), p. 84.

[85] Cf. M. Horten, Die Metaphysik des Averroes (1912), p. 40, l. 1; C. Quirós, Averroes Compendio de Metafisica (1919), Spanish translation, p. 58, § 3; S. van den Bergh, Die Epitome der Metaphysik des Averroes (1924), p. 28, l. 28. Dieterici in Alfarabi's philosophische Abhandlungen, p. 146, correctly translates it by "die doppelsinnigen" but his translation of *al-muttafiqah* by 'analoge' (p. 145) is not quite correct in this instance (cf. above, n. 77, and Baneth, op. cit., p. 34, n. 6). I. Madkour in his L'Organon d'Aristote dans le monde arabe (1934) translates *mushakkik* by "équivoque" (p. 61), which in its strictly technical sense is only a synonym of "homonyme" by which he translates *mushtarak* (p. 62).

ings which in Arabic texts, through the influence of the Greek commentators on Aristotle, we have found to be attached to terms which they describe as ambiguous, so that while in Arabic philosophy 'analogical' terms are included under 'ambiguous' terms, in St. Thomas, quite conversely, 'ambiguous' terms, which he does not specify directly, are included under 'analogical' terms. Thus like the 'ambiguous' terms in Arabic philosophy, the 'analogical' terms in St. Thomas are said (*a*) to be neither 'equivocal' nor 'univocal,'[86] (*b*) to be applied to different things according to the order of priority and posteriority,[87] and (*c*) are illustrated by the example of the term 'being' in its application to 'substance' and 'accident.'[88] One can therefore readily see how translators from the Arabic or the Hebrew who were acquainted with this use of the term 'analogical' in Latin philosophic literature would come to use it as a translation of the corresponding Arabic term *mushakkik* or Hebrew term *mesuppaq*.

To sum up the results of our discussion. We have shown that an intermediate type of term, one that is neither 'equivocal' nor 'univocal,' is mentioned by Aristotle himself in such places as *Topics* II, 3, 110b, 16–17, and *Metaphysics* IV, 2, 1003a, 33–34 and VII, 4, 1030a, 34–35. The name 'ambiguous' was given to it by Alexander in his commentary on the *Topics*. In Aristotle's discussion in *Topics* II, 3, 110b, 16–111a, 7, of what Alexander calls for him ambiguous terms, four types of such terms are enumerated: 1. Terms applied to things having one end or else, according to passages in *Metaphysics* XI, 3, 1061a, 3–5 and *Nicomachean Ethics* I, 6, 1096b, 27–28, proceeding from one source. 2. Terms applied to things which are contraries. 3. Terms applied to certain common accidents which exist in things according to a difference of primariness and subsequency. 4. Relative and hence also analogical terms. 5. A fifth type of ambiguous terms is referred to in *De Anima* I, 1, 402b, 6–8, as interpreted by Alexander, and in many pas-

[86] Contra Gentiles I, 34: "neque univoce neque aequivoce, sed analogice."

[87] I. Sententiarum, Distinct. 35, Quaest. 1, Art 4, Solutio: "Sed duplex est analogia. Quaedam secundum conventiam in aliquo uno, quod eis per prius et posterius convenit."

[88] Contra Gentiles I, 34: "sicut *ens* de substantia et accidente dicitur."

sages in the *Metaphysics*, such as VII, 4, 1030a, 21–22, VII, 1, 1028a, 13–15 and 30–31, namely, that which is used according to priority and posteriority or according to first and next. We have also shown how the various descriptions of ambiguous terms which occur in the writings of Alfarabi, Avicenna, Algazali, Averroes and Maimonides reproduce either one or more than one of those five types of ambiguous terms enumerated by Aristotle. Alfarabi and Avicenna mention 2 (contraries) and 5 (prior and posterior). Algazali mentions 1 (one end and one source), 3 (accident) and 5 (prior and posterior). Averroes mentions 1 (one end and one source or both), 3 (accident), 4 (analogy) and 5 (prior and posterior). Maimonides mentions 3 (accident). We have further shown how the examples used by them in illustration of the various types of ambiguous terms are also derived from Aristotle. Finally, we have shown how under the influence of the terminology of St. Thomas Aquinas, whose term 'analogy' has absorbed what in Arabic philosophy is called 'ambiguous,' the Arabic as well as the Hebrew term for 'ambiguous' is often translated into Latin and modern languages by the term 'analogical.'

23

THE TERMS *TAṢAWWUR* AND *TAṢDĪQ* IN ARABIC PHILOSOPHY AND THEIR GREEK, LATIN AND HEBREW EQUIVALENTS

Throughout the history of Arabic philosophy, beginning with Alfarabi, works on Logic open with the formula that knowledge is divided into *taṣawwur* and *taṣdīq*. These two terms lend themselves to various translations,[1] of which "formation" and "affirmation" are closest to the original Arabic. The distinction, on the whole, corresponds to the distinction usually made by logicians between "simple apprehension" and "judgment." But the origin of these two Arabic terms has baffled modern scholarship for over a century. As to the various explanations which have been offered, we shall enumerate them and comment upon them at the end of the paper, after we have completed our own investigation of the subject.

But let us first get a complete and orderly picture of the manner in which the distinction is used in Arabic philosophy. As the basis of our investigation we shall take eight texts of five Arabic authors: I. Alfarabi's (1) *'Uyūn al-Masā'il*,[2] II. Avicenna's (2) *Shifā'*,[3] (3) *Najāt*[4] and (4) *Ishārāt*,[5] III. Algazali's (5) *Maqāṣid al-Falāsifah*,[6] IV. Shahrastani's (6) *Kitāb al-Milal wal-Niḥal*,[7] and V, Averroes' (7) *Faṣl al-Maqāl wal-Taqrīr mā bain al-Sharī'ah wal-Hikmiah min al-Ittiṣāl*,[8] and (8) *Epitome of the Organon*.[9] Of these eight texts, the *'Uyūn* and the *Maqāṣid* give complete treatments of the subject; the others contain abridged or fragmentary treatments of it.

To begin with, there are two terms which are used in the various Arabic texts as a description of that which is divided into *taṣawwur* and *taṣdīq*. They are the terms doctrine (*ma'rifah*) and discipline (*'ilm*),[10] though sometimes only the term doctrine (*ta'ālīm*)[11] or only the term discipline (*'ilm*)[12] or disciplines (*'ulūm*)[13] is used.

Then, in the various definitions of the *taṣawwur* and *taṣdīq* in these Arabic texts, we find certain characteristic terms which describe the distinction between them. As contrasted with *taṣdīq, taṣawwur* is called the first knowledge *(al-'ilm al-awwal).*[14] It is said to imply that there is (1) a thing *(al-shai,*[15] *res*[16]*)* or a simple thing *(amr sādij)*[17] and that that simple thing is designated by (2) a term *(ism,*[18] *nomen*[19]*)* or by a single term *(dictio separata*[20]*),* which conveys to the mind (3) the meaning *(ma'na,*[21] *intentio*[22]*)* or the essence *(substantia*[23]) of that thing, in which meaning, however, (4) there is no truth or falsehood.[24] In contradistinction to this, *taṣdīq* is said to be the "assertion or the denial of something about something."[25]

Besides the main distinction between *taṣawwur* and *taṣdīq,* each of these two is further subdivided into primary *(awwaliyy)* and acquired *(muktasib).*[26] The primary kind of *taṣawwur* is described as that which "comes to a stop and is not connected with any preceding *taṣawwur,*"[27] whereas acquired *taṣawwur* is that which "is completed only by some preceding *taṣawwur,*"[28] and similarly primary *taṣdīq* is that which "is not preceded by another *taṣdīq* upon which it is dependent," whereas acquired *taṣdīq* is that "which one cannot comprehend without having comprehended some other things." Or, the distinction between primary *taṣawwur* and *taṣdīq* and acquired *taṣawwur* and *taṣdīq* is said to be between "that which is comprehended primarily without investigation and search and that which is obtained only by investigation." There is thus altogether a fourfold division: (1) primary *taṣawwur,* (2) acquired *taṣawwur,* (3) primary *taṣdīq,* and (4) acquired *taṣdīq.*

Each of these four kinds of knowledge is illustrated in the various Arabic texts by certain examples. Let us examine these examples.

Primary *taṣawwur* is illustrated in the *'Uyūn* by the terms "necessity" *(al-wujūb),* "existence" *(al-wujūd)* and possibility *(al-mukn),*[29] and these are described as "self-evident and true concepts which are implanted in the mind."[30] In the *Maqāṣid,* it is illustrated by the terms being *(al-maujūd)* and thing *(al-shai).*[31] Now, the term "that which exists" or "being" (τὸ ὄν, *ens, al-maujūd),* together with the term "unity", is described by Aristotle as one of the most generic terms, transcending even the categories.[32] Similarly the term "thing" *(res)* is included in what in post-Aristotelian philosophy is known as the six *transcendentales,* which, like the terms "being" and "unity" in Aristotle, are described as the most generic terms.[33] Consequently in these Arabic texts, the primary kind of *taṣawwur* refers to those concepts which, like "being" and "one" in Aristotle and like the six *transcendentales* in post-Aristotelian philosophy, are most generic and therefore conceived without the aid of anything prior to them.

The acquired kind of *taṣawwur* is illustrated in the *'Uyūn* by the term body *(al-jism),* which, it says, implies a prior knowledge of the terms "length, breadth and depth,"[34] and to this kind of *taṣawwur* also evidently belong the terms sun, moon, soul and intellect, mentioned there previously as illustrations of the term *taṣawwur* in general.[35] In the *Maqāṣid* it is similarly illustrated by the terms body, tree, jinn, and spirit,[36] for all of these it says, depend upon "the conception of the things which reveal their essences."[37] In the *Shifā',* it is illustrated by the term "man."[38]

The descriptions or illustrations of these two kinds of *taṣawwur* in the other texts are not so clear, but we shall try to explain them in the light of the statements in those texts which we have quoted.

In the *Najāt* it is said that *taṣawwur* is acquired by a definition and what is like it, as, e.g., our forming the concept of the quiddity of a man."[39] This is evidently a description of the acquired kind of *taṣawwur,* though no distinction between these two kinds of *taṣawwur* is made in the *Najāt.* In Shahrastani the expression "definition and what is like it" is definitely used as an illustration of the acquired kind of *taṣawwur.*[40] Similarly in the *Ishārāt,* when "simple *taṣawwur*" is illustrated by "our knowledge of the meaning of the term triangle,"[41] the reference is to the acquired kind of *taṣawwur,* for the term "triangle" implies some prior conception, namely, that of "angles" and "three."

In the *Faṣl, taṣawwur* is illustrated by the terms "[1] the thing itself *(al-shai nafsuhu)* and [2] the image thereof *(mith-*

āluhu)."[42] Here, I take it, the term "the thing itself" should be understood in the sense of "the concept of thing" and as the equivalent of the term "thing" used in the *Maqāṣid,* where, as we have shown, it is used in the sense of what is known as the *transcendentales,* and hence this term should also be understood as being used by Averroes as an illustration of the primary kind of *taṣawwur*. Accordingly, the term "the image thereof" is to be taken here as referring to some perceptible thing, analogous to the term "body" in the *'Uyūn* and the *Maqāṣid,* and hence as being used by Averroes as an illustration of the acquired kind of *taṣawwur*.

If our interpretation of this statement of Averroes is correct, then the terms "the thing itself" and "the image thereof" are survivals of the Platonic philosophic vocabulary in a system of philosophy which is not Platonic. The term *al-shai nafsuhu* reflects exactly such Platonic terms as αὐτὸ τὸ καλόν[43] and πῦρ αὐτό,[44] which in Plato mean "the idea of beauty" and "the idea of fire," and the term *mithāl* is an exact translation of the Greek εἰκών, which is used by Plato as a description of perceptible objects.[45] Furthermore, Averroes' term *al-shai nafsuhu* is an exact literal translation of the term αὐτὸ τὸ πρᾶγμα which occurs in a Stoic fragment in Sextus Empiricus,[46] and which means the concept of a thing. Later, we shall show that some such passage as that recorded in Sextus Empiricus is one of the sources of the discussion of *taṣawwur* and *taṣdīq* in Arabic texts.[47]

The primary kind of *taṣdīq* is illustrated in the *'Uyūn* by the law of excluded middle and by the geometrical axiom that "the whole is greater than the part."[48] In the *Maqāṣid,* it is illustrated by two geometrical axioms and by what Aristotle calls primary premises (ἀρχαί) of which Algazali gives a list of thirteen.[49]

The acquired kind of *taṣdīq* is defined in the *Najāt* and in Shahrastani as that which is obtained by a syllogism *(qiyās)*.[50] In the *'Uyūn* it is illustrated by the proposition that "the world is created."[51] The *Maqāṣid* adds to this the propositions that bodies will be resurrected at the last judgment and that the obedient will be rewarded and the rebellious will be punished.[52] The *Najāt* uses as an illustration the proposition that "for everything there is a beginning,"[53] which is only another way of phrasing the proposition, "the world is created" used in the *'Uyūn,* and the *Ishārāt* uses the proposition that the angles of a triangle are equal to two right angles.[54] In the *Shifā'* the proposition that white is an accident is evidently also used as an illustration of the acquired kind of *taṣdīq*. In the *Epitome of the Organon,* it is illustrated by propositions regarding the existence of a vacuum and the creation of the world.

In the *Faṣl,* no formal distinction is made in *taṣdīq* between primary and acquired. All that Averroes says is that the methods of *taṣdīq* are three: "demonstrative *(al-burhāniyyah),* dialetical *(al-jadaliyyah)* and rhetorical *(al-ḫuṭbiyyah)".*[55] Ostensibly, this statement is based on a passage in *Analytica Posteriora* I, 1, quoted below,[56] where rhetorical persuasion is said to be based on "pre-existent knowledge", inasmuch as it uses "either example, a kind of induction, or enthymeme, a form of syllogism".[57] But, as used here by Averroes, I take it, "demonstrative and dialectical methods" refers to acquired *taṣdīq* and "rhetorical method" refers to primary *taṣdīq*. My reason for this interpretation of the passage is Averroes' explanation of the rhetorical method, in contradistinction to the dialectical and demonstrative methods, as a method which endeavors to establish belief by means of *mathal* and *shibh*.[58] These two terms, I take it, represent respectively the Greek γνώμη, *maxim,* and παράδειγμα, *example,* which, according to Aristotle, are two of the three rhetorical methods of establishing faith (πίστις *taṣdīq),* the third being the enthymeme,[59] which is left out here by Averroes. Now both maxim and example, in contradistinction to enthymeme, are considered by Aristotle as immediate or as non-syllogistic knowledge. Maxims are described by him as "conclusions or premises of enthymemes without the syllogisms"[60] and as being generally known or agreed upon or self-evident.[61] Similarly example is defined by him as a "rhetorical induction"[62] and induction is considered by him as being the opposite of syllogism and demonstration[63] and as depending upon our senses.[64] When therefore Averroes says that the methods of *taṣdīq* are "demonstrative, dialectical and rhetorical", he means thereby that *taṣdīq* is either acquired, such as is obtained syllogistically by arguments, or primary, such as is learned not syllogistically but rather immediately by "maxims" or inductively by "examples".

Here then we have a composite outline of what Arabic philosophers thought of *taṣawwur* and *taṣdīq*, how they defined these terms, how they subdivided each of these terms, and how they illustrated them by examples. We shall now try to show the Greek sources not only of the distinction in general, but of the general scheme of classification and of the examples used, and on the basis of all this we shall establish the origin of the terminology.

II

The key to these Greek sources is furnished by Averroes, who in at least three places in his commentaries on Aristotle connects the Arabic distinction between *taṣawwur* and *taṣdīq* with a particular passage in Aristotle which he happens to discuss.

The first passage in Aristotle with which Averroes connects the distinction of formation and affirmation is *De Interpretatione,* ch. 4. In that chapter, Aristotle makes a distinction between a sentence (λόγος, *qaul)* and a word (φάσις, *lafẓah).*[65] A sentence, he says, if it is enunciative (ἀποφαντικός, *jāzim),* has in it either truth or falsity,[66] whereas a word, though it has meaning (σημαντική), expresses no affirmation or negation.[67]

Commenting upon this, Averroes in the Latin translations of his Middle Commentary on the *De Interpretatione* says that what Aristotle calls "word" is *per modum intelligentiae et conceptionis* (or *intellectus et formationis), non per modum affirmationis et negationis.*[68] The Latin term *conceptio* or *formatio* here reflects the Arabic *taṣawwur.* Thus, according to Averroes' suggestion here, the Arabic distinction between *taṣawwur* and *taṣdīq* corresponds to Aristotle's distinction here between a "word" and an "enunciative sentence." This passage of Aristotle will also explain the use of the terms word *('ibārah, ism,* φάσις) and meaning *(ma'na,* σημαινόμενον) in connection with *taṣawwur* and the expressions affirmation and negation in connection with *taṣdīq.* Still, while the distinction made here by Aristotle undoubtedly corresponds to the distinction between *taṣawwur* and *taṣdīq* in the Arabic texts and while also Aristotle's ἀποφαντικὸς λόγος may explain the use of the term *taṣdīq,* for the ἀποφαντικὸς λόγος is defined as that "in which there is either truth or falsity"[69] and the term *taṣdīq* literally means "to consider truthful" or to "affirm," there is no explanation in this passage for the use of the term *taṣawwur.* Furthermore, Averroes couples here the term *intelligentia* or *intellectus* (= *'aql.)* with the term *conceptio* or *formatio (= taṣawwur).* We should like to know what reason is there for his coupling these two terms.

The second passage in Aristotle with which Averroes connects conception and judgment is *De Anima* III, 6.

In that passage of De Anima, Aristotle says: "The thinking (νόησις) of indivisibles is in those cases in which there is no falsehood; but in cases in which both truth and falsehood are possible, there is already some combining of notions into one."[70] Then later Aristotle explains these two statements. With regard to the second statement, he says: "The assertion (φάσις) of something about something, as, e.g., an affirmation, as well as every composite sentence, is either true or false."[71] With regard to the first statement, he says that in the case of thought (νοῦς), i.e., in the case of thinking (νόησις), "the assertion of the quiddity of a thing is true."[72]

Now in the Arabic translation of the *De Anima,* as may be judged from the Latin[73] as well as the Hebrew[74] translation of it which is included in Averroes' Long Commentary on it, the term νόησις in this passage was translated by *taṣwīr,* for in the Latin it is *formare* and in the Hebrew *ẓayyer.* By *formare* and its underlying Arabic *taṣwīr* is meant here the process of forming a concept in the mind, for in Arabic the term *taṣwīr* by itself may mean both the forming of an image and the forming of a concept,[75] though, through usage, it is more often associated with the formation of images. Commenting on this passage, Averroes identifies Aristotle's distinction between these two actions of the mind, namely, that of thinking (νόησις) of indivisibles, or the thought (νοῦς) of them, and that of the assertion of something concerning something with what he describes as the "more renowned" distinction between *formatio* and *fides*—two terms which reflect respectively the Arabic terms *taṣawwur* and *taṣdīq*.[76] Similarly, in his comment upon the statement in which Aristotle contrasts the "assertion of something about something" and "the assertion of the quiddity of a thing," Averroes refers to these two as *fides* and *formatio,* that is to say, *taṣdīq* and *taṣawwur*.[77] Furthermore, in his comment on Aristotle's expression "thinking of indivisibles," the term indivisibles (ἀδιαίρετα) is explained by him by the term simple things *(res simplices)*.[78] In this passage then, we have the source of the distinction between *taṣawwur* and *taṣdīq* in Arabic texts, the use of the terms "simple" and "quiddity" in the description of *taṣawwur* in some of those texts. Though the *taṣawwur* in the Arabic texts is said to be neither true nor false, whereas the νόησις of simple things is said here by Aristotle to be "in those things in which there is no falsehood," this statement must have been understood by Arabic philosophers to mean that there is in them neither falsehood nor truth. In fact, this is how this statement is interpreted by Averroes.[79] On the basis of this passage, too, we may assume that the Arabic *taṣawwur* is a translation of the Greek νόησις and is the equivalent of νοῦς. This will explain the use of the expression *per modum intelligentiae* (or *intellectus) et conceptionis* (or *formationis)* used by Averroes in the passage of his Middle Commentary on the *De Interpretatione* referred to above. In that passage *conceptio* or *formatio (taṣawwur)* represents νόησις, whereas *intellectus ('aql)* represents νοῦς, both of which are used interchangeably here in *De Anima.*

The third passage in Aristotle with which Averroes connects the distinction between *taṣawwur* and *taṣdīq* is in *Analytica Priora* I, 1-2.

In that passage Aristotle begins with the statement that "all doctrine (διδασκαλία) and all intellectual discipline (μάθησις) arise from pre-existent knowledge (προϋπαρχούση γνῶσις)."[80] The terms "doctrine" and "intellectual discipline" are explained by him to refer to (1) mathematical sciences and other arts, (2) logical reasoning and (3) rhetorical persuasion.[81] Then "pre-existent knowledge" is said by him to be of two kinds: (1) "with some things we must presuppose that they are, but (2) with others we must understand that which is spoken of."[82] As an illustration of the first kind of pre-existent knowledge he quotes the proposition stating the law of excluded middle,[83] and as an illustration of the second kind of pre-existent knowledge he mentions the term triangle.[84] In the course of his discussion he also mentions the geometrical proposition that the angles of every triangle are equal to two right angles as a previously known major premise in a syllogism,[85] but evidently this proposition, though described here as a previously known major premise in a syllogism, is itself subject to demonstration.[86]

In his Long Commentary on this passage Averroes quotes Alfarabi to the effect that the distinction drawn here by Aristotle refers to the distinction between primary and acquired under both *taṣawwur* and *taṣdīq*. Averroes, however, disagrees with him, contending that in the *Analytica Posteriora* Aristotle deals only with *taṣdīq*.[87] In his Middle Commentary, commenting upon Aristotle's two kinds of pre-existent knowledge, he says of the proposition stating the law of excluded middle that it is what is called *verificatio*, i.e., *taṣdīq*, and of the term triangle that it is what is called *formatio*, i.e., *taṣawwur*.[88]

From Averroes' discussion of this passage we may gather that the main distinction between *taṣawwur* and *taṣdīq* is already assumed and that all that this passage does is to introduce the subdivision of "primary" and "acquired" either under both *taṣawwur* and *taṣdīq* according to Alfarabi, or only under *taṣdīq* according to Averroes.

But though the main distinction between *taṣawwur* and

taṣdīq is not based upon this passage, some of the expressions and illustrations found in the Arabic texts we have quoted, in their discussion of this main distinction, are derived from this passage. Thus the terms *ma'rifah* and *'ilm* used in the *Najāt*[89] as that which is divided into *taṣawwur* and *taṣdīq*, and also the term *ta'alīm* used in the *Faṣl*[90] as the equivalent of *ma'rifah*, are literal translations of the terms διδασκαλία and μάθησις διανοητική used in this passage by Aristotle. Similarly the illustration of *taṣawwur* by the meaning of the term triangle,[91] the definition of *taṣdīq* as that which is true or false,[92] the illustration of the primary kind of *taṣdīq* by the proposition stating the law of excluded middle,[93] the definition of the acquired kind of *taṣdīq* as being based upon demonstrative, dialectical and rhetorical arguments,[94] and the illustration thereof by the geometrical proposition that the angles of a triangle are equal to two right angles[95]—all this is to be found in this passage of the *Analytica Posteriora.*

We have now collected from the writings of Aristotle all the strands from which were woven together the various discussions in Arabic literature of the distinction between *taṣawwur* and *taṣdīq*. In Aristotle, too, we have found the prototype of these two Arabic terms. Of *taṣawwur* it is νόησις; of *taṣdīq* it is ἀποφαντικὸς λόγος. But still all this does not seem to us to explain everything. We have a feeling that between the scattered statements in Aristotle and the concise formal distinction which we find in Arabic literature from Alfarabi on, there must have been some intermediate source in which that formal distinction as we find it in Arabic literature is already to be found. Can we find some such source? Then, again, with regard to the term *taṣdīq*, while it may be explained etymologically as having been suggested by the definition of ἀποφαντικὸς λόγος,[96] we have a feeling that there must have already been in Greek one single term which expressed that idea and of which one single term the term *taṣdīq* is a direct translation. Is there such a term to be found in Greek literature?

A passage like the one which we feel must have been the immediate source of the Arabic discussions of *taṣawwur* and *taṣdīq* is to be found, I believe, in Sextus Empiricus.

Speaking in the name of the Stoics, he says: "Three things are connected with each other, the meaning (τὸ σημαινόμενον), that which expresses the meaning (τὸ σημαῖνον) and the thing (τὸ τυγχάνον). Of these, that which expresses the meaning is the spoken word, as the word Dion; the meaning is the concept of the thing (αὐτὸ τὸ πρᾶγμα), which is designated by the spoken word and which, when presented before our mind, is apprehended by us; the barbarians do not understand this, even though they hear a voice; the thing, finally, is that which has external existence, as Dion himself. Of these, two are corporeal, namely, the spoken word and thing, and one is incorporeal, namely, [the concept of] the thing meant (σημαινόμενον πρᾶγμα) and expressed (λεκτόν), and this may be either true or false. This last statement, however, does not apply to all verbal expressions alike, for of verbal expressions some are defective (i.e., words) and others are complete in themselves (i.e., enunciative sentences), the latter kind being called judgment (ἀξίωμα), and it is this latter kind which they (the Stoics) describe by saying: 'Judgment is that which is either true or false'."[97] To this statement of Sextus Empiricus, we may add the fact that in Diogenes' restatement of the teachings of the Stoics, the term φαντασία λογική, *rational imagination,* is used as corresponding to the terms τὸ σημαινόμενον, *the meaning,* and αὐτὸ τὸ πρᾶγμα, *concept of the thing.* But the Stoic φαντασία λογική, we know, is used as the equivalent of what Aristotle calls νόησις.[98] Similarly we know that the Stoic ἀξίωμα is used as the equivalent of what Aristotle calls ἀποφαντικὸς λόγος,[99] and it differs from Aristotle's use of the term ἀξίωμα, with whom it means the indemonstrable premises of a demonstration.[100]

It is some statement like the one quoted in Sextus Empiricus in the name of the Stoics that may be considered as the intermediary source under the influence of which the Aristotelian views on this subject were formulated in Arabic philosophy. Here we get all the four characteristics of *taṣawwur* that we have met with in the Arabic texts, viz., (1) thing,

(2) meaning, (3) word, and (4) neither true nor false. Here, too, we find the single word ἀξίωμα, which can perfectly serve as a model of the Arabic term *taṣdīq*. Diogenes, quoting Chrysippus, says: "A judgment (ἀξίωμα) is that which in and by itself can be denied or affirmed," and then adds: "The Greek word for judgment (ἀξίωμα) is derived from the verb ἀξιοῦν, *to consider worthy,* as signifying acceptance or rejection."[101] The Arabic word for judgment *(taṣdīq),* we may similarly say, is derived from the verb *taṣdīq, to consider truthful,* as signifying acceptance or rejection. We have already called attention to the fact that the term *al-shai nafsuhu* used by Averroes is an exact translation of the term αὐτὸ τὸ πρᾶγμα used in the Stoic quotation in Sextus Empiricus.[102]

In the light of this discussion, let us examine the various explanations of the origin of *taṣawwur* to which we have referred at the beginning of the paper. Schmoelders, who was the first among modern scholars to deal with the subject, merely refers to Aristotle's distinction between axiom or thesis and demonstration.[103] But these terms can at best be used only as source of the distinction between primary and acquired *taṣdīq,* but not of the distinction between *taṣawwur* and *taṣdīq*. Prantl, in the first edition of his work, identified *formatio* and *verificatio* in the Latin translation of Averroes' *Epitome of the Organon* with definition and argumentation respectively, and suggested that the terms *formatio* and *verificatio* were introduced from "Arabic-Jewish" literature.[104] Steinschneider corrected him and added references, but did not explain the origin of these terms.[105] Beer confesses ignorance of the origin of these two terms and suggests that they must have been original Arabic terms coined especially for the purpose of designating the two parts into which logic was usually divided.[106] Nallino positively declares that these terms have no equivalents in Aristotle's logic, and described them as oriental.[107] This, as we have seen, is incorrect. Madkour declares this distinction to be a restatement of what he describes as Aristotle's distinction at the beginning of the *Analytica Posteriora* between "intuition and rational" knowledge.[108] This passage, as we have seen, explains only the origin of the distinction between primary and derivative either under both *taṣawwur* and *taṣdīq,* according to Alfarabi, or only under *taṣdīq,* according to Averroes, but it is not the origin of the main distinction between *taṣawwur* and *taṣdīq*. Kraus suggests the Stoic φαντασία and συγκατάθεσις as the origin of the terms *taṣawwur* and *taṣdīq*.[109] As we have seen, the equivalent of *tasawwur* in Stoic vocabulary is not φαντασία but rather φαντασία λογική, and the opposite of that term in the Stoic vocabulary corresponding to *taṣdīq* is not συγκατάθεσις but rather ἀξίωμα. The term συγκατάθεσις is never contrasted with φαντασία in the same way as *taṣdīq* is contrasted with *taṣawwur.*

In conclusion we may now give the genealogy of these two terms in Greek, Arabic, Hebrew and Latin.

Taṣawwur

Greek—(a) Aristotle: νόησις (b) Stoics: φαντασία λογική.
Arabic—from Greek (a): *taṣawwur.*
Hebrew—from Arabic: *ẓiyyur.*
Latin—(a) from Arabic:
- (1) *imaginatio* (Algazali's *Maqāṣid*).
- (2) *formatio* (Averroes' Long Commentary on *De Anima* III, Comm. 21).
- (3) *informatio* (*Ibid.,* Comm. 26).

(b) from Hebrew:
- (1) *conceptio* (Abraham de Balmes' translation of the Long Commentary on *Analytica Posteriora* I, Comm. 1).
- (2) *formatio* (Burana's translation of the same).
- (3) *notitia* (Mantinus' translation of the same).
- (4) *conceptus* (*ibid.*); also *formatio.*

Taṣdīq

Greek—(a) Aristotle: ἀποφαντικὸς λόγος (b) Stoics ἀξίωμα.
Arabic—from Greek (b): *taṣdīq.*
Hebrew—from Arabic: *ẓidduḳ,* (also *haẓdaḳah, heẓdeḳ*)[110] *immut, ha'amatah* (cf. above n. 76).
Latin—(a) from Arabic:
- (1) *credulitas* (Avicenna's *Shifā'*; Algazali's *Maqāṣid*).
- (2) *fides* (Averroes' Long Commentary on *De Anima* III, Comm. 21 and 26).

(b) from Hebrew:
- (1) *assertio* (Abraham de Balmes, *loc. cit.*).
- (2) *verificatio* (Burana, *loc. cit.*).
- (3) *certificatio* (Mantinus, *loc. cit.*).
- (4) *certitudo* (*ibid.*); also *fides.*

NOTES

1 See list of translations at the end of the paper.

2 F. Dieterici, *Alfārābī's philosophische Abhandlungen,* Arabic, 1890, p. 56; German, 1892, pp. 92-3.

3 Logyca, Prima Pars, fol. 2va, in *Avicennae opera,* Venice, 1508.

4 ed. Cairo, 1331 A. H., pp. 3-4.

5 *Kitāb al-Ishārāt wal-Tanbīhat. Le Livre des théoremes et des avertissements,* ed. J. Forget, 1892, pp. 3-4.

6 *Maqāṣid al-Falāsifah* I, ed. Cairo, no date, pp. 4-5. Latin from quotations in Prantl, *Geschichte der Logik,* II, 2nd ed., 1885, p. 368, nn. 236-7; Hebrew from MS. in the Jewish Theological Seminary.

7 Arabic, ed. Cureton, pp. 348-9; German by Haarbrücker, II, pp. 213-214.

8 ed. M. J. Müller, *Philosophie und Theologie von Averroes,* 1859, p. 19.

9 Latin translation in *Aristotelis opera,* Venice, 1874, Vol. I, Pars II, p. 36B-H. Hebrew translation: *Ḳol Meleket Higgayon,* Riva di Trento, 1559, p. 2a-b.

10 *Najāt,* p. 3, 1. 13. Perhaps, instead of *ma'rifah,* the reading here should be *mu'rifah,* inasmuch as this term here, as we shall show later, is a translation of the Greek διδασκαλία as distinguished from *'ilm,* μάθησις (cf. below at nn. 89 and 90).

11 *Faṣl,* p. 9, 1. 10.

12 *'Uyūn,* p. 56, 1. 3; Shahrastani, p. 348, 1. 17.

13 *Maqāṣid,* p. 4, 1. 7.

14 *Najāt,* p. 13, 1. 14; Shaharastani, p. 348, 1. 18.

15 *Ishārāt,* p. 3, 1. 15.

16 *Shifā',* p. 2va, 1. 27.

17 Shahrastani, p. 348, 1. 18; cf. *Ishārāt,* p. 3, 1. 16; *Epitome of the Organon,* Latin: *intellectus rei* (p. 36E); Hebrew: *habanat ha-dabar* (p. 2a, 1. 20).

18 *Ishārāt,* p. 3, 1. 16.

19 *Shifā',* p. 2va, 11. 28-9.

20 *Epitome of the Organon,* p. 36F; Hebrew: *millah nifredet* (p. 2a, 11.29-30).

21 *Ishārāt,* p. 3, 1. 16.

22 *Shifā',* p. 2va, 1. 30.

23 *Epiome of the Organon,* p. 36E. Hebrew: *'aẓmut* (p. 2a, 1. 21), which reflects the Arabic *dhāt.* Hence the definition of *taṣawwur* in the *Maqāṣid* (p. 4, 11. 8-9) is to be translated as follows: "It is the apprehension of the essence of individual things (*al-dhawat;* Latin: *rerum;* Hebrew: *'aẓmuyyot*) which are designated by single words (*'ibārāt mufradah;* Latin: *singulae dictiones;* Hebrew: *meliẓot nifradot*) as a means of communicating their meaning (*al-tafhīm;* Latin: *ad intelligendum;* Hebrew: *'al derek ha-habanah*) and imparting a knowledge of their true nature (*al-taḥqīq;* Latin: *ad certificandum;* Hebrew: *ha-hit 'atmut*)."

24 *Shifā',* p. 2va, 1. 30: *quamvis non sit ibi veritas nec falsitas.*

25 *Epitome of the Organon,* p. 36E; Hebrew: p. 2a, 11. 23-4; Shahrastani, p. 348, 11. 19-20.

26 Shahrastani, p. 349, 1. 1.

27 *'Uyūn,* p. 56, 1. 8.

28 *Ibid.,* 1. 5.

29 *Ibid.,* § 2, p. 56, 11. 16-7.

30 *Ibid.,* p. 56, 1. 13.

31 *Maqāṣid,* p. 5, 11.4-5.

32 *Metaph.* III, 3, 998b, 17-21.

33 Thomas Aquinas, *De Veritate,* I, 1 c.

34 p. 56, 1. 6.

35 p. 56, 11. 3-4.

36 p. 4, 1. 10; p. 5, 11. 6-7.

37 p. 5, 1. 7.

38 p. 2va, 1. 27.

39 p. 3, 1. 13-p. 4, 1. 1.

40 p. 349, 11. 1-2.

41 p. 3, 1. 16.

42 p. 19, 11. 12-13.

43 *Rep.* VI, 493E.

44 *Tim.* 51B.

45 *Ibid.* 49C; *Soph.* 240B, *et passim.*

46 *Adversus Logicos* VIII (II), 12.

47 Cf. below n. 97.

48 p. 56, 11. 17-18; cf. Euclid, *Elements,* Common Notion 5.

49 p. 5, 11. 7-11; cf. p. 52, 1. 4-p. 57, 1. 17.

50 p. 4, 1. 1; p. 349, 11. 2-3.

51 p. 56, 1. 14.

52 p. 5, 1. 12-13.

53 p. 4, 1. 2.

54 p. 3, 11. 17-18; cf. Euclid, *Elements,* I, 32.

55 *Faṣl,* p. 19, 11. 11-12.

56 Cf. below n. 81.

57 *Anal. Post.* I, 1, 71a, 10-11.

58 *Faṣl,* p. 15, 11. 8-13.

59 *Rhet.* II, 20, 1393a, 23-24.

60 *Ibid.* II, 21, 1394a, 27-28.

61 *Ibid.* II, 21, 1394b, 10-15.

62 *Ibid.* I, 2, 1356b, 4-5.

63 *Anal. Pr.* II, 23, 68b, 13.

64 *Anal. Post.* I, 18, 81a, 38-81b, 9.

65 *De Interp.,* 4, 16b, 26-27. For ϑάσις in the sense of "assertion" see quotation below n. 71 and cf. Bonitz, *Index Aristotelicus,* s. v.

66 *Ibid.,* 17a, 2-3.

67 *Ibid.,* 16b, 27-28.

68 In *Aristotelis opera,* Venice, 1574, Vol. I, Pars I, p. 72E.

69 *De Interp.,* 17a, 3.

70 *De Anima* III, 6, 430a, 26-28.

71 *Ibid.,* 430b, 26-27. In the Latin translation from the Arabic, this passage reads: "Et dicere aliquid de aliquo, sicut affirmatio, et omne compositum est verum vel falsum". In this translation, the Greek πᾶσα (1.27), which underlies the Latin *omne compositum,* was evidently taken by the Arabic translator to refer to λόγος σύνθετος in *De Interp.,* 5, 17a, 22, i.e., a proposition consisting of both an affirmation and a negation, as, e.g., A is B, not C. My translation of this passage follows the Latin translation from the Arabic. Cf. the same passage in English translations of *De Anima.*

[72] *Ibid.*, 430b, 27-29. In the Latin translation from the Arabic (Text. 26) this passage reads: *sed qui dicit quiditatem rei est verus.* Evidently the expression *quiditatem rei* is a translation of the entire Greek expression τοῦ τί ἐστι κατὰ τὸ τί ἦν εἶναι in l. 28. My translation of this passage here follows the Latin translation from the Arabic.

[73] Liber III, Text. 21, in *Aristotelis opera,* Venice, 1574, Vol. VI, p. 165F.

[74] MS. Berlin, Cod. Heb. 1387-8.

[75] Cf. *The Moslem World,* XXXI (1941), 38.

[76] *De Anima,* III, Comm. 21. The corresponding terms in the Hebrew translation are *ẓiyyur* and *ha'amatah* (but *immut* in Comm. 26). St. Thomas, in his restatement of this passage of Averroes (*De Veritate,* XIV, 1 c), has the term *imaginatio* in place of *formatio*: "Unde etiam et apud Arabes prima operatio intellectus vocatur imaginatio, secunda autem vocatur fides, ut patet ex verbis Commentatoris in III. De Anima (com. XXI)".

[77] *Ibid.*, Comm. 26.

[78] *Ibid.*, Comm. 21. Hebrew: *ha-debarim ha'bilti mitḥalḳim.*

[79] *Ibid.*, Comm. 21. But in Comm. 26, Averroes says: "sed actio quae est informatio, est semper vera"—an inconsistency to which attention is called on the margin of the 1574 Venice edition, p. 169B-C.

[80] *Anal. Post.* I, 1, 71a, 1-2.

[81] *Ibid.*, 71a, 3-11.

[82] *Ibid.*, 71a, 11-13.

[83] *Ibid.*, 71a, 13-14.

[84] *Ibid.*, 71a, 14-15.

[85] *Ibid.*, 71a, 19-20.

[86] In Euclid (I, 32) this is given as a geometrical proposition and not as a common notion or postulate. So also in *Metaph.* IX, 9, 1051a, 24-26.

[87] Long Commentary on *Analytica Posteriora* I, Comm. 19, Burana's translation:

"Enuntiatio haec, quemadmodum dixit Abunazar, comprehendit sub subiecto suo omnia, quaecunque sunt in hoc libro et hoc, quia cum dixit: Omnis doctrina et omnis disciplina, comprehendit sub se omnes species quaesitorum, quae procedunt secundum viam verificationis et secundum viam formationis" (p. 12E).

"Sed oportet etiam, ut consyderemus de hac enuntiatione quae dixit Abunazar et alij, an comprehendat verificationem inductam et formationem. Quoniam verba Aristotelis et exempla, quibus utitur, videntur esse ex materia verificationis, non ex materia formationis" (p. 13F).

[88] Middle Commentary on *Analytica Posteriora* I, p. 1E-G, Burana's translation:

"Cognitio autem, quam oportet praecedere in omni eo, quod assequimur per cogitationem ac syllogismum, est duobus modis: aut enim cognoscitur quod res sit, aut non sit, et haec cognitio vocatur verificatio; aut cognoscitur quid significet nomen ipsius, et vocatur formatio. Oportet autem discipulum in quibusdam praecognoscere quod sunt tantum, quemadmodum in propositione, quae dicit de omni vera est aut affirmatio, aut negatio, propterea quod in huiuscemodi propositionibus, opus est, ut cognoscamus veritatem ipsorum tantum, quodque nemo ipso renuit praeter Sophistas. In quibusdam vero oportet ut praecognoscat quid significent nomina eorum tantum, quemadmodum oportet Geometram praecognosccere, quid significet nomen circuli in arte sua, et nomen trianguli."

It is evidently on the basis of this passage of Averroes that Narboni in his Hebrew commentary on the *Maqāṣid,* 1 c. (MS. Jewish Theological Seminary) says: "*Ẓiyyur* (*taṣawwur*) is the knowledge of quiddity; *immut* (*taṣdīq*) is the knowledge of existence".

[89] Cf. above n. 10.

[90] Cf. above n. 11.

[91] Cf. above n. 41.

[92] Cf. above nn. 24, 25.

[93] Cf. above n. 48.

[94] Cf. above n. 55.

[95] Cf. above n. 54.

[96] Cf. above n. 66.

[97] Sextus Empiricus, *Adversus Logicos* VIII(II), 11-12. With this translation of the passage compare the translation by Bury in The Loeb Classical Library and also the Latin translation by Hervetus in ed. Fabricius, Leipzig, 1841.

[98] Cf. Index to Arnim, *Stoicorum Veterum Fragmenta,* sub νόησις.

[99] Cf. *ibid.*, sub ἀξίωμα.

[100] *Metaph.* III, 2, 997a, 7-8.

[101] Diogenes Laertius, VII, 65.

[102] Cf. above n. 46.

[103] *Documenta Philosophiae Arabum,* 1836, p. 88.

[104] *Geschichte der Logik,* II, 1st ed., 1861, p. 385, n. 346. In the 2nd ed. (1885, p. 397, n. 386) Prantl changed his entire treatment of the *Epitome of the Organon,* evidently as a result of Steinschneider's criticism (see next note).

[105] *Al-Farabi,* 1869, pp. 147-148.

[106] *Al-Gazzali's Makasid al-Falasifat,* 1888, pp. 8-9.

[107] "Filosofia 'orientale' od 'illuminativa' d'Avicenna?", *Rivista degli Studii Orientali,* X (1923-25), 460.

[108] *L'Organon d'Aristote dans le monde arabe,* 1934, 54-55.

[109] "Abstracta Islamica", p. 220, in *Revue des Études Islamiques,* 9 (1935). Cf. *The Moslem World,* XXX (1941), 38, and above n. 69.

[110] Cf. Klatzkin, *Oẓar ha-Munaḥim ha-Piloṣofiyyim,* s. v.

24

THE CLASSIFICATION OF SCIENCES IN MEDIAEVAL JEWISH PHILOSOPHY

BETWEEN THE TWO TYPES of classification of sciences traditionally attributed to Plato and Aristotle the basic differences are to be found in the general scheme of the classification as well as in the inclusion and omission of certain sciences. In the so-called Aristotelian classification all the sciences are divided into three main classes, theoretical, *θεωρητική*, practical, *πρακτική*, and productive, *ποιητική*[1], or—as the last is better known by its mediaeval designation—*ars mechanica*. The theoretical is subdivided into physics, mathematics and metaphysics;[2] the practical into politics, economics and ethics.[3] The mathematics of Aristotle's classification was again subdivided by Ammonius Hermiae into arithmetic, geometry, astronomy and music[4]—a fourfold classification which was generally adopted and was known among the Schoolmen as the *quadrivium*. Logic is excluded from this scheme of classification, being considered only as an instrument and as auxiliary to all the other sciences. The classification which is identified with the name of Plato differs from this classification in the following respects. It does not mention the distinction between the theoretical and practical science; it does not number mathematics among the sciences; it includes logic as a co-ordinate science, which, however, it uses in the more general sense of dialectics and as synonymous with metaphysics. The Platonic classification thus falls into three parts: logic, physics and ethics.[5]

[1] *Metaphysics* VI, 1, 1025b, 25.
[2] *Op. cit.*, 1026a, 19.
[3] *Ethics* VI, 9, 1142a, 9–10. See Zeller: *Aristotle* I, p. 186.
[4] See Zeller: *Op. cit.*, p. 181, n. 1.
[5] See Zeller: *Plato*, p. 164.

When we attempt, however, to determine whether any given mediaeval classification of sciences is Aristotelian or Platonic, the task is not so easy. Very often, because of the omission of the general terms distinguishing between the auxiliary, theoretical, and practical sciences, the classification appears as a co-ordinate arrangement of the specific sciences. In a classification which is truly Aristotelian we may, therefore, get a list of sciences among which logic will appear to be included. Again, some lists are only partial and incomplete, thus lacking the characteristic features by which the basis of the classiffication may be determined. Furthermore the original Aristotelian classiffication is sometimes amplified by the additional subdivision of certain sciences into their specific branches, or by the introduction of new religious and practical sciences not found in the original scheme, so that the character of the nuclear classification is lost among the excrescences. Finally, the confusion is sometimes increased by the rearrangement of the parts of the classification, or by the substitution of some specific branches for the general science to which they belong, as, for instance, astronomy for mathematics. Thus in any attempt at determining the basis of a classification all these factors must be taken into consideration. On the whole, the use of logic as a co-ordinate science or the omission of the distinction between theoretical and practical is by itself no proof of a Platonic influence; but, on the other hand, the inclusion of mathematics and the restrictive use of the term logic, or the enumeration of both logic and metaphysics, will be an infallible proof for an Aristotelian origin of any given classification.

Through the translation of Johannes Philoponus' commentary on Porphyry's *Isagoge* the Aristotelian classification was introduced into Arabic philosophy where it became the basis of all the classifications of science.[6] It is the underlying scheme of Alfarabi's classification,[7] though the distinction between

[6] See Grabmann: *Die Geschichte der Scholastischen Methode* II, p. 30.

[7] See Steinschneider: *Die Hebraeischen Uebersetzungen des Mittelalters*, p. 44, n. 7b; Clemens Baeumker: *Alfarabi, Ueber den Ursprung der Wissenschaften* (*De Ortu Sciantiarum*); Carra de Vaux: *Farabi* in Hastings' *Encyclopedia of Religion and Ethics*, V, pp. 557–8; T. J. De Boer: *Philosophy* (*Muslim*), *Ibid.* IX, p. 880.

theoretical, practical and auxiliary is omitted and new religious and linguistic sciences are added. It is literally taken over by Avicenna,[8] Algazali[9] and Averroes.[10]

Slightly modified, but still Aristotelian in principle, is the classification given in the Encyclopedia of the Ihwan al-Safa. This classification is of signal importance for our purpose, as it contains most of the characteristic features which we shall notice in the classifications of Jewish philosophers. Laying out the plan of their encyclopedia after the manner of the French Encyclopedists, the Ihwan al-Safa divide the knowledge of their time into two classes, practical arts (الضنائع العمليّة) and theoretical art (الضنائع العلميّة).[11] Under theoretical the authors include three main divisions:[12] (1) Propaedeutic (الرياضيّة) or literary (الاداب) sciences, such as reading, and writing, etc. (2) Sciences of religious law (النواميس), and (3) purely philosophical sciences (الفلسفيّة الحقيقيّة). Omitting the first two as irrelevant for our purpose, we find under purely philosophical sciences four subdivisions: (1) Mathematics, designated by the same name of propaedeutic (الرياضيّات),

[8] See the following quotation from the Hebrew translation of his *Al-Shafa* published in *Ozar Nehmad* II, pp. 114–115:
חלקי החכמות שלשה. חכמה העליונה, והיא חכמת ענינים אין דבקות להם בחומר, והיא החכמה האלהית. והחכמה התחתונה, והיא חכמת ענינים הם בחומר, והם עם זה בחומר נראים, והיא חכמה הטבעית. וזאת החכמה תחייב העיון בכל הדברים אשר להם חמרים נראים ובכל המקרים אשר להם. ובכאן חכמה אמצעית, יש לה חלקים שבעה, וקצתם חזק היחס לחכמה האלהית, וקצתם חזק היחס לחכמה הטבעית, וזאת היא החכמה הלמודית. וחלקיה: המספר, והתשבורת, והמוסיקא, והמשקלות, והמדות, והמבטים, והתכונה. והנה חכמת המספר (ושאר) חכמת דברים אין המציאות לה שתהיה בחומר, אבל הנה יקרה לה וישיגה שתמצא בחומר במוחלט ולא נראית, והשכל ישולל אותה מן החומר שלילה אמתית, ולכן יש לה יחס לחכמה האלהית מאד. וחכמת התשבורת חכמת דברים אפשר שידומו זולת החומר כמו שחשב, אם כי במציאות דקות השכל ישיג השנה אמתית שהיא לא תהיה כי אם בחומר, אבל היא לא חומר נראה. וחכמת המוסיקא והמשקולת והמדות והמבטים כלם חכמת דברים הם בחומר, ויהיה לאחת על אחת יתרון בקרוב אל החכמה הטבעית והרוחק ממנה, והמזג ביניהם הרבה או מעט. והנה חכמת התכונה מזיגה מטבעית ולמודית, ונושאה הגדול שבכל חלקי החכמה הטבעית ונשואה למודית.

[9] *Makasid al-Falasifah* II, pp. 76–79.

[10] At the beginning of his *Epitome of the Metaphysics*. See Horten: *Die Metaphysik des Averroes*, pp. 1–9.

[11] Dieterici: *Die Logik und Psychologie der Araber*, p. 1; Arabic text, *Idem*: *Die Abhandlungen der Ichwân Es-Safâ*, p. 239.

[12] *Ibid.* p. 10ff. Arabic text, *op. cit.*, p. 246ff.

(2) logic, (3) physics, and (3) theology, each of these being again subdivided into special branches. Theology has five such branches, the fourth of which is described as the science of government (السياسة) and is again subdivided into five parts of which the last three correspond to Aristotle's politics, economics and ethics.

This classification has been characterized as un-Aristotelian,[13] but a closer observation of the plan will reveal that what we have here is really the Aristotelian scheme with certain common modifications the like of which we also find among Aristotle's commentators and the Schoolmen. The distinction between practical and theoretical is easily recognized as Aristotelian. But the Ihwan al Safa use here practical, عمليّة not in the sense of πρακτική but rather in the sense of productive, ποιητική. Such a merging of the terms "practical" and "productive" is also found among the commentators and the Schoolmen.[14] Having thus used up "practical" for the "productive", they place Aristotle's "practical", i. e., politics, economics, and ethics, under theology. This, too. was a common practice among the Schoolmen.[15] By omitting the general terms distinguishing between the theoretical, practical and auxiliary, logic is thus made a co-ordinate branch of the philosophical sciences. There is no need of assuming a Platonic influence, for logic is used here in a strictly Aristotelian sense and the topics enumerated under it are all taken from Aristotle's writings.

The classifications in Jewish philosophical literature follow on the whole the Arabic models and are consequently Aristotelian in principle. Such classifications occur with great frqeuency in Jewish literature.[16] Some of them are formal statements,

[13] See Carra de Vaux: *Philosophy* (*Muslim*) in Hastings' *Enc. of Rel. and Eth.*, IX, p. 880.

[14] See Grabmann: *Die Geschichte der Scholastischen Methode* II, p. 30; Robert Flint: *Philosophy as Scientia Scientarum*, p. 90.

[15] See Flint: *Ibid.*

[16] For "classification of sciences" we have in Hebrew the following expressions: (1) מספר החכמות (Falaquera in *Reshit Hokmah* and Moses da Rieti. See below n. 73) from Alfarabi's احصا العلوم.

others are casual remarks, still others are only indirect implications. The observations which follow are based on a varied collection of sources which, while not complete, is large and representative enough to serve as a basis for a study of the classification of the sciences in Jewish philosophical literature.

One of the earliest classifications is found in Isaac Israeli's introduction to his commentary on the *Sefer Yezirah*.[17] The practical sciences are entirely omitted nor is the distinction between theoretical and practical mentioned, but, dealing only with the theoretical, which is called the "science of philosophy" (חכמת פילוסופיא), he divides it into the three conventional parts of the Aristotelian tradition. Here, again, the general terms mathematics, physics, and theology are omitted, but each is represented by some of the specific sciences which usually go under the main division. Thus for mathematics the quadrivium is given, for physics, medicine is specified, and for theology in general, the science of the unity of God and of the spiritual beings is particularly mentioned.

The term used here for "medicine" will prove of some interest. The passage reads חכמת הטבעים, כלומר חכמת הרפואות. Graetz, who ascribes this commentary to Dunash ibn Tamim, takes the term טבעים in its ordinary sense of "physics", and understands the passage to enumerate "physics" and "medicine" as two

(2) סוגי החכמות (Abraham Shalom, See n. 63). Similarly Ihwan al-Safa: اجناس العلوم (*Op cit.*, p. 246).

(3) מיני החכמות (Abba Mari and Zerahiah Hen. See n. 61 and 72). Similarly Ihwan al-Safa: وانواع تلك الاجناس (*Ibid.*).

(4) חלקי החכמות (Israeli, Avicenna and Bahya: اقسام. See n. 17, 8 and 29).

(5) חלוק החכמות تقسيم العلوم (Algazali: *Makasid al-Falasifah* II, p. 75).

(6) מעלות החכמה (Judah ben Barzilai. See n. 30).

[17] See quotation in *Orient*, *Litteraturblatt*. 1845, p. 562:
אלא למי שהוא בקי בחכמת פילוסופיא ואפני חלקיה השלשה, אשר תחלתם חכמת החשבון, חכמת ההנדסה, וחכמת הגלגל, וחכמת החבור, כלומר המוצקי. ואחריו החכמה השנית, והיא חכמת הטבעים, כלומר הרפואות. ואחר כך ידע את החכמה השלישית, והיא חכמת היחוד להקב"ה והענינים הרוחנים.

separate sciences.[18] The word כלומר, however, makes it clear that חכמת הרפואות is an explanation of חכמת הטבעים. While it is not impossible that in Hebrew, as in other languages, the term "physics" has been used here in the sense of "medicine",[18a] still another explanation of this passage may be suggested. It would seem that the term טבע is not to be taken here as the equivalent of the Arabic طبع but rather of طب, and one is tempted to change the reading טבעים to טיבים. In the Arabic classifications, علم الطب stands for "medicine" and is translated into Hebrew by חכמת הרפואה.[19]

While in this passage Israeli does not give the general term for "mathematics", the deficiency is supplied by him in another passage, where he says of music that "it is the best and last of the four branches of the sciences of טורח": והוא המעולה שבארבעה חכמת הטורח[20]. The meaning of the term טורח has escaped the knowledge of Rappoport and Dukes who rendered it by "Turkey". But Michael Jehiel Sachs has pointed out the incorrectness of the translation, and Senior Sachs has inferred its real meaning from the context, without, however, attempting to explain its etymology.[21] The word טורח would seem to be like הרגל, שמוש and מוסר, which we shall meet in the sequel, a Hebrew translation of the Arabic رياضى, "propaedeutic", which, as we have already seen, is used for mathematics. The Arabic root means "to exercise"; the Hebrew root טרח simiarly means "to exert oneself". All these terms are translations of the Greek *προπαιδεία*, *preparatory training* (or rather of *παιδεία*, without the proposition), which Plato applies to mathematics.[22] It is the interpolation

[18] See *Geschichte der Juden*, 4th ed., vol. V, p. 330.

[18a] Thus Maimonides describes medicine as being based on טבע המציאות (See *Pirush ha-Mishnah*: *Pesahim*, ch. 4).

[19] See *Makasid al-Falasifah* II, p. 78. See below n. 137.

[20] See *Kerem Hemed* VIII, p. 64.

[21] *Ibid.*

[22] *Republic* VII, 536D. The Hebrew הלמודים for mathematics has a different etymology. It is a literal translation of تعليم-*μάθημα*. Cf. Steinschneider: *Al-Farabi*, p. 32, n. 32. Reifmann's conjecture that למודי is a later substitution by Samuel ibn Tibbon for שמושי, הרגלי and מוסרי is wrong (See *Ozar ha-Sifrut* II, p. 48). Samuel ibn Tibbon himself only says that

of a Platonic term in classifications which are basically Aristotelian.

Another classification belonging to the same period is that of David Al-Mukammas, quoted by Judah ben Barzilai (Al-Barceloni) in his commentary on *Sefer Yezirah*.[23] It starts out with what would at first sight seem to be the conventional Aristotelian distinction between theoretical (חכמה ומדע) and practical (אומנות או מעשה). Upon a closer observation, however, it becomes apparent that like the Ihwan al-Safa he substitutes Aristotle's productive, or what may be called applied, science, for practical. He thus says that every science, say geometry, may be either a science (מדע) or an art (אומנות). For this illustration, too, there is a parallel in the Encyclopedia of the Ihwan al-Safa where mathematics is said to be divided into sensible (حسّيّة) and rational (عقليّة), the former leading to the practical arts and the latter to the theoretical.[24]

Taking up the theoretical, Al-Mukammas divides it into three parts. The first and the last correspond to Aristotle's theology and physics respectively. The second, which we would expect to be mathematics, is described in the following terms: **והמעלה האמצעית חכמת המוסר והשכל המאמצת דעות בני אדם והמנהגת להם דרך הבינה**. As the term **מוסר** generally means "ethics", the statement in translation would read as follows: "And the middle grade is the science of ethics and of the mind which streng-

למודים is synonymous with שמושים and הרגלים (See *Pirush meha-Millot Zorot*, under למודים.

[23] *Pirush Sefer Yezirah le-Rabbi Judah b. Barzilai*, Berlin 1885, p. 65: וכתב דוד הבבלי כך: הוי יודע כי גדר החכמה הוא מדע יושר הנמצאות, לעמוד על סוף מחקרם, והיא נחלקת לשני חלקים. יש ממנה מה שסוף מחקרו הוא המדע, ועל דעת תוכן הנמצא ויושר תבניתו יעמוד המחקר ודיו; זהו הנקרא חכמה ומדע. ויש ממנה שסוף בקשתם ואחרית מחקרם הוא מעשה ומלאכה ומציאת דבר לעין, וזה נקרא אומנוה או מעשה. והראה מזה משל בחכמת המדה והמשקל הנקרא בלשון ערבי הנדסה ובלשון יוני גומטריה.... ותמצא חכמה זו בענין הזה עת מתפרדת למדע ואומנות. וכן כל שאר והחכמות. ומשם אמר כי החכמה נפרדת למדע ולמעשה. והמדע נחלקת לשלש מעלות: המעלה הראשונה מדע העליון, הנקרא מדע האלהי, והיא החכמה המשֻבחת להבין יחודו של הב״ה, וחכמת תורתו ומצותיו, והוא הגבוה והמעולה מכל החכמות. והמעלה האמצעית חכמת דמוסר והשכל המאמצת דעות בני אדם והמנהגת להם דרך הבינה. והמעלה השלישית המדע השפל והתחתון, והוא מדע דרך היצורים ותוכן הנבראים.

[24] Dieterici: *Die Propaedeutik der Araber*, p. 24. Arabic text, *Idem*: *Die Abhandlungen der Ichwân Es-Safâ*, p. 293.

thens the opinions of men and guides them in the path of understanding". Both the use of the term מוסר and the description by which it is followed would seem to point to ethics as the middle science, and this is the general understanding of the passage.[25] But taken in this sense, the classification would be thrown out of the framework of both the Platonic and the Aristotelian schemes, which would seem rather strange. An attempt must therefore be made to cast it in one of the traditional forms of classification, and to this end two alternative solutions may be proposed:

First, leaving the term מוסר in the sense of "ethics", we may take the term שכל in the sense of "logic".[26] That שכל could be a Hebrew rendering of the Arabic المنطق, λογική, like מבטא, דבור, and הגיון, is quite clear, for all these terms mean "reason" as well as "speech". In fact, according to Samuel ibn Tibbon the proper designation for logic should have been מלאכת השכל.[26a] The "middle" science would thus be the "science of ethics and of logic". The description which follows may equally apply to both these sciences. The threefold classification would thus in reality be a fourfold classification, containing theology, ethics, logic, and physics. Such a fourfold classification was not unknown among the Aristotelians and is based upon the classification of Aristotle's writings.[27]

Second, the term מוסר, despite its ordinary meaning of ethics, may be another Hebrew translation of the Arabic رياضى, "propaedeutic", i. e., mathematics.[27a] In the *Cuzari* the term

[25] Cf. Kaufmann: *Die Theologie des Bachja Ibn Pakuda* in *Gesammelte Schriften* II, p. 21–22, note; Bernfeld: *Da'at Elohim*, p. 136.

[26] This is how Husik takes it. See *A History of Mediaeval Jewish Philosophy*, p. 18.

[26a] See *Pirush meha -Millot Zorot* under הגיון: ולפי דעתי היה ראוי לקראה מלאכת השכל.

[27] See Zeller: *Aristotle* I, p. 181, n. 1.

[27a] Reifmann takes the passage to refer to mathematics, but, puzzled by the use of the term מוסר, he changes the reading of חכמת המוסר והשכל to חכמה המישרת להשכל. See *Ozar ha-Sifrut* II, p. 50. It is interesting to note that the Hebrew מוסר usually translates the Arabic ادب (See Steinschneider: *Uebersetzungen*, p. 350) and that the Ihwan al-Safa couple الاداب with الرياضيّة

الرياضيّة is translated by both המוסריות and ההרגליות.[28] The expression חכמת המוסר והשכל may be taken as a hendiadys, as if it were written חכמת המוסר השכלי, to be translated "the science of rational mathemathics", that is to say, the "rational mathematics" of the Ihwan al-Safa as contrasted with the "sensible"—a reference to Al-Mukammas' own distinction between the "science" and the "art" of geometry. Now, in the Encyclopedia of the Ihwan al-Safa the difference between "rational" and "sensible" mathematics is described as follows: "The study of sensible mathematics is an aid to the thorough understanding of the practical arts; the study of rational mathematics is a guide to the thorough understanding of the speculative arts, for this science is one of the gates which leads to the knowledge of the substance of the soul. This knowledge is the beginning of the sciences, the constituent element of wisdom, and the root of the practical and theoretical arts".[29] Al-Mukammas' brief description of "the science of rational mathematics," quoted above, claims for it the same excellencies.

The second explanation would seem to be more plausible, for in another passage quoted again by Judah ben Barzilai, Al-Mukammas definitely enumerates mathematics, physics and theology as the three sciences, though he names them in a different order. He says: "Philosophy is the knowledge of all things according to the measure of their form, the secret of their nature, and the veracity of their impartation. We have felt it necessary to use three properties in the definition of philosophy, in order to be able to bring under this definition the three grades of philosophy. Thus the expression 'according to the measures of the form of things' makes this definition include the science which investigates the external form of things and the boundaries of their bodies, as arithmetic and the like. The expression 'the secret of their nature' makes it include the science which investigates the bodies of things and

as a description of their "propaedeutic" sciences exclusive of mathematics (See above p. 265).

[28] *Cuzari* III, 39; V. 12; V. 14. Here too, Reifmann changes מוסריות to מוסדיות (*loc. cit.*). See below n. 32.

[29] Dieterici: *Die Propaedeutik der Araber*, p. 36.

the secrets of their nature, as all the sciences which deal with the structure of heaven and earth and all created beings. The expression 'the veracity of their impartation' makes it include the science which is superior to all other sciences, namely, the science of the Torah by which those who fear God are favored". He then concludes: "In this fashion the grades of philosophy are three and the definition of philosophy as we have given it includes them all, and all these sciences are called the theoretical sciences or the sciences of the mind".[30]

The formal classification of philosophy (חכמה, علم) given by Bahya ibn Pakuda in the Introduction of the *Hobot ha-Lebabot* deals again only with the theoretical part of philosophy and follows Aristotle's threefold division, mentioning under mathematics the quadrivium.[31] There is only one point which must detain us here. In the Hebrew translation the Arabic الرياضى, "propaedeutic", is rendered by השמוש and is followed by the

[30] *Pirush Sefer Yezirah le-Rabbi Judah b. Barzilai*, p. 66:
ואנו פותחים ראשונה ואומרים כי מלת חכמה נאמרת בלשון הקודש על שני ענינים, על החכמה שהיא חכמה ממש, אשר עליה אמר הכתוב, והחכמה מאין תמצא, והחכמה מאין תבא, והיא מדע כל הנמצאות על אומד תבניתם, ותוכן יצירתם, ואומן נתינתם. והוצרכנו לשום בגדר החכמה שלש חוצצים, כדי להכניס בגדר הזה שלש מעלות החכמה. ויהיה אומד תבנית הנמצאות מכניס בגדר הזה החכמה המעיינת בצורות הנמצאות החצונות, ותכלית גופן, כחכמת המנין והדומה לה. ותוכן יצירתם מכניס בו החכמה המעיינת בגופי הנמצאות, וסודי יצירתן, כלל החכמות המדברות על בנין שמים וארץ ושאר היצורים. ואומן נתינתם מכניס בו החכמה המעולה על כל החכמות, והיא חכמת התורה הנתונה ליראי השם... על הדרך הזה היא מעלות החכמה שלש מעלות, והגדר אשר שמנו לחכמה כולל אותם. והחכמות האלה נקראין חכמה שכלנית וחכמת השכל.

I have emended אומר to read אומד in אומד תבניתם.

The term חוצצים is the Arabic خاصّة, *ἴδιον*, *property*, one of the five predicables usually translated into Hebrew by סגולה or, as in *Cuzari* V, 12, מדה מיוחדה (See below n. 162). Kaufmann seems to have confounded it with فصل, *διαφορά*, *difference*, which is usually translated by הבדל, פרק or, as in *Cuzari* V, 12, חלק. (See below n. 162). Cf. Kaufmann's notes on *Pirush Sefer Yezirah le-Rabbi Judah b. Barzilai*, p. 336.

[31] והחכמה מתחלקת לשלשה חלקים. החלק הראשון, חכמת היצירות, שקורין לה בלשון ערב אלע׳לם אלט׳בעי, והיא חכמת טבעי הגופות ומקריהן. והחלק השני היא חכמת השמוש, שקורין לה בלשון ערבי אלע׳לם רי״צי, ויש מי שקראה חכמת המוסר, והיא חכמת המנין והשעורים וחכמת הכוכבים וחכמת הנגון, הנקראת מוזיקא. והחלק השלישי קורין לה בלשון ערבי אלע״לם אל׳די, והיא חכמת האלהות, והוא דעת האל יתברך ודעת תורתו, ושאר המושכלות, כנפש וכשכל וכאישים הרוחניים,

statement ויש מי שקראה חכמת המוסר, which has caused some difficulty to students.[32] It can be shown, however, that the statement is an interpolated gloss. There is nothing in the original Arabic text to correspond to it. In the *editio princeps* of the Hebrew translation, Naples 1489, and in the Venice edition of 1548 it does not occur.[33] It makes its first appearance in the Constantinople edition of 1550.[33a] That מוסר has been used as a Hebrew equivalent of رياضة has already been pointed out, and the ויש מי שקראה probably refers to the Hebrew translation of the *Cuzari*, if not also to Al-Mukammas.

The classification given by the Karaite Nissi ben Noah in his commentary on the Decalogue[33b] is of interest not only for some of the peculiar terms it contains but also for its textual difficulties. The text as it stands would seem to divide philosophy into metaphysics, mathematics and ethics, and this is how Steinschneider seems to understand it.[33c] This would make it a rather unusual arrangement of topics, though made up of parts taken from Aristotle's classification. The passage, however, bears internal evidence of being corrupt, as has already been suspected by Reifmann.[33d] In the first place, it begins with a statement that philosophy is divided into two parts, but mentions only one of these parts. In the second place, it says that the first part of philosophy is to be subdivided into two other parts, but, instead of giving these two parts, it enumerates the three sciences, metaphysics, mathematics and ethics. Evidently there is something missing in the text.

The passage, however, can be completed by filling out the gaps with phrases taken from the passages preceding and

[32] See commentary *Pat Lehem, ad loc.*; Fürstenthal's Hebrew notes *ad loc.;* Reifmann in *Ozar ha-Sifrut* II, pp. 49–50, who changes מוסר to מוסד. See above n. 28. Schmiedl in *Monatsschrift* 1861, p. 186; Kaufmann: *Die Theologie des Bachja Ibn Pakuda* in *Gesammelte Schriften* II, p. 21, note; Senior Sachs; *Kerem Hemed* VIII, p. 64.

[33] Nor does this addition occur in the quotation of this passage in Shabbethai Bass' (Meshorer's) *Sifte Yeshenim*, Zolkiew, 1806, f. 7b.

[33a] The gloss occurs in MS Adler 900 in the Jewish Theological Seminary.

[33b] *Pirush Aseret ha-Debarim* in Pinsker's *Likkute Kadmoniyyot* II, p. 9.

[33c] *Uebersetzungen*, p. 209, n. 734b.

[33d] Cf. *Ozar ha-Sifrut* II, p. 50.

following it. This reconstructed passage would yield us, in the first place, a general division of philosophy into scientific knowledge (דעת) and revealed knowledge (יראת אל שדי),[33e] and then, in the second place, under scientific knowledge, a complete Aristotelian classification with its general distinction of theoretical and practical knowledge and the subdivision of the former into metaphysics, mathematics and physics, and the subdivision of the latter into ethics, economics and politics.[33f]

No formal classification of the sciences is given by Judah ha-Levi. But here and there in his *Cuzari* he gives us snatches of classifications which seem to be torn out of an Aristotelian context, such, for instance, as his casual references to physics,

[33e] The distinction between these two kinds of knowledge is explained by the author in the preceding paragraph as follows:

שהחכמה נודעת משני פנים: הא' חכמה ותושיה נודעת מן הבריאה והיצירה, שהיא עולה במחשבה בהתקששם החכמים בשכלם, כמו ידיעת היוצר מן היצירה, שהתורה והנבואה עדים עליה ומאמינים בה. והשני חכמה ובינה, שהיא התורה והחזות, שניהם בנבואה, שהתורה והחכמה מצדיקים אותה ומאמינים בה,

[33f] The emended passage will read as follows:

והחכמה הזאת מתחלקת, כמו שאבאר למטה: הא' הדעת, והיא מתחלקת על שני חלקים. [הא' הדעת השכלית, והיא על ג' חלקים]: א' מהם דעת העליונה בשכל, כמו שיראה בדעת אל עליון ומלאכים ונפשות ורוחות. והשני, דעת המוסר, והוא נחלק על ארבעה חלקים: הא' דעת הטפחות והמדה. והב' דעת המספר והמנין. והג' דעת החבור והמזלות. והד' דעת העגבים והקולות. והשלישי מהם השכל התחתון, כדעת ארבע מטבעות. [והב' הדעת המעשית], והוא על ג' חלקים: הא' נהילת העדה, כנהילת המלך למדינות ולארצות. והב' נהילת בני הבית, כנהילת המלך בני ביתו וקרוביו. והג' נהילת האיש לנפשו ביותר, כנהילת האיש לנפשו וגופו. [והב' יראת אל שדי]. לפיכך שידענו שיראת אל שדי [ית'] שמו היא ראשית החכמה, וכו'.

In the description of astronomy in this passage, דעת החבור והמזלות, if the term החבור is not a corruption of העבור, *inetrcalation*, then it must be taken in the astronomical sense of *conjunction*, i. e., the conjunction of the moon with the sun, as the equivalent of the more usual term קבוץ. See *Mishneh Torah*: *Kiddush ha-Hodesh* VI, 1:

בזמן שעושין על הראייה היו מחשבין ויודעין שעה שיתקבץ בו הירח עם החמה... ויודעין שעת קבוצן...

The term חבור in the classification of sciences ordinarily means music. See above n. 17.

The expression ארבע מטבעות refers to the four natural elements, היסודות הטבעיים, which is usually mentioned as one of the topics of physics. Steinschneider takes it in the sense of the four qualities of human nature and as referring to ethics (*Uebersetzungen*, p. 209, n. 734b). But see Reifmann in *Ozar ha-Sifrut* II, p. 51.

astronomy and music,[34] to astronomy and physics,[35] and to various topics of physics and to theology.[36] In one place he speaks of the reliability of the philosophers in matters mathematical and logical as contrasted with their unreliability in matters physical and metaphysical,[37] and in another place he enumerates physics, theology, mathematics and astronomy as some of the sciences embodied in the Mishnah and Talmud.[38] A complete classification of the three theoretical sciences and logic with an enumeration of their branches may be derived from his discussion of psychology in his attempt to explain how the hylic intellect comes into possession of rational ideas through application and study.[39]

In one of those mystifying passages in which the works of Abraham ibn Ezra abound some Jewish scholars think to have found a classification of sciences. In his commentary on Ecclesiastes III, 21, Ibn Ezra says as follows: "And the knowledge of the soul is shrouded in mystery, requiring subtle speculations, and nobody can grasp even a small part of its nature except those thinkers whose thought has become clarified in the balance of wisdom and its elements four, of which three are **ספר ספר וספור** and, [the fourth], that which is composed of the two".[40] Friedlaender translates the three Hebrew words by

[34] *Cuzari* II, 64: עלם אלאפלאך–חכמת הגלגלים; אלטביעיה–הטבעיות עלם אלמוסיקא–חכמת המוסיקא.

[35] *Ibid.* IV, 29: עלם אלפלך–חכמות הכוכבים והגלגלים; עלם אלהיה–חכמת התכונה אלעלם אלטביעי–החכמה הטבעית.

[36] *Ibid.* V, 2:
הטבעיים, והאצטגנינים, ובעלי הטלסמאות, והמכשפים, ואנשי הקדמות, והפילוסופים... ההיולי והצורה... היסודות הנקראים בערבי אסטקסאת... הטבע... הנפש... השכל... החכמה האלהית.–אלטביעיין, ואלמנגמין ואלמטלסמין ואלסחרא ואלדהריין ואלמסתלספין... ללהיולי אלמשתרכה... אלאסטקסאת... אלטביעה... אלנפוס... אלעקל... אלעלם אלאלאהי.

[37] *Ibid.* V, 14:
למה שנתברר מהם המופת בחכמות ההרגליות (אלריאציה) וההגיון (ואלמנטק) בטחו הנפשות על כל מה שאמרוהו בטבע (פי אלטביעה) ובמה שאחר הטבע (ופי מא בעד אלטביעה).

[38] *Ibid.* III, 39:
ומי שהוא רוצה להאמין בו יראה חכמת המשנה והתלמוד והם מעט מהרבה מחכמות הטבעיות (אלעלום אלטביעיה) והאלהיות (ואלאלאהיה) והמוסריות (ואלריאציה) והגלגליות (ואלפלכיה).

[39] *Ibid.* V, 12.

[40] ודעת הרוח עמוקה וצריכה לראיות, ולא יוכלו להבין אפילו קצתם, כי אם המשכילים, שהתבררה מחשבתם במאזני החכמה ובארבעה יסודותיה, שהשלשה מהם ספר וספר וספור, ומורכב מן השנים,

"reading, writing and arithmetic".[41] There is, however, no basis for this translation except that the three Hebrew words with their alliteration lend themselves to a rendering into the proverbial three R's. Rosin identifies all the four elements with mathematics, grammar, logic and physics.[42] The difficulty with this rendering is that that it does not correspond to either the Platonic or the Aristotelian classiffication. Furthermore, the expression מורכב מן השנים for Physics is rather far-fetched. Rosin's reference to the Ihwan al-Safa in support of his classification seems to be irrelevant. Besides, we have already seen that their classification of the purely philosophic sciences is strictly Aristotelian. Krochmal conjectures that the four elements refer to the four types of immediate knowledge, namely, sense perceptions, intellectual notions, traditions and general opinions.[43] But he makes no attempt to show how the text can be made to assume this interpretation.

It seems to me that this passage has no reference to the classification of sciences nor to the types of immediate knowledge Its meaning is to be sought elsewhere. The puzzling words ספר ספר וספור in Ibn Ezra are a well known quotation from *Sefer Yezirah* I: וברא את עולמו בשלשה ספרים, בספר וספר וספור Now this in itself would not help much, for the passage in the original source is in itself a conundrum and his been variously interpreted by ancient and modern commentators. But Saadia's interpretation of this passage willl throw light upon the difficulty. Says Saadia:[44] "The expression 'He hath created the world in three books' means to say that all things may be registered in three ways." He then raises the question why only three ways are mentioned, seeing "that the philosophers have enumerated four ways, for they have said that things may exist under four aspects, in their substance, as when we see a man; in spoken words, as when we

[41] M. Friedländer: *Essays in Ibn Ezra*, p. 26, n. 3.

[42] *Monatsschrift* XLII, p. 448.

[43] Extracts from Ibn Ezra's commentary on Ecclesiastes in *Moreh Nebuke ha-Zeman*.

[44] M. Lambert: *Commentaire sur le Séfer Yesira ou Livre de la Creation par le Gaon Saadia de Fayyoum*, pp. 42–43; Arabic text, pp. 22–23.

say, 'man'; in writing, as when we write the latters *m a n*; in thought, as when we form an idea of a man". Explaining why substance is omitted, Saadia concludes: "The author finds that there are three ways in which a thing can be expressed, namely, writing, number, and the spoken word, which, added to substance, make in all four". Saadia further explains that "number" stands here for "thought", for it is a species of thought, and he gives ספר מחשבה וספור as the equivalent of ספר ספר וספור. In the light of this explanation it is clear that Ibn Ezra's mention of the four elements of knowledge refers to the four modes of knowing things enumerated by Saadia, of which he quotes from *Sefer Yezirah*, again following Saadia, the three, namely, סֵפֶר "the written word", סְפָר "the number", i. e., the idea, and סִפּוּר "the spoken word", and adds Saadia's fourth mode, "that which is composed of the two", i. e., substance. Substance, says Aristotle, applies to matter, form, and to the concrete thing which is composed of the two.[45] Ibn Ezra similarly says: "All created beings are composed of two, namely, matter and form."[46] That Abraham ibn Ezra refers here to four modes of knowledge rather than to classes of sciences may be inferred from his use of the expression מאזני השכל. The word מאזני reflects the Arabic ميزان, which, while literally meaning "balance", is also used in the sense of "judgement,"[47] "rule" and "method", and hence the expression מאזני השכל undoubtedly means 'the laws of thought" or "the modes of knowledge."

There is, however, another passage in which Ibn Ezra refers to a classification of sciences. In his commentary on Proverbs 9, 1, he attempts to give a different rendering of the verse which is usually translated: "Wisdom hath builded her house, she hath hewn out her seven pillars". "It may be explained", he says, "that the plural חכמות is used here in order to show that the meaning of the verse is that out of the seven wisdoms she (=wisdom) hath builded her house. This is what is meant by

45 See *Metaphysics* VII, 10, 1035a, 1.

46 See D. Rosin: *Reime und Gedichte des Abraham ibn Ezra*, p. 42, n. 13: והנבראים שנים, שהם עצם וצורה

47 See Munk: *Guide des Égarés*, I, 62, p. 279, n. 1.

'she hath hewn out her seven pillars', 'her pillars' here referring to the pillars of the house, and thus the second strophe is an explanation of 'out of wisdoms she hath builded her house'. Accordingly, the word בית is used here in the feminine gender. Or, 'her pillars' may refer to the pillars of wisdom, and these pillars are the seven branches of wisdom upon which the house of wisdom is erected. Some, however, interpret the number seven here to refer to something else, but *suum cuique* and truth will show the way."[48]

There are several possible lists to which these "seven sciences" may refer, and we shall mention them in the sequel. But here one is inclined to take the number seven to refer to the three branches of the Aristotelian theoretical philosophy, including the mathematical quadrivium, and to logic, thus making in all seven, for under these heads one may arrange all the specific sciences, outside the purely linguistic sciences, which Ibn Ezra enumerates in the first chapter of *Yesod Mora* as prerequisites to the proper understanding of the Bible and the Talmud. They are in the order in which they are first mentioned as follows: Astronomy (חכמת המזלות), geometry (חכמת המדות), psychology (חכמת הנפש), physics (חכמת התולדות, חכמת תולדות השמים והארץ), astrology (משפטי המזלות), logic (חכמת המבטא, חכמת ההגיון), arithmetic (חכמת החשבון), proportion (חכמת הערכים), theology (סוד המרכבה ושעור קומה סוד הנפש ומלאכי עליון והעולם הבא). Elsewhere he also mentions music (חכמת הנגינות).[49] All these may be tabulated according to the Aristotelian classification, making a list of seven sciences, as follows:[50]

1. A. Logic
   B. Theoretical sciences
2. I. Theology (including psychology)[51]

[48] ויתכן לפרש שאמר חכמות להודיע שהחכמה בנתה ביתה מחכמות שבע, וזה טעם חצבה עמודיה שבעה, והם עמודי הבית, והוא הביאור למאמר חכמות בנתה ביתה, ובית לשון נקבה. או עמודיה שבעה, עמודי החכמה, והעמודים הם שבע החכמות שבית החכמה נכון עליהם. ויש מפרשים אלה השבעה על העניינים אחרים, וכל אחד בוחר לעצמו, והאמת יורה דרכו.

[49] M. Friedländer; Essays on Ibn Ezra, Hebrew Text, p. 43.

[50] Contrast with this the classification made by Rosin in *Monatsschrift* XLIII, p. 232.

[51] For the inclusion of psychology within theology see below p. 294.

II. Mathematics
3. a. Arithmetic (including Proportion)
4. b. Geometry
5. c. Astronomy
6. d. Music
7. III. Physics (including Astrology)[52]

Like Judah ha-Levi, Abraham ibn Daud does not give a formal classification of sciences but refers to it incidentally in his description of the gradual stages in which the soul acquires knowledge. He mentions there mathematics (הלמודיות), physics (הטבעיות) and theology (האלהיות).[53] In addition to the specific enumeration of these three sciences, which he does not describe by the general term theoretical, he also speaks of a practical class of philosophy (פילוסופיא מעשית).[54] In another long passage Abraham ibn Daud gives not exactly a classification of sciences but something that may be described as an evaluation of the sciences, especially medicine, philology, mathematics and law.[55] The passage will be reproduced at the end of this paper.

A rather novel classification is given by Joseph ben Isaac Kimhi in the Introduction to his *Sefer ha-Galui*. While on the whole the topics are drawn from the Aristotelian classification, they are grouped differently. All the sciences, according to this author, are divided into three parts. First, those which are useful only for the world to come. Second, those which are useful both for this world and for the world to come. Third, those which are only useful for this world. Under the first he includes theology in all its branches. Under the second he mentions at random astronomy, geometry and medicine, by which he evidently means to include the entire field of mathematics and

[52] Astrology is part of physics according to Algazali's *Tahafut al-Falasifah* quoted by Caleb Afendopolo (See *Monatsschrift* XL, p. 93).

[53] *Emunah Ramah* II, iv, 1, p. 58:
ואחר ילך בהדרגה אל חלוקת ההקדמות, וסדורם על תמונות מה, והולדת התולדות ההם, עד שיגיעו לו החכמות הלימודיות, והטבעיות, והאלהיות.

[54] *Ibid.*, General Introduction, p. 4:
אמנם נושא העיון הזה הנה מבואר שהוא פילוסופיא מעשית.

[55] *Ibid.*, II, Introduction, p. 45.

physics. Under the third he includes the productive arts, or the *artes mechanicae*[55a].

Of all the classifications of sciences the most comprehensive and complete, despite its brevity, and the most truly Aristotelian is that given by Maimonides in the *Millot ha-Higgayon* XIV. We shall reproduce it here with a running commentary.

He begins with a statement as to the use of the term מלאכה. This term may be taken to represent the Arabic صناعة and the Greek τέχνη, meaning "art". Now, τέχνη in Aristotle has, on the whole, two meanings. In *Metaphysics* I, 1, the term τέχνη is used in the sense of θεωρία, *speculation*, and is contrasted with ἐμπειρία, *experience*, and αἴσθησις, *perception*. In *Ethics* VI, 3, however, the term τέχνη is used in the sense of ἐπιστήμη ποιητική, *productive science*, as contrasted with both ἐπιστήμη θεωρητική *theoretical science*, and 'επιστήμη πρακτική, *practical science*. In these two senses the equivalent Arabic term صناعة is used by the Ihwan al-Safa when they divided the sciences into الصنائع العلميّة, *speculative arts*, and الصنائع العمليّة, *productive arts*. As has already been shown, the former stands for both the θεωρητική and the πρακτική, whereas the latter stands for the ποιητική. Referring to this, Maimonides thus says: "The term art is used among the ancients in an equivocal sense and is applied by them to every theoretical science and to all works of production. They thus call every philosophic discipline a theoretical art and every form of carpentry and masonry and their like a productive art".[56]

[55a] *Sefer ha-Galui*, Introduction, pp. 1–2:
ודע כי כל החכמות הנמצאות במדרגת שלש כסאות. החכמה העליונה היושבת בכסא כבוד מראשון היא חכמת אלהות בדעת יחוד הבורא ובתורותיו ובמצותיו להשיג אהבהו לעולם הבא. ואין לזאת החכמה חלק בזה העולם, כי צריך האדם שתהיה כוונתו לעבוד הבורא ולאהוב אותו ולא בעבור העולם הזה. והחכמה היושבת במדרגת השנית היא חכמת הככבים וחכמת השעורים וחכמת הרפואות ודומיהם, שהם נחלקים לצורך העה"ז ולצורך העה"ב, ומותר ליהנות מהם בעה"ז. והחכמה היושבת במדרגה התחתונה היא חכמת המלאכות והאומניות לישוב העה"ז, תקון בתים ושדות וכרמים ומלבושים וכסף וזהב ותקון אבנים טובות ודומיהן.

[56] והשם מלאכה אצל הקודמים שם משתף, יפילוהו על כל חכמה עיונית [Ahitub's translation: חכמה שכלית], ויפילוהו גם כן על כל המעשים המלאכתים. ויקראו כל חכמה מחכמת הפילוסופיא מלאכה עיונית [Ahitub: שכלית], ויקראו כל אחת מהנגרות והחצבות ומה שדומה להן מלאכה מעשית [Ahitub: מלאכה מלאכותית].

Maimonides thus like the Ihwan al-Safa divides the Aristotelian sciences into two parts, calling the *θεωρητική* by its given name and designating both the *πρακτική* and the *ποιητική* by the general name "philosophy", the latter of which he also calls "theoretical art" [שכלית] מלאכה עיונית. Similarly Averroes, in his classification of the sciences, couples "art" and "science" together.[57]

Maimonides now takes up the term "philosophy". This, too, is an equivocal term, for in a general sense it applies to the art of demonstration, מלאכת המופת, i. e., logic, and the special philosophic disciplines.[58] Similarly Averroes, and as we shall see also Aristotle, says that philosophy in a general sense includes also logic. But, properly speaking, says Maimonides, logic is not a philosophic discipline; it is only an instrument (כלי, *ὄργανον*). Thus the term philosophy is to apply only to the theoretical and practical disciplines. We therefore now have a new set of terms, "theoretical philosophy", הפילוסופיא העיונית, and "practical philosophy", הפילוסופיא המעשית, which are not to be confused with "theoretical art", מלאכה עיונית, and "practical art", [מלאכותית] מלאכה מעשית. In Hebrew, it should be noticed, the same term מעשית is used for both *πρακτική* and *ποιητική*. Similarly the Arabic term عمليّة, used by the Ihwan al-Safa, has these two meanings, as has already been pointed out.[59]

The "theoretical philosophy" is divided by Maimonides into the conventional physics, mathematics and metaphysics, mathematics being again subdivided into the quadrivium. Of the subdivisions of "practical philosophy," we shall speak later.

In the literature after Maimonides, the Aristotelian scheme continues to be the model for all classifications. The occasional mention of the sciences in such works as the *Ma'amar Ikkawu ha-Mayim* by Samuel ibn Tibbon,[60] the *Sefer ha-Yareah* by

57 Cf. *Epitome of the Metaphysics*.

58 ושם הפילוסופיא שם משתף, פעמים יקראו בו מלאכת המופת, ופעמים יקראו בו החכמות.

59 See above p. 266.

60 *Ma'amar Ikkawu ha-Mayim*, Ch. XI, p. 54:
וזה המין הוא מה שקורין חכמי המחקר חכמת התכונה, והוא חלק מהחכמות שקורין הרגליות או למודיות.

Abba Mari Don Astruc of Lunel,[61] and the *Nobelot Hokmah* by Joseph Solomon Delmedigo[62] all belong to this category. Of a similar nature is the classiffication given by Abraham Shalom in his *Neveh Shalom*.[63]

It is this Aristotelian classification which forms the groundwork of the encyclopedic works in Hebrew beginning with the thirteenth century, though some confine themselves only to certain selected sciences and other amplify their plan by introducing auxiliary linguistic and religious sciences after the manner of the encyclopedia of the Ihwan al-Safa. Judah ben Solomon ha-Kohen ibn Matkah in his *Midrash ha-Hokmah* enumerates

[61] *Sefer ha-Yareah*, ch. 1, p. 125:
ידוע ומפורסם לחכמים כי מיני החכמות שנים: הא׳ חכמת הטבע, היא חכמה מעשה בראשית, והב׳ חכמת אלהית, והוא מעשה מרכבה. ויש עוד חכמה ג׳ שהיא במדרגה לאלו הב׳, ונקראת חכמה למודית, מפני שהיא מרגלת השכל ומלמדת אותו להשיג האמתיות. ויש לחכמה הזאת כמו מספר תכונה תשבורת, והם שקורין אותה ז׳ חכמות, מהם שהם מדרגות קרובות לחכמות הטבע, ומהם שהם מדרגות קרובות לחכמת האלהית. ואע״פ שהם מדרגות לב׳ החכמות יש לכל אחד תכלית מכוונת לעצמה, המשל בזה מלאכת הרפואה, תכליתה הראשון מכוון לב׳ חלקים. החלק הא׳ שמירת הבריאות. והחלק הב׳ הסרת החולי, ומי שיקרא רופא מסיר החולי כן יקרא רופא שומר הבריאות. והוא שאמר הכתוב: כל המחלה אשר שמתי במצרים לא אשים עליך כי אני ד׳ רופאך, ר״ל שומר בריאותך. וכמו שיש תכלית מכוון למלאכת הרפואה, כן יש תכלית מכוון לשאר החכמות, שהוא גדר וגבול לחכמה ההיא. ויש תועלת גדולה לחכמים יראי ה׳ לכל אחד מהתכליות, כי בהם יבחן האדם סוד המציאות, וידע וישכיל קצת מפליאות ד׳, ויעלה באלה המדרגות עד שיגיע אל ב׳ החכמות העליונות, והם מעשה בראשית ומעשה מרכבה, ומתוך כך ידע ויכיר מי שאמר והיה העולם.

As for the sevenfold division of the mathematical sciences see quotation from Avicenna above n. 8. As for the propaedeutic character which this passage ascribes to mathematics see above n. 22.

[62] *Nobelot Hokmah*, f. 4a:
ועוד יש קדימת הסדר אצל הפילוסופים כאשר יאמר שהדקדוק קודם בסדר הלמוד למלאכת השיר או להלצה ולהגיון, וההגיון לטבעית, והטבעית לאלהית, וחכמת המספר והשעור לתכונה או למיכאניקה או לחכמת הראייה.

[63] *Neveh Shalom* V, 7 f. 74b–75a:
ולפי שסוגי החכמות שבהם ישלים האדם נפשו הם שלש: האחת, הלמודית, והיא ידיעת צורת הגלגלים... והנה סוג אחר נמצא לחכמה והיא הטבעית, ונחלק המדע הטבעי לשמנה חלקים עצומים... ותמצא אלו השמנה חלקים באו בשלמות בתורתנו במעשה בראשית... הסוג השלישי הוא חכמת האלהות.

The term צורה in צורת הגלגלים in this passage is not to be taken as the ordinary translation of صورة, *εἶδος*, but rather as synonymous with תכונה and like the latter may be considered as a translation of هيئة, *διάθεσις*, for the Arabic هيئة literally means not only "dispositions" but also "form" (See below n. 155, 179).

physics, mathematics and metaphysics, to which he adds logic as an instrument to the sciences but not included among them.[64] Shem-tob Joseph Falaquera deals with the classification of sciences in several of his works. In his *De'ot ha-Pilusufim* he deals only with physics and metaphysics and of the latter only with the problem of the active intellect.[65] But his *Reshit Hokmah*, which is devoted to the classification of sciences, contains a complete Aristotelian classiffication. A similar classification is found in his poem at the beginning of the *Reshit Hokma* and parts of it may also be found in his *Mebakesh*. Gershon ben Solomon of Arles in his *Sha'ar ha-Shamayim* deals with the three parts of the Aristotelian theoretical philosophy, physics, mathematics and metaphysics, but in mathematics he confines himself to astronomy and he similarly narrows down the scope of metaphysics to psychology only.[66] A complete classification is given by Caleb ben Elijah ben Judah Afendopolo in his commentary on a Hebrew translation of the arithmetic of Nichomachus of Geresa. It comprises logic and all the branches of theoretical as well as practical philosophy.[67] A somewhat modified plan is found in the encyclopedia *Kelal Kazer mi-Kol ha-Rashum Biketab* by Judah ben Joseph ibn Bulat. He divides all learning into (a) sacred and (b) profane (הלמודיים החצוניים, חולין), a division which is not unknown among the Scholastics.[68] Under profane sciences, however, he enumerates the Aristotelian practical and theoretical philosophy and also logic and linguistics.[69] Similarly Solomon ben Jacob Almoli divides his encyclopedia *Meassef Lekol ha-Mahanot* into speculative sciences and traditional sciences, giving under the former linguistics, logic and the branches of the Aristotelian theoretical and practical philosophy.[70]

A sevenfold classification of science is to be found in the

[64] See Steinschneider: *Uebersetzungen*, § 1.
[65] *Ibid*, § 2.
[66] *Ibid.*, § 3.
[67] Steinscneider: *Monatsschrift* XL, pp. 90–94.
[68] See H. O. Taylor: *The Mediaeval Mind*, II, p. 343.
[69] See Steinschneider: *Uebersetzungen* § 8.
[70] *Ibid.*, § 9.

writings of Zerahiah Gracian (Hen), Moses da Rieti and Leo Hebraeus (Judah Abarbanel). It is significant that all these three lived in Italy and were acquainted with Latin literature. The sevenfold classification must have been introduced by them under the influence of the enumeration of the so-called seven liberal arts which, beginning with Varro, contemporary of Cicero, runs throughout European literature.[71] But these Jewish authors accepted only the number seven, which was not entirely new in Hebrew literature, without its contents. The seven liberal arts are as a rule the trivium, (grammar, logic, rhetoric) and the quadrivium, (arithmetic, geometry, astronomy, music). In all these three Jewish authors, however, the seven sciences are physics, metaphysics, the four branches of mathematics and practical philosophy. Thus Zeraḥiah Gracian in his commentary on Proverbs 9, 1, "Wisdom hath builded her house, she hath hewn out her seven pillars." says as follows: "After he has finished his discourse about Wisdom, he proceeds to mention in passing the classes of science that constitute Wisdom. He says their number is seven, which is well known to students of philosophy. These seven are divided into two parts. The first is mathematics, which includes four disciplines, namely, arithmetic, geometry, music and astronomy. The second part is philosophy and is divided into three branches: physics, theology and politics".[72] The same enumeration is given by Moses da Rieti in his *Mikdash Me'at*.[73]

[71] See Robert Flint: *Philosophy as Scientia Scientiarum*, pp. 88–89.

[72] See *Ha-Shahar* II, pp. 226–7:
חכמות בנתה ביתה חצבה עמודיה שבעה. אחר שכלה לדבר בדבר החכמה בא לזכור לך על צד הרמז מיני החכמות, ואמר שהם שבעה, כמו שזה ידוע אצל אנשי החכמה, והם נחלקים לשני חלקים, האחד הוא הלמודים אשר בכללם ד׳ חכמות, שהם חכמת החשבון, הגמטריא שהוא בערבי אלהנדסה, המוציקא בלשונינו ניגון, וחכמת הכוכבים. והחלק השני הוא הפילוסופיה, ונחלקת לג׳ חלקים, חכמת הטבע, וחכמת האלהות, והנהגת המדינה.

[73] *Mikdash Me'at* I, 3:
במספר החכמות... נלקח מדברי אבונצר אלפראבי ואלגזלי ואבן רשד והרב ז"ל.

הראשונות שבעה למיניהן
תשבורת, מספר, תכונה, נגון,
תחת הלמודים סדורות הן.
הטבעיות–גם בסדר הגון
האלהות והמדות, ובם

In Judah Abarbanel's *Dialoghi di Amore* the same seven sciences are called *arti liberali* of which the Hebrew translator gives the Hebrew equivalent השבע חכמות.[74] A reference to seven sciences is also found in Abba Mari Don Astruc of Lunel's *Sefer ha-Yareah*,[75] but his seven are the seven branches of mathematics enumerated by Avicenna. Similar allusions to the number seven is found in Joseph ben Isaac Kimhi's Introduction to his *Sefer ha-Galui*[76] and in Moscato's commentary *Kol Yehudah* on the *Cuzari*.[76a] Abraham ibn Ezra's reference to the seven sciences has already been discussed above.

The three theoretical sciences are of unequal importance and they are therefore arranged according to a certain gradation of value. Aristotle himself evaluated these sciences, declaring metaphysics to be superior to the others.[77] In Arabic and Jewish philosophy, Avicenna, Algazali, Al-Mukammas and Bahya use the terms "superior", "middle" and "inferior" in the description of metaphysics, mathematics and physics respectively. Accordingly the logical order of arranging these sciences would be either from the highest to the lowest or *vice versa* from the lowest to the highest. And in fact, these two methods of arrangement are found to have been followed indiscriminately by various authors. Thus Algazali and Al-Mukammas (in one instance)[78] begin with the highest, metaphysics, whereas Bahya, Judah ha-Levi (in one instance),[79] Judah ibn Matkah, Solomon of Arles, Abba Mari Don Astruc, Caleb Afendopolo,

חיי הלב ולא יהיה ענון.
. . . .
ושני כלים להם אתה בוחר
דקדוק הלשון גם ההגיון
כי הם לכל כאניות סוחר.

[74] See *Wikkuah al ha-Ahabah*, p. 7b:

ובו נכללו השבע (חכמות), ארטי ליביראלי.

For his entire classification see p. 8b.

[75] See quotation above in n. 61.

[76] מי חכם ויבין אלה ונבון ויתבונן במופלא לחקור ולדרוש בשבעה עמודים שחצבה החכמה.

[76a] See his comment on the enumeration of topics under metaphysics in Book V, section 12: והיא אשר הטביעה אדניהם לעמודיהם שבעה.

[77] *Metaphysics* VI, 1, 1026a, 23.

[78] See quotation in n. 23.

[79] *Cuzari* V, 12.

and Judah ibn Bulat begin with the lowest, physics. In many enumerations, however, we find that the order given is that of mathematics, physics and metaphysics.[80] Thus we find it in the Ihwan al-Safa, Alfarabi, Israeli, Al-Mukammas (in one instance),[81] Judah ha-Levi (in one instance), Abraham ibn Daud, Maimonides, Zerahiah Gracian, Moses da Rieti, Abraham Shalom, and Solomon Almoli. This peculiar phenomenon may be explained by the distinction between the arrangement of these sciences according to the order of importance and their arrangement according to the order of study—a distinction, already pointed out by Reifmann.[82] According to the former method of arrangement, mathematics occupies a place between physics and metaphysics, for reasons which will be made clear in the sequel. But according to the latter method of arrangement, mathematics comes before physics.[83] We have a clear statement on the order of study in Maimonides where warning is given that instruction should not begin directly with metaphysics but should start with logic and should then proceed from mathematics through physics to metaphysics.[84] A similar warning is sounded

[80] This order is followed by Aristotle himself in *Metaphysics* VI, 1, 1026a, 19. In *De Anima* I, 1, 403b, 10–16, however, mathematics is placed between physics and metaphysics. But, on the other hand, physics is sometimes referred to by Aristotle as the "second" philosophy. Cf. Zeller: *Aristotle* I, p. 186.

[81] See quotation in n. 30.

[82] See *Ozar ha-Sifrut* II, pp. 49 and 50.

[83] That the order of study of the sciences was to be distinguished from their mere classification may be derived from the fact that Alfarabi, in addition to his work on the *Enumeration of the Sciences* (במספר החכמות), has also written a treatise on the *Order of the Study of the Sciences* (אגרת בסדור קריאת החכמות). See Steinschneider: *Uebersetzungen*, pp. 293–294. Similarly Averroes, at the beginning of his *Epitome of the Metaphysics*, after classifying the sciences, discusses their proper order of study. See also quotation from *Nobelot Hokmah* above in n. 62.

[84] See *More Nebukim* I, 34:

אי אפשר אם כן בהכרח למי שירצה השלמות האנושי מבלתי התלמד תחלה במלכת ההגיון ואחר כן בלימודיות על הסדר ואחר כן בטבעיות ואחר כן באלהיות.

By על הסדר after לימודיות, Maimonides evidently refers to the four branches of mathematics. See also Maimonides' letter to Joseph ibn Aknin which forms the Itroduction to the *Moreh* where the author refers to having taken him through a course of mathematics and logic in preparation to the

by Judah ha-Levi who criticises the Karaites for plunging directly into metaphysics without first going through the preliminary disciplines.[85] There is no justification however, for Steinschneider's and Kaufmann's attempt to prove the alleged Karaism of Al-Mukammas on the ground of his naming metaphysics first in his enumeration of sciences.[86] Al-Mukammas is simply arranging the sciences in the order of importance, starting with the highest, and his classification was not meant to be taken as a programme of study. In fact, Al-Mukammas himself, as we have seen, in another place, changes the order and names mathematics before physics and metaphysics.[87]

The order of importance of these sciences is determined by the subject matter with which they deal. We thus come to another point in our discussion, namely, the definition of each of these sciences, their subject matter and the special disciplines which they comprise.[88]

Metaphysics[89] seems to have been defined by Aristotle in

study of metaphysics. But later in the same letter, according to a marginal note in Alharizi's translation, Maimonides recommends physics as an additional preparatory study:

ולא יבין זה אלא מי שהקדים לדעת מלאכת ההגיון וטבע המציאות.

This passage occurs neither in the Arabic text nor in Ibn Tibbon's translation. There seems to be, however, an inconsistency in these passages as to whether logic precedes mathematics or *vice versa*.

An outline of a ten year programme of study, attributed to Aristotle, is given in Al-Harizi's translation of Honain ben Isaac's *Musare ha-Pilusufim* I, 11: בסדר למוד עשר החכמות. There mathematics precedes logic.

85 See *Cuzari* V, 2:

לא אנהג בך על דרך הקראים אשר עלו אל החכמה האלהית מבלי מדרגה.

86 See Kaufmann: *Die Theologie des Bachja Ibn Pakuda* in *Gesammelte Schriften* II, p. 21, note, and cf. quotation above in n. 23.

87 See quotation above in n. 30.

88 Thus Algazali, after defining each science, discusses its "subject", موضوع, נושא, and its "branches" فروع, סעיפים. The Ihwan al-Safa speak of the main divisions and the subdivisions of the sciences as the "genera", اجناس and the "species", انواع.

89 "Metaphysics", *μετὰ τὰ φυσικά*, is also called by Aristotle "theology", *θεολογία*, and the "first philosophy", *πρώτη φιλοσοφία* (cf. Zeller: *Aristotle* I, p. 76, n. 1 and 2). All these terms are used in Arabic and Hebrew philosophic literature, as in the following passages:

three ways. First, he describes it as the science which deals with "something which is eternal and immovable and separable [from body]".[90] Second, he characterizes it as the science which deals with "being *qua* being—both what it is and the attributes which belong to it *qua* being".[91] Third, he very often speaks of metaphysics as including the principles of mathematics, logic and physics. He thus says that metaphysics must include "the truths which are in mathematics called axioms;"[92] it must deal with the logical methods of demonstration, for "the philosopher, who is studying the nature of all substance, must inquire also into the principles of syllogism;"[93] and it must also comprise the general principles of physics, such as the four causes and the like.[94] Of these three definitions Algazali reproduces the first,[95] Avicenna the second,[96] and Alfaribi restates the first[97] and the third.[97a].

Maimonides: *Millot ha-Higgayon*, Ch. XIV:

ויקראו גם את החכמה האלהית מה שאחר הטבע.

Algazali: *Makasid al-Falasifah* II, p. 76:

האלהית והפילוסופיא הראשונה, الالهى والفلسفة الاولى

So also Judah ibn Bulat: הלמודים האלהיים and הפילוסופיאה הראשונה, (See *Uebersetzungen*, p. 30, n. 194).

Ibn Bulat uses also the expression החכמה הרבנית, ربّانية (See *Ibid*).

[90] *Metaphysics* VI, 1, 1026a, 10–11. See also *De Anima* I, 1, 403b, 15–16.

[91] *Metaphysics* VI, 1, 1026a, 31–32.

[92] *Ibid.*, IV, 3, 1005a, 20.

[93] *Ibid.*, 1005b, 5–8.

[94] *Ibid.*, I, 3, 983a, 24. cf. Grote: *Aristotle*, II, p. 135.

[95] See *Makasid al-Falasifah* II, p. 78.

[96] See quotation above in n. 8.

[97] See T. J. De Boer: *Philosophy* (*Muslim*) in Hastings' *Encyclopedia of Religion and Ethics*, IX, p. 881: "The doctrine of the existent in general, together with its *accidents*". The word *accidents* is erroneously used here. The existent in general can have no accidents. The underlying Arabic word must have been something meaning *attributes*. Thus in the definition reproduced in Falaquera's *Reshit Hokmah* it is correctly stated והדברים אשר יקראו להם במה שהם נמצאים, i. e., "and the things which are predicated of them *qua* being" and not אשר יקרו להם, i. e., "which are accidental to them *qua* being". See quotation below in n. 102 and reference to Aristotle above n. 91.

[97a] See De Boer, *loc. cit.* and compare Averroes' classification in his *Epitome of the Metaphysics*.

In Jewish philosophy, too, these three definitions of metaphysics are restated in whole or in part. Thus in the *Cuzari* two of these definitions are given. The second is reproduced in the following words: "Things metaphysical, such as the knowledge of the principles of being *qua* being and the attributes which belong to it".[98] The third definition is reproduced later in the same passage as follows: "And the establishment of the principles of the speculative sciences, the mathematical and the physical as well as the logical, which cannot be attained except by this science [i. e., metaphysics]".[99] The first and third definitions are given by Maimonides. He says: "Theology is divided into two parts: First, it is an inquiry into every being that is not material nor a force inherent in a body. . . . The second part of theology is an inquiry into the underlying causes of everything included in the other sciences."[100] The second and third definitions may also be discerned in the vague poetic verses of Moses da Rieti, in the following passages: "Where the mind causes its cloud to rest over absolute being in general and its attributes. . . . And there the Philosopher has shed his light over the principles of demonstration and has spread his pavilion over the other sciences".[101] Abraham Shalom mentions only the

[98] *Cuzari* V, 12:
והצטיירות הדברים האלהיים וידיעת התחלת המציאה בסתם מצד שהיא מציאה והתלויים בה.–ותצור אלאמור אלאלאהיה̈ ומערפה̈ מבאדי אלוגוד אלמטלק מן חית הו וגוד ולואחקה. This definition is almost a verbal reproduction of Aristotle's passage referred to above in n. 91.

[99] Ibid.:
וקיום התחלות החכמות העיוניות מהמוסריות והטבעיות מן הדבריות אשר לא יגיעו אליהם אלא בזאת החכמה.–ואתבאת מבאדי אלעלום אלנטריה̈ מן אלריאציה̈ ואלטביעיה̈ מן אלמנטקיה̈ אלתי לא יתוצל אליהא אלא בהדא אלעלם.

[100] *Millot ha-Higgayon* XIV:
והחכמה האלהית תחלק לשני חלקים, אחד מהם הוא העיון בכל נמצא שאינו גשם ולא כח בגשם, והוא הדבור במה שנתלה באל יתעלה שמו, ובמלאכים גם כן לפי דעתם, כי הם לא יסברו שהמלאכים גשמיים אבל יקראו אותם השכלים הנפרדים. והחלק השני בחכמת האלהית, העיון בסבות הרחוקות מאד מכל מה שיגללו עליו שאר החכמות האחרות [לכל מה שכוללת אותן שאר החכמות האחרות :Ahitub] ויקראו גם כן את החכמה האלהית מה שאחר הטבע.

[101] *Mikdash Me'at* I, 3:

מקום השכל עננו ישרה
על הנמצא המשולח כולל

second but seems to imply that the first is included in it.[101a] All the three definitions are mentioned by Shem-tob Falaquera[102] and Caleb Afendopolo[102a] in their enumeration of the topics of metaphysics.

After the definition of metaphysics and a general description of the subject matter with which it deals there naturally follows an enumeration of the topics which are included under this science. We shall first give a tabulated list of topics mentioned by various authors and then we shall make a few general observations about them.

The Ihwan al-Safa enumerate five topics: (1) The Creator and His attributes, such as unity, existence, knowledge, providence and the like. (2) Spiritual beings (i. e., the Intelligences). (3) Soul. (4) Ethics in its various branches, including the Aristotelian subdivisions of practical philosophy and revealed law. (5) Eschatalogy.[103]

Algazali gives two lists of general concepts, as follows: (a) Unity, cause and effect, likeness and difference, being and privation.[104] (b) Substance and accident, whole and part, one and many, cause and effect, potential and actual, like and dif-

ומשיגיו. . . . .
. . . .
ושם הפלוסוף האיר נרו
על התחלות מופתים ונטה
על יתר החכמות שפרירו.

[101a] *Neveh Shalom* V, 7, f. 75a:
הסוג השלישי היא חכמת האלהות, והוא ידיעת הנמצא במה שהוא נמצא ותארו ומשיגיו וחלקותיו, ונכנס בזה ידיעת השכלים הנבדלים וידיעת תארי האל ומציאותו.

[102] *Reshit Hokmah*, p. 53:
וזו החכמה נחלקת לשלשה חלקים, הראשון יחקור הדברים הנמצאים והדברים אשר יקראו להם במה שהם נמצאים. והשני יחקור בו התחלות המופתים בחכמות העיוניות הפרטיות... והשלישי יחקור הנמצאים אשר אינם בגופים [read: גופים] ולא בגופים.

One is not to be tempted to change in this passage ארש יקראו להם to אשר יקרו להם. See above n. 97.

[102a] See Steinschneider in *Monatsschrift* XL, pp. 93–94: "1. Die separaten (מופשטים) Intelligenzen, 2. Die Wesen in Allgemeinen, ohne Rücksichit auf ihre Körperlichkeit oder Unkörperlichkeit, 3. Principien (? התחלות) der Beweise der besonderen speculativen Wissenschaften".

[103] See Dieterici: *Die Logik und Psychologie der Araber*, pp. 15ff. Arabic text. *Idem: Die Abhandlungen der Ichwân Es-Safâ*, p. 251ff.

[104] *Makasid al-Falasifah* II, p. 76. See n. 117.

ferent, necessary and possible,[105] He ends both lists by saying "and the like".

Among the Jewish philosophers we have the following lists:

Israeli: Unity of God. Spiritual beings.[106]

Al-Mukammas: Unity of God. His laws and commandments.[107]

Bahya: God. His law. Intelligible forms, such as soul, intellect and the spiritual beings (i. e., Intelligences or angels).[108]

Judah ha-Levi: His list is divided into two parts, following his two definitions of metaphysics. Under the first definition, he enumerates the following concepts of being *qua* being: Potential and actual, beginning, cause, substance and accident, genus and species, the opposite and the same in species, likeness and difference, unity and plurality.[109] Under the second definition, he enumerates certain general principles belonging to the various other sciences, as follows: "Proof of the existence of the Prime Creator, the nature of the species [i. e., universals]. the relation of intellect [i. e., rational soul] to the Creator, the relation of the [animal] soul to the intellect, the relation of nature [i. e., vegetable soul] to the [animal] soul, the relation of matter and form to nature, the relation of the spheres, stars and other phenomena to matter and form, the wherefore of their being classified in this manner, the wherefore of their being arranged in this order of anteriority and posteriority, the knowledge of things human and divine, of universal nature, of divine providence."[110]

105 *Ibid.*, p. 77–78. See n. 117.

106 See above n. 17.

107 See above n. 23 and 30.

108 See above n. 31. For "Spiritual beings" Bahya uses the expression האישים הרוחניים; Isaac Israeli: הענינים הרוחניים; Maimonides: השכליים הנפרדים, המלאכים. In Al-Harizi's translation of Honain ben Isaac's *Musare ha-Pilusufim* I, 11, Philosophy, i. e., Metaphysics, is identified with האותות העליונים: חכמת הפילוסופייה והיא חכמת האותות העליונים. The expression on האותות העליונים usually means "meteorology." But the suggestion has been made to change it here to האישים העליונים (See Loewenthal: *Honein ibn Ishak, Sinnsprüche der Philosophen*, p. 69, n. 4).

109 *Cuzari* V, 12. See n. 117.

110 *Ibid.*

בקיום הבורא הראשון, והנפש הכללית, ואיכות המינים, ומדרגת השכל מהבורא, ומדרגת

Abraham Ibn Ezra: God, psychology, angels, eschatalogy.[111]

Joseph ben Isaac Kimhi: Unity of God. His laws and commandments.[111a]

Maimonides: Divine attributes, angels.[112]

Shem-tob Falaquera in his *Reshit Hokmah* and Afendopolo:[113] They both classify the topic of metaphysics into two groups. The first is presented by them as an analysis of Aristotles' *Metaphysics* and contains the following topics: Being *qua* being, principles of the other sciences and a refutation of the false theories of the ancients, God, the Intelligences, the universe in its relation to God. The second group, called by both of them "branches", contains the following: Prophecy, eschatalogy. Afendopolo adds also soul. In his *De'ot ha-Pilusufim* Falaquera deals only with the Active Intellect.[113a]

Gershon ben Solomon of Arles: Psychology.[114]

Moses da Rieti: Like Judah ha-Levi he arranges the topics of metaphysics under its two definitions which he has reproduced. Under the first definition he enumerates the following: Substance and accident, cause and effect, whole and part (or universal and particular), one and many, potential and actual, prior and posterior, finite and its opposite, necessary and possible.[115] Under the second definition he enumerates the following topics: The immaterial Intelligences, God, His attributes, refutation of erroneous views.

הנפש מהשכל, ומדרגת הטבע מהנפש, ומדרגת ההיולי והצורה מהטבע, ומדרגת הגלגלים והכוכבים וההויות מההיולי והצורה, ולמה הוטבעו על המחלוקת הזאת, והקדימה והאיחור, ידיעת האנושות והאלהות והטבע הכללי והשנחה הראשונה.

[111] See *Yesod Mora* I.

[111a] See quotation above in n. 55a.

[112] See quotation above in n. 100.

[113] *Monatsschrift* XL, pp. 93–94.

[113a] See above n. 65.

[114] See above n. 66.

[115] *Mikdash Me'at* I, 3:

. . . . בעצם ומקרה,
וכמו עלה או אשר יעלל,
כולל וחלקיי, אחד ורב.
ובכח ובפעל שם יתגולל.

קודם ומתאחר בם יעורב
והבעל תכלית יסותרו,
ומחוייב ואפשר אחר נקרב.

Abraham Shalom: Essence and attributes of God, angels, sublunar world, soul, prophecy, eschatology.[116]

These topics, as will have been noticed, may be grouped together under the various definitions of metaphysics reproduced above from Aristotle. Some of them are an enumeration of immaterial beings and their attributes, others are general concepts of being *qua* being, still others are principles common to the other sciences.

In Algazali's lists all the topics, sixteen in number, are to be found in the list of terms defined by Aristotle in *Metaphysics* V. Of the fourteen terms given by Judah ha-Levi in the first part of his list, nine are the same as those given by Algazali and the remaining five are to be found in *Metaphysics* V.[117] Thus both lists are based upon *Metaphysics* V.

Similarly, of the sixteen terms enumerated by Moses da Rieti twelve are found in Algazali and Judah ha-Levi and thus go back to the same Aristotelian source. The remaining four are also found in Aristotle, and two of these, *prior* and *posterior*, in *Metaphysics* V (ch. II).

In Israeli and Al-Mukammas there occurs the expression "unity of God" which is to be taken in the general sense of

[116] See quotation above in n. 101a.

[117] The fourteen terms mentioned by Judah ha-Levi are as follows: 1. בכח, באלקוה; 2. בפעל, אלפעל; 3. ההתחלה, אלמבדא; 4. העלה, אלעלה; 5. העצם, אלגוהר; 6. המקרה, אלערץ; 7. הסוג, אלגנס; 8. המין, אלנוע; 9. ההפך, אלמצאדה; 10. הדומה, אלמגאנסה; 11. ההסכמה, אלאתפאק; 12. החלוף, אלאכתלאף; 13. האחדות, אלוחדיה; 14. הרבוי, אלכתרה.

The seven additional terms mentioned by Algazali are as follows: 15. מחוייב, واجبا. 16. אפשר, ممكنا, 17. עלול, معلولا. 18. כולל, كليا. 19. חלקי, جزئيا. 20. המציאות, الوجود. 21. ההעדר, العدم.

The corresponding Greek terms in *Metaphysics* V are as follows:

1. Ch. 12: δύναμις. 3. Ch. 1: ἀρχή. 4. Ch. 2: αἴτον. 5. Ch. 8: οὐσία. 6. Ch. 30: συμβεβηκός. 7. Ch. 28: γένος. 9. Ch. 10: ἀντικείμενον. 10. Ch. 10: ταὐτά τῷ εἴδει. 11. Ch. 9: ὅμοια. 12. Ch. 9: διάφορα. 13. Ch. 6: ἕν. 14. Ch. 6: πολλά. 15. Ch. 5: ἀναγκαῖον. 16. Ch. 12: δύναμις. 18. Ch. 26: ὅλον. 19. Ch. 25: μέρος. 20. Ch. 7: τὸ ὄν. 21. Ch. 22: στέρησις.

Only 2, 8 and 17 are not given in the *Metaphysics*. But they are all implied in their antithetical terms.

divine nature or divine attributes as used by Maimonides and others, for the unity of God is the foundation of all discussions of divine nature and attributes. The use of the expression "unity of God" shows the influence of the Motazilite school one of whose chief dogmas was the principle of the absolute unity of God on which account they were called the partisans of unity. Saadia, too, deals with the problem of attributes in a chapter bearing the title of the unity of God.

In some of these lists (Ihwan al-Safa, Judah ha-Levi, Ibn Ezra, Shem-tob Falaquera, Caleb Afendopolo) certain phases of psychology, especially of the higher faculties of the soul, or human psychology *par excellence*, are included in metaphysics. In Aristotle, psychology is part of physics, and so it is also treated by Avicenna and Algazali. The reason for the inclusion of the treatment of the higher faculties of the soul in metaphysics, or rather theology, is probably due to the close relation of the subject to the problems of religion. Gershon ben Solomon, however, includes the entire subject of pyschology under metaphysics.

The inclusion of ethics under theology, noticeable in the Ihwan al-Safa, Al-Mukammas and Bahya, is probably due to the fact that in ethics the works of the pagan authors were supplemented, and sometimes supplanted, by the revealed writings of religion, and religious subjects as a whole, irrespective of their subject matter, were included under theology or metaphysics. It is for this reason, probably, that in some of these classifications the original distinction between theoretical and practical philosophy is not mentioned. Maimonides, who retains the main division of philosophy into theoretical and practical, includes under the latter, as we shall attempt to show, religious legislation as a special branch of practical philosophy in addition to three Aristotelian branches.[118] Thus also Ibn Daud openly appropriates the expression "practical philosophy"

[118] See *Millot ha-Higgayon* XIV:
ולפילוסופים בכל אלו הדברים ספרים הרבה שכבר יצאו בלשון הערב ואולי לא יצאו יותר מהם [כבר הועתקו אל הערבי ושמא אותם שלא הועתקו יותר רבים :Ahitub] והנה איננו צריכים באלו הזמנים אל כל זה, ר״ל החקים הדתות והנמוסים והנהגת האנשים בעניני אלהיים.

and uses it as a designation for certain principles of religious belief and conduct. He says: "Similarly in the second part we shall explain the origin of evil, which we absolutely deny to proceed directly from God, and we shall explain the nature of prophecy and the different kinds thereof, and what are the attendant conditions of a prophet whom we are under obligation to obey, and we shall also explain what is meant by reward and punishment. This is the method which we intend to follow. The subject matter of this sort of inquiry is obviously of the kind known as practical philosophy, for the same subject which in religion is only a matter of revelation is in true philosophy demonstrated by proof".[119] It is for this reason that purely religious precepts which constitutes religious ethics take the place of Aristotle's practical philosophy and are included under theology.

The inclusion of eschatalogical subjects under theology by Abraham Ibn Ezra[120] and Caleb Afendopolo[121] has its parallel in the Ihwan al-Safa.[122] Algazali includes it under physics together with psychology.

Physics is defined by Aristotle as the science which "deals with things which are inseparable from bodies but not immovable",[123] or as he says in another place, "the physicist deals with all the active properties or passive affections belonging to a body of a given sort and the corresponding matter".[124] This definition runs throughout Arabic and Jewish philosophy. Algazali says it deals with "the bodies of the world in so far as they fall under motion, rest and change".[125] Bahya defines it as "the science

[119] See *Emunah Ramah*, General introduction, p. 4:
וגם כן נבאר במאמר השני מקורי הרעות, אשר נכחיש המשכם מהאל ית' בהכלית ההכחשה, ונבאר הנבואה ומיניה, ותנאי הנביא אשר אנחנו מחויבים לשמוע אליו, ונבאר ענין הגמול והעונש. זה אופן הדרך אשר ניחל ללכת בו. אמנם נושא העיון הזה הנה מבואר שהוא פילוסופיא מעשית, מצד היותה בדת מקובלת ובפילוסופיא האמתית מבוארת במופת.

[120] See *Yesod Mora* I.

[121] See *Monatsschrift*, XL, p. 94.

[122] See Dieterici: *Die Logik und Psychologie der Araber*, p. 17; Arabic text, *Idem*: *Die Abhandlungen der 'Ichwân Es-Safâ*, p. 253.

[123] *Metaphysics* VI, 1, 1026a, 13–14.

[124] *De Anima* I, 1, 403b, 10–12.

[125] *Makasid al-Falasifah* II, p. 78.

of the natures of bodies and their accidents".[126] It also underlies the vague statement of Al-Mukammas when he says that it is "the science which investigates the bodies of things and the secrets of their nature".[127] Maimonides narrows down this definition by distinguishing, again after Aristotle,[128] between works of nature and works of art. He says: "The science of physics inquires into bodies which exist by nature and not by the will of man—such as the various species of minerals, plants and animals. The science of physics thus deals with all these bodies and with everything belonging to them, i. e., their accidents, properties and causes, and also with everything under which they fall, as time, space and motion".[129]

In enumerating the topics of physics two methods are used. The first of these is a classification of the physical writings of Aristotle, and this is done in two ways.

Sometimes the physical writings of Aristotle are referred to by their titles. Thus we find it in Judah ibn Matkah,[130] Shem-tob Falaquera, Abraham Shalom,[131] Caleb Afendopolo,[132] and Judah ibn Bulat.[133] They mention among them the following works of Aristotle, which are sometimes spoken of as the eight books of Aristotle's physical writings:[133a] (1) *Physics*, (2) *De Caelo et Mundo*, (3) *De Generatione et Corruptione*, (4) *Meteorologica*, (5) *De Anima*, with which are sometimes coupled some of the works of *Parva Naturalia*, such as *De Sensu et*

[126] See quotaion above in n. 31.

[127] See quotation above in n. 30.

[128] *Metaphysics* VII, 7; XII, 3.

[129] *Millot ha-Higgayon* XIV:

והחכמה הטבעית העין בגשמים הנמצאים בטבע לא ברצון האדם כמיני המקורים [המחצבים Ahitub:] ומיני הצמחים ומיני בעלי חיים. הנה החכמה הטבעית תעין בכל אלו ובכל מה שימצא בהם, ר"ל במקריהם כלם וסגלותיהם וסבותם, ובכל מה שימצאו הם בו [שימצא בהם Ahitub:] בהכרך כזמן והמקום והתנועה.

See also *Reshit Hokmah*, p. 48ff.

[130] See above n. 64.

[131] See above n. 63.

[132] See above n. 67.

[133] See above n. 69.

[133a] Cf. *Reshit Hokmah*, p. 51:

והספרים המחוברים בשרשים [=בחכמת הטבע] הם שמונה במספר החלקים, וצריך שנזכיר כל אחד מהם בשמו כמו שעשינו בחכמת ההגיון.

Sensibili, De Memoria et Reminiscentia, De Somno, De Somniis, De Longitudine et Brevitate Vitae, (6) *Historia Animalium*, and two spurious works, (7) *De Plantis* and (8) *De Mineralibus*.

Sometimes the physical writings of Aristotle, instead of being mentioned by their titles, are referred to by some description of their contents. Thus Judah ha-Levi describes eight of Aristotle's physical writings as follows: "The explanation of physical notions, as matter, form, privation, nature, time, space, motion (*Physics*); spherical and elementary substances (*De Caelo*); absolute generation and corruption (*De Generatione et Corruptione*); generated phenomena, as the phenomena generated in the air (*Meteorologica*), in minerals (*De Mineralibus*) and on the terrestial globe, as plants (*De Plantis*) and animals (*Historia Animalium*); the essence of man and how the soul knows itself (*De Anima*)"[134] The Ihwan al-Safa enumerate only seven of these works, leaving out *De Anima*, which they include under theology, but describing the *Physics* almost like Judah ha-Levi as the science of the principles of things, matter, form, time, space, motion.[135] The topics mentioned in Maimonides' definition of physics quoted above may similarly be taken to refer to some of the writings of Aristotle.

The second method consists in giving an independent list of topics not based upon Aristotle's writings. Thus Alfarabi enumerates the following eight sciences: *scientia de indiciis* (prognostication), *de medicina, de nigromantia, de imaginibus, de agritultura, de navigando, de alkimia, de speculis*.[136] Similar topics are included in the incompleted list given by Algazali, as follows: (1) medicine, (2) talismanics, (3) conjury, (4) magic.[137]

[134] *Cuzari* V, 12:
ובהתברר אמיתת הענינים הטבעיים, בהיולי והצורה, וההעדר, והטבע, והזמן, והמקום, התנועה, והגרמים הגלגליים, והגרמים היסודיים, וההויה וההפסד המוחלטים, וההויות הנולדות ההוות באויר, וההוות במוצאים, וההוות על כדור הארץ מצמח, וחי, ואמתת האדם, ואמתת הצטיירות הנפש את נפשה.

See commentary *Kol Yehudah, ad loc.*, followed by Cassel, *ad loc.*

[135] Dieterici: *Die Logik und Psychologie der Araber*, p. 13; Arabic text, *Idem: Die Abhandlungen der Ichwân Es-Safâ*, p. 249.

[136] Baeumker: *Alfarabi, Ueber den Ursprung der Wissenschaften* (*De Ortu Scientiarum*), pp. 20 and 12.

[137] *Makasid al-Falasifah* II, p. 78: (1) الطب, הרפואה, (2) الطلسمات, הטלסמאות, (τέλεσμα), (3) النارنجات, אחיזת העינים, (4) السحر, הכשוף.

It is interesting to note that these sorts of practical and magical sciences are mentioned by the Ihwan al-Safa in the class of sciences which they describe as preparatory,[138] and that *de speculis* in Alfarabi's list is usually placed under the mathematical arts.

Sometimes these two methods are combined. Thus Shem-tob Falaquera,[138a] Moses da Rieti[138b] and Caleb Afendopolo,[138c] after naming the eight works of Aristotle's physical writings, proceed to enumerate the branches (Falaquera and Rieti: **ענפים**, Afendopolo: **סעיפים**) of natural science, which branches, remarks Falaquera, are not always mentioned by authors in their classifications of sciences.[139] The branches these three authors mention are on the whole like those given by Alfarabi and Algazali. They all mention medicine, physiognomics, oneirocritics, and alchemy. Rieti has also magic and conjury. Falaquera and Afendopolo include among these also astrology which is given by Rieti and others, and again by Falaquera and Afendopolo themselves, under astronomy. Talismanics, which is omitted here by Rieti, is mentioned by him under the mathematical arts.[140]

As we have already seen, physics is identified with the,

[138] Dieterici: *Die Logik und Psychologie den Araber*, p. 10; Arabic text *Idem: Die Abhandlungen der Ichwân Es-Safâ*, p. 246.

[138a] *Reshit Hokmah*, pp. 48–53

[138b] *Mikdash Me'at* I, 3.

[138c] Cf. Steinschneider in *Monatsschrift* XL, 91–92.

[139] *Reshit Hokmah*, p. 53:
ואלו הענפים לא זכרום מקצת הפילוסופים בזכרם מספר החכמות, ואני כדי שיהיה הספר שלם זכרתים.

These branches are also mentioned by Solomon Almoli in his list which includes physics, medicine, magic, talismanics and alchemy (See above note 70).

[140] The following are the Hebrew terms used by Falaquera, Rieti and Afendopolo for some of the physical sciences they mention:
Physiognomics, F: חכמת ההכרה. R: הכרת הפרצוף. A: חכמת הפרצוף.
Oneirocritics, F and A: חכמת הפתרון. R: פתרון החלומות.
Alchemy, F: אלכימיאה (or קמייא, כמיאא). R: חכמת הצריפה.
Conjury, R: אוחזי העינים (see below n. 137).
Talismanics: F.: חכמת הצלמים. A: חכמת התרפים והצלמים (See below n. 155d).

science of medicine by Isaac Israeli.[141] A formal division of medicine into hygienics and therapeutics is given by Abba Mari don Astruc.[142] A sevenfold division of medicine is given by Rieti, as follows: Anatomy, pathology, diagnostics, pharmacology, dietetics, hygienics and therapeutics.[142a]

Al-Mukammas places under physics the science of the structure of heaven and earth and the other creatures,[143] which, of course, includes almost everything under the sun.

Unlike both physics and metaphysics with regard to the subject matter of which it treats, but standing midway between these two sciences, is mathematics. Aristotle describes it as a science which, in so far as its subject matter is concerned, partakes both of physics and metaphysics. "The attributes which, though inseparable, are not regarded as properties of a body of a given sort, but are reached by abstraction, fall under the province of the mathematician".[144] In another place he seems to suggest that some branches of mathematics are more like physics, with regard to their subject matter, while others are more like metaphysics. He says: "Mathematics also is theoretical; but whether its subjects are immovable and separable from matter, is not at present clear; it is clear, however, that it considers some mathematical objects *qua* immovable and *qua* separable from matter".[145] It is evidently upon the basis of this passage of Aristotle that Avicenna arranges the

[141] See above n. 17.
[142] See above n. 61.
[142a] *Mikdash Me'at* I, 3

ולה ענף חכמת הרפואה,
אשר תועלותיה ספורים,
ושבעה דרכים למוצאה:

ידיעת נתוח האברים,
הבריאות ומחלות הגופים,
והאותות אשר בהם נכרים,

וסמים ומזונות מתחלפות,
ושמירת בריאות נמשך רצוף,
והסרת החולי בתרופות.

[143] See above n. 30
[144] *De Anima* I, 1, 403d, 12–15.
[145] *Metaphysics* VI, 1, 1026a, 7–10.

seven branches of mathematics in order of their growing dependence upon matter, beginning with (1) arithmetic, which he takes to stand nearest to metaphysics, and following it with (2) geometry, (3) music, (4) the theory of weight, (5) the theory of measure, (6) the theory of perspective, and (7) astronomy, the last of which he takes to be nearest to physics.[146] Aristotle's definition is given also by Algazali.[147] In Maimonides it is reproduced as follows: "The science of mathematics does not investigate bodies *qua* bodies, but investigates the attributes abstracted from bodies".[148] Similar definitions are given by other Jewish authors.

The topics of mathematics are seven according to Avicenna, as already mentioned. Alfarabi[149] gives a similar list, but he counts the theories of measure and weight as one and adds technique. Of these topics the quadrivium of arithmetic, geometry, music and astronomy constitutes the "roots", اصول, שרשים, of mathematics whereas the others are called the "branches", فروع, סעיפים. Thus Algazali[150] and, following him, Afendopolo[151] use these terms of differentiation. Similarly Maimonides designates the quadrivium by the term "roots"[152] (Ibn Tibbon: שרשים, Ahitub: עיקרים) and Moses da Rieti applies the term "branches" ענפים, to the other mathematical topics.

In the enumeration of the topics of mathematics, some authors mention only the quadrivium (Ihwan al-Safa, Israeli, Bahya, Maimonides, Zerahiah Gracian), others mention only part of the quadrivium (Al-Mukammas, Gershon ben Solomon of Arles, Abba Mari Don Astruc, Abraham Shalom), still others mention part of the quadrivium and some "branches" (Joseph Solomon Delmedigo), but there are some who mention not only

[146] See above n. 8.

[147] *Makasid al-Falasifah* II, p. 77.

[148] *Millot ha-Higgayon* XIV.
אמנם החכמה הלמודית לא תעיין בנשמים במה שהם עליו, אבל תעין בענינים משללים מחמריהם. [Ahitub: מופשטים]

[149] See Hastings' *Enc. of Relig. and Eth.*, IX, p. 881.

[150] *Makasid al-Falasifah* II, p. 78.

[151] See above n. 67. But Caleb Afendopolo uses also שרשית in the general sense of mathematics: חכמה הרגלית או למודית ותקרא גם כן שרשית. *loc. cit*

[152] *Millot ha-Higgayon* XIV.

the quadrivium and the "branches" but many of the subdivisions of the latter (Falaquera, Rieti, Afendopolo).

The list given by Judah ha-Levi presents some difficulty. The published text of the Hebrew translation would seem to offer arithmetic, mechanical measurement, astronomical measurement, musical measurement and optical measurement.[153] The Arabic original,[154] however, and the Oxford text of the Hebrew translation read here arithmetic, musical measurement and optical measurement.

The classifications of the mathematical sciences given by Falaquera in his *Reshit Hokmah* and by Moses da Rieti show a striking similarity.[154a] The former follows Alfarabi in enumerating the quadrivium and the theory of weight, the theory of perspective and technique.[155] The latter omits perspective

[153] *Cuzari* V. 12.
והצטיירות הדברים המוסריים מהמנינים, והשעורים המלאכיים, והשעורים הכוכביים, והשעורים הנגוניים, והשעורים המראיים.

[154] *Cuzari loc. cit.*
ותצור אלאמור אלריאצ̇יה̈ מן אלעדדיה̈ ואלהנדסיה̈ אללחניה̈ ואלהנדסיה̈ אלמנאטריה̈.

[154a] There is also a close similarity between the classifications of these two and that of Afendopolo.

[155] The following are the Hebrew equivalents for these seven mathematical sciences:

Arithmetic. 1. חכמת החשבון. 2. ח' המניין. 3. ח' המספר.

Geometry. 1. תשבורת. 2. ח' הכדות. 3. גומטריה. 4. ח' השעורים. 5. הנדסה. 6. ח' המדה והמשקל (See n. 21 Text probably corrupt), 7. ח' הטפחות (See n. 33f). 8. תכונה (See below under Astronomy).

But שעורים and the Arabic هندسة are also used in the general sense of measurement in connection with (mechanics, astronomy), music and aspects. See *Cuzari* V, 12, quoted in n. 153 and 154.

Etymologically, חשברת would seem to be connected with the Arabic root شبر, *to measure by the span.*

The commentary *Kol Yehudah* on *Cuzari, loc. cit.*, takes תשבורת in the sense of *arithmetic*: ועל התשבורת אמר והצטיירות הדברים המוסריים מהמניינים. Steinschneider takes תשבורת in the sense of Algebra (*Jüdische Literatur* in Enoch und Gruber, p. 435).

Astronomy, 1. ח' הכוכבים, علم النجوم (See above n. 31). 2. ח' הגלגל, علم الفلك (See above n. 35, 38). 3. ח' המזלות (See above p. 278). 4. ח' החכונה, علم الهيئة, an abridged form of תכונת העולם, هيئة العالم (*Makasid al-Falasifah*

though he mentions it, as does again Falaquera, in enumerating the topics of technique. Both divide each of the quadrivium, with the exception of astronomy, into theoretical, עיוני, and practical, מעשי, which reminds us of the Ihwan al-Safa and Al-Mukammas. Astronomy is subdivided by Falaquera into

II, p. 78, Cf. Steinschneider: *Uebersetzungen* p. 998), i. e., *the disposition or arrangement of the world* (תכונה = هيئة = *διάθεσις*, See below n. 179. 5. ידיעת צורת הגלגלים (See above n. 63).

According to Samuel ibn Tibbon, תכונה is a general term including astronomy as well as astrology. See *Pirush Meha-Millot Zorot* under למודים: וחכמת התכונה הכוללת תכונת הגלגלים והכוכבים ומשפטי הכוכבים.

In Al-Harizi's translation of Honain ben Isaac's *Musare ha-Pilusufim* I, 11, there is the following passage:

אחרי כן בשנה רביעית לחכמת החשבון. אחרי כן בשנה החמישית לחכמת התכונה והמדות. אחרי כן בשנה ששית לחכמת הככבים. . . . . אחרי כן בשנה שמינית לחכמה המוסיקא היא חכמת הנגון.

It is clear that the passage enumerates the quadrivium. The term תכונה, coupled here with מדה, could not evidently mean astronomy, for the latter is mentioned in חכמת הככבים, unless we take תכונה in the specific sense of astronomy and חכמת הככבים in the sense of astrology, which, however, does not seem probable. If תכונה here is synonymous with מדה in the sense of "measurement" and hence "geometry", then it must etymologically differ from תכונה which is used for astronomy. We may thus conclude that the term תכונה has two roots:

(1) The Biblical תכונה from כון, *arrange* which, as a translation of the Arabic هيئة, *arrangement, disposition,* is used for astronomy as well as in the expression תכונת הנפש, *disposition of the soul.*

(2) The same word from תכן, *measure,* like the Biblical תכן, תכנית and מתכנת, used here by Al-Harizi as synonymous with מדה (also שעור, תשבורת) in the sense of *measurement* and hence *geometry.*

As a derivative of כון and the equivalent of هيئة the term תכונה has all the meanings of هيئة. It thus also means "exterior", "appearance", "form". Consequently, Samuel ibn Tibbon translates the Arabic אלשכל, "form", "shape", "figure" (*Moreh Nebukim* II, Prop. 22) by התכונה, which Efodi (*ad loc.*) and Crescas (*Or Adonai* I, i, 22) explain by התמונה Al-Harizi translates it by התבנית.

Again, תכונה in its Biblical sense of "fixed place" is made use of by Al-Harizi when he translates the Arabic אוצע, "position" (*Moreh Nebukim, loc. cit.*) by התכונה המיוסדת. Samuel ibn Tibbon translates it by הנחה which is the equivalent of מצב (Cf. *Or Adonai, loc. cit.*).

Music. 1. ח' הנגון or הנגינות. 2. ח' הלחנים (لحون). 3. ח' החבור (See n. 17), i. e., *composition,* as explained in *Millot ha-Higgayon* XIV by

mathematical astronomy, חכמת הכוכבים הלמודית, and astrology. Rieti, too, has this classification but adds a third part, the art of calendar making, which he characterizes as a particularly Jewish art. Rieti uses the following terms in designating these three parts of astronomy: (1) חכמת החזיון, *the science of observation*, i. e., what Falaquera calls "mathematical astronomy". (2) חכמת הנסיון,[155a] *divination* and hence *astrology*. (3) סוד, העבור, *the secret of intercalation*. Both state that it is only the first which properly belongs to mathematics.[155b] Finally, under *technique* Falaquera includes many branches relating to all the mathematical sciences as well as to the various practical

חכמת חבור הנגונים. But why not the Arabic حبر, *music and dance*? As for חבור in the sense of *astronomy*, See above n. 33f. 4. המוצקי, אלמוסיקה, המוסיקא (See n. 17), המוציקא (See n. 72). 5. (لحون) חכמת הקולות (See n. 33f). 6. חכמת העוגבים (See n. 33f).

Theory of perspective, 1. חכמת המראות or המראים or הראיה (See n. 62). 2. ח' המבטים or ההבטות (Cf. Steinschneider, *Uebersetzubng*, pp. 511–512).

Theory of weight, 1. חכמת הכבדים. 2. ח' המשקולת. (But see *Reshit Hokmah*, p. 47, where the latter is made a branch of the former).

Technique, תחבולות (=حيل). See *Monatsschrift*, XL, p. 93, n. 1.

155a. Afendopolo, too, uses חכמת הנסיון for astrology. See *Monatsschrift*, XL, p. 93.

The division of astronomy, חכמת הככבים, into חזיון and מלאכת הנסיון is also found in Abraham bar Hiyya's *Zurat ha-Arez, Introduction.*

As for the etymology of נסיון, Steinschneider seems to take it from the ordinary meaning of נסה, *try*, and translates it by *Erfahrungskunst*. (*Jüdische Literatur* in Ersch und Gruber, p. 435). But it is hard to see why astrology should have been considered as an art based upon experience. It seems to me, therefore, that נסיון should be taken in the sense of ניחוש, *divination*. Thus in Genesis 30, 27, נחשתי is rendered in the Onkelos Targum by נסיתי. Rashi comments upon it: נסיתי בניחוש שלי, and Ibn Ezra says explicitly: נחשתי כמו נסיתי. Thus when Abraham bar Hiyya says of astrology מפני שראיותיה אינם ראיות נכונות וכולם באות מן הסברות לה והנסיונות the term נסיונות is not to be taken to mean "experiences" but rather "conjectures".

155b Falaquera: "והחלק השני חכמת הכוכבים הלמודים, וזו היא הנמנית בחכמות הלמודיות.

Rieti: ותקרא חכמת החזיון, וזאת אשר בחכמות תתרפק.

Rieti's statement, however, is more reminiscent of Abraham bar Hiyya's characterization of חזיון:

והחלק הזה הוא הנמנה בכל חכמת המדע ומלאכת השכל, וכל ראיותיו וטענותיו ישרות ונאמנות שאין בהם שום ספיקא.

arts and crafts. Among those relating to arithmetic and geometry he mentions algebra and the theory of equations.[155c] He also mentions the art of making metrical, astronomical, musical and optical instruments. He also refers to the making of arms and to architecture, sculpture and painting. Rieti gives a similar list but adds talismanics. This is rather strange, for talismanics is usually placed under physics. An explanation for this, however, may be found, if we assume that Rieti was dependent upon the *Reshit Hokmah*, though he does not mention Falaquera among the authors whom he says he has followed in his classification of sciences. Falaquera speaks of a special branch of *technique* which is the working in גופות וצורות. From the context it is clear that the reference is to sculpture, architecture and painting. He furthermore describes this branch of *technique* as a social art, מלאכה מדינית. Now, the terms צורות and צלמים are often used as the Hebrew equivalents for טלסמאות.[155d] Furthermore in another place Falaquera speaks of astrology (and by the same token of the art of forecasting in general) as a social science, חכמה מדינית (p. 52). It is thus easy to see how Rieti could have taken the following passage of the *Reshit Hokmah*, p. 48:

חכמות תחבולות, והן התחלות המלאכה המדינית המעשית, אשר מלאכתה בגופות והצורות כמו מלאכת הבנין, והדומה לזה.

[155c] *Reshit Hokmah*, p. 47:

ומהם התחבולות החשבוניות על פנים רבים, מהם החכמה הנקראת בלשון הערב אל גבר ואלמקבלה (الجبر والمقابلة) ומה שדומה לה, ואעפ״י שזו החכמה משותפת לחשבון ולתשבורת.

The same Arabic terms are also used by Afendopolo (*Monatsschrift*, XL, p. 93). Similarly in Judah ben Barzilai's *Pirush Sefer Yezirah*, p. 144, the Arabic term for algebra is reproduced without an attempt to translate it into Hebrew.

וכבר דברתי אליהן דבר ארוך בספר אשר כתבתי בחשבונם הנקרא חסאב אלגבאר.

But in *Makasid al-Falasifah* II, p. 78, the Arabic الجبر is translated by the Hebrew חכמת התחבולה. The term תחבולה, as we have seen (n. 155), specifically means *technique* of which Algebra is a subdivision.

[155d] Thus Maimonides *Pirush ha-Mishnah*, *Pesahim* IV: וזו הצורה נקראת בלשון יון טלס״ם. Thus also Samuel ibn Tibbon explains טלסמאות by צורות מדברות (*Moreh Nebukim* I, 63 and cf. Friedlander, *ad loc.*). Afendopolo uses for it the terms החרפים והצלמים (*Monatsschrift* XL, p. 92).

to refer to talismanics and thus paraphrase it by:

ותחבולות נעלמות באות
עם טבע מה וכוח ככבים
בצלמים גם הטלסמאות.

That logic is not to be included among the sciences but is only an instrument of science is dwelt upon by Maimonides, Judah ibn Matkah, Zerahiah Gracian, Moses da Rieti[156] and others. Though Aristotle himself never explicitely designates logic as an organon or instrument,[157] the term is applied to it by Andronicus (early first century B. C.) and Alexander of Aphrodisias (c. 200 A. D.) and is the title by which Aristotle's logical writings have been collectively known. The topics enumerated under logic are usually based upon an enumeration of Aristotle's logical writings which Maimonides says to be eight in number, and gives their titles.[158] The eight books are also named by Alfarabi,[159] Judah ibn Matkah,[160] Falaquera,[160a] Rieti,[160b] and Judah ibn Bulat.[161] All of these authors mention the six books of the Organon: *Categoriae*, *De Interpretatione*. *Analytica Priora*, *Analytica Posteriora*, *Topica*, and *De Sophisticiis Elenchis*, supplemented by the *Rhetorica* and the *Poetica*. Judah ha Levi, here again, instead of naming these eight books

[156] *Millot ha-Higgayon* XIV.:

אמרו מדרגת מלאכת ההגיון מן השכל כמדרגת מלאכת הדקדוק מן הלשון.
ואולם מלאכת ההגיון, הנה אינה אצלם מכלל החכמות, אבל היא כלי לחכמה, אמרו שלא יכשר ללמוד או ללמד על חדר [Ahitub: סדר] כי אם במלאכת ההגיון, כי היא הכלי לכל דבר ולא מן הדבר.

Serahiah Gracian: Commentary on Proverbs IX, 3:

שלחה נערותיה תקרא על גפי מרמי קרת. זה רמז להקדמות הצריכות לדעת תחלה בחכמות, כמלאכת ההגיון בחכמת הטבע ובאלוהות.

Moses da Rieti: *Mikdash Me'at* I, 3:

ושני כלים להם אתה בוחר, דקדוק הלשון גם ההגיון, כי הם לכל כאניות סוחר.

Judah ibn Matkah: See Steinschneider, *Uebersetzungen*, § 1.

[157] See Grote: *Aristotle* I, p. 78, n. a; Zeller: *Aristotle* I, p. 187; Ueberweg-Praechter: *Geschichte der Philosophie des Altertums*, p. 519.

[158] *Millot ha-Higgayon* X and XIV.

[159] Hastings' *Enc. of Rel. and Eth.* IX, p. 880.

[160] See above n. 64.

[160a] *Reshit Hokmah*, p. 37ff

[160b] *Mikdash Me'at* I, 3.

[161] See above n. 69.

by title, refers to them and also to Porphyry's *Isagoge* by describing their contents, as follows: "Logical truths, as general, species, differences and properties (*Isagoge*); the words (i. e., the ten Categories) both simple (*Categoriae*) and combined in the various ways of combination (*De Interpretatione*); syllogims both true and false (*Analytica Priora*); judgments giving rise to conclusions which are necessary and demonstrative (*Analytica Posteriora*) or only dialectical (*Topica*) or rhetorical (*Rhetorica*) or sophistical (*De Soph. Elench.*) or poetical (*Poetica*)."[162]

In all these lists of logical topics, it will have been noticed, the *Rhetoric* and the *Poetics* are included under logic. This is significant. Aristotle himself considered rhetoric as a branch of dialectics and politics.[163] How he would have classified the *Poetics* is unknown. Probably he would have put it under his productive sciences.[164] The Ihwan al-Safa place poetics among the introductory disciplines, together with reading, writing and grammar,[165] and rhetoric is made by them a part of logic.[166]

We have already pointed out that Aristotle's practical philosophy is often identified with religious law and is thus treated as a part of theology. Still in many formal classifications it is given a place by itself as the counterpart of theoretical philosophy. Whatever we have to say on this subject we shall give here in the form of a running commentary on a passage taken from Maimonides' *Millot ha-Higgayon* XIV. The vague meaning of the passage is clear enough. But we shall try to

[162] *Cuzari* V, 12:

האמתות הדבריות, כמו הסוגים [אלאגנאס] והמינים [אלאנואע] והחלקים [אלפצול] והמדות המיוחדות [אלכ̇ואץ̇] והמלות [אלאלפאט̇] הנפרדות והמורכבות בדרכים הנחלקים מההרכבות, וההקשות המחוברות האמתיות והכזביות, והגזרות המולידות תולדות הכרחיות מופתיות או נצחויות או הלציות או הטעיות או שיריות.

See commentary *Kol Yehudah, ad loc.*, followed by Cassel, *ad loc.*

Exactly the same description of the first five of these books is given by the Ihwan al-Safa. See Dieterici: *Die Logik und Psychologie der Araber*, pp. 12–13; Arabic text, *Idem*: *Die Abhandlungen der Ichwan Es-Safa*, pp. 248–249. See also *Millot ha-Higgayon*, ch. X.

[163] See Zeller: *Aristotle* I, p. 185

[164] See *Ibid.*; Ueberweg-Praechter, *op. cit.* p. 281.

[165] Dieterici: *Die Logik und Psychologie der Araber*, p. 10; Arabic text, *Idem*: *Die Abhandlungen der Ichwân Es-Safâ*, p. 246.

[166] *Ibid.*, p. 11; Arabic text *Ibid.*, p. 245.

determine the precise meaning of its terms, to make a translation of parts of the text and to account for the allusions it contains.

What is generally called practical philosophy, המעשית (Ahitub: המלאכותית), says Maimonides, is also known as "human philosophy", פילוסופיא אנושית, and "political science," החכמה המדינית. Both these additional designations may be found in Aristotle. The expression "political science", πολιτική, is sometimes used by him in a general sense and is made to include the science of individual conduct as well as of the state and of the management of a household.[167] Then also Aristotle uses the expression ἀνθρώπινα φιλοσοφία, i. e., "the science of human nature", to designate politics in its widest sense.[168]

Practical philosophy is divided by Maimonides into four parts instead of the three of Aristotelian tradition.

The first is ethics which is described as "man's governance of himself", הנהגת האדם נפשו. The term הנהגה (as well as its equivalent נהילה),[169] which may be translated by "management" or "government" reflects the Arabic تدبير or سياسة.[170] All of these terms may be traced to the Greek νομία which occurs in οἰκονομία. In Arabic and Hebrew, however, the term is also used in connection with ethics and politics and very often by itself as the equivalent of practical philosophy. Thus the Ihwan al-Safa designate practical science by علم السياسة. The expression "of himself" (נפשו) which occurs in Maimonides' definition of ethics, and which is also used by many other authors, may be traced to Aristotle, who, in contrasting ethics with economics and politics, speaks of it as "knowledge for one's self", τὸ αὑτῷ εἰδέναι.[171]

Maimonides' description of ethics which follows is a brief but careful summary of Aristotle's theory of virtue, ἀρετή. Virtue,

167 See Zeller: *Aristotle* I, p. 186, n. 4; p. 187, n. 1.

168 *Ethics* X, 10, 1181b, 15.

169 See quotation above in n. 33f. From passages quoted by Steinschneder it would seem that the term תקון is also used as the equivalent of הנהגה. See *Uebersetzungen*, p. 209, n. 734b.

170 *Makasid al-Falasifah* II, p. 75; Dieterici: *Die Abhandlungen der Ichwân Es-Safâ*, p. 252.

171 *Ehtics* VI. 9. 1141b. 34.

according to Aristotle, is one of the qualities of the soul, but, being neither feeling, πάθη, nor capacity, δύναμις, it is habit, ἕξις.[172] Virtue is not only the result of human actions but, on becoming a habit, it also determines action, for "the virtue of man also must be a habit, from which man becomes good and from which he will perform his work well".[173] The opposite of virtue is vice, κακία, and virtue is "a mean state between two vices, one in excess, the other in defect".[174] These two moral qualities, virtue and vice, are dispositions, διαθέσεις, of the soul.[175] It is according to their virtues and vices that men are either praised or blamed and are called either good or bad.[176] Just as the soul is divided into an irrational, ἄλογον, and a rational, λόγον ἔχον, part so are the virtues divided into moral, ἠθική, and intellectual, διανοητική.[177] Finally, virtue and the moral character of man must be formed by education which is to be enforced by law, νόμος.[178]

This composite statement, made up of passages culled from the *Ethics*, is the literary background of the following passage of Maimonides:

"Man's governance of himself is the science which enables him to develop good qualities and to free himself from bad qualities, if he has already acquired them. Moral qualities are dispositions which gradually become more and more fixed in the soul until they are formed into a habit by which actions are determined. Philosophers describe moral qualities as either excellent or defective. Praiseworthy moral qualities are called virtues; blameworthy moral qualities are called vices. Actions resulting from praiseworthy qualities are called good; those resulting from blameworthy qualties are called bad. Similarly philosophers describe reasoning, i. e., the act of conceiving ideas, as either excellent or defective. We thus speak of in-

[172] *Ibid.*, II, 4, 1105a–b.
[173] *Ibid.*, II, 5, 1106a, 22–24.
[174] *Ibid.*, II, 6, 1107a, 2–3.
[175] *Ibid.*, II, 8, 1108b, 11.
[176] *Ibid.*, II, 4, 1105b, 28–1106a, 13.
[177] *Ibid.*, I, 13, 1103a, 3–10
[178] *Ibid.*, X, 10.

tellectual virtues and intellectual vices. The philosophers have many books on the moral virtues. Every rule of conduct by which one man governs another is called law''.[179]

Maimonides' description of the other two parts of practical philosophy is similarly an analysis of Aristotle's *Economics* and *Politics*.

The *Economics* of Aristotle begins with a discussion of the relation of husband to wife and of master to slave. He also describes the methods to be employed by a household manager in procuring and preserving property.[180] These methods, he further explains by many illustrations, differ with time and place.[181]

This outline is reproduced by Maimonides as follows:

"The management of a household is the science by which the manager knows how the members of the household are to help each other and how they are to be provided for in such a manner that their affairs would be properly conducted in accordance with the means of the household and in accordance with the established standards of a given time and place.''[182]

179 אמנם הנהגת האדם נפשו, הוא שיפנה אותה אל המדות הנכבדות, ויסיר ממנה הפחיתיות, אם היה שכבר הגיעוה. והמדות הן התכונות הנפשיות שתגענה בנפש עד שעור היותם לקנין [טבע Ahitub:] ותסדרנה מהן פעלות. והפילוסופים יתארו המדות במעלות ובפחיתיות. ותקראנה המדות החשובות מעלות המדות [מדות טובות Ahitub:] והמדות המגנות פחיתות המדות [מדות מגונות Ahitub:]. והפעלות הבאות מהמדות החשובות תקראנה טובות, והבאות מהמדות המגנות תקראנה רעות. וכן יתארו הדבור גם כן, והיא ציור המשכלות, במעלות ובפחיתיות. ונאמר מעלות דבוריות ופחיתות דבוריות, ולפילוסופים ספרים רבים במדות. וכל הנהגה ינהיג בה זולתו נקראה חק [הנהגה Ahitub:].

Cf. Rosin: *Die Ethik des Maimonides*, p. 36.

The Greek equivalents of some of the terms in this passage are as follows:

מדות, *ἦθος, manners, moral nature*

תכונה, *διάθεσις, disposition.*

קנין [טבע], *ἕξις, habit.*

מעלות [מדות], *ἀρετή, virtue excellenceé*

פחיתיות [גנות], *κακία, vice.*

דבורי, *διανοητικός, intellectual.*

חק [הנהגה], *νόμος, custom, law, ordinance.*

180 *Oecon*, I, 6.

181 *Ibid*. Bk. II.

182 ואולם הנהגת הבית היא שידע איך יעזרו קצתם את קצתם ובמה יסתפקו עד שיכשר תקון ענינם לפי היכלת ולפי הענינים הראוים בזמן ההוא ובמקום ההוא.

Maimonides' description of politics is a paraphrase of such general statements in Aristotle's *Politics* as that the purpose of society is to attain to some good,[183] and that the best government is that which leads to the attainment of that good,[184] and that there are different kinds of good.[185] Maimonides refers only vaguely to Aristotle's elaborate descriptions and evaluations of the different forms of government.

"As for the governance of the city-state, it is a science which imparts to those who pursue the study thereof the knowledge of true happiness, showing them how to go about in attaining it, also the knowledge of true evil, showing them how to go about in avoiding it, and also the knowledge of how to muster up all their moral qualities in abandoning the pursuit of imaginary happiness to the end that they may have no desire for it and take no pleasure in it. It teaches them also the harmless nature of imaginary evil to the end that they may not be affected by it and that they may take no unnecessary trouble to rid themselves of it. It also prescribes the right methods by which groups of people may organize themselves under a proper form of government."[186]

The fourth class of practical philosophy is described by Maimonides as הנהגת האומה הגדולה או האומות, which would naturally be translated "the government of the great nation or of the nations" and is taken to refer to international politics.[187] The underlying Arabic term for אומה must have been امّة. Later in the passage Maimonides speaks of חכמי האומות השלמות, which, again, would ordinarily be translated "the sages of the perfect nations". However, the Arabic امّة

183 *Politics* I, 1.

154 *Ibid.*, VII, 1.

185 *Ibid.*,

186 ואולם הנהגת המדינה, הנה היא חכמה תקנה בעליה ידיעת ההצלחה האמתית ותראה להם ההתפשטות [Ahitub: ההליכה] בהגעתה, וידיעת הרעה האמתית ותראה להם ההתפשטות [Ahitub: ההליכה] בשמירה ממנה, והשתמש במדותיהם בעזיבת ההצלחה המדמה עד שלא יתאוו אותה ולא יחיו נפשם בה. ותבאר להם הרעה המדמה עד אשר לא יכאבו בה ולא יעזבו אותה. וכן תניח דרכי הישר יסדרו בם קבוציהם סדור נאה.

187 See Mendelssohn's commentary *ad loc.* and Rosin: *Die Ethik des Maimonides*, p. 35.

may also mean a "religion" or a "religious sect". It is probably under the influence of this Arabic meaning of the term that the Hebrew אומה was applied to the Karaites.[188] It would also seem that when Saadia says of the Jews that they are a אומה, امّة, by reason of the Torah, he does not simply mean a "nation" but rather a "religious people".[189] In view of this, Maimonides' fourth class of practical philosophy may be translated: "the government of the great religion or of the other religions". By the "great religion" Maimonides undoubtedly means Judaism. Thus also Abraham ibn Daud calls Judaism "the exalted religion", האמונה הרמה, though the term used by him is عقيدة[189a] When Maimonides later speaks of חכמי האומות השלמות, I should take השלמות as a deliberate mistranslation, though not altogether unjustifiable, of the Arabic مسلمات, *Moslem*, and hence: "the sages of the Moslem sects." In suggesting this rendering of האומות השלמות, I am not unmindful of the fact that such expressions as המדינה החשובה[189b] and האומה החסידה,[189c] which occur frequently in philosophical Hebrew literature, usually refer to the ideal state and government as described by Plato and other philosophers. Maimonides' fourth class of practical philosophy will therefore refer to religious legislation, both Jewish and Moslem. My reason for suggesting this interpretation is briefly as follows: There is nothing in Aristotle to correspond to this class of practical philosophy, whereas we do find such a branch of philosophy, described exactly in the same words, in the the works of Moslem authors.

The Ihwan al-Safa, in their five-fold division of practical philosophy, the last three of which are Aristotelian, the first is called السياسة النبويّة, i. e., "prophetic government". It is described as the study "of religious legislations, النواميس, (νόμος), that is to say, the agreeable divine law, الشرائع المرضيّة, and

188 ותלמידי ענן וכו' ועדיין הם בטעותם ונעשו אומה לעצמן. quoted by Ben Jehuda from *Seder Rab Amram Gaon*.

189 *Enumot ve-Deot* III, 7: ועוד כי אומתנו איננה אומה כי אם בתורותיה.

189a See Steinschneider, *Uebersetzungen*, p. 369.

189b Levi ben Gershon: *Milhamot Adonai* II, 2, p. 97.

189c Isaac ibn Pulgar: '*Ezer ha-Dat* I, 3, p. 11.

pious customs السنن الزكيّة ".[190] Similarly Alfarabi, in addition to politics, mentions "legislative science, i. e., the science of faith and religiou sduty".[191] The underlying Arabic term for "legislative" here must again be the Greek *νόμος*. Furthermore, in Al-Farani's commentary on a work of Alfarabi, the third class of practical philosophy is subdivided into several parts, one of which is "the science of prophecy and divine law" which is called "legisiative science".[192] The term used here, again, is *νόμος*. Maimonides, as will be noticed, also calls this fourth class נמוסים which is again *νόμος*.

From all this it is evident that the fourth class of practical philosophy in Maimonides is the science of religious law, the *νόμος*, of Arabic philosophers. He thus describes it in the following terms:

"Thus the sages of the Moslem sects prescribe customs and usages, each in accordance with his particular belief, and by these their obedient followers guide themselves. These are called religious laws, נמוסים. The different sects are in the habit of regulating their lives according to these religious laws".[193]

The value and importance of each of the sciences is determined not only by the subject matter with which it deals but also by the purpose which it serves. Each science, according to Aristotle, has an end which is called its good, and metaphysics is called the supreme science and the most authoritative of all the sciences because it knows to what end each thing must be done.[194] Unlike all the other sciences, the end of metaphysics, according to Aristotle, is not utilitarian; it is a science which is desirable on its own account and for the mere sake of knowing.[195]

Mediaeval Jewish philosophers, too, speak of the particular end of each science and of the final end of all the sciences[196] which,

[190] Dieterici: *op. cit.* Arabic text, p. 252; German translation, p. 16.

[191] Hastings' *Enc. of Rel. and Eth.*, IX, p. 881.

[192] M. Horten: *Das Buch der Ringsteine Farabis*, pp. 321–322.

[193] וכן חכמי האומות השלמות יניחו הנהגות ודרכים לפי שלמות כל איש מהם, ינהגו בהם עבדיהם הסרים למשמעתם, ויקראו אותם נמוסים. והיו האומות מתנהגים בנמוסים ההם.

[194] *Metaphysics* I, 2, 982b, 4–7

[195] *Ibid.*, 982a. 14–16.

[196] See quotation above in n. 55a and 61.

to them, however, is not, as in Aritsotle, simply knowing for the mere sake of knowing, but knowing God for the sake of knowing and obeying His laws and commandments. Maimonides may affect the Aristotelian manner and begin his discourse by dwelling upon the finality of the contemplative life and upon the superiority of intellectual perfection to moral perfection. But he cannot shake off his belief that obedience to the laws and commandments is indispensable for the life of pure contemplation. He is thus soon forced to admit that the knowledge of God is to be taken to mean the knowledge of God's ways and attributes which ought to serve us as a guide for our actions.[197] Logically, Maimonides could have repeated with Abraham ibn Daud that "the end of all philosophy is right conduct."[198]

This conception of a final end serves as the touchstone by which the particular sciences are tested and evaluated. In Bahya we have a pertinent passage bearing upon this subject. He says: "All the divisions of philosophy as determined by the difference of their subject matter are gates which God has opened to rational beings through which they may attain to a knowledge of the Law and the world. Some of the sciences, however, are more particularly necessary for the understanding of the Law while others are more particularly necessary for the uses of the world. Of those which are more particularly necessary for the world there is first the lowest science, which is the science of the natures of bodies and their accidents, and then the middle science, which is mathematics. These two sciences show the way to all the secrets of this world, its uses, and the advantages that we may gain therein. They also serve as guides to the different arts and crafts which are necessary for the satisfaction of bodily wants and for the acquisition of the various wordly goods. The science which is more particularly necessary for the Law is the highest science, namely, theology. It is our bounden duty to pursue the study of this science in order to attain to a knowledge and understanding of the Law"[199]

Another passage is from Abraham ibn Daud. It is remark-

[197] *Moreh Nebukim* III, 54.
[198] *Emunah Ramah,* General Introduction, p. 4: כי תכלית הפילוסופיא המעשה
[199] *Hobot ha-Lebabot,* Introduction.

able for its freshness and modernity, for its eloquence and worldly wisdom, for its indictment of materialism, pedantry and formalism, for its plea on behalf of the social and liberal aspects of learning and for a higher conception of the religious ideal. Despite its length we shall quote whole sections of it, and with this we shall conclude our paper.

"The sciences are many, ranging one above the other, and the aim of all of them is the knowledge of God. Body is to man only a beast of burden, a stepladder, as it were, by which he may ascend to God. But there are some whose sole ambition is to stuff the beast with plenty of fodder—these are the people whose object in life is eating and drinking. There are others whose desire is to adorn the beast with an ornamental saddle, bridle and blanket—these are the people whose only object in life is to parade in gaudy clothes. Still others waste their entire life in trying to find out what kinds of sickness may befall the beast, how its health may be preserved and how its malady cured, and the nature of herbs and food that are beneficial or hurtful—these are the physicians. I do not mean to say that their art is altogether worthless. Quite the contrary, theirs is an honorable profession, which may do a lot of good in this world now, for through it the worldly life of man may be prolonged so that he may attain perfection and life of a higher kind. This art may also stand its owner in good stead in the world to come, inasmuch as the competent physician may be able to save the lives of God's servants from death and destruction. But I contend that whosoever makes this art the chief aim in life and wastes upon it his entire time does violence to his soul.

There are some who waste their time on something still more worthless, as those who make their chief occupation the art of grammar and of rhetoric, learning it first themselves and then teaching it to others to the end of their days.

Others waste their time in the art of numbers, trying to unravel strange, hypothetical puzzles......the like of which will never happen, and think that thereby they may be accounted as distinguished arithmeticians. Similarly others waste themselves on the subtleties of geometry. Of these sciences only that part is truly necessary which leads to a knowledge of astronomy".

The author then tells the story of a slave who was promised freedom and a kingdom if he went on a pilgrimage to a certain holy place. The slave, instead of hurrying to reach his destination and receive his reward, wasted time and unnecessarily prolonged the journey. The author proceeds:

"Like the wasting of too much time on the preparations for the journey is one's excessive devotion to the arts which are mostly of use to the material world, as medicine and law. By this I mean to refer only to a person who wastes his time in the practice of medicine for the sake of picking up fees rather than for the sake of rendering merciful service, or to a person who similarly wastes his time in the practice of law in order to gain a reputation or to amass a fortune or to display his wit. Both of these sciences have something good in common, for both may be useful in alleviating certain evils. Law may do away with some of the unpleasantness that springs up in the mutual relations of men and may establish friendly intercourse among them. By medicine, too, many of the ills resulting from the discordant rheums and from the inclement seasons of the year may be remedied. There is, however, a difference between these two professions. If all men were honest and did no wrong to each other, there would hardly be any need for the legal profession. But without medicine it would never be possible for mankind to get along......

Like the one who prolongs the journey by making too many unnecessary stops and by pacing slowly with lingering steps is the one who is given too much to the purification of the soul in an effort to cleanse if from the cardinal vices and the offshoot thereof.

Like the arrival at the journey's end is one's attainment of perfection in the knowledge of God".[200]

[200] *Emunah Ramah* II, Introduction, p. 45.

ADDITIONAL NOTES

To the Article on the Classification of Sciences in Mediaeval Jewish Philosophy

P. 496 The confusion of Aristotle's *πρακτική* with his *ποιητική* must have been widespread in Arabic philosophy. Thus the classification given by the unidentified Ali in his *Epistle*, which has been preserved in a Hebrew translation (about which see Steinschneider, *Uebersetzungen*, §204), is based upon the distinction between *theoretical* מלאכת מחשבת and *productive* מלאכת מעשה. The former comprises logic and philosophy in all its main divisions, by which is undoubtedly meant both the *theoretical* and the *practical* philosophy of Aristotle. The latter comprises all the *productive* arts and is subdivided into *commercial* מסחריות and *natural* טבעיות, namely, agriculture, boviculture and hunting, each of these having again many subdivisions.

See אגרת המוסר הכללי לאריסטו in קונטרס דברים עתיקים, ed. Benjacob, Leipzig 1844, p. 15:

אמר עלי הישמעאלי, ואחרי זאת אומר כי המלאכות נחלקות לשני חלקים, חלק מלאכת מחשבת, כגון חכמת הפילוסופיא ושעריה, וחכמת ההגיון ושעריו; והלק מלאכת מעשה. ומלאכת המעשה נחלקת למלאכות טבעיות ומלאכות מסחריות. והטבעיות הם שלש. הראשונה עבודת האדמה להוציא ממנה המחיה והמזון מאכילה ושתיה. והשנית המרעה אשר ממנה תהיה תועלת המקנה הבקר והצאן. והשלישית מלאכת הציד. ובכל אחת מאלו השלש נכללות מלאכות פרטיות רבות.

The same *Epistle* contains another classification which would seem to be based upon Aristotle's threefold division into *theoretical*, *practical* and *productive*, retaining the distinction between the three divisions but giving the last one a new meaning and content. It appears on pp. 12–13:

ובעבור כי לפעמים יחשוב האדם כי מצא האמת רחוקה ממנו, נצרך השכל למלאכה אשר יכיר בה האמת מן הכזב בכל ענין, ויבחן בה בין הטוב והרע במעשים,

וישכיל בה בין הצדק והשוא בדעות, והחכמים הגידו כי זאת המלאכה היא מלאכת ההגיון. והחכם הגיד כי ההצלחה הגמורה נחלקת לשלשה חלקים: החלק הראשון בדעת יסודות השמים והארץ וכל עניניהם, וכי יש להם סבה ראשונה, והוא הוד כבוד עושה הכל ומנהיגו ית׳ שמו, וכי כח השגחתו פושטת והולכת בהם, ועצמו הוא תכלית היסוד המבוקש מהם; ונחלקים גם כן לשלשה חלקים, חלק למודי וחלק טבעי וחלק אלהי. וחלק השני הוא להכיר ולדעת עניני האדם וכל עסקיו ואיזה מהם הוא הטוב; ונחלק ג״כ לג׳ חלקים, חלק תקון המדות והטבעים, וחלק תקון צרכי הבית, וחלק תקון צרכי המדינה. והחלק השלישי ללמוד [הענינים] המביאים החכמה. כגון למלאות חוק האמונה וחוק הנפש ולחובות (?) מסגולות [read: ולהרבות בסגולות] החברים וההון והכבוד והממשלת והשם הטוב.

Though the terms for the general main divisions are not given, the underlying scheme of the classification seems to be as follows: [*Propaedeutic*]: Logic. [*Theoretical*]: Mathematics, Physics, Metaphysics. [*Practical*]: Ethics, Economics, Politics. [*Productive*]: Practical rules for conduct in personal, domestic and social life. It is quite obvious that the last is meant to reproduce Aristotle's *productive* arts. The difference between the *Practical* and the *Productive* in this classification is made clear from the context as that between the *descriptive* and the *normative* phases of the sciences of ethics, economics and politics.

P. 498 The Hebrew מוסר as a translation of the Arabic رياضى and hence the Greek προπαιδεία, or rather παιδεία, has its analogy in the Septaugint where מוסר is often translated by παιδεία.

P. 504 n. 33f. The conjecture that חבור in the passage of Nissi ben Noah is to be taken in the same technical sense as קבוץ in the expression קבוץ הירח עם החמה finds corroboration in Cuzari IV, 29:

כי לא ישלם בירור הליכת הירח והתחלפות הליכתו לברר עת התחברו (אגתמאעה) עם השמש והוא המולד.

P. 509, n.52. While Algazali, Abraham Ibn Ezra and Afendopolo include astrology under physics, Abraham bar Ḥiyya, Falaquera and Rieti make it a co-ordinate branch of astronomy and put it under mathematics. This difference of opinion may perhaps be traced to Aristotle's question whether astrology (ἀστρολογία) is different from physics or is a part of it (*Physics* II, 1, 193b, 26). While ἀστρσλογία here means "astronomy," it is possible that it was taken by some in the sense of משפטי احكام النجوم הכוכבים (astrology) instead of חכמת הכוכבים علم النجوم (astronomy).

P. 513, n. 68. A list of Hebrew terms for "secular" sciences has been collected by Dr. Ignácz Hirschler in the Hungarian *Festschrift* in honor of Moses Bloch (pp. 107–114), Budapest 1905. (I am indebted for this reference to Dr. George A. Kohut).

P. 513-5. A new classification of the "seven sciences" is given in the poem *Al-Saba'niyyah* by Abu 'Imran Moses Tobi with its Hebrew translation and commentary *Batte ha-Nefesh* by Solomon ben Immanuel Dapiera (published by Hartwig Hirschfeld in the *Report of the Judith Montefiore College*, 1894). The poem speaks of the sciences as being "seven" in number (§30), but the enumeration of the particular sciences in the Hebrew translation does not agree with that of the Arabic original. In the Arabic (p. 20) the seven sciences are: (1) Religion אלעלום אלאדיאן, §25. (2) Medicine עלם אלטב, §25. (3) Physics עלם אלטביעה, §26. (4) Metaphysics ומן בעדה, §26. (5) Logic קאנון אלברהאן, §27. (6) Astronomy עלם אלהאיה, §28. (7) Geometry עלם אלמקדאר, §28.

In the Hebrew translation (pp. 35–38) they are: (1) Theoretical Medicine חכמת הרפואה....חלקה הראשון שהיא החכמה העיונית §25. (2) Practical Medicine כי זה תכלית הרפואה ר"ל המעשה שהוא חלק השני, §25. (3) Physics החכמה הטבעית, ידיעות טבעיות §26. (4) Metaphysics החכמה האלהית, ידיעות אלהיות §26. (5) Logic ההגיון §27. (6) Mathematics למודיות §28. (7) Astronomy חכמת ככבים, §29.

P. 527. In the Iḥwan al-Safa's and Judah ha-Levi's analyses of Aristotle's *Physics* the following topics are enumerated: 1. Matter. 2. Form. (3. Privation). 4. Nature. 5. Time. 6. Space. 7. Motion. The first three topics clearly refer to Book I of the *Physics*, 4 to Book II, 5 and 6 to Book IV, and 7 to Book III. The question may be raised, Why is Book III placed after Book IV and why are Books V—VIII omitted? The answer would seem to be that "Motion" in these analyses does not only refer to Book III but also to Books V—VIII. Aristotle's *Physics* was originally divided into two distinct treatises, the first consisting of Books I—VI (or I—V) and the second of V, VI, VIII (or VI—VIII). Aristotle usually refers to the first group as the *Physics* or the book *On Nature*, and to the second as the book *On Motion* (See W. D. Ross, *Aristotle*, p. 11). It is also possible that in early Arabic versions of the *Physics* Book III was placed after Book IV together with the other books on motion.

P. 530. Avicenna's characterization of some branches of mathematics as being more closely connected with physics may have its origin in Aristotle's description of perspectives, music and astronomy (literally, astrology) as the more physical branches of mathematics (*Physics* II, 2, 194a, 7–8).

P. 533, n.155. In the Hebrew commentary on the *Al-Sab-a'niyyah* (p. 37) the term משקולות is used in the sense of music: וחכמת המוסיקא והיא חכמת משקלי הלחנים והניגונים, והן חכמת המשקולות נאמר עליהם נעימות וראויות. Literally the expression משקלי הלחנים means "the rhythm of sounds."

P. 533, n.155. The query raised by me as to whether חבור could not be taken as the Arabic جبر is to be dismissed. The explanation in the *Millot ha-Higgayon* XIV: חכמת חבור הנגונים, is not a Hebrew gloss but a translation from an Arabic expression. The expression occurs in the Arabic original of the *Hobot ha-Lebabot* (p. 4, 1.9) تاليف اللحون وهو الموسيقى. The term חבור is a literal translation of the Greek ἁρμονική.

P. 541. In corroboration of my conjecture that Maimonides' fourth branch of practical philosophy is the science of religious legislation called נימוסים we may quote the following passage from Falaquera's *Reshit Hokmah*, pp. 58–59:

וכל זה [i.e. ethics, economics, politics] נזכר בספר אפלטון וארסטו בהנהגה. ומה שהוא נתלה בה מהנבואה והדת כמו שנזכר בספריהם בנימוסים. והפילוסופים אינם רואים מה שיחשבו אותם ההמון כי הנימוס הוא הפיתוי והתחבולה אלא הנימוס אצלם הוא הדין והדבר הקיים ברדת הנבואה, והערביים קורים למלאך המוריד הנבואה נימוס. וזה החלק מהחכמה המעשית תודיע מציאות הנבואה וסגולת כל דת ודת כפי עם ועם וזמן וזמן, וההפרש אשר בין הנבואה האלהית ובין המתנבאים לשקר.

It has already been established that the Arabic ناموس has two etymologies and two distinct meanings: 1. As the Greek *νόμος* it means "law." 2. As an original Arabic word it means "secret" and hence "revelation." (See Dozy, *Supplément aux*

Dictionaries Arabes, under ناموس). These two meanings have often been combined in Arabic, and this passage of Falaquera seems to show that a similar combination of the two meanings had been imported into the Hebrew נימוס (cf. Leopold Dukes, *Philosophisches aus dem Zehnten Jahrhundert*, p. 89, n.5).

25

NOTE ON MAIMONIDES' CLASSIFICATION OF THE SCIENCES

In his classification of political science (החכמה המדינית) in his *Millot ha-Higgayon*, Ch. 14, Maimonides enumerates four disciplines, of which the third is "the government of the city" (הנהגת המדינה) and the fourth is "the government of the great nation or of the nations" (הנהגת האומה הגדולה או האומות). Rosin suggests that the three terms used here by Maimonides, מדינה, אומה and אומות, correspond respectively to Alfarabi's classification of states into small, middle-sized and great.[1]

Before taking up the discussion of the question of the relation of Maimonides' classification to that of Alfarabi, I shall comment briefly upon the Aristotelian origin of Alfarabi's classification. "Of human aggregates," says Alfarabi,[2] "some are great, some are middle-sized, and some are small. As for the great aggregates, they are aggregates of many nations who league together and help each other.[3] As for the middle-sized, it is the nation. As for the small, it is that which is limited by the city . . . Of nations, some are great and some are small." This classification, it seems,

[1] David Rosin, *Die Ethik des Maimonides*, p. 35, n. 5.

[2] *Sefer Hatḥalot ha-Nimẓa'im*, pp. 32–33, in Filipowsky's *Sefer ha-Asif*, 1894; German translation from the Arabic in Dieterici-Brönnle, *Die Staatleitung von Alfarabi*, 1904, pp. 50–51. A parallel statement is also found in Alfarabi's *Al-Madīnah al-Fāḍilah* in Dieterici, *Alfarabi's Abhandlung der Musterstaat*: Arabic text, 1895, p. 53; German translation, 1900, p. 85.

[3] The Hebrew text reads ויפזרו which is evidently a corruption of ויעזרו. The text should read: ויעזרו קצתם לקצתם.

is based upon a passage in Aristotle's *Politics*, II, 2, 1261a, 24–29. Aristotle refers there to three kinds of associations: (1) the confederacy, συμμαχία, (2) the nation, ἔθνος, and (3) the city, πόλις. The connection between Alfarabi's middle-sized and small associations and Aristotle's "nation" and "city" is evident, for the Arabic terms used by Alfarabi, *ummah* and *madīnah*, are the same as the Greek terms used by Aristotle. The great state, however, is not described by Alfarabi by any specific term, for the same term *ijtimāʻ*, literally, "aggregation," is used by him in the general sense of "association" or "community," corresponding to Aristotle's κοινωνία, as well as in the specific sense of this particular kind of association which he calls "great." Still his definition of the great state suggests Aristotle's definition of a confederacy. According to Aristotle, a confederacy is that which "is naturally formed for the sake of *help*—βοηθείας" (ibid., 26–27). Similarly Alfarabi in his definition of his great state or aggregate of nations, as we have seen above, uses the expression "and *help* each other."

That Maimonides' classification of political science reflects on the whole Alfarabi's distinction between *madīnah* and *ummah* is quite clear. But what use Maimonides makes of that distinction is not quite so clear. Alfarabi himself, it must be observed, does not make use of his own threefold classification of states in his own formal classification of the sciences in his treatise *Iḥṣāʼ al-ʻUlūm*.[4] With the exception of his use of the terms "cities and nations" (*al-mudun wal-umam*) in his description of *al-ʻilm al-madīniyy*, he treats of political science as one discipline without subdividing it in accordance with his threefold division of states. Maimonides, too, it will be noticed,

[4] Arabic text with Latin and Spanish translations by Ángel Gonzáles Palencia, *Alfarabi Catálogo de las Ciencias*, Madrid, 1932.

adds only one discipline to that of the government of the city. The question may therefore be raised whether the two terms האומה הגדולה and האומות which he includes in his fourth discipline correspond to Alfarabi's national state and confederate state or whether they have some other meaning.

Now, if we assume with Rosin that Maimonides' "great nation" (האומה הגדולה) refers to Alfarabi's national state (*ummah*), the question may be raised, why does he qualify it by the adjective "great"? Indeed Alfarabi says that nations are either great or small. But why should Maimonides confine this discipline of political science only to the government of a *great* nation? Nor can we assume, as a modification of Rosin's view, that או האומות is used here only as an alternative term for האומה הגדולה, so that both these terms refer to Alfarabi's confederate state, for the terms used by Alfarabi in describing a confederacy are *jamā'ah*, *ijtimā'*, *ahl*, but never *ummah*. On the contrary, a "nation" is defined by Alfarabi as a group which is homogeneous either in racial characteristics or in language, whereas a confederacy is defined by him as being composed of different nations.[5] Furthermore, Maimonides himself in *Moreh Nebukim*, II, 29, uses the term אומה in (מלה עטימה) אומה גדולה in the sense of nation as distinguished from דולה (Ibn Tibbon: עם; Ḥarizi: מלכות) by which he means an empire made up of different nations or a dynasty ruling over different nations.[6] By the same token, the term האומות cannot refer, as it does according to Rosin, to a confederacy, unless it is taken as an abbreviation of קבוץ האומות. If Maimonides' classification is to reflect that of Alfarabi, we will have to assume that the plural

[5] Cf. *Sefer Hatḥalot ha-Nimẓa'im*, p. 33. German translation, p. 51.
[6] Cf. Munk, *Guide des Egarés*, II, p. 211, n. 1.

האומות is used by him here distributively in the sense of Alfarabi's national state (*ummah*) and that in האומה הגדולה the underlying Arabic is not *ummah* but rather some such term as Alfarabi's *jamā'ah* or *ahl* or Maimonides' own *daulah* of *Moreh Nebukim*, II, 29, quoted above, so that האומה הגדולה would refer to Alfarabi's confederate state. That the Arabic term underlying האומה may have been different from that underlying האומות in this passage is to be inferred from the fact that in Aḥitub's version the former is translated by עם whereas the latter is translated by the term האומות as in Moses ibn Tibbon's version. It will be noticed that in *Moreh Nebukim*, II, 29, the term *daulah* is translated in Samuel ibn Tibbon's version by both עם and אומה.[7]

But it would seem that while the difference between Maimonides' third and fourth disciplines may have been suggested by Alfarabi's distinction between city-state and the other kinds of states, the difference within the fourth discipline between האומה הגדולה and האומות is not that between Alfarabi's national state and confederate state. It is rather that between the Jewish nation and the heathen nations.[8] The contrast between האומה and האומות as a contrast between Jews and non-Jews is common in Hebrew literature and it occurs frequently in the writings of Maimonides. Thus in *Moreh Nebukim*, II, 29, he says: כאשר התחיל לספר איך היתה חולשת האומה (אלמלה̈) . . . שאנחנו לא נירא כשימותו האומות (אלמלל). Similarly in *Iggeret Teman* the expres-

[7] *Moreh Nebukim*, II, 29: כשהגיד על נתיצת עם (דולה̈) and בהתחדש הצלחת אומה (דולה̈). Ḥarizi in both instances: מלכות. But עם represents Arabic *ummah* in *Kuzari*, II, 56: ואנחנו אין אנו נקראים עם (אמה̈) משה אלא עם (אמה̈) ה' and III, 50: וידע כי בעמים (אלאמם) הרבה אנשים.

[8] My discussion here supplements, and in a few details revises, my discussion of the same suggestion in "The Classification of Sciences in Mediaeval Jewish Philosophy," *Hebrew Union College Jubilee Volume* (1925), pp. 310–312. Above, pages 493–545. Cf. especially discussion of האומות השלמות.

sion בלשון האומה[9] is used with reference to the Jews and האומות[10] is used with reference to non-Jews. So also in *Ma'amar Teḥiyyat ha-Metim* Maimonides refers to the Jews as האומה in the expression מבוארת גלויה באומה.[11] The Arabic terms underlying האומה and האומות in this passage of *Millot ha-Higgayon* would accordingly be *millah* and *milal*[12]—terms generally used by Maimonides throughout his writings—and not *ummah* and *umam* which are used by Alfarabi in his discussion of political science. The qualifying adjective "great" (הגדולה; Aḥitub: הרב, which may be a corruption of הרם) may mean here "excellent"—the equivalent of the Arabic *fāḍilah* (Hebrew: החסידה, המעולה, החשובה),[13] which is used by Alfarabi in the expression *al-ummah al-fāḍilah*, "the excellent nation," and which to Maimonides, of course, would primarily apply to the Jews. Thus also in his *Iggeret Teman*, evidently drawing upon Alfarabi's expression *al-ijtimā' al-fāḍil*, "the excellent community," Maimonides refers to the Jews as "the divine excellent community" (הקבוץ האלהי המעולה).[14] The distinction between the third and fourth disciplines in Maimonides' classification of political science would thus be not only that between a city-state and a national state but also

[9] *Ḳobeẓ*, II, p. 2b, col. 1; p. 7a, col. 2.

[10] Ibid., p. 2b, col. 1.

[11] Ibid., p. 7b, col. 2. Arabic אלמלה in unpublished text, according to a communication by Dr. J. Finkel.

[12] In *Moreh Nebukim* the Arabic *millah* is usually translated by אומה. But in Ibn Tibbon it is also translated by אמונה and דת. Cf. III, 29: ידוע שאברהם אבינו ע"ה גדל באמונת (מלה) הצאבה and וספר יצחק הצאבי בטעון שהשם בחרם לעם בעבור דת (מלה) הצאבה. In Kuzari, I, 95, the passage (חזבא) ולאומה (ואמה) מבין אומות (מלל) העולם would seem to indicate that *ummah* was used for Jews and *millah* for non-Jews. But throughout the *Kuzari*, *ummah* is used also for non-Jews; *millah* is used for Jews in II, 32: האומות (אלמלל) המתות אשר חשבו להדמות לאומה (אלמלה) החיה.

[13] Cf. Steinschneider, *Al-Farabi*, pp. 66, 68–69.

[14] *Ḳobeẓ*, II, p. 2a, col. 2. Cf. Alfarabi, *Al-Madīnah al-Fāḍilah*, p. 54, l. 8.

that between a civil state and a religious state. The inclusion of religious government within the scheme of Aristotle's practical philosophy and by the side of his ethics, economics and politics is common in Arabic philosophy. Alfarabi himself, in his *Iḥṣā' al-'Ulūm*, conjoins the knowledge of religious law (*fiḳh*) with that of political science, and in his discussion of religious law he uses the term *millah* in place of the term *ummah* which he invariably uses in his discussion of political science.[15]

The plausibility of this suggestion may perhaps be strengthened by a study of Maimonides' subsequent description of his third and fourth disciplines which he places under one general heading ואמנם הנהגת המדינה.

The first half of this description can be shown to be based upon the description of *al-'ilm al-madīniyy* in Alfarabi's *Iḥṣa' al-'Ulūm*. Alfarabi himself, in summarizing his description, divides political science into two parts. To quote: "This science falls into two parts. The first part consists of the knowledge of happiness and the distinction between true happiness and imaginary happiness . . . The second part consists of the method of properly arranging these virtuous dispositions and habits in cities and nations."[16] Exactly these two divisions are also to be discerned in Maimonides' description of הנהגת המדינה. Corresponding to the first part of Alfarabi's description, Maimonides says: "As for the government of the city-state, it is a science which imparts to those who pursue the study thereof the knowledge of true happiness . . . and of imaginary happiness." Corresponding to the second part of Alfarabi's description, Maimonides similarly says: "It also lays down right methods by which their communities may be arranged

[15] Op. cit., Arabic text, p. 56.
[16] Ibid., Arabic text, p. 54; Latin text, p. 169.

properly." It will be noticed that in Maimonides' דרכי עיקרים של צדק היושר יסדרו בם קבוציהם סדור נאה (Aḥitub: שיסתדר בהם קבוצם) the terms דרכי (עיקרים) and . . . יסדרו סדור נאה (יסתדר) correspond exactly to Alfarabi's وجه ترتيب.[17]

But Maimonides then adds to this summary of Alfarabi's description of הנהגת המדינה a statement of his own which was evidently meant by him to be particularly a description of his fourth discipline הנהגת האומה הגדולה או האומות. He describes the nature of this fourth discipline by referring to the legislation of certain nations who in Moses ibn Tibbon's version are called "perfect nations" (האומות השלמות) and in Aḥitub's version are called "bygone nations" (האומות שכבר כלו). The discrepancy between these two versions can be explained by the assumption that the underlying Arabic expression was אלמלל אלסאלפה̈, i. e., *bygone* or *ancient nations*, but that in the Arabic text used by Moses ibn Tibbon, the term אלסאלפה̈, by a slight corruption of one letter, was changed to read אלסאלמה̈. Now this very same Arabic expression אלמלל אלסאלפה̈ is used by Maimonides in *Moreh Nebukim*, II, 39,[18] with reference to the heathenish nations of antiquity. As to who these ancient heathenish nations were, Maimonides mentions there specifically the Sabeans and the Greeks,[19] and among them, he says, there were also philosophers who had no accurate understanding of God.[20] The laws of

[17] Aḥitub invariably uses in Ch. 14 עיקרים where Ibn Tibbon uses דרכים. The underlying Arabic term in all these instances must have been وجوه, which means both.

[18] Munk's Arabic text, p. 85b, l. 19. Samuel ibn Tibbon's and Ḥarizi's (Ḥarizi: הסכלות) האומות הסכליות reflects, according to Munk (p. 304, n. 3), the Arabic reading אלג̇אהליה̈.

[19] Cf. *Moreh Nebukim*, II, 39 end.

[20] Cf. ibid., III, 29: ותכלית מה שהגיע עליו עיון מי שהתפלסף בימים ההם שידמה שהשם רוח הגלגל.

these ancient heathenish nations are described by Maimonides by the plural of the Arabicized form (*nawāmīs*, Hebrew נימוסים) of the Greek word for law (νόμος). To quote: נימוסי (נואמים) האומות הסכליות (*Moreh Nebukim*, II, 39); נימוסי (נואמים) היונים (ibid.); נימוסי (נואמים) הצאבה ופרטי דתם וחגיהם וקרבניהם ותפלותיהם וזולתו מענייני דתם (ibid., III, 29). So also here in *Millot ha-Higgayon* Maimonides says that the sages of these bygone nations describe their practices and principles (הנהגות ודרכים, Aḥitub: הנהגות ועקרים) by the term [*nawānīs*] נימוסים. Furthermore, in *Moreh Nebukim*, III, 29, Maimonides gives a list of books of the Sabeans and concludes that they "have been translated into Arabic, and there is no doubt that they form a small portion in comparison to that which has not been translated." Similarly here Maimonides says that "the philosophers have many books on all these matters, some of which have already been translated into Arabic, and perhaps those which have not been translated are more numerous."[21] Finally, in *Moreh Nebukim*, II, 39 f., Maimonides contrasts the laws of these bygone nations with the laws of the Jewish religion, referring to the former as human legislation הנהגות הנימוסים המונחים and to the latter as divine law הנהגות התורה האלהית (ibid., II, 40). Similarly here Maimonides concludes: "We nowadays are not in need of all these books, that is to say, these books on customs, doctrines, laws and the conduct of men in matters divine" (ר"ל החקים הדתות והנימוסים והנהגת האנשים בעניינים אלהיים). The implication of this statement is that the Jewish religious books have nowadays taken the place of those ancient

[21] Alfarabi in *Iḥṣa' al-'Ulūm* (Arabic, p. 55; Latin, p. 170) only mentions Aristotle's *Politics* and Plato's *Politics* (i.e., *Republic*) and refers in a general way to "works of Plato and others."

heathenish books.[22] Now, inasmuch as in Maimonides' description of the fourth discipline of political science there is a contrast between Jews and heathens, we have reason to believe that in his general statement of this fourth discipline there is a similar contrast; furthermore, inasmuch as the "bygone nations" in that description undoubtedly refers to "the nations" in the general statement, we may also assume that the "we" of the former refers to "the great nation" of the latter.

In the light of the foregoing discussion we may be justified in assuming that Maimonides' fourth discipline of political science reflects a complexity of considerations. Maimonides must have started with Alfarabi's distinction between city and nation (*ummah*)—Alfarabi's other distinction between one single nation and a confederacy of many nations being to him only a subdivision of nation as contrasted with city. Then, on account of the customary inclusion of religious law within political science and on account also of the fact that the Arabic word *ummah* as well as *millah* means both nation and religious community, the original distinction between city and nation assumed in his mind the meaning of a distinction between a civil community and a religious community. Substituting therefore for the term *ummah*, which is used by Alfarabi in his classification of states in the sense of a racial or linguistic group, the term *millah*, which is used by Alfarabi in his classification of the sciences in the sense of a religious group, he distinguished within the latter between Jews and ancient heathens.

[22] The "we nowadays" may perhaps also include Mohammedans and Christians inasmuch as they, too, are contrasted by Maimonides with the Sabeans in so far as they acknowledge the truth of the Jewish Scriptures (*Moreh Nebukim*, III, 29).

NOTE

In the Arabic text of the *Millot ha-Higgayon*, edited by Mubahat Turker (in the *Review of the Institute of Islamic Studies*, Publications of the Faculty of Letters, Istanbul University, Vol. III, parts 1-2, 1950-1960), p. 109, last line, the Arabic underlying Ibn Tibbon's השלמות is not, as suggested by me, אלסאלפה̈ corrupted into אלסאלמה̈, but אלכ̇אליה̈ corrupted into אלכ̇אלמה̈. Cf. I. Efros, *JQR*, N. S., 53: 272 (1962-1963).

26

NOTES ON PROOFS OF THE EXISTENCE OF GOD IN JEWISH PHILOSOPHY

OF THE MANY HISTORICAL PROOFS for the existence of God—the three from speculative reason enumerated by Kant, the cosmological, the ontological, and the teleological, and others like universal assent and the innateness of the idea of God—only the cosmological type of argument was pressed into service by Jewish theologians. The arguments from universal assent and the innateness of the idea of God were omitted for very good reasons, and the argument from design, though not overlooked completely, was not used as an independent proof for the existence of God. As for the ontological argument, an eminent scholar to the contrary notwithstanding, it is entirely absent, though some of the ingredients of which it is made up were not unknown, as, for instance, the identity of essence and existence in God which is the basis of the ontological proof as given by Spinoza. Of these general remarks, which summarize the situation, the discussion which follows is an enlargement.

It was Kaufmann who invited us to be astounded at the failure of our religious thinkers to turn to account, as did Christian and Moslem theologians, the ancient, classical argument of universal assent.[1] When we scrutinize, however, the nature of that argument and all it implies, instead of being surprized at their remissness we shall have to admire their circumspection. The argument from universal assent, it might

1 *Attributenlehre,* p. 2, n. 4.

be said, reflects a polytheistic background of religious belief, or, at best, a stage in the development of the conception of divine unity which is sometimes described by the term henotheism. In a religious tradition where the recognition of one spiritual deity as supreme did not mean the branding of all others as false, there was indeed a certain cogency in the argument from universal assent, for all mankind, to be sure, acknowledged the existence of some kind of god. It was thus well for Roman Cicero[2] to declare that all men had an idea of god and prove thereby his existence. It was thus also with the heathen converts to Christianity and Islam when they began to prove the existence of the Jewish God by arguments taken from classical philosophy. When Jewish theologians, however, in the tenth century, found it necessary to prove the existence of God, the situation was entirely different. They were called upon to prove the existence of a God who in the consciousness of his believers was the only true God, besides whom all the other gods were vain and false idols. It was hardly possible for them to appeal to the general persuasion of mankind as to His existence. To them, quite the contrary, mankind denied the existence of God, and it was only by a special act of grace that a single chosen people had come to know him by means of a direct revelation. It was therefore not to a universal assent that Jewish philosophers appealed but rather to a national assent, or tradition, as they call it, a tradition based upon the evidence of a direct experience shared by the entire race at the foot of Sinai. The argument from tradition, it might therefore be said, is the Jewish equivalent of the classical argument from assent. I hope to show elsewhere, that in Anselm, too, we may identify under the guise of tradition the argument from assent and thus prove that his famous ontological proof was only meant to be considered as ancillary to the proof of *consensus gentium*.

No more inexplicable is another difficulty, again raised by Kaufmann, as to the failure of Jewish theologians to present the argument of the innateness of the idea of God in the

[2] *De Natura Deorum* II. 4.

human mind as proof for His existence.[3] The term innate idea is used in two senses. It is sometimes used in a rather loose and general sense merely as the denial of an external, sensible source to certain ideas, assigning to them, however, some external, super-sensible source. In this sense, Plato's theory of reminiscence, which ascribes to knowledge an external, super-sensible source, is often spoken of as a theory of innate ideas.[4] But the term is also used in the more specific sense of knowledge coming entirely from within, as something constitutional with the mind, having no external source whatsoever, sensible or super-sensible. In this sense it was that Cicero conceived of innate ideas of which the idea of God he declared to be one.[5] Now, taken in the first sense, Jewish philosophers did not fail to mention that the idea of God might be innate in man. The knowledge of God arrived at by revelation or through prophetic insight, the basis of tradition, may be said to represent knowledge of that kind. When Maimonides, for instance, declares that the knowledge of the existence of God may be obtained either by demonstrative reasoning or by direct revelation,[6] this revealed idea of God may be called innate in the same sense as the awakened memories of Plato. Taken in the second sense, however, God as an innate idea, to be sure, was not urged by Jewish philosophers as a proof for His existence, and for the very good reason that in their theory of knowledge innate ideas of this kind had no existence. Characteristic of the theory of knowledge commonly held by Jewish philosophers, to whatever school of thought they might otherwise belong, is its essential empiricism. Not that they were empiricists in the sense that all knowledge was to be derived from sensuous experience, but in the sense that it had to be acquired from *without* and could never rise from *within*. The external sources of knowledge were either the impressions of the external world upon the senses or the operation of some

3 *Attributenlehre*, p. 2, n. 4.

4 See, for instance, Janet and Sérailles, *A History of the Problems of Philosophy*, I. 82.

5 *De Natura Deorum* II. 4.

6 *Moreh Nebukim* II. 33.

immaterial agency, as the Active Intellect, for instance, upon the human mind.

That this is the general character of the theory of knowledge held in common by Jewish philosophers may be gathered from their respective classifications of the sources of knowledge. There is a uniformity of principle underlying all these classifications which unmistakably betokens a common origin. Whatever difference they display is rather in the use of terms and in the manner of arrangement, which, however, can all be reduced to a common type.

Saadia enumerates four sources of knowledge:[7] (1) Sense perception. (2) Knowledge of reason,[8] by which he means, to judge from Bahya's paraphrase of this expression, the self-evident truths, the first principles, ἀρχαί, and the immediate propositions, πρότασις ἄμεσος, of Aristotle. (3) Necessitated knowledge,[9] i. e., knowledge by logical inference. (4) Tradition.

Bahya's classification is somewhat vague in its preliminary statement.[10] But subsequent explanatory remarks, which occur in the course of his discussion, render it quite clear. It resembles Saadia's classification in its main outline. Saadia's first three classes are reduced to two, the antithesis of knowledge of the senses and knowledge of reason.[11] Sensible knowledge is then

7 *Emunot ve-Deot*, Introduction.

8 Saadia calls it מדע השכל the equivalent of which in Bahya's classification is שהוא משיג הדברים המושכלים בעצמו (see below note 13). The fact that Saadia illustrates it by such judgments as that truth is good and a lie is horrid, שהצדק טוב והכזב מגונה, does by no means limit this kind of knowledge to judgments of value only. It is rather two examples taken at random. The immediate propositions (πρότασις ἄμεσος, *Anal. Post.* I. 2, 72a, 7) of Aristotle include all the self-evident truths of mathematics, logic, physics, metaphysics, and ethics. Algazali, in his *Makasid al-Falasifah* I. 51–58, enumerates thirteen kinds of immediate propositions among which are included such judgments of value as given here by Saadia, illustrated by the same example of a lie being horrid, الكذب قبيح (p. 55). He describes such judgments as "general opinions", المشهورات, המפורסמות (see below note 20).

9 מדע הכרחית. Joseph ibn Zaddik, however, uses this term to designate direct knowledge in general. See quotation below in note 19. (Cf. Brüll's JJGL IV. 137.)

10 *Hobot ha-Lebabot* I. 10.

11 *Ibid.* האחד מהם הרגשותינו הגשמיים . . . והשני בדרך שכלנו.

subdivided into perceptions of the external senses and representations of the internal senses.[12] Knowledge of reason is subdivided, after the manner of Saadia, into primary notions and logical inference.[13] His classification therefore runs as follows: (1) Sensible knowledge, subdivided into (a) perceptions and (b) representations. Rational knowledge, subdivided into (a) primary notions and (b) inferences. (3) Traditions.

Judah ha-Levi, in his general treatment of the soul,[14] follows Bahya in his main classification, dividing knowledge, barring tradition, into sensible and rational.[15] The former he subdivides into (a) the perceptions of the five external senses, and (b) the representations formed by the common sense out of material furnished by the external senses. Such representations are the common sensibles, τὰ κοινά, such as figure, number, size, motion, rest.[16] Rational knowledge he subdivides, like Bahya, into (a) primary notions and (b) logical inferences.[17]

The contrasts between sensible and rational, direct and indirect knowledge cross each other in Joseph ibn Zaddik's classification. He divides knowledge, first, into (a) sensible and (b) rational,[18] and, then, into (a) necessitated, by which he means, unlike Saadia, any kind of direct knowledge be it

12 *Ibid.* ויתבאר אצלך מענין החושים הגשמיים אשר זכרנו והחושים הנפשיים.

13 *Ibid.* וכן נאמר בשכל שהוא משיג הדברים המושכלים בעצמו ובדרך הראיות.

14 *Cuzari* V. 12.

15 *Ibid.* This formal division may be inferred from the following statement: זה היוצא לנו מדברי האנשים האלה במה שלמטה מהנפש המדברת. ואמרו במדברת וכו'.

16 *Ibid.* החושים החמשה ידועים, ומושגיהם ידועים, באמצעותם [ובאמצעות ההרגשה המשתתפת] תושג הדמות והמנין והגודל והתנועה והמנוחה. התבאר מצוא ההרגשה המשתתפת מאשר אנחנו דנין על הדבש, דרך משל, כשנראהו, שהוא מתוק. That the term באמצעותם does not mean that the five senses are the sole and direct means whereby the "common sensibles" are perceived may be gathered from *De Anima* III. 1, 425a, 14 seq. and II. 6, 418a, 17–19. Hence the bracketed remark within the quotation.

17 *Ibid.* ויהיו בו הצורות המושכלות, אם בלמוד אלהי ואם בקנין. ואשר הם בלמוד הם המושכלות הראשונות, אשר ישתתפו בהם כל בני אדם אשר על המנהג הטבעי, ואשר בקנין הם בהקשה ובחדוש המופתי.

18 *Olam Katan* I. 1. האדם ישיג המושגות בשני ענינים, האחד בהרגש והאחר בשכל.

sensible or rational, and (b) logical inference.[19] Necessitated knowledge is subdivided by him into four kinds: (a) sense perceptions, (b) general opinions, (c) traditions, and (d) primary notions.[20] In addition, he mentions also the knowledge of spiritual beings which the soul perceives immediately.[21]

Like Joseph ibn Zaddik, Maimonides contrasts in a general way direct knowledge with knowledge by logical inference.[22] Of direct knowledge he gives us two classifications, which are mutually complementary. One is to be found in te *Millot ha-Higgayon*,[23] where it is divided into (a) perceptions, (b) primary notions, (c) general opinions, and (d) traditions. The other, in the *Moreh Nebukim*,[24] has the following divisions: (a) primary notions, (b) perceptions, and (c) and what is almost as nearly evident as perceptions. By this he undoubtedly means the "common sensibles" mentioned by Judah ha-Levi. He describes it as follows: "Such are the existence of motion, of man's free will, of phases of production and destruction, and of the natural properties of things perceived by the senses, e. g., the heat of fire, the coldness of water, and many other similar things."

This is a well-night exhaustive list of the sources of knowledge enumerated by the most representative Jewish philosophers. Now, which of these kinds of knowledge could by any show of reason be claimed as innate? Some scholars are inclined

19 *Ibid.* ונדבק לענין זה מה שראוי לו במדע ההכרח ומדע הראיה . . . המדע המוכרחי, אשר הוא מוכרח לאדם להודות אותו ולא יוכל לכפור אותו . . . . נאמר עתה כי המדע המופתי והוא מדע הראיה . . . . הוא בנוי על המדע המוכרחי. Cf. above note 9.

20 *Ibid.* הנה עתה מיני הדברים המושכלים בעצמם ארבעה מינים, מורגשות ומפורסמות ומקובלות ומושכלות ראשונות. All these four kinds of immediate sources of knowledge are included among the thirteen immediate propositions enumerated by Algazali. See above note 8.

21 *Ibid.* אבל הדברים הרוחניים תשינם הנפש החכמה בעצמה בלא אמצעי שום דבר, לפי שהוא דומה להם ברוחניות ובדבקות.

22 See, e. g., *Moreh Nebukim* II. 33, where המפורסמות והמקובלות are contrasted with המושכלות. The term המושכלות is the equivalent of what he describes previously as כל מה שיודע במופת אמנם שאר הדברות הם מכת המפורסמות והמקובלות לא מכת המושכלות.

23 Chapter 8.

24 Part I, Chapter 51.

to take the primary notions as kind of innate knowledge. Thus Kaufmann identifies Saadia's knowledge of reason with innate ideas.[25] Friedländer translates Maimonides' מושכלות ראשונות by "innate notions".[26] Neither of these, however, is right.

First, with regard to Saadia's knowledge of reason. There are two parallel classifications in the philosophic encyclopedia of the Brethren of Purity which would seem to throw light upon the nature of this kind of knowledge. One of these passages tries to explain knowledge of reason as the knowledge which Plato held to be attainable through an awakening of the slumbering ideas by means of reflexion and thought.[27] The other passage simply describes it in the general familiar terms in which are usually described the functions of Aristotle's *sensus communis* and of Avicenna's internal senses.[28] However that many be, knowledge of reason cannot be innate. Even Platonic recollections are not innate ideas in the strict sense of the term, for while indeed they are not derived from perception they are still derived from an external source, namely, the world of pure ideas.[29]

Second, with regard to the "primary notions". The term מושכלות ראשונות, "primary notions", would seem to be a translation of Galen's ἀρχαὶ λογικαί and are akin to Aristotle's ἀρχαί and to the προλήψεις and κοιναὶ ἔννοαι of the Stoics. None of these are known to be innate[30] in the strict Ciceronian sense

25 *Attributenlehre*, p. 3, n. 3.

26 *Guide of the Perplexed* I. 51.

27 Cf. Dieterici, *Die Anthropologie der Araber im X. Jahrhundert*, p. 40 "Die Form der Dinge wird im Wesen und die Bedeutung alles Vorhandenen wird uns in der Substanz der Seele klar. Sie ist die Fundgrube der Wissenschaft und die Stätte der Formen, wie Plato sagt, daß alle Wissenschaft in der Seele der Kraft nach sei; wenn du über ihr Wesen nachdenkst und es erkennst, so sind alle Wissenschaften in ihr durch die Vernunft."

28 Cf. Dieterici, *Die Lehre von der Weltseele bei den Arabern im X. Jahrhundert*, 38. "Oder zweitens durch die Vernunftkraft, das ist durch Nachdenken Anschauung, Verständnis, Unterscheidung, richtige Vermutung und klaren Scharfsinn." This passage is referred to by Kaufmann evidently to prove that by knowledge of reason is meant innate ideas.

29 Cf. Zeller, *Ecclecticism*, 159; Windelband, *A History or Philosophy*, 119.

30 Zeller, *Aristotle*, I. 200–203, *Stoics, Epicureans and Sceptics*, 79–80,

of the term. Furthermore, in the discussion of the nature of the primary notions by early Jewish philosophers, it is generally assumed that they have an external source, albeit a super-sensible external source. Thus both Judah ha-Levi and Abraham ibn Daud ascribe them to divine inspiration.[31] But to say that they are divinely inspired is simply another way of saying that they are acquired from *without* and consequently are not innate.

The existence of innate ideas of the Ciceronian type was thus unknown to the Jewish philosophers. They could not therefore be expected to argue that God was such an innate idea.

The argument from design, which is ascribed to Socrates by both Xenophon[32] and Plato[33] and was also used by Cicero,[34] is not altogether absent in Jewish philosophy. But it was used for purposes other than to prove the existence of God. It was used either as a reinforcement of the cosmological argument from creation or as evidence of divine goodness, unity, intelligence, and the like, after existence had already been demonstrated on some other ground. Bahya introduces the argument from design as a refutation of those who "had maintained that the world came into being by accident".[35] The allusion is no doubt to the Epicurean view,[36] which, while

Ecclecticism, 159, 363; Ritter, *The History of Ancient Philosophy*, III. 59; Grote, *Aristotle*, I. 256, 369–371.

31 Cf. *Cuzari* V. 12, quoted above in note 17, and *Emunah Ramah* II. iv. 1. p. 58. וכמו אלה המשפטים הנקראים ראשונים, המגיעים בהתעוררות אלהי, בלי מחשבה ועיון. See also p. 60.

32 *Memorabilia* IV. 3.

33 *Phaedo* 96 seq.

34 *De Natura Deorum* II. 5.

35 *Hobot ha-Lebabot* I. 6. ויש בני אדם שאמרו שהעולם נהיה במקרה מבלי בורא שהתחילו ויוצר שיצרו. The commentary *Marpe la-Nefesh, ad loc.* explains it: שאמרו שהעולם קדמון, which, of course is wrong. See Azriel's *Ezrat Adonai*, p. 2. ואם תאמר שלא כיון בבריאותו, א"כ היתה העולם במקרה, וכל דבר הבא במקרה אין לו סדר, ואנו רואים כי הנבראים יש להם סדר, ועל סדר הם מתקיימים ועל סדר הם מתבטלים ועל סדר הם מתחדשים.

36 Cf. Lucretius, *De Rerum Natura* V. 416–431; *Emunot ve-Deot* I. 3 והדעת התשיעי דעת המקרה; *Moreh Nebukim* II. 20, and Narboni *ad loc.* על מי שחשב מן הראשונים — רמוז בזה על אפיקורוס.

admitting a temporal beginning of the world, denied the existence of a Creator, explaining the origin of the world as the result of the interaction of blind mechanical forces. The argument is thus used by Bahya in conjunction with creation; in no way does he attempt to prove thereby the existence of God if the world were assumed to be eternal. Likewise Judah ha-Levi[37] makes the argument dependent upon creation, proving thereby, after having shown that the world was created and that consequently there must be a Creator, that creation was an act of wisdom and will and justice and not merely that of blind chance and accident. Averroes and Maimonides, too, use design as evidence of divine knowledge, unity, and the purposiveness of creation.[38] Joseph Albo puts the situation in a nutshell when he says something to the effect that the act of creation itself proves the existence of God; the fact that creation was performed after a certain manner proves that it was an act of purpose and forethought.[39] Thus when Kant argues that the "physico-theological" proof must rest upon some other proof, his argument can hardly be used as a criticism of Jewish philosophers, for they have never used design as an independent proof.

The absence of the ontological proof in Jewish philosophy was called in question by Guttmann who believes to have found it foreshadowed in Abraham ibn Daud.[40] His belief, however, would seem to be based upon a rather loose interpretation of the Avicennean type of the cosmological proof. He seems to think that the crux of Avicenna's argument is the contention that an absolutely necessary being must have existence involved in its essence. That this is not so is quite evident from all the texts which produce Avicenna's proof.

37 *Cuzari* III. 11, and V. 20.

38 Cf. *Happalat ha-Happalah*, Disputation IV (MS. Bodleian 1354) שהסדר אשר בעולם יראה ממנו שהמנהיג לו אחד, כמו שהסדר אשר בצבא יראה שהמנהיג לו אחד והוא שר הצבא, and *Moreh Nebubim* II. 20.

39 *Ikkarim* II. 4. ממה שנזכר שם יציאת הדברים מן הכח אל הפועל יש ראיה על מציאות הפועל המוציא אותם אל הפועל, וממה שנזכר מיציאתם אל הפועל בזמנים מתחלפים, והם ששת ימי בראשות, יש ראיה על מציאות הפועל בכונה ורצון.

40 Cf. *Die Religionsphilosophie des Abraham ibn Daud aus Toledo*, p. 121.

Avicenna's argument from possibility, like Aristotle's argument from motion, is grounded upon the view that any series of causes and effects must somehow come to an end. It simply argues to the effect that given a series of caused causes, i. e., possible beings, it cannot go on to infinity, and must therefore end at an uncaused cause, i. e., an absolutely necessary being. That absolutely necessary being, to be sure, must have existence involved in its essence, but this identity of essence and existence follows only as an inference from its nature as an uncaused cause.[41] In fact, Algazali questions the validity of that inference, contending that the proof whereby the existence of an uncaused cause is established warrants only the denial of external causation and does not necessarily exclude a logical distinction of essence and existence in its nature.[42] Guttmann cites the following passage from Abraham ibn Daud in support of his view. **והנמצא, אשר מציאותו מחוייב, עצמותו מספיק במציאות עצמותו**. He seems to take the term **עצמות** in this passage in the technical sense of "essence", as the equivalent of **מהות** and the opposite of **מציאות**, "existence". He thus renders the meaning of the passage as follows: "Ein Wesen von Nothwendiger Existenz, sagt A. b. D., ist ein solches, in dessen Wesen schon die Existenz seines Wesens inbegriffen ist". But **עצמותו** here is simply a reflexive pronoun, the passage simply aiming to assert that an absolutely necessary being cannot have a prior cause but must be the cause of itself. Of course, the idea of an uncaused cause whose essence involves existence was later made by Spinoza the basis of his ontological proof. But neither Avicenna nor any of his Jewish followers tried to prove the existence of that uncaused cause ontologically; they all proved it cosmologically.

It is the cosmological argument, therefore, based upon the principle of causality, that became the standard proof of the existence of God in Jewish philosophy. There it is found to

41 See *Moreh Nebukim* I. 57, אמנם מי שאין סבה למציאותו, והוא השם יתעלה ויתרומם לבדו, כי זה הוא ענין אמרנו עליו יתעלה שהוא מחוייב המציאות, תהיה מציאותו עצמו ואמתתו ועצמו מציאותו.

42 See JQR N. S. VII. 25ff.

have undergone three stages of development. The first may be called the Platonic; the second is the Aristotelian; the third is associated with the name of Hasdai Crescas.

The cosmological proof in its first stage is known in Jewish literature as the proof from creation. The existence of God is made a corollary to the creation of the world. Prove that the world came into being and, by the principle that every thing that comes into being must have a cause, you conclude that there is a God. It is essentially the same as Plato's proof from efficient causation,[43] though the relation between these two proofs does not seem to have been generally known. Maimonides as well as Averroes speaks of it as something invented by the Mutakallimun and entirely unknown to the ancients.[44] Moses Narboni, however, distinctly recognized its Platonic origin.[45] The popularity of this type of cosmological argument, the readiness with which it was generally accepted, was due to the fact that it chimed in with the traditional method of reasoning which had come down from the Scriptures. To argue from the fact that the world had come into existence to the existence of a Creator was simply to translate into a syllogistic formula the first verse of the book of Genesis or to rationalize the emotional appeal of the Prophets to look up into heaven and ask who had created it all. It is thus that for a long time this argument passed for the standard proof of the existence of God and God's existence was made dependent upon a belief in a created world. This indirect method of proving the existence of God is followed by Saadia,[46]

43 *Timaeus* 28.

44 See *Happalat, ha-Happaıah*, Disputation I, ולכן מי שהשתדל מזה הצד קיום הפועל הנה הוא מאמר ספוקי הלצי נצוחי לא מופתי. ואם יחשב כאבונצר ובן סיני שהם הלכו בזה הדרך בקיום שכל פעל יש לו פועל והוא דרך לא דרכו בה הקודמים ואמנם נמשכו שני אלה האנשים בו אל המדברים מאנשי אמונתנו, and *Moreh Nebukim* I. 74 end. אלו הם אמתות דרכי המדברים בקיום הדוש העולם, וכאשר תתקיים אצלם באלו הראיות שהעולם מחודש יתחייב בהכרח שיש לו פועל חדשו בכונה ורצון וחדוש.

45 Commentary on *Moreh Nebukim* II. 2, הנה רבינו משה רמז הנה על המחלוקת אשר בין כת אפלטון וכת ארסטו׳, כי אפלטון שיאמין בחדוש יצטרך בהכרח להניח לעולם פועל עושה חדשו.

46 *Emunot ve-Deot* I. 2.

Bahya,[47] Judah ha-Levi[48] in his restatement of philosophy, and Joseph ibn Zaddik.[49] It should be further noted that the proof from creation was made to rest upon the theory of creation in general and not necessarily upon *creatio ex nihilo*.[50] In this it had retained its original Platonic character. Crescas was quick enough to take Maimonides up on this point and build around it his criticism, when the latter attempted to make use of this proof.[51]

The Platonic stage of the cosmological argument, as we have seen, is based upon two principles. First, the principle of causality, the assertion that nothing can change or come into existence without a cause. Second, the principle that the world did come into existence. With the denial of a created universe by Aristotle, the argument enters upon its second stage. The first principle of causality is still retained, but the second principle of creation is replaced by the principle denying the possibility of an infinite regress. In Jewish philosophic literature, the cosmological argument in its second stage occurs under three forms. One is couched in terms of motion, another in terms of potentiality and actuality, and a third in terms of possibility and necessity. The first of these is Aristotle's argument from motion given in the eighth book of the *Physics*, to which we shall hereafter refer as the first proof from motion. The second may be likewise traced to Aristotle.[52] The third is associated with the name of Avicenna, although it is also

47 *Hobot ha-Lebabot* I. 4—6.

48 *Cuzari* II. 50 and V. 18.

49 *Olam Katan* III (p. 49, ed. Horovitz).

50 In Saadia this point is clearly brought out. He first proves creation in general, whence he derives the existence of God, and then proceeds to prove that creation must have been *ex nihilo*. The others likewise proceed immediately from creation in general to the existence of God.

51 Cf. *Or Adonai* I. 11. 20. ועוד שלא יתחייב מהחלוקה, שאם היה הוה ונפסד שיהיה מתהוה אחר הפסד בדרך שנצטרך לממציא, וזה שכבר אפשר, שיהיה הוה ונפסד בהמשכות כענין באישי המין. Crescas, as he very often does, has left out here the most essential point of his argument. But his criticism would have been entirely unwarranted, if the argument from creation had assumed *creatio ex nihilo*.

52 Cf. *Metaphysics* IX. 8. 1049b, 24 seq. and XII. 7. 1072b, 3 seq.

found in Alfarabi.[53] All these three arguments are in fact only different forms of one and the same argument. They are all based upon the two principles mentioned above, causality and the impossibility of an infinite regress. Motion, potentiality, and possibility are all forms of causality and they are in a way interchangeable terms. In Greek the same term δύναμις means both potentiality and possibility, and Aristotle defines motion as the actuality of that which is potential so far as it is potential[54] and also as the actuality of that which is movable so far as it is movable.[55] A hybrid form of the cosmological proof, made up of the Platonic principle of creation and of the Aristotelian principle as to the impossibility of an infinite regress, is to be found in Bahya.[56]

In addition to the argument from motion already mentioned, Aristotle has another argument, also based upon motion, but without involving the principle of infinity. It may best be described in the words of Gomperz as a postulate of logical symmetry.[57] From the fact that there are things which are moved but do not move, and there are things which both move and are moved, he infers that there must be something which moves but is not moved.[58] This argument, too, has found its place in Jewish philosophy, and together with the previous three forms of the Aristotelian cosmological proof makes up Maimonides' four proofs for the existence of God.[59]

The literary treatment of these proofs in Jewish philosophic texts might become an interesting subject of investigation in a comprehensive study of the proofs of the existence of God. But even in such a summary sketch as this it will not be altogether out of place to discuss at some length the different

53 Guttmann, *Die Religionsphilosophie des Abraham ibn Daud aus Toledo*, p. 120.

54 *Physics* III. 1. 201a, 10—11.

55 *Physics* III. 2. 202a, 7—8.

56 *Hobot ha-Lebabot* I. 5.

57 *Greek Thinkers* IV. 219.

58 Cf. *Metaphysics* XII. 7. 1072a, 20, *Physics* VIII. 5. 256b, 23; *De Anima* III. 10. 433b, 13.

59 *Moreh Nebukim* II. 1

usages made by Abraham ibn Daud and Maimonides of Aristotle's two proofs from motion. Abraham ibn Daud it was who for the first time introduced the second stage of the cosmological proof in Jewish philosophy. In his work it is found in two of its forms, motion and possibility.[60] He has also reproduced Aristotle's second argument from motion, although with a slight verbal modification;[61] but, curiously enough, unlike Maimonides, he does not employ it as a proof for the existence of God. He uses it only to prove the immovability of the Intelligences. The question naturally arises, why did not Abraham ibn Daud use the second proof from motion as a proof for the existence of God?

It will be rather difficult to answer this question properly without having to turn for a while from the main read of our inquiry and into some of its intricate byways. The philosophy we are here considering now is a close-knit system and it is well-nigh impossible to probe a single point and not be obliged to overhaul the entire structure. It is often the despair of the student to find an effective way of isolating a problem without having to wander far off into devious directions to trace the paths where its roots lie concealed. Perhaps, the best and most economic way of attacking our present problem would be to preface the discussion by a few general remarks.

There is, to begin with, the controversy with regard to the relation of God to the Intelligences and the celestial spheres with which many names are associated but which we shall present here under the names of its two chief exponents, Averroes and Avicenna.[62] According to Averroes, God is one of the many Intelligences which preside each over its respective sphere. He is the Intelligence of the outermost, all-encompassing, inerratic sphere, the first heaven, so called. He

60 *Emunah Ramah* II. 1, pp. 47—48.

61 *Op. cit.* II. iv. 2, p. 61, הנה במציאות שלשה מיני מניעים: אחד מהם מניע יניע מבלתי ידיעה, כמו מניע האבן אל המטה. והמין השני מניע בידיעה והוא עם זה מתנועע. ..... והמין השלישי מניע יניע מבלי שיתנועע.

62 Moses ha-Lavi in his *Ma'amar Elohi* (MS. Bodleian 1324. 5) alligns on the side of Avicenna also Alexander Aphrodisiensis, Themistius and Alfarabi. He himself joins this group. See also *Or Adonai* IV. 12.

moves that sphere directly in the same manner as the other Intelligences move their own respective spheres, as a final cause as well as an efficient and formal cause, and it is through this motion, which God imparts directly to the outermost sphere, that He becomes the mover of the entire universe. He differs from the other Intelligences only by reason of His priority in degree and importance, being the cause of the Intelligences not only but also of the spheres, all of which proceed from Him simultaneously and not by way of succession, one from the other. On all these points Avicenna has entirely different views. God, according to him, is a being beyond the Intelligences. He does not move directly any of the spheres, but as a remote cause He may be said to be the mover of the universe in so far as He is the object of desire and thought of all the Intelligences. The proximate cause of the motion of the outermost sphere is an Intelligence, who is an emanation from God, the first and only emanation from God; all the other Intelligences and spheres proceed from that first Intelligence by way of succession, one from another.[63] It may be said that after a manner Avicenna conceives God as a transcendent being, Averroes conceives Him as an immanent being.

Then there is a second point. Both Avicenna and Averroes agree that the Intelligences are not moved reciprocally and accidentally by the spheres in which they produce motion. Though in a general sense the Intelligences constitute an internal principle of motion in the spheres analogous to the soul in living beings, still, unlike souls, they receive no accidental motion in return, and this because of the peculiar relation the Intelligences bear to the spheres. Avicenna explains their relation as that of the Active Intellect to the human mind.[64] Moses Narboni, speaking for Averroes, explains it after the manner of the relation of the Acquired Intellect to man in Maimonides's psychology.[65]

63 See commentaries on *Moreh Nebukim* II. 1. 4, 22, especially Shem-Tob.

64 See Horten, *Die Metaphysik Avicennas*, 593. "Daher besitzt also jede Sphäre einen unkörperlichen, für sich bestehenden Geist, der sich zu ihrer Seele verhält, wie der aktive Intellekt zu unserer Seele."

65 See Narboni on *Moreh Nebukim* II, Introduction, Proposition XI. כ״

A third point is as follows. The divergent views of Avicenna and Averroes were meant to be interpretations of Aristotle's discussion of the First Mover. The controversy is therefore sometimes reduced to the question whether Aristotle's arguments from motion, whereby he proves the existence of a first immovable mover, was meant to prove the existence of God or was only meant to prove the existence of an immovable first Intelligence who is not God. According to Avicenna, the immovable First Mover which, in *Metaphysics* XII. 7, Aristotle identifies with God is not the immovable first mover the existence of which he establishes by his arguments from motion. The latter is only the first Intelligence.[66] It will be noted in that in *Physics* VIII Aristotle never explicitly identified his elicited first mover with God. According to Averroes, identifying as he does the Intelligence of the first sphere with God, the proofs from motion naturally constitute proofs for the existence of God.

Finally, as a result of this interpretation of Aristotle, Avicenna makes no use of the arguments from motion as proofs of the existence of God but invented in their stead the argument from possibility and necessity. Furthermore, the Avicenneans are rather chary of the use of the expression first mover as a designation of God inasmuch as according to their interpretation the term in its more rigid sense is used by Aristotle

השכל זה ענינו שהוא נקשר עם הגלגל הקשר צורה נפרדת, ר"ל הקשר מציאות לא עירוב, ואיננו מתנועע במקרה. וככה השכל הנקודה [הנקנה] לפי דעת רבינו משה אשר חבר שיחסו לאדם יחס השכל הנבדל אל איש העולם.

66 See Moses ha-Lavi, *Ma'amar Elohi.* מאמר אלהי לחכם הפילוסוף האלהי משה ב"ר יוסף הלאוי, בקיום שמניע הגלגל האחרון עלול מהסבה הראשונה ית'. אמר ירחמנו האל, הכונה בזה המאמר בקיום מציאות הסבה הראשונה וסתירה מי שטעה בזה... והביא המופת על שהוא זולת המניע הראשון, ושהמניע הראשון עלול לו... הפילוסוף מקיים מציאות מניע ראשון בשמיני מהשמע.... אבל הוא מביא שמה מופת רק על מציאות מניע ראשון ולא עלה בחקירתו אל סבת המניע הראשון והוא ד'. See also remark of Isaac Albalag in his commentary on Alazali's *Makasid* II, quoted by Steinschneider in his *Übersetzungen*, p. 116, note 61 ואני זה כמה ימים לא זזתי מלעיין בס' השמע, ולא מצאתי ראיות אריסטו מבוארות לא למציאות מניע ראשון אינו גוף ולא כח בגוף, אבל לא נתבאר שם אם הוא האלוה או זולתו and Shem-Tob on *Moreh Nebukim* I. 69. אמנם כפי דעת הרב הלקוח מדברי ב"ס באלשפ"א ואלנ"גי, לא מה שהתנוהו שרשי אריסטו אשר האמין כי המניע הראשון אינו האלוה, כי זה לא יניע הגלגל.

as a designation of the First Intelligence. More frequently do they designate God by the expressions First Cause, סבה ראשונה, and the Necessary Existent, מחוייב המציאות.

Now, both Abraham ibn Daud and Maimonides are followers of Avicenna with regard to the transcendency of God and the process of emanation. They differ, however, as to the immovability of the Intelligences and it is here that the reason for the different usages they make of the second argument from motion is to be found.

Abraham ibn Daud leaves us in no doubt as to his belief in the immovability of the Intelligences. Again and again he states with great precision and with much emphasis that the Intelligences are as immovable as God himself.[67] He explains the reason for their immovability in terms used by Avicenna, namely, that they are related to the spheres after the manner of the Active Intellect to the human mind.[68] This together with his Avicennean conception of a God transcending the Intelligences would naturally make it impossible for him to use the second argument from motion as a proof for the existence of God. The argument, as may be recalled, established only the existence of an immovable mover, but, according to Abraham ibn Daud, the Intelligences are no less immovable than God.

If, however, Abraham ibn Daud was justified in not using the second argument from motion as a proof for the existence of God, how then could he use as such the first argument from motion? That argument, too, establishes only the existence of an immovable mover which to him must not necessarily be God. Neither Avicenna nor Averroes claim anything more for it. If Averroes makes it a proof for the existence of God, it is only because he identifies God with the Intelligence of

67 *Emunah Ramah* II. iv. 2, p. 62. ולשואל שישאל ויאמר, כבר הסכימו האנשים על שהמניע אשר לא יתנועע אחד, ועתה יאמרו שלנפש כל רקיע מניע לא יתנועע, א״כ המניעים אשר לא יתנועעו רבים — והתשובה שהאנשים אמנם סברו שהמניע הראשון אשר לא יתנועע הוא אחד, וזה האחדות שב אל הראשון, לא אל אשר לא יתנועע, אבל העצמים אשר לא יתנועעו רבים מסודרים, כמו שגשמי השמים מסודרים. See also pp. 64, 66, 68.

68 *Emunah Ramah* II. iv. 2, p. 62. ובכאן עצמים פשוטים מדרגתם מן העצמים אשר הם לשמים כמו (הנפשות), מדרגת השכל הפועל אל הנפש האנושית.

the outermost sphere. But Abraham ibn Daud stretches the argument to prove the existence of a first mover which he identifies with Avicenna's Necessary Existent, calling the Intelligence of the outermost sphere a second mover, as may be inferred from his statement that the second Intelligence is a third mover.[69] Now, it must be admitted that Aristotle's first proof from motion could be easily modified and made to prove the existence of Avicenna's God. Maimonides, as we shall presently see, did so modify it. Nor would it be impossible to discover traces of such a modification in Abraham ibn Daud's restatement of the argument, or, better still, to read into it some new meaning. Nowhere, however, does he give us the slightest hint or suggestion of a conscious effort to justify his position. It is well to acclaim Abraham ibn Daud as the first to introduce the proof from motion in Jewish philosophy, but was he justified in doing so? Does he speak the language of a pioneer whose innovations, when unaccompanied by a statement of reasons and explanations, would only tend to land him in a maze of inconsistencies? All this would seem to point to the conclusion that Abraham ibn Daud was blindly following a certain literary source, unknown to me at the present writing, where the application of the argument from motion as a proof of the existence of the Avicennean God was fully and satisfactorily accounted for.

The case of Maimonides is much clearer. He uses both the first and the second arguments from motion as proofs for the existence of Avicenna's God, and he does so without involving himself in any inconsistencies, owing to his particular theory of the movability of the Intelligences.

Maimonides happens to be of the opinion, in which he seems to be alone, that the Intelligences have accidental motion. He conceives the Intelligences to be related to the sphere neither as the Active Intellect to the human mind nor as the Acquired Intellect to the human body. The Intelligences are indivisible forces within the spheres as is the hylic intellect in the human body, as a result of which they are moved accident-

[69] *Emunah Ramah* II. iv. 3, p. 64. ואחר כן זה היציאה יציאה ראשונה מן הראשון ית׳ וית׳ הוא נ״כ במאמרם מניע לא יתנועע, ויצא ממנו מניע שלישי לא יתנועע.

ally. It is this theory, which he states elsewhere,[70] that makes him say, in his discussion of his first proof, as follows: "As for the fourth case, namely, that the [ultimate] mover of the sphere be an indivisible force residing in it in the same manner as the human soul resides in man, it is likewise impossible that this mover alone, even though indivisible, should be the cause of the perpetual motion. For if this were its first mover [*par excellence*], that mover would have an accidental motion."[71] Again says he: "It is inadmissible that the Intelligence which moves the uppermost sphere should be the Necessary Existent."[72] He therefore concludes that the first immovable mover which is identified with God is not the proximate motive agent of the outermost sphere but rather the remote and final cause: "And this is God, praised be His name, that is to say, the First Cause which moves the sphere."[73] It is this First Cause of motion, the only immovable mover, whose relation to the world is described by Maimonides after the analogy of the relation of the Acquired Intellect to the human body.[74]

Thus Maimonides' reason for converting Aristotle's proofs from motion into proofs for the existence of Avicenna's God

70 *Moreh Nebukim* I. 72. ויהיה דמיון הכח הדברי כשכלי הגלגלים אשר בגופות. Cf. Narboni on *Moreh Nebukim* II, Introduction, Proposition XI, ואשר צריך שתדעהו שכל זה הביאו אליו למה שחשב הרב . . . כי השכל הוא כח בגוף, רק בלתי מתפשט, כענין בשכל האדם, ולפי שהוא כח בגוף יתנועע במקרה.

71 *Moreh Nebukim* II. 1, First Proof. Maimonides seems to be using the term "first mover" מניע ראשון in two senses. First, specifically with reference to God, as in the following passage: יתחייב בהכרח שימצא מניע לא יתנועע כלל וזהו המניע הראשון. (*Moreh Nebukim* II. 1, Second Proof.) Second, in the general sense of an internal principle of motion, as in the following passages: והחום הטבעי הניעתהו הצורה [=הנפש החיונית] אשר בו והוא המניע הראשון. (*Ibid.*, First Proof. See Munk, *Guide*, II. 30, n. 4. Friedländer's note 5, on p. 12, is quite off the mark.) והנפש היא המניע הראשון בעצם . . . . . . יתחייב אם כן שתהיה למניע ההוא הראשון סבה אחרת בהכרח חוא מן הכלל המורכב ממניע וממתנועע . . . . ולזאת הסבה לא ינועו גופות בעלי חיים תמיד ואף על פי שבכל אחד מהם מניע ראשון. (*Ibid.*) Hence the bracketed additions within the translation of the passage quoted in the text.

72 *Moreh Nebukim* II. 4.

73 *Moreh Nebukim* II. 1, First Proof.

74 *Moreh Nebukim* I. 72. ודע שראוי היה שנדמה יחס האלוה ית' לעולם יחס השכל הנקנה הנאצל לאדם אשר אינו כח בגוף והוא נבדל מן הגוף הבדל אמתי ושופע עליו.

is quite clear. But the question may now be raised, was Maimonides justified in transforming the argument of Aristotle in the face of the declaration by both Avicenna and Averroes that it was meant to prove only the existence of an immovable Intelligence of the outermost sphere? Or, to put in other words, is Maimonides' restatement of Aristotle's first proof from motion a perversion of the original Aristotelian proof or is it a legitimate interpretation thereof? The object of my subsequent remarks is to show that Maimonides was fully justified in setting his new construction on Aristotle's argument and that it was fully warranted by the original text of the eighth book of the *Physics*.

Aristotle's first argument from motion aims to prove two things: First, that there is a first mover. Second, that the first mover is immovable. The first point is proved by the denial of an infinite regress; the second point is based on the eternity of motion. The successive stages of the argument are as follows. It begins with the proposition that everything which is moved is moved by something else *externally*.[75] As this, however, cannot go on infinitely, it is concluded that there must be something which is first moved without being moved by anything else *externally*.[76] This marks the end of the first part of the argument, and in the seventh book of the *Physics*, assuming that book to be Aristotelian, Aristotle stops at that. In the eighth book, however, the argument is carried on further. For what the argument has thus far established is the fact that in a series of *mota* and *moventia* we must ultimately arrive, owing to the impossibility of an infinite regress, at a *motum* which has not external *movens* and which must, however, have an internal *movens*. Or, in other words, the argument at this point has shown that the outermost sphere must be a self-moving body, its moving agent being an inner principle, related to the body of the sphere, in a general way, after the analogy of the soul to the body of living beings. This inner principle of motion is what Aristotle calls the first mover. But here a

75 Cf. *Physics* VII. 1, 241b, 24, and VIII. 4, 256a, 2–3.
76 *Op. cit.* VII. 1. 242a, 19–20, and VIII. 5. 257a, 17–21.

new question comes up. Motion, according to Aristotle, is eternal, and eternal motion cannot be explained except on the assumption of a first mover who is absolutely immovable.[77] Now, in living beings, says Aristotle, the internal moving principle, namely, the soul, while immovable *per se*, is moved *per accidens* by the motion of the body.[78] The first mover, however, he argues, cannot be like that; it must be absolutely immovable, inasmuch as the motion it produces is eternal.[79]

With this statement of facts, Aristotle terminates his argument. We are thus left to ourselves to draw our own conclusions. All we have to guide us are the following three statements: (1) There is a first mover. (2) The soul of living beings is moved accidentally. (3) The first mover, unlike the soul, must be absolutely immovable. When we attempt, however, to draw the conclusion, we are confronted with the possibility of two interpretations. According to one possible interpretation, Aristotle's three statements might be connected as follows: (1) There is a first mover, namely, the Intelligence of the first sphere, who is related to the sphere, in a general sense, as the soul is related to the body. (2) Though the soul of living beings is moved accidentally, (3) still the first mover, namely, the Intelligence, is absolutely immovable, because its specific relation to the sphere is like that of the Active or Acquired Intellect to man. According to another possible interpretation, the three statements would be connected as follows: (1) There is a first mover, namely, the Intelligence of the first sphere, who is related to the sphere, specifically, as the hylic intellect is related to man. (2) Inasmuch as the soul of living beings, including the hylic intellect of man, is moved accidentally, (3) consequently, the first mover, who must be absolutely immovable, cannot he the Intelligence of the first sphere, but must be something transcendent. The interpretation of Aristotle will thus depend upon the view one happens to hold with regard to the movability of the Intelligences. Maimo-

77 *Op. cit.* VIII. 6. 258b, 10–12.
78 *Op. cit.* VIII. 6. 259b, 14–20.
79 *Op. cit.* VIII. 6. 259b, 20 seq.

nides, therefore, believing as he did in the movability of the Intelligences—a view which is closely bound up with a particular phase in his system of psychology—was justified in following the second interpretation and prove by Aristotle's first argument from motion the existence of Avicenna's transcendent God.

It would take us too far afield to treat here, with all the fullness it deserves, of the third stage of the development of the cosmological proof ushered in by Crescas. The present writer hopes to submit the result of his studies on this subject in a work entitled *Crescas's Critique of Aristotle and Maimonides*. But it would seem fitting to conclude this concatenation of notes on the proofs of the existence of God with an observation on the historical confusion displayed in a statement by Spinoza as to the development of the cosmological proof. Spinoza, speaking with approval of Crescas's elimination of the impossibility of an infinite regress from the cosmological proof, expresses himself this wise: "But I should like first to observe here, that the later Peripatetics have, I think, misunderstood the proof given by the ancients who sought to demonstrate the existence of God. This, as I find it in a certain Jew named Rabbi Chasdai, runs as follows."[80] The implication of this passage is that the cosmological proof as given by the ancients, that is, Aristotle, was vitiated by the later Peripatetics, that is, the mediaeval Aristotelians, but was restored to its pristine, genuine form by Rabbi Chasdai. This is not exactly what we know of the history of the proof. Fritz Mauthner wisely remarks in a recent publication: "Spinoza and Kant (von Sokrates and Platon nicht zu reden) wußten wenig von der Geschichte der Philosophie."[81]

80 Epistola XII (olim XXIX).

81 *Spinoza*, p. 24, Dresden 1921.

27

THE DOUBLE FAITH THEORY IN SAADIA, AVERROES, AND ST. THOMAS

In a paper published in 1942, I tried to show how the question discussed in Judaism, Christianity, and Islam as to the relation of their respective Scriptures to philosophy, commonly known as the problem of faith and reason, turns upon a conception of a twofold meaning of the term faith analogous to the twofold meaning of the term faith as used by Aristotle, namely, faith in the sense of the acceptance of the truth of a proposition as self-evident and faith in the sense of the acceptance of the truth of a proposition as established by demonstration. On the basis of this twofold meaning of the term faith, I suggested that all the various views on the problem of faith and reason, however they may be expressed, could be grouped together into three main theories, namely, (1) the double faith theory, according to which the teachings of any of the three Scriptures are to be accepted both as self-evident truths and as rationally demonstrated truths; (2) the single faith theory of the authoritative type, according to which the teachings of any of the three Scriptures are to be accepted primarily as self-evident truths; (3) the single faith theory of the rationalistic type, according to which the teachings of any of the three Scriptures are to be accepted primarily as demonstrated truths.

The paper published in 1942 bore the title "The Double Faith Theory in Clement, Saadia, Averroes, and St. Thomas." The first two sections of that paper, namely, "The Aristotelian 'Faith' and the Stoic 'Assent' " and "Clement of Alexandria," were republished, with many revisions, in my PHILOSOPHY OF THE CHURCH FATHERS, I (1956, third revised edition 1970), to which were added a section on the double faith theory in Augustine, a section on the single faith theory of the authoritative type in Tertullian, and a section on the single faith theory of the rationalistic type in Origen.

Saadia

From the Church Fathers, through personal contact between Moslems and Christians, the problem of the relation of faith to reason was introduced into Islam during the Umayyad period. Later, with the rise of the Mu'tazilite sect, under the second of the Abbasid rulers, speculations about faith and reason developed into a system. But in the writings which record the theological discussions among the Moslems before the time of Saadia (882–1042), with all their wealth of material on particular problems, there is to be found no extensive discussion of the general problem of the relation of faith to reason. Of the Mu'tazilites we know in a general way that they considered it as a "duty" to arrive at the "knowledge of God" by "speculation and proofs"[73] or "by reason,"[74] and from what is known of their general attitude it may be inferred that they held a single faith theory of the rationalist type. Similarly from what is known about the Ash'arites we may gather in a general way that they held a single faith theory of the authoritarian type. In Saadia's *Emunot ve-De'ot*, therefore, we find the first extensive discussion of the relation of faith to reason in Arabic philosophy, whether its Moslem or its Jewish branch.

The view represented by Saadia, we shall try to show, is that of the double faith theory, like that we have met with in Clement. As a purely epistemological term, we shall try to show, the term faith is used by him in the sense of a judgment of the truth of both immediate and derivative knowledge. As a religious term, we shall also try to show, it is used by him in the sense of the judgment of the truth of Scriptural teachings both with demonstration and without demonstration, and, moreover, both these two kinds of faith in its religious sense are considered by him as of equal degrees of perfection, each of them being the perfect religion for those to whose needs it is adapted. In presenting now Saadia's view on faith and reason, we shall therefore pursue the method which we have chosen to follow throughout this study, namely, to state first his conception of faith as a purely epistemological term and then his conception of it as a religious term, though in his own discussion the two aspects of the term are merged together.

Logically, though not actually, the starting point of his

[73] Shahrastani, p. 62, ll. 19–20.
[74] Ibid., p. 87, l. 17.

discussion is his formal classification of the types of knowledge.[75] These types of knowledge are divided by him into three, corresponding to what Aristotle would call (1) sensation, (2) primary premises and (3) scientific knowledge. Though this threefold classification of the types of knowledge was already a commonplace by the time of Saadia,[76] still the terminology used by him needs some comment.

Sense perception is described by him as the knowledge of that which is visible.[77] The term visible here reflects the Greek ὁρατόν, which is used as a description of corporeal objects which are perceptible by the senses.[78] Then, what Aristotle would call primary premises Saadia calls "the knowledge of the intellect."[79] This evidently reflects Aristotle's statement that it is the intellect (νοῦς) which apprehends the primary premises,[80] on account of which, in his various classification of types of knowledge, Aristotle himself describes intuitive knowledge by the term νοῦς.[81]

[75] *Emunot ve-De'ot, Hakdamah* (ed. Josefov, 1885), § 5, pp. 43 f. (Arabic, ed. Landauer, p. 12, ll. 17 f.).

[76] Cf. references to the Ikhwan al-Ṣafa (Arabic in Dieterici, *Die Abhandlungen der Ichwân es-Safă in Auswahl*, pp. 196, 212, 521) in Guttmann, *Die Religionsphilosophie des Saadia*, p. 22, n. 5.

[77] *Emunot ve-De'ot*, loc. cit., p. 43 (p. 12, l. 20– p. 13, l. 1): علم الشاهد : ידיעת הנראה.

[78] See, e. g., *Timaeus* 46D. The same term is also used by the Ikhwan al-Ṣafa in their description of this kind of knowledge; cf. op. cit., p. 196, ll. 4–5; p. 212, l. 21; p. 521, l. 4. In Arabic philosophy this term as a description of sensible things has gained currency evidently through the additional fact that it is used in that sense in the Koran 9.95.

[79] *Emunot ve-De'ot*, loc. cit. (p. 13, l. 4): علم العقل : מדע השכל.

[80] *Anal. Post.*, II, 19, 100b, 12. But in *Emunot ve-De'ot, Hakdamah*, § 2, p. 37 (p. 2, l. 12) the term المعرفة العقلية : המדע השכלי, as may be judged from the context, is used in the sense of ratiocinative thinking, the term عقل : שכל in that passage, unlike the same term in this passage, thus reflecting the Greek λόγος rather than νοῦς; cf. a similar double use of the Latin term *intellectus*, below § 5, n. 154.

[81] *Anal. Post.*, II, 19, 100b, 7–8; *De An.*, III, 3, 428a, 4–5; *Eth. Nic.*, VI, 3, 1139b, 16–17.

Finally, what Aristotle calls scientific knowledge (ἐπιστήμη), which is identified by him with conclusions of demonstrations, Saadia calls "a certain knowledge which necessity leads up to"[82] or "the knowledge of necessary things."[83] This expression, too, reflects a passage in Aristotle which states that "a demonstration is a necessary thing, because the conclusion cannot be otherwise, if there has been demonstration in the full sense; and the causes of this necessity are the first premises, i. e., the fact that the propositions from which the syllogism proceeds cannot be otherwise."[84]

Now these three types of knowledge, as will be noticed, fall into two groups, of which one, that which includes sensation and primary premises, is immediate knowledge, and the other, that which includes logical conclusions, is derivative knowledge. Consequently, when Saadia, previous to his classification of the types of knowledge, comes to define faith as the judgment of the truth of knowledge, he has two definitions of it, one with reference to immediate knowledge and the other with reference to derivative knowledge.

With reference to knowledge that is immediate, he defines faith as "a concept which arises in the soul of anything known according to the condition in which it really is."[85] In this definition, the expression "a concept which arises in the soul," I take it, refers to both sense-perception and

[82] *Emunot ve-De'ot*, loc. cit. (p. 13, l. 1): علم ما دفعت الضرورة اليه: ידיעת מה שההכרח מביא אליו.

[83] Ibid. (p. 13, ll. 5–6): علم الضروريات: מדע ההכרחית.

[84] *Metaph.*, V, 5, 1015b, 6–9; cf. above § 1, n. 14; § 2, n. 53, and below § 5, n. 160.

[85] *Emunot ve-De'ot*, loc. cit., § 4, p. 42 (p. 11, ll. 4–5): אנחנו צריכים לבאר מה היא האמונה (الاعتقاد). ונאמר כי היא ענין (معنى) עולה בלב (نفس = נפש) לכל דבר ידוע בתכונה אשר הוא עליה.

primary premises, reflecting Aristotle's statement about sensation that out of particular sense-perceptions a universal concept (καθόλου) is formed in the soul (ἐν τῇ ψυχῇ),[86] and also his statement about primary premises that it is the mind (νοῦς) which apprehends them.[87] The expression "of anything known according to the condition in which it really is" is the conventional restatement of the correspondence theory of truth as given by Aristotle.[88]

With reference to derivative knowledge, he defines faith in the following figurative language: "When the cream of speculation is extracted, the intellect takes it under its wings, folds itself around it, causes it to penetrate into the soul and to become intermingled so that man becomes thereby a believer in the concept thus arrived at and he keeps it in reserve for some later occasion or occasions."[89] In this passage, the opening statement "when the cream of speculation is extracted" means when by an act of speculation a conclusion is derived from primary premises. The remaining part of the passage means to say that the conclusion, which technically speaking is a "second notion," derived by demonstration from a primary premise or a "first notion," may itself, after it has been fully approbated and accepted by the mind, become a primary premise out of which other conclusions may be derived.[90] In Aristotle there is an allusion to the use of conclusions of one demon-

[86] *Anal. Post.*, II, 19, 100a, 16.

[87] Ibid., 100b, 12.

[88] Cf. *Metaph.*, IV, 7, 1011b, 27.

[89] *Emunot ve-De'ot*, loc. cit. (p. 11, ll. 5–8): וכאשר תצא חמאת העיון יקבלנה השכל ויקיפנה ויכניסנה בלבבות (نفوس=נפשות) ותמזג בהם ויהיה בהם האדם מאמין בענין אשר הגיע אליו ויצניעהו לעת אחרת או לעתים.

[90] On this meaning of "second notions," see *Millot ha-Higgayon*, Ch. 8, and *Ruaḥ Ḥen*, Ch. 3; *Milḥamot Adonai*, Introduction (p. 4). It differs from the scholastic term "*secundae notiones*; cf. my *The Philosophy of Spinoza*, II, pp. 121–22.

stration as a premise in another demonstration in his reference to the geometrical proposition that "the angles of every triangle are equal as two right angles" as something which a student "knew beforehand" (προῄδει),[91] that is to say, as something to be used as a premise in a demonstration. Now the equality of the angles of a triangle to two right angles is not a self-evident primary premise; it is deduced, as Aristotle himself says elsewhere, from the proposition that a straight line set up on a straight line will make angles equal to two right angles[92] or, in other words, it is the conclusion of a demonstration.

Saadia then proceeds to show, in true Aristotelian fashion, how each of these three types of knowledge may be either true or false. In the case of the sense of sight, for instance, he says, the knowledge arrived at by it is true when there is a real external object which we see, for, in that case, our knowledge corresponds exactly to reality, inasmuch as our organ of sight is assimilated to the perceptible object and becomes identical with it, and this on account of the likeness between the combining ratios of the same four elements which constitute the forms of both the perceptible objects and the organ of sight.[93] It is untrue, when we see the image of an object reflected in a mirror or in water and

[91] *Anal. Post.*, I, 1, 71a, 19 ff.

[92] Cf. *Metaph.*, IX, 9, 1051a, 24–26, and Euclid, I, 32 and I, 13; cf. also *Phys.*, II, 9, 200a, 16–18, with Ross's Commentary ad loc.

[93] *Emunot ve-De'ot*, loc. cit., p. 45 (p. 15, ll. 15–16): ונאמר כי מדע החוש כל אשר יפול חושנו האמתי בדבוק אשר בינינו וביניו ראוי שנדע שהוא הוא באמת כאשר השגנוהו; cf. I, 3(8), p. 74 (p. 20, ll. 7–8): וידוע שעינינו אינם משינים כי אם מה שהוא מאלה הארבעה יסודות כי טבעיהם מתחברים עם טבעי עינינו; II, 12, p. 102 (p. 106, ll. 9–11): שהדברים אינם נראים כי אם במראים הנראים בשטחיהם המיוחסים אל הארבעה טבעים ומתחברים עם הכחות אשר בראות העין ממיניהם באמצעות האויר ויראו.

All this is based upon Aristotle's statement in *De An.*, II, 5, 418a, 5–6, with regard to the sensitive faculty, that "when once it has been acted upon, it is assimilated and has the same character as the sensible object."

think that that reflection is a real object.[94] Similarly in the case of primary notions, he maintains, "all those which are formed in our mind when in a wholesome state are true and not subject to any doubt, provided only that, after we know how to form by speculation such notions, we do form them in a perfect manner."[95] As an example of perfectly formed and hence true notions he mentions such a generally accepted ethical notion as that "truth is good and falsehood is horrid."[96] Now these generally accepted ethical notions belong to what Aristotle calls maxims (γνῶμαι) in rhetoric,[97] describing them as being generally known or agreed upon or self-evident,[98] corresponding to primary premises in demonstrative syllogisms, except that they deal "with objects of human actions, and with what should be chosen or avoided with reference to them."[99] In fact, Arabic logicians include such maxims under what they call by the general term "primary premises,"[100] describing them specifically as "generally known primary premises."[101] But, on the other hand, he continues, there are also imperfectly formed and hence untrue notions in

[94] Ibid. (p. 15, ll. 18–21): ולא נטעה בהם כעם אשר חשבו כי הצורה אשר תראה במראה כי היא צורה ברואה שם באמת... ולא כעם אשר שמו הקומה אשר תראה במים נהפכת שהוא אמת תברא בעת ההיא.

[95] Ibid. (p. 16, ll. 4–6): אך המושכלות כל אשר יצטייר בשכלנו הנצל מכל פגע והוא מדע אמת אין בו ספק, אחר שנדע איך נעיין (ننظر) ואחר כן נשלים העיון (النظر).

I take it that the terms ننظر : נעיין and النظر : העיון in this passage do not mean the art of speculation or of reasoning but rather the formation of concepts in the mind. In the passage quoted below in n. 113, the expression مناعة النظر : מלאכת העיון refers to the art of reasoning, i. e., logic.

[96] Ibid., p. 43 (p. 13, l. 5): כמו שהצדק טוב והכזב מגונה.

[97] *Rhet.*, II, 20, 1393a, 23–24.

[98] Ibid., II, 21, 1394b, 10–15.

[99] Ibid., II, 21, 1394a, 24–26.

[100] Cf. Algazali, *Maqaṣid al-Falāsifah*, I, p. 52, l. 4: الاوليات.

[101] Ibid., p. 55, ll. 9 ff.: المشهورات; cf. *Millot ha-Higgayon*, 8: מפורסמות.

our mind, to which he refers as "phantasms and dreams."[102] These he describes as being due sometimes to "the thoughts which happened to cross through the mind during the past day" and sometimes to "the foods, with reference to their having been hot or cold, much or little," and sometimes to "the humor which happens to gain dominance over the mixture; the warm and moist become the dream-images of merriment and pleasure; the cold and dry become the dream-images of grief and mourning."[103] Finally, in the

[102] *Emunot ve-De'ot*, loc. cit., p. 45 (p. 16, ll. 6–7): ונשמר מן הדמיונים [التخيلات] והחלומות (والاحلام). These terms evidently reflect Aristotle's statement that "every image (φάντασμα) in sleep is a mere dream (ἐνύπνιον)" (*De Somniis*, 1, 458b, 24).

[103] Ibid. (p. 16, ll. 9–15 ff.): ולא ידעו כי קצתם יהיה מעניני היום החולף אשר עברו על המחשב . . . וקצתם מפני המזונות וחומם וקורם ורובם ומעוטם . . . וקצתם מפני המסך (الكيموس = χυμός) הגובר על המזג (المزاج) והחום והלח ידמה (يخيل) שמחות ומיני שחוק והקור והיבש ידמה אבל (ماتم) ודאגות (احزانا).

From the fact that in this passage, the كيموس : מסך, which happens to become predominant in the مزاج : מזג, is said to be either hot or moist, cold or dry, it is evident that it refers to one of the four humors, for the four humors correspond to the four primary qualities of the elements (cf. *Hippocratis de humoribus liber et Galeni in eum commentarius*, I, in *Galeni opera*, ed. Kühn, XVI, 23–24). The literal Hebrew translation of χυμός, كيموس, *juice, humor*, is ליחות. But, inasmuch as in Arabic the common word for humor is خلط, literally, *mixture*, κρᾶσις, μῖξις, the translator renders كيموس here by מסך, *mixture*. Conversely, too, we find that the Hebrew ליחות, literally, *juice*, is used as a translation of the Arabic خلط, literally, *mixture*. For examples see the quotations in Klatzkin, *Oẓar ha-Munaḥim ha-Pilosofiyyim*, s. v. All this interchange of terms is due to the fact that the terms *humor* and *mixture of humors* became interchangeable, owing to the fact that usually in every mixture of humors one particular humor predominates and lends its name to the mixture as a whole.

But see another interpretation of the term מסך here in Philipp Bloch, *Vom Glauben und Wissen*: *Saadiah's Emunoth we-Deoth*, München, 1879, p. 27, n. 1, which is adopted by Klatzkin, op. cit., sub מסך.

The second and third causes of dreams mentioned here by Saadia are also given by Abraham Ibn Ezra in his commentary on Eccl. 5.2: כשיהיה החולם מעורב מענינים רבים ידוע שהוא מתערובת המאכלים והתגבר אחת מן הארבעה שרשים לא יהיה לו פתרון ולא יורה על טוב ורע כי הבל הוא.

case of derivative knowledge, he concludes, it is true when, as in the case of what Aristotle calls scientific knowledge, it follows certain rigid logical rules of demonstration. It may be false, however, when, as in the case of what Aristotle calls opinion, there is some laxity in those rules of demonstration, and Saadia thereupon enumerates five such rules that are to be observed in demonstrative reassuring.[104]

Since both immediate and derivative knowledge may be either true or false, faith with reference to both these kinds of knowledge may be either true or false. In Clement, as will be recalled, there is a similar distinction between faith of scientific knowledge, which is true, and faith of opinion, which may be false.[105] Drawing upon the terms used in the definition of the correspondence theory of truth, Saadia defines these two kinds of faith as follows: "True faith means that a thing is known to be as it really is, the many to be many, the few to be few, the white to be white, the black to be black, the existent to be existent and the nonexistent to be nonexistent. False faith means that a thing is known to be the opposite of what it really is, the many to be few, the few to be many, the white to be black, the black to be white, the existent to be nonexistent and the nonexistent to be existent.[106]

This, then, is Saadia's restatement of Aristotle's double faith theory as a purely epistemological concept. Let us now see how he treats of the same theory as a religious concept.

Besides these three types of knowledge which may be

[104] Ibid., p. 46 (p. 18, ll. 16 ff.): וכיון שבארנו איך יהיה המדע ההכרחי צריך שנזכיר מה שישמרהו מן ההפסד.

[105] Cf. above § 2, n. 56.

[106] *Emunot ve-De'ot*, loc. cit., § 4, p. 42 (p. 11, ll. 10–14): והאמונה האמיתית הוא שידע הדבר כאשר הוא, הרב רב והמעט מעט, והלבן לבן והשחור שחור, והנמצא נמצא והנעדר נעדר. והאמונה השקרית הוא שידע הדבר בהפך מה הוא, הרב מעט והמעט רב, והלבן שחור והשחור לבן, והנמצא נעדר והנעדר נמצא.

either true or false, Saadia mentions a fourth type of knowledge, which he considers as being unqualifiedly true. He calls this fourth kind of knowledge "true tradition" and by this he means the teachings of Scripture as well of those of the oral Jewish tradition which are supplementary to Scripture.[107] Now these teachings of Scripture and of the oral Jewish tradition may be accepted by the believer as true without any demonstration, in the same way as one accepts the truth of indemonstrable primary premises. But they may also be demonstrated by reason and thereby become accepted as true in the same way as one accepts conclusions of syllogistic proofs as true. To Saadia both these kinds of acceptance of the truth of these teachings constitute faith in the religious sense of the term. The former is described by him as the faith of him "who believes by tradition" and the latter as the faith of him "who believes by speculation and understanding."[108] Thus, as in Clement, we have here a double faith theory in the religious sense of the term.

Moreover, again as in the case of Clement, both these kinds of faith are regarded by Saadia as of equal perfection. Against those who might think that the religion of the simple believer is inferior to that of the philosopher, Saadia briefly declares that the religion of those who are incapable of speculation is "perfect."[109] But being more concerned with those who in his own time objected to the use of philosophy in connection with religion, he undertakes to

[107] Ibid., p. 44 (p. 14, ll. 2 ff.): אבל אנחנו קהל המיחדים מאמינים באלה השלשה משכים אשר למדעים ונחבר אליה משך רביעי הוצאנו אותו בשלש ראיות ושב לנו שרש והוא ההגדה הנאמנת (الخبر الصادق); cf. the use of the terms ההגדה הנאמנת and הגדה אמתית (خبر صحيح) in III, 6, pp. 113, 114 (p. 126, l. 13; p. 127, l. 4).

[108] Ibid., § 2, p. 39 (p. 6, l. 7): וישוב המאמין בקבלה להאמין בעיון ובהבנה.

[109] Ibid., § 6, p. 51 (p. 25, l. 18): ומי שיהיה מן הנשים או הנערים ומי שלא ידע לעיין תהיה דתו שלמה.

refute all the popular prejudices against the application of reason to Scripture and, moreover, to show on many grounds that the application of reason to Scripture is desirable.[110] But while philosophic speculation about matters of faith are permissible and while also such speculations, if they are sound and founded on true principles, cannot conceivably be in disagreement with the teachings of Scripture,[111] one is not to make his belief in these teachings dependent upon the outcome of one's own rational investigation nor is one to relax in one's belief pending the outcome of such personal investigation. "We are not allowed," he says, "to put the books of the prophets aside and to rely upon what may occur to the mind of each one of us by his own reasoning when taking up for consideration such questions, for instance, as the beginnings of place and time. For he who employs speculation in matters religious in this manner may by himself either hit the right belief or miss it. Consequently, until he hits the right belief, he will be without belief. And if he happens to hit a right belief and gets hold of it, he will not be sure of himself that he will not part from it at the rise of some doubt in his mind, and thus his belief will be ruined for him."[112] Belief, Saadia would say, is a habit as well as a conviction, and such a habit can be formed by a decision of the will and cultivated by practice.

With his conception of the equality of undemonstrated faith and demonstrated faith, Saadia raises the question, which we have already met with in Origen, as to what

[110] Ibid., p. 48 (p. 20, l. 18– p. 21, l. 22).

[111] Ibid., p. 49 (p. 22, ll. 6–10): והודיענו כי כאשר נעיין ונחקור יצא לנו הברור השלם בכל שער כאשר הודיענו על יד נביאו והבטיחנו, כי לא יתכן שיהיה לכופרים עלינו טענה בתורתנו ולא ראיה למספקים באמונתנו.

[112] Ibid. (p. 21, ll. 15–20): אבל מנעו שנעזוב ספרי הנביאים לצד ושנסמך על מה שיצא לכל אחד ואחד בדעת עצמו בהעלותו על דעתו התחלות הזמן והמקום, כי כל המעיין מן הצד הזה אפשר שימצא ואפשר שיטעה, ועד שימצא יהיה בלא דת, ואם ימצא הדת ויחזיק בה לא יבטח מהעתקתו ממנה בספק שיעמוד לפניו, ויפסיד עליו אמונתו.

need was there for revelation, when men can attain to the same truth by their own reason. His answer is like that given by Origen. Speculative faith, he says, may indeed be suitable for those persons who by natural ability, training and leisure are able to carry through a logical argument to a successful conclusion. But there are those who, for various reasons, are lacking either the leisure or the ability to reason out for themselves the truths of religion. "God in his wisdom," he says, "knew that problems which are to be solved by the art of speculation can be brought to a conclusion only after the passage of some tract of time. Consequently, if God were to refer us to the art of speculation for a knowledge of His Law, we would each have to remain without the Law throughout the time that we were engaged in gaining proficiency in that art and perfection in the use of it. And perchance many among us would never become proficient in the art of speculation on account of some deficiency in them; or they would never become perfect in the use of that art on account of some aversion to it which might overtake them or of some doubts which might overpower and perplex and bewilder them. From all these troubles God has quickly saved us by sending to us His prophets."[113]

Thus, as in Clement, revelation is to Saadia a short-cut to salvation, and the short-cut and the long road both lead to faiths which are of equal perfection. For the perfection of faith, argues Saadia in effect, consists in the certainty

[113] Ibid., p. 51 (p. 24, l. 19– p. 25, l. 5): ונאמר מפני שידע בחכמתו כי המבוקשים המוצאים במלאכת העיון לא ישלמו כי אם במדה מן הזמן, כי אם ימחה אותנו בידיעת תורתו עליה, נעמוד זמן בלא תורה, עד שתשלם המלאכה, ויתם העסק בה. ושמא רבים ממנו לא תשלם בו המלאכה בעבור חסרון שיש בו, או שלא ישלם לו להתעסק בה בעבור שיקיץ בה (لضجر يلحقه), או מפני שהספקות שולטים עליו ומבלבלים אותו, ושמרנו הבורא מכל אלה הטרחים כלם במהרה ושלח לנו שלוחיו.

The Hebrew קוץ in Gen. 27.46, Num. 21.5, and Prov. 3.11, is translated by Saadia himself by ضجر. For מדה מן הזמן, see *Eth. Nic.* II, 1, 1103a, 15–17: Acquisition of intellectual virtue requires time.

and strength of one's conviction in the truth of what is believed, irrespective of the manner by which that truth was arrived at. The ideal believer is described by him as "he who has arrived at the truth and knows it and rejoices in it."[114] Imperfection of belief, similarly, is not to be identified either with a person's lack of rational arguments in support of his faith or with his use of such arguments. Nor is it even to be identified exclusively with a person's belief in what is not true, or with his lack of decision as to what beliefs are true. A person's faith may be called imperfect also if he lacks firm conviction in what he has chosen to believe, even though he happens to have chosen a belief which is true. He thus distinguishes from the type of the perfect believer quoted above three types of imperfect believers. These are first, "he who has arrived at the truth but he is still doubtful about it, being neither assured of it nor holding fast to it."[115] Second, "he who assures himself of that which is false on fancying that it is true, so that he clings and holds to falsity and abandons that which is right."[116] Third, "he who preoccupies himself with a certain view for some time, but gives it up on account of a certain defect he notices in it. He then transfers himself to another view for some time, but parts from it on account of something in it of which he disapproves. He then transfers himself to still another view for some time, but after

[114] Ibid., § 2, p. 38 (p. 3, l. 22– p. 4, l. 1): מי שהגיע אל האמת והוא יודע אותה ושמח בה.

[115] Ibid. (p. 4, l. 3): מי שהגיע אל האמת והוא מסתפק בה ואיננה מתאמתת אצלו ולא מחזיק בה.

[116] Ibid. (p. 4, ll. 5–6): ומהם מי ש(לא מתאמת אצלו ומחזיק בה ו)הוא אומר השקר וחושב שהוא אמת והוא מחזיק בשוא (بالزور) ומניח השוה (المستوى)، ועליו נאמר (איוב ט״ו, ל״א) אל יאמן בשו נתעה כי שוא תהיה תמורתו. The השוא in the printed text is to be read השוה. In his translation of, and commentary on Job, Saadia takes the שו in the verse of Job quoted by him here as being the equivalent of שוה; cf. Bacher's in *Version Arabe Du Livre de Job de R. Saadia ben Josef al-Fayyūmī*, Paris, 1899, p. 51; cf. also D. Kaufmann, *Gesammelte Schriften*, III, p. 439–40.

a while he rejects it on account of something which has rendered it faulty in his eye. And thus he vacillates from one view to another throughout his lifetime."[117]

Averroes

The development of the problem of the relation of faith to reason in the Moslem branch of Arabic philosophy was the reverse of that of its Jewish branch. Arabic Jewish philosophy started with Saadia's double faith theory, then developed, in Hallevi, a single faith theory of the authoritarian type, and ended up with Maimonides' single faith theory of the rationalist type. Arabic Moslem philosophy, on the other hand, started with the Mu'tazilite view of a single faith theory of the rationalist type, then developed, in Algazali, a single faith theory of the authoritarian type, and ended up with Averroes, a contemporary of Maimonides, with a double faith theory like that of Saadia and Clement of Alexandria.

Unlike Saadia who takes as the subject of his discussion the term *i'tiqād*, faith, Averroes takes as the subject of his discussion the term *taṣdīq*, which from its original meaning "the consideration of a thing as true" it came to mean also "affirmation" and "belief" and "judgment." We shall try to explain Averroes' use of this term before we undertake to explain his double faith theory.

Early in the history of Islam there appeared the question as to what constitutes religious faith (*imān*), by virtue of which a believer could be properly called a Moslem. Some said that faith is only a confession (*iqrār*) of the tongue of certain articles of the creed, even it were not

[117] Ibid. (p. 4, ll. 7–10): ומהם מי שמנהיג את עצמו בדעת מן הדעות ואחר כך מאסו בעבור דבר שראה בו, והעתיק ממנו אל דעת אחרת אחר זמן ומאסו בעבור דבר מגונה בעיניו בו, ואחר כך העתיק ממנו אל דעת אחרת אחר זמן ועזבו בעבור ענין שהפסיד אותו בעיניו, וזה בהתהפכות כל ימיו.

accompanied by a sincere conviction of the truth of the creed. Others said, quite on the contrary, that it is a belief (*taṣdīq*) in the heart. Still others said that it is a combination of the two. There were finally others who said that in addition to the confession of the tongue and the belief of the heart, it is also the performance of good works.[118]

Now all this was a problem of practical religion, which concerned itself with the question as to what were the duties required of a true Moslem. Historically, it would seem to be a repercussion within Islam of certain discussions among the Christians with whom Moslems had come in contact, which had their origin in such New Testament statements as "That if thou shalt confess with thy mouth . . . and shalt believe in thine heart . . . thou shalt be saved"[119] and "faith without works is dead."[120] It had nothing to do with the problem of the relation of faith to reason. The expression "belief of the heart," which may also mean "the conviction of a truth in the heart" had no implication that that conviction must be based upon reason and demonstration. We may gather this from the fact that such exponents of opposite views with reference to the relation of faith and reason as the Mu'tazilite al-Najjār and Al-Ash'arī both declare that faith is a belief (*taṣdīq*) of the heart.[121]

Now, Averroes happens to believe that faith is not only confession or good works but also a belief of the heart. Accordingly he uses the term *taṣdīq* instead of *imān* or *i'tiqād* in his formal discussion of the relation of faith to reason.

With this preliminary comment, we shall now try to

[118] Cf. L. Krehl, *Beiträge zur Charakteristik der Lehre von Glauben im Islam*, pp. 7 ff.; F. A. Klein, *The Religion of Islam*, pp. 39 ff.

[119] Romans, 10.9.

[120] James, 2.20.

[121] Shahrastani, p. 62, l. 20; p. 73, ll. 2–3.

recast Averroes' entire discussion of the relation of faith to reason, in his special treatise devoted to this problem,[122] in the general pattern of the problem as we have presented it in this paper. We shall discuss first Averroes' conception of faith in its general epistemological meaning and then we shall discuss his conception of the term in its special theological meaning.

Epistemologically Averroes starts his discussion of the meaning of the term faith with the statement with which all Arabic works on logic usually begin, which in his version reads: "Instruction is of two kinds, namely, simple apprehension (*taṣawwur*) and belief (*taṣdīq*), as the masters of the science of the Kalam have explained." He then proceeds to say that the methods of *taṣdīq* are "demonstrative, dialectical and rhetorical."[123] Now we are going to show that in this threefold division of the methods of *taṣdīq* Averroes means to say that *taṣdīq* may refer either to belief in immediately known truths or to belief in demonstrated truths. In Arabic philosophic literature prior to Averroes, the term *taṣdīq* is said to be of two kinds, the primary (*awwaliyy*) and the acquired (*muktasib*),[124] the former being a judgment which is "not preceded by another judgment upon which it is dependent"[125] or which is "with-

[122] *Kitāl Faṣl al-Maqāl wal-Taqrīr mā bain al-Sharī'ah wal-Ḥikmah min al-Ittiṣāl*, in J. M. Müller's *Philosophie und Theologie von Averroes*, Arabic: 1859; German: 1875; French by L. Gauthier, *Accord de la Religion et de la Philosophie: Traité d'Ibn Rochd (Averroès)*, in *Recueil de Mémoires et de textes publié en l'honneur du XIVe Congrès des Orientalistes par les professeurs de l'École Supérieure des Lettres et des Médersas*, Alger, 19C5, pp. 269–318; English by M. J. Rehman, *The Philosophy and Theology of Averroes*, Bardoa, 1921.

[123] *Faṣl*, p. 19, ll. 10–12. This passage of Averroes is discussed more fully by the present writer in a paper on the terms *taṣawwur* and *taṣdīq* to be published in *The Moslem World*.

[124] Shahrastani, p. 349, l. 1.

[125] Alfarabi, *'Uyūn al-Masā'il*, in *Alfārābī's philosophische Abhandlungen* by F. Dieterici, p. 56, l. 16.

out investigation and research,"[126] the latter being a judgment "which one cannot comprehend without having comprehended beforehand some other things"[127] or "which is obtained only by investigation."[128] As illustrations of the primary kind of judgment, in Alfarabi and Algazali, mention is made of certain common notions in geometry or, in general, of primary premises in logical demonstrations,[129] and as illustrations of the acquired kind of judgment mention is made of several propositions which are arrived at only by demonstration as conclusions from primary premises.[130] Since, therefore, *taṣdīq* is said in Arabic philosophy to be either primary or acquired, when Averroes says here that the methods of *taṣdīq* are "demonstrative, dialectical and rhetorical," he undoubtedly means to say that *taṣdīq* may be either primary or acquired. As to how this distinction of primary and acquired is used by Averroes here with regard to *taṣdīq* may be gathered from a further study of what he says subsequently about the rhetorical method of *taṣdīq* as distinguished from the demonstrative and the dialectical method.

The rhetorical method of *taṣdīq* is said by Averroes to be a method which endeavors to establish belief by means of *mathal* and *shibh*.[131] These two terms, I take it, represent respectively the Greek γνώμη, *maxim*, and παράδειγμα, *example*,[132] which, according to Aristotle, are two of the three rhetorical methods of establishing faith (πίστεις), the third being the enthymeme (ἐνθύμημα).[133] Now both

[126] Algazali, *Maqāṣid al-Falāsifah* I, p. 5, l. 4.

[127] Alfarabi, op. cit., p. 56, l. 13.

[128] Algazali, op. cit., p. 5, l. 5.

[129] Alfarabi, op. cit., p. 56, ll. 17–18; Algazali, op. cit., p. 5, ll. 7–11.

[130] Alfarabi, op. cit., p. 56, l. 14; Algazali, op. cit., p. 5, ll. 12–13.

[131] Cf. *Faṣl*, p. 15, ll. 8–13, quoted below in n. 144.

[132] Müller's "Bilder und Gleichnisse," Gauthier's "des figures et des symboles" and Rehman's "examples and parables" have all missed the technical use of these two Arabic terms here.

[133] *Rhetorica*, II, 20, 1393a, 23–24.

the maxim and the example, in contradistinction to the enthymeme, are considered by Aristotle as immediate kinds of knowledge. Maxims are described by him as "conclusions or premises of enthymes without the syllogisms"[134] and as being generally known or agreed upon or self-evident.[135] They are in fact like the immediately known primary premises of demonstrative syllogisms, except that they deal "with objects of human actions, and with what should be chosen or avoided with reference to them.[136] Similarly the example is defined by Aristotle as a "rhetorical induction,"[137] in contradistinction to the enthymeme which is a "rhetorical syllogism," for induction is considered by Aristotle as being the opposite of syllogism and demonstration[138] and as a primary but indirect sort of knowledge based upon our senses.[139] When therefore Averroes says that the methods of *taṣdīq* in the sense of belief are "demonstrative, dialectical and rhetorical," he means thereby that belief may be either 'acquired,' such as are obtained syllogistically by arguments, or 'primary,' such as are learned not syllogistically but rather directly by 'maxims' and indirectly by 'examples.'

Belief or faith, then, in its general epistemological sense of the term, is used by Averroes in its two Aristotelian senses. In the first place, it is the judgment of the truth of undemonstrated knowledge, such as the truth of ethical maxims or generally known primary premises. In the second place, it is the judgment of the truth of conclusions which have been arrived at by demonstration. Like Clement, therefore, Averroes applies the term faith to

[134] Ibid., II, 21, 1394a, 27–28.
[135] Ibid., II, 21, 1394b, 10–15.
[136] Ibid., II, 21, 1394a, 24–26.
[137] Ibid., I, 2, 1356b, 4–5.
[138] *Anal. Pr.*, II, 23, 68b, 13.
[139] *Anal. Post.*, I, 18, 81a, 38–81b, 9.

scientific knowledge, i. e., to conclusions which follow by necessity from their premises. But he differs from Clement in his description of the nature of this kind of faith. According to Clement, as we have seen, faith of any kind, even faith with reference to scientific knowledge, is an act of free will.[140] Averroes, in contradistinction to this, explicitly says that "the belief which arises in the soul of the truth of a thing by reason of a proof is something compulsory and not voluntary, that is to say, we have not the power to consider that thing as untrue or as true in the same way as we have the power to rise or not to rise."[141]

Coming now to his conception of faith in its theological sense, we find that Averroes starts with the common assumption of all religious philosophers ever since Philo, in asserting about the Koran what both Jews and Christians asserted about the Hebrew Scripture and what Christians asserted also about the Greek Scripture, namely, "that this our divine Law is true."[142] Faith, then, in the religious sense, means the acceptance of the teachings of the Koran as true. Now as to the question whether one is to accept the truth of the teachings of the Koran without investigation or whether one should try to demonstrate them by reason, his answer is like that of Clement and Saadia. Each man is to have a faith according to his capacities. "The natures of men," he says, "differ with reference to their conviction of the truth of a thing. One will be convinced of the truth of a thing through demonstration.

[140] Cf. above § 2, text at n. 53 f.

[141] *Faṣl*, p. 13, ll. 18–20. Horten (*Texte zu dem Streite zwischen Glauben und Wissen im Islam*, p. 16) is not right, I think, in inferring from this statement that "faith," according to Averroes, is a voluntary act and hence essentially different from "reason." What this statement means is that, though scientific truth is not voluntary, still the term faith can be applied to it. See discussion on this point in St. Thomas, below § 5.

[142] Ibid., p. 6, ll. 14–15.

Another will become convinced of the truth as a result of dialectical arguments, just as the former becomes so by demonstration, and this because he is by his nature incapable of more than that. Still another will become convinced of its truth as a result of rhetorical arguments, just as the master of demonstration becomes so by demonstrative arguments."[143] The same view is expressed by him elsewhere. "With regard to things," he says, "which on account of their abstruseness cannot be known except by demonstration, God has shown his favor to those of his servants who have no access to demonstration, either because of their natural predispositions or because of their habits or because of their lack of means to instruct themselves, by making use for their benefit of maxims (*amthal*) and examples (*ashbāh*) of these things, and with these maxims he has invited them to faith, for with these maxims one can attain faith by the use of arguments which are commonly accessible to all, that is to say, by dialectical and rhetorical arguments.[144]

In still another place, after mentioning the three methods of convincing people of the truth of a thing, namely, the demonstrative, the dialectical and the rhetorical methods, he says: "Inasmuch as not all men are by their natural dispositions capable of mastering the art of reasoning by arguments, not even reasoning by dialectical arguments and still less so reasoning by demonstrative arguments, in addition to the intrinsic difficulty of the task of learning these demonstrative arguments and the length of time it

143 Ibid., p. 6, ll. 17–21.

144 Ibid., p. 15, ll. 8–13. Strictly speaking, "dialectical" arguments are not based upon "maxims" and "examples." But Averroes' coupling here of Rhetoric and Dialectic reflects Aristotle's statement that "Rhetoric is a counterpart of Dialectic; for both have to do with matters that are in a manner within the cognizance of all men and not confined to any special science" (*Rhet.*, I, 1, 1354a, 1–3).

must take those who are capable of learning them, and inasmuch also as the Law has no other purpose than to instruct all the people, the Law of necessity has to include all the various methods of affirmation or belief and all the various methods of simple apprehension."[145]

So far, then, we have in Averroes a double faith theory like that in Clement, in Origen and in Saadia. There is one truth underlying both forms of faith, the truth of the revealed teachings of the Koran. There is only a difference in the method by which different believers arrive at that truth. Some accept it implicitly and hence take the teachings of the Koran literally; others are supported in their acceptance of it by demonstration and hence understand some of those teachings as interpreted philosophically. To the former, the truth of the teachings of the Koran is like an indemonstrable primary premise or a maxim or an example; to the latter, it is like the conclusion of a syllogism.

But as Averroes goes on in the development of his double faith theory he advances a view which is unique with him. The two conceptions of faith are not only defended and justified as true types of faith for those who by their capacities and opportunities happen to hold them, but they are set apart from each other as the only types of faith for their respective possessors. The simple believer is not only assured that his simple belief is good enough for him, but he is prohibited from trying to profess a belief as it is understood by philosophers, and the latter are not only allowed to rationalize about certain religious beliefs, but they are also prohibited from trying to profess such beliefs in the manner in which they are understood by the common people. In the case of such statements, he says, as can be understood either literally or rationally, as, e. g., the statements that God "proceeded to the heaven"[146] or that

[145] *Faṣl*, p. 19, ll. 13–17. [146] Surah, 2.27.

he comes down every night to the earth,[147] "for philosophers to take them according to their external literal meaning it is disbelief, and similarly for those who are not masters of demonstration to interpret them and to take them out of their literal sense it is accounted as disbelief or heresy.[148] Moreover, not only must each particular class of believers keep to its own kind of belief, but it is also not allowed for philosophers to propagate their rational beliefs among the common people, or to expound them in popular books which may be read by the common people,[149] and this prohibition applies even to philosophic interpretations which are true, not to mention those which are untrue.[150] He justifies this position of his by the analogy of medicine where, he says, it is commonly considered improper to discuss in popular work medical problems which might lead the common people to disregard the practical prescriptions of physicians for the preservation of health.[151]

Now this is a new element introduced by Averroes into the double faith theory. When one considers the political conditions that existed in Moslem Spain under the Almohad rule during the time of Averroes one cannot help feeling that this element of his view was dictated by political necessity. But his essential view as to the relation between faith and reason, apart from the rigid boundary he has set up between the two camps of believers, is nothing but the old double faith theory, which, as we have shown, has its basis in the Aristotelian epistemological conception of faith.[152]

147 Cf. M. J. Müller, *Philosophie und Theologie von Averroes*, German translation, p. 8, n. 1, for the source of this statement in Moslem tradition.

148 *Faṣl*, p. 16, ll. 2–4.

149 Ibid., p. 17, ll. 13 ff.

150 Ibid., p. 23, ll. 15 ff.

151 Ibid., p. 22, ll. 7 ff.

152 A historical survey of the various interpretations of Averroes' conception of the relation of faith to reason is to be found in L. Gauthier, *La Théorie d'Ibn Rochd (Averroès) sur la Rapports de la Religion et de*

In Latin philosophy throughout the twelfth century the pendulum was swinging between the two extreme single faith theories. As the exponent of the one extreme single faith theory, that of rationalism, is Abelard; as exponent of the other extreme single faith theory, that of authoritarianism, is St. Bernard of Clairvaux.[153] Among the exponents of this latter view the chief contention was that the term faith cannot be applied to knowledge the truth of which is either self-evident or demonstrated by reason — a view unlike that maintained by Clement, Saadia and Averroes. This contention is expressed rather vaguely by St. Bernard. Evidently using the term intellect (*intellectus*) in the sense of the Aristotelian primary premises as well as scientific knowledge (ἐπιστήμη, *scientia*) and defining it as "certain and manifest knowledge of anything whatever invisible,[154] he refuses to apply the term faith to it, but defines faith rather as "a voluntary and sure foretaste of truth which has not yet been made manifest."[155] The salient point of this definition is that faith must apply to something of which the truth is not manifest. His disciple, William of St. Thierry, using more technical language, rephrases this

de la Philosophie, Paris, 1909, with a bibliography on pp. 185–95. The myth of the so-called Averroes' double truth theory has been exploded by M. Asin y Palacios in his "El Averroismo Teológico de Santo Tomas de Aquino," in *Homenaje á D. Francisco Codera*, Zaragoza, 1904, pp. 271–331.

[153] Cf. J. G. Sikes, *Peter Abailard*, pp. 31–60; G. B. Burch, *The Steps of Humility, by Bernard, Abbot of Clairvaux*, pp. 268–74.

[154] *De Consideratione*, V, 3, 6 (*MPL*, 182, 791A): Intellectus est rei cujuscunque invisibilis certa et manifesta notitia.

For the use of the term *intellectus* (νοῦς) in the sense of both primary premises and demonstrated scientific knowledge, see the parallel case of the same double use of the Arabic *'aql* (νοῦς) in Saadia above § 3, n. 80.

[155] Ibid.: Fides est voluntaria quaedam et certa praelibatio necdum propalatae veritatis.

definition of his master to read that faith is "a voluntary assent of the mind with regard to those things which are from God,"[156] from which we gather that the "foretaste" of St. Bernard is but another word for "assent." That faith is not to be identified with demonstrated scientific knowledge is also insisted upon by Hugo of St. Victor in his statement that "faith is a certain certitude of the soul concerning absent things which is placed above opinion and below knowledge,"[157] that is to say, faith, while it is above mere opinion, is not to be applied to scientific knowledge.

Now St. Thomas sets out to combine two tendencies in Christianity with regard to the relation of faith and reason. Essentially he wants to establish a double faith theory like that of Clement, that is to say, the equality of undemonstrated and demonstrated belief in the teachings of Scripture. But on the other hand, he wants to retain the definition of faith as given by St. Bernard, William of St. Thiery and Hugo of St. Victor, namely, that faith is a voluntary assent to a truth which is neither self-evident nor the result of demonstration. So what does he do? He tries to show that not even Aristotle applies the term faith, in its purely epistemological sense, to something the truth of which is either self-evident like primary premises or absolutely established by demonstration like scientific knowledge.

Let us then see first how he works out his definition of faith as a purely epistemological term.

[156] *Speculum Fidei* (*MPL*, 180, 370D): Deo enim inspirante fit in nobis voluntarius mentis assensus in his quae de ipso sunt . . . et ipsa est fides.

[157] *De Sacramentis fidei Christianae*, I, 10, 2 (*MPL*, 176, 330C): Fidem esse cercitudinem quamdam animi de rebus absentibus, supra opinionem et infra scientiam constitutam. The expression "absent things" reflects the definition of faith as "the evidence of things not seen" in Hebrews 11.1.

Following the tradition which has existed in Christian philosophy ever since Clement of Alexandria, that of combining Aristotle's faith with the Stoic assent, he says: "Faith implies assent of the intellect to that which is believed."[158] Externally this definition would seem to be a reproduction of the definition used by Clement of Alexandria and all those who followed him. But upon a closer observation one notices in it a significant change. To Clement and others, faith is identical with assent; to St. Thomas it is not identical with assent. The latter to him is a more general term than faith; it indeed includes faith, but it includes also that which is not faith. Assent, he says, may apply to the first premises in demonstrations, which are immediately known to be true, and also to conclusions in demonstrations, the truth of which follows by necessity from the first premises. The assent to neither of these implies free choice, for the assent forces itself upon us in either of these two cases. Consequently, this kind of assent is not faith, for faith, by the definition as already formulated by Clement of Alexandria, must be an act of free choice. Faith is to be found only in cases where after some doubt and hesitation and indecision the mind is satisfied with the preference of one side to all the other sides and makes a voluntary decision, and that decision once made is sure and free of all doubt.[159] In his definition of faith therefore the term 'assent' is used by him as a genus and the term 'voluntary' is used by him as a specific difference.

Analyzing this definition of faith, we find in it a combination of elements which have been discussed by earlier philosophers, with some of which St. Thomas agrees and with others he disagrees.

His statement that assent may be either voluntary or

[158] *Sum. Theol.*, II, II, 1, 4c.
[159] Ibid.

involuntary may be taken as an interpretation of the statements of his predecessors who speak of faith as a voluntary assent. St. Thomas seems to have understood these statements to mean that while faith is a voluntary assent, assent is not always voluntary, though the Stoics who first introduced the term assent probably meant that assent is always voluntary, in the sense in which they understood the term voluntary.

Then, his statement that scientific knowledge is necessary and not voluntary reflects exactly Aristotle's statement to the effect that conclusions follow from primary premises by necessity.[160] We have seen above, how Saadia similarly describes conclusions as "a certain knowledge which necessity leads up to" or as "the knowledge of necessary things."[161] Averroes, too, as we have seen, describes scientific knowledge as necessary.[162]

Finally, his statement that because faith is a voluntary assent it cannot apply to scientific knowledge is at variance with the view of Clement, who defines faith as a voluntary assent, and still takes it to apply to scientific knowledge,[163] though, it must be added, he does not explicitly say that scientific knowledge is by necessity. It is at variance also with the views of Saadia[164] and Averroes,[165] both of whom explicitly say that scientific knowledge is by necessity and yet they apply to it the term faith, though, here again it must be added, they do not explicitly say that faith is a voluntary assent.

St. Thomas seems to have considered his exclusion of the use of the term faith with reference to scientific knowledge

160 Metaph., V, 1015b, 6–9; cf. above § 1, n. 14; § 2, n. 53; § 3, n. 84.
161 Cf. above § 3, nn. 82–83.
162 Cf. above § 4, n. 141.
163 Cf. above § 2, nn. 49–54.
164 Cf. above § 3, nn. 82, 83, 108.
165 Cf. above § 4, n. 141.

as representing the view of Aristotle. We may gather this from his comment on a passage in the *Nicomachean Ethics*, where Aristotle, after enumerating the five modes in which the soul reaches truth in affirmation and negation, namely, art, scientific knowledge, prudence, wisdom, reason, adds, "assumption (ὑπόληψις) and opinion (δόξα) I do not include, because by these one may go wrong."[166] In the Latin translation used by St. Thomas the term ὑπόληψις is rendered by *suspicio*, which is evidently taken by St. Thomas in the sense of *fides*.[167] Accordingly, in commenting upon this passage, he says that "the faith of which the Philosopher speaks is based on human reasoning in a conclusion which does not follow of necessity from its premises and which may be false."[168] The meaning of this statement is that Aristotle himself uses the term faith only with reference to conclusions which do not constitute scientific knowledge.

Now in so far as St. Thomas deals with the application of the term faith to scientific knowledge, his statement about Aristotle may be literally true, for, as we have pointed out above, the term faith is never explicitly used by Aristotle with reference to scientific knowledge, though, as we have pointed out, there is no logical reason why he could not have used it with reference to it, for faith is never defined by Aristotle as a voluntary act.[169] But St. Thomas goes still further to say that, on the ground that faith is a voluntary assent, it is not used by Aristotle even with reference to primary premises which are immediately known as true. This would seem to be not in accordance with what Aris-

[166] *Eth. Nic.*, VI, 1, 1139b, 17–18.

[167] *S. Thomae Aquinatis expositio in libros ethicorum ad Nicomachum*, VI, Lect. III.

[168] *Sum. Theol.*, II, II, 4, 5, ad 2.

[169] Cf. above § 1, nn. 18, 19, 20.

totle actually says, for, as we have seen above, Aristotle does actually say with regard to primary premises that "things are true and primary which obtain faith not on the strength of anything else but of themselves."[170] St. Thomas' proof-text for his interpretation of Aristotle would seem to be the latter's statement quoted above, that faith is a "vehement assumption" (ὑπόληψις σφοδρά),[171] which is quoted by St. Thomas in Latin as *opinio vehemens*.[172] From this passage he evidently infers that faith must be an 'opinion' which becomes 'vehement' by voluntary assent, but not a conclusion of a demonstration to which the assent cannot be voluntary.

The Aristotelian definition of faith as interpreted by St. Thomas may still be described as a double faith theory. For it still applies to knowledge which is either immediate or derivative. The interpretation given by St. Thomas does not abolish that double nature of faith. The new element that his interpretation introduces into the definition is only the view that the knowledge of which faith is the judgment of truth, whether it is immediate or derivative, must not be absolutely certain on purely intellectual grounds. Intellectually there must be some element of uncertainty and doubt about it. Only by an act of the will does it become certain knowledge. Faith to St. Thomas still applies to immediately known propositions and to conclusions, but the immediately known propositions are those which, on purely intellectual grounds, Aristotle would call probabilities (ἔνδοξα),[173] and the conclusions are those

[170] *Top.*, I, 100a, 30–100b, 18; cf. above, § 1, n. 7.

[171] Ibid., IV, 5, 126b, 18.

[172] *Sum. Theol.*, II, II, 129, 6c: fides dicitur etiam opinio vehemens. Cf. ibid., I, II, 67, 3c: fides autem medio modo se habet: excedit enim opinionem, in hoc quod habet firmam inhaesionem; deficit vero a scientia, in hoc quod non habet visionem.

[173] *Top.*, I, 1, 100b, 21–23.

which Aristotle would call opinions,[174] or rather vehement assumptions,[175] which fall short of scientific knowledge.

With this conception of faith as a purely epistemological term, St. Thomas approaches his discussion of it as a religious term. Faith in its religious sense means a voluntary assent to the teachings of Scripture about which intellectually the mind may be in doubt but which are still accepted by a voluntary assent. The test of such faith is the certainty which follows the assent. The essential points in this definition are three: (1) that there must be no intellectual compulsion in the acceptance of these teachings, (2) that their acceptance must be a pure voluntary assent, and (3) that the assent must be complete and absolute so that no doubt remains in the mind and no suspicion and no hesitancy. This definition of faith in its religious sense is not only taken by St. Thomas to be based on what he considered to be the Aristotelian definition of faith in its epistemological sense, but it is also taken by him to be the true meaning of St. Augustine's definition that faith is "to think with assent."[176] Ostensibly the word "to think" would imply speculative reasoning which determines with certainty the truth of knowledge and, taken in that sense, it would seem to be the opposite of St. Thomas' definition. But, argues St. Thomas, "to think" (*cogitare*) in this definition is to be understood to mean the act of the "deliberating intellect" (*intellectus deliberans*) or of the "cogitative power" (*virtus cogitativa*), which involves some doubt and uncertainty before final certitude is attained, and that the assent is to be given by free choice and not by the compulsion of logical demonstrations.[177] His main

[174] *De An.*, III, 3, 428a, 19–23; cf. above, § 1, nn. 9, 10.
[175] *Top.*, IV, 5, 126b, 18; cf. above n. 171.
[176] *De Praedestinatione Sanctorum*, c. 2, 5 (*MPL*, 44, 963): quanquam et ipsum credere, nihil aliud est, quam eum assensione cogitare.
[177] *Sum. Theol.*, II, II, 2, 1c.

support, however, is the statement of John of Damascus that "faith is assent without investigation."[178]

But in Scripture there are certain beliefs which St. Thomas, following the commonly accepted view among all philosophers, considers as being demonstrable by reason and at the truth of which one could arrive by mere reason. Now that one is allowed to demonstrate these doctrines by reason is taken by St. Thomas for granted.[179] But still by its technical definition faith applies only to an assent to something which has not been demonstrated by reason. How can these two be reconciled? St. Thomas finds a way of reconciliation by maintaining, in a manner similar to that of Saadia,[180] that logical demonstration of beliefs which can be demonstrated should come after one has first accepted those beliefs voluntarily. A person must accept by faith even those things which can be demonstrated by reason,[181] and only after he has accepted them should he look for reasons to establish them on rational grounds.[182] When reasons are found, then those beliefs which were at first accepted by voluntary assent will, of course, become necessary conclusions for those who have demonstrated them by reason, but they will still remain mere objects of belief for those who have not demonstrated them by reason. That the same doctrines should with some people remain only an object of voluntary assent and with others, as a result of demonstration, should become scientific knowledge, is no cause for any difficulty, for, says St. Thomas, "it may happen that a thing which is an object of vision or science for one, is believed by another."[183]

178 *De Fide Orthodoxa*, IV, 11 (*MPG*, 94, 1128D), quoted in *Sum. Theol.*, II, II, 2, 1, obj. 1: Fides est non inquisitivus assensus.

179 *Cont. Gent.*, I, 8; I, 9; *Sum. Theol.*, I, 1, 8.

180 Cf. above § 3, n. 112.

181 *Sum. Theol.*, II, II, 2, 4c.

182 Ibid., II, II, 2, 10c.

183 Ibid., II, II, 1, 5c.

The term faith in its religious sense as defined by St. Thomas may still be characterized as a double faith theory. For it still applies to the acceptance of the teachings of Scripture either as immediately known propositions or as demonstrated conclusions. All that he insists upon is that however those teachings are accepted, their truth and certainty should not be logically compelling at the time they are accepted. One's voluntary assent to them, despite one's intellectual uncertainty of them, is that which constitutes faith in the technical sense of the term — a faith, which, once established as a mere voluntary assent, may be later transformed into intellectual certainty. Like Clement, he could call the second stage of faith "scientific faith."

There is also another aspect of the double faith theory which is retained by St. Thomas, and that is the equality of demonstrated faith and undemonstrated faith. In the case of St. Thomas, this will mean the equality of the faith at the time it is only a voluntary assent and of the faith when, as a result of subsequent demonstration, it becomes an intellectual conviction. The matter is discussed by him in the form of a question "whether reasons in support of what one believes lessen the merit of faith."[184] Now Gregory the Great, who held a single faith theory of the authoritarian type, definitely says that "faith has no merit when human reason gives proof."[185] St. Thomas, however, as an adherent of the double faith theory disagrees with this view, and comes out in support of the view which we have met with in Clement and Saadia and Averroes, namely, that there is an equality of perfection between the two kinds of faith. To the question quoted above, his answer is that if the reasons are used merely to support

[184] Ibid., II, II, 2, 10.

[185] *XL Homiliarum in Evangelia*, XXVI (*MPL*, 76, 1197c): nec fides habet meritum, cui (ubi in St. Thomas' quotation of it) humana ratio praebet experimentum, quoted in *Sum. Theol.*, I, 1, 8, Obj. 2.

that which has already been assented to voluntarily, they do not exclude the merit of faith; on the contrary they are a sign of greater merit.[186] So then, while the term faith technically refers to assent without demonstration, such assent still remains faith even when fortified by demonstration.

As in every theology which recognizes that certain beliefs are based upon reason and can be arrived at by reason, the question is raised by St. Thomas why should such matters have been revealed to men and why should they not have been left to be discovered by human reason. The answer given by him is like that we have already met with in Origen, Saadia and Averroes. "*Three* disadvantages would result," he says, "if this truth were left solely to the inquiry of reason." *One* of these disadvantages is that only a few men would have knowledge of God, inasmuch as some men are hindered from gathering the fruit of diligent inquiry by "an indisposition of temperament," others by "the needs of household affairs," and still others by their "laziness" to go into the study of all the preliminary disciplines necessary as preparations for the study of metaphysics and theology. "The *second* disadvantage is that those who would arrive at the discovery of the aforesaid truth would scarcely succeed in doing so after a long time," for this truth is so profound that (1) it requires long practice before it can be grasped, (2) it must be preceded by many preliminary studies and (3) it requires maturity of mind which man does not possess in his youth. The *third* disadvantage is the weakness of the human intellect which makes it impossible for it to arrive at a pure truth without some adulteration of falsehood.[187]

Now the classification of these reasons as well as the terms used reflect the reasons we have reproduced from

[186] *Sum. Theol.*, II, II, 2, 10c.

[187] *Cont. Gent.*, I, 4; cf. *Sum. Theol.*, II, II, 2, 4.

Origen, Saadia and Averroes.[188] But St. Thomas himself has in some of his other writings reclassified the three reasons given by him in *Contra Gentiles* and *Summa Theologica* for the need of a short-cut of revelation to the knowledge of God into five reasons. These five reasons are acknowledged by him to have been taken directly from Maimonides' enumeration of five reasons why instruction in philosophy should not begin with metaphysics.[189]

Conclusion

Let us now summarize the result of our discussion. We have shown how in Aristotle the term faith is used as a judgment of the truth of either immediately known primary premises or of conclusions derived by demonstration from those premises. As a judgment of truth, faith, according to him, belongs to the theoretical intellect and is outside the function of will which belongs to the practical intellect. For the judgment of the practical intellect and the choice of the will with regard to what is good and desirable, Aristotle uses in one single passage the term assent in its verb form. Then the Stoics, adopting the term assent, use

[188] Here is a list of parallel expressions from St. Thomas (*Cont. Gent.*, I, 4, and *Sum. Theol.*, II, II, 2, 4), Origen (cf. above § 2, n. 72), Saadia (cf. above § 3, n. 113) and Averroes (cf. above § 4, n. 144):

I. *St. Thomas*: "indisposition of temperament"; "dullness of mind." *Origen*: "weakness of men." *Saadia*: "some deficiency." *Averroes*: "natural predisposition"; "habits."

II. *St. Thomas*: "the needs of household affairs"; "occupations and temporal needs." *Origen*: "necessities of life." *Averroes*: "lack of means to instruct themselves."

III. *St. Thomas*: "after a long time"; "until late in life." *Origen*: "until they could give themselves to a thorough examination of reasons." *Saadia*: "only after the passage of some tract of time." *Averroes*: "the length of time it must take."

[189] *De Veritate*, XIV, 10; cf. Jacob Guttmann, *Das Verhältniss des Thomas von Aquino zum Judenthum und zur jüdischen Litteratur*, p. 37, n. 1.

it also as a judgment of the true, and describe assent, even as a judgment of the true, as an act of the will. However, the term will which the Stoics use, even though it is described by them as free will, does not mean absolutely undetermined freedom. With Clement of Alexandria, the term assent of the Stoics becomes combined with the term faith of Aristotle and from that time on faith is defined as assent and as an act of the will. In Clement, however, the term will is used in the sense of absolutely undetermined freedom. Now just as faith in Aristotle and assent in the Stoics applies either to self-evident true knowledge or to demonstrated true knowledge, so also faith in the teachings of Scripture comes with Clement to mean either assent to them as a self-evident revealed truth or assent to them as a demonstrated truth, and both these kinds of faith are of equal perfection and merit. This view is followed, on the whole, by Saadia, Averroes and St. Thomas, but with the following difference. To Clement, Saadia and Averroes, both in their interpretation of Aristotle's use of faith as a purely epistemological term and in their own use of it as a religious term, faith applies to something which on purely intellectual grounds is absolutely true either as an immediate truth on the order of Aristotelian primary premise or as a demonstrated truth on the order of Aristotelian scientific knowledge. To St. Thomas, both in his interpretation of Aristotle's use of faith as a purely epistemological term and in his own use of it as a religious term, faith applies only to something which on purely intellectual grounds is only of uncertain truth, such as primary premises which Aristotle would call probabilities, and conclusions which Aristotle would call vehement opinion. The certainty which faith must necessarily contain is that which is acquired by it through the voluntary assent of the believer. Then also between Clement and Averroes, and perhaps also Saadia, there is the following difference. To Clement, faith in demonstrated scientific knowledge, though intellectually compelling, may still be called voluntary, because the will could still refuse assent to it, despite its intellectual compulsion. To Averroes, and perhaps also to Saadia, faith in scientific knowledge, which is intellectually compelling, cannot be called voluntary, inasmuch as according to him it is not within the power of the will to refuse assent to it.

INDEX

Abarbanel, *see* Abrabanel
Abba Mari Don Astruc of Lunel, 512, 515, 529–530
Abelard, Peter, 605
Abrabanel, Isaac, 446–447
Abrabanel, Judah, *see* Leo Hebraeus
Abraham bar Hiyya, 547
Abraham de Balmes, 396, 433, 437–439, 490
Abraham di Benevento, 448–449
Abraham ibn Daud, *see* Ibn Daud, Abraham
Abraham ibn Ezra, *see* Ibn Ezra, Abraham
Abraham Shalom, *see* Shalom, Abraham
Abū Hāshim, 163–165
Abu 'Imran Moses Tobi, 548
Abukrat, *see* Hippocrates
Aëtius, 28, 35, 40
Afendopolo, Caleb ben Elijah, 513, 515, 520, 522, 524–526, 528, 530–531, 547
Aḥitub, 530, 537, 554–555, 557–558
Ahmed Fouad El Ahwani, 436
Albertus Magnus, 146, 294–301, 305, 317, 326, 383
Albinus, 115, 117–126, 129, 131–135, 137–138, 141, 150, 389
Albo, Joseph, 569
Aldabi, Meir, *see* Meir Aldabi
Alexander Aphrodisiensis, *see* Alexander of Aphrodisias
Alexander of Alexandria, 208
Alexander of Aphrodisias, 131, 140, 156, 244, 386, 394, 395, 413–414, 443, 449, 455–460, 463, 467, 469, 476, 535; souls of the spheres, 24, 25, 27–32, 34–38, 40–45, 47–48, 54
Alfarabi, 12, 395, 443, 573, 600; ambiguous (amphibolous) terms, 456–461, 466, 473, 477; attributes, 144, 146, 148–154, 158; classification of sciences, 494, 516, 527–528, 530–531, 535, 542; creation, 210–211, 214, 216–217, 231, 235, 375–376; internal senses, 274–276, 282–283, 288, 310, 319, 327, 329, 332, 336–338, 342–343, 355, 357, 368–370; political science, 551–557, 559; souls of the spheres, 45–46; Taṣawwur and Taṣdīq, 478–482, 486, 490
Algazali, 393–395; ambiguous (amphibolous) terms, 456–457, 461–463, 466, 468–475, 477; attributes, 144, 149, 152–154, 158–162, 164–166, 168; classification of sciences, 495, 515, 518, 520, 523–525, 527–528, 530, 547; creation, 244, 376–377; existence of God, 570; faith, 596, 599; internal senses, 282–285, 292, 295–299, 301, 322; prime mover, 406, 413, 417; souls of the spheres, 44, 46, 50; Taṣawwur and Taṣdīq, 478–479, 490
Ali, 546
Allāf, 162–163
Almanzi, Joseph, 434
Almoli, Solomon ben Jacob, *see* Solomon ben Jacob Almoli
Altmann, Alexander, 229–230, 331
Ambiguous (amphibolous) terms, 455–477
Ammonius Hermiae, 493
Ammonius Saccas, 12, 146–147, 387, 472
Anatolio, Jacob, 431
Anaxagoras, 25, 174
Andreas Torresanus de Asula, 437
Andronicus, 535
Apollinaris, 92–93
Apollonius of Tyana, 263–264
Apologists (Church Fathers), 80, 177
Apostolic Fathers, 80
Aristotle: ambiguous (amphibolous) terms, 455–464, 466–474, 476–477; attributes, 115, 120–121, 128–129, 131–134, 137, 140–141, 145–151, 154–158, 166–169; Averroes, 371–374, 378–381, 383–390, 393–395; Church Fathers, 77–79, 84–87, 90–94; classification of sciences, 493–497, 499–500, 502–504, 506–508, 510–513, 515, 517–518, 522–530, 535–543, 546–548; commentary of Averroes on, 430,